CARCHEMISH IN CONTEXT

Themes from the Ancient Near East BANEA Publication Series, Vol. 4

CARCHEMISH IN CONTEXT
THE LAND OF CARCHEMISH PROJECT, 2006–2010

Edited by

TONY J. WILKINSON, EDGAR PELTENBURG
AND ELEANOR BARBANES WILKINSON

Oxbow Books
Oxford & Philadelphia

British Association for Near Eastern Archaeology (BANEA)

Published in the United Kingdom in 2016 by
OXBOW BOOKS
10 Hythe Bridge Street, Oxford OX1 2EW

and in the United States by
OXBOW BOOKS
1950 Lawrence Road, Havertown, PA 19083

Hardcover Edition: ISBN 978-1-78570-111-5
Digital Edition: ISBN 978-1-78570-112-2

A CIP record for this book is available from the British Library

Library of Congress Cataloging-in-Publication Data

Names: Wilkinson, T. J. (Tony J.) | Peltenburg, E. J. | Wilkinson, Eleanor
    Barbanes. | British Association for Near Eastern Archaeology.
Title: Carchemish in context : the Land of Carchemish Project, 2006-2010 /
    edited by Tony J. Wilkinson, Edgar Peltenburg and Eleanor Barbanes
    Wilkinson.
Description: Oxford : Oxbow Books, 2016. | Series: Themes from the ancient
    Near East (BANEA publication series) ; vol. 4 | "British Association for
    Near Eastern Archaeology (BANEA)." | Includes bibliographical references.
Identifiers: LCCN 2015046547 (print) | LCCN 2015047903 (ebook) | ISBN
    9781785701115 (hardcover) | ISBN 9781785701122 (digital) | ISBN
    9781785701122 (epub) | ISBN 9781785701146 (pdf) | ISBN 9781785701139 (
    mobi)
Subjects: LCSH: Carchemish (Extinct city) | Iron Age--Turkey--Karkami?s
    Region. | Iron Age--Syria--Jar?abulus Region. | Excavations
    (Archaeology)--Turkey--Karkami?s Region. | Excavations
    (Archaeology)--Syria--Jar?abulus Region. | Land of Carchemish Project. |
    Archaeological surveying--Turkey--Karkami?s Region. | Archaeological
    surveying--Syria--Jar?abulus Region. | Karkami?s Region
    (Turkey)--Antiquities. | Jar?abulus Region (Syria)--Antiquities.
Classification: LCC DS156.C32 C27 2016 (print) | LCC DS156.C32 (ebook) | DDC
    939.4/202--dc23
LC record available at http://lccn.loc.gov/2015046547

Printed in Malta by Melita Press

For a complete list of Oxbow titles, please contact:

UNITED KINGDOM
Oxbow Books
Telephone (01865) 241249, Fax (01865) 794449
Email: oxbow@oxbowbooks.com
www.oxbowbooks.com

UNITED STATES OF AMERICA
Oxbow Books
Telephone (800) 791-9354, Fax (610) 853-9146
Email: queries@casemateacademic.com
www.casemateacademic.com/oxbow

Oxbow Books is part of the Casemate Group

Front cover: Carchemish from the south-east. Photo: P. Newson
Back cover: Ceramic lion head found during 2006 survey at site LCP 6. Photo: E. Wilkinson

The Land of Carchemish Project was the last regional survey conducted by T.J. Wilkinson, and this volume was one of the last that he brought to completion. Tony's vision, hard work, and expertise shaped the entire project, and every field season benefitted from his steady guidance, boundless enthusiasm and inclusive humour.

This book is dedicated to Tony, who left us much too soon.

CONTENTS

LIST OF CONTRIBUTORS

Michael Brown
Dept of Archaeology, Durham University

Emma Cunliffe
School of Archaeology, University of Oxford

Jesper Eidem
Netherlands Institute for the Near East, Leiden

J.D. Hawkins
School of Oriental and African Studies, University of London

Dan Lawrence
Dept of Archaeology, Durham University

Paul Newson
Dept of History and Archaeology, American University of Beirut

Edgar Peltenburg
School of Classics, History and Archaeology, University of Edinburgh

Andrea Ricci
German Archaeological Institute (DAI), Berlin

Stefan L. Smith
Dept of Archaeology, Durham University

Mark Weeden
School of Oriental and African Studies, University of London

Eleanor Wilkinson
Dept of Archaeology, Durham University

Tony J. Wilkinson
Dept of Archaeology, Durham University

LIST OF ABBREVIATIONS

AS	Algaze's survey along the banks of the Euphrates in Turkey (Algaze *et al.* 1994) see Chap. 1 bibliography	KOS	survey conducted by Mehmet Özdoğan and Necmi Karul in the Birecik district to the east of the Euphrates (Özdoğan and Karul 2002) see Chap. 1 bibliography
BRB	Bevelled-rim bowl	LBA	Late Bronze Age
DEM	Digital Elevation Model	LC	Late Chalcolithic
DGAM	Directorate General of Antiquities and Museums in Syria	LCP	Land of Carchemish Project
EBA/EB	Early Bronze Age	LLC	Local Late Chalcolithic
EBSE	other Euphrates surveys in Syria by Moore and Sanlaville and McClellan and Porter	MBA/MB	Middle Bronze Age
		MP	McClellan and Porter survey
EME	Early Middle Euphrates period	RIMA	Royal Inscriptions of Mesopotamia (Grayson 1991, 1996 in Chap. 3 bibliography)
ESA	Eastern Sigillata A		
FCP	Fragile Crescent Project	SAA	State Archives of Assyria.
GIS	Geographical Information System	SCM	Sanlaville, Copeland and Moore survey
GPS	Global Positioning System	SRTM	Shuttle Radar Topographic Mission
GPCC	Global Precipitation Climatology Centre	WP	GPS waypoint on geographical location in the field
IA	Iron Age		
KCG	Karkemish Cist Grave		

1

INTRODUCTION

T.J. Wilkinson and Edgar Peltenburg

Carchemish can be regarded as one of the iconic sites in the Middle East, a mound complex known both for its own intrinsic qualities as the seat of later Hittite power and Neo-Hittite kings, but also because its history of excavations included well known historical figures such as Leonard Woolley and T.E. Lawrence. According to Irene Winter (1982, 177):

> "Perhaps no other site in the region of northern Syria and south-eastern Anatolia played as important a role in the history of the early first millennium B.C. as Carchemish, 'on the banks of the Euphrates.' It is one of the best-documented sites of the period, due to a combination of Neo-Assyrian references and the excavated material of the site itself, including inscriptions, reliefs and large-scale architectural projects initiated by the rulers of Carchemish. All of these documents attest to its immense wealth and power."

However, because of its location within the military zone of the Turkish-Syrian border the site itself has been inaccessible to archaeologists for more than 90 years since the cessation of the British Museum's excavations there in 1920. What is less well known is that some 40% of the total site area remains within Syria, in the form of the Iron Age "Outer Town" as defined and mapped by P.L.O. Guy with Sir Leonard Woolley in 1920. Although part of this important settlement is buried beneath the modern Syrian town of Jerablus, a significant part remains within pistachio nut orchards and gardens adjacent to the border. Our aim in *Carchemish in Context* is therefore to summarize the results of regional investigations conducted within the Land of Carchemish Project in Syria, as well as other archaeological surveys in the region, in order to provide:

- a regional context for the development of the city;
- a summary of changes in the settlement and landscape of the region;
- an archaeological assessment of the 40 ha remains of the Outer Town within Syria;
- an historical context for Carchemish through a summary of the textual sources for the site, as well as an assessment of what is meant by the term "Land of Carchemish."

Chapter 8 of this volume provides the history of archaeological exploration and excavations at Carchemish. In this Introduction, we examine descriptions and commentary made by early archaeologists and travellers concerning the site, the surrounding landscape, and its broader geographical context. Sir Leonard Woolley, T.E. Lawrence, David Hogarth, and P.L.O. Guy all published useful background material on the geography. It is important to appreciate that during their campaigns the early British Museum teams devoted a great deal of time to exploring the area, amassing a considerable amount of background information, and their valuable records have informed our own investigations. The chapters in the present volume follow this lead, in part to re-create a balanced perspective on the sites and its region. *Carchemish in Context* provides a counterbalance to the tendency over the past 40 years for scholars to see the city of Carchemish through the lens of ever diminishing scales of analysis that have been focused upon primarily the reliefs and inscriptions of the area between the Water Gate and the King's Gate and the associated Long Wall of Sculpture, the Herald's Wall and the Temple of the Storm God. Because these areas fall within modern Turkey and because they have been covered by a number of recent analyses (Hawkins 2000; Harmanşah 2013; Gilibert 2011) and especially by the new investigations of the "Turco-Italian Joint Project at Karkemish" which started in 2011 (Marchetti 2012, 2014) we have chosen to focus upon a summary of the inscriptions, the latest evidence from the Outer Town as well as a geographical analysis of the region.

The Euphrates valley has, throughout history, held strategic value both as a border and as a corridor of communication, and it has long been a popular route for travellers. Consequently, numerous individuals and groups have traversed the region and some of them have left behind useful accounts which are particularly relevant to our study. For example, in 1879 Eduard Sachau journeyed southward from Carchemish to "Sreisat" (Land of Carchemish Project (henceforth LCP) Site 1; see Appendix A for site numbers) and noted rice and Durra growing in marshy surrounds in the vicinity of Carchemish, many wild pig in the Euphrates valley by Jerablus and, further south in the plain, well-watered areas for the rice (Sachau 1883, 169–174). Also, in his *Personal Narrative of the Euphrates Expedition*, Ainsworth (1888) provides insightful comments on the location of one of our main sites, LCP 1, known as Seraisat. Not only is this site identified to the north of the area of Mughar and the River Sajur (Ainsworth 1888, 224), he also notes the presence of the fragmentary remains of an ancient town now known as Sarisat (*sic*), which he identifies as Ceciliana of the classical itineraries (Ainsworth 1888, 224). Whether this identification is correct is not certain, but it is significant that our survey discovered not only major multi-period settlements at the modern village (LCP 1), but also an adjoining Classical Roman site (LCP 18) which clearly extended as major buildings and cultural accumulations onto the flood plain where they had been trimmed and eroded by the Euphrates.

In her pioneering surveys through Syria Gertrude Bell (1924, 34) provides an excellent description of the Roman architecture as it remained on the surface of the Inner Town of Carchemish:

> "The northern mound is covered with the ruins of the Roman and Byzantine city, columns and moulded bases, foundations of walls set round paved courtyards, and the line of a colonnaded street running across the ruin field from the high ridge to a breach that indicates the place of a gate in the southern face of the enclosing wall. A couple of carved Hittite slabs, uncovered during Henderson's excavations and left exposed at the mercy of the weather, bear witness to the antiquity of the site."

Thanks to its fortuitous presence within what was the inaccessible Turkish military zone, much of this pattern still remains visible to the sensors of high resolution satellite imagery such as GeoEye.

Earlier visitors also supply useful observations on the Byzantine lower town at Qara Qozaq (Bell 1910, 516), a late Antique Islamic canal south of Carchemish previously published (Wilkinson *et al.* 2007; P.L.O. Guy map), cemeteries at Tell Amarna and its neighbourhood and the site of Deve Höyük (located just north of the border in Turkey; Moorey 1980). They also remind us of the fact that Carchemish was not always a major centre and that its fortunes were subject to the vagaries of geo-politics, communications and other impacts. In the 19th century AD, the Aleppo–Birecik route was one of the main routes to the

Fig. 1.1 The Euphrates near the junction with the Sajur River, south of Carchemish (by Gertrude Bell in February 1909); with thanks to Bell Archives: J117

east, bypassing the ruins of Carchemish which so attracted those interested in antiquity (Sachau 1883, 160–161 and map). Birecik was the political and commercial capital of the region, and it was to Birecik that Woolley and Lawrence repaired in order to obtain the necessary *firman* (permit) from the Ottoman authorities to carry out their excavations at Carchemish.

Perhaps surprisingly, the bare un-wooded landscape, which is quite evident on Bell's photographs of the area (Fig. 1.1), contrasts markedly with the verdant, partially wooded appearance of the valley floor landscape evident today. Such valley floor woodland is partly a bi-product of the high water levels raised behind the modern Tishrin Dam downstream as well as recent settled conditions, population growth and need for more farming and poplars for roofing. This riparian vegetation is complemented today by the increasingly orchard-covered slopes which result from the copious planting of olive trees on the dry uplands over the past 20 years.

In addition, more recent investigations have made a major contribution to our understanding of the region. These include the French and British surveys of the late 1970s (Sanlaville *et al.* 1985), the survey conducted by Tom McClellan and Ann Porter of the greater Tishrin Dam area, as well as the survey of rock-cut features and Classical remains by Vivancos (2005). All supplied a foundation for the later investigations of the Land of Carchemish Project which were conducted between spring 2006 and July 2010. Although the Project was intended to be more intensive, it fell somewhat short of this goal because of the growth of civil unrest in Syria after 2011, and it must be emphasized that the results presented in this report are hardly comprehensive; rather, they are the synthesis of the results achieved up until the beginning of the current Syrian conflict.

The location of the site

As one of the most significant urban centres in the ancient

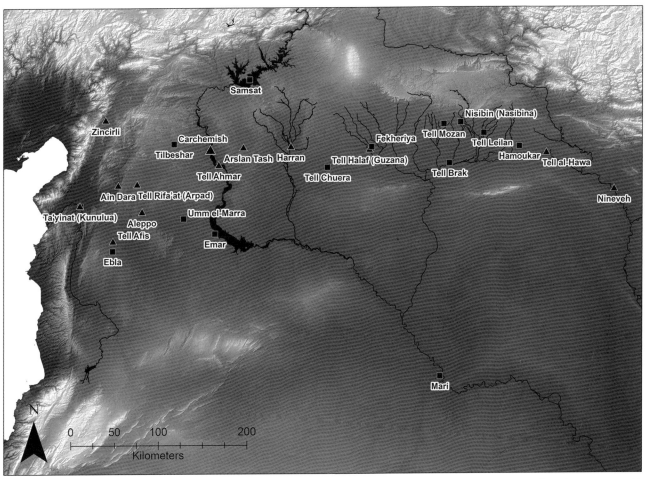

Fig. 1.2 Carchemish located within an arc of major sites between the Tigris and the Mediterranean. ▲: major Iron Age sites or with significant Iron Age occupation; ■ other significant sites discussed in text

Near East, Carchemish is characterized by not only a long history of occupation, but also by its prominence as a subject of investigation dating back to the pioneering days of Near Eastern archaeology. Perhaps in part due to the sheer volume of scholarly and popular studies, over the decades many generalizations have been made about the site, and some of these seem to be based more on speculation or conjecture than on actual archaeological evidence. One such generalization is that the city was situated at a major, well-used crossing point of the Euphrates (Chapter 5). In fact, as will be discussed in Chapters 3, 4 and 5, the more accurate characterization may be that the ancient city was situated within a broad arc of communication routes which, during the Iron Age, appear to have connected the Assyrian heartland at Nineveh through Tell Halaf, Harran, Arslan Tash, Carchemish, Rifa'at, Ain Dara and Ta'yinat to the Mediterrranean coast (Fig. 1.2). Unfortunately, only parts of this corridor can be recognized from its physical traces (Chapters 3 and 5), and it is clear that because of local political contingencies and centres of power, campaign

routes by the Assyrian kings did not always follow the regularities of functionalist logic or "least-cost" pathways.

The topography of Carchemish includes three major components: a citadel mound or 'acropolis', an attached and ramparted Inner Town, and beyond it, the Outer Town mentioned above (see Fig. 8.1). The citadel mound presents a commanding position on the west (right) bank of the Euphrates overlooking a broad and fertile plain to the south and a somewhat narrower plain to the north. The semi-arid high terraces of the Euphrates and associated limestone uplands seem to have restricted settlement away from the river, although as the survey has made clear, in fact both uplands and the tributary valley floors away from the river to the west were rather well settled by relatively small communities back to at least the Halaf period.

Today the landscape has been dissected, disturbed and transformed by constant human intervention. The Aleppo-Baghdad railway cuts through the Outer Town of Carchemish to form the de-facto frontier; major dams create reservoirs to the north of the site (Birecik and Carchemish Dams), as

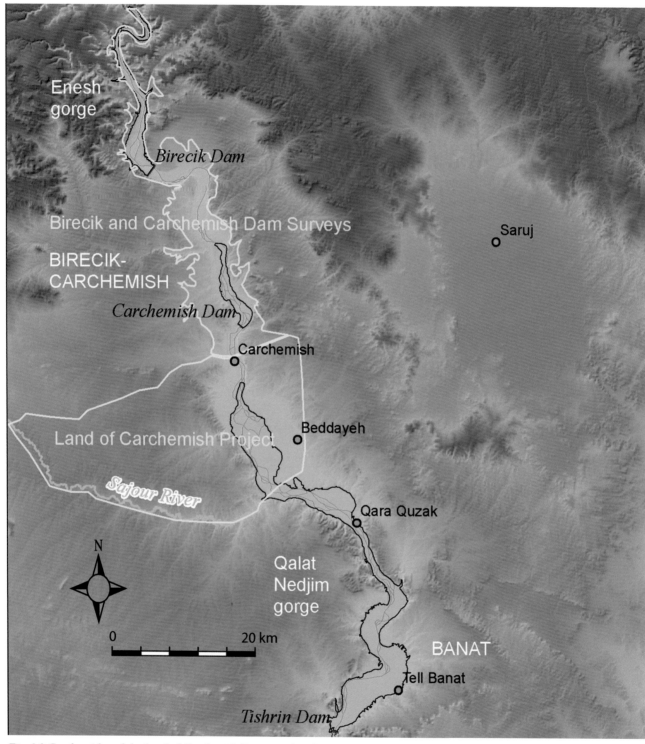

Fig. 1.3 Carchemish and the Land of Carchemish Project within the Middle Euphrates in Syria and Turkey (based on an original map by Niko Galiatsatos for the Fragile Crescent Project)

well as further to the south (Tishrin Dam; Fig. 1.3), and growing towns such as Jerablus are threatening to engulf parts of the Outer Town (Chapter 10). As a result of the dams the river has been effectively tamed and it is now difficult

to appreciate how it may once have threatened many sites with flooding, or indeed how at other times the floodplain itself *may* have been settled and cultivated (Chapter 5). Until 2010, the frontier zone was perforated by minefields which have been recognized and partly cleared to enable archaeological investigations and tourism to go ahead; but because of uncertainties related to the present Syrian conflict it is unclear how the area will develop in the near future. Because the site and region of Bronze Age Carchemish has been treated in an earlier volume (Peltenburg 2007), there is no reason to present detailed appraisals of the region during this period. Rather this volume acts as a complement to earlier publications which often lacked the resources such as remote sensing, GIS and digital elevation models that make it possible to analyze large areas relatively quickly.

The origins of the Land of Carchemish Project

The origin of the LCP lies in the excavations at Tell Jerablus Tahtani conducted by Edgar Peltenburg from 1992 to 2004, and specifically from 2003 when both Tony and Eleanor Wilkinson joined him at the Department of Archaeology, Edinburgh University. At the outset, it was clear that although during the rescue project's excavation results were appearing thick and fast, most were concentrated along the edge of the Euphrates on the lower terraces and there was little perspective on the nature of settlement away from the river. Therefore following an initial visit in 2004 by Tony Wilkinson to the post-excavation project at Jerablus, we initiated formal surveys in the spring and early summers of 2006, 2008 and 2009 (Chapters 4 and 5), with detailed investigations of Carchemish Outer Town in 2009 and 2010 (Chapter 8). Unfortunately, the initiation of civil unrest and the following Syrian conflict from spring 2011, made it impossible to continue fieldwork in that summer as planned. Therefore since 2011, the team has been engaged in compiling the collected data for this monograph.

Much ink has been spilt on the political geography of the Hittite and Neo-Hittite kingdoms. With the introduction of remote sensing as a significant survey tool, the Land of Carchemish Project has added a new dimension to previous surveys of the region, especially with respect to the identification of smaller or flat sites. The increased range of information garnered in this way is not simply more of the same, but informs on a variety of landscape uses and site contexts. It enables several contributors to this volume to make detailed contributions to the subject of the political geography of Carchemish and its hinterland, a goal that could only be tackled in a general manner with the kind of information available to earlier surveyors.

One period that all surveys have called particular attention to is the Early Bronze Age. In Chapter 4, Lawrence and Ricci show that the number of sites in the Birecik-Carchemish region expanded significantly during the 3rd millennium, in line with a general increase of settlements in Northern Mesopotamia. Additional insights into this phenomenon are provided by texts found in the ruins of palace G at Ebla,

some 170 km south of Carchemish. They cover some two or three generations before its destruction, c. 2300 BC, and hence they provide a fleeting snapshot into what seems to have been volatile times.

During the 25th century BC, the general political situation in Northern Mesopotamia started to shift from largely independent polities to growing regional states (Archi 1996). Shortly thereafter the Carchemish area first appears in historical documentation. Iblul-Il, a king of Mari, apparently conquered several cities in the region of the Big Bend of the Euphrates, including Emar, Abarsal and Hassuwum. He was not the first Mariote king to venture into the Middle Euphrates valley and this has led some authorities to claim a Mari supremacy in the area of Carchemish prior to the expansion of Ebla (Archi and Biga 2003, 1–3). Discussion of the location of these cities epitomizes a general problem, namely, the location of places for which we have few pieces of independent corroboratory evidence. Abarsal is a case in point. Opinions range from locations to the north of Carchemish, to the east as far as the Khabur River catchment and even just some 20 km south of Carchemish, at Tell Ahmar (Milano and Rova 2000, 8, fig. 3; Bunnens 2007, 48–50 with references). If, as many assume, it lies to the east of the Euphrates, perhaps at Tell Chuēra, it is conceivable that the Euphrates River formed the border between Ebla and Abarsal in the vicinity of Carchemish or further south.

In contrast to Abarsal, there is some consensus about the location of *Gàr-gàr-mi-iš*[ki] at Carchemish and that it was included within Ebla's territory (Archi 2011, 5; Biga 2014). The city served as a distribution centre for Eblaite textiles, Ebla gave certain residents gifts that included textiles, bracelets and other metals, and the city in turn provided food for Ibrium, the vizier of Ebla, and his army. That it was a regional centre of strategic value is suggested by the fact that kings and officials from several cities came to it to receive gifts from the envoy of the king of Ebla (Biga 2014, 76–79). Unlike many cities in this part of the Ancient Near East, however, Carchemish lacked a king or named ruler. It may have been a trading gateway rather than one possessed of political power, and if so, it may have had a distinctive relationship with smaller sites in the area. Be that as it may, we are still uncertain as to what it actually meant to be under the control of Ebla. Although individuals at the court of Ebla held estates far and wide, with land allocations on the Euphrates near Emar to the south of Carchemish, for example, a centralised state system seems unlikely. The situation was fluid and hegemony may have been more as Liverani characterizes: "the definition of boundaries not as lines but as lists of settlements politically and economically oriented toward the respective royal palaces" (quoted in Lafont 1999, 52 n. 25).

A general consensus that touches on the political geography of our region is the existence of several places with high ranking officials known as *badalum*. The title refers to the king's substitute, or merchant, or trader, and they are found in cities in the area between Urfa and Gaziantep, immediately north of Carchemish. This *badalum* region with its distinctive political structure may have come into existence because of the intermediary role played by kingdoms there in the metals exchange system (Bonechi 1998, 235).

A polity that seems to have been located in this region of Syro-Anatolia had an organisation that suggests the co-existence of yet other political systems. *Luatum* apparently did not have a king, but was controlled by a group of elders. It was situated to the east, between Ebla and Abarsal (Archi 1989) or on the west bank of the Euphrates, south of the confluence between it and the Sajur (Milano and Rova 2000, 722–723, fig. 3). The polity possessed 52 forts (*bàd^{ki} - bàd^{ki}*). They may be no more than small strongholds, perhaps just fortified villages, but they suggest that some relatively minor polities included a network of defended sites and so held coherent territory. Such a configuration may have a bearing on our understanding of the proliferation of small sites in the region of Carchemish in the second half of the 3rd millennium BC.

In sum, with their focus on trade and conflict, the Ebla texts, considered together with the many heavily defended Early Bronze Age sites in the Middle Euphrates valley, have led some scholars to conclude that our region was a politically fragmented buffer zone and a 'theatre of war' (Milano and Rova 2000, 735–738).

As part of the post-survey investigations we organized a special session on the Land of Carchemish Project for the annual British Association of Near Eastern Archaeologists (BANEA) conference in Manchester, 8–10 June 2012. This provided the opportunity for many of the authors listed in this volume to present initial findings and obtain some feedback. We then supplemented this list with additional papers on the Land of Carchemish: these include the Neo-Hittite period (Brown and Smith, Chapter 3), the Classical, Roman, Late Antique and Roman periods (Newson, Chapter 9), and the destruction of archaeological sites (Cunliffe, Chapter 10). Here we have no intention of summarizing the detailed sequence of the part of the site that is within Turkey, because, as mentioned above, this work is currently ongoing (Marchetti 2012, 2014). However, we are grateful to Dr Marchetti for sending a presentation on the latest results which was read by Mark Weeden at the June 2012 BANEA meeting.

Layout of the volume

This volume commences with a summary and synthesis of the history of Carchemish by J.D. Hawkins and Mark Weeden, beginning with the period in which it was the seat of the Hittite viceroy in Syria and ending with the

termination of Neo-Assyrian occupation, when the textual references for the site diminish (Chapter 2). Here it is necessary to make a clarification of the spelling: although Carchemish, rather than Karkamish/Karkemish, is used throughout most of the chapters in this volume, because epigraphic convention tends to prefer Karkamish or Turkish usage Karkemish, Karkamish has been used in Chapter 2. However, it has been necessary to retain the spelling of Carchemish for the remaining chapters because this was the name of the original field project beginning in 2006, and The Land of Carchemish Project (LCP) has been used for all subsequent field records and publications.

The volume continues with a regional overview of the Land of Carchemish as it is defined by archaeological features and key historical references through to the early Iron Age (Chapter 3, by Brown and Smith). Importantly, these observations provide insightful snapshots of the dynamics of an ancient state which can now be seen to have fluctuated dramatically in size throughout some 700–800 years, in part depending upon the power of the king of Carchemish or the aggressions of external powers.

Chapter 4 presents the major results from the Land of Carchemish Project to provide an overview of the main trends of settlement in the region over some 8000 years. Importantly, and building upon the PhD theses of Dan Lawrence and Andrea Ricci, the authors chart settlement from a combination of survey data bases to both north and south of the Syrian-Turkish border. Key to the success of this synthesis has been the help supplied by Professor Guillermo Algaze (Birecek-Carchemish Dam surveys; Algaze *et al.* 1994) and the survey conducted by Mehmet Özdoğan and Necmi Karul in the Birecik district to the east of the Euphrates (hereafter KOS) (Özdoğan and Karul 2002). In Chapter 4 the focus is upon the earlier phases of settlement from the Neolithic until the end of the Bronze Age (LBA) when Carchemish became an outpost of the Hittite empire.

The regional perspective on settlement continues in Chapter 5, beginning with a discussion of the physical and cultural landscapes of the Land of Carchemish Project. Following a summary of the geomorphology of the region and its relationship to the issue of site survival, this chapter focuses upon the Iron Age, a period blessed by numerous historical records, some blood-thirsty, others prosaic, some of which can be traced in the modern landscape. In addition, Chapter 5 discusses the Classical and later landscapes as they have been explored using off-site survey and related techniques.

Chapter 6, by Jesper Eidem, is the first of a series of more focussed chapters which explore site-specific aspects of the regional archaeology. In this chapter, Eidem draws particular attention to a series of important sites along the southern boundary of the survey area on the Sajur river, some of which were positioned along the main campaign routes of the Assyrian kings. Not only does this chapter contribute fundamental insights into the nature of boundaries in the region, it also provides crucial anchor points for the archaeology.

In Chapter 7, Edgar Peltenburg discusses the close relationship between the Early Bronze Age (EBA) site of Tell Jerablus Tahtani and Carchemish, located some 5 km to the north. Although the precise size and archaeological sequence of the city of Carchemish during the 3rd millennium BC remains unclear it is suggested that during phases when Tell Jerablus Tahtani was abandoned (specifically around 2250 BC) the city of Carchemish itself expanded to accommodate the additional population.

Chapter 8, by Eleanor Wilkinson and Andrea Ricci, summarizes the results from the Carchemish Outer Town survey conducted in 2009 and 2010. These campaigns, which took place in the 40 ha outer town as defined by the British Museum team, provide important new data sources regarding the layout, defences and dates of occupation of this significant part of the city as well as a reassessment of the original town plan produced by C.L. Woolley and P.L.O. Guy in 1920.

The latest phases to be discussed, namely the periods of the Classical, Roman, Byzantine and Early Islamic occupations, are presented by Paul Newson as Chapter 9. In addition to discussing the later history of the city of Carchemish, this chapter describes and discusses the later stages of settlement and material culture of the land of Carchemish Project area.

It is important to appreciate that the exploration and investigations of Carchemish have taken place within dynamic and sometimes tempestuous economic and political climates: e.g. the growth of mechanized agriculture, the construction of railways, two World Wars, the creation of both the Syrian and the Turkish states together with their borders, as well as the current Syrian conflict. The conflicts, together with the intervening periods of political stability, have resulted in a considerable attrition of the archaeological features. Therefore in Chapter 10, Emma Cunliffe summarizes the evidence for this attrition mainly for the past fifty years (based upon Cunliffe 2013).

The overall narrative is brought to a close by a discussion (Chapter 11) which emphasizes the main results of the LCP campaigns and how they illuminate the historical context of Carchemish. Although the project may be seen as representing many sites and periods, it also was based upon a significant degree of inter-disciplinary research which crossed many chronological, academic and geographical boundaries. We therefore hope that this final Chapter brings out insights and connections which might otherwise have been lost.

Finally, we include an Appendix, in the form of a gazetteer, which summarises the basic details of the sites (LCP 1–80) recorded by the Land of Carchemish Project survey, together with locational and other relevant data on Table A.1. This Appendix is not intended to act as a final report on the survey, but rather to provide the basic data which will allow readers to check on site details not covered in the preceding chapters.

Acknowledgements

The Land of Carchemish Project was made possible though the kind permission of the Directorate General of Antiquities and Museums, Syria. We are very grateful to Directors General, Dr. Tammam Fakouche and Dr. Bassam Jamous, and to the Director of Excavations, Dr. Michel al-Maqdissi for their wise advice and valued support. We benefitted greatly from the efforts and energies of the staff of the National Museum Aleppo, especially Dr. Nadim Faqish, Dr. Joussef Kanjo, and our Government Representative, Mohammed Ali, all of whom were enormously helpful in facilitating our fieldwork.

The Project was fortunate to receive financial support from the British Academy, the Council for British Research in the Levant and the Global Heritage Fund.

We extend special thanks to Andrew Moore for further information on his survey material and permission to study it in the National Museum. We would also like to thank the CBRL, especially Bill Finlayson and Nadja Qaisi, for their expertise and administrative assistance.

The LCP was very much a team effort. The editors warmly thank our colleagues who participated in the field and in post-survey analysis of recovered material. They include: Emma Cunliffe (2010), Maria Bianca D'Anna (2010), Danny Donoghue (2010), Michael Brown (2006), Dan Lawrence (2009–10), Niko Galiatsatos (2010), Andrew McCarthy (2006–09), Paul Newson (2006–2010), Silvia Perini (2006–09), Louise Rayne (2010), Andrea Ricci (2008–10), Miranda Semple (2006), Stefan L. Smith (2008), Leigh Stork (2009), and Dan Thompson (2010).

Bibliography

Ainsworth, W.F. (1888) *A Personal Narrative of the Euphrates Expedition*. London, Kegan Paul and Co.

Algaze, G., Breuninger, R. and Knudstad, J. (1994) The Tigris–Euphrates archaeological reconnaissance project: final report of the Birecik and Carchemish Dam survey area. *Anatolica* 20, 1–96.

Archi, A. (1989) La ville d'Abarsal. In M. Lebeau and P. Talon (eds) *Reflets des deux fleuves: volume de mélanges offerts à André Finet*. Akkadica Supplementum VI, 15–19. Leuven, Peeters.

Archi, A. (1996) Polity interaction in the age of Ebla. In F. Ismail (ed.) *Proceedings of the International Symposium on Syria and the Ancient Near East 3000–300 BC*, 13–18. Aleppo, University of Aleppo.

Archi, A. (2011) In search of Armi. *Journal of Cuneiform Studies* 63, 5–34.

Archi, A. and Biga, M.G. (2003) A victory over Mari and the fall of Ebla. *Journal of Cuneiform Studies* 55, 1–44.

Bell, G.L. (1910) The east bank of the Euphrates from Tell Ahmar to Hit. *Geographical Journal* 36 (5), 513–37.

Bell, G.L. (1924) *Amurath to Amurath*. London, Macmillan.

Biga, M.G. (2014) Karkemish in the Ebla texts: some new data. In N. Marchetti (ed.) *Karkemish. An Ancient Capital on the Euphrates*. Orient Lab 2, 75–80. Bologna, Ante Quem.

Bonechi, M. (1998) Remarks on the III millennium geographical names of the Syrian Upper Mesopotamia. In M. Lebeau (ed.) *About Subartu: Studies devoted to Upper Mesopotamia*. Subartu 4 (1), 219–241. Turnhout, Brepols.

Bunnens, G. (2007) Site hierarchy in the Tishrin Dam area and third millennium geopolitics in Northern Syria. In E. Peltenburg (ed.) *Euphrates River Valley Settlement. The Carchemish Sector in the Third Millennium BC*. Levant Supplementary Series 5, 43–54. Oxford, Oxbow Books.

Cunliffe, E. (2013) *Satellites and Site Destruction: An Analysis of Modern Impacts on the Archaeological Resource of the Ancient Near East*. PhD Thesis, Durham University.

Gilibert, A. (2011) *Syro-Hittite Monumental Art and the Archaeology of Performance: The Stone Reliefs of Carchemish and Zincirli in the Earlier First Millennium BC*. Berlin, Walter de Gruyter.

Harmanşah, Ö. (2013) *Cities and the Shaping of Memory in the Ancient Near East*. Cambridge, Cambridge University Press.

Hawkins, J.D. (2000) *Corpus of Hieroglyphic Luwian Inscriptions. vol. 1–3. Inscriptions of the Iron Age*. Berlin, de Gruyter.

Lafont, B. (1999) Le proche-orient à l'époque des rois de Mari: un monde sans frontières? In L. Milano, S. de Martino, F. Fales and G. Lanfranchi (eds) *Landscapes, Territories, Frontiers and Horizons in the Ancient Near East (Part I: Invited lectures)*. Papers presented to the XLIV Rencontre Assyriologique Intrernationale Venezia, 7–11 July 1997, 47–55. Padova, S.A.R.G.O.N.

Marchetti, N. (2012) Karkemish on the Euphrates. Excavating a City's History. *Near Eastern Archaeology* 75 (3), 132–147.

Marchetti, N. (ed.) (2014) *Karkemish. An Ancient Capital on the Euphrates*. Orient Lab 2, Bologna, Ante Quem.

Milano, L. and Rova, E. (2000) Ceramic provinces and political borders in Upper Mesopotamia in the late Early Dynastic period. In S. Graziani (ed.) *Studi sul Vicino Oriente Antico dedicati alla memoria di Luigi Cagni*, 709–749. Napoli, Istituto Universitario Orientale.

Moorey, P.R.S. (1980) *Cemeteries of the First Millennium BC at Deve Höyük near Carchemish Salvaged by T.E. Lawrence and C.L. Woolley in 1913*. Oxford, BAR 887.

Özdoğan, M. and Karul, N. (2002) Birecik – Suruç Arkeolojik Envanter Raporu. In *Birecik – Suruç Türkiye Kültür Envanteri Pilot Bölge Çalışmaları*. Istanbul, Arkeoloji ve Sanat Yay. TÜBA TÜKSEK yay, 1–101.

Peltenburg, E. (ed.) (2007) *Euphrates River Valley Settlement: The Carchemish Sector in the Third Millennium BC*. Levant Supplementary Series 5. Oxford, Oxbow Books.

Sachau, E. (1883) *Reise in Syrien und Mesopotamien*. Leipzig, F.A. Brockhaus.

Sanlaville, P. (ed.) (1985) *Holocene Settlement in north Syria: résultats de deux prospections archae archéologiques effectuées dans la région du nahr Sajour et sur le haut Euphrate syrien*. Oxford, BAR S238.

Vivancos, A.E. (2005) *Eufratense et Osrhoene: poblamiento Romano en el alto Éufrates Sirio*. Murcia, Universidad de Murcia, Servicio de Publicaciones.

Wilkinson, T.J., Peltenburg, E., McCarthy, A., Wilkinson, E.B. and Brown M. (2007) Archaeology in the Land of Carchemish: landscape surveys in the area of Jerablus Tahtani, 2006. *Levant* 39, 213–247.

Winter, I.J. (1983) Carchemish *ša kišad puratti*. *Anatolian Studies* 33, 177–197.

Sketch history of Karkamish in the earlier Iron Age (Iron I–IIB)

J.D. Hawkins and M. Weeden

The city of Karkamish had served as the seat of the Hittite viceroy in Syria, where a line of direct descendants of the Hittite Great King Suppiluliuma I had administered Hittite rule in Syria since the mid-14th century BC. The end of the Hittite Empire remains a complex of events that is largely shrouded in mystery. Building on a narrative mainly constructed from Egyptian sources historians had until recently seen the Hittites engulfed in the flames of widespread upheavals associated with large-scale population movements and multiple destructions of sites along the Levantine littoral and in northern Syria.[1] More recent appraisals of events towards the end of the Hittite capital at Hattusa (modern Boğazkale/-köy) in central Anatolia have suggested rather that the city was abandoned in a more or less organised way before any destruction by fire occurred (Seeher 1998, 515–523). It has also been clear since the discovery of the seal of Kuzi-Teššub, king of Karkamish and son of the last known Hittite viceroy at Karkamish, that some kind of continuity exists between the end of the Late Bronze Age Hittite Empire and its Iron Age successor state in northern Syria (Hawkins 1988). Everything else, however, is entirely unclear.

The early 20th century excavations at Karkamish revealed next to no Late Bonze Age remains, a state of affairs which has even of late led to suggestions that the Hittite imperial seat was not situated at the site of the Iron Age city (Summers apud Aro 2013; Summers 2013, 316). At the time of writing new excavations conducted by N. Marchetti have not yet conclusively answered this challenge, but the material evidence for significant Late Bronze Age occupation at the site is growing (Marchetti 2012; Marchetti 2013). The extent of Hittite imperial control in the areas beyond the central Anatolian heartland is also

a matter of discussion. Some scholars refrain from using the word "Empire" to describe the political form taken by Hittite hegemony whether in Syria or elsewhere, eschewing the notion of a centralized economic and administrative unit for that of a network of interlocking and competing interest groups.[2] The suddenness of the disappearance of Hittite control could be explained from this perspective by the fragility of its grip on the areas subordinated to it (Summers 2013, 316).

Against this view is ranged the picture of a rump state of the Hittite Empire in Northern Syria that survived the fall of the Empire and carried on using the same instruments of propaganda, Hieroglyphic Luwian inscriptions, the same religious and military ideology, and a similar set of titles and offices as those that characterized Late Bronze Age Hittite state, society and culture. This rump state, however, at least by the 11th century BC, would not have had its capital at Karkamish, but further to the West in the Amuq plain, centred around the newly re-settled Kinaliya (Tell Tayınat), just opposite the site of a massive LBA Hittite fortress at Alalakh (Tell Atchana).[3] During this period Karkamish is supposed to have been weak. The scarcity of specifically Early Iron Age (Iron Ia) material culture at the site is also surprising, whether or not one can link this to any kind of political inferiority. From the 10th century down to its annexation by the Neo-Assyrian Empire in 717 BC Karkamish remained the centre of a thriving, wealthy and international trade network with a monumental culture itself befitting the centre of an Empire rather than the hub of a small state on the fringes of one. Its changing geographical boundaries and enduring topographical features are explored in the paper by M. Brown and S. Smith in this volume (Chapter 3).

The 12th century BC

Despite the declaration of Ramesses III to the contrary, it does not appear archaeologically to be the case, nor is it apparent from external textual records, that Karkamish was destroyed around the end of the Late Bronze Age.[4] The attestation of Kuzi-Teššub, king of Karkamish, son of Talmi-Teššub, King of Karkamish, both on seal-impressions from Northern Syria and in a cuneiform text at Boğazköy, has been held to indicate a continuity of rule at Karkamish beyond the fall of the central Hittite Empire.[5]

More information concerning the end of the Hittite Empire around 1192 BC is now available from as yet unpublished cuneiform tablets found at the Assyrian outpost at Tell Ṣabi Abyad on the Balih river in northern Syria. In one letter references are made to a presumably recent conflict between the former Hittite dependency of Emar on the Middle Euphrates and Karkamish.[6] The conflict would appear to have been resolved. A further letter asks for information concerning the "Land of Hatti", which must refer to the central Anatolian Hittite state.[7] This must be around the time of Kuzi-Teššub himself.

Possibly shortly after this, cuneiform texts from Emar mention a people referred to as the *tár-wa*, who have besieged the town (Arnaud 1991, no. 25 and 44; Singer 2000, 25). This must be from a time shortly before the destruction of Emar in 1175 BC, a date arrived at on the basis of a date-formula using the name of the Kassite king Meli-Šipak on a tablet from Emar (Cohen 2004, 95). The famous Ankara Silver Bowl may also belong in this period, with its dating by means of the phrase "in the year that T[udhaliya] Labarna smote the Tarwean land".[8] "Labarna", a Late Bronze Age Hittite royal title, would appear to indicate a supreme executive of some kind in the imperial Hittite tradition, but it is unclear where this character, T[udhaliya] (?), would have been located.[9] The inscription itself commemorates the fashioning, purchase or dedication, depending on interpretation, of the bowl on which it is found "in the presence of king Maza/i-Karhuha" by an individual called Asmaya. Maza/i-Karhuha contains as a theophoric element a divine name which is only ever found at Karkamish and in the immediate vicinity (Tell Ahmar), written with a sign (*kar*) that is only otherwise used to write the name of Karkamish. This person was thus likely to have been king there. It is possible that the relationship "Labarna: King" in some way prefigures the relationship "Great King: Country Lord" which is found at Karkamish from the 10th century BC onwards, where it seems likely that both the "Country Lord" and his "Great King" would have been located at Karkamish, although this is not definitively secure. Might one also have had a "Labarna" and a separate "King" in the 12th century at Karkamish?[10]

G. Summers argues that the Late Bronze Age Hittite grip on the region from Malatya down to Karkamish was weak, due to lack of Late Bronze Age occupation at Lidar Höyük and now, as currently seems to be the case from the latest readings of the dendrochronological data, also at Tille Höyük (Summers 2013). Here the current interpretation of the archaeological record would seem to be in conflict with that won from texts, where Kuzi-Teššub, a figure straddling Late Bronze and Early Iron Ages, is certainly attested at Lidar.

Kuzi-Teššub, is not only known from impressions of his elaborate seal found at Lidar Höyük, but also from the inscriptions of the kings of Malatya, two of whom claim to be his "grandson" or "descendant" (Hawkins 1988; 2000, 285–287). The earliest Malatya inscriptions are dated to the late 12th or early 11th century BC on this basis, although the dating has recently been questioned (Singer 2012, 471). Lidar Höyük is itself halfway upstream from Karkamish towards Malatya along the Euphrates. A viable route between Karkamish and Malatya may have run along the river a certain way by boat, but is made virtually impassable by a deep gorge just before Malatya. The intervening terrain is mountainous and difficult to traverse, but roads did and do exist. Are we then to understand that Karkamish and Malatya formed some kind of political unit in the Early Iron Age? Or is it merely that the local kings legitimized their claims via the king of Karkamish as direct descendant of the Great Kings of Hattusa?

Doubtless belonging to the same geography as Malatya on topographical grounds is the Karahöyük-Elbistan stele, to be dated to sometime in the 12th century BC, in which a local official called Armanani apparently celebrates the visit of a "Great King" Ir(i)-Teššub to a country the name of which cannot yet be read due to being written logographically.[11] T.R. Bryce has supposed that the "Great King" in Karahöyük-Elbistan would have come from Karkamish, which is certainly worthy of consideration and F. Giusfredi suggests that the name is a by-form of the ancestral Karkamish ruler's name Ini-Teššub, predecessor of Talmi-Teššub king of Karkamish from the Empire Period (Bryce 2012, 86; Giusfredi 2010, 41). It is unlikely, however, that this name would have been misspelled in this way.

Palaeographically the inscription shows a number of similarities with those of the "Great King" Hartapu at Karadağ-Kızıldağ and Burunkaya on the southern Anatolian plateau, in particular in the shape of the sign/*sa*/.[12] These latter are almost certainly to be associated either directly with the late 13th century and possibly even still post-Hittite Empire kingdom of Tarhuntassa (classical Rough Cilicia), or with its successor state. Quite what form and extent such an Anatolian rump state of the Hittite Empire would have had, if it in fact existed, is currently difficult to determine on archaeological grounds, as well as being beyond the scope of this contribution. Thus in both these cases, Karkamish-Malatya and Elbistan-Tarhuntassa, the style and/or content of inscriptional evidence seems to hint at units of some kind existing over and above what might be considered to be "natural" geographical boundaries. In the current state of our knowledge it is impossible to say whether these units were political in any sense.[13]

11th century BC

The annals of Tiglath-Pileser I of Assyria (r. 1114–1086 BC) document for the year 1100 BC an encounter with a king called "Ini-Teššub, king of the land of Hatti".[14] Although not explicitly stated in the text, it is commonly assumed that this must have taken place at Karkamish itself. The names Karkamish and Hatti are frequently used interchangeably in Neo-Assyrian documents. The city may have inherited the toponymic designation of the Late Bronze Age Hittites. The assumption that the Ini-Teššub encountered by Tiglath-Pileser I was at Karkamish carries with it the implicit acceptance of a hypothesis that Karkamish continued as a Hittite capital throughout the 12th and into the 11th century. This must, however, be reconcilable with the fact that material remains for Iron I are poorly represented at the site.

A further variant of the rump state continuity view sees the Hittite centre shift south-west towards the Amuq and the kingdom of Walastin most likely centred at Tell Tayinat. In the 11th century a king of this "land of Palastin" had influence over the temple of the storm-god at Aleppo, only *c.* 100 km to the south-west of Karkamish. Two inscriptions of Taita, king of Palastin, dated to the 11th century on palaeographic grounds, were found in the Aleppo Temple (Hawkins 2011). One of these not only mentions Karkamish, but also Egypt.[15] The immediate context for mentioning Karkamish is damaged. There is no agreement that such a mention in an inscription of Palistin implies that Karkamish was in any way subjugated to this potentially larger territory at this stage (Hawkins 2011, 53; Weeden 2013, 17). See the accompanying contribution by M. Brown and S. Smith (Chapter 3) for consideration of the expanding and shrinking physical borders of Karkamish, especially in their relationship to the Quweiq valley and Aleppo.

Consideration of the status of Karkamish at this stage may also be tied in with that of Malatya and the intervening area of the Euphrates states, as in the previous century. The latest archaeological research at Malatya indicates that the city experienced degradation to a "squatter" occupation during the mid-11th century, which lasted until its eventual re-flowering in the 9th century BC (Liverani 2012; Frangipane and Liverani 2013). The late 12th and early 11th centuries, on the other hand, saw Malatya exhibiting a flourishing monumental culture and two of its kings claiming descent from Kuzi-Teššub, king of Karkamish. At the time of the encounter between Tiglath-Pileser I and Ini-Teššub of Hatti (= Karkamish) the ruler of Malatya was known as Allumari according to Assyrian royal inscriptions.[16] In the Assyrian

royal view at least these were separate entities, both of which had sufficient status to warrant being mentioned in the course of campaign narrative.

The area between Karkamish and Malatya may itself have experienced a renaissance of sorts during the mid-12th century, before falling into decline in the early 11th century. Summers also notes that the 12th century architecture of Tille Höyük, in particular the gate, does not appear to be "imperial", although he associates it with a supra-regional state on the North Syrian Euphrates that reached as far as Malatya (Summers 2013, 317). Whatever we conclude from this, a similar development of decline during the 11th century both at Malatya and at Tille can be observed. Whether this was a regional phenomenon and whether that reached as far as Karkamish are both points which are unclear.

10th century BC

From the 10th century at the latest and through the early 9th Karkamish was ruled by a dynasty of so-called "Country Lords", during the earlier part of this period also in some sort of tandem with a "Great King" (Hawkins 1995; Payne 2014). The chronological framework for these rulers is delimited at the lower end of the period by the encounter of the Assyrian king Shalmaneser III with "Sangara the Karkamishean" as part of an anti-Assyrian coalition including Gurgum, Sam'al and Patin in 858 BC.[17] This Sangara is not yet mentioned in any of the published native inscriptions and is thus assumed to be later than them. The two earliest inscriptions belong to a father and son, one stela erected by Suhi I "Country-Lord" and one by his son, the "Priest of Kubaba". The texts appear to be almost identical in content and are both dedicated to Ura-Tarhunda, "Great King, Hero, King of the Land of Karkamish, son of Sapaziti, Great King, Hero".[18] We thus have a Great King, a Country Lord and a priest of Kubaba, with inscriptions only being prepared by the last two, who were also related.

Suhi I calls himself a *muwida* of the king, using a logogram that is otherwise also found in the early Malatya inscriptions and is shown by later usage to have the afore-mentioned phonetic form.[19] The precise meaning is unclear, but a translation "seed(?)" is currently the best available, indicating that the Country Lord was possibly a distant blood relative of the Great King. The later inscription of KELEKLİ, from the reign of the grandson of Suhi I, Suhi II, indicates that intermarriage was also possible between the lines of "Great Kings" and "Country Lords" (Hawkins 2000, 93).

The earliest two inscriptions mention a conflict that came from the land of Sura. It has recently been proposed to identify this Sura with the designation "Leukosyroi" given by Greek authors to the Cappadocians and to assume that it was the native designation of the land called Tabal by the

Neo-Assyrians (Simon 2012). This proposal is essentially without foundation in the native inscriptions. The toponym Sura is more conventionally equated with Assyria, as unequivocally demonstrated by the correspondence between a toponym 'šr in the Phoenician text of the 8th century BC ÇİNEKÖY Bilingual and Sura in the Hieroglyphic Luwian of the same text.[20] This identification has to contend with the consideration that Assyria was apparently weak in military and economic terms at the end of the 11th/beginning of the 10th century BC and might not have been expected to be conducting campaigns as far west as the Euphrates. Assyrian activity is attested on the Habur during this period (Grayson 1991, 126-127, Weeden 2013, 10).

The first longer narrative inscription was written by Suhi II, son of Astuwalamanza, grandson of Suhi I, and erected to accompany the Long Wall of Sculpture at Karkamish sometime during the 10th century BC.[21] It concerns injury done to and revenge exacted on behalf of the Storm-god of S(a)mar(i)ka, which H.C. Melchert compared with the Late Bronze Age Hittite toponym Ismerikka (Melchert 1988, 37). Siverek in the direction of Diyarbakir has often been identified with Ismerikka, although this identification is tentative.[22] The place-names Alatahana and Hazauna, which are mentioned in a hostile context by Suhi II in his inscription, have also not been located.[23] It is thus not possible to assess the extent of any military campaign in which Suhi II may have been involved. The mention of Hazauna, however, is closely followed by a fragmentary reference to a "grandfather" and "(of) my city", so it is possible that Suhi was re-asserting earlier territorial claims.[24]

The son of Suhi II, Katuwa, is by far the most prolifically attested among the authors of inscriptions. In the inscription KARKAMISH A11b+c we learn of an apparent transaction, according to the latest interpretation of the verb in question, (LOCUS)*pit(a)haliya*, between Katuwa and the "Grandsons of Ura-Tarhunda".[25] This may refer to the same Ura-Tarhunda who was "Great King" at the time of Suhi I, the great-grandfather of Katuwa. However, if the grandsons of Ura-Tarhunda are at all related to the Great Kings of the reigns of Suhi I and II, they are not given that title and this is the last we hear of them.

The passage is disputed, but the latest interpretation, offered by H.C. Melchert, implies that "this city", i.e. Karkamish, had both been empty for some time and previously belonged to a man called Ninuwi. Katuwa is supposed by Melchert to have rebuilt it, possibly exchanging it with the grandsons of Ura-Tarhunda for land-holdings of some kind in two other towns, Ipani and Muzik (Melchert 2011, 75–77). The latter of these might be associated with the Mount Munziganni to the west of Karkamish encountered by Aššurnaṣirpal II in 870 BC (Hawkins 2000, 105). While this interpretation is philologically possible, it is historically unlikely given the significant building activity at Karkamish registered by Katuwa's predecessor, Suhi II.

Katuwa almost certainly experienced a revolt at some time in his reign, presumably by relatives of his, who are referred to as the 20-*tá-ti-zi* in KARKAMISH A11a §5–6 (Hawkins 2000, 97). Comparison with occurrence of the same word in TELL AHMAR 1 makes it likely that these are "relatives",[26] while the verb used (*ARHA* CRUS+*RA/I*) suggests "secession" when compared with similar Late Bronze Age Hittite locutions.[27] Rather than these "relatives" being identical with the grandsons of Ura-Tarhunda, as previously assumed (Hawkins 2000, 97) it is possible that these latter helped Katuwa regain the city from the secession of the former, with the verb (LOCUS)*pit(a)haliya-* referring to the manner in which this occurred, whatever that was. An etymological explanation does not suggest itself, nor is it necessary. The further mention of the particular kind of land-holdings in the cities of Ipani and Muzik may then refer to additional confiscations, rather than gifts in exchange. Here the verb is lost in a break.[28]

Indeed, the narrative continues with further military achievements which took place in the year in which Katuwa completed the building of the "upper floors" for his wife which the inscription is commemorating.[29] These consist of "I carried/moved the chariotry of the city *Kawa/i*", and of the standard trope of marching further than any of one's ancestors.[30] This ethnic adjective *Kawiza-* has been interpreted as corresponding to the Assyrian provincial place-name Que (Plain of Cilicia), which is occasionally spelled Qaue in Assyrian cuneiform.[31]

However, it remains rather problematic why Karkamish inscriptions should refer to this place as *Kawa/i* when the Cilician ÇİNEKÖY inscription from the 8th century BC and now the two new stelae from ARSUZ from the 10th century BC, which commemorate a victory of the Walastinean king Suppiluliuma in the region, refer to the area as Hiyawa.[32] One would have to hypothesize that Karkamish, concomitant with its geographical location, uses a form of the name that was more usual either further to the east, possibly even forming the point of departure for the Assyrian borrowing of the name Q(a)ue itself, or in Aramaic.[33] Until the place-name Hiyawa is found on inscriptions from Karkamish, thus excluding that *Kawa/i* refers to the same area, the matter cannot be considered closed.

An identification of *Kawa/i* with Que, or at least with part of it, also tallies with the apparently western focus of the previous engagements, if Muzik can be associated with Mount Munziganni. It is thus interesting that both the land of Walastin and the land of Karkamish had military engagements with Que/Hiyawa during the 10th and early 9th centuries BC. This is doubtless to be seen in the light of the increasing wealth and resources that accrued to the diverse Neo-Hittite states during an economic upturn after the Early Iron Age period. Increased resources mean increased potential for the exercise of expansionist tendencies. It is into this heating cauldron of conflicting territorial interests that the Assyrians marched in the second quarter of the 9th century BC.

9th century BC

For the bulk of the 9th century, inscriptions from Karkamish are lacking, although Katuwa might well fit into the beginning of this period and its end may accommodate the earlier inscriptions of the next dynasty to rule the city that is known from native inscriptions. Most of our information during this period is to be found in Assyrian royal inscriptions.

Neo-Assyrian policy towards Karkamish follows an interesting pattern of isolation, Karkamish being the last Neo-Hittite territory in Northern Syria to be annexed to the Assyrian Empire in 717 BC. By this time all the other Neo-Hittite states had first been reduced to vassal-status and then annexed to the Empire and provided with an Assyrian governor.

When Shalmaneser III (859–824 BC) crossed the Euphrates in 858 BC he seems to have done so to the north of Karkamish into the territory of Kummuh, and then moved around it into Gurgum and then Sam'al, where he met the forces of an anti-Assyrian alliance including Karkamish (Yamada 2000, 92). When he receives the tribute of the defeated enemies in the next year at Dabigu, after apparently dealing with Til-Barsip and the lands of Bit-Adini to the south and south-west of Karkamish, Karkamish itself is conspicuously absent from the list of tributaries recorded on the stone slab from Fort Shalmaneser.[34] According to the reconstruction of Shigeo Yamada this recalcitrance prompts an approach towards Karkamishean territory at Sazabê, "a fortified city of Sangara the Karkamishean".[35] The Kurkh monolith records the receipt of tribute by all the fearful "kings of the land H[atti]" after this action, including that of Karkamish, thus conflating the submission of tribute by Karkamish with that of the other states.[36]

Sangara appears already in the Balawat Bronze Bands of Aššurnaṣirpal II (883–859 BC) as a tributary of the Assyrian king, probably at some time between 875 and 868 BC (Yamada 2000, 74–75). He also appears in years 1, 2, 6, 10 and 11 of Shalmaneser III (859–824 BC) (Yamada 2000, 117 fn. 146). In the last of these Shalmaneser boasts of capturing 97 of his cities.[37] This does not necessarily indicate that Karkamish was any bigger than any of its neighbours. Certainly, however, the above-noted initial hesitancy of Shalmaneser in dealing with the state of Karkamish, and the apparent re-focussing of the narrative of the second regnal year in the Kurkh Monolith to place the panic of the "Kings of H[atti]" after the attack on Sazabê are both indications that the Assyrians perceived the "Land of Karkamish" as the strongest and most important of the Neo-Hittite states during the 9th century BC. If there ever

had been any competition with the "Land of Walastin" (= Patin) during earlier centuries, this had been entirely overcome by now. Sangara himself, however, is likely to have been so tested by his Assyrian adversaries that he failed to leave any clearly identifiable inscriptional traces at the city of Karkamish itself.

Late 9th to 8th centuries BC

Apart from a brief mention by Samši-Adad V (824–811 BC), Karkamish does not appear in Assyrian sources from the mid-9th until the mid-8th century BC.[38] This is peculiar, as the Assyrians were clearly established very close by, only 20 km downstream, at Kar-Shalmaneser (formerly Til-Barsip, modern Tell Ahmar) during the whole of this period. Karkamish is not mentioned in the Pazarcık stela from 805 BC which includes details of pitched battle between Adad-Nerari III and an alliance of Ataršumki of Arpad and eight other kings at nearby Paqirahubuna.[39] Adad-Nerari III and his commander (*turtānu*), Šamši-ilu, established a border between Ataršumki of Arpad and Zakur of Hamath around 796 BC according to the Eponym Chronicle and the Antakya stele, an event probably to be related to that narrated in the Aramaic stele of the same Zakur from Tell Afis.[40] Here we are told that Bar-Guš (=Ataršumki of Bit-Agusi) had attacked Zakur at the instigation of Hazael of Damascus in an alliance with kings of Que, Unqi, Gurgum, Sam'al, Melid and two or three other names which are lost in damage to the text. It would be strange if Karkamish were not mentioned here. However, the city is also not mentioned in the alliance led by Urartu and Arpad which was defeated by Tiglath-Pileser III in 743 BC, nor in any of the successive Assyrian actions against Arpad (742–740 BC) and Unqi (739–738 BC), but a king Pisiri of Karkamish does finally appear in the list of tributary kings from 738 BC.[41] This same Pisiri appears to have still been in power in 717 BC when Sargon II had him removed and deported to Assyria for colluding with Mita of Muski, and finally annexed the land of Karkamish to the Assyrian Empire.[42]

However, the period of the late 9th and first half of the 8th centuries coincides with a renewal of activity in the inscriptions and building work at Karkamish. Possibly Assyria was consciously leaving Karkamish alone during this period, a policy hardly fit to be mentioned in royal inscriptions, or there were yet other reasons for the Assyrian silence. Karen Radner has identified an Assyrian imperial tendency to leave major trading centres to their own devices, as long as politically expedient, in order to be able to profit from their already established and functioning networks and infrastructures.[43] Certainly Karkamish appears to have been left until last among all the Neo-Hittite states before being turned into a province.

During this period we find three generations of builders

and inscription-makers at Karkamiš. A king Astiruwa is referred to in the inscription of KÖRKÜN (Hawkins 2000, 171), who is then succeeded by a regent, Yariri, calling himself "ruler" (*tarwani-*), who appears to be a eunuch and has responsibility for the care of Astiruwa's son, Kamani, as well as for the rest of the family. Kamani apparently presides as "ruler", "country-lord" (REGIO.DOMINUS), and also once as "king", over a short-term expansion or consolidation of Karkamishean influence towards the Quweiq river, as possibly evidenced in the inscription found at Cekke, and is later replaced by an Astiru, who is not his son, but that of his vizier, Sastura. New evidence indicates that there may have also been a son of Kamani, called Atika, who for some reason did not become king or ruler (Akdoğan 2013; Hawkins *et al.* 2013). It is possible, but not certain, that the final king, Pisiri, known from the royal inscriptions of Tiglath-Pileser III and Sargon II, may also have had his name on a preserved monument at Karkamish.

The inscriptions of Yariri, who was regent while Kamani was a child, are among the most impressive and detailed from Karkamish. He was responsible for the Royal Buttress, a series of sculptures and inscriptions on orthostats added to a structure built by Katuwa beside the King's Gate. One of Katuwa's own inscriptions was thereby removed and re-used as paving slabs in the floor of the King's Gate. In the sculptures Yariri is shown, beardless and carrying a sceptre upside-down, leading Kamani by the arm, followed by the other children of Astiruwa. This depiction may suggest that he is a eunuch, as is further corroborated by the use of the word *wasinasi-* illustrated by the beardless bodyguards depicted on the Royal Buttress.[44] The word clearly refers in another context to (male) offspring who have been turned into eunuchs.[45] The structure itself is referred to as the ("MENSA.SOLIUM")*asa-*, possibly just a "seat (?)", to which Kamani used to run and where Yariri "seated him on high".[46]

International relations are prominent in the inscriptions of Yariri. On the inscription attached to the Royal Buttress he boasts that his name was heard "in Egypt, in Babylon(?), among the Musa, Muska and Sura".[47] The Musa and Muska are usually associated with Lydians (Mysioi) and Phrygians (Greek Moschoi, Assyrian Muški), but the precise associations of those terms are rather unclear. Even less clear is the identity of the Sura, supposed variously to be Urartians or the Anatolian Neo-Hittite group of states which was referred to by the Assyrians as Tabal.[48] The intended rhetorical opposition appears to be between Egypt and possibly Babylon on the southern field of the compass (west and east), and a suitably broad geographical sweep encompassing the corresponding world to the north-west and north-east of Karkamish. This understanding of the references in the inscription would make Urartu still the best candidate for Sura in this text.[49]

Another text written on a statue-base of Yariri found out of its original context refers to different types of writing and languages, after a break in the narrative:

> "… in the City's writing, in the Tyrian writing, in the Assyrian writing and in the Taimani writing, and I knew 12 languages. By means of travelling my lord *selected* every country's son for me because of language."[50]

Again, the precise the referents of the types of writing are not all agreed, in particular whether "S/Zurawani" in the text refers to Tyre (i.e. Phoenician) and whether Taimani refers to Teima and a very early stage of Early North Arabian Script, or to Aramaic via a similar-sounding tribal name known from Assyrian texts.[51] Yet the passage is clearly intended to highlight the pre-eminent position of Karkamish in the mercantile world (Radner 2004, 158). Multilingualism and knowledge of scripts rather than military engagements and conquests are here the currency in which Yariri's achievements are valued. One should be careful not to generalize from this depiction and infer a time of peace and prosperity in a military and political vacuum corresponding to silence in the Assyrian sources.

An unfortunately very broken text found among other stones at the bottom of the Great Staircase appears to have been attached to another statue of Yariri and explicitly refers to conflict with Assyria.[52] It is not entirely clear from the preserved fragments that Yariri was directly involved in the conflict, although he was active in some fashion and the context of a commemorative statue can only suggest that it was celebrating his or his lord's deeds. There is some clearly negative military action either on the part of mounted troops (?) towards a city called Parnassa, or directed by someone at mounted troops (?) from a city called Parnassi, after which Yariri becomes active in some way.[53] Then we have a clear historical reference, which has unfortunately not been identified in accounts from any of the other powers of the time: "[Wh]en(?) the Assyrian king *carried* off Halabean Tarhunzas, and he *smote* Assyria with a *firebrand* ... Kubaba (nom. or acc.) brought forth … [and Assyr]ia(?) she x-ed away"[54]

The passage is not only badly broken but also peppered with *hapax legomena*, which hinder a clear understanding beyond the relatively secure reference to what Yariri thought was an Assyrian defeat. This would presumably be far too early to refer to the defeat inflicted on Assur-Nerari V by Sarduri II of Urartu in 754 BC, only 16 years before Pisiri is attested in Assyrian Annals as king of Karkamish. It seems likely that it would have been Urartu once again which punished the Assyrians for transgressing against the Storm-God of Aleppo, but another agent of his divine displeasure cannot be ruled out. One can only speculate on the circumstances behind this tantalizing reference.

There are three monuments which explicitly belong to the reign of Kamani: the Kubaba stele with appended inscription detailing the building of her temple; the storm-god stele from

Cekke, located further to the south-west towards the Quweiq valley; and a drum commemorating a property transfer which refers to Kamani as "king" (Hawkins 2000, 140–154). In the Cekke stela, Kamani is referred to as "Country Lord of the cities Karkamish and Ma(li)zi (=Malatya?)", "ruler" and he is acting in concert with his "first servant" Sastura.[55] In the Kubaba-stele, of which the beginning is currently broken, he only refers to himself as "ruler (*tarwani*)".[56] A fragment referring to a "...] Country Lord, the Hero, son of Astiru" is also likely to be attributed to him, despite the use of the archaizing title "Hero".[57]

The reference to Malatya, although in an irregular writing which only occurs in one other Karkamish inscription, might recall the possible connection between Karkamish and Malatya which we noted during the 12th century BC and thus be a memory of much earlier dynastic claims. The Kubaba stele mentions expansionist activity: "I subjected the Pinatean fortresses to Karkamish and [resettl]ed (?) the devastated areas."[58] Unfortunately we have no idea where Pinata was located. Furthermore, the phenomenon of CEKKE itself, planted outside of the central Karkamish area, needs to be taken into consideration.

The inscription of CEKKE was set up by a "servant of Sastura" and commemorates the purchase of a town called Kamana, presumably in the region of Cekke itself, by Kamani and Sastura. The town is acquired from a group of Kanapuweans, presumably either residents of a nearby settlement which had previously exercised some sort of property rights over Kamana, or more likely previous residents of Kamana itself, which may formerly have been called Kanapu.[59] The city is "to be bound as a *kitri* (donation?)" for 20 *TAMI* and ten children, where the term *TAMI* is not understood, and a mayor and "Great Ones" are also mentioned.[60] Then "*frontier stelae*" are "to be engraved and bound as a *kitri* (donation?)" for 15 fathers and sons from a list of unidentified towns: Zilaparha (vel sim.), Hawara-, Lutapa (vel sim.), Apakuruta, Zarahanu, Sarmuta, Isata, Huhurata and Satarpa.[61] Some of the language of the stele has been supposed to reflect the language of Assyrian border-markers such as the Antakya-stele (Hawkins 2000, 147). The settlement of men and their sons in the area, after its purchase by Kamani and Sastura, may be as a reward for services rendered. See further M. Brown and S. Smith, Chapter 3, in this volume.

A damaged relief with an archaizing inscription by an author whose name is broken preserves almost exactly the same title as Kamani had on CEKKE: "... Hero, Country Lord of the city Karkamish and the land of Malatya, beloved of Kubaba".[62] However, the inscription also refers to "my father Sastu(ra)". It is possible that this is the same Sastura as the "first servant" of Kamani from the CEKKE inscription. A further fragment may fit at the beginning of the inscription, although this is not assured, and would in this case supply the name of the inscription's author: Astiru. We would then have an Astiru II, son of Sastura succeeding Kamani as ruler of Karkamish (and Malatya).[63]

From another fragmentary inscription attached to a colossal figure of a seated ruler from the South Gate we learn of a further ruler "beloved of Kubaba", whose name is broken, but whose filiation is "son of Astir[u]".[64] It is a reasonable but tentative hypothesis that we are here dealing with the last king at Karkamish, Pisiri, who is otherwise known only from Assyrian inscriptions and must have ruled for at least 21 years before the city's annexation in 717 BC. This interpretation of the inscription from the South Gate would mean that Astiru II succeeded to rule Karkamish after Kamani, despite being the son of Kamani's "first servant", and that then his son succeeded him. However, the inscription could also date to Kamani, son of Astiru(wa) I, and indeed this is supported by the script style (Hawkins 2000, 168).

Unequivocal evidence for the existence of an Astiru II is provided by a new stele allegedly from the Karkamish area but now in Adana Museum, belonging to one Atika, "son of K[am]ani, [be]loved servant of Astiru, hero [Country] Lord of Kar[kamish]".[65] It does, however, create further problems for our understanding of the sequence, especially if this Astiru is the son of Sastura. The change in line from Kamani to Sastura's son, Astiru II, might have been more easily intelligible if Kamani had had no male issue. Why did Kamani's son not succeed him, becoming instead the servant of Sastura's son? The first inscription on the Cekke stele was written by a servant of Sastura, who clearly had important executive powers while still being the "first servant" of Kamani. Indeed, the act of purchasing the city of Kamana is performed by Kamani and Sastura together. The circumstances surrounding the switch in line from Astiruwa (Yariri his servant) – Kamani (Sastura his servant) to Astiru II (son of Sastura, Atika, son of Kamani his servant) – [Pisiri?] son of Astiru, remain a matter of speculation for the moment.

Nevertheless, the complex relations of the last attested rulers of Karkamish, with some apparent fluctuation between the lines of rulers and those of their servants, may be a distant echo of the political set-up involving Great Kings and Country Lords in Karkamish from the 10th to early 9th centuries. Such a two-tier system of government may indicate a division of functions, such as responsibility for foreign *vs* domestic policy (see Astiruwa *vs* Yariri above), or ceremonial *vs* executive offices. Comparable cases where a high-ranking official or vizier succeeded to royal or supreme power are known, for example in New Kingdom Egypt, but any explanation remains currently unverifiable in the absence of further data.

717 to 605 BC

The period after the Assyrian take-over in 717 BC is not well known. Few Assyrian finds have been documented at Karkamish itself, the early excavations producing one Neo-Assyrian cuneiform economic tablet, a fragment of an inscribed stele, inscribed bricks of Sargon, a fragment of an Assyrian relief, an inscribed Lamaštu amulet and a Pazuzu head.[66] The tablet concerns the organization of tanners and other workers as part of the *iškāru*-service of the king in the nearby town of Elumu and is of some importance for the understanding of Neo-Assyrian administration of Empire.[67] The 2013 excavations produced a literary cuneiform tablet in Neo-Assyrian ductus from the building associated with the Royal Buttress, but this appears to belong to the period before the Assyrian occupation.[68]

Assyrian documentation from Nineveh and Kalhu (Nimrud) mentions Karkamish with reference to the "Mina of Karkamish", which appears to have been a unit of measurement used not only in the west but also closer to the Assyrian heartland. The governor of Hamath, Adda-Hati, collects silver tribute from the local population according to the "mina of Karkamish" in a letter found at Kalhu dating to the reign of Sargon II.[69] It is unclear whether this letter dates from before or after 717 BC, but it demonstrates the importance that Karkamish's position as a trade hub and its political pre-eminence among the Neo-Hittite states had for the Assyrians in implementing their imperial administration.[70] Dated documents referring to the mina of Karkamish as the unit of payment are:

Text	Find-city	Location concerned	Year
SAA 6.17	Nineveh	Du'ua	747
SAA 6.26	Nineveh	—	711
SAA 6.34	Nineveh	—	709
SAA 6.39	Nineveh	—	694
SAA 6.40	Nineveh	—	693
SAA 6.41	Nineveh	—	693
SAA 6.81	Nineveh	Aššur	694
SAA 6.104	Nineveh	—	690
SAA 6.107	Nineveh	—	686
SAA 6.90	Nineveh	Nabur	683
SAA 6.108	Nineveh	—	683
SAA 6.45	Nineveh	—	682
SAA 6.91	Nineveh	Talmusu	681
SAA 6.110	Nineveh	—	681

Assyrian documents thus use the term "mina of Karkamish" both before and after 717 BC. The significance

of this unit may be less geographical than to do with the fact that the mina of Karkamish represented a different amount to the regular Assyrian mina, possibly even a continuation of the Late Bronze Age Hittite mina, which consisted of 40 as opposed to 60 shekels, although the details of precisely what weight of shekel would be appropriate for which weight of mina still need to be worked out.[71] Why the Assyrians should have occasionally used this weight rather than the regular Assyrian mina is unclear. The chariot driver Šumma-ilani, who frequently uses the mina of Karkamish in his business dealings, does appear to have some direct contact to an official in the city (see below).[72]

A badly broken document from Nineveh lists deliveries of "red wool" and "madder" from 14 western provinces, as far as the tablet is preserved.[73] Among these Karkamish sends in more than three times as much of the item being counted as do the other provinces for which the figures are preserved. It is therefore possible that Karkamish continued to play a key role in the textile industry and trade while part of the Assyrian Empire, although one should be wary of the evidence provided by a single, isolated and broken document. There was a relatively seamless transition between the economic roles of "tribute" (*mandattu*) paid by a client ruler and the various kinds of taxes that a province would pay via its governor once annexed to the Assyrian Empire (Radner 2006, 226–7). Here one might recall the tribute that Sangara paid to Shalmaneser III (859–824 BC) according to the Kurkh monolith, which included: "20 talents of red purple wool, 500 garments ... and 5,000 sheep."[74] Each of these elements was also present in the tribute of Qalparunda of Patin from the same year, so textiles cannot be said to be a particular speciality of Karkamish.

One other Assyrian letter may, according to S. Parpola's interpretation, give details of the Assyrian administration of Karkamish, although it is unclear whether the letter should be dated before or after the Assyrian takeover. The reference to a "(king of) Karkamish", in Parpola's translation might indicate that he favours a dating before 717 BC, and the reference to Arpad as a place of refuge for those trying to escape corvée-labour (*ilku*) may well support this, given that Arpad participated in a rebellion against Sargon II at the beginning of his reign.[75] It is, however, not clear that the letter is written from the perspective of Karkamish in the first place, and the king of Karkamish is not specifically mentioned, merely "Karkamishean(s)".[76] A further letter deals with the arrest and delivery to the king of a group of people from Karkamish who had arrived illicitly in another town.[77]

We only know the names of two governors who were installed in Karkamish by the Assyrians on the basis of their appearance as limmu-officials for the years 691 and 649 BC.[78] A "major-domo of Karkamish" ([lú]GAL É) called Aššur-bēl-uṣur is attested on a legal document from Nineveh loaning oil from the above-mentioned chariot driver Šumma-ilani.[79] The tablet is dated to late in the reign of Sennacherib, 681 BC. One of the witnesses on the document has a name written [1.d]*kù*-KÁ-*sa-pi*, which can be normalized as Kubaba-sapi.[80] The Karkamish tablet dealing with the organization of *iškāru*-service of the king in the town of Elumu mentions a "captain" (*rab kiṣri*) called Šarri-taklak who may well be stationed in Karkamish (Postgate 1974, 362).

The last chapter in the history of the Karkamish before its classical resettlement is the role it played in the fall of the Neo-Assyrian Empire. It is thought that the Assyrians and their Egyptian allies fell back to Karkamish after they had been driven out of Harran by Babylonian forces in 610 BC, although this is not certain. By 607–6 BC a Babylonian Chronicle implies that the Egyptian army was already stationed in Karkamish, from where it was routed and chased as far as Hamath by the Babylonian Nebuchadnezzar in 605 BC, the last year of his father Nabopolassar, as a further chronicle tablet informs us.[81] The garrison of the Egyptian army in Karkamish also finds some support from reports in the Old Testament.[82] Interestingly, House D in the Outer Town, in which the Pazuzu-head mentioned above was found, also contained Egyptian and Egyptianizing artifacts (Woolley 1921, 126, 127 fig. 43; Holloway 2002, 214 fn. 448).

The prime location of Karkamish for trade and its historical political importance ensured that it remained a regionally defining city in northern Syria throughout the earlier Iron Age, with a possible although undemonstrated decline during the 11th century BC. It functioned not only as a wealthy trade hub, but was also seen as the ancestral seat of Hittite power in the region, an association which clearly had an enduring ideological appeal. Among all the Neo-Hittite states Karkamish was virtually avoided by the Assyrians until the late 8th century BC, although it is not possible to exclude that this was part of a wider Assyrian strategy. After its annexation to the Assyrian Empire it appears to have left an imprint on the formation of trade and collection of tribute through the measurement known as the mina of Karkamish, which was used not only in the west as far as Hamath but apparently also in contracts regarding areas nearer the Assyrian heartland, although this may be partly due to the contracting parties having western connections. The period immediately after the fall of the Assyrian Empire saw some of the key power-struggles for the domination of the whole of the area formerly controlled by Assyria played out there.

Notes

1   See Weeden 2013 for a recent summary of some of the vast previous literature on this topic.

2   Glatz 2009, as a model for understanding ancient Empires in general. An intermediate form of external control referred to as 'Intensive Hegemony' on the Middle Euphrates (*ibid.*,

138) is contrasted with a more 'hands-off' approach to rule at Ugarit.

3   Harrison 2013, 61. Alalakh is now thought to have been deserted much earlier in the 13th century than previously thought, which should change significantly our assessment of its significance at the end of the Hittite Empire (Yener 2013; Akar 2013).

4   This statement may naturally be subject to revision in the course of the new excavations at the site conducted since 2011 by the Universities of Bologna, Istanbul and Gaziantep under the directorship of N. Marchetti.

5   E.g. Hawkins 1988; Güterbock 1992.

6   T96-1, cited at Cohen and d'Alfonso 2008, 14–15.

7   T93-12, cited at Cohen and d'Alfonso 2008, 15 n. 54.

8   Publication Hawkins 2005; for the connection of the Emar *Tarwa* with the bowl's *tarwiza* ("Tarwean") see Mora 2007, 519.

9   See Oreshko 2012 for a a rejection of the reading of "T[udhaliya] Labarna". Oreshko reads instead "Mount Labarna", which he equates with Mount Lebanon, which is not convincing. In the reading MONS[.*tu*] (= Tudhaliya) the *tu* is restored because the area is covered with modern solder. For the location of this Tudhaliya (V) on the central plateau see Simon 2009. For his location in Karkamish see Giusfredi 2013.

10   Giusfredi 2013, followed by Oreshko 2012, reads the title of the figure named Asmaya on the silver bowl as "Country Lord", rather than "man of the land of Hatti" (Hawkins 2005), a reading which is not defensible

11   KARAHÖYÜK §1: POCULUM.PES.*67(REGIO). Hawkins 2000, 291. The reading of the name Ir(i)-Teššub is also not secure, as it is written half-logographically. See Simon 2013, 827–828 for a summary of suggestions.

12   Hawkins 2000, 291. See Simon 2013, 824–826 for the arguments (a) that KARAHÖYÜK belongs stylistically to the Karkamish group, which is not substantiated, (b) that the stylistic similarities with inscriptions from the central plateau are not indicative of geographical grouping, but merely of archaism, (c) that the style of the Karkamish inscriptions developed more slowly than in Malatya, for which this is the only evidence, (d) that the king Iri-Teššub is identical with the king of "Karkamish" Ini-Teššub encountered by Tiglath-Pileser I in 1100 BC (*ibid.*, 828). The specific form of the sign /*sa*/ is not addressed in the discussion of (a) and (b). The evidence for n/r rhotacism at this date needed to explain (d) is not sufficient.

13   Simon (2013, 824) argues that Iri-Teššub must have been king of Karkamish because otherwise the dominion of Malatya over Karahöyük-Elbistan, allegedly demonstrated by an inscription of PUGNUS-*mili* from the end of the 12th century, is unexplained (MALATYA 9, Hawkins 2000, 284). This timeframe does not exclude that the "Great King" of the KARAHÖYÜK inscription is an earlier Great King from the central plateau area.

14   A.0.87.3, 28 (Grayson 1991, 37).

15   ALEPPO 7, 5 §7 (Hawkins 2011, 48).

16   It is notable, although not clear from the composite transliteration by Grayson (1991, A.0.87.4, 31) that the name Allumari is not spelled out completely in any of manuscripts

but always appears in a break. It is thus a reconstruction. See Hawkins 1998, 66 fn. 15.

17 RIMA A.0.102.1, 55', 67' (Stone slab from Fort Shalmaneser).

18 KARKAMIŠ A4b (Hawkins 2000, 80–82); Dinçol *et al.* 2012.

19 Dinçol *et al.* 2012.

20 ÇİNEKÖY Luwian §6–7 = Phoenician 8–9; Payne 2012, 43.

21 KARKAMIŠ A1a. Hawkins 2000, 87–91. Astuwalamanza now is re-read from previous Astuwatamanza.

22 See Del Monte and Tischler 1978, 149 for literature. One should of course be wary of associations made on the basis of an alleged phonetic similarity to a modern Turkish name, especially one containing a common Turkish morpheme like —*erek*, but the Armenian name Sevovorak implies a greater age to the formation. Two monuments with hieroglyphic Luwian inscriptions have been found in the Siverek area, although their content is not known (Çelik 2005; Kulakoğlu 2003).

23 KARKAMISH A1a §9, §12 (Hawkins 2000, 88).

24 KARKAMISH A1a §14 (Hawkins 2000, 88).

25 KARKAMISH A11b+c §4, §31; Edition at Hawkins 2000, 101–108; interpretation at Melchert 2011, 75–77.

26 TELL AHMAR 1, §11 (Hawkins 2000, 242).

27 KARKAMISH A11a §5 (Hawkins 2000, 95, 97).

28 KARKAMISH A11b+c §5 (Hawkins 2000, 103).

29 *ibid.*, §15.

30 *ibid.*, §7–8.

31 Hawkins 2000, 105, with question mark.

32 *Kawa/i ≠ Que* at Giusfredi 2010, 50 fn. 68; Simon 2011, 260; Gander 2012, 292.

33 Simon (2011, 261 fn. 19) argues on phonetic grounds against **Kawa/i* being a "dialect form" of *Hiyawa*. The difference in form could be areally rather than dialectally conditioned, however, or could have been generated through an Aramaic transmission (see *qwh* in the inscription of Zakkur of Hamath, Donner and Röllig 1962–64, 202 A6, albeit almost a century later). Simon (*ibid.*, 261) further sees **Kawa/i* in A11b+c as referring to the place–name *kw* mentioned in the Phoenician inscription of Cebel İres Dağı (Mosca-Russell 1987, 5–6), which would itself be located in Hiyawa! This may be supported by the fact that **Kawa/i* in Karkamish A11b+c is given the determinative "city". For the purposes of assessing the extent of Katuwa's military reach it is irrelevant whether one interprets **Kawa/i* as referring to the area *Que* or to a city *kw* in the area *Hiyawa* (= *Que*).

34 RIMA A.0.102.1, 93'–95' (Grayson 1996, 11)

35 RIMA A.0.102.2 ii 19 (Grayson 1996, 18); Yamada 2000, 117. See Chapter 5 for possible location of Sazabê.

36 RIMA A.0.102.2 ii 27–9 (Grayson 1996, 18)

37 RIMA A.0.102.6 ii 69 (Grayson 1996, 38)

38 The extent of Assyrian rule is delimited towards the west by Kar-Shalmaneser (= Tell Ahmar), "which is opposite Karkamish" A.0.103.1, 9–10 (Grayson 1996, 184). See Radner 2004, 158 fn. 21 for a more sinister explanation of this phrase.

39 A.0.104.3, 12 (Grayson 1996, 205).

40 Donner and Röllig 1962–4 no. 202, A1, 1–9.

41 Tiglath-Pileser III 11, 9; 14, 11; 27, 4; 32, 3; 35 iii 16 (Tadmor and Yamada 2011).

42 *Annals* 72–76 (Fuchs 1994, 88, 316).

43 Radner 2004, 158–159. The "Phoenician" ports of Tyre and Sidon provide a parallel (*ibid.*, 159–162).

44 KARKAMIŞ A6, §30, referring to sculpture KARKAMIŞ B4–5 (Hawkins 2000, 128, also p. 78 fn. 64).

45 MARAŞ 4, §12–14 (Hawkins 2000, 257, see also *ibid.*, 266).

46 KARKAMIŞ A6 §8 (Hawkins 2000, 126).

47 KARKAMIŞ A6 §6 (Hawkins 2000, 126).

48 Hawkins 2000, 126; Simon 2012.

49 It may be tempting to understand the name *Sura* here as Assyria, but this is unlikely given the fact that Yariri otherwise spells Assyria as *a-sú+ra/i-* KARKAMIŞ A15b §19 (Hawkins 2000, 131).

50 KARKAMIŞ A15b §19–21 (Hawkins 2000, 131).

51 Hawkins 2000, 133; Starke 1997, 388–92.

52 KARKAMIŞ A24a (Hawkins 2000, 135).

53 KARKAMIŞ A24a §3 (Hawkins 2000, 135).

54 KARKAMIŞ A24a §6–7 (Hawkins 2000, 135).

55 CEKKE §6a (Hawkins 2000, 145).

56 KARKAMIŞ A31 §7 (Hawkins 2000, 142).

57 KARKAMIŞ A27e frag. 1 §1 (Hawkins 2000, 166, where dated to Kamani).

58 KARKAMIŞ A31 §5 (Hawkins 2000, 142).

59 CEKKE §6b–12 (Hawkins 2000, 145).

60 CEKKE §13–14 (Hawkins 2000, 145).

61 CEKKE §15–17o (Hawkins 2000, 145–146).

62 KARKAMIŞ A21+A20b §1 (Hawkins 2000, 160). Dated to Pisiri on the basis of sculptural style at Hawkins 2000, 159, 162, also 79).

63 KARKAMIŞ A21 frag. 1. It is also possible that the fragment belongs to the genealogy of the author (Hawkins 2000, 162).

64 KARKAMIŞ A13 c1, See Hawkins 2000, 168. A number of fragments from Karkamish A13, thought to be lost, were re-discovered during the 2013 season at Karkamish.

65 Akdoğan 2013; Hawkins, Tosun, Akdoğan 2013. Clearly the evidence from this stele has no bearing on the question of the ascription of KARKAMIŞ A13 to either Kamani or Pisiri.

66 See Hawkins 1976–80, 446. Lamaštu (BM 1177587) Holloway 2002, 212 fn. 447. Pazuzu: Woolley 1921, 127 fig. 43, Holloway 2002, 214 fn. 448.

67 BM 116230, Postgate 1974, 95, 216, 226, 360–62; dated to 702 BC at Fales 1973, 108 fn. 102 due to partially restored eponym; Holloway 2002, 419 fn. 526. The same town is the subject of a land-grant during the reign of Aššurbanipal (SAA 12.90, Kataja and Whiting 1995, 110–112).

68 See Marchesi 2014.

69 SAA 19.173, 6–7 = SAA 1.176 (Parpola 1987). For Adda-Hati see Radner 1998: 45.

70 An as yet unverified proposal in the literature has been that the mina of Karkamish formed the basis for the "light" mina of Assyria (*c.* 500gm). Powell 1987–90, 516 with further literature.

71 Van den Hout 1987–1990, 525–527; Vargyas 1996. Middle and Late Bronze Age evidence for Karkamishean weights is discussed at Vargyas 1998. If the "light" mina and the mina of Karkamish are identical (cf. fn. 70 above), the question becomes rather why specific Assyrian texts opt for calling this weight the mina of Karkamish.

72 SAA 6.34; 39; 40; 41; 45; 46; 53; 54 (Kwasman and Parpola 1991). It is notable that all of these transactions concern traffic

in slaves. Šumma-ilani does not use the mina of Karkamish in his property transactions, for example (SAA 6.37; 42). This restriction to transactions concerning slaves does not apply to other individuals who use the mina of Karkamish.

73 SAA 7.116 obv. 4': Karkamish delivers 100+2 talents; also recorded are 30 talents from Arpad (*ibid.*, 3'), 30 from Que (*ibid.*, 5'), 15 from Megiddo (*ibid.*, 6'), [1]5 from Manṣuate (*ibid.*, 7').

74 A.0.102.2 ii 28 (Grayson 1996, 18). One should note that the terms translated "red wool" in SAA 7.116 rev. 4' (ḪÉ.MED) and "red purple wool" in the Kurkh Monolith (SÍG ZA.GÌN SA₅), while both being wool, appear to denote different types of wool or wool products.

75 SAA 1.183, 10', 16' (Parpola 1987, 146). Parpola points out that Sargon imposed *ilku*-duties on Karkamish in his 5th year (718 BC).

76 The letter could have been written by an Assyrian governor or magnate in a neighbouring area, e.g. Kar-Shalmaneser on the other side of the river, as the reference to people crossing the Euphrates to go to Arpad might indeed indicate (SAA 1.183, 16'). For an Assyrian governor of Kar-Shalmaneser during the reign of Sargon II see Radner 2006.

77 SAA 5.243, 13–18. The editors suppose on the basis of the handwriting that the sender "may be identical with the governor of Mazamua" who authored SAA 5.199 (Lanfranchi and Parpola 1995, 175). If so, this incident did not happen locally to Karkamish.

78 Hawkins 1976–80, 446; Radner 2006–2008, 58. A further unnamed governor of Karkamish is mentioned in SAA 7.136 rev. i 3', a list of food provisions from Nineveh presumably for rather than from the governors of eight provinces as preserved (Fales and Postgate 1992).

79 SAA 6.46, obv. 1 (Kwasman and Parpola 1991, 47); Radner 1998, 175.

80 SAA 6.46, rev. 5 (Kwasman and Parpola 1991). The goddess Kubaba with the same writing appears in the curses attached to Esarhaddon's loyalty oath (SAA 2.6, 469) where she may be responsible for causing venereal disease, depending on interpretation (Parpola and Watanabe 1988).

81 Written ᵘʳᵘ*gal-ga-meš*. Glassner 2004: 226–7, Chronicle 23, Nabopolassar; ibid. 227–8, Chronicle 24, late Nabopolassar/ early Nebuchadnezzar II. The latter text also mentions a campaign by Nebuchadnezzar II as far as Karkamish in *Hattu* (i.e. northern Syria) in 596 BC.

82 II Chronicles 33, 20 (cf. II Kings 23, 29); Jeremiah 46, 2. Hawkins 1976–80, 446.

Bibliography

Akar, M. (2013) The Late Bronze Age Fortresses at Alalakh. Architecture and Identity in Mediterranean Exchange Systems. In K.A. Yener (ed.) *Across the Border: late Bronze–Iron Age relations between Syria and Anatolia*, 37–55. Leuven, Peeters.

Akdoğan, R. (2013) Adana Müzesinde Luwi Hiyeroglif Yazıtlı Stel. *Aktüel Arkeoloji* 35, 14.

Arnaud, D. (1991) *Textes syriens de l'Age du Bronze Récent.* Barcelona, Aula Orientalis Supplementa 1.

Aro, S. (2013) Carchemish before and after 1200 BC. In A. Mouton, I. Rutherford and I. Yakubovich (eds) *Luwian Identities. Culture, Language and Religion Between Anatolia and the Aegean*, 233–276. Leiden-Boston, Brill.

Bryce, T. (2012) *The World of the Neo-Hittite Kingdoms.* Oxford, Oxford University Press.

Çelik, B. (2005) A new stele base of the Late Hittite period from Siverek-Şanlıurfa. *Anadolu/Anatolia* 28, 17–24.

Cohen, Y. (2004) Kidin-Gula – The foreign teacher at the Emar scribal school. *Revue d'Assyriologie* 98, 81–100.

Cohen, Y. and d'Alfonso, L. (2008) The duration of the Emar archives. In L. d'Alfonso, Y. Cohen, and D. Sürenhagen (eds) *The city of Emar among the Late Bronze Age Empires, History, Landscape and Society. Proceedings of the Konstanz Emar conference 25–26.04. 2006*, 3–25. Münster, Alter Orient und Altes Testament 349.

Dinçol, A., Dinçol, B. Hawkins, J.D. and Peker, H. (2012) At the origins of the Suhi-Katuwa Dynasty. *Near Eastern Archaeology* 75/3, 145.

Donner, H. and Röllig, W. (1962–4) *Kananäische und Aramäische Inschriften Vol. I.* Wiesbaden, Harrassowitz.

Fales, M.F. (1973) *Censimenti e catasti di epoca neo-assira.* Centre per le antichita e la sto- ria dell'arte del Vicino Oriente: Studi economici e technologici 2. Rome, Centro per le antichita e la storia dell'arte del Vicino Oriente.

Fales, F.M. and Postgate, J.N. (1992) *Imperial Administrative Records, Part I. Palace and Temple Administration* State Archives of Assyria 7. Helsinki, Helsinki University Press.

Frangipane, M. and Liverani, M. (2013) Neo-Hittite Melid: continuity or discontinuity? In K.A. Yener (ed.) *Across the Border: late Bronze–Iron Age relations between Syria and Anatolia*, 349–372. Leuven, Peeters.

Fuchs, A. (1994) *Die Inschriften Sargons II. aus Khorsabad.* Göttingen, Cuvillier.

Gander, M. (2012) Aḫḫiyawa – Ḫiyawa – Que: Gibt es Evidenz für die Anwesenheit von Griechen in Kilikien am Übergang von der Bronze- zur Eisenzeit. *SMEA* 54, 281–309.

Glassner, J.-J. (2004) *Mesopotamian Chronicles* Writings from the Ancient World. Atlanta, Society for Biblical Literature.

Glatz, C. (2009) Empire as network: Spheres of material interaction in Late Bronze Age Anatolia. *Journal of Anthropological Archaeology* 28, 127–141.

Giusfredi, F. (2010) *Sources for a Socio-Economic History of the Neo-Hittite States.* Heidelberg, Texte der Hethiter 28.

Giusfredi, F. (2013) Further considerations on the Ankara Silver Bowl. In L. Feliu, J. Llop, A. Millet Albà and J. Sanmartin (eds) *Time and History in the Ancient Near East. Proceedings of the 56th Rencontre Assyriologique Internationale at Barcelona, 26th–30th July 2010 at Barcelona*, 665–680. Winona Lake IN, Eisenbrauns.

Grayson, K. (1991) *Assyrian Rulers of the Early First Millennium BC (1114–859 BC).* Toronto, Royal Inscriptions of Mesopotamia, Assyrian Periods 2.

Grayson, K. (1996) *Assyrian Rulers of the Early First Millennium BC II (858–745 BC).* Toronto, Royal Inscriptions of Mesopotamia, Assyrian Periods 3.

Güterbock, H.G. (1992) Survival of the Hittite Dynasty. In W.A. Ward and M.S. Joukowsky (eds) *The Crisis Years: The 12th Century B.C. From Beyond the Danube to the Tigris*, 53–55. Dubuque, Kendall/Hunt.

Harrison, T.P. (2013) Tayınat in the Early Iron Age. In K.A. Yener (ed.) *Across the Border: late Bronze–Iron Age relations between Syria and Anatolia,* 61–87. Leuven, Peeters.

Hawkins, J.D. (1976–80) Karkamiš. In *Reallexikon der Assyriologie und Vordersiatischen Archäologie* 5, Ia ... *Kizzuwatna,* 426–446. Berlin, De Gruyter.

Hawkins, J.D. (1988) Kuzi-Tešub and the 'Great Kings' of Karkamiš. *Anatolian Studies* 38, 99–108.

Hawkins, J.D. (1995) "Great Kings" and "Country Lords" at Malatya and Karkamiš. In Th. van den Hout and J. de Roos (eds) *Studio historiae ardens. Ancient Near Eastern Studies Presented to Philo H.J. Houwink ten Cate on the Occasion of his 65th Birthday* PIHANS 74, 73–86. Leiden, NINO.

Hawkins, J.D. (1998) Hittites and Assyrians at Melid (Malatya). In H. Erkanal, V. Donbaz and A. Uğuroğlu (eds) *XXXIVème Rencontre Assyriologique Internationale, Istanbul, 6–10/VII/1987,* 63–77. Ankara, Türk Tarih Kurumu Basımevi.

Hawkins, J.D. (2000) *Corpus of Hieroglyphic Luwian Inscriptions Vol. I.1–3: Inscriptions of the Iron Age.* Berlin, de Gruyter.

Hawkins, J.D. (2004) A Hieroglyphic Luwian inscription on a silver bowl in the museum of Anatolian civilisations Ankara. *Studia Troica* 15, 193–205.

Hawkins, J.D. (2011) The inscriptions of the Aleppo temple. *Anatolian Studies* 61, 35–54.

Hawkins, J.D., Tosun, K. and Akdoğan, R. 2013: a new hieroglyphic Luwian stele in Adana Museum. *Höyük* 6, 1–13.

Holloway, S.W. (2002) *Aššur is King! Aššur is King! Religion in the Exercise of Power in the Neo-Assyrian Empire.* Culture and History of the Ancient Near East 10. Leiden-Boston-Köln, Brill.

Hout, Th. van den (1987–1990) Masse und Gewichte Bei den Hethitern. In *Reallexikon der Assyriologie und der vorderasiatischen Archäologie* 7, 517–527. Berlin-New York, De Gruyter.

Kataja, L. and Whiting, R. (1995) *Grants, Decrees and Gifts of the Neo-Assyrian Period,* State Archives of Assyria 12. Helsinki, Helsinki University Press.

Kwasman, T. and Parpola, S. (1991) *Legal Transactions of the Royal Court of Niniveh,* Part 1: *Tiglath-Pileser III through Esarhaddon,* State Archives of Assyria 6. Helsinki, Helsinki University Press.

Kulakoğlu, F. (2003) Şanlıurfa'da Son Yıllarda Keşfedilen Geç Hitit heykeltıraşlı Merkezleri ve Eserleri, *2002 Yılı Anadolu Medeniyetleri Müzesi Konferansları,* 65–87. Ankara: T.C. Kültür Bakanlığı Anıtlar ve Müzeler Genel Müdürlüğü Anadolu Medeniyetler Müzesi.

Lanfranchi, G.B. and Parpola, S. (1990) *The Correspondence of Sargon II, Part II: Letters from the Northern and Northeastern Provinces.* State Archives of Assyria 5. Helsinki, Helsinki University Press.

Liverani, M. (2012) Melid in the Early and Middle Iron Age: Archaeology and History. In G. Galil, A. Gilboa, A.M. Maeir and D. Kahn (eds) *The Ancient Near East in the 12th to 10th Centuries BCE: Culture and History. Proceedings of the International Conference held at the University of Haifa, 2–5 May, 2010,* AOAT 392, 327–344. Münster, Ugarit-Verlag.

Marchesi, G. (2014) A Bilingual Literary Text from Karkemish Featuring Marduk (with contributions by Werner R. Mayer and Strahil V. Panayotov). *Orientalia* 83/4, 330–340 (Tab. XXXII-XXXIV).

Marchetti, N. (2013) The 2011 Joint Turco-Italian Excavations at Karkemish, in *34. kazı sonuçları toplantısı, 28 mayıs–1 haziran 2012, Çorum. 1. cilt,* 349–364. Ankara, T.C. Kültür ve Turizm Bakanlığı.

Marchetti, N. (2012) Karkemish on the Euphrates: Excavating a City's History. *Near Eastern Archaeology* 75 (3), 132–147.

Melchert, H.C. (1988) "Thorn" and "Minus" in hieroglyphic Luvian orthography. *Anatolian Studies* 38, 29–42.

Melchert, H.C. (2011) Enclitic subject pronouns in hieroglyphic Luvian. *Aramazd, Armenian Journal of Near Eastern Studies* 6 (2), 73–86.

Monte, G. del and Tischler, J. (1978) *Die Orts-und Gewässernamen der hethitischen Texte.* Repertoire Géographique des Textes Cunéiformes 6 (BTAVO, Reihe B7). Wiesbaden, Harrassowitz.

Mora, C. (2007) Three Metal Bowls. In: M. Alparslan, M. Doğan Alparslan, H. Peker (eds) *VITA – Festschrift in Honor of Belkis Dinçol and Ali Dinçol.* Istanbul, Ege Yayınları 515–521.

Mosca, P.G. and Russell, J. (1987) A Phoenician inscription from Cebel İres Dağı in Rough Cilicia. *Epigraphica Anatolica* 9, 1–28.

Oreshko, R. (2012) Hieroglyphic Luwian Inscription on the Ankara Silver Bowl: an essay of epigraphic and historical re-interpretation (in Russian with English summary). *Vestnik Drevnej Istorii* 2012 (2), 3–28.

Payne, A. (2012) *Iron Age Hieroglyphic Luwian Inscriptions.* Writings from the Ancient World 29, Atlanta, Society for Biblical Literature.

Payne, A. (2014) Zum Herrscherhaus von Karkamiš. In C. Brosch and A. Payne (eds) *Na-wa/i-VIR.ZI/A MAGNUS SCRIBA Festschrift für Helmut Nowicki zum 70. Geburtstag,* 149–156. Dresdner Beiträge zur Hethitologie. Wiesbaden, Harrassowitz.

Parpola, S. (1987) *The Correspondence of Sargon II, Part I: Letters from Assyria and the West.* State Archives of Assyria 1. Helsinki, Helsinki University Press.

Parpola, S. and Watanabe, K. (1988) *Neo-Assyrian Treaties and Loyality Oaths.* State Archives of Assyria 2. Helsinki, Helsinki University Press.

Postgate, J.N. (1974) *Taxation and Conscription in the Assyrian Empire.* StPSM 1. Rome, Pontificial Institute.

Powell, M.A. (1987–90) Masse und Gewichte. In *Reallexikon der Assyriologie und der Vorderasiatischen Archäologie* 7, 457–517. Berlin-New York, De Gruyter.

Radner, K. (ed.) (1998) *The Prosopography of the Neo-Assyrian Empire Vol. I Part I: A.* Helsinki, Neo-Assyrian Text Corpus Project.

Radner, K. (2004) Assyrische Handelspolitik: die Symbiose mit unabhängigen Handelszentren und ihre Kontrolle durch Assyrien. In R. Rollinger und C. Ulf (eds) *Commerce and Monetary Systems in the Ancient World. Means of Transmission and Cultural Interaction. Proceedings of the Fifth Annual Symposium of the Assyrian and Babylonian Intellectual Heritage Project. Held in Innsbruck, Austria, October 3rd–8th, 2002,* 152–169. Stuttgart, Franz Steiner Verlag.

Radner, K. (2006) Aššur-dūr-pānīya, Statthalter von Til-Barsip unter Sargon II. von Assyrien. *Baghdader Mitteilungen* 36, 185–195.

Radner, K. (2006–8) Provinz C. Assyrien. In *Reallexikon der Assyriologie und der vorderasiatischen Archäologie* 11. *Prinzessin ... Samug,* 43–68. Berlin, De Gruyter.

Radner, K. (2007) Abgaben an den König von Assyrien aus dem

In und Ausland. In H. Klinkott, S. Kubisch and R. Müller-Wollermann (eds) *Geschenke und Steuern, Zölle und Tribute. Antike Abgabenformen in Anspruch und Wirklichkeit*, 213–230. Leiden-Boston, Brill.

Seeher, J. (1998) Neue Befunde zur Endzeit von Hattuša: Ausgrabungen auf Büyükkaya in Boğazköy. In S. Alp and A. Süel (eds) *Acts of the IIIrd International Congress of Hittitology, Çorum, September 16–22, 1996*, 515–523. Ankara, publisher unknown.

Simon, Zs. (2009) Die ANKARA-Silberschale und das Ende des hethitischen Reiches. *Zeitschrift für Assyriologie und Vorderasiatische Archäologie* 99 (2), 247–269.

Simon, Zs. (2011) The Identification of Qode. Reconsidering the Evidence. In J.-P.Mynářová and V. Maříková (eds) *Egypt and the Near East – The Crossroads. International Workshop on the Relations between Egypt and the Near East in the Bronze Age*, 249–269. Prague, Czech Institute of Egyptology, Charles University.

Simon, Zs. (2012) Where is the land of Sura of the Hieroglyphic Luwian inscription KARKAMIŠ A4b and why were Cappadocians called Syrians by Greeks? *Altorientalische Forschungen* 39 (1), 160–180.

Simon, Zs. (2013) Wer war der Großkönig I(a)+ra/i-TONITRUS der KARAHÖYÜK-Inschrift. In L. Feliu, J. Llop, A. Millet Albà and J. Sanmartin (eds) *Time and History in the Ancient Near East. Proceedings of the 56th Rencontre Assyriologique Internationale at Barcelona, 26th–30th July 2010 at Barcelona*, 823–832. Winona Lake IN, Eissenbrauns.

Singer, I. (2000) New evidence on the end of the Hittite Empire. In E. Oren (ed.) *The Sea Peoples and Their World: A Reassessment*, 21–33. Philadelphia PA, University of Pennsylvania Press.

Singer, I. (2012) The Philistines in the North and the Kingdom of Taita. In G. Galil, A. Gilboa, A.M. Maeir, and D. Kahn (eds) *The Ancient Near East in the 12th to 10th Centuries BCE: Culture and History. Proceedings of the International Conference held at the University of Haifa, 2–5 May, 2010*, 451–472. AOAT 392. Münster, Ugarit-Verlag.

Starke, F. (1997) Sprachen und Schriften in Karkamiš, in P. Pongratz-Leisten, H. Kühne and P. Xella (eds) *Ana šadî Labnāni lū allik. Beiträge zu altorientalischen und mittelmeerischen Kulturen (= Festschrift Wolfgang Röllig)*, 381–395. AOAT 247. Kevelaer, Butzon und Bercher and Neukirchen-Vluyn, Neukirchener Verlag.

Summers, G.D. (2013) Some implications of revised C14 and dendrochronological dating for the "Late Bronze levels" at Tille Höyük on the Euphrates. In K.A. Yener (ed.) *Across the Border: late Bronze–Iron Age Relations between Syria and Anatolia*, 311–328. Leuven, Peeters.

Tadmor, H. and Yamada, Sh. (2011) *The Royal Inscriptions of Tiglath-pileser III (744–727 BC) and Shalmaneser V (726–722 BC), Kings of Assyria*. Royal Inscriptions of the Neo-Assyrian Period 1, Winona Lake IN, Eisenbrauns.

Vargyas, P. (1996) The Mina of Karkemiš in the Neo-Assyrian Sources. *State Archives of Assyria Bulletin* 10 (2), 9–14.

Vargyas, P. (1998) Talent of Karkamish and Talent of Yamhad. *Altorientalische Forschungen* 25, 303–311.

Weeden, M. (2013) After the Hittites: the Kingdoms of Karkamish and Palistin in Northern Syria. *Bulletin of the Institute of Classical Studies* 56 (2), 1–20.

Woolley, C.L. (1921) *Carchemish: Report on the Excavations at Jerablus on Behalf of the British Museum, Part II: The Town Defenses*. London, British Museum.

Yamada, Sh. (2000) *The Construction of the Assyrian Empire. A Historical Study of the Inscriptions of Shalmaneser III (859–824 BC) Relating to His Campaigns to the West*. Leiden–Boston, Brill.

Yener, K.A. (2013) New Excavations at Alalakh: The 14th–12th Centuries BC. In K.A. Yener, (ed.) *Across the Border: late Bronze–Iron Age Relations between Syria and Anatolia*, 11–35. Leuven, Peeters.

The Land of Carchemish and its neighbours during the Neo-Hittite period (*c.* 1190–717 BC)

Michael Brown and Stefan L. Smith

Introduction

With the collapse of the Hittite empire in the early decades of the 12th century BC, the city-kingdom of Carchemish became the main political power amongst the former imperial possessions of north Syria and south-east Anatolia along the west bank of the Euphrates. The subsequent era of Neo-Hittite rule at Carchemish lasted nearly half a millennium, coming to an end in 717 BC as the result of an Assyrian invasion. Although the influence exerted by Carchemish over its neighbours varied considerably during the intervening Iron Age I–II period, it remained throughout an important regional centre of the Neo-Hittite world.

In the following, an attempt has been made to define the nature and extent of this jurisdiction, and understand how it changed over time. The approach in this chapter is to employ archaeological features in association with historical reference points to roughly define areas that lay a) within the land of Carchemish, b) approximated to the shifting border zone, and c) were demonstrably outside the land of Carchemish at the time in question. Emphasis is placed throughout on the wider landscape context in which overlapping spheres of Neo-Hittite, Assyrian and Aramaean territoriality developed (for history of the capital itself see Chapter 2).

Pottery recorded during survey is the main category of archaeological evidence for mapping patterns of settlement in the hinterland of Carchemish. This diverse landscape has been investigated with varying degrees of intensity by du Plat Taylor *et al.* (1950); Perrot (1962); Archi *et al.* (1971); Matthers (1981); Sanlaville (1985); Algaze *et al.* (1994); Özgen *et al.* (2001, 2002); Kulakoğlu (2006) and Wilkinson *et al.* (2007 and this volume). In most instances, however, it is only possible to identify a general Iron Age phase of occupation, as opposed to more specific material criteria for

Neo-Hittite period settlement. This lack of chronological resolution is due to the predominance in survey collections of local wares and forms, which often cannot be readily distinguished from earlier second and later 1st millennium BC assemblages. It is compounded by a paucity of better dated imports.

Identification of Iron Age I–II settlement within the territory of Carchemish must therefore rely on correlation with written sources that provide a more precise historical and geographical context. These primarily take the form of Assyrian annals recording military campaigns west of the Euphrates, and monumental Luwian inscriptions which attest to the shifting extent of political control exercised by Carchemish over surrounding areas. Assyrian, Luwian and Aramaic texts provide further points of reference for neighbouring polities. Major studies concerning this corpus include those of Hawkins (2000) and Grayson (1996, 1991).

Iron Age political territories in north Syria and south-east Anatolia are outlined in Figure 3.1. A proposed map of the land of Carchemish itself is presented in Figure 3.2. This includes all features used to define its territory, together with a tentative reconstruction of maximum and minimum territorial extent. For corresponding patterns of settlement, a distinction is made between Iron Age sites where there is possible evidence of Neo-Hittite period occupation, and those sites where archaeological and/or textual evidence permits more precise identification. Select sites in adjacent regions are also indicated where relevant to the following discussion. The contents of Figure 3.2 are listed in Table 3.1 at the end of this chapter.

Historical sources for the land of Carchemish

At the beginning of the Neo-Hittite period in the early 12th

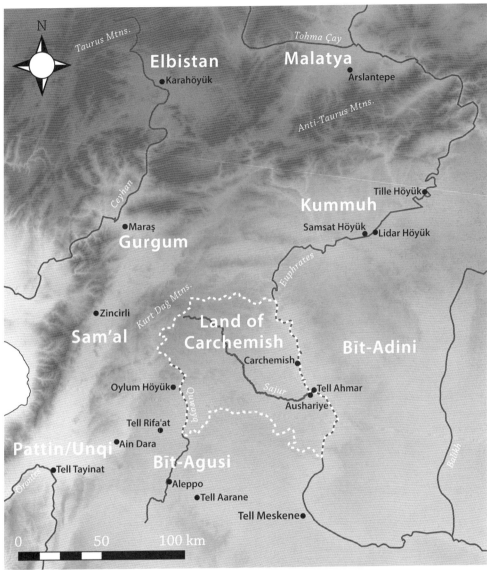

Fig. 3.1 North Syria and south-east Anatolia

century BC, the city-kingdom of Carchemish controlled a vast swath of territory along the west bank of the Euphrates, from the Sajur valley in the south to the Malatya plain in the north (Fig. 3.1). These lands were to a large extent defined by continuity in systems of governance established with the Hittite conquest under Suppiluliuma I during the later 14th century BC. Beyond those areas directly administered by Carchemish, this extensive dominion was divided between two main subordinate kingdoms; Kummuh based at Samsat Höyük, and Malatya/Melid with its capital at Arslantepe. In several instances the 'Country Lords' who ruled these lands were blood relations of the 'Great Kings' at Carchemish, who themselves shared an uninterrupted lineage with their Late Bronze Age viceroyal predecessors (Hawkins 1995a and Chapter 2).

Fragmentation of this expansive territory may be

associated with an Assyrian invasion under king Tiglath-Pileser I during the late 12th–early 11th century BC (Grayson 1991, 37). It is, however, entirely plausible that both Kummuh and Malatya had already become independent by this stage. The latest possible indication of expansion by Carchemish to the far north-west comes from the site of Karahöyük-Elbistan, where a stele commemorates the (re)foundation by Ir-Teššub of a city called POCULUM (Özgüç and Özgüç 1949; Hawkins 2000, 288–295). This 'Great King' is identified by Bryce (2012, 85–86) as the second ruler of Neo-Hittite Carchemish who reigned during the later 12th century BC; *cf.* Hawkins (2000, 283) who associates this inscription with the ruling dynasty of Tarhuntassa in Cilicia.

From the 10th century BC the ruling 'Great King' dynasty at Carchemish, claiming descent from Kuzi-Teššub, shared

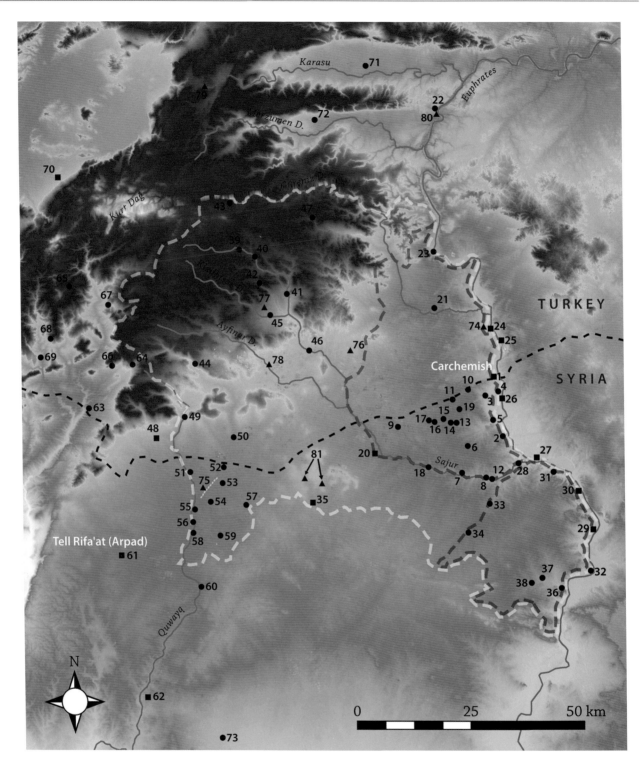

Fig. 3.2 The land of Carchemish in the Neo-Hittite period. Numbered sites refer to Table 3.1

power with a second line of 'Country Lord' rulers beginning with Suhi I. These two roles appear to have initially co-existed, perhaps in the relationship akin to that between a sovereign and a prime minister (Dinçol *et al.* 2014, 130). An inscription from Carchemish dating to the reign of Katuwa during the late 10th–early 9th centuries BC raises the possibility that its immediate hinterland later became divided for a time between these competing dynasties (Hawkins 2000, 101–108). This change in nomenclature also potentially reflects the diminished authority of Carchemish over neighbouring polities. The Kelekli stele (Fig. 3.2, no. 74) indicates control of the Euphrates valley *c.* 11 km to the north of Carchemish by Suhi II during the 10th century BC (Hogarth 1909, 173; Hawkins 2000, 92–93). In *c.* 870 BC the city of Carchemish submitted and paid a substantial tribute to the Assyrian king Aššurnāṣirpal II (Grayson 1991, 217), in an episode which may have weakened the city's influence over surrounding areas still further.

The principal historical source for the political geography of Carchemish and its neighbours during the 9th century BC are Assyrian annals recording campaigns against cities controlled by Ahuni, ruler of the Aramaean kingdom Bīt-Adini, between 858 and 855 BC (Yamada 2000, 77–142; Grayson 1996). These holdings appear to have surrounded Carchemish in all directions, and likely represent the minimum extent of its territory during the Neo-Hittite period.

In 857 BC Shalmaneser III laid siege to Til Barsip [modern Tell Ahmar], before proceeding across the Euphrates and west along the Sajur to conquer six fortified cities of Ahuni, including Til Bashere and Dabigu, and destroy a further 200 'cities' in their environs. After receiving tribute at Dagibu from the rulers of Pattin/Unqi, Gurgum, Sam'al and Bīt-Agusi, the forces of Shalmaneser III returned east, destroying the fortified city of Sazabê located on or near the frontier of the land of Carchemish (Yamada 2000, 108–120).

In the latter half of the 9th century BC Carchemish appears to have benefited from the elimination of Bīt-Adini as a geopolitical rival. The Cekke stele (Fig. 3.2, no. 75; Fig. 3.3), erected in *c.* 775 BC and found approximately in-situ, is the foundation charter for the city of Kamana, established by the Carchemishite ruler Kamanis supported by his vizier Sasturas (Dunand 1940; Hawkins 2000, 143–151). A stele found close to the village of Körkün near Gaziantep (Fig. 3.2, no. 77) with an inscription by Kazupis, a high ranking servant of the Carchemishite king Astiruwa, indicates that the region was under the latter's control during the late 9th century BC (Kalaç 1969; Hawkins 2000, 171–175).

Expansion of Carchemish's western hinterland during the second half of the Neo-Hittite period was probably a reassertion, in part, of earlier territorial claims. When Aššurnāṣirpal II passed through Bīt-Adini territory on the way to Carchemish between 876–868 BC, the description does not include any cities west of the Euphrates (Grayson

Fig. 3.3 The Cekke stele (Dunand 1940, pl. I)

1991, 216–217). Bīt-Adini's control over territory in the Quwayq valley and further north appears therefore to have been a relatively short-lived phenomenon (Hawkins 1995b, 91). In 848 BC the annals of Shalmaneser III record the conquest of 97 towns belonging to Sangar(a), ruler of Carchemish (Yamada 2000, 170–171).

Discovery of an inscribed Luwian funerary stele at Tilsevet [alias Ekinveren] (Fig. 3.2, no. 76) with crenulations representing a tower, a style otherwise unique to Carchemish and dated on typological grounds to the 8th century BC, may suggest the western extent of the capital's own immediate hinterland at this time (Kalaç 1968; Hawkins 2000, 178–180).

Neo-Hittite rule at Carchemish came to an abrupt end in 717 BC when the city was captured by the Assyrians. Justification for this attack by Sargon II was an apparently treacherous communication between his vassal Pisiri, the last king of Carchemish, and the Phyrgian ruler Mita, whose growing influence threatened Assyria's control over south-east Anatolia. Assyrian annals record that a significant proportion of the city's population, including the royal family and its entourage, were deported and replaced by settlers from Mesopotamia (Hallo and Younger 2000, 293).

Archaeological sites in their topographical context

The political landscape outlined above corresponds to a diverse geographic region, within which numerous archaeological correlates for textual sources can plausibly be identified. Remote sensing and paleoenvironmental studies provide further insights into overland communications and potential land use.

The main agricultural hinterland of Neo-Hittite Carchemish would have been, as in preceding and subsequent periods, the adjacent flood plain and low river terraces on the west bank of the Euphrates River. This area presents a notable concentration of multi-period mounds and upland sites, reflecting significant Iron Age occupation. Alluviation also obscures numerous pre-Roman features along the valley floor (Wilkinson *et al.* 2007, 220–223 and Chapter 5). Cultivation of the Euphrates floodplain around Emar [modern Tell Meskene] is known from textual sources to have been underway by the late 2nd millennium BC (Mori 2003). Paleoenvironmental evidence demonstrates this was not incompatible with the contemporary existence of riverine gallery forest (Deckers 2005). Analysis of wood charcoal from Tilbesar and Horum Höyük indicates that extensive oak stands have become almost completely denuded since the Bronze Age (Willcox 2002, 143). To what extent this occurred during the Neo-Hittite period is unclear, although agriculture, charcoal production for smelting, and Assyrian timber exports could all have contributed towards deforestation. Wood may also have been exported locally to more degraded areas of adjacent steppe. Much of the Gaziantep plain west of Carchemish would, as today, have been suitable for dry farming. While intensive modern irrigation and canalization of the Quwayq River obscures its underlying fluvial morphology, the area surrounding Cekke was likely also a focus for agricultural activity during antiquity (Dorrell 1981, 75–76). Charred remains of barley were recovered from Iron Age contexts at nearby Tell Rifa'at (Hillman 1981).

Around Cekke numerous sites with Iron Age occupation have been identified through archaeological survey in the Quwayq valley (Matthers 1981, 415–418, 435). The site of Tell Dabiq (Fig. 3.2, no. 56) is commonly associated with ancient Dabigu, variously described in Assyrian annals of Shalmaneser III's 857 BC campaign as one of "the fortified cities of Adini", and "the fortress in the land of Hatti". This difference in nomenclature reflects both geographical conventions for territory west of the Euphrates, and perhaps also a changing geopolitical reality (Yamada

2000, 112–113) . The specific association between ancient Dabigu and Tell Dabiq can be questioned on the basis of survey by Matthers (1981) which has not found any evidence for an Iron Age settlement at that site. Such occupation is recorded, however, immediately to the north at Douabiq (Fig. 3.2, no. 55), which likely represents a variant on the same original toponym. This site is also located on the east side of the Quwayq River, forming a natural boundary with the adjacent Aramaean territory of Bīt-Agusi based at Tell Rifa'at [ancient Arpad] (Fig. 3.2, no. 61). The Assyrian conquest of Dabigu is depicted on Balawat Bronze Band IV (King 1915, pls xix–xxiv).

The fortified city of Sazabê belonging to "Sangara the Karkamishean", attacked by Shalmaneser III on his return journey from Dabigu in 857 BC, can plausibly be associated with Tell al-Qana (Fig. 3.2, no. 20). Extensive scatters of Iron Age ceramics were present at this *c.* 17 ha site which was informally visited in 2009 (Chapters 4 and 5). A probable mention in the Balawat reliefs to an earlier attack on Sazaba/ê by the Assyrian king Aššurnāsirpal II in *c.* 870 BC (Yamada 2000, 74) also favours a location in close communication with the Euphrates (see 'Lands beyond Carchemish' section below). For the Sajur's longstanding role as a political frontier see Peltenburg *et al.* (2012, 213–214) and Chapter 6.

Identification of hollow ways emanating from the fortified Iron Age lower town at Tell Rifa'at [ancient Arpad] by Casana (2013, 261–262) provides diagnostic criteria for other possible contemporary examples elsewhere in the Quwayq valley and surrounding areas. A nearby hollow way with comparable morphology, orientated NE-SW and *c.* 60–80 m in width, is visible on CORONA imagery for *c.* 5.5 km to the south of Cekke (Fig. 3.4). A shorter section of hollow way is also visible immediately north of the village. It can be speculated that the Cekke stele was positioned along a road between Iron Age settlements at Douabiq and Tell Battal Shomali (Fig. 3.2, no. 55+52). Based on the close correspondence of this hollow way to a least-cost path from Carchemish to Tell Rifa'at, it is possible that it also formed part of a long-distance connection between these two cities (Fig. 3.5). Modified projection of this hypothetical route, taking into account likely crossing points over the Sajur River, further suggests that it may have run adjacent to Tell al-Qana (see also Wilkinson and Wilkinson forthcoming).

North of Cekke, the Quwayq River probably continued to mark the border of Carchemish territory. Extensive Iron Age occupation has been recorded in this region by Özgen *et al.* (2001; 2002). This includes the large mound of Oylum Höyük (Fig. 3.2, no. 48) with its excavated Iron Age I-II settlement (Özgen *et al.* 1997). Although direct evidence pertaining to the beginning of the Neo-Hittite period is lacking, it is possible that the Quwayq River represents the original line of control between (post) viceroyal Carchemish and Aleppo. Monumental reliefs found at the temple of

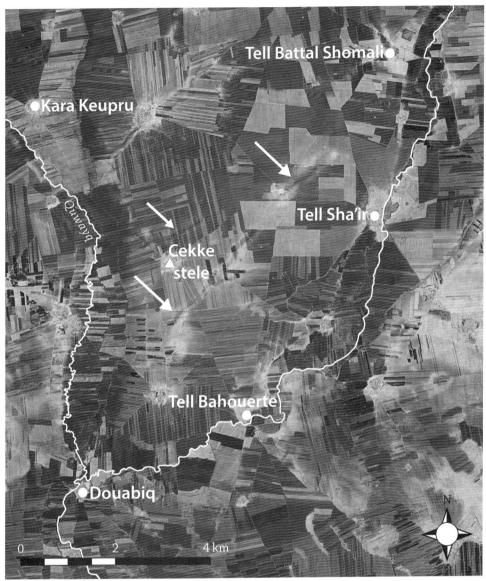

Fig. 3.4 Corona satellite image (November 1968) of hollow ways in the east Quwayq valley showing relationship with Cekke stele and nearby Iron Age settlements (image courtesy of US Geological Survey). Hollow ways identified with arrows

the Storm God in Aleppo (Fig. 3.2, no. 62) featuring king Taita, suggest that city had come under the influence of Pattin/Unqi by the 11th–10th century BC (Hawkins 2009, 169–171; Kohlmeyer 2009).

It seems unlikely that the Neo-Hittite territory of Carchemish could have extended any further south than where the Quwayq valley narrows adjacent to Tell Nef (Fig. 3.2, no. 60). As noted by Matthers *et al.* (1978, 146–147), above the 450 m contour line valley systems to the east become isolated, and are perhaps more closely associated with the adjacent Jabbul plain that was at least partially under the control of Bīt-Agusi. For Iron Age occupation in this region see Schwartz *et al.* (2000, 452–453; see also Yukich 2013) and Maxwell Hyslop *et al.* (1942).

Settlement in the extended western hinterland of Carchemish otherwise corresponds in geographical terms to the watershed of the Sajur River and its tributaries, chiefly the Kızılhisar Çay and Ayfinar Çay. Uplands surrounding these fertile valleys alternate between pasture and eroded Eocene limestone hills. The site of Tilbeshar is conventionally associated with ancient Til Bashere (Fig. 3.2, no. 46), listed in itineraries of Shalmaneser III's campaign against Bīt-Adini in 857 BC. It should be noted, however, that no archaeological evidence of Iron Age occupation has yet been found (see Kepinski 2005 for summary of fieldwork results). In the vicinity of Gaziantep, several sites with Iron Age occupation (Fig. 3.2, no. 39–42) were recorded by du Plat Taylor *et al.* (1950). The nearby site

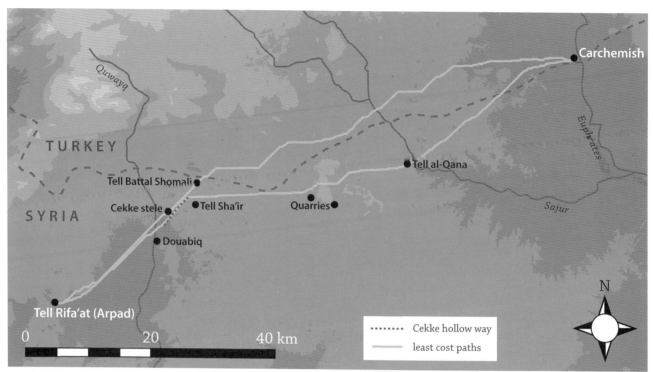

Fig. 3.5 Projected least-cost route corridor between Carchemish and Tell Rifa'at incorporating probable Iron Age hollow way near Cekke

of Sārīn [alias Sazgın] (Fig. 3.2, no. 45) is associated by Lipiński (2000, 178) with ᵘʳᵘ*Su-ú-ru-nu* of the Assyrian annals. Approximately 10 km north of Gaziantep, Iron Age occupation has been recorded by Perrot (1962, 18) at Dülük Höyük [ancient Doliche] (Fig. 3.2, no. 43), which is known from classical sources to have been a major crossroads in antiquity (Dussaud 1927, 479–479).

With the exception of Lidar Höyük (Fig. 3.1), where seal impressions were found belonging to Kuzi-Teššub (Sürenhagen 1986; Hawkins 2000, 574–575), there is no indication that the jurisdiction of Carchemish extended east beyond the Euphrates during the Neo-Hittite period. A defining feature of this boundary was paired settlements on opposite banks of the river; e.g. for the crossing at Samsat Höyük-Şaşkan Küçüktepe which linked Kummuh with Aramaean territory (Til-Abne?) east of the Euphrates see Wilkinson (1990, 113, 101). The extent of direct geopolitical control exercised by Carchemish would most probably have been restricted to the north by a pronounced narrow section of the Euphates valley which separates it from the Adıyaman basin. This naturally defined frontier potentially corresponds to a river crossing at Tilmusa Höyük (Fig. 3.2, no. 23), where Algaze *et al.* (1994, 32–33) documented Iron Age III occupation together with numerous coarsewares of possible earlier date. A crossing at this point would have linked major overland communications west towards Dülük Höyük with a clear route north-east towards Samsat. Closer to Carchemish, the location of Şaraga Höyük (Fig. 3.2,

no. 24) where Luwian hieroglyphic inscriptions have been found, relative to Harabebezıkan Höyük (Fig. 3.2, no. 25) downstream on the opposite bank, again suggests a paired west-to-east river crossing.

Lands beyond Carchemish

In addition to those features outlined above which provide direct evidence for geopolitical control by Carchemish, the changing extent of its jurisdiction can also be deduced by way of reference to neighbouring areas demonstrably outside the land of Carchemish during the period under review. Along the east bank of the Euphrates, cities belonging to Bīt-Adini included Burmarina [modern Tell Shioukh Fawqani], which was the nearest major river settlement opposite and downstream from Carchemish (Fig. 3.2, no. 26). Accounts of Shalmaneser III's first year campaign in 858 BC record crossing the Euphrates, either at Burmarina itself or further north (Yamada 2000, 90–91). A boatman named Šin-zabad is mentioned in a 7th century BC Aramaic tablet from Tell Shioukh Fawqani (Fales *et al.* 1996, 90, 104–105).

Prior and subsequent to its takeover by Bīt-Adini, the site of Til Barsip [modern Tell Ahmar] (Fig. 3.2, no. 27) was the capital of an independent kingdom called Masuwari ruled by a Neo-Hittite dynasty, latterly under the supervision of an Assyrian governor when the site is also known as Kar-Shalmaneser. On the opposite west bank at the confluence of the Euphrates and Sajur Rivers, ancient Pitru/Ana-Assur-uter-asbat has been convincingly identified with the site of Aushariye/Aushar Bujak (Fig. 3.2, no. 28), which preserves the root 'Assur' (Eidem and Pütt 2001, 86 and Chapter 6). This strategically important region for overland and riverine communications periodically came under Assyrian control, firstly during the reign of Tiglath-Pileser I (r. 1114–1076 BC), before its loss to an unknown Aramaean king during the reign of Ashur-Rabi II (r. 1013–973 BC) (see Fig. 3.2 'Assyrian occupation'). Following the Assyrian recapture of Til Barsip in 856 BC, and the flight of its Aramaean ruler Ahuni, several former Bīt-Adini possessions including Pitru and Nappigi [modern Membij] (Fig. 3.2, no. 34) were settled with colonists from elsewhere in the empire (Grayson 1996, 19). Iron Age occupation has also been identified along the Wadi Membij at the intermediate site of Houdhoud (Fig. 3.2, no. 33). As noted by Eidem and Pütt (2001, 85, 87), the equidistant location of small Iron Age sites along the river bank south of Aushariye is suggestive of inter-visible communication. Wadi Abu Qalqal surveyed by Mottram and Menere (2005) also presents a notable concentration of Iron Age settlements including those shown (Fig. 3.2, no. 36–38).

Direct annexation of territory by the Assyrians south-west of the Sajur River contrasts with other former Bīt-Adini areas west of the Euphrates, where there is no firm archaeological or textual evidence for a continuing permanent presence. At the beginning of the Neo-Hittite period the region south of the Sajur River would have been ruled by either Carchemish, or perhaps a local Aramaean group who had come to control the area following the destruction of Emar [modern Tell Meskene] and other settlements in the land of Aštata by c. 1175 BC. The earliest evidence for reoccupation at Tell Meskene is a fragmentary decorated object with a short Aramaic inscription, attributed on typological grounds to the 8th century BC (Margueron and Teixidor 1983).

West of the Quwayq river was the Aramaean territory of Bīt-Agusi. Foundation of its principal settlement at Arpad [modern Tell Rifa'at] is dated historically to the 9th century BC (Matthers et al. 1978, 144). An earlier 'Akhlamu-Aramaean' occupation at Tell Rifa'at has also been suggested by Seton Williams (1967, 19) on the basis of limited excavation. The tell and fortified Iron Age lower town at Arpad encloses an area of c. 120 ha (Casana 2013, 5). This bears comparison with Iron Age Carchemish at c. 100 ha, suggesting a similar level of urban development (see Chapter 8 for discussion of the Outer Town area).

To the north-west of the land of Carchemish was the Neo-Hittite kingdom of Gurgum with its capital at Maraş. In the far west, where the Kurt Dağ range [Assyrian Mt. Atalur?] meets the Islahiye plain, was the Aramaean kingdom of Sam'al based at Zincirli Höyük (Fig. 3.1). Above c. 1500 m the intervening foothills of the Kurt Dağ mountains present a natural barrier to occupation with thin soil cover and much exposed bedrock. Iron Age occupation within the

Islahiye-Kahramanmaraş region is recorded in surveys by du Plat Taylor et al. (1950), Alkım (1969), Carter et al. and Garrard et al. (see Swartz Dodd 2003).

Of particular interest is Coba Höyük/Sakçagözü (Fig. 3.2, no. 70) excavated by du Plat Taylor et al. (1950). This site is commonly identified with Lutibu on the northern frontier of Sam'al, which Shalmaneser III attacked in 858 BC (Yamada 2000, 95). As well as potentially guarding the adjacent border with Gurgum, this large fortified settlement was located in close proximity to a major passage through the Kurt Dağ mountains, along the route of the modern Gaziantep-Osmaniye road. The strategic location of Sam'al, which also controlled overland communications with Cilicia and the Amuq plain, was noted by its king Kulamuwa (c. 840–810 BC) who records hostilities with surrounding larger neighbours that perhaps included Carchemish (Hallo and Younger 2000, 147). Prior to the foundation of Sam'al by an Aramaean dynasty in the late 10th century BC, the region may have been home to a Neo-Hittite population referred to by king Kulamuwa as Mškbm (Lipiński 2000, 236).

At various times during the Neo-Hittite period the land of Carchemish was bordered to the north by Bīt-Adini, Kummuh, and probably the city-kingdom of Paqarhubuni. The Kızkapanlı/Pazarcık stele (Donbaz 1990) marked the north–south border between Kummuh to the east and Gurgum to the west (Fig. 3.2, no. 79). According to its two inscriptions this boundary was initially established in 805 BC and confirmed again in 773 BC. The stele is believed to have been found in situ, next to the village of Kızkapanlı in a narrow side valley east of the Maraş plain (Donbaz 1990, 8–10). By far the most direct route between Gurgum and the core territory of Kummuh around Samsat is via the Karasu valley which adjoins the west bank of the Euphrates. It can therefore be surmised that in the first quarter of the 8th century BC this valley formed a district of Kummuh, thus providing a maximum northern limit for the contemporary land of Carchemish which likely did not reach further north than the Güreniz-Nizip Dere (see Fig. 3.2. 'maximum Carchemish control').

The Kızkapanlı/Pazarcık stele text records a large battle between the Assyrians and a coalition of Syrian armies on the outskirts of a city called Paqarhubuni in 805 BC. Paqarhubuni is also mentioned in the context of two other Assyrian campaigns during the 9th century BC (Grayson 1996, 15–16, 38–39, 66, 205). The city of Paqarhubuni was the setting for a large battle in 858 BC, when it is clearly identified as a possession of Bīt-Adini. During the year 847 BC, the land of Paqarhubuni was the sole target of Shalmaneser III's twelfth campaign, at which time it appears to have become independent following the defeat of Ahuni in 855 BC (Yamada 2000, 178–179; cf. Hawkins 2000, 75 who suggests Paqarhubuni was subsequently absorbed into the territory of Carchemish). Potential candidates for Paqarhubuni include the large multi-period site of Araban

(Fig. 3.2, no. 71) in the middle of the Karasu valley (Archi *et al.* 1971, 49–51), or Yavuzeli Höyük (Fig. 3.2, no. 72) in the adjacent Merzumen valley where possible Iron Age occupation has been recorded by Perrot (1962, 141).

Association of a site in the Karasu-Merzumen region with Paqarhubuni receives circumstantial support from the Assyrian description of Bīt-Adini's northern geography contained within the Kenk gorge inscription (Fig. 3.2, no. 80), made following the siege of Mount Shitamrat in 855 BC (Taşyürek 1979). This fortress of Ahuni is described as being on the west bank of the Euphrates, "hovering like a cloud suspended from heaven" (Yamada 2000, 137). Shitamrat is tentatively identified with the fortified Iron Age site of Kaleboyu (Fig. 3.2, no. 22), located *c.* 1 km north of Kenk on high cliffs overlooking the river (Comfort and Ergeç 2001, 27).

Both proposed identifications for Shitamrat and Paqarhubuni rely upon the presumption that the places named in the Pazarcık/Kızkapanlı and Kenk texts are to be found in the near vicinity. Omission of Paqahubuni from the aforementioned Assyrian campaign itinerary of 857 BC, which very likely includes sites controlled by Bīt-Adini in the vicinity of Gaziantep, arguably does not support an alternative location in this area (*cf.* Streck 2004). A close territorial relationship between Paqarhubuni and Shitamrat has previously been suggested by numerous authors including Yamada (2000, 137–139) and Dion (1997, 91).

Reconstructing patterns of settlement

The map of the land of Carchemish presented in Figure 3.2 shows the relationship between features used to define its territory and corresponding patterns of settlement. As noted above, due to the paucity of clear diagnostic wares in archaeological survey assemblages, it is only possible in the majority of instances to identify a general Iron Age phase of occupation. More specific identification of Iron Age I–II remains relies on correlation with historical texts featuring known locations, and/or artefacts that can be dated on typological grounds to between the 12th and 8th centuries BC. Lack of clearly differentiated ceramic forms in survey assemblages also means that sites founded after the Assyrian conquest of Carchemish in 717 BC may have inadvertently been included in the possible Neo-Hittite period category, although the number is likely to be low due to more visible imports from Mesopotamia at this time. The distribution of sites shown in Figure 3.2 within the proposed territory of Carchemish should therefore be viewed as an approximation rather than a direct representation of settlement during Iron Age I–II.

A major reason underlying this lack of chronological resolution is the dearth of comparanda for archaeological surface collections from stratified excavations. Within the

proposed territory of Carchemish, only at the capital itself have Neo-Hittite period settlement remains been exposed. While the situation is somewhat better for neighbouring areas where significant Iron Age I–II occupation has been documented at sites including Tille Höyük, Lidar Höyük, Oylum Höyük and Tell Ahmar, other important regional centres such as Tell Rifa'at [ancient Arpad] have only been subject to very limited investigation (see Table 3.1 for site references). For a review of research on Iron Age ceramics in north Syria and south-east Anatolia see contributions in Hausleiter and Reiche (1999).

For most if not all of the archaeological survey areas covering the proposed territory of Carchemish, poor recognition of Iron Age I–II ceramics constitutes a potential source of bias when reconstructing settlement patterns. This may account in part for the apparent discrepancy between the 200+ cities in the environs of Til Bashere – Dabigu mentioned in Assyrian annals of 857 BC, and the comparatively small number of sites recorded through archaeological survey in the Quwayq and Sajur valleys. By way of example, several additional Iron Age sites along the Sajur valley have been proposed by Morandi Bonacossi (2000, 379) based on a re-examination of the survey pottery published by Moore and Copeland in Sanlaville (1985) (see also Chapter 4). When considering the extent of this disparity, it is worth bearing in mind the propagandistic nature of the Assyrian sources, in which description of 'cities' is known to include smaller settlements and nomad encampments.

Divergent methodologies employed by different survey teams also hinder comparison between archaeological data-sets. This concern is exemplified by overlapping areas to the south of Gaziantep investigated by Archi *et al.* (1971) and Özgen *et al.* (2001, 2002). Whereas the former was concerned solely with mounded sites identified prior to survey using a topographic map, the latter attempted to document a comprehensive range of occupation types. While both studies indicate the predominance of höyüks within the Iron Age settlement landscape, a greater number and diversity of sites was recorded by Özgen *et al.*, largely as a result of the more intensive mode of survey employed. In Figure 3.2 only those sites in the Quwayq-Afrin area listed by Özgen *et al.* as having definite Iron Age occupation are shown. If sites with possible Iron Age occupation recorded by Özgen *et al.* are also included, this suggests a much more densely populated landscape (Fig. 3.6).

At a broader regional scale, the focus in recent decades on rescue projects concurrent with dam construction has led to bias in coverage towards the Euphrates flood plain. In terms of comparison between archaeological surveys covering the proposed territory of Carchemish, those investigations conducted by du Plat Taylor *et al.* (1950), Perrot (1962), Archi *et al.* (1971) and Kulakoğlu (2006) are limited to site reconnaissance. Investigations by Copeland and Moore published in Sanlaville (1985) systematically examined sites

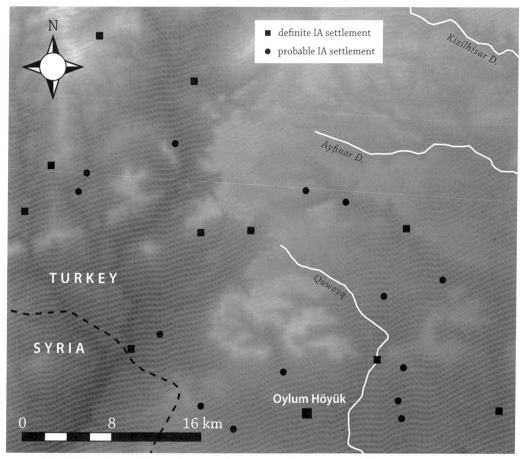

Fig. 3.6 Iron Age settlement density in the Quwayq-Afrin area (after Özgen et al. 2001, 2002)

within their environmental context, but were constrained by limited recognition of Iron Age ceramic types at the time of publication. The results of more intensive survey by Özgen *et al.* (2001, 2002) are presently only available in preliminary form. Reports by Matthers (1981), Algaze *et al.* (1994) and Wilkinson *et al.* (2007 and this volume) provide the most comprehensive account of their respective survey areas.

Concepts of territoriality

In addition to elucidating the changing extent of Carchemish's political control over surrounding areas during the late 2nd to early 1st millennia BC, the various sources outlined above highlight common and contrasting concepts of territoriality held by Neo-Hittite, Assyrian and Aramaean populations. Evidence from archaeological survey indicates that permanent Iron Age settlement in the land of Carchemish was predominantly, although not exclusively, located on and/ or around tells. This continuing occupation of multi-period sites suggests a significant degree of demographic overlap across the Bronze-to-Iron Age transition. At Carchemish this extended to an unbroken tradition of political organisation.

It can thus be inferred that conceptual and administrative definitions of territory would have been well established amongst most sedentary communities by the Neo-Hittite period.

The CEKKE and TÜNP 1 stelae (Fig. 3.2, no. 74 and 77), and the KARKAMIS A4a text from the capital itself, all record property transactions during the first half of the 8th century BC (Hawkins 2000, 143–156). This legal framework for land ownership would have been central to the collection of tax. Primacy of local rulers in this process offers an explanation as to how cities in the western hinterland of Carchemish were able to switch back and forth between its own sphere of control and that of Bīt-Adini during the 9th century BC. Acquisition of taxation rights, in addition to land assets, was probably the overall purpose behind the various payments listed in the Cekke text, which commemorates the purchase of the city (re)founded as Kamana from the "men of Kanapu". As well as illuminating the practicalities of property transaction, the Cekke text also reflects a more archaic sense of territorial entitlement through references to Kamanis as Country Lord of both Carchemish and Maliz/ Malatya, a claim based upon a much earlier geopolitical reality (Hawkins 2000, 147–148 and Chapter 2).

For the Assyrians, territory west of the Euphrates was regarded as the 'Land of Hatti', a traditional designation dating back to the initial establishment of Hittite control over north Syria and south-east Anatolia in the later 14th century BC. This conceptual division between what Postgate (1992) termed "the land of Assur and yoke of Assur" meant that, prior to the mid-8th century BC, Assyrian involvement west of the Euphrates was characterized by temporary incursions to extract tribute from conquered lands. With the probable exception of the relatively small area between Pitru [modern Aushariye] and Nappigi [modern Membij], there is no archaeological or textual evidence to suggest a permanent Assyrian presence beyond a few isolated outposts. Carchemish and neighbouring states were rather subject to client agreements that were enforced where necessary through the threat or exercise of military force. The political geography of the Assyrian empire in the northern Levant and Euphrates region can be viewed as a network of overland communications, which facilitated the movement of material goods and troops through independently governed territories (Liverani 1988, 86; Chapter 5). Subsequent assimilation of Carchemish and its territory into the Assyrian provincial system formed part of a wider trend towards direct rule, beginning with the conquest of Arpad/Bīt-Agusi under Tiglath-Pileser III in 740 BC. The final conquest of Neo-Hittite Carchemish by the Assyrians in 717 BC reflects the transition from a network to land based empire west of the Euphrates.

The meaning and expression of territoriality on the part of Aramaean populations would have changed significantly during the period under review, concurrent with the shift from semi-nomadic to sedentary patterns of occupation. At the beginning of the Neo-Hittite period the mobile nature of the Akhlamu-Aramaeans appears to have caused particular problems for the Assyrians under Tiglath-Pileser I (r. 1114–1076 BC), who records 28 military campaigns across the Euphrates River (Grayson 1991, 43). By the 10th century BC several Aramaean states with defined territories bordered the land of Carchemish; principally Bīt-Agusi, Sam'al, and Bīt-Adini which before the 9th century BC was restricted to east of the Euphrates. In several instances this transition appears to reflect the ascendancy of a pre-existing demographic component. Population migration also very likely played a role in the expansion of Aramaean groups into areas such as the north Quwayq valley, which latterly became the centre of Bīt-Agusi territory (Schwartz 1989). As well as changing over time, the nature of territorial possessions varied between Aramaean groups. Whereas the inhabitants of Bīt-Agusi likely shared for the most part a common sense of tribal identity, those cities west of Carchemish held by Bīt-Adini during the mid-9th century BC probably owed their affiliation to military conquest.

The common array of material culture associated with Neo-Hittite and Aramaean groups in particular highlights their interconnected, as opposed to exclusive, spheres of material and social engagement (e.g. for Tell Ahmar see Bunnens 2009; Harmanşah 2013, 68–69). A degree of symbiosis between sedentary communities and mobile pastoralists would normally be expected through exchange of agricultural surplus and animal products (Wilkinson 2007, 28–29). In times of environmental stress this relationship may have turned to one of conflict between Neo-Hittite/ Assyrian and Aramaean groups over food (for adjacent areas of Mesopotamia see Kirleis and Herles 2007). As noted by Seton Williams (1961, 70) in relation to modern Bedu settlement at Tell Rifa'at, major loss of livestock through drought can quickly force nomadic groups to adopt a more settled lifestyle, placing further stress on finite resources. South of the Sajur and east of the Quwayq valley, possible fluctuations in the zone of rainfed cultivation during the late 2nd–early 1st millennia BC could have made agriculture more marginal (Wilkinson and Barbanes 2000, 398–400 and Chapter 5). Transfer of Bit Agusi's capital from Arne [modern Tell Aarane?] to Arpad [modern Tell Rifa'at] can plausibly be associated with ecological stress; the two sites being respectively situated below and within the optimal zone for rainfed cultivation (Fig. 3.2, no. 73+61).

The equidistant location of basalt sculpture quarries at Sikizlar-Zilfe (Fig. 3.2, no. 81) between Arpad and Carchemish, approximately 45 km as the crow flies in either direction, also raises the possibility that this prestige resource was in some way shared across political borders. Transportation of monumental artworks to these centres could have been by way of the hypothetical long-distance route corridor shown in Figure 3.5. Exploitation of the quarries is dated on stylistic grounds to between the 10th–8th centuries BC (Mazzoni 1986–87, 270; Orthmann 1974), suggesting they fell at various times within and outside the proposed jurisdiction of Carchemish.

Summary and conclusions

The above review of archaeological and textual sources suggests five distinct phases in the development of the Neo-Hittite land of Carchemish in relation to its neighbours;

Phase 1. [*c.* 1190–1100 BC]: At the beginning of the Neo-Hittite period Carchemish maintained sovereignty over lands west of the Euphrates stretching from Malatya in the north to the Sajur valley in the south. The imposing natural topography separating Carchemish from the Adıyman region suggests that riverine communications along the Euphrates would have been particularly important at this time. Practicalities of long-distance Euphrates navigation by the Assyrians are discussed in Fales (1993). Textual evidence for Malatya founding its own satellite settlements in the 11th century BC (Hawkins 1995b, 89) supports the view that the secession of Kummuh and Malatya was a gradual process. This period likely represents the maximum extent of the land of Carchemish during the Neo-Hittite period (see Fig. 3.2 'maximum Carchemish control').

Phase 2. [*c.* 1100–870 BC]: Excavations at Carchemish show extensive urban renewal during the late 11th to early 10th centuries BC, indicating a period of economic prosperity. This correlates with circumstantial evidence for an extensive western hinterland. In wider north Syria and south-east Anatolia, this period sees major urban development at sites including Zincirli and Arpad (Mazzoni 1995, 181–182). The switch from 'Great King' to 'Country Lord' dynasties at Carchemish probably reflects the reduced geopolitical role of its rulers when compared to the preceding post-viceroyal era.

Phase 3. [*c.* 870–855 BC]: Begins with Assyrian subjugation of Carchemish, and is characterised by a period of ensuing weakness when the city loses control over most of its western hinterland to the Aramaean ruler Ahuni of Bīt-Adini. This period likely represents the minimum extent of the land of Carchemish during the Neo-Hittite period (see Fig. 3.2 'minimum Carchemish control').

Phase 4. [*c.* 855–717 BC]: Following the Assyrian defeat of Bīt-Adini, the city-kingdom of Carchemish gradually reasserts influence over its extended western hinterland, including the (re)acquisition of land around Cekke, and the probable (re)establishment of the Quwayq river as its south-eastern frontier.

Phase 5. [717 BC+]: End of Neo-Hittite rule at Carchemish with Assyrian conquest of the city, and absorption of its territory into the Assyrian provincial system. Archaeological survey along the banks of the Euphrates north of Carchemish suggests that repopulation of the city recorded in the Assyrian annals may have extended to surrounding areas, potentially resulting in an increase in the density and distribution of settlement under radically altered geo-political conditions (Algaze *et al.* 1994, 19; Chapter 4). For possible identification of the Neo-Hittite Outer Town wall destroyed by the Assyrians see Chapter 8.

This historical sequence describes a geopolitical territory, which both overlaps with and is distinct from contemporary settlement landscapes known from archaeological survey. Whereas the former has its origins in the preceding Hittite era, the latter also constitutes part of a longer tradition of societal development. This underlying lineage is reflected most clearly in the archaeological record through conservative retention of ceramics technologies, and continuous occupation of multi-period mounded sites.

In addition to clear similarities between the Iron Age I–II territory of Carchemish and that of the preceding Late Bronze Age (Brown forthcoming), a comparable sphere

of regional engagement from the Euphrates west towards Oylum Höyük has been proposed as far back as the 3rd millennium BC (Özgen and Helwing 2003, 74). While Carchemish itself did not develop as a significant urban centre until the later 3rd millennium BC at the earliest (Peltenburg 2010 & Chapter 7), this similarity in network orientation does reflect basic common dynamics, namely routes of overland communication, land use and associated population distribution.

It should be emphasized that the proposed map of the land of Carchemish (Fig. 3.2) represents the maximum and minimum extent of geopolitical control exercised by the city-kingdom at various points during the Neo-Hittite period, and does not in the vast majority of instances show a defined border. While the existence of frontier-markers such as the Kızkapanlı/Pazarcık stele demonstrates that set definitions of territoriality did exist, these notions were inconsistently applied across the landscape, and were undoubtedly contested between sometimes overlapping population groups (for comparable discussion concerning the Amuq valley see Osborne 2013). As highlighted above, several outstanding issues are also apparent with the present reconstruction associated with the resolution, coverage and convergence of the various data-sets involved. The common geographic framework established in this study provides a basis for future reassessment of archaeological evidence, in light of much needed refinements to regional ceramic typologies (for preliminary analysis of Iron Age II–III ceramics from the 2011 Turkish–Italian excavations at Carchemish see Bonomo and Zaina 2014).

Table 3.1. List of sites with definite [■] or possible [●] Neo-Hittite period settlement (Iron Age I–II) as shown in Fig. 3.2 ('LCP' = Land of Carchemish survey)

Euphrates and Sajur valleys
1. ■ Carchemish (excavated: Woolley 1921; Woolley and Barnett 1952; Marchetti 2014; Outer Town surveyed by Wilkinson *et al.* Chapter 8) [LCP site no. 46]
2. ● Khirbet Seraisat (surveyed: Wilkinson *et al.* Appendix A) [LCP site no. 1]
3. ● Tashatan/Marm al-Hajar (surveyed: Wilkinson *et al.* Appendix A) [LCP site no. 5]
4. ● Jerablus Tahtani Village (surveyed: Wilkinson *et al.* Appendix A) [LCP site no. 6]
5. ● Tell Amarna (surveyed: Wilkinson *et al.* Appendix A; see also Tunca 1999) [LCP site no. 21]
6. ● Tell Dabas (surveyed: Wilkinson *et al.* Appendix A) [LCP site no. 24]
7. ● Dadate North (surveyed: Wilkinson *et al.* Appendix A) [LCP site no. 37]
8. ● Tell Sha'ir [Sajur] (surveyed: Wilkinson *et al.* Appendix A) [LCP site no. 38]

9. ● Boz Höyük/Tell al-Akhbar (surveyed: Sanlaville 1985; Wilkinson *et al.* Appendix A) [LCP site no. 47]
10. ● al-Hajalliya (surveyed: Wilkinson *et al.* Appendix A) [LCP site no. 54]
11. ● al-Hilwaniya/Duknuk (surveyed: Sanlaville 1985; Wilkinson *et al.* Appendix A) [LCP site no. 55]
12. ● Majra Saghir West/al-Tukhar (surveyed: Wilkinson *et al.* Appendix A) [LCP site no. 56]
13. ● Yousuf Bek (surveyed: Sanlaville 1985; Wilkinson *et al.* Appendix A) [LCP site no. 59]
14. ● Yousuf Bek SW (surveyed: Wilkinson *et al.* Appendix A) [LCP site no. 62]
15. ● Koundouriye/al-Ghoundariya (surveyed: Sanlaville 1985; Wilkinson *et al.* Appendix A) [LCP site no. 60]
16. ● Nahr Bash (surveyed: Wilkinson *et al.* Appendix A) [LCP site no. 66]
17. ● Nahr Bash West (surveyed: Wilkinson *et al.* Appendix A) [LCP site no. 65]
18. ● Arab Hassan (surveyed: Sanlaville 1985; Wilkinson *et al.* Appendix A) [LCP site no. 68]
19. ● al-Haimar (surveyed: Wilkinson *et al.* Appendix A) [LCP site no. 78]
20. ■ Tell al-Qana [ancient Sazabê?] (surveyed: Wilkinson *et al.* Chapters 4 & 5)
21. ● Kuru Höyük (surveyed: Perrot 1962, 17)
22. ● Kaleboyu [ancient Shitamrat?] (surveyed: Comfort and Ergeç 2001)
23. ● Tilmusa Höyük (surveyed: Algaze *et al.* 1994)
24. ■ Şaraga Höyük (excavated: Sertok *et al.* 2008)
25. ■ Harabebezıkan Höyük (surveyed: Algaze *et al.* 1994)
26. ■ Tell Shioukh Fawqani [ancient Burmarina] (excavated: Bachelot & Fales 2005)
27. ■ Tell Ahmar [ancient Masuwari?/Til Barsip/Kar-Shalmaneser] (excavated: Bunnens 1997)
28. ● Aushariye/Aushar Bujak [ancient Pitru?/Ana-Assur-uter-asbat?] (excavated: Eidem & Pütt 2001 and Chapter 6)
29. ■ Tell Jurn Kabir (excavated: Eidem & Pütt 1999)
30. ■ Tell Qadahiye (excavated: Eidem & Pütt 1999)
31. ● Hammam Kebir North (surveyed: Eidem & Putt 2001)
32. ● Sandaliye Kebir/Maqbara (surveyed: Eidem & Putt 2001)
33. ● Tell Houdhoud (surveyed: Sanlaville 1985)
34. ● Membij [ancient Nappigi] (surveyed: Maxwell Hyslop *et al.* 1942)
35. ■ Tell Sanndi (surveyed: Mazzoni 1986-7)
36. ● Tell Halula (surveyed: Mottram & Menere 2005)
37. ● Tell el-Homr (surveyed: Mottram & Menere 2005)
38. ● Tell Abu Qalqal (surveyed: Mottram & Menere 2005)

Gaziantep region

39. ● Gaziantep (surveyed: du Plat Taylor *et al.* 1950)
40. ● Homanus/Hümaniz Höyük (surveyed: du Plat *et al.* 1950; Archi *et al.* 1971)
41. ● Hagar/Hacar Höyük (surveyed: du Plat *et al.* 1950; Archi *et al.* 1971)

42. ● Camus/Cansiz Höyük (surveyed: du Plat *et al.* 1950; Archi *et al.* 1971)
43. ● Dülük/Keber Höyük [ancient Doliche] (surveyed: Perrot 1962)
44. ● Müşetil Höyüğü (surveyed: Özgen *et al.* 2001)
45. ● Sārīn/Sazgın [ancient Suúrunu?] (surveyed: Archi *et al.* 1971)
46. ● Tilbeshar [ancient Til Bashere?] (see Kepinski 2005)
47. ● Arıl Höyük (surveyed: Kulakoğlu 2006; Archi *et al.* 1971)

Quwayq valley

48. ■ Oylum Höyük (excavated: Özgen *et al.* 1997)
49. ● Sinnep Höyük North (surveyed: Özgen *et al.* 2001)
50. ● Çatalhöyük East (surveyed: Ozgen *et al.* 2001)
51. ● Kara Keupru (surveyed: Matthers 1981)
52. ● Tell Battal Shomali (surveyed: Matthers 1981)
53. ● Tell Sha'ir [Quwayq] (surveyed: Matthers 1981)
54. ● Tell Bahouerte (surveyed: Matthers 1981)
55. ● Douabiq [ancient Dabigu?] (surveyed: Matthers 1981)
56. ● Tell Dabiq (surveyed: Matthers 1981)
57. ● Tell Aar (surveyed: Matthers 1981)
58. ● Tell Archaq (surveyed: Matthers 1981)
59. ● Tell Akhterine (surveyed: Matthers 1981; see van der Meer & Hillen 1952)
60. ● Tell Nef (surveyed: Matthers 1981)
61. ■ Tell Rifa'at [ancient Arpad] (excavated: Seton Williams 1967; 1961)
62. ■ Aleppo [ancient Halab] (excavated: Kohlmeyer 2009)

Afrin valley

63. ● Bekere Höyüğü (surveyed: Özgen *et al.* 2001)
64. ● Çörten Tepesi (surveyed: Özgen *et al.* 2001)
65. ● Körahmet Höyüğü (surveyed: Özgen *et al.* 2002)
66. ● Hennis Pınar Höyüğü (surveyed: Özgen *et al.* 2002)
67. ● Beientepe (surveyed: Özgen *et al.* 2002)
68. ● Musabeyli Höyüğü (surveyed: Özgen *et al.* 2002)
69. ● Zengül Höyük (surveyed: Özgen *et al.* 2002)

Neighbouring regions

70. ■ Coba Höyük/Sakçagözü [ancient Lutibu?] (excavated: du Plat Taylor *et al.* 1950)
71. ● Araban/Altintaş (surveyed: Archi *et al.* 1971)
72. ● Yavuzeli Höyük (surveyed: Perrot 1962; Archi *et al.* 1971)
73. ● Tell Aarane [ancient Arne?] (surveyed: Matthers *et al.* 1978; 1981; Maxwell Hyslop *et al.* 1942)

Other man-made features of the Neo-Hittite period [▲]

74. ▲ Kelekli stele (Hogarth 1909)
75. ▲ Cekke stele (Dunand 1940)
76. ▲ Tilsevet/Ekinveren funerary stele (Kalaç 1968)
77. ▲ Körkün stele (Kalaç 1969)
78. ▲ Tünp 1 stele (Kalaç 1965)
79. ▲ Kızkapanlı/Pazarcık stele (Donbaz 1990)
80. ▲ Kenk inscription (Taşyürek 1979)
81. ▲ Sikizlar-Zilfe quarries (surveyed: Mazzoni 1986-87; Orthmann 1974)

Acknowledgements

We would like to extend our thanks to David Hawkins and Mark Weeden for their expert advice concerning the use of historical sources. The responsibility for any conclusions drawn in this regard rests solely with the present authors. Thanks are also due to Tony and Eleanor Wilkinson for stimulating discussions during the preparation of this chapter, and to Marco Nebbia for help with least-cost path projections.

Bibliography

Algaze, G., Breuninger, R. and Knudstad, J. (1994) The Tigris–Euphrates archaeological reconnaissance project: final report of the Birecik and Carchemish Dam survey area. *Anatolica* 20, 1–96.

Alkım, U.B. (1969) The Amanus region in Turkey: new light on the historical geography and archaeology. *Archaeology* 22, 280–289.

Archi, A., Pecorella, P.E. and Salvini, M. (1971) *Gaziantep e la sua regione: uno studio storico e topografico degli insediamenti preclassici.* Incunabula Graeca 48. Rome, Edizioni dell'Ateneo.

Bachelot, L. and Fales, F.M. (eds) (2005) *Tell Shiukh Fawqani 1994–1998.* Monograph VI (1–2), History of the Ancient Near East. Padova, S.A.R.G.O.N.

Bonomo, A. and Zaina, F. (2014) The Iron Age II–III pottery assemblage from Karkemish and Yunus. In N. Marchetti (ed.) *Karkemish. An Ancient Capital on the Euphrates.* OrientLab 2, 137–144. Bologna, Ante Quem.

Brown, M. (forthcoming) Carchemish and the Hittite Empire in the Middle Euphrates Valley. In D. Lawrence, M. Altaweel and G. Philip (eds) *New Agendas in Remote Sensing and Landscape Archaeology in the Near East: Studies in Honor of Tony J. Wilkinson.* Chicago, Oriental Institute Publications.

Bryce, T. (2012) *The World of the Neo-Hittite Kingdoms: A Political and Military History.* Oxford, Oxford University Press.

Bunnens, G. (2009) Assyrian Empire building and Aramization of culture as seen from Tell Ahmar/Til Barsib. *Syria* 86, 67–82.

Bunnens, G. (1997) Til Barsib under Assyrian domination: A brief account of the Melbourne University excavations at Tell Ahmar. In S. Parpola and R. Whiting (eds) *Assyria 1995: Proceedings of the 10th Anniversary Symposium of the Neo-Assyrian Text Corpus Project, Helsinki, September 7th–11th, 1995,* 17–28. Helsinki, Neo-Assyrian Text Corpus Project.

Casana, J. (2013) Radial route systems and agro-pastoral strategies in the Fertile Crescent: new discoveries from western Syria and southwestern Iran. *Journal of Anthropological Archaeology* 32 (2), 257–273.

Comfort, A. and Ergeç, R. (2001) Following the Euphrates in antiquity: north–south routes around Zeugma. *Anatolian Studies* 51, 19–49.

Deckers, K. (2005) Anthrocological research at the archaeological site of Emar on the Middle Euphrates, Syria. *Paléorient* 31, 152–166.

Dinçol, A., Dinçol, B., Hawkins, J.D., Marchetti, N. and Peker, H. (2014) A new stele from Karkemish: at the origins of the Suhi–Katuwa Dynasty. In N. Marchetti (ed.) *Karkemish. An Ancient Capital on the Euphrates.* OrientLab 2, 127–131. Bologna, Ante Quem.

Dion, P.-E. (1997) *Les Araméens à l'age du fer: histoire politique et structures socials.* Études bibliques nouvelle série 34. Paris, Gabalda.

Donbaz, V. (1990) Two Neo-Assyrian Stelae in the Antakya and Kahramanmaraş Museums. *Annual Review of the Royal Inscriptions of Mesopotamia Project* 8, 5–24.

Dorrell, P. G. (1981) The Qoueiq valley: the physical background. In J. Matthers (ed.) *The River Qoueiq, northern Syria, and its catchment,* 75–80. Oxford, BAR S98.

Dunand, M. (1940) Stèle Hittite a L'Effigie de Adad-Teshoub. *Bulletin du Musée de Beyrouth* 4, 85–92; pl. I–II.

du Plat Taylor, J., Williams, M. and Wachter, J. (1950) The excavations at Sakce Gözü. *Iraq* 12, 53–138.

Dussaud, R. (1927) *Topographie Historique de la Syrie Antique et Médiévale.* Paris, Geuthner.

Eidem, J. and Pütt, K. (2001) Iron Age Sites on the Upper Euphrates. *Les Annales Archéologiques Arabes Syriennes* 44, 83–96.

Eidem, J. and Pütt, K. (1999) Tell Jurn Kabir and Tell Qadahiye. Danish Excavations in the Tishrin Dam Area. In G. Del Olmo Lete and J.-L Montero Fenollós (eds) *Archaeology of the Upper Syrian Euphrates. The Tishrin Dam Area. Proceedings of the International Symposium held at Barcelona, Jan. 28th–30th, 1998,* 193–204. Barcelona, Editorial Ausa.

Fales, F.M. (1993) River transport in Neo-Assyrian letters. In J. Zablocka and S. Zawadzki (eds) *Šulmu IV. Everyday Life in the Ancient Near East,* 79–92. Poznań, UAM.

Fales, F.M., Bachelot, L. and Attardo, E. (1996) An Aramaic tablet from Tell Shioukh Fawqani (Syria). *Semitica* 46, 81–121.

Grayson, A.K. (1996) *Assyrian Rulers of the Early First Millennium BC II (858–745 BC).* Royal Inscriptions of Mesopotamia Asyrian Periods 3. Toronto, University of Toronto Press.

Grayson, A.K. (1991) *Assyrian Rulers of the Early First Millennium BC I (1114–859 BC).* Royal Inscriptions of Mesopotamia Assyrian Periods 2. Toronto, University of Toronto Press.

Hallo, W.W. and Younger, K.L. (eds) (2000) *The Context of Scripture II. Monumental Inscriptions from the Biblical World.* Leiden, Brill.

Harmanşah, Ö. (2013) *Cities and the Shaping of Memory in the Ancient Near East.* Cambridge, Cambridge University Press.

Hausleiter, A. and Reiche, A. (eds) (1999) *Iron Age Pottery in Northern Mesopotamia, Northern Syria and South-Eastern Anatolia: papers presented at the meetings of the international "table ronde" at Heidelberg (1995) and Nieborów (1997) and other contributions.* Altertumskunde des Vorderen Orients 10. Münster, Ugarit-Verlag.

Hawkins, J.D. (2009) Cilicia, the Amuq, and Aleppo. *Near Eastern Archaeology* 72 (4), 164–173.

Hawkins, J.D. (2000) *Corpus of Hieroglyphic Luwian Inscriptions. Volume I: Inscriptions of the Iron Age.* Berlin, de Gruyter.

Hawkins, J.D. (1995a) "Great Kings" and "Country-Lords" at Malatya and Karkamish. In T. van den Hout and J. De Roos (eds) *Studio Historiae Ardens: Ancient Near Eastern Studies Presented to Philo H. J. Houwink ten Cate on the Occasion of his 65th Birthday,* 73–85. Istanbul, Nederlands Historisch-Archeologisch Instituut in Het Nabije Oosten.

Hawkins, J.D. (1995b) The political geography of North Syria and South-East Anatolia in the Neo-Assyrian Period. In M. Liverani (ed.) *Neo-Assyrian Geography*, 87–102. Quaderni di Geografia Storica 5. Rome, Università di Roma "La Sapienza".

Hillman, G.C. (1981) The barleys from Iron Age Rifa'at. In J. Matthers (ed.) *The River Qoueiq, northern Syria, and its catchment*, 508–510. Oxford, BAR S98.

Hogarth, D.G. (1909) Carchemish and its neighbourhood. *Liverpool Annals of Archaeology and Anthropology* 2, 165–184; pl. xxxvi.3.

Kalaç, M. (1969) Körkün de Bulunan hiyeroglifli Havatanrisi Steli (Die Wettergott Stele mit Hieroglyphen aus Körkün). *Athenaeum* 57, 160–163.

Kalaç, M. (1968) Hiyeroglif Araştırmaları. *Belleten* 32, 315–330.

Kalaç, M. (1965) *Tünp Hiyeroglif Yazıtı/Die hieroglyphische Inschrift aus Tünp*. Istanbul, Fakülteler Matbassı.

Kepinski, C. (2005) Tilbeshar – A Bronze Age city in the Sajur Valley (southeast Anatolia). *Anatolica* 31, 145–159.

King, L.W. (1915) *The Bronze Reliefs from the Gates of Shalmaneser III, King of Assyria B.C. 860–825*. London, British Museum.

Kirleis, W. and Herles, M. (2007) Climatic change as a reason for Assyro-Aramaean conflicts? Pollen evidence for drought at the end of the 2nd millennium BC. *State Archives of Assyria Bulletin* 16, 7–37.

Kohlmeyer, K. (2009) The Temple of the Storm God in Aleppo during the Late Bronze and Early Iron Ages. *Near Eastern Archaeology* 72 (4), 190–202.

Kulakoğlu, E. (2006) Gaziantep ve Adıyaman illeri kültür envanteri projesi 2005 yılı çalişmalari sonuç raporu. *Araştırma Sonuçları Toplantısı* 24 (2), 325–334.

Lipiński, E. (2000) *The Aramaeans: Their Ancient History, Culture, Religion*. Leuven, Peeters.

Liverani, M. (1988) The growth of the Assyrian Empire in the Habur/Middle Euphrates area: a new paradigm. *State Archives of Assyria Bulletin* 2, 81–98.

Marchetti, N. (2014) *Karkemish. An Ancient Capital on the Euphrates*. OrientLab 2. Bologna, Ante Quem.

Margueron, J. and Teixidor, J. (1983) Un objet à legend araméenne provenant de Meskéné-Emar. *Revue d'assyriologie et d'archéologie et d'archéologie orientale* 77, 75–80.

Matthers, J. (1981) *The River Qoueiq, Northern Syria, and its Catchment: Studies arising from the Tell Rifa'at survey 1977–79*. Oxford BAR S98.

Matthers, J. *et al.* (1978) Tell Rifa'at 1977: Preliminary Report of an Archaeological Survey. *Iraq* 40 (2), 119–162.

Maxwell Hyslop, R., du Plat Taylor, J., Seton Williams, M.V. and Waechter, J.D'A. (1942) An Archaeological survey of the Plain of Jabbul, 1939. *Palestine Exploration Quarterly* 74 (1), 8–40.

Mazzoni, S. (1995) Settlement pattern and new urbanization in Syria at the time of the Assyrian conquest. In M. Liverani (ed.) *Neo-Assyrian Geography*, 181–191. Quaderni di Geografia Storica 5. Rome, Università di Roma "La Sapienza".

Mazzoni, S. (1986–7) A Sculptures Quarry in Sikizlar. *Annales Archéologiques Arabes Syriennes* 36/37, 268–275.

Morandi Bonacossi, D. (2000) The Syrian Jezireh in the Late Assyrian Period: a view from the countryside. In G. Bunnens (ed.) *Essays on Syria in the Iron Age*. Ancient Near Eastern Studies Supplement 7, 349–396.

Mori, L. (2003) *Reconstructing the Emar landscape*. Quaderni di Geografia Storica 6. Rome, Università di Roma "La Sapienza".

Mottram, M. and Menere, D. (2005) Preliminary surface investigations in the Wadi Abu Qalqal region, North Syria. *Mediterranean Archaeology* 18, 161–174; pls 17–20.

Orthmann, W. (1974) Der Löwe von Zilfe. In K. Bittel, P.H.J. Houwink ten Cate and E. Reiner (eds) *Anatolian Studies Presented to Hans Gustav Güterbock on the Occasion of His 65th Birthday*, 239–43; pls xxvi–xxviii. Istanbul, Nederlands Historisch-Archaeologisch Institut in Het Nabije Oosten.

Osborne, J.F. (2013) Sovereignty and territoriality in the city-state: A case study from the Amuq Valley, Turkey *Journal of Anthropological Archaeology* 32 (4), 774–790.

Özgen, E. and Helwing, B. (2003) On the shifting border between Mesopotamia and the West: Seven seasons of joint Turkish–German excavations at Oylum Höyük. *Anatolica* 29, 61–85.

Özgen, E., Helwing, B. and Engin, A. (2001) The Oylum Regional Project: archaeological prospection 2000. *Araştırma Sonuçları Toplantıları* 19 (2), 217–229.

Özgen, E., Helwing, B. and Tekin, H. (1997) Vorläufiger Bericht über die Ausgrabungen auf dem Oylum Höyük. *Istanbuler Mitteilungen* 47, 39–90.

Özgen, E., Helwing, B., Herling, L. and Engin, A. (2002) The Oylum Regional Project: results of the 2001 Prospection Season. *Araştırma Sonuçları Toplantıları* 20 (2), 151–159.

Özgüç, T. and Özgüç, N. (1949) *Türk Tarih Kurumu Tarafından Yapılan Karahöyük Harfiyat Raporu 1947 (Ausgrabungen in Karahöyük)*. Ankara, Türk Tarih Kurumu Yayınları.

Peltenburg, E. (2010) The emergence of Carchemish as a major polity: Land of Carchemish Survey (Syria) 2006. In P. Matthiae, F. Pinnock, L. Nigro and N. Marchetti (eds) *Proceedings of the 6th ICAANE Conference, May 5th–10th 2008, Rome, vol. 2*, 539–552. Wiesbaden, Harrassowitz Verlag.

Peltenburg, E., Wilkinson, T. J., Ricci, A., Lawrence, D., McCarthy, A., Wilkinson, E. B., Newson, P. and Perini, S. (2012) The Land of Carchemish (Syria) Project 2009: The Sajur Triangle. In R. Matthews and J. Curtis (eds) *Proceedings of the 7th ICAANE Conference, April 12th–16th 2010, London, vol. 3*, 209–221. Wiesbaden, Harrassowitz Verlag.

Perrot, J. (1962) *Reconnaissance Archeologique en Turquie Meridionale 1961*. Jerusalem, Centre national de la recherché scientifique.

Postgate, J.N. (1992) The Land of Assur and the Yoke of Assur. *World Archaeology* 23 (3), 247–263.

Sanlaville, P. (ed.) (1985) *Holocene settlement in north Syria: résultants de deux prospections archéologiques effectuées dans la région du nahr Sajour et sur le haut Euphrate syrien*. Oxford, BAR S238.

Schwartz, G.M. (1989) The origins of the Aramaeans in Syria and northern Mesopotamia: research problems and potential strategies. In O.M.C. Haex, H.H. Curvers and P.M.M.G. Akkermans (eds) *To the Euphrates and Beyond: Archaeological Studies in Honour of Maurits N. van Loon*, 275–291. Rotterdam, A.B. Balkema.

Schwartz, G.M., Curvers, H.H., Gerritsen, F.A., MacCormack, J.A., Miller, N.F. and Weber, J.A. (2000) Excavation and survey in the Jabbal Plain, Western Syria: The Umm el-Marra Project 1996–1997. *American Journal of Archaeology* 104 (3), 419–462.

Sertok, M.K., Kulakoğlu, F., Squadrone, F.F. (2008) Şaraga Höyük Salvage Excavations. In H. Kühne, R.M. Czichon and F.J. Kreppner (eds) *Proceedings of the 4th ICAANE Conference, March 29th–April 3rd 2004, Berlin, vol. 2*, 411–418. Wiesbaden, Harrassowitz Verlag.

Seton Williams, M.V. (1961) Preliminary Report on the Excavations at Tell Rifa'at. *Iraq* 23, 68–87.

Seton Williams, M.V. (1967) Preliminary Report on the Excavations at Tell Rifa'at. *Iraq* 29, 16–23.

Streck, M.P. (2004) Paqarhub/puni. *Reallexikon der Assyriologie und Vorderasiatischen Archäologie* 10 (5–6), 332.

Sürenhagen, D. (1986) Ein Königssiegel aus Kargamis. *Mitteilungen der Deutschen Orient-Gesellschaft zu Berlin* 118, 183–190.

Swartz Dodd, L. (2003) Chronology and continuity in the Early Iron Age: the north eastern side of the Amanus. In B. Fischer, H. Genz, É. Jean and K. Köroğlu (eds) *Identifying Changes: the Transition from Bronze to Iron Ages in Anatolia and its Neighbouring Regions*, 127–136. Istanbul, Ege Yayınları.

Taşyürek, O. A. (1979) A rock relief of Shalmaneser III on the Euphrates. *Iraq* 41 (1), 47–53.

Tunca, Ö. (1999) Tell Amarna: Présentation sommaire de sept campagnes de fouilles (1991–1997). In G. del Olmo Lete and J-L Montero Fenollós (eds) *Archaeology of the Upper Syrian Euphrates. The Tishrin Dam Area*. Aula Orientalis Supplementa 15, 129–136. Barcelona, Editorial Ausa.

van der Meer, R. and Hillen, C. (1952) Reis in Irâq en Proefgraving in Syrië in 1951. *Jaarbericht Ex Oriente Lux* 12, 191–207.

Wilkinson, T.J. (2007) Archaeological regions in the neighbourhood of Carchemish. In E. Peltenburg (ed.) *Euphrates River Valley Settlement: the Carchemish Sector in the Third Millennium BC*, 27–42. Oxford, Oxbow Books.

Wilkinson, T.J. (1990) *Town and country in SE Anatolia I: Settlement and land use at Kurban Höyük and other sites in the Lower Karababa Basin*. Chicago IL, Oriental Institute Publications 109.

Wilkinson, T.J. and Barbanes, E. (2000) Settlement patterns in the Syrian Jazira during the Iron Age. In G. Bunnens (ed.) *Essays on Syria in the Iron Age*. Ancient Near Eastern Studies Supplement 7, 397–422.

Wilkinson, T.J. and Wilkinson, E. (forthcoming) The Iron Age of the Middle Euphrates in Syria and Turkey. In J. MacGinnis (ed.) *The Provincial Archaeology of the Assyrian Empire*. Cambridge, Cambridge University Press.

Wilkinson, T.J., Peltenburg, E., McCarthy, A., Wilkinson, E.B. and Brown, M. (2007) Archaeology in the land of Carchemish: landscape surveys in the area of Jerablus Tahtani, 2006. *Levant* 39, 213–247.

Willcox, G. (2002) Evidence for ancient forest cover and deforestation from charcoal analysis of ten archaeological sites on the Euphrates. In S. Thiébault (ed.) *Charcoal Analysis: Methodological Approaches, Palaeoecological Results and Wood Uses. Proceedings of the Second International Meeting of Anthracology, Paris, September 2000*, 141–145. Oxford, BAR S1063.

Woolley, C.L. (1921) *Carchemish. Report on the excavations at Jerablus on behalf of the British Museum, Part II: The Town Defences*. London, British Museum.

Woolley, C.L. and Barnett, R. (1952) *Carchemish. Report on the excavations at Jerablus on behalf of the British Museum, Part III: The Excavations in the Inner Town and the Hittite Inscriptions*. London, British Museum.

Yamada, S. (2000) *The Construction of the Assyrian Empire: A Historical Study of the Inscriptions of Shalmanesar III (859–824 B.C.) Relating to His Campaigns to the West*. Culture and History of the Ancient Near East 3. Leiden, Brill.

Yukich, S.T.K. (2013) *Spatial dimensions of social complexity: environment, economy and settlement in the Jabbul plain 3000–550 BC*. Unpublished PhD thesis, Johns Hopkins University, Baltimore.

Long-term settlement trends in the Birecik-Carchemish Sector

Dan Lawrence and Andrea Ricci

Introduction

Over the past three decades the construction of the Birecik and Carchemish Dams in Turkey and the Tishrin Dam in Syria has led to an explosion of archaeological work along the Middle Euphrates valley. More recently, scholars have begun to investigate the landscapes outside the river valley, increasing our understanding of settlement dynamics in the wider region. This paper makes use of remote sensing techniques, published excavation and survey reports and recent archaeological survey undertaken as part of the Land of Carchemish Project to reconstruct settlement and landscape trajectories to the north and south of Carchemish, across the modern border between Turkey and Syria. Using a conceptual framework based on the idea of landscapes as inherently stable systems punctuated by periodic structural transformations (Casana 2007; Wilkinson 2003) we seek to place the urban development at Carchemish in its wider settlement context throughout its long occupational history. As such, the paper is designed to complement the more historically specific treatments of the site and its surroundings provided elsewhere in this volume.

Data sources and methods

The primary dataset used in this study consists of three archaeological surveys: Guillermo Algaze's survey along the banks of the Euphrates in Turkey (hereafter AS) (Algaze *et al.* 1994), the survey conducted by Mehmet Özdoğan and Necmi Karul in the Birecik district to the east of the Euphrates (hereafter KOS) (Özdoğan and Karul 2002) and the on-going Land of Carchemish Project (hereafter LCP) directed by Tony Wilkinson and Edgar Peltenburg in Syria (Wilkinson *et al.* 2007; Peltenburg *et al.* 2012) which covers

a triangle between the Sajur and Euphrates rivers and the Syro-Turkish border (see Fig. 4.1). Though the modern border has little physical geographical significance, none of the surveys could explore the areas north and south of this boundary in the frame of a single study. This research collates and analyses archaeological data produced by the projects in both Turkey and Syria in order to overcome this modern political division. Comparing and combining survey data can be problematic due to differences in goals, methods and chronological frameworks. Although the research histories of the three surveys are not identical, with the AS a rescue survey in advance of the construction of the Birecik and Carchemish dams and the LCP and KOS aimed at pure research, the goals of both were to maximize the recovery of sites from all periods. Furthermore, all three projects involved some form of pedestrian survey and a degree of off-site investigations (see Fig. 4.2 for the areas covered in the LCP) which, along with their relatively similar size and survey intensity, render the datasets broadly comparable. The participation of the authors in the LCP and the reanalysis of the KOS field collections by Ricci over the course of his PhD[1] mean that the chronological phases attributed to individual sites in those two surveys are readily comparable. Although the original ceramics collected by the AS team are no longer available (Algaze pers. comm. November 2010), the phasing used in the final publication is sufficiently similar to that used in the LCP to make reasonable comparisons, with some exceptions which will be discussed below. Two additional vehicle-based survey projects, one by Sanlaville, Copeland, and Moore in the 1970s (hereafter SCM) (Copeland and Moore 1985; Sanlaville 1985) and the other by McClellan and Porter in the 1980s (hereafter MP) (McClellan and Porter in press), have also been used to provide further evidence where necessary (these are collectively labeled EBSE in the below figures), but the scale, methods, chronology and fragmentary nature of the data available for both datasets render them rather less useful (see below and Table 4.1).

We will also discuss recent excavations at a number of sites in the Euphrates valley on both sides of the border. The majority of these began as rescue projects in advance of the construction of major dams in both Syria and Turkey and have not yet been fully published (see, for example, papers in del Olmo Lete and Montero Fenollós 1999 and Peltenburg 2007b), although excavations have continued at sites such as Shiukh Fawqani which were not inundated when the reservoirs were filled. Finally, remote sensing data, including CORONA and high resolution modern imagery, have been used. In the case of the LCP, CORONA was used from the outset as a prospection tool to locate sites and features which could be visited in the field. This resource was not utilized by any of the other surveys, and we have used it to re-interrogate the original survey data sets, allowing us to reinterpret known sites and also discover new potential occupations in the wider area. As well as locating sites and features, remote sensing data such as Landsat imagery and Digital Elevation Models (DEMs) have been used to place the archaeological remains in their wider landscape and environmental context.

The physical environment

The region under study is a sub-basin of the Middle Euphrates River Valley defined as the Birecik-Carchemish sector (see Wilkinson 2007). It is located in Upper Meso-potamia between the southern piedmont of the Anti-Taurus range and the Syrian steppe. The modern Turkish town of Halfeti, where Algaze and colleagues started their survey in 1989 (Algaze *et al.* 1994, 2) sets the northern limit, whilst an ideal line extending from the Qara Qozaq/Qalat Nedjim Gorge over the Sajur-Euphrates junction and along the Sajur Valley sets the southern limit. The study area is 65 km from north to south, although the actual length of the Euphrates is approximately 84 km. Broadly speaking, rainfall decreases from north to south, in modern times ranging from 480 mm per year to below 300 mm, with marked inter-annual fluctuations (Besancon and Sanlaville 1981). This places the region close to the limit for sustainable dry farming agriculture, especially to the south of the Sajur river which falls within the so called 'zone of uncertainty', where cultivation is a risky undertaking and may be supplemented by increased use of pastoral resources and irrigation (Wilkinson 2000; Wilkinson *et al.* 2012). The physical context of the LCP on the Syrian side of the study area is discussed in detail in a recent article and in this volume (Wilkinson *et al.* 2012, Wilkinson in Chapter

5). Several geomorphological zones have been recognised and these can be extended to the Turkish side of the border through topographical and geomorphological observations and remote sensing analysis to produce the following classifications (see Figure 4.3):

Land unit 1: Euphrates alluvial plain composed of Holocene alluvial terraces at different levels. In the Birecik district, a few 4th and 3rd millennium BC occupations (Şeraga Höyük; Şavi Höyük I; Tilmusa Höyük) have been documented on the terraces immediately above the valley bottom (Kuzucuoğlu *et al.* 2004, 203). More settlements may have been present but the low lands of this landscape of destruction suffered numerous "cycles of erosion and sedimentation and the […] archaeological record [is] lost" (Wilkinson *et al.* 2012, 147).

Land unit 2: Pleistocene terrace complexes above land unit 1 accommodate several Chalcolithic, Bronze Age and later sites as well as modern settlements. Examples are the Horum and Jeralbus Plains. The Euphrates discharge occasionally reached this higher terrace complex and various flood events are recorded at different relative heights during the 4th and 3rd millennium BC.

Land unit 3: Rolling eroded limestone hills and associated incised river valleys. In the Birecik district, this unit extends to the east towards the Soruç Plain, whereas in Syria, to the west of the Euphrates, it stretches towards the uplands of the Quwayq-Gaziantep-Nizip Plain. Land unit 3 might be further subdivided into the actual limestone slopes and hilltops (3a) and the valleys of larger Euphrates tributaries (3b). Sub-unit 3a offers good conditions for grazing but is of limited agricultural potential. Several tells and other occupations are located in the valley bottoms (3b) that provide more favourable conditions for cultivation.

Land unit 4: Eastern fringes of the Quwayq-Gaziantep-Nizip Plain. This high plain is flat and is covered by red *terra rossa* soil. This unit provides a stable environment offering good conditions for agriculture.

Land unit 5: Basalt sheet formations located at the north-eastern edges of the Soruç Plain in Turkey and to the west of the Sajur Basin in Syria. Sites and landscape features (field systems, cairns) are known on and around these basalt formations, but have not been thoroughly investigated. This land unit must have been an important source for basalt procurement.

A more detailed discussion of the geomorphological make-up of the Land of Carchemish project area is provided by Wilkinson in Chapter 5.

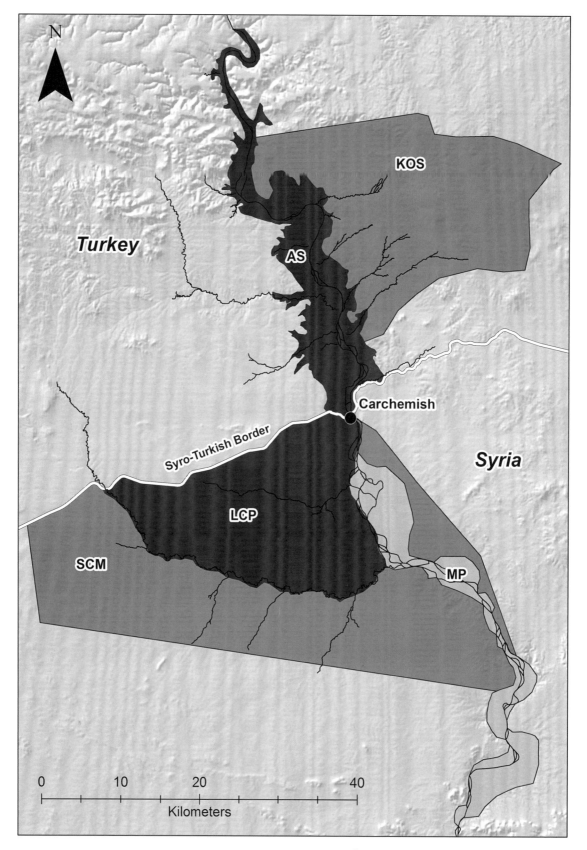

Fig. 4.1 Map of key survey areas. Survey acronyms: AS – Algaze Survey, KOS – Özdoğan and Karul Survey, LCP – Land of Carchemish Project, SCM – Sanlaville, Copeland, and Moore Survey, MP – McClellan and Porter Survey

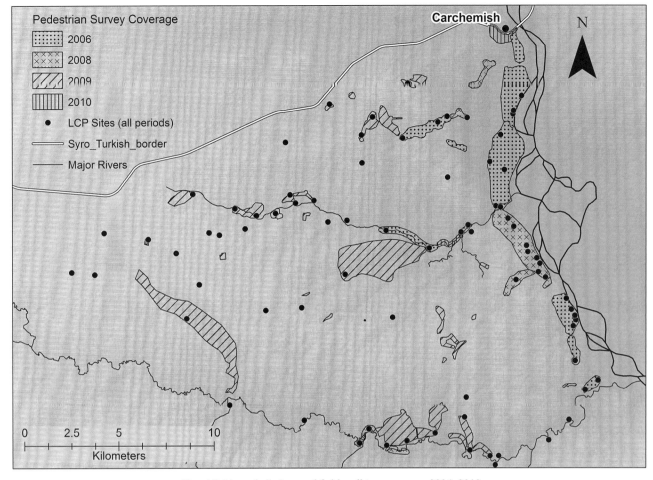

Fig. 4.2 Map of all sites and field walking coverage 2006–2010

The archaeological landscape

The land unit classification is critical to the interpretation of the archaeological record because each unit has different geological, geomorphological and settlement histories, and these in turn have profound effects on the preservation of sites and features. Land unit 1, for example, has experienced significant erosional episodes throughout the Holocene as the Euphrates shifted course, meaning any sites located on the flood plain would have been destroyed. Where relic floodplains do survive in land unit 2 they often contain sites. If there were periods when settlement was possible in land unit 1, therefore, we may be missing a significant proportion of the original settlement pattern, especially for earlier phases. Land unit 3 also represents an unstable erosional environment which could potentially lead to the attenuation of sites and features, but the low numbers of sites in this area could also be related to the relatively poor soils and lack of water sources outside the river valleys. Land units 4 and 5, by contrast, offer fairly stable geomorphological environments; the attenuation of the archaeological record

here is more likely to be related to the destructive effects of later occupations, particularly recent ploughing in land unit 4 and bulldozing in land unit 5 (see Chapter 10).

The archaeological landscape can be divided into two classes of site and a variety of off-site features. As in other surveys in the region, mounded tell sites are common, and whilst there are a variety of morphological variations the majority of these are round and conical shaped. The second class of site includes simple artefact scatters with thin cultural deposits and little or no topographical expression. These can be defined through the extent of the distribution of the artefacts (usually ceramics) and occasionally by soil colour and low mounding. Some of these 'flat' sites are in fact slightly mounded, but are clearly very different from the more substantial tells. The distinction between tells and flat sites is important because of the likelihood of earlier occupations being buried below later ones on the tell sites. This process is likely to have had significant implications for the reconstruction of settlement patterns in the earlier periods, and will be discussed in more detail below. Off-site

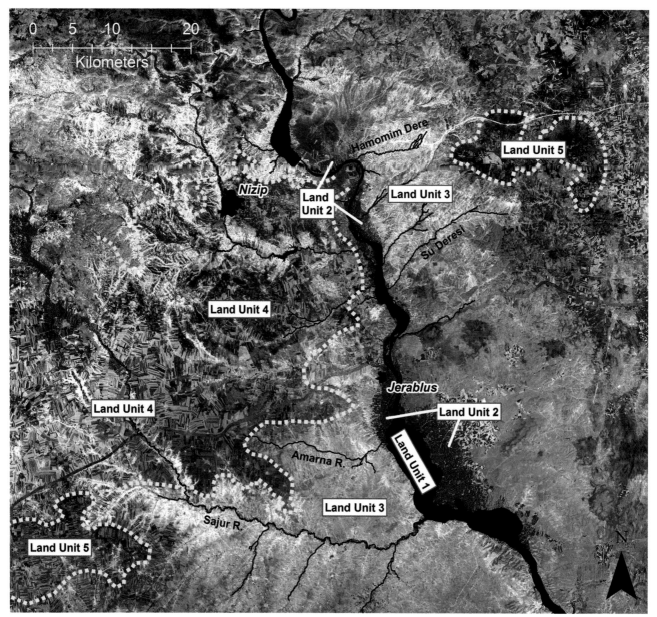

Fig. 4.3 Map of land unit areas described in text. Background: Landsat 7 ETM+ Image with band combination 4-3-2. Note that areas of high vegetation show up as bright red, lower vegetation as green and limestone as white

features include the remains of water management systems, in this case comprising canals, qanats and cisterns, and burial features such as cemeteries, rock-cut tombs and subterranean graves (see Chapters 5 and 10). Unlike in the Jazira to the east, extensive transect walking has revealed a patchy coverage of off-site sherd scatter with small concentrations separated by broad areas free of sherds. Evidence for the ancient route networks visible as hollow ways in both the Jazira (Ur 2003; 2010b) and the Qoueiq plain to the west (Casana 2013) is similarly rare. In fact, clear hollow ways are not present in any of the surveyed areas, with only four

possible linear features visible on the CORONA imagery in the extreme west of the LCP in land unit 4. Whilst the patchy occurrence of surface scatters most probably reflects the localized presence of the sorts of ancient manuring practices which created the scatters visible elsewhere (see Chapter 5), the lack of hollow ways is more likely related to a combination of the geomorphological make-up of the area and later destructive processes such as intensive ploughing, with the former probably accounting for their absence in land units 1–3 and the latter in land unit 4.

Late Pleistocene/Early Holocene

The Palaeolithic landscape of the study area has not been systematically investigated by the Land of Carchemish Project (although see brief discussions of individual sites in Nymark Jensen 2011; Shaw 2012). Despite the presence of 'abundant' surface remains the AS team did not include a lithic specialist and therefore did not collect any data on the periods prior to the Neolithic (Algaze *et al.* 1994, 8). The LCP recovered a single Upper Paleolithic/Early Neolithic site, Jebel al-Mitraz (LCP 13), a small scatter of lithics on a hill-top overlooking the Euphrates valley. Three sites which may date to the PPNB and early ceramic Neolithic are known in the area, two in the AS, Teleilat Höyük (AS 46) and Akarcay Tepe (AS 73), and one in the LCP, Mughar Seraisat (LCP 20). The two AS sites are notable for their rather large size, reaching 7 and 5 hectares respectively in the PPNB, and are low mounds situated on relict river terraces within the Euphrates river valley (Algaze *et al.* 1994). In contrast to this, Mughar Seraisat is a flat site with very shallow deposits (0.5–1 m) situated on a hill-top on the bluffs immediately adjacent to the Euphrates, a similar situation to Jebel al-Mitraz. Although documented as somewhat smaller than the AS sites at under 1 hectare, continuing scatter on a slope to the northeast may be the remains of an extension of the site (Wilkinson *et al.* 2007, 225). The absence of Neolithic sites away from the Euphrates valley is puzzling, and may be a result of the burial of sites under later occupations, destruction through natural and cultural landscape change or a real absence of settlement. At this stage it is difficult to make any statements about the landscapes of this period beyond noting the importance of the Euphrates and the presence of both hill-top and lowland settlement.

Halaf and Ubaid

The reconstruction of the Halaf and Ubaid landscapes of the area is hampered by the burial of ceramics under later occupations. At Tell Jerablus Tahtani (LCP 22), for example, three Halaf sherds were recovered from secondary contexts but the large scale excavations at the site did not recover any occupation layers pre-dating the LC 3, despite reaching natural deposits in several areas (Peltenburg, pers. comm. March 2014). The AS survey recovered Halaf sherds from only two sites, AS 23 and AS 45, during the original fieldwork but subsequent excavations revealed Halaf layers at three further sites, AS 10, AS 33 and AS 73, all of which had substantial later occupations (Marro *et al.* 2000; Balkan Atlı *et al.* 2002; Özbaşaran *et al.* 2004; Fuensanta 2007). Given the small number of sites discovered by the AS, even the addition of a further three alters the interpretation of the settlement pattern during this period. Algaze had suggested little settlement continuity between the Halaf and the Ubaid as the two sites discovered in the AS were single period occupations with no relation to later Ubaid occupations,

yet all three of the excavated sites also contained Ubaid sherds. Overall, the Halaf period marks the beginning of recognizable settlement patterns across the area, with nine sites occupied in the LCP and five (including the three identified through excavation) in the AS (Fig. 4.4). The first recorded occupation at Carchemish also dates to this period, with Halaf sherds recovered in secondary contexts in soundings on the main citadel mound, as well as at the village of Yunus, approximately one kilometer to the northwest (Woolley 1934). All of these occupations were small, with none larger than two hectares, and all are located close to water sources, either in the Euphrates river valley in the case of the AS sites, Carchemish and Jerablus Tahtani, or on the larger side tributaries such as the Amarna (LCP 19, 21, 50 and 60). Only two of the Halaf occupations were not mounded, AS 23 and LCP 19. The latter, excavated by a Belgian team, has been heavily disturbed by the erosional activities of the Wadi Amarna, but appears to have been fairly short-lived (Cruells 2004). Of the other occupied sites, it is worth noting that Halaf sherds were recovered from several of the largest tells in both the AS and LCP surveys. This may be an indicator of the long-term success of the locations chosen for settlement during the Halaf, but may also again be related to ceramic recovery. Larger tells tend to experience greater erosion due to the volume of water falling on larger areas and their steeper and longer slopes, meaning older sherds are more likely to be washed out. In this regard it is significant that a Halaf presence was also visible at the small mound of Tell Tashatan (LCP 5) which was cut by a number of modern pits around its lower edges.

The transition to the Ubaid period, as mentioned above, included elements of continuity as well as settlement increase. Ten of the Halaf sites continued to be occupied, whilst eleven new Ubaid sites were founded. As in the Halaf, most of these new sites were located close to water sources and in areas of high soil fertility, Land units 3b and 4 (Fig. 4.4). The Ubaid occupations were generally less than two hectares and evenly dispersed across the landscape with no apparent site hierarchy. Soundings on the citadel at Carchemish also contained a small number of Ubaid sherds along with the Halaf (Woolley 1934; Algaze *et al.* 1994) and it is likely that the site remained occupied across both periods. Sites are generally situated at a distance ranging between 3 km and 5 km from each other, sufficient space for agricultural independence but easily within one or two hours walk. Regular local contacts and small-scale economic exchanges may have been established between sites located on opposite banks of the Euphrates. The presence of a late Ubaid occupation at Duluk (LCP 2), at the junction of the Euphrates with the Sajur River, can be associated with the long-lasting Ubaid settlement of Tell al-'Abr (EBSE 5). The two sites are located directly opposite one another across the Euphrates in an area where the morphology of the valley offers favourable conditions for crossing. Clay boat models have been discovered at Ubaid sites in both Southern and Northern Mesopotamia, as for example at Tell Mashnaqa (Thuesen 1996, 52–53; 2000, 77) and more recently in a domestic context at Tell Zeidan on the Balikh (Stein 2011, 126, fig. 25). These small boats, probably built of reeds and waterproofed on the outside, could transport one or two people and may have been similar to those that navigated the marshlands of Southern Mesopotamia until recent times. Such boats could have been used to cross the river, as well as for fishing activities with the use of small nets (Parker 2010, 356). Furthermore, the Ubaid occupations recorded at Tell Amarna (LCP 21), at the narrow access of the Amarna valley, and at Tell Hudhud (SCM 12), some 10 km away from the Euphrates and approximately 6.5 km upstream from the junction of the Sajur with the Wadi Membij, confirm the importance of east-west contacts and movement towards western Syria. It is possible that incipient site specialisation might have arisen during the Ubaid period, as recognised in other Northern Mesopotamian regions (Carter and Philip 2010, 9). Populations located along the rivers could exploit the richness of both the alluvial lands for agriculture and the rivers for fishing activities, as well as managing the crossing of the waterways. Communities on the internal plains concentrated more on rural resources, but also played a role in managing areas more suitable for animal husbandry and routes of movement across that landscape. However, as no centre of economic or political power is recognizable in the area under investigation, we have to assume that each site was an independent unit, with its own sustaining area and distinctive availability of natural resources integrated into a local system of equal relations and frequent exchanges. This local network was also connected to a broader system of more distant Northern Mesopotamian Ubaid interaction.

Late Chalcolithic and Uruk

Both the AS and KOS surveys were undertaken before the widespread adoption of the Santa Fe chronology which divides the period between the end of the Ubaid and the Early Bronze Age into five separate phases, LC 1–5, with the last two based on intrusive Uruk ceramic types (Rothman 2001; Wright and Rupley 2001). The adoption of the Santa Fe chronology in the LCP has allowed for a more fine-grained analysis of settlement change in comparison to the earlier surveys which do not distinguish between LC 1–2 and LC 3 occupations. In fact, with the exception of the LCP, all of the projects determined Local Late Chalcolithic (LLC) occupation solely on the basis of what we now know to be LC 3 artifacts. It might therefore be assumed that the available evidence reflects the actual LC 3 regional settlement pattern rather than an amalgamation of all of the sites occupied between the LC 1 and LC 3. As a result, LC 1–2 occupation remains poorly understood outside the LCP, a situation further compounded by the fact that no excavation

has reached undisturbed contexts of this period. Excavations at Horum Höyük (AS 10) have recovered evidence of LC 1–2 ceramics in secondary deposits, as well as LC 3 types, whilst at Uçtepe Höyük 1 (KOS N40A041.001) and Gre Gavuran (KOS O40A022) re-examination of the collected pottery has confirmed LC 1–2 occupation at the former and the presence of both LC 1–2 and LC 3 at the latter. For the Uruk period, the LCP also distinguished between LC 4 (Middle Uruk) and LC 5 (Late Uruk) occupations, although this was not possible for all sites. This again represents a higher level of precision than the other surveys, which generally categorised the Uruk as a single phase. However, the subsequent excavation of a number of sites in the AS area allows for a more nuanced treatment of this period. The discovery of new LC occupations through excavation provides further evidence for the impact of later occupations on the recovery of prehistoric ceramics during survey. As in the Halaf and Ubaid, it is therefore likely that the LC is underrepresented.

The division between LC 1–2 and LC 3 ceramics is important because within the LCP we can see variations between the phases. Settlement expanded significantly during the LC 1–2 phase, with seven new sites founded, whilst occupation continued at all of the Ubaid sites. The new sites were mostly along the two major inland tributaries, the Amarna and Sajur rivers, and particularly the former. The presence of ceramics comparable to the 'Western Horizon' assemblages at Oylum Höyük and Arslantepe (period VIII; Frangipane 2012) suggests that this settlement pattern may be a reflection of stronger contacts to the west and north-west during this period. In contrast to the LC 1–2, the LC 3 phase sees a contraction of settlement, from 13 to nine sites, with the abandonment of several of the new foundations in the central part of the Amarna valley and two new sites appearing, one in the uplands between the Euphrates and Amarna valleys (LCP 78) and one on the plain further to the West (LCP 53). Tell Jerablus Tahtani (LCP 22) in the Euphrates Valley was also first settled at this time and may have been part of a pairing with Shiukh Fawqani (EBSE 1) on the opposite bank. The absence of settlement at Tell al-'Abr (EBSE 5) during the LC 1–2 and 3 phases might, therefore, be related to a shift in crossing points from the Sajur pairing further north to the Jerablus plain. This in turn may be a reflection of the growing importance of Carchemish during this period. It is likely that the entire citadel mound was occupied by the LC 3 (see Woolley and Barnett 1952), making Carchemish a relatively large site at approximately four hectares. North of Carchemish, it is clear that the LLC period saw an increase in settlement numbers and perhaps complexity. Although the AS documented fewer occupations than in the preceding Ubaid (six in the LLC compared to nine in the Ubaid), the evidence from the KOS suggests an increase in small sites away from the river valley (Fig. 4.5). Excavations at the 3.3 ha mound of

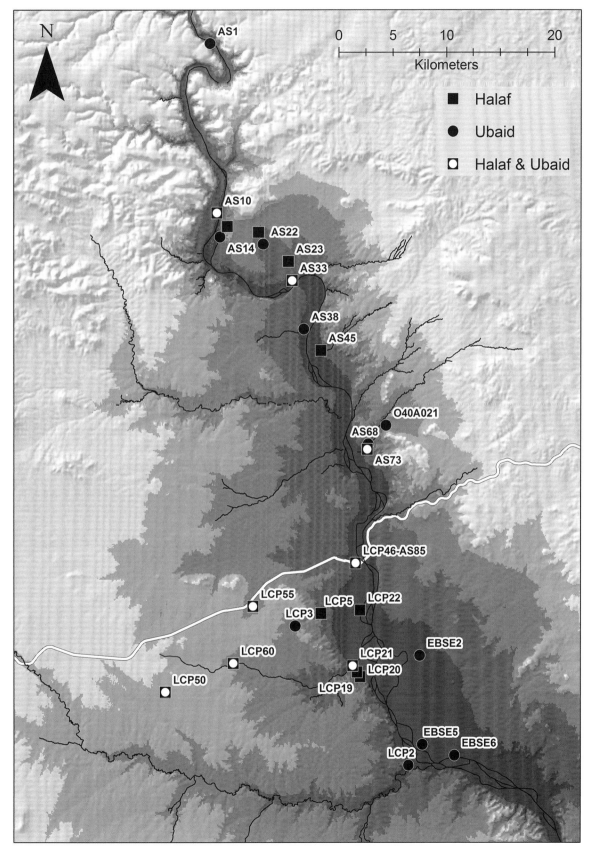

Fig. 4.4 Settlement pattern during the Halaf and Ubaid periods. Background: SRTM with 50 m contour intervals and hillshade

Hacınebi (AS 28) have revealed LC 3 building levels with monumental architecture and possible storage facilities, as well as evidence for prestige goods and metallurgical and administrative activities, suggesting a degree of social differentiation amongst the inhabitants (Stein 1999). The settlement pattern might be interpreted as further evidence of an incipient hierarchy, with slightly larger sites such as Hacınebi, Şadi Tepe (AS 76), Akarçay Tepe (AS 73) and possibly also Zeytinli Bahçe (AS 44), situated in the fertile Euphrates river valley and more specialised pastoral sites on the uplands to the east and west. If this interpretation is correct, we might consider Carchemish at this time to be one of a group of larger villages in the region beginning to establish wider spheres of influence.

Uruk materials have been recovered from 43 sites within the Birecik-Carchemish region, only six more sites than the combined total for the LLC. However, this apparent stability masks a profound change in settlement organisation, with 19 new foundations and the development of a clear site hierarchy (Fig. 4.5). After his initial survey, Algaze identified the area from Jerablus Tahtani to the northern part of his survey area as one of several Uruk 'settlement complexes' along the Euphrates, representing intrusive communities of Southern Mesopotamian settlers, or at least individuals with strong links to the southern alluvium (Algaze 2005 [1993]). New information from excavations within the AS, as well as the LCP, allows us to add to this picture. It is possible to distinguish an emerging three tiered hierarchy, along with a set of relations which point to specialisation and differentiation based on a variety of site characteristics, including topographic location, presence or absence of earlier settlement and artefactual evidence such as cones or administrative devices. In terms of size, the majority of the sites (21) are smaller than 1.5 ha, with 17 medium sized occupations (1.5–4 ha) and two or three larger centres (Şadi Tepe (AS 76) 8 ha; Tiladir Tepe (AS 82) 12.2 ha; and possibly Kum Ocağı (AS 80) 6.3 ha). Small sites at lower locations were not independent, but had close relationships with the larger centres. For instance, Komeçli Höyük (AS 74) and Şadi Tepe, both LC 4 (Middle Uruk) foundations, are spatially very close but may have had different functions. Komeçli Höyük is located on a low alluvial terrace less than a kilometre north-west of the 50 m high limestone bluff on which the larger Şadi Tepe is found. Away from the river, small Uruk sites punctuate the KOS and the LCP areas. The nature of the relations between these smaller communities and the system of larger Uruk settlements along the Euphrates is difficult to assess at this stage. However, the absence of bevelled-rim bowls (BRBs) west of Tell Haimer (LCP 78) and on all the KOS sites might hint at a rather low degree of economic and political control by the larger sites over the non-riverine settlements. Indeed, BRBs are documented only along the Euphrates, where they have been recovered on the great majority of

sites. Here, the centralised, redistributive system required the use of such vessels to organise labour and to sustain unequal relationships of interdependency among larger and smaller sites. Conversely, the sites east and west of the Euphrates accommodated smaller communities, possibly only a few families, and the local economy seems to have lacked centralised administrative authorities.

The integrated system of Uruk settlements along the Euphrates River certainly required upstream and downstream communications, but a series of sites distributed every 3–6 km on the opposite banks of the river also facilitated its crossing and highlights the significance of east–west communication networks. Six to seven Uruk paired sites (AS 33–AS 36, AS 43b–AS 44, AS 71–AS 72, AS 80–AS 82, LCP 22–EBSE 1, LCP 2–EBSE 5; possibly AS 10–AS 14) indicate the likely locations of crossing points. The pairing between Jerablus Tahtani and Shiukh Fawqani (LCP 22 and EBSE 1) is particularly significant because of the nature of the occupation at the former and the orientation of the settlement pattern further inland. Investigations in 2006 revealed Uruk ceramics in well sections in an extended area around Jerablus Tahtani, interpreted at the time as evidence for an 'extended activity area' of some 12 ha below the main tell (Wilkinson *et al.* 2007, 228). Test trenches in the same areas did not reveal any substantial remains (Peltenburg *et al.* 2000), whilst a further program of auguring and test pitting in 2009 point to discontinuous occupation. Inland from Jerablus Tahtani, an alignment of six sites (moving westwards, LCP 5, LCP 3, LCP 78, LCP 60, LCP 65 and LCP 50), all 2–4 km apart from one other may be taken as evidence for an inland routeway relating to east–west movements.[2] This communication route may have been established as early as the LC 4 (Middle Uruk) period, because materials of this phase have been recovered from at least four of the seven sites. Taken together, the expanded site at Jerablus Tahtani and the possible route-way demonstrate the importance of *both* river-based movement *and* contacts further inland. The continuing importance of such a trade route in close proximity to Carchemish is also worth noting.

Early Bronze Age

Over the course of the Early Bronze Age (EBA), Carchemish expanded to become the pre-eminent site in the Birecik-Carchemish region, and one of the largest sites in Northern Mesopotamia outside the Khabur basin. This expansion most probably occurred in the second half of the EBA (see below), and the Early EBA site probably remained at around four hectares. In the wider landscape, twenty two new sites were founded in the Early EBA, all below 4 ha in size, whilst occupation continued at 31 Uruk sites (Fig. 4.6). Excavations at Zeytinli Bahçe (AS 44) and Jerablus Tahtani (LCP 22) have documented uninterrupted sequences

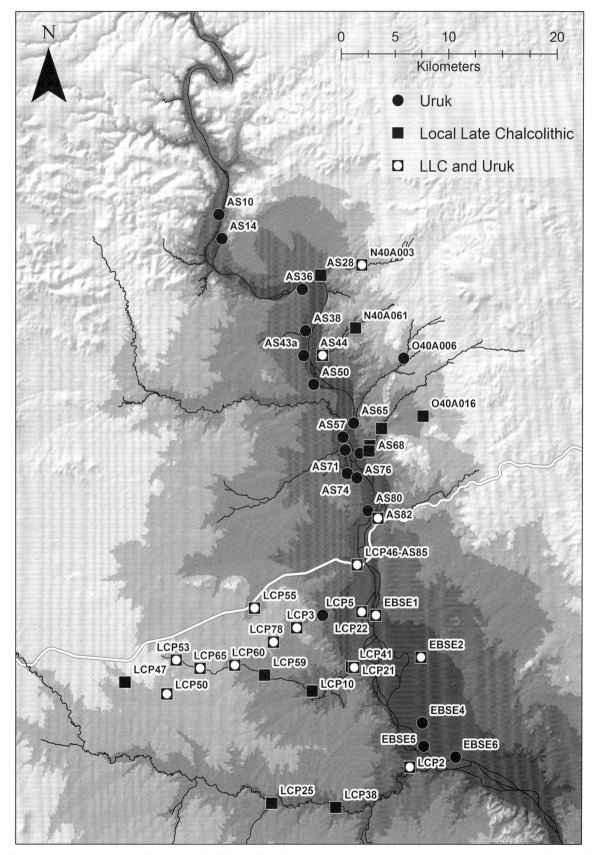

Fig. 4.5 Settlement pattern during the Late Chalcolithic and Uruk periods. Background: SRTM with 50 m contour intervals and hillshade

and gradual transformations in material culture. The nature of the changes which occurred towards the end of the Uruk period and in the Early EBA are therefore difficult to interpret, but it seems that in the Birecik-Carchemish sector the transformation was rather more incremental than has previously been considered. Changes in the location of settlement did occur, however, with the large Uruk sites of Şadi Tepe (AS 76) and Kum Ocağı (AS 80) in the central part of the study area being abandoned and the entire area not resettled until the end of the EBA. A similar pattern is visible in the Tabqa dam, where the area surrounding the Uruk sites of Tell Sheikh Hassan, Habuba Kabira South and Jebel Aruda was abandoned, whilst new paired settlements at Tells Hadidi and es-Sweyhat and Selenkahiye and Halawa were located some distance to the north and south (Wilkinson *et al.* 2012, 169–170). Overall, the transition from the Uruk phase to the Early EBA resulted in a more ruralized settlement pattern (Fig. 4.6), and perhaps a simplification of social structure (Algaze 1999, 544–546). The settlement pattern appears less structured and hierarchical than during the Uruk phase. Although the alignment of sites inland from Jerablus Tahtani is still present, the re-emergence of settlement along the Nahr al-Amarna might represent a competing route-way. Rescue excavations at the so-called "Birecik cemetery", some 800 m southwest of the eponymous Dam, have unveiled over 300 cist and *pithoi* burials containing weapons, jewellery and copper objects (Sertok and Ergeç 1999). Rich Early EBA graves are also known at the northern edge of the citadel of Carchemish (Woolley and Barnett 1952) and there are 25 cist graves at Hacınebi (AS 28), where no associated Early EBA settlement was established (Stein *et al.* 1997). Grave goods found in these necropolises emphasise the physical strength, leadership and warrior qualities of high status male individuals, who were often buried with weapons and copper tools. In the dispersed non-urbanized Early EBA settlement pattern, family ties became stronger and groups legitimized their power on the basis of ancestral ties, whilst claims to territories were increasingly contested (Cooper 2006; Chapter 9; Peltenburg 2007–8, 2013; Helwing 2012). Occupation at Carchemish was most likely still confined to the citadel mound (Falsone and Sconzo 2007), and as a 4 ha settlement with associated graves the site would represent one of several larger villages in a wider network.

The second half of the EBA saw a massive expansion in settlement on a regional level. The timing and degree of expansion at Carchemish is still a matter of considerable debate as a result of the lack of access to the lower town. For the purposes of this article we follow Falsone and Sconzo (2007) and McClellan (1999) in assuming that the entire lower town was occupied from the Middle EBA onwards. This gives a total occupied area for Carchemish during the second half of the third millennium of 44 ha and is based on isolated finds at various points across the inner

town, including the main city gates (Woolley 1921, 79) and the presence of domestic architecture in the Lower Palace Area (Woolley and Barnett 1952, 230–236; Falsone and Sconzo 2007, 88–90). This dating places the development of Carchemish firmly within the wider phenomenon known as the 'second urban revolution' (Akkermans and Schwartz 2003, 233), during which unequivocally 'urban' centres emerged across the Northern Fertile Crescent at a density that was not matched until the 20th century (Ur 2010a) and included large public buildings, city walls, and evidence for social differentiation and mass production of goods. Morphologically, Carchemish fits with the wider pattern of 'citadel cities' visible in the Middle Euphrates at sites such as Titriş Höyük and Tell es-Sweyhat which are comprised of a high citadel with an extensive lower town surrounded by large fortification walls (Lawrence 2012; Wilkinson *et al.* 2012).

The development of Carchemish coincides with a peak of settlement in the Birecik-Carchemish region (Fig. 4.7). Seventy three occupations are recorded with sites evenly distributed along the course of the Euphrates and the valleys of the larger tributaries. Taken together, the growth at Carchemish and in the surrounding area comes to 73 ha of additional settlement, implying rapid demographic change. Sites seem to control an immediate catchment area which may have provided primary economic support. A three tiered site hierarchy may be visible, with Tiladir Tepe (AS 82), Surtepe Höyük (AS 33) and Tell Taslihöyük (KOS N40A035) in the north and Tell Amarna (LCP 21), Arab Hassan (LCP 68) and Tell Beddayeh (EBSE 3) in the south occupying a middle layer beneath Carchemish. Examples of fortifications are known at several sites and cities, regardless of their size, along the Northern Syrian Euphrates Valley (Cooper 2006; Chapter 4; Peltenburg 2013). At Jerablus Tahtani (LCP 22), by the mid-3rd millennium the population had retreated into the central part of the tell, inside a complex rampart and glacis defensive system built in a few phases over a short period (Peltenburg *et al.* 1996, 2000, Peltenburg, Chapter 7). The erection of these structures substantially altered the internal organisation of the settlement and the morphology of the tell, which rose higher with steeper sides. Many of the tells in the Birecik-Carchemish region, and in fact across the western part of Northern Mesopotamia, still display this 'conical' morphology (Lawrence 2012, 149–151), which may have resulted from similar building activities. This phenomenon had a dramatic impact on the perception of the mounded sites, which appeared more visible in the landscape (Peltenburg 1999, 109), but also less accessible. Well organised political authority, capable of mobilising significant labour forces, planned and realised these protective structures, which represented an effort to erect a physical and psychological barrier between the settlement mound with its inhabitants, houses, activities and products, and the land and communities beyond it.

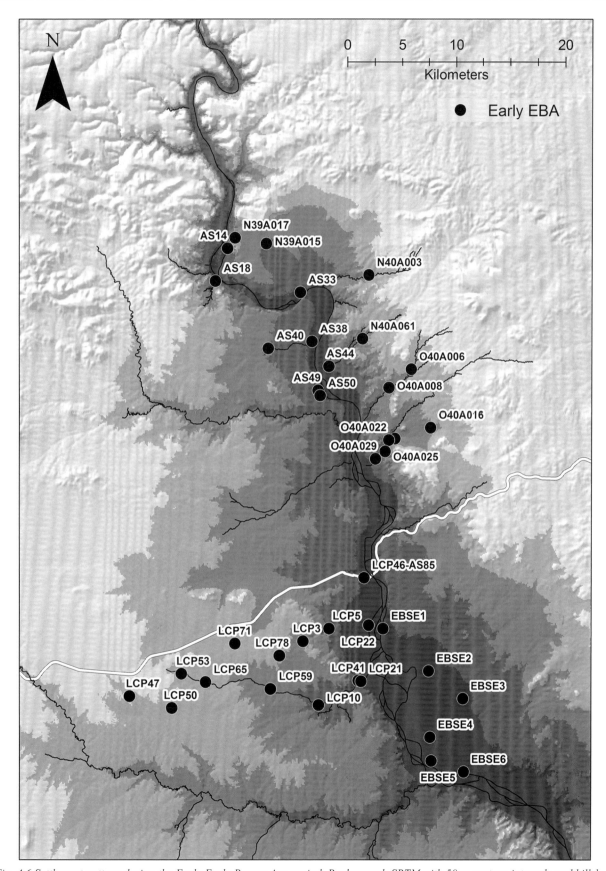

Fig. 4.6 Settlement pattern during the Early Early Bronze Age period. Background: SRTM with 50 m contour intervals and hillshade

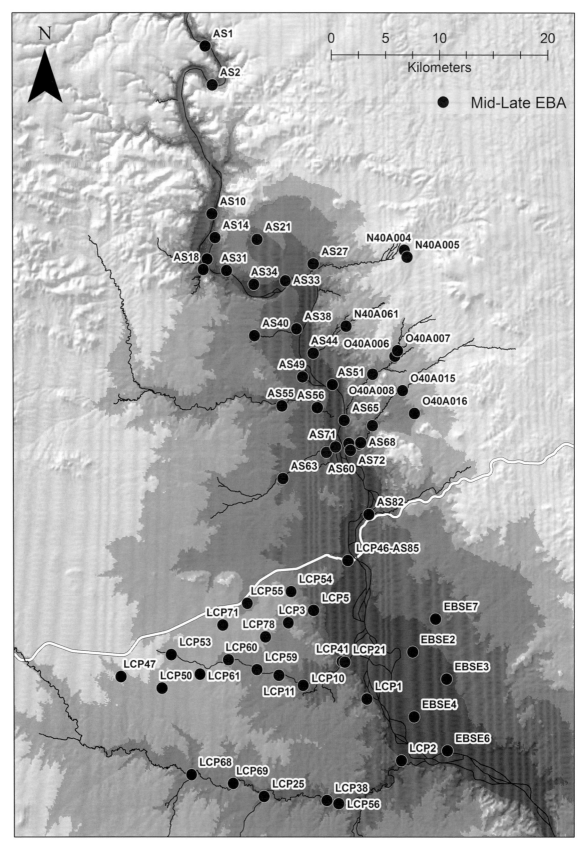

Fig. 4.7 Settlement pattern during the Middle and Late Early Bronze Age periods. Background: SRTM with 50 m contour intervals and hillshade

At the end of the EBA, both the number of sites and the estimated occupied area dropped. Carchemish remained inhabited and probably continued to be the principal regional centre, but significant depopulation occurred around the site. Forty sites were abandoned, and the total number of occupied sites halved, whilst the total settled area decreased by *c.* 25%. Almost 90% of Late EBA settlements continued to occupy the same Middle EBA locations, with only five new Late EBA foundations (Fig. 4.7). Settlement stability was stronger along the river in the Birecik sector, but the dating of the AS Late EBA sites is to some degree questionable (see below). More evident is the abandonment of sites in the LCP and KOS areas. Population decline specifically affected the small sites, under 2 ha in size, while settlement generally continued at the larger occupations. This trend might reflect a structural change at the village level rather than a total collapse of the settlement system. It is also possible that a more gradual expansion at Carchemish might have drawn in local populations, as has been suggested for the inhabitants of Jerablus Tahtani (Peltenburg 1999, 103). Excavations at Şeraga Höyük (AS 71) and Jerablus Tahtani (LCP 22) have documented major flooding events of the Euphrates towards the end of the Middle EBA period (Peltenburg *et al.* 1996, 14–15; Peltenburg *et al.* 1997, 15–16; Sertok *et al.* 2007, 345–349). These natural violent episodes might have prompted local inhabitants to abandon settlements along the river, though the most dramatic decline in terms of number of sites occurred in the tributary valleys. More generally, climate proxy records indicate that climatic conditions had become drier, at least by 2300–2200 BC (Staubwasser and Weiss 2006; Kuzucuoğlu 2007). Declines in settled population at the end of the EBA have also been recorded in other regions of northern Mesopotamia (Akkermans and Schwartz 2003, 282–287; Lawrence 2012; Wilkinson *et al.* 2012) and sites that had expanded into more marginal zones during the Middle EBA declined by the end of the 3rd millennium BC. The precise nature, and ultimate causes, of this "Late Third Millennium Crisis" continue to be debated, with scholars generally blaming some combination of environmental and socio-economic factors (Staubwasser and Weiss 2006; Kuzucuoğlu and Marro 2007; Wossink 2009).

Middle and Late Bronze Age[3]

The assessment of settlement trends during the Middle and Late Bronze Age in the Carchemish sector is particularly complex due to the difficulties in understanding the ceramic chronology for these phases. Both the AS and SCM surveys documented significant rises in settlement during the MBA which are not reflected in the data from the LCP, and this requires some discussion. It must be appreciated that the AS and SCM surveys were conducted at a time when the ceramic chronology of the Middle Euphrates was much less well known than it is today, and in the case of the SCM that

the primary periods of interest of the surveyors lay within the prehistoric periods. Within the LCP there is a degree of ambiguity in the assessment of the ceramics from individual sites and we therefore present the results as a range between minimum and maximum counts rather than single figures. Algaze and his team distinguished a combined Late EBA–MBA phase, in which the number of sites and total occupied area increased dramatically. However, we now know that the production of some of the types used to identify this phase, such as the so called 'champagne cups', ended before the last quarter of the 3rd millennium (Peltenburg 2007a; 2007b). It is possible that the expansion of settlement documented by the AS during the Late EBA and MBA is at least in part a misinterpretation of an earlier phenomenon, perhaps the Middle EBA expansion which was recognised in the LCP. In the case of the overlapping areas of the SCM and LCP, we can directly compare the assemblages recovered from individual sites and the counts derived (Fig. 4.8). Bearing in mind that the SCM survey covers a much larger area than the LCP, the two surveys show roughly comparable numbers of EBA sites, a much larger number of MBA sites for the SCM and a significantly diminished number of LBA sites. The LCP also showed significantly more Iron Age sites than the SCM survey, especially when the survey areas are taken into account, and this again may be a result of Iron Age types being misattributed in the SCM chronology (see Morandi Bonacossi 2000, 379). Overall, because of their conspicuous appearance and the fact that the recognition of prehistoric occupations was one of the main aims of the SCM survey, Halaf and Ubaid sites appear to be quite accurately represented. However, because there is no Late Chalcolithic in the SCM periodization it appears that distinctly LC and Uruk sherds are included in the EBA I–III. This is evident in de Contenson's rather detailed report on the material culture from the survey which shows, for example, a BRB on fig. 5:11 (from Tell Ibr/al-'Abr), and a good group of LC forms on fig. 6, specifically 7–15. In fact, a brief perusal of figs. 5 & 6 of de Contenson's report (de Contenson *et al.* 1985), suggests that early EBA forms (*cyma recta*; cooking wares, and Early EBA jars as found in the Tabqa area) are distinctly under-represented. This therefore suggests that the period EBA I–III, roughly equivalent to the Early and Middle EBA in the LCP, includes the LC, back to at least LC 3. On the other hand, EBIV appears to be quite a good representation of wares of the later third millennium BC (Late EBA in the LCP sequence).

The over-representation of the MBA (Bronze Moyen) becomes apparent from the notes on the sites by Copeland as well as from de Contenson's report. In the former the Bronze Moyen is particularly well represented on most sites: 37 sites were reported for this period, representing more than double that for any other period before the Hellenistic/Roman. In fact the site descriptions of Copeland state "the usual Middle Bronze Age" for the site of Tellik

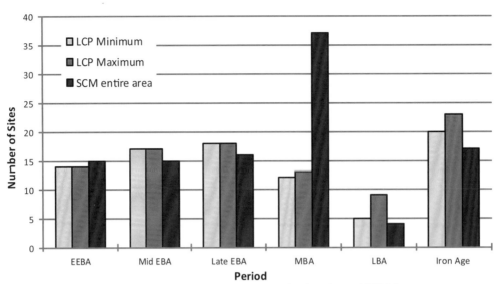

Fig. 4.8 Graph of site counts by phase from the Early EBA to the Iron Age for the LCP and SCM Surveys

(94). Several sites, such as Maazale (SCM 41; LCP 11) are described as MBA only, whereas the LCP, despite several visits, only managed to recover a small collection with no definitive MBA. This is not to say that the SCM survey recognition of MBA at Maazale is wrong; collecting at an earlier period when the pottery on the site may have been more visible, can be an advantage. However, it does suggest that the SCM team, working at the time when the ceramic periodization was less well known, was over-representing this period. Particularly relevant is the site of Tell Jerablus Tahtani (SCM 96; 22 of Moore) which according to the SCM survey included MBA (at least four forms were illustrated as Moyen Bronze). However, Peltenburg's major excavations at the site demonstrated that occupation terminated there in the mid-third millennium and did not resume until the Iron Age (perhaps as a burial area). Of the types illustrated by de Contenson (de Contenson *et al.* 1985), two (fig. 11: 4 and fig. 12: 11) are difficult to assign to any phase whereas two, figs. 13 nos 24 and 25, are probably EBA wares. Both the excavations and this interim re-appraisal of the survey pottery therefore suggest that Tell Jerablus Tahtani was not occupied in the Middle Bronze Age.

Of the other SCM sites recollected by the LCP, 'Ain al Beydar (LCP 10), Chemal (Jemal, LCP 23), Tell Halwanji, Dadate and Arab Hassan are not incompatible with our own pottery assessments suggesting these sites all had some MBA occupation. However, the presence within the published Bronze Moyen pottery plates of a mix of MBA, LBA, Iron Age and perhaps even occasional EBA sherds, suggests that an overly wide range of ceramic types have been included in the Bronze Moyen category in the SCM, meaning that it actually represents pottery over a range of some 1000 to 1500 years. Among the Bronze Moyen figures, figure 11 from de Contenson's report (de Contenson *et al.* 1985) shows a series

of Iron Age bowls (nos. 21–24); on figure 12 are two forms which are likely to be LBA (fig. 12: 16, 20), and two more Iron Age forms on figure 13 (nos 13 and 15). However, figure 14 of the same report is characterized by a group of good MBA parallels (fig. 14: 1–9). Of these, 1 is from al-Qana, which supports Eidem's suggestion (this volume Chapter 6) that this major Early Iron Age site extended back to the MBA. However, other illustrated sherds from this site (e.g. fig. 11: 8; fig. 12: 9) (de Contenson *et al.* 1985) are probably Iron Age and LBA respectively, whilst some (figs 13: 10–13) are of uncertain date but can probably be attributed to some point in the MBA-Early Iron Age.

Overall, and as in the AS, the high count of sites with MBA occupation in the SCM can be explained by the generous range of types employed in this category. The inadvertent inclusion of Iron Age, LBA and perhaps late EBA types within the MBA category has probably resulted in the under-representation of Iron Age and LBA sites, and perhaps also sites of Later EBA date. The data from the SCM survey therefore needs to be treated cautiously. The increase in MBA settlement, especially to the south of the Sajur has been explained as follows:

"According to its excavator, Jesper Eidem, Qala'at Halwanji c. 15 km west of the Euphrates above the south bank of the Sajur, an imposing MB II, short-lived fort with administrative materials was established by one of the regional powers. This was most likely situated within the territory of Yamhad, and so the foundation of so many new sites may be associated with the expansion of that state up to the Sajur. Indeed, so remarkable is this growth that we should not rule out a deliberate settlement policy for the consolidation of its territories, at least near its frontiers." (Peltenburg *et al.* 2012, 196)

However, taking the re-evaluation of our own collections into account, as well as those of the SCM survey, suggests the following more cautious interpretation. Throughout the entire area the SCM survey exaggerates the number of sites with MBA settlement and under-represents those with EB IV, LBA and Iron Age occupations. The re-assessment of the LCP data suggests that the situation in the LCP area was somewhere between virtually stable settlement (18 EBA *vs.* 17 MBA sites) and slight decline (from 18 to 12 sites). In the LBA there was a further decline from the MBA varying between a precipitous drop of 17 (MBA) to five (LBA) sites, to a rather more conservative decline from 12 (MBA) to nine (LBA) sites. Although we have not been able to re-assess the SCM sites from the greater area, including those to the south of the Sajur, the problems in the dating of ceramics for the SCM Bronze Moyen suggests that over-counting of this period also occurred in the greater SCM region.

We can therefore suggest that for the LCP the gradual decline in rural settlement visible in the Later EBA continues into the MBA and LBA. As in the Late EBA, it is possible that this decline may have been the result of the drawing in of populations to Carchemish, which continued to be an order of magnitude larger than any other site in the region. Occupation during the MBA continued to be concentrated on previously settled tells, although the movement away from the east–west alignment and the Amarna valley might suggest a greater emphasis on north-south routes (Fig. 4.9). More significant reorganization occurred along the Sajur where three large sites were founded, including two probable fortresses, Qala'at Halwanji and Aushariye, and al-Qana on the upper Sajur (see Chapter 6), whilst another large site, Arab Hassan (LCP 68), may have been fortified through the construction of a stone enclosing wall. All of these sites are on the southern side of the river whilst settlement on the northern side was limited, with only one small tell immediately opposite Qala'at Halwanji occupied. As Peltenburg *et al.* (2012) have suggested, albeit for different reasons, it is possible that the Sajur operated as some kind of political boundary during this period and that the heavily fortified positions on the south bank were related to either local rivals to Carchemish or the extent of the power of the polity of Carchemish itself.

Information from textual sources has allowed for the reconstruction of the political history of the Carchemish polity from the LBA onwards (Bryce 2005 [1998], see also this volume Chapters 2 and 3). The relationship between material culture and wider political and cultural changes is extremely complex, and beyond the scope of this chapter, but we can say that there do not appear to be significant shifts in the ceramic assemblage over the course of this relatively short (1600–1200 BC) phase. The gradual decline in settlement which began in the Late EBA and MBA is again visible in the LBA in the LCP but the change from the combined Late EBA–MBA phase to the LBA in the AS is rather more drastic, with only one site occupied (Fig. 4.9). However, this again

may be a result of the pottery types used to identify LBA occupations in the AS (Algaze *et al.* 1994, 18). Settlement was still overwhelmingly concentrated on the long-lived tell sites which had characterized the preceding phases. This continuity of occupation is particularly striking since it persists throughout the turbulent period of political and cultural transformations which occurred with the collapse of the Hittite empire, when Hittite, Hurrian, Mitannian and local groups sought to control the Euphrates Valley. For example, there is no evidence from the surveys for the sorts of population influxes envisioned by Bryce into the Carchemish area (2005 [1998], 350) or for settlement shifts during the expansions and contractions of the Carchemish polity documented by Brown and Smith (Chapter 3). Part of the reason for this may have been the strength of the cultural sphere around Carchemish itself. A recent article by Şerifoğlu (2009) identifies a distinct ceramic 'province' around Carchemish from Qara Quzaq to Şaraga Höyük (AS 71), with a large Mittani and Assyrian influenced province to the north and east and a Levant influenced one to the west and along the Euphrates valley. The Carchemish province approximates well to the area of stable settlement visible in the LCP and AS. We therefore have two lines of evidence, ceramics and settlement patterns, which point to some degree of autonomy in the region of Carchemish during the LBA, in which rural life continued to operate much as it had done for the previous two millennia. However, the slight decline in settlement may also be taken as evidence of the notion suggested elsewhere that during the LBA, i.e. during the period when Carchemish was an administrative outpost of the late Hittite empire, the rural landscape was more sparsely settled, and that some of the population may have settled into nucleated fortified settlements that occurred at intervals along both banks of the river (Wilkinson *et al.* 2004, 187–188). A similar argument has been made for the Altinova plain (Turkey) where, from the 14th century BC, the switch from local to Hittite rule led to the concentration of population at fewer larger settlements (Müller 2003).

Iron Age

The Iron Age settlement of the Carchemish region is covered elsewhere in this volume (see Chapters 2, 3 and 5) and this section is intended as a summary of the interpretations available from survey evidence. As in the LBA, our current understanding of changes in ceramic production during the Iron Age cannot match the detail provided by the textual sources, particularly in relation to chronological precision. The AS distinguished between an earlier and later Iron Age based on the presence or absence of Late Assyrian ceramics but it is possible that these types might not be recovered at all sites occupied during this period. The LCP did not attempt broad uniform divisions for the Iron Age assemblages, although individual sites have been more precisely dated

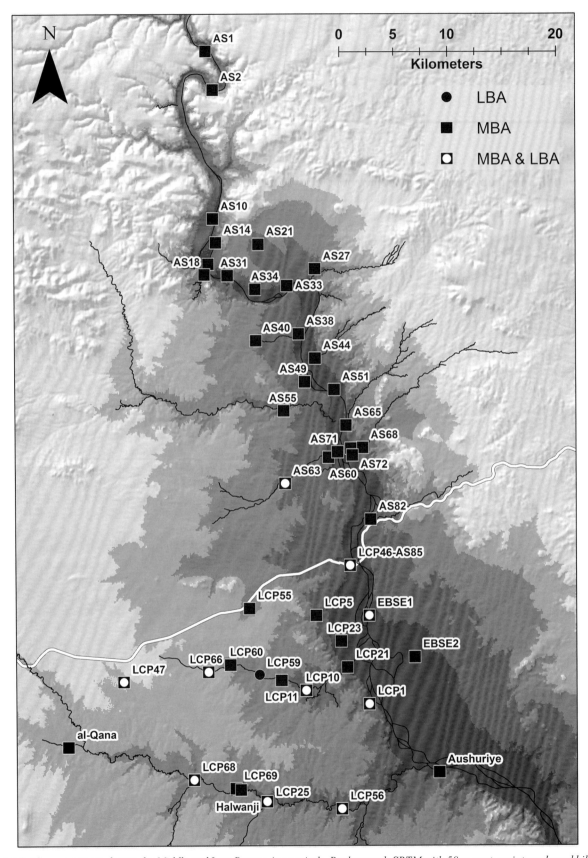

Fig. 4.9 Settlement pattern during the Middle and Late Bronze Age periods. Background: SRTM with 50 m contour intervals and hillshade

where possible. Despite these chronological issues, it is possible to make some general statements on the Iron Age occupation of the area. It is clear from both the LCP and the AS that settlement expanded during the period, with both the number and the total area of occupation increasing (Fig. 4.10). Carchemish also expanded as the lower town became settled, resulting in a total settled area of some 100 ha (see Chapter 8). It is interesting that the two phases of growth at Carchemish, the Middle EBA and Iron Age, were both characterized by a simultaneous rise in rural settlement. Occupation continued at a number of the long-lived tell sites in both the LCP and AS, whilst tells abandoned during the MBA and LBA were reoccupied. The Iron Age also marks the beginning of a new phase of settlement foundation away from the traditional tell-based landscape. The majority of these sites in both the LCP and AS are small and flat but some represent larger settlements, of which LCP 6 is a good example (see Wilkinson *et al.* 2007 for a full discussion of this important site). As in the MBA, the Sajur valley seems to have been militarily important, with the fortresses of Al-Qana and Aushariye situated on the western and eastern ends respectively. Tell Ahmar, on the opposite bank of the Euphrates to Aushariye, was also an important centre of the Hittite Bit-Adini polity, and later the Assyrian Empire, during this period (see Chapter 3). Analysis of CORONA satellite imagery at Al-Qana has revealed a lower town bounded by a substantial outer wall, a similar configuration to the excavated site of Tell Ahmar (Fig. 4.11). It is likely that the Iron Age also saw the first significant investments in landscape infrastructure, particularly canals. Although notoriously difficult to date, canals associated with Iron Age sites are visible in the Jerablus plain (see Chapter 5) and in the Sajur valley close to LCP 56. Overall, Iron Age settlement appears to have remained predominantly tell-based, although the number of small dispersed settlements increased slightly in comparison to previous periods, whilst large centres were located at strategic points.

Classical and Islamic periods

A full treatment of the Hellenistic, Roman and Byzantine landscapes of the LCP and wider area is provided by Newson (Chapter 9), whilst aspects of the Classical landscape are also discussed by Wilkinson (Chapter 5). Here we therefore concentrate on the major trends in settlement. In both the LCP and the AS, the later Roman and Byzantine periods represent a peak of settlement unmatched until modern times. The number of sites and total area of occupation expanded enormously and the settlement pattern became increasingly dispersed (Fig. 4.12). Many of the high tells which had been occupied for millennia were abandoned, although often settlement continued in the same general location in lower towns at the foot of the mounds. During the Hellenistic period a new site founded to the north of Carchemish, Seleukia on the Euphrates, began to rival Carchemish in size and importance. This site, also known as Apamea and Zeugma during the Roman and Byzantine periods, eventually supplanted Carchemish as the main crossing point of the Euphrates, as well as being a nexus of north–south routes (Comfort *et al.* 2000; Comfort and Ergeç 2001). Several medium sized towns are known from this period, including Khirbet Seraisat (LCP 1), where a substantial lower town developed below the EBA tell during the Late Roman period. Similar extensive settlements were discovered at Horum Höyük, probably dating to the Hellenistic period and situated upstream of Seleukia in the AS, and Gırlavık and Tihabes close to Carchemish, both of which were founded slightly later during the Early Roman period (Algaze *et al.* 1994, 23). Larger villages have been discovered away from the river in the LCP, as well as the numerous small farmsteads spread across the landscape in all three surveys. The Classical period also saw significant investment in landscape infrastructure such as canals, qanats and road networks. Small canals and conduits have been recovered on both the Sajur and the Amarna rivers, and qanat shafts have also been found cut into the limestone at various points along the Sajur, many of which can probably be dated to the Hellenistic–Roman period (Wilkinson and Rayne 2010). South of the Sajur, several larger qanat systems are visible on the Corona imagery, some of which stretch for many kilometers towards Membij.[4] Unfortunately the shafts and up-cast remains of these features are particularly susceptible to destruction through ploughing and other agricultural practices, and attempts to visit their locations in the field have not as yet been successful. Other landscape features include numerous rock cut tombs, many with multiple chambers, as well as a rock cut road at Khirbet Seraisat and two possible water mills (Vivancos 2005, Wilkinson *et al.* 2007, 239–240; see also this volume Chapters 5 and 9).

Settlement during the Islamic period is difficult to interpret (Fig. 4.13). The brittlewares used as type fossils for the Byzantine occupations continued to be in use into the Early Islamic phase, and it seems likely that there was some degree of continuity in settlement throughout this period. Early Islamic occupations were recorded at the large Roman–Byzantine towns of Zeugma and Khirbet Seraisat but the occupation appears to have been greatly reduced at both sites. By the Middle Islamic period (equivalent to the Medieval in the AS) settlement seems to have reduced in both the LCP and AS, with only a few small sites occupied. In the LCP these include some of the larger tell sites, but in most cases only a few sherds were recovered. Many of the Middle and Late Islamic occupations are likely buried or destroyed beneath modern villages, and this may account for the apparent decline in settlement visible in these phases.

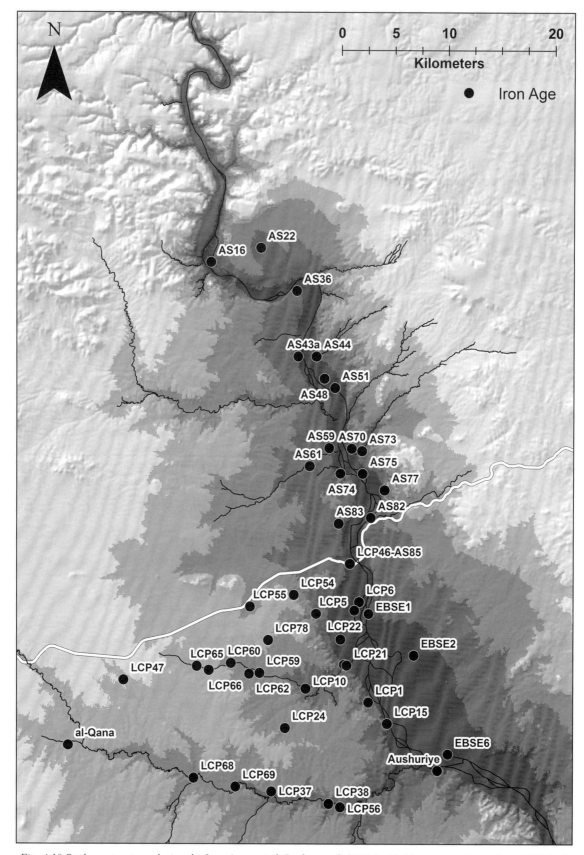

Fig. 4.10 Settlement pattern during the Iron Age period. Background: SRTM with 50m contour intervals and hillshade

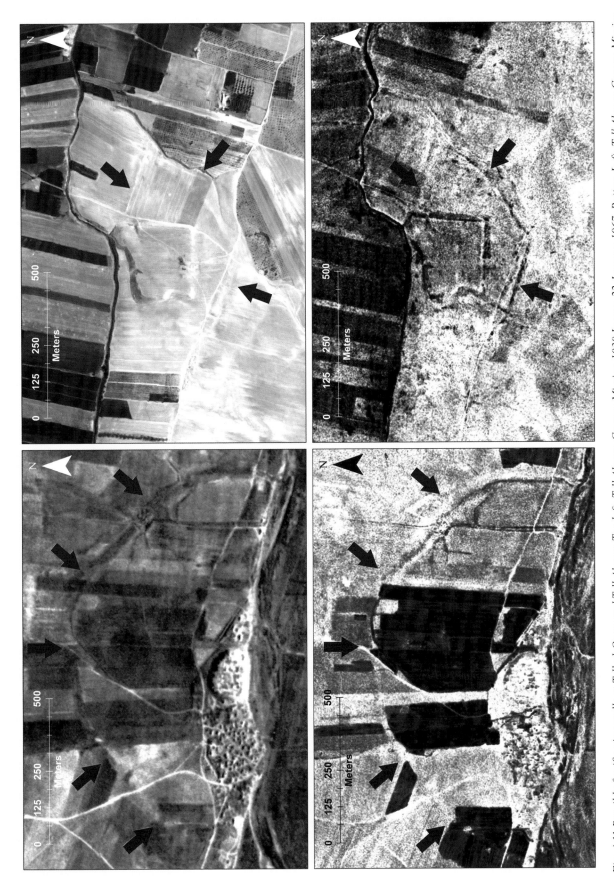

Fig. 4.11 Possible fortification walls at Tell al-Qana and Tell Ahmar: Top left: Tell Ahmar, Corona Mission 1038 Image, 22 January 1967. Bottom Left: Tell Ahmar, Corona Mission 1104 Image, 8 August 1968. Top Right: Tell al-Qana, Corona Mission 1104 Image, 8 August 1968. Bottom Right: Tell al-Qana, GeoEye-1 Image, 19 April 2010. Black arrows indicate likely fortification walls

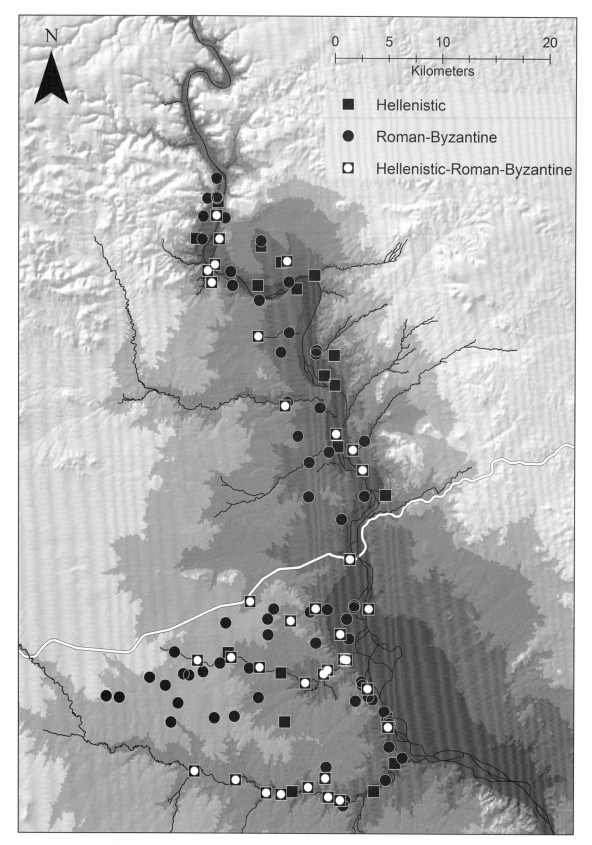

Fig. 4.12 Settlement pattern during the Hellenistic and Late Roman-Byzantine periods. Background: SRTM with 50 m contour intervals and hillshade

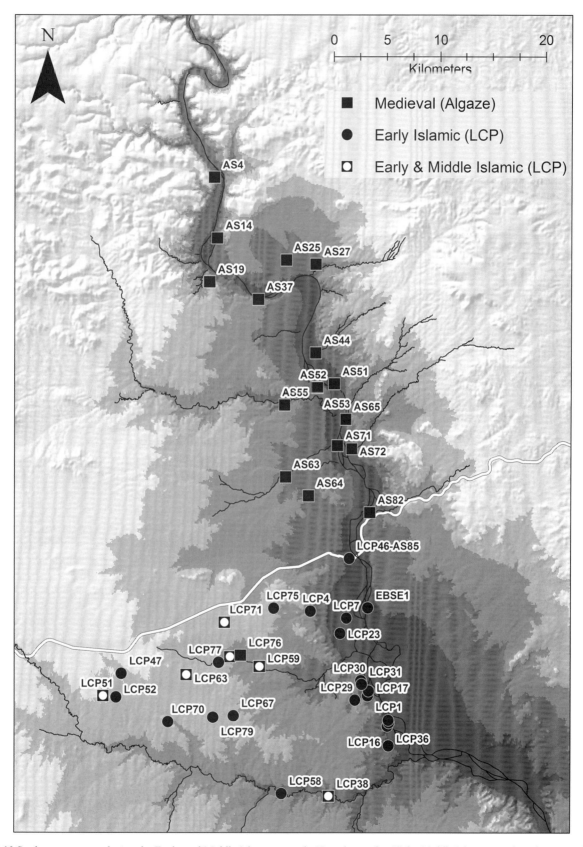

Fig. 4.13 Settlement pattern during the Early and Middle Islamic periods. Note that in the AS the Middle Islamic is referred to as Medieval. Background: SRTM with 50 m contour intervals and hillshade

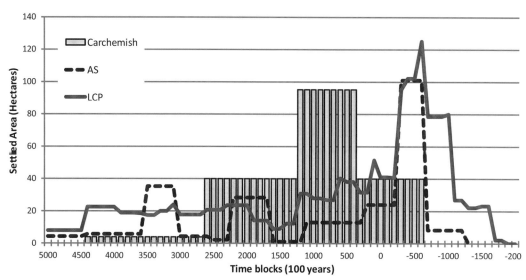

Fig. 4.14 Graph of total settled area for the AS, LCP and site of Carchemish displayed by 100 year time blocks. Note the AS line excludes the 137 ha settlement of Zeugma during the Hellenistic and Roman–Byzantine periods.

Discussion: structural transformations and urban development in the long term

Having discussed the settlement patterns of individual periods we can now draw out trends in settlement and landscape use in the long term. Figure 4.14 shows the density of occupation for the LCP and AS surveys, along with the occupied area of Carchemish, over the last 7000 years. Due to the slight differences in chronology between the AS and the LCP and the variation in dating individual sites within the LCP, the phase-based chronology has been converted into time blocks of 100 years using the Fragile Crescent Project database (see Lawrence 2012; Lawrence *et al.* 2012). The figures for Carchemish should be taken as only very rough approximations given our understanding of the site but these fit with the results from the excavations and Outer Town Survey (see Chapter 8). We have also excluded the site of Seleukia/Apamea/Zeugma from the Algaze survey since the addition of the 137 ha site skews the data for the Hellenistic and Roman periods enormously. Given that Carchemish has also been treated separately from both surveys it makes sense to remove the other large urban site, meaning the lines on the graph represent total rural settlement. The KOS and SCM data have not been processed as there is insufficient information available on site size. Displaying the data in this way allows for the comparison of the AS and LCP surveys with one another, the comparison of both datasets with the trajectory of Carchemish and the examination of overall trends in the Birecik-Carchemish sector. It is clear from the graph that the surveys show a broadly similar pattern, with low levels of settlement in the prehistoric period, gradually increasing occupation from the beginning of the Iron Age and a significant increase in the Hellenistic and Roman periods, before a decline towards the present day. Two notable peaks of settlement are visible in the AS, during the Uruk period and the Late EBA–MBA. The latter of these can be related to problems with the ceramic chronology of the AS, and it is likely that this peak should in fact be spread over the whole EBA (see above). The Uruk peak is more likely to represent a real difference in settlement between the surveys. This difference is probably in part due to the concentration of Uruk settlement, and especially the larger sites, along the banks of the Euphrates, and therefore the area covered by the AS.

In order to make sense of the large amount of data and significant time depth available, we draw on the idea of structural transformations as a useful framework for analysis. This approach takes landscapes to be inherently stable entities subject to periodic shifts in organization which can be related to combinations of environmental and social factors (Casana 2007). In a study of the Amuq plain in southern Turkey, Casana identifies two major structural transformations over the course of the Holocene, with a shift from small dispersed settlements in the prehistoric periods to a 'landscape of tells' from the EBA to the end of the Iron Age, followed by a second phase of dispersal at a much higher density than before. These changes are observable across the Northern Fertile Crescent, although there are differences in the precise timing of the second transformation, Wilkinson's 'great dispersal', which began in the Late Bronze Age in the Jazira but did not take place in the Amuq until the end of the Iron Age (Wilkinson 2003; Chapters 6 and 7; Casana 2007; Lawrence 2012). The general settlement patterns of the Birecik-Carchemish sector visible in Figure 4.14 do broadly conform to this wider pattern. One of the most striking trends is the long-term stability of settlement from the beginning of the Late

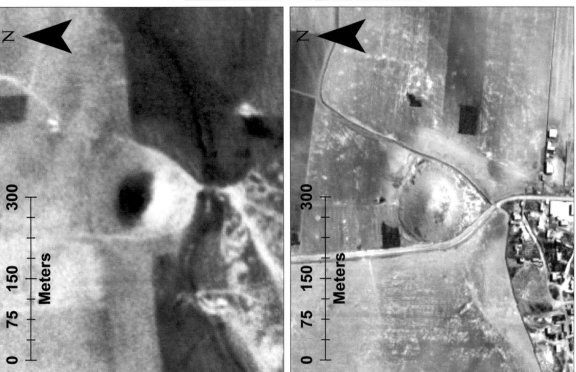

Fig. 4.15 Example of a typical conical tell, LCP 60 Tell Koundariyeh. Top Left: Corona Mission 1038 Image, 22 January 1967. Bottom Left: GeoEye-1 Image, 19 April 2010. Centre Right: Photograph taken in the field by Ricci, July 2009

Chalcolithic to the end of the Bronze Age, especially in the LCP. A small number of site locations formed the basic units of the settlement pattern and were continuously, or near continuously, occupied for many thousands of years, forming settlement mounds or tells. In the LCP, these tells have a distinct conical morphology visible in the field and on satellite imagery (Fig. 4.15) which may be the result of the construction of walls or glacis on the outer edge. The longevity and stability of this tell landscape in the Birecik-Carchemish area is exceptional. As discussed above, several of the larger tells were first occupied during the Halaf and Ubaid periods, meaning we can project the roots of the system back to the Late Neolithic. Even during the Uruk 'impact', a relatively innovative period in terms of material culture and social organization which may have seen an influx of population from Southern Mesopotamia, half of the settlements were located on previously occupied sites.

The continuation of this system is even more remarkable in the context of the urban development at Carchemish during the second urban revolution. Elsewhere in the Middle Euphrates the expansion of sites such as Titriş Höyük and Tell es-Sweyhat saw a similar growth in rural population, with new sites founded and, in the Titriş area at least, the development of a three tiered site hierarchy (Wilkinson *et al.* 2012). In the Jazira, by contrast, urbanization processes at sites such as Tell Hawa during the same period drew in local populations resulting in rural depopulation (Lawrence 2012; Wilkinson *et al.* 2014; Lawrence and Wilkinson in press). The trajectory of Carchemish does not fit either model. The site appears to have been one of a series of medium sized villages during the Late Chalcolithic and into the Early EBA but the settling of the lower town during the second half of the 3rd millennium BC does not appear to have had much of an effect on the settlement pattern, especially to the south in the LCP. This incredible longevity is difficult to explain. In the wider Fertile Crescent, the continuity of occupation on tell sites has been linked to systems of land tenure and management which discouraged individuals from moving away from nucleated communities (Wilkinson 2010), whilst defense may also have been a consideration during the later periods (Cooper 2006; Peltenburg 2013). The success of the smaller settlements is also mirrored by Carchemish once it reached urban proportions. Unlike the other large sites in the Euphrates Valley, our current understanding of Carchemish suggests it did not decline at the end of the EBA and continued to be of significant size during the MBA and LBA. Certainly the political and cultural power provided by the Hittite Empire during the later part of this period must have played a part in this apparent continuity, whilst the political instability of the period combined with the increasing proficiency of standing armies may have resulted in rural population decline as people sought protection in the well-defended regional capital and perhaps other fortified centres in certain periods such as the LBA.

The long-standing system of tell based settlement began to change during the Iron Age and by the Classical period sites had spread across the landscape. The timing of this 'Great Dispersal' is interesting in the light of trends in settlement visible to the east and west, and at Carchemish itself. Dispersal in the Jazira began as early as the Late Bronze Age but is also associated with the later territorial empires of the Iron Age, and especially the Assyrians (Wilkinson *et al.* 2005; Ur 2010b). In the west, tell-based settlement patterns persist until the Seleucid period, when a much more dramatic shift saw an increase in rural settlement and the occupation of previously unsettled upland areas (Casana 2007, 2012). Carchemish seems to fit between these two models, with a gradual abandonment of tells and expansion of settlement over the course of the Iron Age before a more significant shift in the Classical period (Fig. 4.16). Again, expansion at Carchemish itself, which took place at some point during the Iron Age when the entire lower town was occupied, did not involve drawing in the local rural population, and if anything settlement increased in line with the centre. Given the strong tradition of tell-based occupation visible in the previous periods, it is not surprising that the shift to a dispersed landscape was not immediate. However, the lack of the sort of highly organized landscapes seen in parts of the Jazira during the later Iron Age does suggest that Late Assyrian influence over rural populations was not as strong as in the core area of the 'Land of Assur' closer to the imperial capitals. By the Classical period the density of settlement in the AS and LCP had increased dramatically, whilst for the first time in nearly two millennia Carchemish was not the pre-eminent settlement in the Birecik-Carchemish sector, having been surpassed by Seleukia/Zeugma/Apamea. As in western Syria, occupation extended into previously under settled zones, in the case of the Birecik-Carchemish sector including Land Units 3a and 5, the limestone and basalt uplands. Similar patterns are also visible in the limestone uplands in the Wadi Abu Qalqal region close to Membij (Mottram and Menere 2005, 2008), the next large Hellenistic-Roman period town along the Euphrates to the south of the LCP. Combined with the growing evidence for landscape investment in the form of water systems and road networks, it seems likely that the Hellenistic and especially Roman period saw the development of a highly structured landscape designed to maximize agricultural efficiency (Fig. 4.17 and see Chapter 9). This fits well with our understanding of the area as a frontier province of the Roman and Byzantine empires with a relatively high degree of centralized organization focused on the urban centres.

Conclusion: Carchemish in context

The longevity of occupation at Carchemish and its prolonged period as a significant urban centre place it in a very small group of sites within the Northern Fertile Crescent. Most

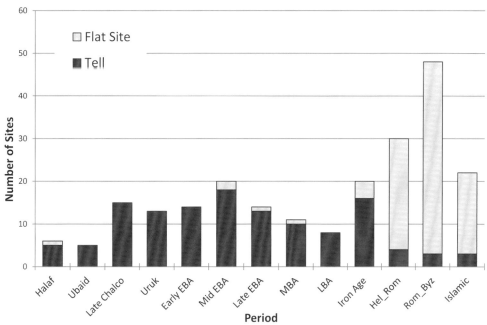

Fig. 4.16 Graph of number of sites by period in the LCP divided between tell and non-tell occupations

Fig. 4.17 Qanats in a village to the south of the LCP. These are part of a larger system which converges on the city of Menbij. Corona Mission 1038 Image, 22 January 1967

Table 4.1: Key information for major surveys used in this study

	Algaze Survey (AS)	Özdoğan and Karul Survey (KOS)	Moore and Sanlaville-Copeland (EBSE sites)	McClellan and Porter (EBSE sites)	Land of Carchemish Project (LCP)
Survey dates	1989	2001	1977, 1979	1987–1989	2006, 2008–2010
Number of Seasons	1	1	2	3	5
Area investigated (km²)	260	525	1350	150	375
Number of Surveyed Sites	84	159	78	34	79
Density of Sites (per 10 km²)	3.23	3.02	0.58	2.27	2.11
Use of Satellite Imagery	Minimal	N	N	N	Y
Use of GPS	N	Y	N	N	Y
Use of 1:25000 topographic maps	Y	Y	N	N	N
Research Design	Rescue	Research	Research	Rescue	Research

of the sites which grew rapidly during the second urban revolution of the Middle and Late EBA declined similarly rapidly after only a few hundred years, whilst only Aleppo and perhaps Hama in Western Syria and Samsat/Samosata on the Euphrates in Turkey continued to be important regional centres into the Iron Age and Classical periods. How can we explain the success of Carchemish in the long term? Part of any explanation must be related to specific historical circumstances, such as the decision by the Hittites to situate a regional capital at Carchemish during the Late Bronze Age. However, the sheer duration of the site's importance argues for the involvement of more structural factors. The location of Carchemish at the nexus of both north-south and east-west trade and exchange networks must be considered integral. As early as the Uruk period there is clear evidence that the Jerablus plain was an important crossing point of the Euphrates, evidenced by the Jerablus Tahtani-Shiukh Fawqani site pairing and the alignment leading inland. The Euphrates itself was a key conduit for the movement of people and goods which Carchemish was in a prime position to exploit and even control. Given our limited understanding of the archaeological sequence at the site itself, especially during the crucial Uruk and early EBA periods before the emergence of the urban centre during the later EBA, it is difficult to make any strong statements about the relationship between long-distance trade networks and the development of Carchemish during prehistoric times beyond noting this general close proximity to likely route systems. It is important to stress that the local landscape also played a part, with the agricultural potential of the fertile plains of Land Units 3b and 5 combined with opportunities for grazing afforded by the upland areas in Land Unit 3a enabling a mixed subsistence strategy. During the Uruk period the diverse environments offered within this landscape may have resulted in a degree of site specialization, with Carchemish representing one of several larger agricultural villages at the apex of a hierarchy including smaller villages and perhaps pastoral focused sites which were less well integrated into the regional economy. Whilst we still have

some way to go in understanding the relationship between stable rural settlement and urban emergence and longevity in the region, it is notable that the boom and bust settlements of Titriş and Sweyhat experienced rapid changes in their surrounding settlement (Lawrence and Wilkinson in press). It is possible that the long-term stability of the small tells around Carchemish provided a solid base from which to extract surpluses of labour and staple products, and therefore contributed to the overall stability of the system as a whole. During the later periods, the persistence of Carchemish as an urban centre can be related to its location in relation to the later territorial empires. Whilst Carchemish's strategic importance in the Hittite state meant an increase in resources during a period of wider settlement decline, its position on the periphery of later empires was significant. This may have saved it from the large-scale re-organizations visible in the Late Assyrian period in the Jazira and the Seleucid and Roman period in the West, resulting in more incremental changes in settlement structure which could be more easily negotiated by the inhabitants of the region. Support for this point is provided by the final decline of Carchemish, which occurred simultaneously with the dissolution of the highly structured landscape of the Late Roman-Byzantine period. Throughout its existence Carchemish was a settlement intimately connected with its surrounding landscape.

Notes

1   We would like to thank Edgar Peltenburg and Tony Wilkinson for allowing us to take part in the Land of Carchemish Project and Mehmet Özdoğan and Necmi Karul who generously granted access to their unpublished archives and to the collections of their 2001 survey in the Birecik district.

2   This alignment of Uruk period sites is discussed in greater detail in Ricci's 2013 PhD thesis.

3   This section was written by the authors in conjunction with T.J. Wilkinson. The majority of the ceramic analysis for the Middle and Late Bronze Age pottery in the field was conducted by T.J. Wilkinson with Silvia Perini.

4   These will be discussed further in a future publication.

Bibliography

Akkermans, P.M.M.G. and Schwartz, G. (2003) *The Archaeology of Syria: From Complex Hunter-Gatherers to Early Urban Societies (ca. 16,000–300 BC)*. Cambridge, Cambridge University Press.

Algaze, G. (1999) Trends in the archaeological development of the Upper Euphrates Basin of South-Eastern Anatolia during the Late Chalcolithic and Bronze Ages. In G. del Olmo Lete and J.-L. Montero Fenollós (eds) *Archaeology of the Upper Syrian Euphrates: The Tishrin Dam Area*, 535–572. Barcelona, Ausa.

Algaze, G. (2005 [1993]) *The Uruk World System: The Dynamics of Expansion of Early Mesopotamian Civilization, Second Edition*. Chicago IL, University of Chicago Press

Algaze, G. Breuninger, R. and Knudstad, J. (1994) The Tigris Euphrates archaeological reconnaissance project: Final report of the Bireçik and Carchemish Dam survey areas. *Anatolica* 20, 1–96.

Balkan Atlı, N. Borrell, F. Buxó, R. Duru, G. Ibáñez, J. J. Maede, O. Molist, M. Özbaşaran, M. Piquet, R. Sana, M. and Wattez, J. (2002) Akçay Tepe 2000. In N. Tuna and J. Velibeyoğlu (eds). *Ilısu ve Karkamış Baraj Gölleri Altında Kalacak Arkeolojik ve Kültür Varlıklarını Kurtarma Projesi 2000 Yılı Çalışmaları – Salvage Project of the Archaeological Heritage of the Ilısu and Carchemish Dam Reservoirs Activities in 2000*, 309–318. Ankara, METU Centre for Research and Assessment of the Historic Environment (TAÇDAM).

Besancon, J. and Sanlaville, P. (1981) Aperçu géomorphologique sur la vallée de l'Euphrate syrien. *Paleorient* 7 (2), 5–18.

Bryce, T. (2005 [1998]) *The Kingdom of the Hittites*. Oxford, Oxford University Press.

Casana, J. (2007) Structural transformations in settlement systems of the North Levant. *American Journal of Archaeology* 111 (2), 195–221.

Casana, J. (2012) Site morphology and settlement history in the northern Levant. In R. Matthews and J. Curtis (eds) *Proceedings of the 7th International Congress on the Archaeology of the Ancient Near East, 12 April–16 April 2010, the British Museum and UCL, London*, 593–608. Wiesbaden, Harrassowitz Verlag. Volume 1 Mega-cities and Mega-sites, The Archaeology of Consumption and Disposal, Landscape, Transport and Communications.

Casana, J. (2013) Radial route systems and agro-pastoral strategies in the Fertile Crescent: new discoveries from western Syria and southwestern Iran. *Journal of Anthropological Archaeology* 32 (2), 257–273.

Comfort, A. Abadie-Reynal, C. and Ergeç, R. (2000) Crossing the Euphrates in antiquity: Zeugma seen from space. *Anatolian Studies* 50, 99–126.

Comfort, A. and Ergeç, R. (2001) Following the Euphrates in antiquity: north–south routes around Zeugma. *Anatolian Studies* 51, 19–49.

Cooper, L. (2006) *Early Urbanism on the Syrian Euphrates*. London, Routledge.

Copeland, L. and Moore, A.M.T. (1985) Inventory and description of sites. In P. Sanlaville (ed.) *Holocene Settlement in North Syria: résultats de deux prospections archéologiques effectuées dans la région du nahr Sajour et sur le haut Euphrate syrien*, 41–98. Oxford, BAR S238.

Cruells, W. (2004) Area L: the soundings. In Ö. Tunca and M. Molist (eds) *Tell Amarna (Syrie) I: La Période de Halaf*, 15–36. Louvain, Peeters.

de Contenson, H. Copeland, L. Moore, A. and Sanlaville, P. (1985) Index. In Sanlaville, P. (ed.) *Holocene Settlement in North Syria: résultats de deux prospections archéologiques effectuées dans la région du nahr Sajour et sur le haut Euphrate syrien*. Oxford, BAR S238.

del Olmo Lete, G. and Montero Fenollós, J.-L. (eds) (1999) *Archaeology of the Upper Syrian Euphrates: The Tishrin Dam Area*. Barcelona, AUSA.

Falsone, G. and Sconzo, P. (2007) The 'champagne cup' period at Carchemish. In E. Peltenburg (ed.) *Euphrates River Valley Settlement*, 73–93. Levant Supplementary Series 5. Oxford, Oxbow Books.

Frangipane, M. (2012) "Transitions" as an archaeological concept. Interpreting the final Ubaid-Late Chalcolithic transition in the Northern periphery of Mesopotamia. In C. Marro (ed.) *After the Ubaid. Interpreting Changes from the Caucasus to Mesopotamia at the Dawn of Urban Civilization (4500–3500BC). Papers from The Post-Ubaid Horizon in the Fertile Crescent and Beyond, International Workshop held at Fosseuse, 29th June–1st July 2009*, 39–64. Istanbul/Paris, IFEA–De Boccard. Varia Anatolica XXVII.

Fuensanta, J. G. (2007) The Tilbes Project (Birecik Dam, Turkish Euphrates): the Early Bronze evidence. In E. Peltenburg (ed.) *Euphrates River Valley Settlement*, 142–151. Levant Supplemetary Series 5. Oxford, Oxbow Books.

Helwing, B. (2012) An age of heroes? Some thoughts on Early Bronze Age funerary customs in northern Mesopotamia in P. Pfälzner, H. Niehr, E. Pernicka and A. Wissing (eds) *(Re-) Constructing Funerary Rituals in the Ancient Near East: proceedings of the First International Symposium of the Tübingen Post–Graduate School "Symbols of the Dead" in May 2009*, 47–58. Wiesbaden, Harrassowitz. Qatna Studien Supplementa Band 1.

Kuzucuoğlu, C. (2007) Climatic and environmental trends during the third millennium B.C. in Upper Mesopotamia. In C. Kuzucuoğlu and C. Marro (eds) *Sociétés Humaine et Changement Climatique à la Fin du Troisième Millénaire: Une Crise a-t-elle eu Lieu en Haute Mésopotamie?*, 459–480. Istanbul, Institut Français d'Études Anatoliennes George Dumezil.

Kuzucuoğlu, C. and Marro, C. (eds) (2007) *Sociétés Humaine et Changement Climatique à la Fin du Troisième Millénaire: Une Crise a-t-elle eu Lieu en Haute Mésopotamie?* Istanbul, Institut Français d'Études Anatoliennes George Dumezil.

Lawrence, D. (2012) *Early Urbanism in the Northern Fertile Crescent: A Comparison of Regional Settlement Trajectories and Millennial Landscape Change*. PhD Thesis. Durham, Durham University.

Lawrence, D. Bradbury, J. and Dunford, R. (2012) Chronology, uncertainty and GIS: A methodology for characterising and understanding landscapes of the Ancient Near East. In W. Bebermeier, R. Hebenstreit, E. Kaiser and J. Krause (eds) *Landscape Archaeology. Proceedings of the International Conference Held in Berlin, 6th–8th June 2012*, 353–359. Berlin, Excellence Cluster Topoi. Special Volume 3.

Lawrence, D. and Wilkinson, T.J. (2015) Hubs and Upstarts: pathways to urbanism in the northern Fertile Crescent. *Antiquity* 89, 328–344.

Marro, C. Tibet, A. and Bulgan, F. (2000) Fouilles de sauvetage de Horum Höyük (Province de Gaziantep): Quatrième rapport préliminaire. *Anatolia Antiqua* 8, 257–278.

McClellan, T.L. (1999) Urbanism on the Upper Syrian Euphrates. In G. del Olmo Lete and J.-L. Montero Fenollós (eds) *Archaeology of the Upper Syrian Euphrates: The Tishrin Dam Area*, 413–425. Barcelona, AUSA.

McClellan, T.L. and Porter, A. (in press) Archaeological surveys of the Tishreen Dam Flood Zone. *Les Annales Archéologiques Arabes Syriennes*.

Morandi Bonacossi, D. (2000) The Syrian Jazireh in the Late Assyrian Period: a view from the countryside. In G. Bunnens (ed.) *Essays on Syria in the Iron Age*, 349–396. Louvain, Peeters Press. Ancient Near Eastern Studies 7.

Mottram, M. and Menere, D. (2005) Preliminary surface investigations in the Wadi Abu Qalqal Region, North Syria. *Meditarch* 18, 161–174.

Mottram, M. and Menere, D. (2008) Wadi Abu Qalqal Regional Survey, Syria. Report from 2006. *Meditarch* 21, 79–104.

Müller, U. (2003) A Change to continuity: Bronze Age traditions in the Early Iron Age. In B. Fischer, H. Genz, E. Jean and K. Köroğlu (eds) *Identifying changes: the transition from bronze to Iron Ages in Anatolia and its neighbouring regions. Proceedings of the International Workshop Istanbul, November 8–9, 2002*, 137–149. Istanbul, Türk Eskiçağ Bilimleri Enstitüsü Yayınları.

Nymark Jensen, A. (2011) *Insights into Middle Palaeolithic Technological Practices at Qala'at Halwanji, Syria: a Technological Analysis of a Surface Scatter*. PhD Thesis. Copenhagen, University of Copenhagen.

Özbaşaran, M. Duru, G. Balkan Atlı, N. Molist, M. and Bucak, E. (2004) Akarçay Tepe 2002. *Kazı Sonuçlar Toplantısı*, 303–310. Ankara, Republic of Turkey, Ministry of Culture, General Directorate of Monuments and Museums.

Özdoğan, M. and Karul, N. (2002) Birecik – Suruç Arkeolojik Envanter Raporu. In N. Başgelen (ed.) *Birecik – Suruç Türkiye Kültür Envanteri Pilot Bölge Çalışmaları*, 1–101. Istanbul, Arkeoloji ve Sanat Yay. TÜBA TÜKSEK yay.

Parker, B.J. (2010) Networks of Interreginal Interaction during Mesopotamia's Ubaid Period. In R. Carter and G. Philip (eds) *Beyond the Ubaid: Transformation and Integration in the Late Prehistoric Societies of the Middle East*, 339–360. Chicago IL, Oriental Institute of the University of Chicago.

Peltenburg, E., Wilkinson, T.J., Ricci, A., Lawrence, D., McCarthy, A., Wilkinson, E., Newson, P. and Perini, S. (2012) The Land of Carchemish (Syria) Project: The Sajur Triangle. In R. Matthews and J. Curtis (eds) *Proceedings of the 7th International Congress on the Archaeology of the Ancient Near East, 12 April–16 April 2010, the British Museum and UCL, London*, 191–204. Wiesbaden, Harrassowitz Verlag. Volume 3 Fieldwork and Recent Research.

Peltenburg, E. (1999) Tell Jerablus Tahtani 1992–1996: a summary. In G. del Olmo Lete and J.-L. Montero Fenollós (eds) *Archaeology of the Upper Syrian Euphrates: The Tishrin Dam Area*, 97–105. Barcelona, AUSA.

Peltenburg, E. (2007a) Diverse settlement pattern changes in the Middle Euphrates Valley in the later third millennium B.C.:
the contribution of Jerablus Tahtani. In C. Kuzucuoğlu and C. Marro (eds) *Sociétés Humaine et Changement Climatique à la Fin du Troisième Millénaire: Une Crise a-t-elle eu Lieu en Haute Mésopotamie?*, 247–266 Istanbul, Institut Français d'Études Anatoliennes George Dumezil.

Peltenburg, E. (2007b) New perspectives on the Carchemish sector of the Carchemish river valley in the 3rd Millennium BC. In E.J. Peltenburg (ed.) *Euphrates River Valley Settlement, 3–24*. Levant Supplemetary Series 5. Oxford, Oxbow Books.

Peltenburg, E. (2007–8) Enclosing the ancestors and the growth of socio-political complexity in Early Bronze Age Syria. In G. Bartoloni and M.B. Benedettini (eds) *Atti del Convegno Internazionale "Sepolti tra i vivi. Buried among the living. Evidenza ed interpretazione di contesti funerari in abitato"*, 215–247. Rome, Istituo Poligrafico e Zecca dello Stato – Libreria dello Stato. Scienze dell'Antichità. Storia Archeologia Antropologia.

Peltenburg, E. (2013) Conflict and exclusivity in Early Bronze Age societies of the Middle Euphrates Valley. *Journal of Near Eastern Studies* 25 (2), 233–252.

Peltenburg, E., Bolger, D., Campbell, S., Murray, M. and Tipping, R. (1996) Jerablus Tahtani, Syria, 1995: Preliminary Report. *Levant* 28, 1–25.

Peltenburg, E., Campbell, S., Carter, S., Stephen, F.M.K. and Tipping, R. (1997) Jerablus-Tahtani, Syria, 1996: Preliminary Report. *Levant* 29, 1–18.

Peltenburg, E., Eastaugh, E., Hewson, M., Jackson, A., McCarthy, A. and Rymer, T. (2000) Jerablus Tahtani, Syria, 1998–9: Preliminary Report. *Levant* 32, 53–75.

Ricci, A. (2013) *An Archaeological Landscape Study of the Birecik-Carchemish Region (Middle Euphrates River Valley) during the 5th, 4th and 3rd Millennia BC*. PhD Thesis. Kiel, Christian-Albrechts-Universität.

Rothman, M.S. (ed.) (2001) *Uruk Mesopotamia and its Neighbours: cross-cultural interactions in the era of state formation*. Santa Fe NM, School of American Research Press.

Sanlaville, P. (ed.) (1985) *Holocene Settlement in North Syria: résultats de deux prospections archéologiques effectuées dans la région du nahr Sajour et sur le haut Euphrate syrien*. Oxford, BAR S238.

Şerifoğlu, T.E. (2009) An attempt to identify the Late Bronze Age cultural provinces of the Carchemish-Harran Area. *Akkadica* 130, 167–187.

Sertok, K. and Ergeç, R. (1999) A new Early Bronze Age cemetery: excavations near the Birecik Dam, southeastern Turkey. Preliminary report (1997–98). *Anatolica* 25, 87–107.

Sertok, K., Kulakoğlu, F. and Squadrone, F. (2007) Living along and together with the Euphrates. The effects of the Euphrates on a long-life settlement as Şaraga Höyük. In C. Marro and C. Kuzucuoğlu (eds) *Sociétés Humaine et Changement Climatique à la Fin du Troisième Millénaire: Une Crise a-t-elle eu Lieu en Haute Mésopotamie?*, 341–353. Paris, De Boccard.

Shaw, A. (2012) *The Earlier Palaeolithic of Syria: Reinvestigating the evidence from the Orontes and Euphrates Valleys*. Oxford, BAR S2341.

Staubwasser, M. and Weiss, H. (2006) Holocene climate and cultural evolution in later prehistoric–early historic West Asia. *Quaternary Research* 66, 372–387.

Stein, G. (1999) Material culture and social identity: the evidence for a 4th millennium BC Mesopotamian Uruk colony at Hacinebi, Turkey. *Paleorient* 25 (1), 11–22.

Stein, G. (2011) Tell Zeidan (2010). *Oriental Institute Annual Report 2010–2011*, 121–113.

Stein, G., Boden K., Edens, C., Pearce Eden, J., Keith, J., McMahon, A. and Özbal, H. (1997) Excavations at Hacınebi, Turkey 1996: Preliminary Report. *Anatolica* 23, 111–171.

Thuesen, I. (1996) Tell Mashnaqa. *Syrian-European Archaeology Exhibition: Working Together*. Damascus, Institut Française d'Etudes Arabes de Damas.

Thuesen, I. (2000) Ubaid Expansion in the Khabur: New evidence from Tell Mashnaqa. In O. Rouault and M. Wäfler (eds) *La Djéziré et l'Euphrate Syriens de la protohistoire à la fin du IIe millénaire av. J.-C.: Tendances dans l'interprétation historique des donnés nouvelles*, 71–79. Turnhout, Brepols.

Ur, J. (2003) CORONA satellite photography and ancient road networks: a northern Mesopotamian case study. *Antiquity* 77, 102–115.

Ur, J. (2010a) Cycles of civilisation in Northern Mesopotamia, 4400–2000 B.C. *Journal of Archaeological Research* 18, 387–431.

Ur, J. (2010b) *Urbanism and Cultural Landscapes in Northeastern Syria: The Tell Hamoukar Survey, 1999–2001*. Chicago IL, Oriental Institute Publications.

Vivancos, A.E. (2005) *Eufratense et Osrhoene: poblamiento Romano en el alto Éufrate Sirio*. Murcia, Universidad de Murcia, Servicio de Publicaciones.

Wilkinson, T.J. (2000) Settlement and Landuse in the Zone of Uncertainty in Upper Mesopotamia. In R. Jas (ed.) *Rainfall and Agriculture in Northern Mesopotamia: Proceedings of the Third MOS Symposium (Leiden 1999)*, 3–35. Leiden, Nederlands Instituut voor het Nabje Oosten.

Wilkinson, T.J. (2003) *Archaeological landscapes of the Near East*. Tucson AZ, University of Arizona Press.

Wilkinson, T.J. (2007) Archaeological regions in the neighborhood of Carchemish. In E. Peltenburg (ed.) *Euphrates River Valley Settlement: the Carchemish sector in the Third Millennium BC*, 27–42. Levant Supplementary Series 5. Oxford, Oxbow Books.

Wilkinson, T.J. (2010) The Tell: social archaeology and territorial space. In D. Bolger and L. Maguire (eds) *The Development of Pre-State Communities in the Ancient Near East: Studies in Honour of Edgar Peltenburg*, 55–62. BANEA Publications Series 2. Oxford, Oxbow Books.

Wilkinson, T.J. and Rayne, L. (2010) Hydraulic landscapes and imperial power in the Near East. *Water History* 2, 115–144.

Wilkinson, T.J., Galiatsatos, N., Lawrence, D., Ricci, A., Philip, G. and Dunford, R. (2012) Late Chalcolithic and Early Bronze Age landscapes of settlement and mobility in the Middle Euphrates: a reassessment. *Levant* 44 (2), 139–185.

Wilkinson, T.J., Miller, N.F., Reichel, C.D., and Whitcomb, D. (2004) *On the margin of the Euphrates: settlement and land use at Tell es-Sweyhat and in the upper Lake Assad area, Syria*. Chicago IL, Oriental Institute Publications 124.

Wilkinson, T.J., Peltenburg, E., McCarthy, A., Wilkinson, E.B. and Brown, M. (2007) Archaeology in the Land of Carchemish: landscape surveys in the area of Jerablus Tahtani, 2006. *Levant* 39, 213–247.

Wilkinson, T.J., Philip, G., Bradbury, J., Dunford, R., Donoghue, D., Galiatsatos, N., Lawrence, D., Ricci, A., and Smith, S. (2014) Contextualizing early urbanization: settlement cores, Early States and agro-pastoral strategies in the Fertile Crescent during the fourth and third millennia BC. *Journal of World Prehistory* 27 (1), 43–109.

Wilkinson, T. J., Wilkinson, E., Ur, J. and Altaweel, M. (2005) Landscape and settlement in the Neo-Assyrian Empire. *Bulletin of the American Schools of Oriental Research* 340, 23–55.

Woolley, C.L. (1921) *Carchemish. Report on the excavations at Jerablus on behalf of the British Museum, Part II: The Town Defences*. London, British Museum.

Woolley, C.L. (1934) The prehistoric pottery of Carchemish. *Iraq* 1, 146–162.

Woolley, C.L. and Barnett, R. (1952) *Carchemish, Report on the excavations at Jerablus on behalf of the British Museum, Part III: The Excavations in the Inner Town and the Hittite Inscriptions*. London, British Museum.

Wossink, A. (2009) *Challenging Climate Change: Competition and cooperation among pastoralists and agriculturalists in northern Mesopotamia (c. 3000–1600 BC)*. Leiden, Sidestone Press.

Wright, H.T. and Rupley, E. (2001) Calibrated radiocarbon age determinations of Uruk-related assemblages. In M.S. Rothman (ed.) *Uruk Mesopotamia and Its Neighbours*, 85–122. Santa Fe NM, School of American Research Press.

5

The landscapes of Carchemish

T.J. Wilkinson

Introduction and previous investigations

Settlement in the Land of Carchemish has already been discussed in Chapter 4, and the task of this Chapter is first to provide a summary of the physical landscape, and second to outline the range of evidence for the landscapes of the later periods (roughly post-Late Bronze Age) when landscape features become better preserved. Here emphasis is upon the Iron Age, not only because this was a major period of occupation at Carchemish itself, but also because the frequent passage of the Assyrian kings through the area lends an element of human agency to the landscape, which is not as apparent during earlier periods. Although these campaigns were not always successful, they did provide information via place names and itineraries which can now be recognized and placed within their landscape context.

Following the collapse of the Assyrian empire, between 612 and 609 BC, the archaeological record becomes more difficult to discern. Then, as a result of the developments ushered in by the Seleucid and Roman empires we see a significant increase in the impact of humans on the landscape. Some of these features are discussed by Paul Newson in Chapter 9; however, here the implications of the Hellenistic to Late Antique impacts on the landscape are discussed in more detail with specific reference to off-site features, quarries, water channels, and agricultural installations.

This chapter effectively starts with the transition from a tell-based landscape in the 4th, 3rd and 2nd millennium BC, when the landscape was apparently rather stable and well vegetated, to a post-Late Bronze Age phase growth in the number of settlements when there was increased settlement dispersal across the landscape. Although the Iron Age can be seen as a transitional phase in this dispersal, the textual records discussed below and in Chapters 2 and 3 make it worthy of specific attention.

The physical environment

Climate

According to data on mean annual rainfall (Fig. 5.1), Carchemish is located where rainfall is sufficient, in most years, for rain-fed cultivation. Estimates of the mean annual rainfall for Carchemish are variable: recent estimates include roughly 340 mm per annum (Kuzucuoğlu and Marro 2007, map 1) or *c.* 400 mm per annum (from a 31 year record compiled by the Global Precipitation Climatology Centre: GPCC). This places the city in roughly the same rainfall zone as Nineveh (Mosul) in northern Iraq, and with significantly more than Tell Brak, near Hasseka. Moreover, with mean inter-annual rainfall variability of around 27%, the rainfall at Jerablus/Carchemish is slightly more reliable than at Mosul (*c.* 32%) or Hasseka (35%).[1]

Significantly, the Sajur, which defines the southern edge of the survey area, according to GPCC estimates, falls roughly on the 300 mm mean annual isohyet and the "desert line" as defined by Lewis from historical records. This places the project area north of the so-called "zone of uncertainty" and within the area where sustained long-term settlement is possible (Wilkinson *et al.* 2012, fig. 4). Of course, rainfall has varied historically, and here it is simply necessary to point out that not only has rainfall declined in northern Syria over the last 30 years, culminating in a very dry episode between 2007 and 2009 (Kaylici 2013, fig. 5.4; Trigo *et al.* 2010), but also for a longer span, a relatively dry trend that started towards the end of the 3rd millennium BC, has continued for the remainder of the late Holocene. Consequently conditions for the last 3000 years under consideration were probably somewhat drier than those of much of the 4th and earlier 3rd millennium BC.

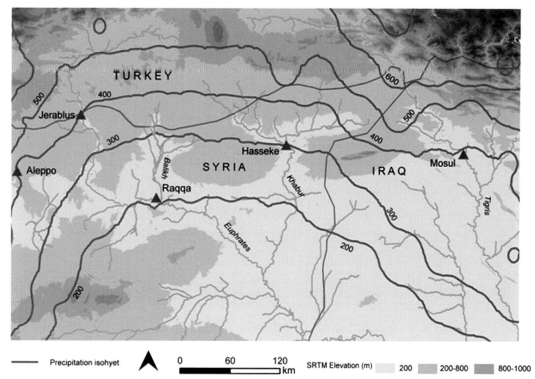

Fig. 5.1 Mean annual rainfall in northern Syria. Data from last 31 years GPCC data, compiled by Louise Rayne

Vegetation

Thanks to painstaking work on the charcoal and carbonized plant remains from excavated sites it is now possible to estimate the main vegetation zones of the middle Euphrates during the Bronze Age (Deckers and Pessin 2011 and references therein). Here key plant indicators, based upon Deckers and Pessin (2011, table 1) are employed to sketch the specific vegetation indices, namely open park woodland, woodland steppe (primarily deciduous Oak), and riverine forest zones (*Salix* and *Populus*) for the sites of Tilbeshar, Horum Höyük, Tell Jerablus Tahtani, Tell Shiukh Fawqani and Tell Emar/Balis. Also plotted are indicators of Mediterranean agriculture: olive and grape vine (Tables 5.1 and 5.2).

The two northern sites of Tilbeshar and Horum Höyük, located in the uplands and elevated plains where rainfall is today close to 400 mm per annum, exhibited large amounts of oak charcoal, sparse to moderate *Salix/Populus*, but also high amounts of olive, suggestive of an oak park woodland with some olive trees. On the other hand, the area of Carchemish, represented by Tells Jerablus Tahtani and Shiukh Fawqani, had only moderate amounts of oak (or the sites had ready access to these types of wood); this dearth was clearly compensated for by significant amounts of *Salix/Populus* woodland in the riverine zone. Here both olive and vines were also present, although these plants were not recorded on the east bank at Tell Shiukh Fawqani (either because they were not there or simply were not

Table 5.1. Oak and Salix/Populus charcoal fragments (from Deckers and Pessin 2011, table 1)

SITE	Mean rainfall per annum	Quercus Mean	Salix/Populus mean
Tilbeshar	390	280.75	13.1
Horum Hk	370	377.8	25.8
Tell Jerablus T	300	25.75	583.25
Tell Shiukh F	300	39	207.7
Balis/Emar	200	1.5	4074.5

Table 5.2. Olive and grape vine charcoal fragments (from Deckers and Pessin 2011, table 1)

Site	Rainfall	Olea Mean	Vitis mean
Tilbeshar	390	19.25	6.375
Horum Hk.	370	118.5	2.5
Tell Jerablus T.	300	8	5.5
Tell Shiukh F.	300	0	0
Balis/Emar	200	2.5	1

encountered). It would therefore appear that the Carchemish area fell within an oak/pistacia steppe, and one is tempted to speculate that the upland plain (zone 4, see below) to the west may have been perhaps the better wooded part of the area. Moreover, the Tilbeshar area, together with a broad region from Samsat to Carchemish through to Ebla, has

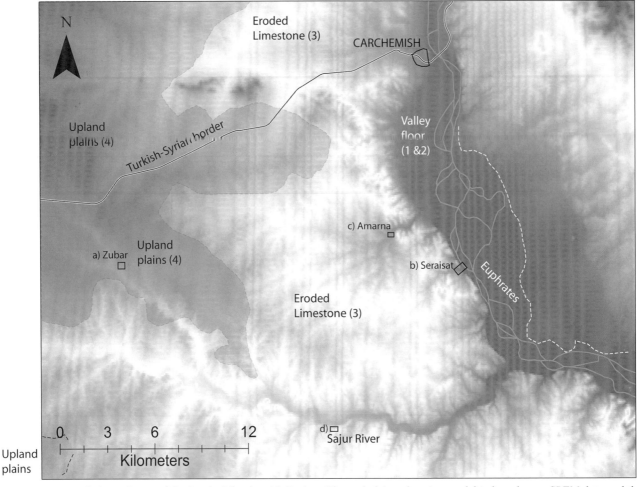

Fig. 5.2 Geomorphological map of the Land of Carchemish Project. The underlying elevation model is based upon SRTM data and the upland plains (zone 4) from Geoeye (compiled by Dan Lawrence and T.J .Wilkinson). a–d) indicate the locations of the four sections discussed in the text

been suggested as having specialized in olive oil and wine production (Kepinski 2007, 159).

In contrast, the great bend of the Euphrates in the vicinity of Emar/Balis showed minimal evidence for the presence of oak, probably because it was an area of pistacia /almond wooded steppe, but with dense areas of riverine woodland (some irrigated in the Late Bronze Age), but also limited amounts of olive and grapes.

Although based upon only five sites, and averaged over more than a millennium, these data allow Deckers and Pessin (2011, 39, 45) to suggest that during the Bronze Age woodland spread significantly further south than is the case today, that riverine woodland was more diverse, and that there has been significant degradation of woodland since the early Bronze Age. Moreover, they argue that the riverine vegetation was cleared first, to be followed by the clearance of woodland steppe on the uplands later. Just as oak woodland was more predominant in the moister north,

as the climate showed some degree of drying during the second millennium, there appears to have been an increase in pistacia woodland during the later stages of the Bronze Age (Deckers and Pessin 2011, 41).

Geomorphology

The geomorphology of the Middle Euphrates is here presented from the perspective of those land units and processes that are particularly relevant to human living conditions and the preservation of archaeological sites (Wilkinson *et al.* 2007). "Stages" of Quaternary development, which have received particular attention over the last thirty years are provided elsewhere in Minzoni-Deroche and Sanlaville (1988), Demir *et al.* (2008), Cremaschi and Maggioni (2005), and Kuzucuoğlu *et al.* (2004).

The area between Carchemish and the Sajur Valley can be sub-divided into four broad land units (Wilkinson *et al.*

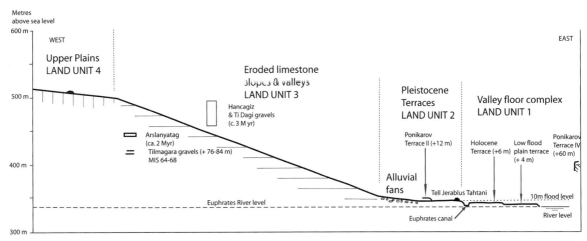

Fig. 5.3 Schematic section across the four geomorphological zones of the Land of Carchemish Survey area

2012, 145–147) although, as discussed in Chapter 4, the greater region includes an additional unit of plateau basalts (5). It is also possible to provide additional sub-divisions to the valley floor lands based upon areas downstream within the Tabqa area (Wilkinson *et al.* 2004 and Fig. 5.3). The following land units are dealt with from lowest (*i.e.* youngest) to highest (oldest) (Figs 5.2 and 5.3):

1) The Euphrates floodplain between Carchemish and Tabqa comprises a low terrace at *c.* 4 m above river level and a slightly higher terrace at *c.* 6 m which together correspond to the "lower fluvial complex" of Cremaschi and Maggioni 2005, 2). During the Bronze Age these lowest floodplain lands probably included alignments of riverine gallery woodland (Miller 1997; Deckers and Pessin 2010), and around Emar Mori has used Late Bronze Age cuneiform texts to demonstrate the presence of cultivated and irrigated fields (Mori 2003; Arnaud 1991). Unfortunately, the flood plain near Carchemish appears to have been so heavily scoured by the river that very little of the original flood plain remains. However, the presence of what appears to be the remains of a major canal at flood plain level, possibly dated to the Neo-Hittite period, suggests the that the western elements of the flood plain may remain from the early 1st millennium BC (see below).

Upstream of Carchemish the "low" sites at Şaraga and Şavi exhibit pre-Uruk and Middle EBA occupation *below* the pre-dam river level (Kuzucuoğlu *et al.* 2004, 203). Such low sites are particularly significant because they imply that the flood plain level has risen and that parts of the floodplain were occupied during the 4th and 3rd millennia BC (see also Wilkinson *et al.* 2004, 22–23). Subsequently these valley bottom lands have

been eroded and/or buried over numerous cycles of erosion and sedimentation and any archaeological record has been lost (Wilkinson 1999; Akkermans 1999).

2) Near Carchemish the main lower Euphrates terrace, probably of Late Pleistocene date, outcrops some 10 m above river level and 3–4 m above the above mentioned 6 m floodplain terrace (the Intermediate terrace of Cremaschi and Maggioni 2005, 1–2). The robust conglomerates of this terrace were referred to by Woolley as "puddingstone" (Woolley 1921, 34, 41 and 53). Not only did this terrace provide the foundation for most riverine settlement during the Holocene (*e.g.* Tells Jerablus Tahtani, Amarna and Shiukh Fawqani), south of Carchemish the terrace exhibited a low-density scatter of artefacts ranging in date from the Uruk to the Late Antique (Wilkinson *et al.* 2007; see below).

3) On CORONA satellite images Zone 3 appears as a broad pale-coloured area of chalk-like limestone dissected by numerous valleys, the largest being the Nahr al-Amarna and the Sajur. This geomorphologically unstable limestone terrain is veneered by thin calcareous soils and cut by numerous wadis. This area of very active erosion appears particularly vividly on SRTM imagery as a dendritic pattern of wadis (Fig. 5.2). Erosion of these valleys appears to have contributed to the alluvial fills which included significant amounts of pale-coloured limestone debris presumably eroded from the wadi slopes rather than the high plains above which consisted of different lithological units. Most Bronze Age sites within Zone 3 were confined to the valleys, but by Roman–Byzantine times settlement had dispersed away from tells into some minor valleys and on to hill-slopes of Zone

West   East   Wadi Zubar (WP 1152; 1237)

Pale reddish brown loam with
calcrete crust. Matrix: 7.5YR 5/4

Medium-coarse gravels in
brown sand.
Irregular & unbedded;
Mainly limestone, rare
basalt.

Occasional small cobbles of
basalt (decayed) in limestone gravel
with flint, chert, greenstones.
Cemented by calcium carbonate;
beds dip to east.

Basalt cobbles (decayed) in
limestone gravel, some calcium
carbonate cement.

WELL-BEDDED LIMESTONE AT
ca. 6m BELOW GROUND SURFACE

ca. 10 m

Fig. 5.4 Section through the high plains at Wadi Zubar (Zone 4), a little below the plateau surface. Scale 2 m (photo by T.J. Wilkinson).

3. Because Bronze Age and Chalcolithic settlement is confined to a few sites along major tributaries, there appears to be a real fall-off in settlement away from the Euphrates. However, to the west, settlement of all periods again became both dense and widespread within Zone 4.

4) Occupying elevations of some 500 m above sea level, the high western plains are covered in red *terra rossa* type soils more typical of western Syria than the Euphrates Valley. More generally, Zone 4 is part of the extensive Gazientep/Quwayq/Nisip upland plain that extends towards Aleppo to the south-west as well as into Turkey, and which forms a broad zone of long-term settlement (Wilkinson 2007). The upland plains around Carchemish correspond roughly to the early Pleistocene or late Pliocene Qf terrace of Minzoni-Deroche and Sanlaville (1988) as well as the very highest terraces defined by Demir *et al.* (2008, fig. 16: the Hancağiz and Ti Dağ units on Fig. 5.3). As indicated on the Wadi Zubar section, these broad upland plains are underlain by local basalt and limestone gravel, cemented by calcium carbonate, overlain by a *terra rossa* type soil (Fig. 5.4). Above these plains rise occasional outcrops of low

calcrete hills. The upland plains, which have been occupied for at least seven millennia, represents a very different environment, and appear almost steppe-like during some seasons. In contrast to the more humid valley floor land of the Euphrates valley, these plains must have provided an excellent resource for both grazing and cultivation.

Of the above zones, the most stable is Zone 4, whereas Zone 3 is dynamic so that the wadis are progressively incising in response to the movements of the Euphrates, and valley slopes are being eroded, if not constantly, then at least as cyclical pulses that result in abundant limestone debris being supplied to the valley floors. Equally, the flood plain lands of the Euphrates (Zone 1) are geomorphologically dynamic, are without known archaeological sites, and are constantly being eroded and obscured by sediment.

Zone 2, on the other hand, upon which have developed most of the sites along the river, appears relatively stable. This main low terrace (termed the "Flood Plain Terrace" in Wilkinson *et al.* 2007, 221) forms an extensive plain, well-suited for cultivation and pasture, situated some 3–4 m above the active floodplain of the Euphrates. Alluvial fans have accumulated along the western edge of the terrace (Wilkinson 2007, fig. 2.6), whereas alongside the

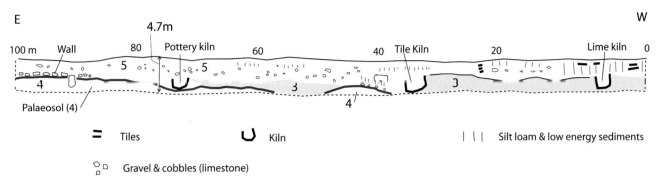

Fig. 5.5 100 m long sketch section through the deposits of the Wadi Seraisat near its junction with the Euphrates (by T.J. Wilkinson and Andrew McCarthy). Section depth at pottery kiln c. 4.7 m. 3: Moderately-bedded medium-coarse limestone gravel in reddish matrix; the lime and tile kilns are cut into this. 4: Palaeosol: of brown silt loam, with calcium carbonate flecks and some cultural material. The upper part was interpreted as mixed by cultivation. 5: High-energy coarse gravel and cobbles of limestone to 25 cm, in cream silt and sand matrix. Post-dates and overlies the kilns and wall

Euphrates floodplain, Richard Tipping's investigations at Tell Jerablus Tahtani suggest that the eastern parts of that site have experienced occasional high mega-floods from the Euphrates (Peltenburg *et al.* 1996, 1997). Although there is no explicit evidence on the terrace for such events, the presence of patches of Uruk and occasionally early Early Bronze Age (EBA) ceramics, at approximately 1–1.5 m depth beneath fine-grained sediments, suggests that there has been significant post-occupational deposition. In the cases of well holes 215 and 223 north-west and west of Tell Jerablus Tahtani, Uruk and early EBA pits cut the calcium carbonate horizon and are covered by roughly 1 m of soil (Wilkinson *et al.* 2007, fig 4). On the other hand, well 222 (north of Tell Jerablus Tahtani) shows pottery below the calcium carbonate horizon, whereas in well 226 (to the south-west of the site) the equivalent sherds are within the horizon. In the above cases a cultural horizon has accumulated and then low-energy sedimentation has occurred over it. These overlying deposits have then been subsequently transformed into a soil horizon, evidenced by the calcium carbonate accumulation and the blocky structure of the upper soil. Where a pit has been cut into the calcium carbonate horizon it appears that the carbonate horizon was in existence first. However, because calcium carbonate horizons can form within the last 5000–6000 years (Wilkinson 1990b), and occurred under relatively stable conditions, it is not possible to use these horizons as definitive chronological markers, but only as indicators that soil formation is of considerable antiquity.[2] Although there is no direct evidence to link this aggradation with Tipping's flood horizon, this appears to be likely.

In summary, although the main Euphrates terrace (Zone 2) is essentially a stable feature it shows evidence for episodic minor depositional phases. Despite the investigation of scores of well holes in the region of Tell Jerablus Tahtani and south of Carchemish, we found no evidence for a Uruk palaeochannel posited by Cremaschi and Maggioni to be west of Tell Jerablus Tahtani (2005, 2 and fig. 4).

Wadi fills

In contrast to Zone 2, the west bank tributaries of the Euphrates which drained the eroded limestone belt (Zone 3) showed very dynamic phases of alluvial sedimentation, in part because they drained terrain characterized by steep slopes and high rates of runoff. In addition, where the distal ends of wadis reached the Euphrates flood plain, they were constantly being eroded by the river, resulting in increased wadi gradients which resulted in erosion and further incision. Summary sequences of the main recorded sections are presented on Table 5.3; the long-term effects of these erosional processes are clearly evident on the geomorphological image (Fig. 5.2). Two sections of the resultant wadi fills were described and illustrated in an earlier report (Wilkinson *et al.* 2007, fig. 5). Both show that relatively high-energy wadi gravels or colluvium accumulated rapidly over Roman or late Roman levels. In the case of the Wadi Seraisat sequence, an entire "industrial area" to the south of Khirbet Seraisat (LCP 1) had been buried by high-energy wadi gravels (Fig. 5.5, layer 5). In addition to the pottery kiln noted in the first report (Wilkinson *et al.* 2007, fig. 5), buried installations include a tile kiln, a lime kiln and the wall of an indeterminate building, in all stretching along *c.* 100 m of the wadi (Fig. 5.5).

Overall, the Wadi Seraisat sequence suggests that initial settlement contemporaneous with palaeosol 4 occurred in a stable environment presumably adjacent to an earlier bed of the Wadi Seraisat. Subsequently moderate-energy limestone gravels (3) accumulated and were cut into by all three kilns. This gravel deposit (3) is estimated to be of 1st millennium BC date or slightly later. Following the construction of the Roman-Byzantine kilns, the area was overlain by high-energy gravel and cobbles (5) suggesting a significant increase in flow energy and perhaps a decrease in perennial flow.

The Wadi Amarna upstream of Tell Amarna (LCP

Table 5.3 Holocene valley fills

Location	Date	Stratigraphic sequence	Max erosion
Sajur: S bank. Fig. 5.2d.	Pleistocene - Holocene	Holocene colluvium Early Holocene palaeosol Late Pleistocene colluvium	???
Sajur: N bank	Post EBA	Post-Iron Age colluvium & wadi gravel Wall & low-energy soil wash (Bronze-Iron Age) Grey-brown clay loam palaeosol (early-mid Holocene)	Post-Iron Age
Wadi Amarna 317. Fig. 5.2c.	Mainly Roman-Late Antique	Modern ploughwash (upper colluvium = 2) Upper palaeosol (3) gravel colluvium (4) lower palaeosol (6) Late Roman-Byzantine horizon w. charcoal (8) Wadi Amarna high energy gravels (Hellenistic-Roman = 11)	Post-Roman
Wadi Amarna 295	Mainly Roman-Late Antique	Cream coloured Wadi Amarna silt (1) Wadi Amarna high-energy gravel (3) & local wadi gravel (11) Hellenistic-Roman canal / conduit Palaeosol (early-mid-Holocene)	Post-Hellenistic Roman
Wadi Seraisat WP 340-343. Fig. 5.2b.	Mainly Roman-Late Antique	High-energy wadi gravel (5) Roman-Byzantine kilns & moderate energy wadi gravel (3) Early-Mid-Holocene palaeosol (4)	Post-Byzantine
Seraisat LCP 18	Hellenistic-Roman	Post-Roman wash Post Hellenistic/ Roman wadi fan (gravel)	Post-Hellenistic

21) revealed similar accumulations of high-energy wadi gravel and cobbles. A section through south bank colluvia illustrated here in revised form (Fig. 5.6: WP 317), shows two distinct phases of stability represented by palaeosols at 1 and *c.* 2.2 m depth, overlying a silt loam with charcoal flecks and containing a single Late Antique tile (Fig. 5.6). Although it is evident from the section that high-energy floods characterised the valley before the Late Antique period (11: Fig. 5.6), these gravels continued to be deposited after as well. This is supported by the presence of limestone gravels overlying the conduit on the North bank. Overall, section WP 317 indicates that an episode of Hellenistic-Roman high-energy flow was overlain by the accumulation of colluvium washed from slopes to the south. The first appeared in or shortly after the Late Antique period, followed by an episode of stability (6) followed by the accumulation of gravelly colluvium (4) and then a later palaeosol (3), in turn, by more colluviation (2). Colluvium 2 may therefore be ascribed to the post-Ottoman period when there was a great increase in ploughing on the limestone uplands, whereas colluvium 4 represents a medieval phase of erosion. As in the Wadi Seraisat, high-energy wadi gravels appear to be Hellenistic and Roman in date.

In addition to the above, a drawn section along the north bank of the Wadi Amarna demonstrates a well-developed palaeosol, above which was constructed a *c.* 1.45 m wide conduit (Table 5.3: Wadi Amarna WP 295). This was in, turn, covered by a complex of limestone gravel (perhaps derived from a tributary wadi), which graded into moderately bedded medium-coarse limestone gravel deposited by high-energy episodic flow of the Wadi Amarna, overlain by cream-coloured low-energy silts. As in the Wadi Seraisat, there was a shift from a stable ground surface (the palaeosol) followed by increased high energy deposits, in this case from both the tributary and the main channel.

In contrast to the Wadi Amarna wadi fills, the perennial Sajur River provided few sections, and there is less evidence for a shift from low- to high-energy episodic flow. Unfortunately, the sequence illustrated on the south bank of the river east of Dadate lacks dating evidence (Fig 5.7). Nevertheless, what appears to be a late Pleistocene colluvium (lower colluvium on Fig. 5.7) is followed by a long period of stability (perhaps early Holocene) followed, in turn, by a prolonged accumulation of some 2 m of upper colluvium, which accumulated as a result of slope and soil wash from the slopes to the south.

When considered in terms of long-term trends in settlement, the three sequences of high-energy aggradation from the Wadis Amarna and Seraisat correspond to the phase of settlement expansion and dispersal of the Hellenistic,

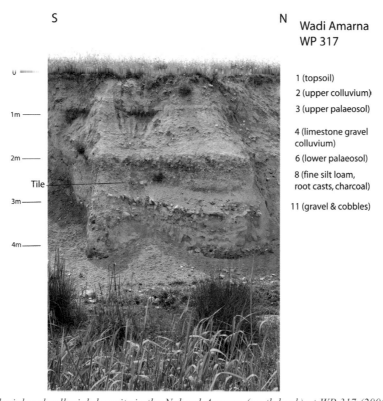

S
N
Wadi Amarna
WP 317
0
1m
2m
Tile
3m
4m
1 (topsoil)
2 (upper colluvium)
3 (upper palaeosol)
4 (limestone gravel colluvium)
6 (lower palaeosol)
8 (fine silt loam, root casts, charcoal)
11 (gravel & cobbles)

Fig. 5.6 Section through alluvial and colluvial deposits in the Nahr al-Amarna (south bank) at WP 317 (2006). Photo by T.J. Wilkinson

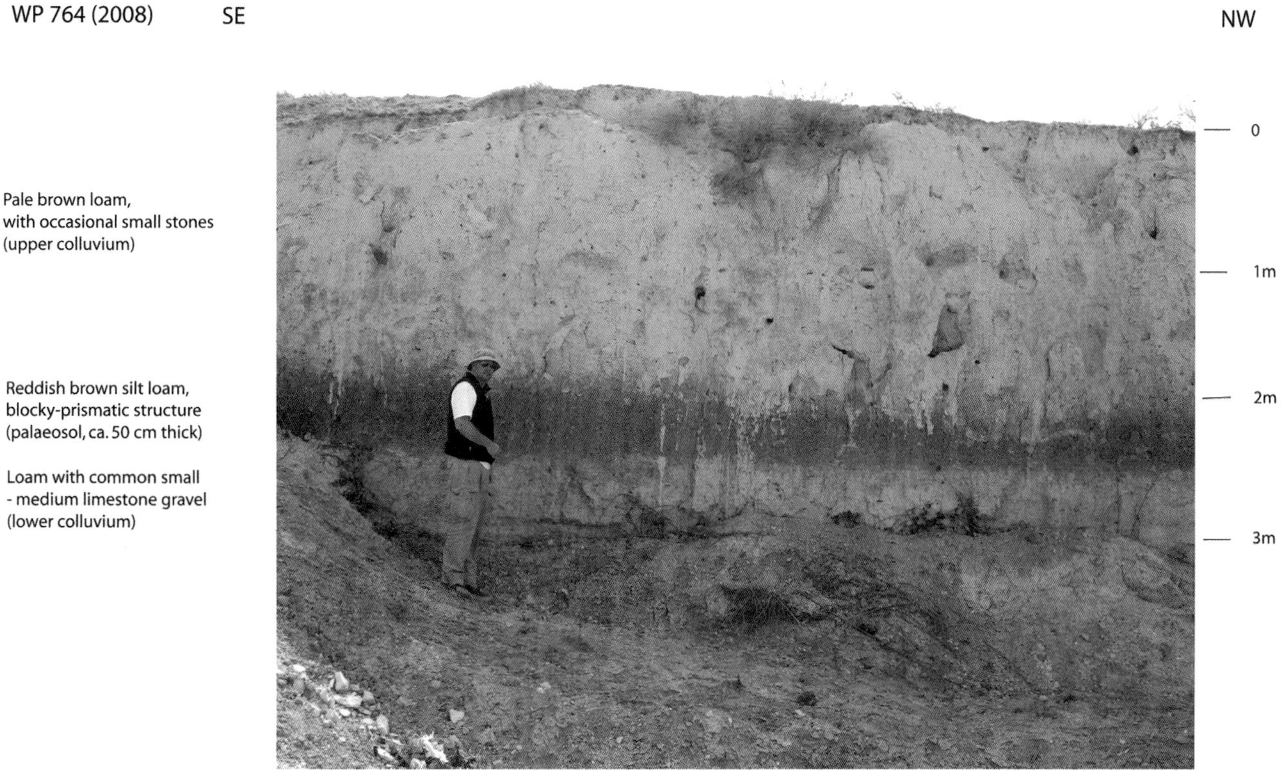

WP 764 (2008)
SE
NW
Pale brown loam,
with occasional small stones
(upper colluvium)
Reddish brown silt loam,
blocky-prismatic structure
(palaeosol, ca. 50 cm thick)
Loam with common small
- medium limestone gravel
(lower colluvium)
0
1m
2m
3m

Fig. 5.7 Section through alluvial and colluvial sediments along the south bank of the Sajur, east of Dadate. Andrew McCarthy for scale. Photo by T.J. Wilkinson

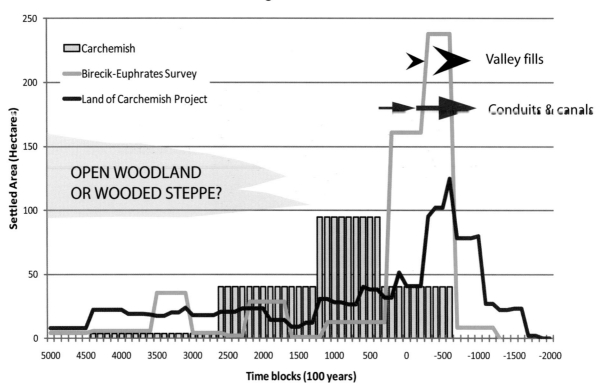

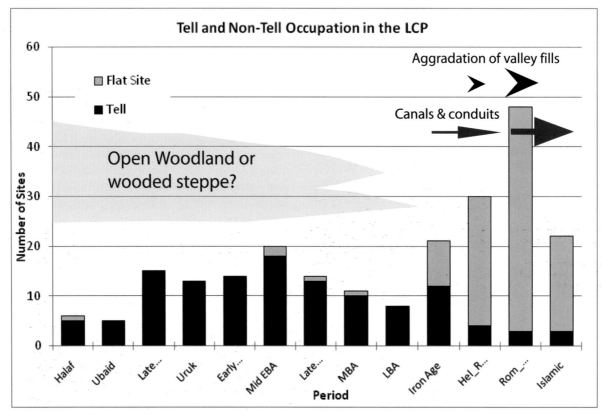

Fig. 5.8 Soil erosion phases in the Land of Carchemish survey in relation to long-term trends in settlement (by Dan Lawrence). a) according to aggregate settlement area; b) type of site

Roman and Late Antique periods (Fig. 5.8a and b). This is equivalent to a similar phase of late Holocene high-energy sedimentation recognized in the Kurban Höyük area of Turkey and elsewhere in the Middle East (Wilkinson 2010, 139–141). However, because high-energy deposits have also accumulated close to major Early Bronze Age centres such as Titriş Höyük (Rosen and Goldberg 1995), it would be premature to argue that the sequences illustrated here represent the only phase of Holocene accelerated erosion. Nevertheless, it does imply that settlement expansion onto limestone slopes, increased use of the area for quarries, cultivation and fuel for kilns, as well as increased abstraction of water from wadis (see below), together resulted in a shift away from a more stable cultural landscape towards a regime of increased run-off, more soil erosion and less perennial flow.

From the above it is evident that the Land of Carchemish is characterised by an increased intertwining of physical and cultural processes during the later Holocene. Because the main features of Chalcolithic and Bronze Age settlement have been considered in Chapter 4, the remainder of this chapter will focus upon the last three thousand years when the area was intermittently under the control of expansive empires and the city of Carchemish was at its maximum extent.

The Iron Age landscape

Historical context

Following the fall of the Hittite empire around 1200 BC, the Land of Carchemish developed into an extensive "Neo-Hittite" state centred on Carchemish under the control of Kuzi-Teššub, extending along the Euphrates from Melid (Malatya) south to Emar (Hawkins 1995, 90–91; Blaylock *et al.* 1990, 103; Bunnens 1999; see Chapters 2 and 3).

This large polity then appears to have split into several smaller Neo-Hittite states, including Carchemish and Kummuh (centred on modern day Samsat: Fig. 5.9). These varied in size during the 9th and 8th centuries BC, until both Carchemish and Kummuh were eventually incorporated into the Assyrian Empire by Sargon II.[3] When the city of Carchemish was captured by Sargon, an Assyrian governor was installed and its territories absorbed within the Assyrian provincial system. Incorporation into the Assyrian empire was not without cost, and Pisiri – the last independent king of Carchemish – together with his family were taken together with his principal courtiers to Assyria as prisoners (Hawkins 1980, 445; Bryce 2012, 98). Elements of the history of the Land of Carchemish are aligned with the archaeology in Chapter 3 of this volume; further discussion regarding the role of Carchemish within the Assyrian provinces is provided in Wilkinson and Wilkinson (forthcoming).

Although it is possible to simplify the political history of the middle Euphrates into independent city states on the west and north banks (*i.e.* right bank) of the Euphrates and Assyrian lands to the east and south (*i.e.* left bank), the complexities of political relations, Assyrian campaigns, and coalitions of Aramaean and Neo-Hittite states against Assyria resulted in a complex sequence of polity developments on both sides of the river (Bunnens 1999). For example, in the 9th century BC Ahuni of Aramaean Bīt Adini held cities on the west bank of the Euphrates thereby circumscribing the land of Carchemish (Hawkins 1995, 91; Chapter 3, this volume). Nevertheless, the role of the Euphrates as a frontier was always significant throughout the Assyrian empire and the crossing of the river was a significant act and tended to receive mention in the campaign annals (Yamada 1998). Ultimately, when what had been Neo-Hittite polities then became provinces of the Neo-Assyrian Empire, they survived under its administration for more than a century until the collapse of the empire in 612 BC and immediately after.

Although we do not know much about the pattern of settlement from the Assyrian sources, there are occasional mentions of the capture of towns, sometimes by name, as well as the deportation of people and the founding of new settlements. For example in the 9th century BC Shalmaneser III claims to have destroyed 200 ālāni ša limēti of Bīt Adini and 97 villages belonging to Carchemish (Grayson RIMA II, 69–70; Morandi 2000: 378). From the topographical context of Shalmaneser's campaigns, Morandi deduces that some of these villages must have been situated within the Sajur valley. From the mis-match between the textual attestations and the surveys of Sanlaville and colleagues, Morandi concludes that the earlier surveys have under-represented the record of Iron Age sites, a point which is supported by results of the Land of Carchemish Project survey.

The survey regions

Because archaeological and historical evidence draw from very different types of source material, bringing them into alignment can be challenging. Whereas the evidence from landscape archaeology can be rather poorly dated when compared with the textual record, surveys can provide a plethora of information on, for example, the number and size of settlements as well as their precise geographical locations, which tend to be under-represented in texts. Conversely, the Assyrian texts provide rather precise records of the timing of campaigns, the routes used, and cities captured and destroyed (Bryce 2012). These two contrasting records can, however, be brought together for certain types of features such as named sites, the presence of crossing points, and perhaps as discussed below, some temporary camps that were used by the Assyrian kings on their campaigns. More inferentially, we can suggest whether Iron Age settlements

78 T.J. Wilkinson

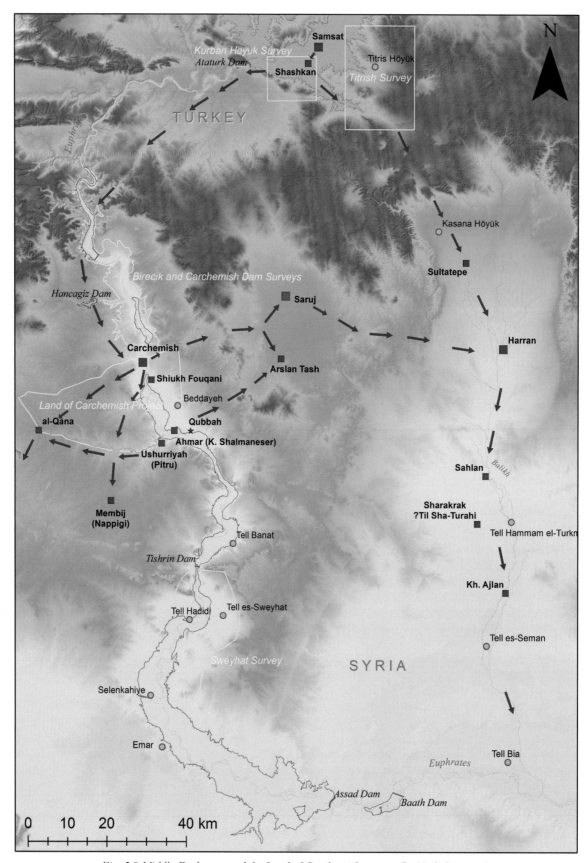

Fig. 5.9 Middle Euphrates and the Land of Carchemish survey (by N. Galiatsatos)

were inhabited by local populations with deep "roots" in the area or were new, perhaps deliberate, foundations.

Such inferences depend upon dating evidence. In the discussions that follow, site distributions for the Land of Carchemish and Biricik/Carchemish Dam surveys are presented as Iron Age (Figs 5.10 and 5.12). This corresponds broadly to the period between 1200 and 500 BC, but in most cases between around 1000 and 600 BC. Although not consistently reliable, local details can be illuminating as is evident from excavated sequences provided by excavations such as Aushariye (Pitru, see Chapter 6) or surface evidence from sites such as Tell Arab Hassan (LCP 68). Although archaeological surveys have supplied ceramic types that relate to both Neo-Hittite and Assyrian occupations, emphasis is placed here on those that yield pottery of recognizably Neo-Assyrian type.

Unfortunately, the location of Carchemish on the modern Turkish-Syrian border means that any archaeological investigations of the "Land of Carchemish" should ideally take place in both countries. This chapter, as well as others in this volume therefore adopt the expedient of combining the data from the Land of Carchemish Project (Wilkinson *et al.* 2007) with that from Algaze's survey of the area that was flooded by the Biricik and Carchemish Dams (Algaze *et al.* 1994).

Land of Carchemish Survey (Syria)

Crucial to estimating the period of occupation of the sites is the dating of surface pottery. Although Iron Age ceramics are relatively easy to recognize, many forms, such as the shallow platters mentioned in Chapter 8 (Figs 8.31, nos 15–20 and 8.34, nos 10–12) have a long life span, and are therefore weak indicators of specific phases. On the other hand, a range of later bowls, common in the 8th and 7th centuries BC are suggestive, but not proof of Assyrian occupation. Specifically Neo-Assyrian forms occurring in the 7th century levels at Tell Ahmar are particularly useful (Jamieson 2012). Among these are the grooved or beaded rim bowls (Fig. 8.30, nos 1–3), and a range of "hammer head" and externally thickened rim bowls common at nearby Shiukh Fawqani in 8th–7th century levels (Figs 8.30 and 8.33).[4] The important sequence at both east bank sites of Shiukh Fawqani (Makinson 2005; Luciani 2005) and Tell Ahmar (Jamieson 2012), together with the west bank site of Jurn Kabir (Eidem and Ackermann 1999) provide valuable assemblages that help narrow down the survey collections.

The Land of Carchemish project area covered some 375 sq km of land on the west bank of the river, south of the Turkish-Syrian border (Figs 5.9). As well as investigating the surface archaeology of the Carchemish outer town (E. Wilkinson *et. al.* 2010; Chapter 8), the survey also recovered evidence for Iron Age settlement from at least 20 sites (Fig. 5.10).[5] This produced an estimated site density of approximately 5.3 sites per 100 sq km.

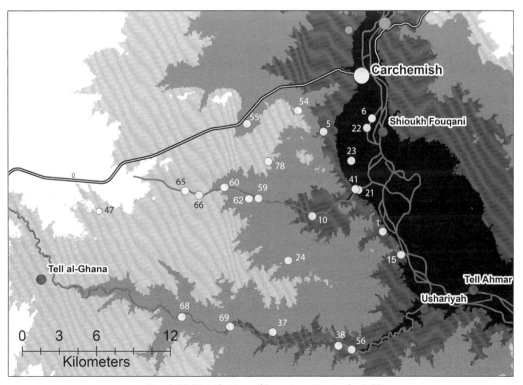

Fig. 5.10 Distribution of Iron Age sites in the LCP

Table 5.4 Morphology of Iron Age sites in the LCP and associated ceramic types

LCP site no. & name	Type of site	Record on survey sheet	Record on drawing & from other sources
1: Seraisat	Tell	Iron Age ?	3 Iron Age bowls from C
5: Tashatan	Tell	Iron A bowls, jars	Jars (9); bowls (10); 2 platters
6: Jerablus Tahtani vill.	Flat site	Iron Age; post Ass.	Jars (13); Bowls (10)
10: 'Ain al Beydar	Tell	? Iron Age	Platter (1); bowls (1–2)
21: Tell Amarna	Tell	Published	Tunca 1999, 134
22: Tell Jerablus Tahtani	Tell	Objects only	No actual occupation reported, Peltenburg (1999, 103)
23: Jemal	Low mound	?Iron Age	Bowls (4), confirmed by Morandi (2000, 388)
24: Tell Dabas	Fort?	?Iron Age	Bowls (4); jar (1)
37: Dadate North	Low mound	Iron Age	Platter (1); Bowls (11); Jars (2); Pithoi (4)
38: Tell Sha'ir (Sajur)	Tell	Iron Age	Bowls (6), incl. 1 Assyrian; 1 platter
41: Amarna cemetery	Lower town	?Iron Age	Bowls (2)
46: Carchemish	Tell L town	–	Chapter 8
47: Boz Höyük	Tell	Iron Age	Bowls (2–3, but not certain)
54: Hajaliyyeh	Fort	Iron Age	Bowls (8); Jars (2); 1–2 other Iron Age
55: Douknouk	Tell	Iron Age	Bowls (3) incl. 1 ?Assyrian
56: Tukhar Saghir W	Tell (dest.)	Iron Age	Iron Age bowls (4); 1 platter
59: Yousuf Bek	Tell	Iron Age	1 impressed cordoned pithos; Bowls (1–2). IA uncertain according to Morandi (2000, 388).
60: Koundouriye	Tell	Iron Age	Iron Age sherds (25). Confirmed by Morandi (2000, 388).
65: Nahr Bash W	Tell	Iron Age	Bowls (9); Platters (1)
66: Nahr Bash	Flat site	LBA/ & Iron Age?	Possible Iron Age (platter)
68: Arab Hassan	Tell	Iron Age	Iron Age sherds (30). Confirmed by Morandi (2000: 389)
69: Tell Halwanji (W)	Tell	?Iron Age	Bowls (1-2); Cordoned pithoi (3). Iron Age uncertain, according to Morandi (2000: 389).
78: Haimer	Low mound	?Iron Age	Bowls (1?)
Total no. of sites	*23*		*Considered in analysis: 20*

Sites with good Assyrian ribbed or grooved bowls: LCP 38; 55; 68; Tells with significant Iron Age: 5; 38; 55; 60; 65; 68. With some Iron Age: 1; 10, 21; 47; 56; 59; 69. 6+7 = 13; Low mounds or flat sites (roughly single period): 6; 23; 37; 78 = 4; Possible Forts: 24; 54 = 2 That is 19 sites plus Carchemish (= 20)
Amarna cemetery (41) is classed with 21 because it appears to be the lower settlement of that site.
Good examples of Iron Age local occupations on tells: LCP 60; LCP 68.

In addition to the above sites, some of which have also been mentioned in Morandi (2000, 388–389), three other sites, 2 Iron Age and 1 possibly Iron Age, were reported by Morandi and Cornet (Morandi 2000, 388–389). These were: Nisel Hussain, and Cornet *et al.* site 54 and 55. In addition, the tells at Dadate (LCP 25) and al-Qana (al-Ghana on Figs. 5.10 and 5.12, this volume) were reported as having possible Iron Age, but this was uncertain. Of these, Dadate is not included in the analysis and al-Qana is discussed in the text.

Accordingly, each site would have had access to approximately 18.8 sq km of land, equivalent to an area of 2.4 km radius around each settlement. Because the distribution of sites was uneven, however, each site would have had access to rather different areas of land. If this averaged area is applied to the nineteen sites recorded, each would have had sufficient land to support a community of moderate size, their flocks and some pasture, together perhaps with any associated woodland and scrub.

A significant feature of Iron Age settlement in the LCP survey area is that pottery of this date was collected from both multi-period tells as well as from low mounds or flat sites, the latter lacking evidence for prolonged occupation. Although many sites were diagnosed as being occupied during the Iron Age, the collections were frequently neither sufficiently large nor distinctive to enable them to be allocated to specific phases of the Iron Age. In this explicitly landscape analysis I therefore illustrate and discuss the significance of sites within their landscape rather than attempting a finely sub-divided record of settlement ebb and flow. Three classes of site characterize the range of site morphology (Table 5.4):

- Tells with either significant or moderate amounts of Iron Age occupation.
- Low mounds or flat sites with evidence for Iron Age occupation.
- Specialized Iron Age sites along inferred routes, and, which from their distinctive morphology or locations could have operated as forts.

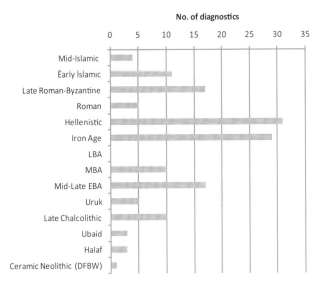

Fig. 5.11 The ceramic sequence at LCP 60 (Koundouriye) according to key diagnostic types

Tells

As is evident on Table 5.4, the majority of Iron Age occupations, namely 13 out of 19, were recognized to be on or associated with tells. Whereas most tells were located on agriculturally productive plains or within river valleys, a minority, specifically Seraisat (LCP 1), Tashatan (LCP 5) and Tell Sha'ir, Sajur (LCP 38) occupied low hilltops or limestone bluffs.

Of the tell occupations, two sites, Koundouriye (LCP 60) and Arab Hassan (LCP 68), are illustrative of Iron Age occupations on tells. At Koundouriye Iron Age pottery was collected on the slopes and in cuts in the lower part of the site, but not on the surrounding fields. This implies that Iron Age settlement, rather than being on the tell summit, was around the edges of the tell, a common location for traditional near eastern villages. On the other hand, at Arab Hassan (LCP 68) Iron Age occupation appears to have been on both the upper and lower parts of the tell as well as within the lower slopes apparently within the outer defensive walls. Particularly significant at both sites was that the Iron Age occupation formed part of an almost continuous occupation; in the case of Arab Hassan this was from probably the at least the mid-3rd millennium BC (Table 5.5), and Koundouriye from at least the 6th millennium BC (Halaf or Amuq B/C: Fig. 5.11). At both sites, the Iron Age occupation appears to have included material from both the earlier (Neo-Hittite) and later (Neo-Assyrian) phases. Although phase-specific diagnostics are not well represented, a single example of a Neo-Assyrian grooved bowl from the upper tell at Arab Hassan (LCP 68A), indicates that this site was probably occupied in both phases (Table 5.5). The presence of Iron Age pottery within these long-lived tell-based occupations implies that they formed part of the prolonged "local"

settlement development, and arguably therefore can be seen as perhaps local communities. In the case of the sequence at Koundouriye, such a local community can be inferred to have been in residence, at least intermittently, over some 7000–8000 years, with only the Late Roman Byzantine period showing any deviation, when the occupation, although present on the tell slopes, apparently also moved out on to the surrounding land.[6]

Although the case for these Iron Age settlements being local communities is only circumstantial, these sites contrast remarkably with the situation further east in the Khabur basin and north-west Iraq, where most settlement was not on high mounds, but was either in the form of lower settlements adjacent to the tell, or took the form of low mounds in the countryside away from them (Wilkinson *et al.* 2005, 37–41).

Here we have presented the evidence for those tells which have yielded large collections of ceramics, and which have been recorded in some detail. However, the other tells illustrated on Table 5.4 also include Iron Age occupation within long-established sites. Again, these can be inferred to be possibly "local" communities.

Low mounds or flat sites

As indicated on Table 5.4, only about four occupations were on low mounds or flat sites. Of these, two – Jerablus Tahtani village site (LCP 6) and Dadate North (LCP 37) – yielded evidence for only Iron Age occupation, both probably of the 8th–7th centuries BC.[7] The other sites of this group, at Jemal (LCP 23) and Haimer (LCP 78) are more difficult to characterize because of their small and rather indistinct Iron Age collections. However, both LCP 6 and 37 are distinctive, the former because of its Euphrates-side location a little to the north-west of Tell Shiukh Fawqani, and LCP 37, because of its position where the inferred route from Carchemish to Membij (Neo-Assyrian Nanpig, Fig. 5.9) crossed the Sajur. In fact its morphology atop bluffs overlooking the Sajur suggests it might have even been fortified, although no evidence for this was recognized in the field.

After three years of archaeological survey (2006, 2008 and 2009) there is no evidence of a general dispersal of low mounds or flat sites across the terrain as becomes so evident further east in the Jazira during the Iron Age, or in the west in the Late Roman and Byzantine periods. In fact, although many of these Late Antique sites were subjected to quite intensive collection, and some re-visits, none showed signs of having been initially occupied in the Iron Age.

Specialized sites or forts

Two sites were recognized, by either their morphology or topographic location, to be possible Iron Age forts. Of these, Tell Dabas (LCP 24), with a roughly square plan but without clear evidence of a fortification wall, yielded a small

Table 5.5. Pottery types from Tell Arab Hassan. Listed in approximate chronological order

LCP 68 A	LCP 68 B	LCP 68 C	LCP 68 D	Period total
			1 Late Antique tile (disposed of).	1
			Late Antique buffware handles: × 6 (total no.)	6
Coarse brittleware handle, 72	Brittle ware, 14			2
Terra Sig. rim: 5				1
Hellenistic incurved-rim bowls, 7, 11.				2
Hellenistic jar, 53				1
Hellenistic fish plate, 22		Hellenistic Coarse fish plate, 142		2
		Hellenistic fold-over rim, 389, 103; variants, 88, 100, 105		5
Neo-Assyrian grooved rim bowl, 31				1
12+ variants on Iron Age bowls (recorded by EBW)	Iron Age bowls, 36, 11 and ? 8	Iron Age bowls, 4, 29, 29, 45, 49, 83, 97, 117, 120, 125		25
		Platters, 23, 70, 92, 119, 121, 122, 129, 140		8
		Iron Age pithoi, 31, 46, 47, 63		4
		LBA square-rim jars: 18, 26		2
		MBA jars w. grooved rims: 22, 24, 37, 52, 54, 64, 134		7
Mid/Late EBA fineware bowls, 6, 57,		Late EBA bowl, 53		3
Mid-Late EBA cooking pot, but without lug, 36		Mid-Late EBA cooking pot, but without lug, 41		2
Mid-late EBA small bowl, 71		Mid-Late EBA bowls: 136, 145		3
		Hama J goblet 98		1
		EBA open bowl 130		1
		Mid-Late EBA small ring base, 12		1
		Mid EBA pedestal based fine ware, 108		1
		Early EBA pedestal base		1
		LC/early EBA cooking pot, 5, 20, 29, 89		3

Area A: upper tell (slopes + summit); Area B: lower tell; Area C: base of lower tell cut by field terraces and dirt tracks; Area D: two fields (without crops) NE of tell. WP 1147 to WP 1150
Numbers in columns 1–4 refer to LCP archive drawing numbers; all counts preliminary

group of Iron Age sherds. The other site, Hajalliya (LCP 54) re-occupied an Early Bronze Age hilltop site, and yielded a range of Iron Age wares of no specific phase. Both sites were adjacent to what were probably major routes out of Carchemish, Dabas being located on what appears to have been the southern route between Carchemish and Membij, and Hajalliya the western route towards Tell Rifa'at and the Amuq (see below: routes). Although cuneiform texts supply illuminating information about the construction and

Table 5.6 Site types in the Biricik and Carchemish Dam surveys (source: Algaze et al. 1994, Fig. 5.12)

	Tells	Flat sites, low mounds	Indeterminate
Surveyed sites	16, 44, 51	22, 36, 43, 48, 59, 70, 61, 74, 75, 77, 82, 83	73
Excavated sites	71, 51, 44, 65	75, 48	0
Totals	5	12	1

function of some Assyrian forts (Parker 1997), unfortunately those in the LCP area have yielded few insights into any of the features referred to in the texts, such as horse troughs or bitumen.

In sum, unlike areas within the Land of Assur, such as the Beydar, Hamoukar, or North Jazira surveys (Wilkinson *et al.* 2005; Ur 2010, 161–163; Wilkinson and Tucker 1995), where the pattern of Neo-Assyrian settlement consisted of low mounds dispersed across the landscape, settlement in the Land of Carchemish was mainly occupied by local or long-lived communities, though with a small, but significant, number of sites that were new foundations or re-settlements closely related to networks of communication. Of these

sites, despite the paucity of recognizable early Iron Age pottery, it is possible that many of the tells were among the 97 settlements destroyed by Shalmaneser III during his campaigns, as noted above.

Biricik and Carchemish Dam Surveys

North of the Syrian-Turkish border, the Biricik and Carchemish Dam surveys show a contrasting pattern to that south of Carchemish (Algaze *et al.* 1994, Fig. 5.12). These surveys, which yielded a moderate number of Iron Age sites (classified as period 10 in the Algaze Survey: 1100–333 BC), demonstrate an increase in settlement over that of the Late

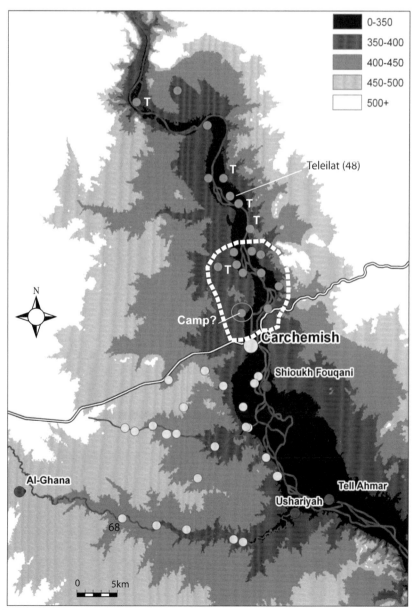

Fig. 5.12 Distribution of Iron Age sites in the combined LCP and the Carchemish-Biricek Dam survey areas. Broken line = Neo-Assyrian enclave (?)

Bronze Age. There was, however, a dearth of early Iron Age occupations, either because settlement was limited at that time, or because of a lack of recognition of diagnostic pottery types. On the other hand, the region was well settled in the later Iron Age, corresponding to the Neo-Assyrian period (c. 8th–7th centuries BC). Of the 16 recorded sites (in addition to Carchemish), only five were associated with long-lived occupation on tells, whereas 12 were settlements on low mounds or flat sites representing relatively short duration occupations (Table 5.6). Most were relatively small settlements of c. 0.5–1.0 ha, with only one recorded site, Şara Harabe (Site 53), extending over a larger area (3–4 ha).

Particularly noteworthy is Aktaş Tarlası (Algaze site 83), which subsequent satellite imagery research has shown, appears to be situated within a large circular feature, perhaps the remains of an Assyrian camp (see below). Because the surface collection showed evidence of Iron Age occupation, this is suggestive of prolonged residence as discussed below.

When data from archaeological survey and subsequent excavations are combined, Iron Age occupations associated with tells can be seen to occur at intervals throughout the area, but with a slight concentration in the northern survey area (Fig. 5.12: T = tell). On the other hand, occupations on low mounds or flat sites were concentrated towards the south (Table 5.1 and Fig. 5.12). In addition, at Mezraa-Teleilat (Algaze site 48) a monumental Neo-Assyrian building or palace, measuring 37 × 30 m, was built on a pre-existing Neolithic site. This suggests that there was a significant Assyrian presence at the northern end of the scatter of low Iron Age sites.[8]

In contrast with the area south of Carchemish, the area north of the border shows a concentration of later Iron Age (i.e. presumably Assyrian sites) a short distance north of Carchemish. This concentration appears to have been framed by the putative Assyrian camp to the southwest and the Assyrian monumental building at Teleilat a little beyond and to the north (Fig. 5.12). Therefore, whereas the land south of Carchemish was characterised mainly by long-lived, and arguably local communities, to the north a possible enclave of Neo-Assyrian settlement is apparent, a point that is returned to below.

Iron Age routes

It has frequently been argued that Carchemish was situated at a major crossing point of the Euphrates (Winter 1983; Kuhrt 1995, 411, 416). However, the actual field evidence for this and for other routes with their associated crossing points needs to be demonstrated and aligned with the evidence from texts. Ancient routes can be inferred from several forms of archaeological evidence: the physical traces of the routes themselves (e.g. from hollow ways), alignments of sites along presumed routes, historically attested sites upon assumed routes, the location of city gates such as at Carchemish, and topographic alignments (such as when lower terrain provides evident of "least cost" pathways). In addition, crossing points of rivers can be inferred from paired sites which appear to have developed where settlements developed at ferries or fords. For the area of Carchemish a range of field and landscape evidence has been used to infer the southern and western routes out of the city. In addition I summarize the archaeological evidence for significant Euphrates crossing points. It must be emphasized that other routes or crossing points may have existed, but the archaeological evidence for them is lacking.

It is significant that both the possible forts (LCP 24 and LCP 54: Fig. 5.10) and at least two of the flat sites or low mounds were associated with apparent ancient routes. In addition to Dabas and Hajalliya mentioned above, Jerablus Tahtani village site (LCP 6) was located at a likely Euphrates crossing point and Dadate north (LCP 37) was south of Dabas (LCP 24) on the route to Membij. This implies that the non-tell occupations, rather than being part of a process of deliberate re-settlement and dispersal in the countryside, developed or were established as special-purpose sites on routes or at crossing points of rivers. Such network locations differ from contemporary low or flat settlements in the Khabur region and north-west Iraq which occupied locations both on and off routes.

Also potentially related to the operation of Assyrian networks is the occurrence of a distinctive Neo-Assyrian pottery form, the bead-rim or grooved rim bowl, dated to the 7th century BC.[9] Although present at Carchemish (Chapter 8), these forms are rare within the survey area, being found only at Tell Sha'ir, Arab Hassan and Duknuk (LCP 38, 68 and 55 respectively). Interestingly, two of these sites are situated on the Sajur river, a favourite passageway for the Assyrian army (as discussed below). The other site, Duknuk, is adjacent to the present Syrian–Turkish border over looking the Değirmen Dere stream that leads east to Carchemish.

Whereas most sites in the Land of Carchemish survey were of modest size, between 0.1 (LCP 54) and 2.8–3.00 ha (LCP 6 and 37), Carchemish, at approximately 100 ha, was the dominant site in the region and must have formed a major hub in the communication network (Fig. 5.9). Other important sites, although not surveyed by the Land of Carchemish Project, are the sites of Aushariye and Khirbet al-Qana, located along the south bank of the Sajur River (Chapter 6) on important lines of communication. These sites can be placed within their historical context, because this area was the locus of numerous Neo-Assyrian campaigns (Yamada 2000, 116; Winter 1983).

Of several possible Euphrates crossing points, that most frequently mentioned in the Assyrian records was that from Tell Ahmar (Til Barsip) on the east bank of the Euphrates to Aushariye (Pitru) on the south (right) bank of the Sajur at its junction with the Euphrates (Fig. 5.10; Bunnens 1999, 615; Eidem and Pütt 2001).

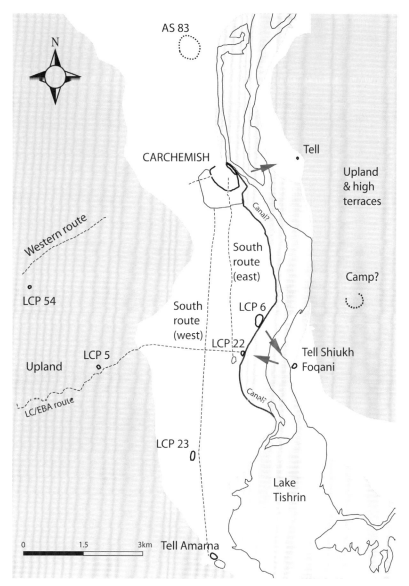

Fig. 5.13 Map of routes, crossing points and possible Assyrian camps in the immediate area of Carchemish

The role of the Euphrates as a long-term boundary of the Assyrian empire is implied in the following passage from Shalmaneser III's campaign in 853 BC:

> "... I approached the city of Kar-Shalmaneser [Til Barsip]. I crossed the Euphrates, which was in flood, for a second time in rafts (made of inflated) goatskins. In the city Ana-Assur-uter-aṣbat, which is by the opposite bank of the Euphrates on the Sagura (and) which people of the land of Hatti call Pitru, I received tribute from the kings on the opposite bank of the Euphrates, from Sangara the Carchemishite ...". (Grayson 1996, 63; cited by Eidem and Pütt 2001, 86)

In other words, Shalmaneser crossed from Tell Ahmar[10] to the modern village tellingly known as Aushar (Assur) Bujak or Aushariye. Identified by Eidem and Pütt as Pitru, the site

has yielded a long sequence of Iron Age pottery dating from *c.* 1100 to *c.* 700/600 BC (Chapter 6).

Additional toponyms from the Assyrian campaigns include that of Burmarina (Tell Shiukh Fawqani), which Shalmaneser claims to have besieged following his departure from Til Barsip. After leaving a pile of 300 heads outside the town (Yamada 2000, 89), Shalmaneser crossed the river from Burmarina on boats. From the pairing of Tell Jerablus Tahtani and Tell Shiukh Fawqani (Fig. 5.13), such a crossing point may have been in operation from at least the fourth millennium BC. However, unlike Shiukh Fawqani, Tell Jerablus Tahtani was not occupied in the Iron Age,[11] therefore it is likely that boats may have crossed to LCP Site 6 to the north-west instead (Fig. 5.13).

Fig. 5.14 Possible southern route leading out of Carchemish Inner Town (see Fig. 8.18 for schematic map of same area)

The Sajur Valley

After crossing the Euphrates between Til Barsip (Tell Ahmar) and Aushariye (Pitru) the Assyrian army would move along the Sajur Valley to campaign against the Aramaean and Neo-Hittite states to the west, thereby avoiding the immediate territory of Carchemish. Although we lack any direct evidence, the Sajur in Syria appears to have formed both a boundary (to the Land of Carchemish at its minimum extent) as well as a thoroughfare. In addition to Pitru (Chapter 6), the sites of Tell Sha'ir (Sajur = LCP 38) and Tell Arab Hassan (LCP 68) both yielded examples of beaded or grooved-rim bowls, suggesting that they had active links with the Assyrian empire. Although Dadate North (LCP 37) lacked distinctive Assyrian diagnostics, its assemblage of 8th and 7th century BC sherds again suggests that it was inhabited during the period of Assyrian domination.

By following the Sajur valley to the northwest, invading Assyrian armies avoided the land of Carchemish, as well as confrontations with the king, and were able to campaign in Nappigi (Membij), Bīt Agusi and lands to the west (Fig.

5.11; Winter 1983; Yamadi 2000, 116). Iron Age sites along the Sajur included the fortified site of Khirbet al-Qana, located to the south and west of the Sajur. Khirbet al-Qana, a roughly square and tabular 5 ha main mound rising some 5 m above the plain, is surrounded by a partial outer rampart enclosing some 17 ha (Chapter 4, Fig. 4.11; Chapter 6, Fig. 6.14 and 6.15). After Carchemish and Tell Ahmar, al-Qana is one of the most impressive Iron Age sites in the region and when visited, it revealed abundant Early Iron Age and Late Bronze Age pottery suggesting that it was probably a major Late Bronze Age and Neo-Hittite centre,[12] possibly corresponding to Sazabu – the fortified city of Sangara (?) the Carchemishite.[13] Although precise geographical information is elusive, after Shalmaneser conquered "the 6 fortified cities of Ahuni"[14] and destroyed 200 cities in their environs (Annals 3 ii 16b–30a): "The king approached Sazabe, the fortified city of Sangara the Carchemishite, besieged the city, conquered it, and destroyed the city in its environs" (Yamada 2000, 109–110).

Because Bryce places Sazabu within the land of Carchemish, probably on its frontier (Bryce 2012, 223), and Yamada (2000, 117) situates it two parasangs from Carchemish, al-Qana makes a likely candidate for the city.[15] Whereas Pitru was evidently occupied by the Assyrians (Chapter 6; Eidem and Pütt 2001), and Tell Arab Hassan has yielded at least one distinctive Neo-Assyrian potsherd amongst a larger Iron Age assemblage (above), al-Qana appears to have been bereft of Neo-Assyrian pottery. This implies that when al-Qana was abandoned, probably in the early Iron Age, it was not resettled, perhaps echoing the destruction of Sazabu by Shalmaneser.

The evidence for a crossing point at Carchemish itself, despite frequent mention in many publications, has less archaeological support (Peltenburg Chapter 7). Nevertheless, the presence of a small, but undated, tell on the east bank within the village at Zor Mughar, suggests that twin sites also existed at this point. Because most tells in the region were occupied in the Bronze Age, and many in the Iron Age as well, this implies the existence of an active crossing point at least during the Bronze Age. From Zor Mughar, a potential route can be inferred to follow the Turkish–Syrian border to a low saddle in the hills east of the river, after which it would have split, with one route leading to Assyrian Saruj (Sarugi), the other leading to Arslan Tash. Nevertheless, the archaeological evidence for this route is meagre (Fig. 5.9).

The southern routes from Carchemish

Conventionally, the southern route from Carchemish may be considered to lead from the south gate of the outer town, as identified by the British Museum team (Chapter 8, with references) to eventually link with the straight modern road which leads southwards out of the town of Jerablus [Fig. 5.13: south route (west)]. Although this is a plausible route because the modern road arguably follows what appears to be a Roman road and also lines up well with the south gate of the Outer town, its date is less clear.

In addition, the south gate of the Inner Town follows a north–south alignment which leads not towards the south gate of the Outer Town, but rather towards a kink in the outer wall on the bluffs of the low terrace (*i.e.* the line of masonry leading due south from the south gate on the 1879 map of Chermside, in Chapter 8). Although not identified as a gateway by Woolley, this distinctive kink resembles a gate (Chapter 8), and being directly south of the Inner Town south gate would follow the logical north–south alignment of the principal colonnaded axis of the Roman Inner town [Fig. 5.13: south route (east) and see Fig. 8.18]. Significantly, a broad, dark soil or vegetation mark within a pistachio orchard to the south of the south gate of the Inner town may represent an area of land, hollowed by use and the passage of people and animals. This curving feature is roughly aligned on the feature identified in the town wall as a possible south gate (Fig. 5.14). This, in turn, is aligned with the edge of the low terrace, which is followed today by

a small track oriented on both the south gate of Carchemish and the possible gate in the outer ramparts. This track, which is parallel to and east of the modern main road, leads directly towards the Late Antique outer town of Tell Jerablus Tahtani and its associated Uruk-period lower activity area.

This implies that Tell Jerablus Tahtani, as well as being one tell of a paired crossing place of the Euphrates, may also have developed at a cross-roads where a north-south route from Carchemish met a roughly east–west route from the Euphrates which then followed the alignment of Late Chalcolithic and Bronze Age sites described in Chapter 4. Although there is no evidence for any relict route system immediately south of Tell Jerablus Tahtani, to the south of Tell Dadate and LCP 37 (Fig. 5.13) a hollow way appears alongside the modern Membij road. Evident in the field as a shallow valley which follows parallel and east of the road, and on CORONA images as a dark soil mark roughly parallel to it, this feature cannot be dated, but appears to represent an earlier stage of the present route. To the north, Tell Dabas and Dadate North (LCP 24 and 37), both of Iron Age date and along the modern road between the Sajur and Tell Ain al-Beydar, suggests that this road follows an earlier route of at least Iron Age date. Together, the above route, being based upon an assemblage of rather inconsequential features, cannot be considered as entirely robust. Nevertheless, these features, especially when anchored by the city gates, supply a compelling argument for the existence of two possible routes leading out of the city, with at least one, or perhaps both, combined leading via Amarna, and Dadate (North) to the Iron Age site of Nappigi (Membij) (Figs. 5.9 and 13).

The western route from Carchemish

A western route from Carchemish can be inferred to have led from the west gate of the Inner Town and through the now destroyed west gate of the outer town (see Chapter 8). About 1 km west of the outer town, a faint line of a dirt track, against which several field boundaries abut, is evident on Geoeye and some CORONA images (Fig. 5.15a). Although not followed by the modern road from Jerablus town, this line which appears to represent a relict route, parallels it and leads westwards towards a gap between two low, but distinctive limestone hills (Fig. 5.15b).[16] Significantly, the southern of these hills is the location of the small EBA and Iron Age site of Hajalliya (LCP 54). Interpreted from its hilltop position as a fort, Hajalliya may have been constructed to have oversight over the main western route out of Carchemish. The significance of this route becomes apparent because, although there is no further evidence of it beyond Hajalliya, the route does fall on a general alignment of sites: al-Qana, Sekizlar quarries, and Tell Rifa'at, ultimately leading towards Ta'yinat in the Amuq (Patin or Amqi) (Chapter 3). Although a single large hollow way near the Quwayq River, and others radiating from Rifa'at, suggest the existence of a major route,

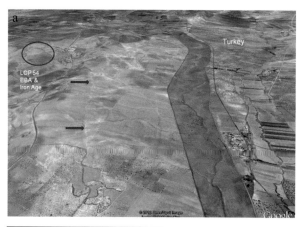

Fig. 5.15 The proposed western route leading out of Carchemish: a) Google earth 3-D; b) sketch from the same

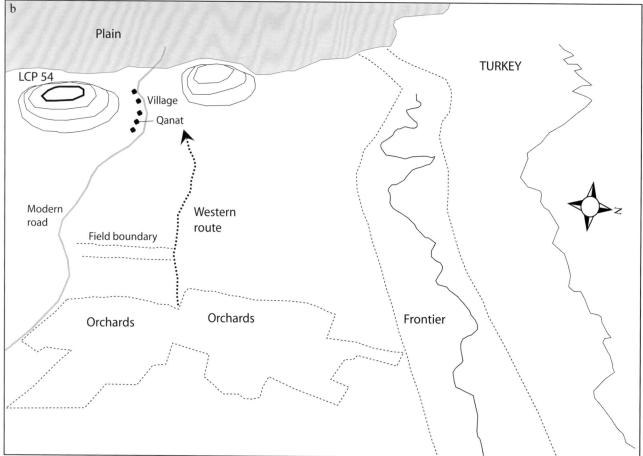

no other specific features provide tangible evidence for the existence of such a road. Nevertheless, the presence of the landscape alignment between Carchemish and Hajalliya, and the alignment of sites from Carchemish to Ta'yinat suggests the existence of a broad corridor of movement along this ENE–WSW axis.

Overall, the route systems around Carchemish appear to fall into two classes, one a local system dominated by Carchemish itself, and a second corridor used by the Assyrian army that avoided Carchemish altogether and led along the Sajur ultimately towards Bīt Agusi, Patin and Hamath. Presumably, when Carchemish was incorporated into the Assyrian empire, the emphasis on the Carchemish crossing point may have increased.

Possible Assyrian camps

More speculative than route systems, but ultimately compelling in terms of Assyrian geography, is the evidence for possible Assyrian camps. Assyrian camps are difficult to recognize archaeologically, because although having a distinctive form, they were probably originally less durable than long-occupied sites and have therefore left a lighter imprint on the land. Like their counterparts in the Roman world, they would be more likely to survive if they were constructed in "landscapes of survival" or were of sufficient duration and robustness to be incorporated into later landscapes. An example of survival in less intensively cultivated areas, is the circular feature visible on CORONA satellite imagery near the Atatürk Dam (Fig. 5.16). On the other hand, where camps were constructed within long cultivated areas, such as the Euphrates terraces, their presence can be inferred only from the patterning of modern land-use which appears to form a pseudomorph of the original feature.

Atatürk Dam

The most convincing example of a possible Assyrian camp is a circular feature evident on a CORONA image close to the Karababa (Atatürk) Dam in Turkey, to the south-west

of the Kurban Höyük survey region (Fig. 5.16). Originally noted by David Kennedy (1998, fig. 6) it was independently discovered by Nikolaos Galiatsatos as part of his research for the Fragile Crescent Project. The feature, which forms an almost perfect circle approximately 400 m in diameter and appears pale-coloured against the background of modern fields, also exhibits light coloured features around the perimeter which feasibly could be relict towers. The one possible feature within the interior is a pale-coloured area west of the central point. Little else can be said about this possible camp, but in addition to being located close to the Euphrates, it probably was also positioned on a probable route leading from Samsat (Kummuh) and the major Iron Age site of Şaşkan Küçüktepe westward towards the Euphrates (Fig. 5.9).

Aktash Tarlası

Whereas the Atatürk Dam feature has not been visited in the field, an enigmatic feature recognized on Geoeye and Corona images and located 3 km north of Carchemish,

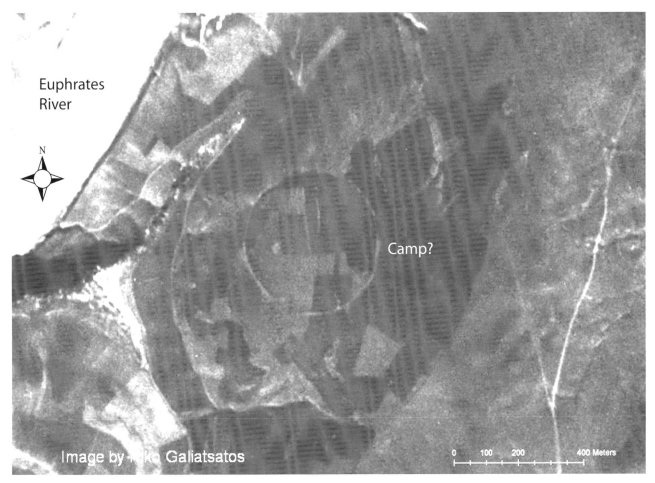

Fig. 5.16 Trace of possible Assyrian camp near the Atatürk Dam (by N. Galiatsatos; CORONA image courtesy of USGS)

Outer
earthworks

Fig. 5.17 Aktash Tarlisi (AS 83): possible Assyrian camp (image)

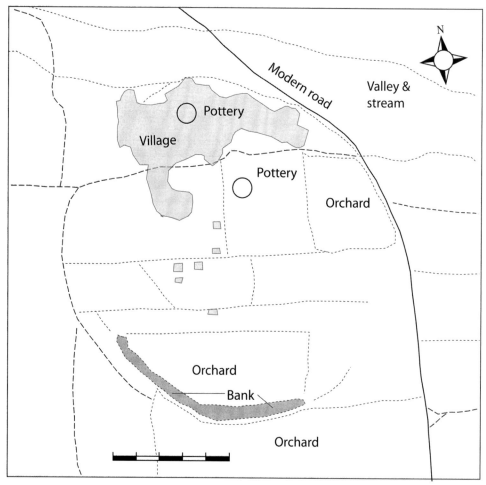

Fig. 5.18 Aktash Tarlisi (AS 83): possible Assyrian camp (map)

surrounds the site of Aktash Tarlası (Algaze site 83, Fig. 5.17). In the field this site, located on a Pleistocene terrace sloping towards the Euphrates river, was recorded as a "flat scatter, single-period site" of *c.* 0.8 ha, with a few Iron Age sherds (Algaze *et al.* 1994, 60). On both the CORONA and Geoeye images, the surrounding feature forms an arc of a roughly circular structure. Equally important, however, is that the site appears to have remained fossilised within the landscape because field boundaries, tracks and orchards mainly respected it as a feature (Fig. 5.18). Specifically note how the orchards to the north and south of what appears to be a semi-circular bank on both Geoeye and CORONA images respect the alignment of this feature, as do the modern road to the east and the earthen track to the west. Algaze's survey collection area for Site 83 falls within the interior of the circle and includes a small collection of Iron Age pottery (Algaze *et al.* 1994, fig. 29). Although by no means certain as an Assyrian camp, this roughly circular feature of some 500 m diameter, provides a compelling example of a "ghost" of what might have been a temporary camp overlooking Carchemish about 3 km to the south.

Shiukh Fawqani

A second enigmatic feature is evident as a partial circle located *c.* 2 km north-east of Tell Shiukh Fawqani on both CORONA and Geoeye imagery (Fig. 5.13). Its partial circular form appears to be the result of head-ward erosion of a Euphrates tributary gully along a line of weakness represented perhaps by an infilled ditch enclosing a camp. Although resembling a wadi meander, the radius of this feature is considerably greater than meanders of minor wadis in the area and arguably, it may be the erosional trace of a ditched enclosure surrounding an Assyrian camp.

East of Carchemish

Additional arc-shaped features are evident on 1969 CORONA images, and less clearly on Google Earth, approximately 3 km east of the Euphrates and south of the modern Turkish border. However, the two features in question may equally result from land use patterns that follow the distinctive stratigraphy of the limestone bedrock which creates arc-shaped configurations.

Significantly, the features north of Carchemish and north-east of Shiukh Fawqani are respectively 3.5 km and 2 km from the two sites. Because these distances approximate to the inferred limits of cultivated fields of the two settlements (Fig. 5.14), if they are Assyrian camps, their location suggests that the Assyrians positioned their camps not immediately outside the city or town, but close to the outer limits of their fields.

To conclude, with the exception of the Atatürk Dam feature, all of the above must be regarded as tentative.

Nevertheless, taken together, they suggest that satellite imagery can provide a valuable tool for locating these elusive, but historically important, features and that although no single feature might be considered as robust evidence of relict camps, there is a chance that one or two of them are. Their subtle imprint on the landscape suggests that the general lack of evidence of Assyrian camps may be because, in such "landscapes of destruction" it is necessary to interpret them in terms of the features that have had to conform to them, rather than their visible morphology. Significantly the feature at Aktash Tarlası, although virtually without morphology when surveyed, suggests that there was sufficient surface pottery to imply that occupation was prolonged. This raises the question whether selected camps continued to be used in order to play some sort of administrative function in areas of Assyrian settlement.

The status of the settlements

Although most of our investigations of Iron Age settlement derive from fieldwork, Liverani's classification of non-Assyrian cities provides insights into how sites in the area may have been perceived by the Assyrians (Liverani 1992, 125; also Ikeda 1979).

Building upon the terminology of Ashurnasirpal II, Liverani groups the local (*i.e.* non-Assyrian) settlement into hierarchical classes of: walled towns which formed the residence of the king ("royal city" or *āl-šarrūti*); walled cities which perhaps formed the residence of a local chief ("fortified cities" *ālāni dannūti*); and "cities in the neighbourhood". In addition, Liverani allows for un-walled villages (*kapru*). Unfortunately this classification cannot be readily applied to the Carchemish area, in part because Carchemish is not listed as a royal city (Liverani 1992, 128; Ikeda 1979, table ii); on the other hand, Til Barsip is mentioned as both a royal and a fortified city (Ikeda 1979, tables i and ii; Hawkins 1995, 91). Sazabu, however, suggested here as al-Qana, is named in Shalmaneser's annals as a fortified city (Ikeda 1979, table i; Yamada 2000, 110). This is clearly the case with al-Qana because its central site is fortified and there are signs of arc-shaped outer ramparts beyond (Fig. 4.11, Chapter 4). Unfortunately, no other settlements can be classified according to this system, which again indicates an enduring problem of relating historical attestations to archaeological data.

Comparative studies

Iron Age settlement density, expressed in terms of the number of sites per 100 sq km of survey area, suggests that the Middle Euphrates region was considerably less densely populated than the core Assyrian lands of northwest Iraq and north-east Syria (Table 5.7). Although estimates derived from archaeological surveys indicate that settlement

Table 5.7. Site density, normalized to number of sites per 100 sq km from north-west Iraq (North Jazira) to west of the Euphrates (Biricik-Carchemish and Land of Carchemish)

Survey Area	Sites/100 km²
Hamoukar	17.6
North Jazira	16.4
Beydar	7.5
Biricik-Carchemish Dams	6
Titriş Höyük	6
Land of Carchemish	5,3
Kurban Höyük	1.75

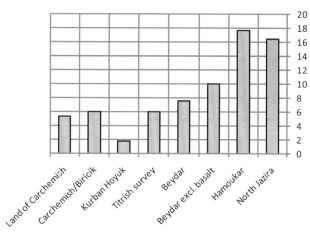

Sites / 100 sq km

Fig. 5.19 Iron Age site density from east (North Jazira) to west (Land of Carchemish) arranged according to geographical location

densities were quite variable, they generally appear to have diminished from east to west (Fig. 5.19). The Middle Euphrates lands were only slightly less densely settled than those in the Beydar area in the western Khabur, which had a settlement density between 7.5 or 10 sites per 100 sq km, depending upon whether the sparsely populated basalt plateau is included. Whereas the lands around Kurban Höyük were sparsely settled, the neighbouring Titriş survey approximated to those north and south of Carchemish.

While these differences may partly be accounted for by the amount of little-settled upland in areas such as around Kurban Höyük, those areas within the "Land of Assur" and closer to the Assyrian capitals clearly exhibited a significantly higher settlement density than those further west. This picture of increased density towards the Assyrian capitals is now supported by the latest results of archaeological survey around Erbil, which demonstrates even higher settlement densities than in the Iraqi north Jazira and around Hamoukar (Ur *et al.* 2013). The only part of the Middle Euphrates with densities approaching those of the Khabur and east of the Tigris, is the enclave immediately north of Carchemish, which, as suggested above, may have been re-settled as a result of Neo-Assyrian policy. With a settlement density of 10–11 sites per 100 sq km, this enclave exhibited a site density equivalent to the lower (non-basalt) areas of the Beydar area, but was considerably lower than the core areas such as the North Jazira and Hamoukar within the Land of Assur.

Post-Assyrian landscapes

After the fall of the Assyrian empire, we enter a period of uncertainty, because the ceramic types in the area did not necessarily change in lock-step with shifts in state power, and some Iron Age forms persisted over many centuries, as mentioned in Chapter 8; it is therefore difficult to determine how much of the region was occupied during the periods of Neo-Babylonian/Median or Achaemenid rule. By the Hellenistic period, however, the highly visible ceramics provide a much clearer perspective on the pattern of settlement, as discussed in their long-term context by Lawrence and Ricci in Chapter 4 and by Paul Newson

in Chapter 9. The following review of the post-Assyrian landscapes seeks to complement those chapters by outlining and discussing the off-site features that demonstrate the broad pattern of activity in the countryside, namely: off-site sherd scatters, quarries, wine presses and evidence of water management.

Off-site sherd scatters

Although as stated in Chapter 4, off-site artefact scatters were rare, the site notebooks reveal the presence of occasional small-scale artefact scatters which might be explained as a result of several mechanisms, as suggested by Bintliff and Snodgrass (1988), but which in the Carchemish area must have included the remains of single small farmsteads, usually of Late Antique date. In addition, a subtle, albeit persistent, feature of the main plain between Carchemish and Tell Jerablus Tahtani were sparse sherd scatters extending between the main occupation sites. These are common features of Mediterranean and Middle Eastern landscapes (Wilkinson 1982; Bintliff and Snodgrass 1988) and one of the goals of the project was to sample such scatters by means of transect surveys in order to define them, establish their date range, and see if they included sites not recognized by more extensive survey techniques. Collections were made in 2006 in the northern part of the plain between Carchemish and Tell Jerablus Tahtani (Wilkinson *et al.* 2007), and subsequently in 2008 additional transects were collected both in the northern area near Carchemish, as well as on a number of fields towards the south end of the plain.

Techniques

In the spring many fields were under either growing cereal

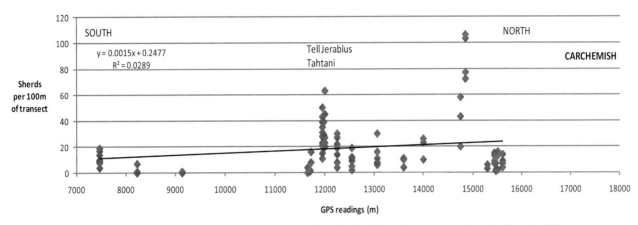

Fig. 5.20 Sherd scatter density plot from transects for the Carchemish plain (data from 2006 and 2008)

crops or early stages of cotton cultivation, therefore only fields that were under fallow or ploughed could be sampled. One hundred metre transects were walked within any one field, with usually 3–4 field walkers spread across the field some 10–20 m apart. Following preliminary counting of sherds, all collected materials were taken back to the project house for washing and processing

Figure 5.20 shows the final results of the collections when plotted in terms of their GPS northing coordinates, and Figure 5.21 shows the estimated date of the sherds according to key diagnostic types.[17] Despite the caveats, a number of trends are evident. The number of pot sherds per 100 m transect[18] range from zero to a maximum of 106, although there is a distinct clustering in the range 0–20 sherds (Fig. 5.22).[19] Although a wide range of chronological diagnostics are present, Late Antique types, specifically Brittle Wares dominate, which is a common feature of sherd scatters in other parts of the Levant, Syria and southern Turkey (Wilkinson 1990a; Newson *et al.* 2007). Although there were a significant number of Bevelled-Rim Bowl sherds together with other Uruk types, these were clustered around Tell Jerablus Tahtani where the lower activity area is demonstrably of Uruk and early 3rd millennium BC date (Wilkinson *et al.* 2007 and Chapter 4).

Other significant types include a small number of rather generic Iron Age bowl rims, and a well-documented range of Late Roman forms and fabrics. Also noteworthy is a small, but significant, number of Early and Middle Islamic types. Although the high sherd counts (in excess of 100 sherds per transect), implies the presence of at least one site within the otherwise rather amorphous scatters,[20] confirmation that these were indeed occupation sites is limited. However, in the vicinity of 14,750–14,850 north a modern well adjacent to the area of highest sherd densities (WP 294) confirms the presence of pottery within the soil down to depths of 2.00–2.40 m. Judging from the diagnostics present in the

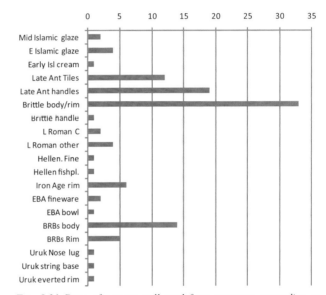

Fig. 5.21 Date of pottery collected from transects according to diagnostic types

surface scatters, this would appear to be a small site of Late Roman-Byzantine date, but without surface expression.

The other anomaly evident on Figure 5.20 is the concentration of surface material around Tell Jerablus Tahtani. In addition to the outer occupation scatter of Uruk date, this area also included a Late Antique outer settlement situated within and around the modern graveyard. Without these two distinct anomalies, sherd scatters would have been modest, persisting between zero and 20 sherds per 100 m, but with significantly lower scatters south of Tell Jerablus Tahtani. Significantly, pottery counts rise to the south in the vicinity of the major multi-period Tell Amarna (LCP 21, Fig. 5.20). Although similar low-density scatters have been recorded

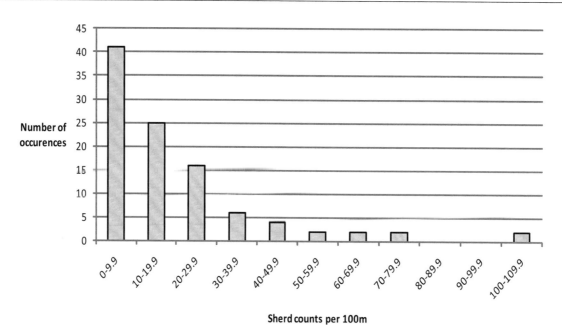

Fig. 5.22 Bar chart showing the number of sherds per 100 m from transects on the Carchemish plain

intermittently on the high plains (region 4) they are by no means continuous.

Overall, it appears that the sherd scatters south of Carchemish represent a field scatter of off-site material, predominantly of Late Antique date. This is suggestive of the application of settlement-derived midden material as fertilizer, punctuated by a small number of sedentary occupations. The latter are either isolated Late Roman or Late Antique period sites and off-site occupations, specifically around Tell Jerablus Tahtani. Away from the river, off-site scatters although present, were more patchy suggesting that land-use practices were only occasionally intensive in those areas. Unfortunately, the curtailment of fieldwork meant that it was not possible to determine the extent or densities of such scatters.

Canals and water supply

Because Carchemish is situated where rainfall is sufficient for cereal cultivation, as well as various types of fruit orchards, it might be expected that water management did not play a major role in the local economy. Although that appears to have been the case for the Bronze Age, there is increasing evidence for water management during the past three thousand years (Rayne 2014). Following a rather speculative interpretation concerning Iron Age canals, I assemble the evidence for systems of the Hellenistic through Islamic periods, which demonstrates that the region was the beneficiary of a considerable degree of water management. Here the evidence is presented in terms of: a) large longitudinal canals of the Euphrates floodplain, b)

small lateral channels (mainly conduits), c) qanats, and d) other features such as cisterns.

Large canals along the Euphrates

It is commonly accepted that because of the high peak flows and erosive nature of the Euphrates River, that early canals did not take their water from the Euphrates; rather they took their flow from the more reliable and controllable flows of tributary wadis (Van Liere 1963). Hence, for example, the "Mill Stream" north of Carchemish, can be seen on one of the Carchemish maps as supplying water for a canal that winds around the east side of the citadel mound immediately below Woolley's water gate to bring water to the appropriate level of the plain south of Carchemish. However, drawing water from tributaries places an inevitable constraint on the amount of water that can be tapped, and it is significant that two canals (Fig. 5.23: C1 and 2; Table 5.8) not only flowed on the floodplain or lower terraces following the main axis of the valley, but also appear to have taken their water from the main river.[21]

A 3–5 m wide channel still flowing today alongside the eastern outer wall of Carchemish, by LCP 6 and also Tell Jerablus Tahtani, was described as "ancient and pre-French" by the local inhabitants (Fig. 5.23: C1). Because this canal is not clearly associated with any specific sites or agricultural areas, its date cannot be determined. However, it is tempting to interpret it as one of the irrigation works claimed to have been built around Carchemish by the 8th century BC Neo-Hittite king Yariri (Bryce 2012, 96; Hawkins 2000, 131). If it was built in the Neo-Hittite period, it seems to have

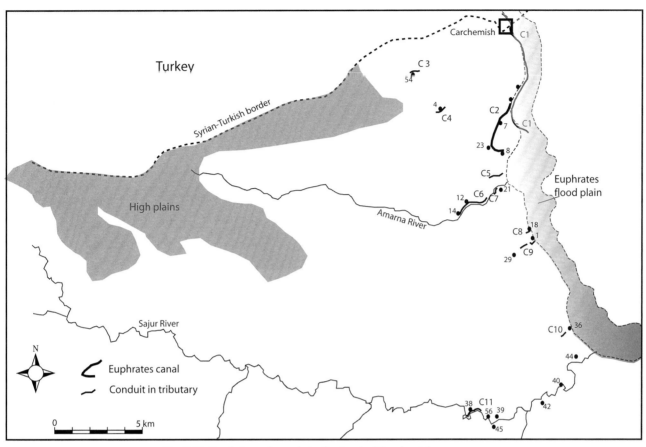

Fig. 5.23 Conduits and canals in the Land of Carchemish survey area

Table 5.8: Conduits and canals

Name of canal (no.) see Fig. 5.23)	Estimated date	Approximate size (W × D)	Type	Comments or reference
Jemal Canal (2)	Late Antique-Early Islamic	9–14 m wide (surface)	Euphrates canal	Wilk *et al.* 2007, figs 14–15
Jerablus Tahtani canal (1)	Iron Age		Euphrates canal	
Hajaliyyeh (3)	Late Antique?		Rock-cut qanat	
Wadi Sha'ir (4)	Late Antique?	50 cm wide	Open channel	Wilk *et al.* 2007
al-Gini' at (5)	Late Antique?		Rock-cut qanat	Wilk *et al.* 2007
Nahr al-Amarna-1 (6)	Hellenistic–Late Antique?	1st phase: 3–4 m W × 2.3 m (or 1.45 m W) 2nd phase: 0.80 × 1.3 m	Earthen canal followed by stone & rock conduit (N bank)	Wilk *et al.* 2007
Nahr al-Amarna-2 (7)	Late Antique		Rock-cut conduit (on S bank)	
LCP 18 (8)	Hellenistic–Roman		Rock-cut conduit	
Wadi Seraisat (9)	Late Antique		Rock-cut conduit	
Kirk Maghara (10)	Late Antique		Rock-cut conduit	Vivancos (2005, 213)
Sajur (11)	Late Antique & later			2008 season
Sajur (11)		1.2 m depth ??	Qanats	Corona & Geoeye

been designed to irrigate, not the slightly raised terraces of the main terrace (upon which Tell Jerablus Tahtani and the other sites in the vicinity developed), but rather the flood plain itself.[22] This of course has significant implications for our interpretations of the local economy, because it would mean that the flood plain was irrigated and there may have been more settlements than are apparent today. Because the more elevated parts of the floodplain have been settled

Fig. 5.24 Blocks fallen from the major north-bank conduit along the Wadi Amarna. Photo T.J. Wilkinson

Fig. 5.25
a) Small conduit into limestone bedrock in the Wadi Seraisat, ca. 1 km W of the village. Photo T.J. Wilkinson

b) Two conduits, both subterranean at this point on the north bank of the Wadi Amarna. Photo T.J. Wilkinson

and cultivated in the 20th century AD, and there is good information from Late Bronze Age Emar for canals and fields at the level of the flood plain, we should also allow for such possibilities in the region of Carchemish. However, because the canal is completely un-dated, and there is no remaining evidence for settlement on the existing flood plain, this must remain speculation.

The second longitudinal canal is the distinctive feature mapped in 2006 between Tell Jerablus Tahtani and Jemal (Fig. 5.23: C2). From the associated sites, this feature is probably Late Antique or early Islamic in date (Wilkinson *et al.* 2007). Whether it was intended to irrigated the area around Tell Jerablus Tahtani, or lands further south around Tell Amarna remains unclear.

Lateral conduits in the tributary valleys

Much more common, and more typical of the survey area, are numerous, small conduits cut either into the limestone bedrock, or made of well-cut stone blocks. These features, between 40 cm and 80 cm wide and of similar depth, appear in virtually every significant tributary wadi of the Euphrates (Wilkinson *et al.* 2007; Wilkinson and Rayne 2010). In style they resemble Classical, Late Antique or Islamic conduits recognized in many parts of the Near East, and in many cases they can be indirectly related to sites of this date. Specifically, numbers C4, C6/7, C8, C9 and C10 on Figure 5.23 all flowed alongside or towards sites with a date range between Hellenistic/Roman to Late Antique/early Islamic. In most of the associated valleys, this is the period when settlement was at its long-term peak. This is

also the case for the conduits along the Sajur, which showed a significant growth of farmsteads and other settlement from the Hellenistic period (Chapter 9).[23]

The conduits recorded show a variation in size around those expected for small Classic-Islamic examples in the Middle East, but significantly there appears to be some historical variation within specific conduits. For example, the large conduit flowing along the north side of the Nahr al-Amarna upstream from Tell Amarna (Fig. 5.23: C6; Fig. 5.24 and 5.25b) appeared to have developed out of an earlier earthen channel which was exposed by two cross sections along the Nahr al Amarna (Wilkinson *et al.* 2007, fig. 16). Although the channel cross-section appeared 3–4 m wide, specifically one section showed the bed width downstream as 1.45 m. Depth and therefore the cross section area (and discharge) could not be estimated, but it appears that the width diminished from 1.45 m to 0.8 m from the early to the later phase of use. Similarly, a well crafted small "canal" recorded in the Wadi Yurum near Kirk Maghara (LCP 36) appears to have been cut in two stages: an initial stage of *c.* 40 cm wide, and a later one a mere 16 cm wide (Vivancos 2005, 213).

With few exceptions, every side valley of the Euphrates had its own Classical/Roman Late Antique settlement, and each of these its own conduit which gathered water from either the ground water, or abstracted it from the perennial flow of the stream. This must have placed a considerable pressure on the local water resources, perhaps to the degree that flow in the Wadis Amarna and Yurum was reduced so that the channel conveying the water had to be diminished in size.[24] The above record of conduits must, however, be

Fig. 5.26 Openings of two bottle-shaped cisterns cut into limestone at LCP 18 (Seraisat)

regarded as a minimum because many of the observed features have been partially eroded away (Fig. 5.25 a and b). It is therefore likely that even more conduits had been in use than were recorded by the survey; this is especially the case for the Sajur valley, where several canals or conduits were recorded on CORONA images, but have not been recorded in detail.

Qanats

Underground channels designed to capture ground water, often from alluvial fans, form a common feature of the hydraulic landscapes of Middle East. Whereas some of the above-mentioned conduits exhibited underground sections marked by circular or rectangular ventilation shafts, most of these were simply underground manifestations of what were generally open channels. In addition, however, a large number of what appeared to be genuine qanat shafts have been observed and mapped along the Sajur Valley and its tributaries.[25]

Cisterns

Although rock-cut cisterns are a common feature of the Classical-Late Antique landscape of the Levant, only one example of cisterns was recorded in the Land of Carchemish Project. These were at the Hellenistic-Roman site of Seraisat (LCP 18, Fig. 5.23: C8) where two bottle-shaped cisterns, measuring some 80 cm at the opening and 2.8 m deep (Fig. 5.26) existed side by side with small local channels. Presumably these cisterns had been dug to collect and store local runoff if the nearby small open channels ran dry.

Overall, the water supply systems within the Land of Carchemish Project indicate that from perhaps the Iron Age, and certainly the Hellenistic period, there was a substantial demand for water and that significant efforts were made to construct large Euphrates canals, open-channel and underground conduits as well as rock-cut cisterns. The one or two Euphrates canals (C1 and 2, Table 5.8) were probably primarily intended to supply water for irrigation on the lower terraces and floodplain, with the Jerablus Tahtani canal (C1), perhaps being intended for transport as well. The conduits along the tributary valleys were probably constructed for the combined purpose of irrigating nearby areas of the lower terraces, for supplying water for domestic use and for livestock. In addition, water mills were probably present at, for example, Khirbet Seraisat (LCP 1) where the foundations of a destroyed water mill were noted. Additional examples can be inferred to have existed on the Değirman (=Mill) Chai, north of Carchemish, as well as, according to a local resident, north of the village of Jamel (LCP 23).

Although the increased abstraction and management of water might have been a response to a drying late Holocene climate, more likely it was to increase the productivity of agricultural land: either to make the growing of vegetables and orchards more productive, or to make yields more stable and predictable for purposes of taxation. Certainly, by tapping significant amounts of water from all available sources, it is likely that the base-flow of the natural channels was significantly reduced, as has been demonstrated for the Balikh River to the east (Wilkinson 1998).

Threshing floors

Although threshing floors are probably a common feature of all periods back to at least the 3rd or 4th millennium BC, they are remarkably invisible in the landscape. However, a sparse Late Roman pottery scatter, characterized by a few small basalt fragments, on the limestone bluff west of Jamel (LCP-33, Bayrzakli) might be the remains of a threshing floor. This is because small basalt fragments are sometimes used in the base of threshing sleds to seperate the grain from the husk.

Wine presses

In contrast to the southern Levant and north-west Syria, where wine presses are relatively common, they appear quite scarce within the mid-Euphrates region. However, some examples were recorded near Tell Sweyhat (Wilkinson et al. 2004, 76–78) and, on Christmas day, 2009, the team was rewarded with the discovery of a single rock-cut wine-press on the limestone slopes below LCP 38 adjacent to the Sajur River (Fig. 5.27). With a treading floor of estimated dimensions 300 × 500 cm, this appears to have had a significantly higher production capacity than those along the Euphrates near Tell es-Sweyhat.

Although no other wine presses have been recognized during survey, this is probably because of their preferred location on slopes or by wadis and streams, which results in them being eroded away or obscured by sediment. Their occurrence clearly indicates that the Carchemish region was a wine producing area when they were in use. Unfortunately, there is no direct dating evidence for the features, although from the form of the above example, it was probably in use at some time during the Hellenistic to Late Antique periods.

Quarries, tombs and other rock-cut features

Quarries were very much part of the landscape of the last 3000 years (Wilkinson et al. 2007, 239). Although the monumental architecture of Carchemish would have demanded basalt of appropriate quality, unfortunately all basalt outcrops were located outside the survey area. For example, the major Neo-Hittite period stone quarries at Sikizlar were situated some 40 km to the south-west of Carchemish, and these must have been a major source of

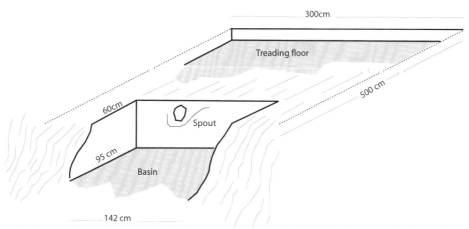

Fig. 5.27 Rock-cut wine-press on the limestone slopes below LCP 38 adjacent to the Sajur River

basalt to the city (Chapter 3), perhaps being shared with other cities in the region such as Tell Rifa'at and Aleppo.

Of the 16 groups of quarries recorded between 2006 and 2009, virtually all were located within the limestone slopes and wadis of zone 3, being most common on limestone hills and Euphrates bluffs (nine examples), within the limits of Hellenistic–Late Antique sites (2) or in wadi floors (5). Quarries were evident, either because of the straight cuts into the limestone, the presence of chisel and other characteristic markings, or when found on hilltops, because the shallow pits were incised by the deep rock-cut grooves created for the removal of the blocks (Fig. 5.28). Although few could be dated directly, one large quarry at 'Ain Abed (WP 196) in the Wadi-Sha'ir was inscribed towards its south end by a highly weathered and illegible inscription in Latin.

In general, the landscape between the sites, especially in the rocky landscape of zone 3, was peppered by occasional quarries and tombs. Tombs are especially frequent in valleys close to where they entered the Euphrates river, specifically near the sites of Kirk Mughara (LCP 36), Seraisat (LCP 18) and Tell Amarna (LCP 21 and 41). Rock-cut features include not only tombs, but other subterranean rock-cut complexes interpreted by Vivancos as monasteries or churches (Iglesia; Monasterio: Vivancos 2005, 278–279 ff.). All three types of rock-cut features were particularly common along the eastern Sajur valley between Tujar and Aushariye (Vivancos 2005, 277–304).

Opposite Dadate within a large quarry immediately below LCP 37, what has been described as a *columbario* was identified by Vivancos (2005, fig. 209). Because *columbaria* can be interpreted as roosts for pigeons or recesses for cremation urns, their interpretation remains ambiguous. Nevertheless, the location of Dadate on what was probably the line of the Ayyubid-Mamluk "pigeon post" between Damascus-Aleppo and Yeni Kale on the Turkish Euphrates, suggests that this distinctive feature (Fig. 5.29) may in fact have been pigeon roosts to service this major communication route with carrier pigeons.[26]

Hellenistic–Islamic settlement along the Euphrates fringe

The quantity of settlement along the edge of the Euphrates Valley, particularly of the Hellenistic–Islamic periods, raises the perennial question, namely to what degree did settlement and agriculture extend on to the flood plain. Because the dynamic fluvial environment of the Euphrates has destroyed all but rare islands of settlement, as discussed above (also Wilkinson *et al.* 2004, 20–24), it is virtually impossible to make inferences about levels of human activity in this verdant part of the valley. Nevertheless, the texts from Emar suggest that during the Late Bronze Age (as indeed during the 20th century AD), this area was an active zone of garden and field agriculture (Mori 2003). Moreover, in the same region prior to the construction of the Tabqa Dam, archaeological sites, truncated by the river could be clearly seen to have once extended on to the flood plain. Similarly, along the Euphrates bluffs south of Tell Amarna (LCP 21) the plethora of human activity hinted that settlement originally spread on to the flood plain. This was vividly evident in the vicinity of Seraisat (LCP 18) where some 3 m of cultural deposits: major walls, associated floors, kilns and various cultural deposits of Hellenistic and Roman date, extended down to the present level of Lake Tishrin. The overlying 1 m of wadi gravels demonstrates that occupation in this area appears to have been abandoned, and then covered by high-energy flood deposits. There is no evidence that occupation continued into the Late Antique or Islamic period, and instead the locus of settlement appears to have shifted to the hills and the valley of Khirbet Seraisat to the south.

The deep cultural deposits at flood plain level at Seraisat

Fig. 5.28 Quarries on hilltops in hills south of Tashatan (LCP 5) indicated by deep grooves cut into limestone. Photo T.J. Wilkinson

(LCP 18), together with the concentration of funerary, quarrying and settlement activity towards the bluffs and in the downstream reaches of the Sajur and Wadi Amarna, all imply that indeed the floodplain was settled, at least during the Hellenistic-Late Antique periods. This may also have been the case as early as the Iron Age when perhaps the major Jerablus canal was in place. It is therefore necessary to allow for the possibility that a large sector of valley floor settlement and agricultural land is missing from the archaeological record.

The last thousand years

The history of settlement over the last thousand years can be sketched using a combination of historical sources and extrapolations from them. In addition, evidence from western travellers, who either visited the area or witnessed it as a result of occasional visits from their residences in Aleppo are harnessed (Lewis 1987). Archaeology provides little evidence for this period, despite the fact that the material culture for at least part of this long period is quite well known (Redford 1998; Wilkinson 1990a, 129). It is, of course, possible that a considerable amount of evidence for Late Antique and Islamic settlement is obscured by modern villages; however, frequently when tantalizing hints of pre-modern settlement were followed up in the field, the architectural elements in question proved to have been introduced from a neighbouring site rather than being part of any settlement beneath the village.

Despite their limitations, the narratives of early travellers,

Ottoman records and early Islamic sources enable the following picture to be sketched. Earlier phases of Islamic settlement, for which we have a moderate number of sites, were brought to a catastrophic end by the Mongol invasions of the mid-13th century AD. These involved massacres at Harran, Urfa, Raqqa, Saruj, Membij, Balis and Qalat Jabr, all in the region of Jerablus, and resulted in most of the towns on both sides of the Euphrates being "devastated and deserted" (Ashtor 1976, 251 and note 5). Although the severity of the Mongol invasions are often exaggerated, it seems likely that the lack of evidence for Middle and Late Islamic settlement may well be because of these.

From the 13th to the 16th centuries AD the area appears to have been lightly settled, until the Ottoman empire ushered in a period of relative, albeit fluctuating, security in at least parts of northern Syria (Hütteroth 1990). Nevertheless, the Membij and Jerablus areas were probably sparsely settled until around 1836 when Ibrahim Pasha (1831–40) re-settled at least part of the steppe between the Euphrates and the Sajur (Lewis 1987, 39).[27] This may have been the time when some of the villages north of the Sajur were settled again (see map 3 of Lewis 1987). Somewhat later, at the close of the 19th century, Sultan Abdul Hamid (1876–1909) laid out numerous estates in what was unregistered and uncultivated land to the south of the Sajur in the vicinity of Membij. As a result of these actions, by the close of his reign some 270,000 ha of land in 333 villages between the Euphrates and al-Bab had been brought into agricultural use. Consequently western travellers were able to report that by the first decade of the 20th century the area was well settled

Fig. 5.29 Columbario (pigeon roost?) on north bank of Sajur near Dadate, cut into limestone face of relict quarry. Photo T.J. Wilkinson

by villages occupied by Turkish, Kurdish or Arabic speakers whose villages formed islands in a sea of cultivation; this combination of languages is reflected by the inhabitants of the modern villages as recorded in the LCP field notes. There were also many more villages lying within "rich ploughed lands" than had been recognized by earlier travellers (Lewis 1987, 54-55; Sykes 1915; Hogarth 1908, 563).

A more singular history was noted by T. E. Lawrence during his time at Carchemish as it has been re-told by Hogarth (1914, 24):

> "The last great head of the combined clans, Akhras Oglu, is nine generations back, and after his time his people lost their hold of the district. Amarna was founded by Turks, and Chakar Oglu (Karanfil), Yarymdja, and Yunnus (Eminik) were built by Kurds and Turks in the fig and mulberry-growing valley of the mill stream. The hill-sides were once all planted with vineyards, whose boundaries are yet known. The Kala'at proper [Carchemish citadel] passed out of occupation finally about fifty years ago, and ten years later was granted by the tribe of Djerablus to Hussein Mahli, a Barak Turk."

This provides not only antecedents for the existing communities, but it also underscores how with the intervention of humans the landscape could be made verdant. Overall, the re-settlement of the region appears, according to Lewis, to have taken place during times of security, namely when the Ottoman administration had a strong hold over the area and there was an incentive to settle it. In contrast, during times when imperial administration was weak, the region became the realm of groups of mobile pastoralists, some of whom were able to benefit from Aleppo's role as a major market for sheep and wool. Consequently, during the secure episodes of the Ottoman administration settlement extended well beyond the desert line (as recognized by Lewis) into areas more marginal for cultivation (Lewis 1987, map 3).

Overview and discussion

As noted by Lawrence and Ricci (Chapter 4), the region experienced a significant change in the structure of settlement from one based around the tell during the Chalcolithic and Bronze Ages and a later phase, from the 1st millennium BC onwards, when settlements started to disperse into the countryside. Although this transformation commenced during the Iron Age, within the Land of Carchemish survey it was spatially patchy, with settlement continuing on tells throughout much of the 1st millennium BC. In contrast, what may have been a deliberate phase of Neo-Assyrian re-settlement occurred to the north of Carchemish. Nevertheless, by the Hellenistic, and especially the Late Roman/Byzantine period, the area witnessed the considerable growth of settlement as outlined by Lawrence and Ricci in Chapter 4 and Newson in Chapter 9. In other words, the area appears to have experienced a structural transformation which, in part, resembled that of the land of Assur, when settlement dispersal took place during the 1st millennium BC, and in part that of western Syria, where the equivalent phase of settlement took place during the Hellenistic to Late Antique periods. This was not simply because the Carchemish region occupied a zone of transition, but rather because it was located to the west of the Euphrates in a region that was only intermittently under the rule of the Assyrian administrations in Nimrud, Khorsabad and Nineveh.

The Land of Carchemish survey area was not densely settled during the Iron Age if compared to areas of re-settlement in the Land of Assur, and this goes some way to suggesting that perhaps the empire was acting to draw in population from the provinces and periphery to re-settle them in the lands near the capital cities where they could be productive, subject to taxation and support the needs of the king and his administration.

Although only a few valley fills have been dated,[28] it appears from the limited evidence available that the main phase of valley fills accumulated during the last two millennia, that is when aggregate settlement area of surveyed sites had increased, and small settlements and villages had dispersed into the countryside. There was probably also a secondary phase of erosion and aggregation when the area was re-settled during the late Ottoman period and the 20th century. Although the evidence for prehistoric and Bronze Age woodland, sketched on Figure 5.8, can only be regarded as tentative (Tables 5.1 and 5.2), the removal of such woodland (perhaps during the growth phases of the city of Carchemish) is likely to have stimulated increased erosion. This would have been compounded by the increased disturbance of the terrain that resulted from the development of settlements in the surrounding countryside during the Classical and Late Antique periods, as well as the associated increase in runoff and sediment removal to the recipient valleys.

A complementary process was also underway with virtually an explosion in the construction of conduits, underground water channels and canals. Although the dating evidence for these is limited, in terms of style, relation to dated settlements and stratigraphy, most appear to conform to a broad phase of the Hellenistic, Roman, Byzantine and early Islamic periods. Their presence in virtually every significant tributary valley of the Euphrates implies that groundwater was lowered and the base flow of the wadis and springs must have been depleted significantly, which would have amplified further the episodic and flashy flow regimes of the wadis.

Together, these processes: loss of woodland, increased dispersal of settlement, off-site activities into the countryside and depletion of bases flow of wadis, together could have contributed to a more erratic and peaked flow regime for the Euphrates tributaries than would have been the case during the well-settled but more stable occupations of the Bronze Age,

when a significant amount of woodland probably remained.

In sum, when the Land of Carchemish is viewed from the perspective of the communities that occupied the area, it would appear that, away from Carchemish itself, the landscape was dominated by small nucleated strongholds, which not only continued for long periods of history, but also probably occupied by long-lived communities that possessed a strong local identity (Chapter 7). In contrast to the Jazira, where such local identities appear to have been disrupted by the re-settlement schemes of the Assyrians, as well as newly created estates and spontaneous settlements, in the Land of Carchemish survey area, local communities appear to have continued throughout the Iron Age and even into the Hellenistic-Roman era (Chapter 9). It follows, that local identities also persisted, an interpretation which is reinforced by the presence of local Iron Age ceramic types which continued and were somewhat different from those to the east of the Euphrates. As the Hellenistic, Roman, and Byzantine empires extended their influence throughout the area, the resultant dramatic transformation of settlement may have resulted from both the re-settlement of new people, perhaps when the area lay on the Euphrates frontier with Parthia, as well as the movement of local people into lands that provided new opportunities for settlement.

Notes

1 Data on rainfall inter-annual variability and mean rainfall figures (Fig. 5.1) kindly provided by Louise Rayne (Rayne 2014).

2 For the dating and interpretation of this outer activity area, see also Chapter 4 of this volume and an extended discussion in Ricci 2013.

3 Carchemish was incorporated in 717 BC and Kummuh in 708 BC (Hawkins 1980, 445; 1995, 92).

4 Luciani 2005: externally thickened rim bowls: pls. 13 & 14; hammer-head bowls: pl. 43, nos. 500, 501; beaded rim or grooved rim bowls: pl. 37, 453, 454; pl. 39, no. 469, pl. 43, no. 498; related bowl forms on pl. 43. Also common are simple jar forms on pl. 46. See also Chapter 8 for discussion of grooved ring bowls and their parallels.

5 Together with Carchemish to make 20 sites, in this analysis.

6 Of course, there probably were gaps in the sequence that were not recognized in the ceramic sequences, but how such gaps may have affected the local communities remains unknown.

7 With LCP 6 perhaps continuing into the 6th century BC (Wilkinson *et al.* 2007, 230–233).

8 Reported in Karul, Ayhan and Özdoğan 2002. The building in Level 1B, is reported to be of a characteristic Neo-Assyrian plan, but contained very few finds from the building itself. However, Neo-Assyrian artefacts and pottery came from associated pits (p. 133) and there were also Iron Age pits and burials (p. 134).

9 Luciano's "projecting rim": 2005: nos 453–454 and 469.

10 Aramaic Til Barsip, Neo-Hittite Mazuwari, Neo-Assyrian Kar-Shalmaneser.

11 According to Peltenburg (1999, 103), the Iron Age (period III) is only attested by objects and graves, not evidence for *in situ* occupation.

12 Khirbet al-Qana was not within the Land of Carchemish survey area and therefore has not been allocated a LCP site number, but the site was briefly visited in 2009, where the abundance of early Iron Age pottery was noted. We are grateful to Jesper Eidem for confirming the dating evidence of this site (discussed further in Chapter 6), which appears also to have been occupied in the Middle Bronze Age. Descriptions and dimensions are based on the authors' field visit in 2009 and on measurements from Google Earth.

13 The city has been variously spelled Sazabe (Yamada 2000), or Sazabu (Bryce 2012).

14 Namely: Tagi, Surunu, Paripa, Til-bashere and Dabigu.

15 The distance from al-Qana to Carchemish is *c*. 30 km or 19 miles, which is somewhat further than the estimate in parasangs (*c*. 8 miles).

16 There is no evidence of this being a hollow way, however. Overall, the absence of hollow ways in the Carchemish area may be because ploughing and associated soil erosion over the last few hundred years (or more) has probably erased most of the evidence for ancient hollow ways. This contrasts with much of the Khabur region, where the impact of later agricultural practices has been relatively light (Wilkinson 2003, 107).

17 These dates are based on the analysis of the 2006 collections only. Because of the battered nature of most of the sherds, significant numbers could not be classified to types (we did not include, *e.g.* possible EBA or possible Iron Age bowls, *etc*). Figure 5.21 therefore only included those ceramic types that were readily recognizable in the field (or after cleaning in the project sherd yard). Hence Figure 5.21 can only be regarded as a partial assessment of the surface pottery.

18 Because the pragmatic viewing tract of each walker was roughly equivalent to a swathe of field of about 1 m each side of the line of sight, this could be taken as rather greater coverage than would be walked in a 10 × 10 m sample square by means of ten sweeps. These Jerablus figures may therefore be somewhat higher than those from earlier sample square surveys by the author.

19 A total of six transects registered zero sherd counts.

20 Together with a second site recovered in 2008 in Transect 25 (WP 895–897) about 1.5 km south of Carchemish.

21 Because the canal off-takes are not visible, this should remain an inference, rather than a fact.

22 Alternatively it may have been employed solely for transport, but even if it was used for transport, a dual use would seem more likely.

23 Because canal construction continued into Ottoman times, as well as the French colonial period, later construction and use must be considered as well. This is particularly so for C11 along the Sajur (Table 5.8) where one particularly impressive length of rock-cut canal near Tell Sha'ir was described by local people as being dug during the French period. Nevertheless, even this might have been re-excavated from an earlier Classical predecessor.

24 Alternatively, in the case of the earthen feature in the Wadi Amarna, it is possible that the earlier earthen feature was less efficient and suffered from leakage and seepage, or was tapping the flood flow of the Nahr. However, despite its lower capacity, the later built feature may have been a more efficient channel.

25 These qanats (see Chapter 4), recorded by Nikolaos Galiatsatos, Dan Lawrence, and Louise Rayne, will be published in the near future (see also Rayne 2014).

26 A paper presented by K. Franz, at the First International Workshop on the Materiality of the Islamic Rural Economy (Copenhagen August 2012) demonstrated the alignment of the main pigeon post routes which connected the capital and provincial centres and frontier towns. I am grateful to Dr Franz for providing information on other pigeon roosts in the region.

27 Lewis mentions that some 226 faddans of land were newly cultivated in 22 villages, a faddan being roughly the amount of land that could be ploughed by an ox team in one day (Lewis 1987, 39).

28 This is, in part, because the second stage of the project which was planned to include the collection of datable samples from alluvial sediments, could not take place.

Bibliography

Akkermans, P.M.M.G. (1999) Pre-pottery Neolithic settlement patterns along the Balikh and the Euphrates, fact or fiction? In G. del Olmo Lete and J-L. Montero Fenollós, (eds) *Archaeology of the Upper Syrian Euphrates, The Tishrin Dam Area*, 523–533. Barcelona, Aula Orientalis Supplementa 15.

Algaze, G., Breuninger, R. and Knudstad, J. (1994) The Tigris–Euphrates archaeological reconnaissance project: final report of the Birecik and Carchemish Dam survey area. *Anatolica* 20, 1–96.

Algaze, G., Goldberg, P., Honça, D., Matney, T., Mısır, A., Rosen, A.M., Schlee, D. and Somers, L. (eds) (1995) Titrish Höyük, a small urban center in SE Anatolia: the 1994 season. *Anatolica* 21: 13–64.

Arnaud, D. (1991) *Textes Syriens de l' Age du Bronze Récent*. Barcelona, Editorial Ausa.

Ashtor, E. (1976) *A Social and Economic History of the Near East in the Middle Ages*. London, Collins.

Aushariye web site: http://aushariye.hum.ku.dk/english/topgrafik/navnetraek.jpg/

Bachelot, L. and Fales, F.M. (eds) (2005) *Tell Shiukh Fawqani 1994–1998*. Monograph VI/1–2, History of the Ancient Near East. Padova: S.A.R.G.O.N.

Bintliff, J. and Snodgrass, A.M. (1988) Off-site pottery distributions: a regional and inter-regional perspective. *Current Anthropology* 29, 506–513.

Blaylock, S.R., French, D.H. and Summers, G.D. (1990) The Adiyaman Survey: an interim report. *Anatolian Studies* 40, 81–135.

Bryce, T. (2012) *The World of the Neo-Hittite Kingdoms: A Political and Military History*. Oxford, Oxford University Press.

Bunnens, G. (1999) Aramaeans, Hittites and Assyrians in the Upper Euphrates Valley. In G. del Olmo Lete and J.-L. Montero Fenollós (eds) *Archaeology of the Upper Syrian Euphrates:*

the Tishrin Dam Area, 605–624. Barcelona, Aula Orientalis Supplementa 15.

Copeland, L. and Moore, A.M.T. (1985) Inventory and description of sites. In P. Sanlaville (ed.) *Holocene settlement in north Syria: résultats de deux prospections archéologiques effectuées dans la région du nahr Sajour et sur le haut Euphrate syrien*, 41–98. Oxford: BAR S238.

Cremaschi, M. and Maggioni, S. (2005) The geomorphological background and formation processes at Tell Shiukh Fawqani. In L. Bachelot, and F. M. Fales (eds) *Tell Shiukh Fawqani 1994–1998. History of the Ancient Near East/Monographs VI/1–2*, 1–18. Padova, S.A.R.G.O.N.

Deckers, K. and Pessin, H. (2011) Riverine development in the Tell Hamidi surroundings. In K. Deckers (ed.) *Holocene Landscapes Through Time in the Fertile Crescent*, 85–96. Subartu 27. Turnhout, Brepols.

Deckers, K. and Pessin, H. (2010) Vegetation development in the Middle Euphrates and Upper Jazireh (Syria/Turkey) during the Bronze Age. *Quaternary Research* 74, 216–226.

Demir T., Seyrek, A., Westaway, R., Bridgland D. and Beck, A. (2008) Late Cenozoic surface uplift revealed by incision by the River Euphrates at Birecik, southeast Turkey. *Quaternary International* 186, 132–163.

Eidem, J. and Ackermann, R. (1999) The Iron Age ceramics from Jurn Kabir. In A. Hausleiter and A. Reich (eds) *Iron Age Pottery in Northern Mesopotamia, Northern Syria and South-Eastern Anatolia*, 309–324. Münster, Ugarit Verlag.

Eidem, J. and Pütt, K. (2001) Iron Age Sites on the Upper Euphrates. *Les Annales Archéologique Arabes Syriennes* 44, 83–96.

Grayson, A.K. (1996) *The Royal Inscriptions of Mesopotamia. Assyrian Periods. Vol. 2. Assyrian Rulers of the Early First Millennium BC II (858–745 BC)*. Toronto, University of Toronto.

Hawkins, J.D. (1980) Kargamiš. In E. Ebeling and B. Meissner (eds) *Reallexikon der Assyriologie und Vorderasiatischen Archäologie*, 426–446. Berlin, Walter Gruyter.

Hawkins, J.D. (1995) The political geography of North Syria and South-East Anatolia in the Neo-Assyrian period. In M. Liverani (ed.) *Neo-Assyrian Geography* 87–101. Quarderni di Geografia Storica 5. Rome, University di Roma.

Hawkins, J.D. (2000) *Corpus of Hieroglyphic Luwian Inscriptions. vol. I: Inscriptions of the Iron Age*. Berlin, De Gruyter.

Hogarth, D.G. (1908) Problems in Exploration. I. Western Asia. *Geographical Journal* 32 (6), 549–63.

Hogarth, D.G. (1914) *Carchemish, Report on the excavations at Jerablus on behalf of the British Museum, Part I: Introductory*. London, British Museum.

Hütteroth, W.-D. (1990) Villages and tribes of the Jezira under early Ottoman administration (16th century), a preliminary report. *Berytus* 38, 179–184.

Ikeda, Y. (1979) Royal cities and fortified cities. *Iraq* 41(1), 75–87.

Jamieson, A. (2012) *Tell Ahmar III. Neo-Assyrian Pottery from Area C*. Leuven, Peeters.

Karul, N., Ayhan, A. and Ozdoğan, M. (2002) Mezraat-Teleilat 2000. In N. Tuna and J. Velibeyoğlu (eds) *Salvage Project of the Archaeological Heritage of the Ilisu and Carchemish Dam Reservoirs: Activities in 2000*, 130–141. Ankara, METU, TAÇDAM.

Kalaycı, T. (2013) *Agricultural production and stability of settlement systems in Upper Mesopotamia during the Early Bronze Age (Third Millennium BCE)*. PhD dissertation, Department of Anthropology, University of Arkansas.

Kennedy, D. (1998) Declassified satellite photographs and archaeology in the Middle East: case studies from Turkey. *Antiquity* 72, 553–561.

Kepinski. C. (2007) Dynamics, diagnostic criteria and settlement patterns in the Carchemish area during the Early Bronze Age period. In E. Peltenburg (ed.) *Euphrates River Valley Settlement – The Carchemish Sector in the Third Millennium BC*, 152–163. Levant Supplementary Scrics 5. Oxford, Oxbow Books.

Kuhrt, A. (1995) *The Ancient Near East ca. 3000–330BC* (2 vols). London, Routledge.

Kuzucuoğlu, C. and C. Marro (eds) (2007) *Sociétés humaines et changement climatique à la fin du trosième millénaire: une crise a-t-elle eu lieu en haute Mésopotamie? Actes du Colloque de Lyon, 5–8 décembre 2005*. Paris, De Boccard Édition-Diffusion.

Kuzucuoğlu, C., Fontugne, M. and Mouralis, D. (2004) Holocene terraces in the Middle Euphrates Valley, between Halfeti and Karkemish (Gaziantep, Turkey). *Quaternaire* 15 (1–2), 195–206.

Lewis, N. (1987) *Nomads and Settlers in Syria and Jordan 1800–1980*. Cambridge, Cambridge University Press.

Liverani, M. (1992) *Studies on the Annals of Ashurnasirpal II. vol 2. Topographical Analysis*. Quaderni di Geografia Storica 4. Rome, Universita de Roma "La Sapienza".

Luciani, M. (2005) The Iron Age productive area (period IX) and the inhumation cemetery (period X). In L. Bachelot and F.M. Fales (eds) *Tell Shiukh Fawqani 1994–1998*, 719–996. Monograph VI (1–2), History of the Ancient Near East. Padova, S.A.R.G.O.N.

Makinson, M. (2005) Le chantier F, archéologie. La strartigraphie general et l'occupation de l'âge du fer (architecture et material). In L. Bachelot and F.M. Fales (eds) Tell Shiukh Fawqani 1994–1998, 411–580. Monograph VI (1–2), History of the Ancient Near East. Padova, S.A.R.G.O.N.

Miller, N.F. (1997) Farming and herding along the Euphrates: Environmental constraint and cultural choice (fourth to second millennia B.C.). In R. Zettler (ed.) Subsistence *and Settlement in a Marginal Environment: Tell es-Sweyhat, 1989–1995 Preliminary Report*, 123–32. MASCA Research Papers in Science and Archaeology 14. Philadelphia PA, University of Pennsylvania, University Museum.

Minzoni-Deroche, A. and Sanlaville, P. (1988) Le Paléolithique Inéfrieur de la région de Gaziantep. *Paléorient* 14, 87–98.

Morandi Bonacossi, D. (2000) The Syrian Jazireh in the Late Assyrian Period: a view from the countryside. In G. Bunnens (ed.) *Essays on Syria in the Iron Age*, 349–96. Ancient Near Eastern Studies 7. Louvain, Peeters Press.

Mori, L. (2003) *Reconstructing the Emar Landscape*. Rome, Quaderni di Geografia Storica 6.

Newson, P., Barker, G., Daly, and Gilbertson, D. (2007) The Wadi Faynan field systems. In G. Barker, D. Gilbertson and D. Mattingly (eds) *Archaeology and desertification: The Wadi Faynan Landscape Survey, Southern Jordan*, 141–174. Oxford, Oxbow Books.

Parker, B.J. (1997) Garrisoning the Empire: aspects of the construction and maintenance of forts on the Assyrian Frontier. *Iraq* 59, 77–87.

Peltenburg, E. (1999) Tell Jerablus Tahtani 1992–1996: a summary. In G. del Olmo Lete and J.-L. Montero Fenollós (eds) *Archaeology of the Upper Syrian Euphrates, The Tishrin Dam Area*, 97–105. Aula Orientalis Supplementa 15. Barcelona, Editorial Ausa.

Peltenburg, E., Bolger, D., Campbell, S., Murray, M.A. and Tipping, R. (1996) Jerablus-Tahtani, Syria, 1995: preliminary report. *Levant* 28, 1–25.

Peltenburg, E., Campbell, S., Carter, S., Stephen, F.M.K. and Tipping, R. (1997) Jerablus-Tahtani, Syria, 1996: preliminary report. *Levant* 29, 1–18.

Rayne, L. (2014) *Satellite remote sensing and the water management systems in the northern Fertile Crescent*. PhD thesis, Durham University.

Redford, S. (1998) *The Archaeology of the Frontier in the Medieval Near East: Excavations at Gritille*. Philadelphia PA, University Museum Publications, University of Pennsylvania.

Ricci, A. 2013. A*n Archaeological Landscape Study of the Birecik-Carchemish Region (Middle Euphrates River Valley) during the 5th, 4th and 3rd Millennium BC*. PhD Dissertation, Christian-Albrechts-Universität, Kiel, Germany.

Rosen, A.M. and Goldberg, P. (1995) Palaeoenvironmental Investigations. In Guillermo Algaze *et al*. Titrish Höyük, a small urban center in SE Anatolia: the 1994 season. *Anatolica* 21, 32–37.

Sykes, M. (1915) *The Caliphs' Last Heritage*. London.

Trigo, R.M., Gouveia, C.M. and Barriopedro D. (2010) The intense 2007–2009 drought in the Fertile Crescent: Impacts and associated atmospheric circulation. *Agricultural and Forest Meteorology* 150, 1245–1257.

Tunca, Ö. (1999) Tell 'Amarna. Présentation sommaire de sept campagnes de fouilles (1991–1997). In G. del Olmo Lete and J.-L. Montero Fenollós (eds) *Archaeology of the Upper Syrian Euphrates, The Tishrin Dam Area*, 129–36. Aula Orientalis Supplementa 15. Barcelona, Editorial Ausa.

Ur, J.A., de Jong, L., Giraud, J., Osborne, J. F. and MacGinnis, J. (2013) Ancient cities and landscapes in the Kurdistan region of Iraq: The Erbil Plain Archaeological Survey 2012 season. *Iraq* 75, 89–117.

Ur, J.A. (2010) Cycles of Civilization in northern Mesopotamia, 4400–2000 BC. *Journal of Archaeological Research* 18, 387–431.

Van Liere W. J. (1963) Capitals and citadels of Bronze and Iron Age Syria in their relation to land and water. *Les Annales des Archéologique de Syria* 13, 109–122.

Vivancos, A.E. (2005) *Eufratense et Osrhoene: poblamiento Romano en el alto Éufrates Sirio*. Murcia, Universidad de Murcia, Servicio de Publicaciones.

Wilkinson, E.B., Wilkinson, T.J. and Peltenburg, E. (2011) Revisiting Carchemish: the Land of Carchemish Project in Syria, 2009 and 2010. http://www.antiquity.ac.uk/projgall/.

Wilkinson, T.J. (1982) The definition of ancient manured zones by means of extensive sherd-sampling techniques. *Journal of Field Archaeology* 9, 323–333.

Wilkinson, T.J. (1990a) *Town and Country in SE Anatolia vol.1: Settlement and Land Use at Kurban Höyük and Other Sites in the Lower Karababa Basin*. Chicago IL, Oriental Institute Publications 109.

Wilkinson, T.J. (1990b) Soil development and early land use in the Jazira region, Upper Mesopotamia. *World Archaeology* 22 (1), 87–102.

Wilkinson, T.J. (1998) Water and human settlement in the Balikh Valley, Syria: Investigations from 1992–1995. *Journal of Field Archaeology* 25, 63–87.

Wilkinson, T.J. (1999) Holocene valley fills of southern Turkey and NW Syria. Recent geoarchaeological contributions. *Quaternary Science Reviews* 18, 555–572.

Wilkinson, T.J. (2003) *Archaeological Landscapes of the Near East*. Tucson AZ, University of Arizona Press.

Wilkinson, T.J. (2007) Archaeological regions in the neighbourhood of Carchemish. In E. Peltenburg (ed.) *Euphrates River Valley Settlement – The Carchemish Sector in the Third Millennium BC*, 27–42. Levant Supplementary Series 5. Oxford, Oxbow Books.

Wilkinson, T.J. (2010) Empire and environment in the northern Fertile Crescent. In I.P. Martini and W. Chesworth (eds) *Landscapes and Societies – Selected Cases*, 135–151. Springer, Dordrecht.

Wilkinson, T.J. and Rayne, L. (2010) Hydraulic landscapes and imperial power in the Near East. *Water History* 2 (2), 115–144.

Wilkinson, T.J. and Tucker, D.J. (1995) *Settlement Development in the North Jazira, Iraq. A Study of the Archaeological Landscape*. Warminster, Aris and Phillips.

Wilkinson, T.J. and Wilkinson, E.R. (forthcoming) The Iron Age Of The Middle Euphrates In Syria And Turkey. In J. MacGinnis (ed.) *The Provincial Archaeology of the Assyrian Empire*. Cambridge, Macdonald Institute.

Wilkinson, T.J., Miller, N., Reichel, C. and Whitcomb, D. (2004) *On the Margin of the Euphrates: Settlement and land use at Tell es-Sweyhat and in the Upper Lake Tabqa Area, Syria*. Chicago IL, Oriental Institute Publications 124.

Wilkinson, T.J., Wilkinson, E., Ur, J.A., and Altaweel, M. (2005) Landscape of empire: the Assyrian countryside in context. *Bulletin of the American Schools of Oriental Research* 340, 23–56.

Wilkinson, T.J., Peltenburg, E., McCarthy, A., Wilkinson, E.B. and Brown, M. (2007) Archaeology in the Land of Carchemish: landscape surveys in the area of Jerablus Tahtani, 2006. *Levant* 39, 213–247.

Wilkinson, T. J., Galiatsatos,N., Lawrence, D., Ricci, A., Dunford, R. and Philip, G. (2012) Late Chalcolithic and Early Bronze Age Landscapes of Settlement and Mobility in the Middle Euphrates: A Re-assessment. *Levant* 44 (2), 139–185.

Winter, I.J. (1983) Carchemish ša kišad puratti. *Anatolian Studies* 33, 177–197.

Woolley, C.L. (1921) *Carchemish, Report on the excavations at Jerablus on behalf of the British Museum, Part II: The Town Defences*. London, British Museum.

Woolley, C.L. and Barnett, R. (1952) *Carchemish, Report on the excavations at Jerablus on behalf of the British Museum, Part III: The Excavations in the Inner Town and the Hittite Inscriptions*. London, British Museum.

Yamada, S. (1998) The manipulative counting of the Euphrates crossings in the later inscriptions of Shalmaneser III. *Journal of Cuneiform Studies* 50, 87–94.

Yamada, S. (2000) *The Construction of the Assyrian Empire: A Historical Study of the Inscriptions of Shalmaneser III (859–824 BC) Relating to his Campaigns in the West*. Leiden, Brill.

6

The scent of empires on the Sajur

Jesper Eidem

Introduction

Archaeological sites in the Sajur Valley attracted some attention from early travellers who passed through the valley en route from Aleppo to reach Jerablus/Carchemish or destinations further removed on the Euphrates and in Anatolia (Sachau 1883; Hogarth 1909; Sayce 1911). The early interest did not, however, inspire further investigations for many decades. The apparent lack of large, historically documented sites left the valley more or less to itself until the 1960s and 1970s when survey teams made an effort to chart ancient settlement, both on the Turkish (Archi *et al.* 1971) and the Syrian Sajur (Sanlaville 1985), the latter work with specific emphasis on prehistoric settlement. Publication of the results obtained on the Syrian Sajur occurred just as the Upper Syrian Euphrates became an acute focus for archaeological research with the inception of the Tishrin Dam Salvage Project (Del Olmo Lete and Montero Fenollós 1999). This project perhaps postponed any follow-up to the new information on the Sajur, but on the other hand logically inspired fresh interest in the area as the hinterland for sites excavated on the Euphrates, as witnessed by the work discussed below, and not least "The Land of Carchemish Project" (Peltenburg *et al.* 2012).

Our Danish expedition to the Tishrin Dam area uncovered a rare sequence of local Iron Age material at the site of Jurn Kabir. Since the Iron Age was poorly documented both in the Tishrin and Sajur areas we decided to conduct two consecutive reconnaissance-type surveys (Fig. 6.1). The first, in April 1998, explored sites on the west bank of the Euphrates within the Tishrin Dam zone, and this led to the discovery of Tell Aushariye, a hitherto poorly known[1] hill-top site at the confluence of the Sajur and Euphrates. This site may, rather confidently, be identified with a fortress mentioned in Assyrian sources. In July 1999

a second brief survey covered part of the Sajur region, not as a comprehensive effort, but to test the apparent lack of Iron Age occupation evident from the earlier surveys.[2] Checking only sites recorded previously this exercise did not identify Qala'at Halwanji, another unrecognised hill-top site, some 15 km upstream from the confluence, and which was only discovered accidentally in June 2007. Both Tell Aushariye and Qala'at Halwanji have subsequently been the focus of excavations, and the present contribution will highlight some selected results which pertain to the theme of the paper: traces of imperial imposition on the Valley, focusing on three scenarios: the Assyrian "West Expansion", the Middle Bronze Age forts in the valley, and a peculiar topographical feature of perhaps Early Bronze Age IV date.[3]

Assyrian "west expansion"

In the year 856 BC the Assyrian king Shalmaneser III campaigned in Syria and conquered Til Barsip on the east bank of the Euphrates. Til Barsip was renamed Kar-Shalmaneser. The king then crossed the river and, according to the text of the Kurkh stela, seized a place, locally known as Pitru, which his ancestor Tiglath-pileser I had once occupied, and which was located on the river Sajur.

> "At that time the city of Ana-Assur-uter-asbat, which the people of Hatti call Pitru (and) which is on the Sajur river [on the other side] of the Euphrates, and the city of Mutkinu, which is on this side of the Euphrates, which Tiglath-pileser (I), a forefather, a prince, my predecessor, had occupied, but (which) at the time of Assur-rabi (II), king of Assyria, the Arameans had seized by force - these cities I restored (and) settled Assyrians therein." (Grayson 1996, p. 19, A.0.102.2)

This marked the first time for several centuries that the

Fig. 6.1 Map of Sajur region with sites mentioned in text

Fig. 6.2 The Early Iron Age (Level III) enclosure at Tell Jurn Kabir, cut by stone foundations of Level II

Assyrians were able to cross the Euphrates and establish a base on the west bank.[4] Shalmaneser was evidently proud that he could restore ancient Ana-Assur-uter-asbat, and thus match an achievement by his famous predecessor in the 11th century BC.

In the spring of 1998 our team surveyed part of the west bank of the Euphrates and here discovered the site of Tell Aushariye (Eidem and Pütt 2001). The topography of the site immediately suggested a role as fortress or stronghold. Aushariye is really a tell placed upon a high limestone cliff, in clear view from Til Barsip/Tell Ahmar. The high part is only about one hectare in area and basically follows the triangular shape of the cliff. In a house near the site we discovered two large fragments of a basalt stele with remains of cuneiform inscription, authored by none other than Shalmaneser III. The owner of the fragments told us that he had found them in the Sajur close to the site, and they almost certainly came from there. So it seemed highly probable that Aushariye was ancient Pitru/Ana-Assur-uter-asbat.[5]

This identification promised some very clear and precise historical connections to the archaeological levels in Aushariye, and this was particularly interesting to us. When we found Aushariye we were close to finishing our first excavation within the Tishrin Dam area, at Jurn Kabir, also on the west bank of the Euphrates, some 20 km south-south-east of Aushariye. Jurn Kabir, which has since been completely flooded by the Tishrin Lake, was a small, low site with mainly Iron Age occupation (Eidem and Pütt 1999). This fact allowed us to examine not just the usual late Neo-Assyrian and post-Assyrian levels, which are quite common at other Iron Age sites in the region, but also to

Fig.6.3 Tell Aushariye. SW corner (Area G). Stone foundations of Level VIII visible

Fig. 6.4 The MB II (Level VIII) stone terracing/glacis in Area O step-trench at Aushariye, covering/cutting earlier brick enciente of Level IX (upper center), and overlaid by Early Iron Age brick terrace (upper right)

reach and expose large parts of the older levels. The earliest level was very badly eroded, but the next, Level III, still preserved enough to reconstruct some interesting building plans (Fig. 6.2). The buildings were unfortunately almost empty of objects, but the characteristic ceramic material of Level III provided a date in the 11th century BC, with the best parallels found at sites on the Upper Syrian and Lower Turkish Euphrates. Level III is therefore a local horizon, broadly contemporary with the time of Tiglath-pileser I (Kehlet 2004). Since the site was not far from his Ana-Assur-uter-asbat what might the possible connections have been?

Moving our work in the Tishrin Dam area to Aushariye was therefore not least to investigate what material impacts Assyrian presence had in a place where this seemed historically assured, in contrast to Jurn Kabir, which produced no inscriptions or other types of finds providing a precise historical context. Excavations at Aushariye began in 2000, and continued through 2007, with a final season in 2010 (Fig. 6.3). The first seasons made it clear that the upper levels on the high plateau dated to the late Neo-Assyrian and early Post-Assyrian periods. These levels were deeper and more destructive of earlier remains than was the case in Jurn Kabir. In several places, however, we managed to reach the earlier Iron Age. On the south slope of the site a 100 m step trench revealed a section through the fortifications of Level III, which corresponds to Jurn Kabir Level III. At this time the steep slope of the site was supplied with a massive brick terrace (Fig. 6.4). Was this then the work of Tiglath-pileser I? Perhaps, but the associated ceramics were fairly exactly like those we had excavated at Jurn Kabir. In fact nothing appeared anywhere on the site that could be securely connected to a late Middle Assyrian presence. Also the level directly above, which structurally is very similar to Level III, and which should correspond to the reoccupation by Shalmaneser III, had local Iron Age materials, which was

Fig. 6.5 Site 9 (=6501; Eidem and Pütt 2001, 90) from SW (May 2005)

puzzling. An obvious solution of course would be that the site after all was not ancient Pitru or Ana-Assur-uter-asbat, and this we can not entirely exclude. But where would the true Pitru then be? The landscape can be deceptive, and hill-top sites easily missed by more extensive surveys, as our own experience with Aushariye and Qala'at Halwanji

Fig. 6.6 Middle Assyrian sealing fragment from Aushariye (AU.7502-4)

shows, but the fact is that we know of no other convincing candidate for Pitru in the area close to the mouth of the Sajur. Upstream from Aushariye there are few sites with Iron Age material for quite a distance, and virtually the only alternative possibility would be a site *c.* 7 km south-east of Aushariye, near Hammam Saghir (Fig. 6.5; Eidem and Pütt 2001, 90, site 9 (= 6501) and 94, fig. 5-6), but this site has at least on the surface only the local Iron Age, and is not nearly as impressive as Aushariye.

Since the identification after all remained convincing we were obliged to think of how a realistic scenario could be imagined more concretely. As pointed out by Postgate (1985) the Middle Assyrian presence at Pitru, which lasted for some 100 years, until removed by Aramaeans in the time of Assur-rabi, would have remained pretty isolated from its base to the east, which later in the reign of Tighlat-pileser I suffered serious Aramaean incursions to the extent that even the core of Assyria was affected. It would appear more realistic therefore to think that Assyrian strongholds on the middle Euphrates were founded and maintained in some kind of cooperation with the local Hittite-Luwian principalities, foremost that of Karkemish (Carchemish). Tiglath-pileser's efforts to curtail Aramaean incursion, including his famous multiple crossings of the Euphrates, would of course have served his own purposes, but in the end also those of the local non-Aramaeans, who were no doubt equally disturbed. As such, supported by centres like Carchemish, strongholds like Pitru could have functioned

for some time. Such an establishment would have provided symbolic and real political importance as part of an Assyrian "network". Viewed in this perspective one may concretely imagine that Tiglath-pileser I was supported logistically in the establishment of Ana-Assur-uter-asbat, and that perhaps only a small core of actual Assyrians were settled there. This could help explain why materially the early Assyrian presence at Aushariye is virtually invisible, and would only be detected in the shape of inscriptions, tablets, seals or sealings, and decidedly elite items, which Assyrians had brought with them, and quite likely removed again when leaving.

Without any secure solution to this problem we turned our attention to the earlier Bronze Age levels at Aushariye, and worked to establish a sequence and understanding of the overall history of the site. In 2008 we moved some 15 km up the Sajur river, to Qala'at Halwanji, a fortress of the Middle Bronze Age, and devoted two seasons to preliminary investigations there. In 2010, however, we went back to Aushariye for a final season to round off work there before moving the team definitively to large-scale exposures at Halwanji. Among the last operations we did at Aushariye was to enlarge exposure at the southwest corner of the site, where we had earlier excavated a massive wall of Level III, potentially belonging to a gate-structure. The new operation exposed stone foundations of the wall turning north and cutting structures from the Late Bronze Age. Close to the surface, in old wash, we found a group of tablet fragments with writing which can be dated to the Middle Assyrian period. The date is supported by a fragment of a Middle Assyrian sealing found in the same deposit (Fig. 6.6). The fragments cannot be joined and must come from several different tablets, and as such they yield little concrete information, but important implications. The find does not prove that Aushariye is ancient Pitru, nor our theory of how that site may have functioned as an establishment of Tiglath-pileser I, but it does provide encouraging support for these assumptions. Control of the west bank of the Euphrates was a tentative and ephemeral undertaking, which left only a few isolated material remains. Indeed the establishment of Jurn Kabir and other contemporary Iron Age sites nearby, like Tell Qadahiye, with a sequence similar to Jurn Kabir, might, but need not, be related to the same scenario.

Middle Bronze Age Forts on the Sajur

Aushariye

There is another aspect of this however. The Assyrian name of Pitru, Ana-Assur-uter-asbat, means "He reconquered for Assur", but since the inscriptions of Shalmaneser III indicate that he himself did not give it this name, it should be Tiglath-pileser I who did it, which again means that it

Fig. 6.7 Tell Aushariye, Area G: Burnt Late MB room (Level VII) built up against unfinished fortification structure (upper right)

Fig. 6.8 Selection of 17th cent. (MB IIB) ceramic vessels from burnt Level VII rooms (Tell Aushariye)

must have been considered Assyrian once before his reign. Does this refer to an earlier and otherwise unknown Middle Assyrian possession or to an even older one? Regarding the archaeological sequence at Aushariye it is tempting to suggest that the relevant period was the Middle Bronze Age, and that the first "Assyrian" possession was during the reign of Shamshi-Adad I in the early 18th century. Indeed we know that this king famously established two fortresses in the kingdom of Jamhad (Yamkhad), thus formally west of the Euphrates in 1786 BC (Middle Chronology), but lost them again six years later (Ziegler 2009). While the precise location of these forts is unknown, it is generally assumed that they should be sought somewhere close to the Euphrates, and between Carchemish and Emar. Let us take a brief look at the evidence from Aushariye.

A prominent feature of the slopes of Aushariye is the eroded lines of stone-settings irregularly preserved on the surface virtually on its entire circumference. From the excavations in Areas G and O we know that this feature represents a massive stone terracing constructed in the mature MB period (Fig. 6.4). At the edge of the slope parallel lines of foundations for the system cut deeply into earlier levels, but at a higher level merged to form a sloping surface. Far down the slope, in Areas O and S, we have exposed the inner edge of a stone feature resting immediately on the rock, and it seems likely that this represents the lowest part of the terracing, and that this formed a glacis. The stone foundations at the edge of the plateau cover or cut three earlier levels with mud-brick *encientes*, and the numerous sherds in the foundation fills range from late EB to MB II. No super-structures for this construction (Level VIII) are preserved on the edge of the slope. Instead the inner edge of the upper stone setting was reused for a series of small rooms in Level VII. Parts of five of these rooms have been excavated in Area G (Fig. 6.7), and the corresponding Level

(VII) reached in Areas O and C. While the rooms in Area G were burnt, with numerous ceramic vessels and other items left *in situ,* this destruction is not in evidence in the other areas. Although clearly domestic in character the rooms must be viewed as part of a larger system, since details of construction, wall sizes, brickwork and plaster, are the same across the different excavation areas. The burning only found in Area G may relate to its location at the corner of the site, where the plateau is most easily accessed, and where an attack may have been focused. However that may be, the numerous reconstructable vessels from the Level VII rooms in Area G (Fig. 6.8) have close parallels at other Euphrates sites, like Saraça Höyük north of Carchemish (Sertok and Kulakoğlu 2002), and apparently Tell Ahmar (Bunnens 2010), and can be securely dated to the 17th century BC (Jacobsen 2011). The general picture then is of a really substantial project to create new massive fortifications at Aushariye at some point probably in the 18th century BC, but the project was apparently quickly abandoned and never brought to conclusion.

Qala'at Halwanji

This scenario might of course fit the brief episode of the two forts established by Shamshi-Adad. Moreover, some 15 km up the Sajur river is the EB IV and MB II site of Qala'at Halwanji (Figs 6.9 and 6.10), which we accidentally discovered in 2007, and where we were able to make some preliminary test excavations in 2008 and 2009 (Eidem 2013; Maqdissi 2013; Ishaq 2013). Immediately under the modern surface the site has remains of a Middle Bronze Age II fortress which existed only briefly before it was burnt down in a cross-site event and never occupied again. Ceramics and sealings found provide a fairly precise date in the 18th century BC. A fairly close parallel to one seal image from

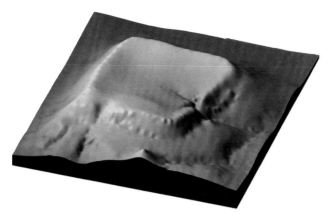

Fig. 6.9 Qala'at Halwanji: model

Fig. 6.11 Seal impression from Level I (MB II) at Qala'at Halwanji (see Eidem 2013)

Fig. 6.10 Qala'at Halwanji: Google image

Fig. 6.12 Tell Arab Hassan (LCP-68)

Halwanji, for instance, is found on an envelope from Level Ib at Kultepe/Kanish dated to 1776 BC (Fig. 6.11; cf. Eidem 2013, 12). What role did such a site play in this region? Who founded it and why? Much of the Sajur region in Syria was recently surveyed by the "Land of Carchemish" project (Peltenburg *et al.* 2012; Chapter 4), and the new evidence suggests that settlement on the Sajur itself in the Middle Bronze Age either remained stable or registered a slight decline (Chapter 4). Nevertheless, there continued a significant presence of MBA sites along the Sajur. A possible background for this development could be the formation of a small local polity which offered relative security. A few kilometres upstream from Qala'at Halwanji is the probably most imposing site in the Sajur region, namely Arab Hassan (LCP 68, Fig. 6.12) (Sanlaville 1985, 74). This site has mainly Bronze Age levels and given its size and central position in the region it seems reasonable to suppose that it could have been the capital of local polities for periods in the 3rd and 2nd millennia BC.[6]

Given the proximity to Arab Hassan, however, it does not seem likely that the Middle Bronze Age fortress at Halwanji was a new military capital for a local ruler – rather it was placed there to control the valley and its central site. From Old Babylonian Mari we have an interesting model for rampart construction on an exercise tablet (Charpin 1993). The text contains calculations of the volumes of earth needed for each side of a rectangular rampart and the number of man-days necessary for the work. Unfortunately the text does not provide dimensions of the walled area or indeed a name of the place, and is clearly an abstract exercise. The calculations, however, are probably fairly realistic and given the quantities of earth calculated, the model must have had dimensions fairly similar to Halwanji. Obviously the Mari text does not represent a model specifically for Halwanji, but a sort of standard model for a medium-sized, fast-to-build fortification of this period, which we must anyway assume existed. A rampart of this type, according to the Mari text, demanded some 27,000 workdays, and so could be completed by, for instance, a workforce of 1000 men in just one month.

Even so, such a project would, in total, represent a considerable investment and this, plus the maintenance of a garrison force, would no doubt have been beyond the resources available to a small local ruler. Regarding the regional context it is clear that Qala'at Halwanji could be related to an episode in the history of Carchemish, located as it is, more or less where the south-western border of the kingdom may have been. In this perspective the fortress could have been intended to mark control in relation to another regional power, like Jamhad (Yamkhad) to the west, or a kingdom to the north-west, perhaps with its centre in modern Tilbeshar, located near Gaziantep in Turkey (Kepinski 2010). This site, which was almost 60 ha in the Middle Bronze Age, may be identical with ancient Haššum, mentioned, although infrequently, in the sources from Mari (Ziegler 2009, 201f.). These sources do not mention any direct confrontations between Carchemish and Haššum, but it seems logical that both kingdoms may have wanted to control as much of the fertile Sajur Valley as possible.

Moving some 17 km west of Halwanji we find Tell Algane (al-Qana), with a very similar size and shape, and MB II occupation. Are the two sites somehow connected, perhaps marking control points of Carchemish and Haššum respectively? Without more evidence this must of course remain speculation, and we may finally turn to the possible international context for Halwanji.

Neither Aushariye nor Halwanji have produced any inscriptions or other evidence which can serve to establish a firm connection to Shamshi-Adad or his Kingdom of Upper Mesopotamia. The investigations at Halwanji were in an early stage when halted by the tragic unrest in Syria, but had produced only ceramics and other materials of local styles. In this situation nothing is really sure. A few years ago A. Otto (2009) and N. Ziegler (2009) suggested that the two fortresses established by Shamshi-Adad could be identified with the sites of Tell Bazi and al-Qitar, located on opposite banks of the Euphrates some 20 km south of Aushariye. Their arguments are good, but not compelling, and also the sites they favour have not yet produced any specific evidence to support the connection. This is not the occasion to discuss all the arguments in favour of either of these two or other possibilities, since only new evidence can provide a firm solution. For the time being however, the situation at Aushariye and the site of Halwanji shows that something important, but fairly ephemeral, was at work on the Sajur more or less at the relevant time. The apparent fact that Pitru was an Assyrian establishment at some time before the reign of Tiglath-pileser I seems to me a good argument that the Aushariye and Halwanji sites had some connection with the forts of Shamshi-Adad. In his known inscriptions Tiglath-pileser I makes no explicit reference to Shamshi-Adad, but in practice he certainly seems to have

Fig. 6.13 "Monument" at Qala'at Halwanji

attempted to emulate or even extend the geo-political reach of this illustrious predecessor, and among other things, like Shamshi-Adad, paid a symbolic visit to the Mediterranean coast. Surely oral traditions and sources now lost or as yet unrecovered kept the memory of Shamshi-Adad and his exploits alive also in Middle Assyrian times. The idea of such a legacy is not new, but worth stressing. At the roots of Assyrian power was the Old Assyrian system of elite families organising international trade, overlaid by a brief imperial episode organised by Shamshi-Adad. His foreign dynasty was expelled, but it retained sufficient prestige to provide throne names for a series of subsequent Assyrian kings.

Monument Valley(?)

Just outside the south-east corner of Qala'at Halwanji is a conspicuous feature: a small, but fairly regular, conical hill, its shape now somewhat blurred by erosion (Fig. 6.13). It is almost certainly not natural, but man-made. No sherds are visible on the surface and a few, shallow robber pits reveal only limestone gravel under the surface. The investigations in 2008–9 did not allow occasion to work on this hill, which we have provisionally referred to as the "Monument", superficially inspired by the remarkable "White Monument" near Tell Banat (McClellan 1998). This is located some 200 m north of the large 3rd millennium BC site of Banat/Bazi, no doubt a major regional center,[7] and is *c.* 20 m high and with a diameter of *c.* 100 m in its latest phase. The excavators estimate that it had no built structure on its small summit, and thus in fact was a "monument", or more precisely a "monumental tumulus":

> "while no true burials or tomb chambers have been found inside or on top of the White Monument, several discrete deposits of human skeletal parts, some animal bones, and pottery were cut into or placed onto the sloping sides of the monument, and then encased within layers of earth and marl (Porter 2002b, 160–1). It has been conjectured that such bone deposits represent the final stage of a multi-stage burial practice, in which the skeletal remains were taken away from their original burial place and

Fig. 6.14 Tell al Qana from SE

returned with others in a collective, anonymous mass of bones." (Cooper 2006, 237–8)

The Banat "Monument" seems unlikely to have been unique, and its exposure has inspired the search for similar mounds in Syria. One example, Tell Menkout, is located just 1 km west of the site of Mari, and variously suggested as a parallel to the White Monument, or as part of religious ceremonies performed at equinox (Butterlin 2007). The quest for parallels is hampered by the obvious fact that many smaller sites in Northern Syria are small, fairly steep, conical hills, in many cases no doubt a result of an initial (often 3rd millennium BC) function as a rural, heavily fortified, stronghold, but not comparable to the Banat example. Potential candidates must be examined on the ground and carefully considered as per topography, surface remains *etc.* With this caveat in mind, however, it seems appropriate to mention two potential parallels to the Halwanji "Monument" in the Syrian Sajur valley, both sites which I have personally visited, and which exhibit suggestive features.

The clearest of the two examples is Tell al Qana (Figs. 4.11, 6.14, 6.15), located *c.* 17 km upstream from Halwanji.[8] It has a shape and size closely similar to that of Halwanji, although founded on the plain and not on a cliff. On a visit to the site in spring of 2009 we found much of the surface completely covered by modern cultivation, but strewn with large fragments of basalt blocks, evidently the remains of substantial ancient structures. Sherds observed, mostly around the edges of the sites, were predominantly of Late Bronze Age/early Iron Age date, but included a few clear examples of MBA material. The 'touristic' nature of the visit did not allow any comprehensive assessment, and so it remains uncertain whether the site was occupied also in the EBA period. Nevertheless the anomalous, circular attachment to the northeast corner of the otherwise very regular site is suggestive of a possible "monument", later merged with the site by erosion. Figure 4.11, Chapter 4 shows the character of this feature.

The other example is the site of Molla Assad (Figs 6.16 and 6.17), located on a small tributary of the Sajur some 6 km south-west of Aushariye and some 12 km south-east of Halwanji (Sanlaville 1985, 76f.). This site is rather complex

Fig. 6.15 Tell al Qana: Google image (c. 1 km altitude) (see site plan, Chapter 4)

Fig. 6.16 Tell Molla Assad from N

and in spite of several visits to it we have failed to reach any clear understanding of its occupational history. The northern end of the site, however, is clearly a tall, separate, conical hill. At its base are cut burnt layers of Neolithic date from which flint and obsidian tools and numerous animal bones have eroded. Higher up the hill has steeper slopes, and the only surface sherd retrieved on our visits was a rim fragment from a Hama-type beaker. Clearly added to this hill is a fairly large, roughly rectangular mound extending south and with a size of *c.* 250 × 150 m. We have found very few diagnostic sherds on this mound, and cannot say what may be the main period(s) of occupation. A few clear examples of MB and late Iron Age sherds, however, have been observed.[9]

In sum, these two sites, although with a longer and more complex settlement history, may exhibit a feature similar to the Halwanji "Monument". This observation of course in no way provides an answer to the central question about the function of the "Monument", but only serves to suggest

Fig. 6.17 Tell Molla Assad: Google image (c. 1 km altitude)

that it was a fairly common feature of Bronze Age Syria. It is unfortunate that none of the three examples can be securely dated. The Halwanji "Monument" should be EB IV or MB II, while the other two examples only potentially are contemporary with it. If, however, we tentatively accept a late EB to MB date of these "monuments", how can they be explained? The Banat "White Monument", as well as other contemporary burial complexes, are clearly part of a "mortuary landscape" of EB Syria, designed to mark, venerate, and appropriate ancestors (*e.g.* Schwartz 2007). In the case of Halwanji, however, which appears to have been a fortress, although this function cannot yet be ascertained for the earlier EB IV phase, I think other possibilities should be considered. One such possibility is offered by the textually documented, but as yet not archaeologically identified "Victory Monument", known from Old Akkadian sources. Old Akkadian kings claim to have raised tumuli over the corpses of defeated enemies, a feature described with the term *birûtum*, recently studied by Marti (2005). In early 2nd millennium Syria the generic term for "commemorative monument", *humūsum*, is apparently used to describe a similar feature (Durand 2005, 93–141). Unfortunately the textual evidence is not very specific as to the material manifestation of these "monuments", but

especially the Mari evidence provides some tantalising information. It would seem that such "monuments", once erected, were intended to stay, and in some measure respected even by the defeated. As such they would have represented a particularly macabre aspect of the "mortuary" and "ancestral" landscape, representing simultaneously a triumphal and a heroic history.[10] If such speculation regarding the Sajur valley monuments has any merit it might further be conjectured that they could potentially mark the battles of a single imperial campaign in the Valley, by some unidentified external power.[11]

Epilogue

The three "scents" of imperial imposition discussed in this paper are based on concrete archaeological evidence, which, however, does not easily translate into the kind of firm historical information we would prefer. While the more precise identifications elude us, we are at least presented with glimpses of substantial activities which must have shaken the otherwise humdrum ancient life in the Sajur Valley: the "Assyrianisation" in the 1st millennium BC, the substantial military activity of the MB II period, and the admittedly more speculative "invasion" of the late 3rd millennium, or whatever spurred the considerable energy needed to construct the alleged "monuments" described above, and others as yet unidentified. Qala'at Halwanji was never occupied again after its destruction in the 18th century BC, and a high-intensive surface sampling conducted in 2008 retrieved only a few traces of transient activity, like a couple of Roman coins and Late Ottoman objects (Weideman 2011).[12] Tell al-Qana, which may owe its very regular outline to an MB project, accommodated important occupation in the late 2nd–early 1st millennium, while Tell Aushariye at the Euphrates junction saw intermittent occupation in the LB and Iron Age periods. Like the travellers of a century or so ago, many ancients followed routes through the valley, and left impacts of varying degrees, some now archaeologically retrievable, and enabling us to grasp the outlines of imperial episodes, easily described as "transient", since only briefly did these endeavours persist, before collapsing or moving decisively beyond the Valley, as was the case of the Neo-Assyrian expansion. Intermediate phases between material remains and the ephemeral, often ideologically charged, historical record, remain difficult to reconstruct in this marginal context.

Notes

1 An earlier visitor must have been the famous T.E. Lawrence, who acquired several objects said to have come from "Oshariye" (but probably came from robbed EB IV tombs at the nearby site of Nizel Hussain), and indeed marked the site as "Osherye" on a map of "Crusader Castles" (Lawrence 1986, 2nd map after preface), although unfortunately without any further mention or description.

2 An initially more ambitious plan for the survey eventually had to be abandoned, and the fieldwork reduced to a single week with only on-site study of surface ceramics. Many sherds, however, were recorded/drawn on-site, and a considerable amount of evidence documented. Although adding important specifics to previous results, the survey confirmed the relative paucity of Iron Age settlement in the region.

3 I am grateful to the conveners of the BANEA meeting in Manchester for their kind invitation to the conference and their subsequent acceptance of this modest contribution to the proceedings, although the subject deviates somewhat from that presented in Manchester. The archaeological work in Syria reported here proceeded with the gracious permission of – and in cooperation with the DGAM of The Syrian Arab Republic. It was funded by a number of Danish Foundations, and supported by the host institutions of the author (University of Copenhagen 1993–2007, The Excellence Cluster TOPOI (Berlin) 2008–9, and NINO (Leiden) 2010). Needless to say numerous collaborators, European and Syrian, contributed to the results, and for this deserve my warm thanks.

4 The Assyrian expansion towards the west has been the subject of numerous recent studies: see for instance Bagg 2012 for the historical evidence; for a very complete survey of the Middle

Assyrian expansion from an archaeological and historical perspective see Tenu 2009.

5 For more information on the stela fragments, and the site in general I refer to the website: www.aushariye.hum.ku.dk

6 See Chapter 5 for more complete periodisation.

7 A. Otto (2006) has argued for an identification with ancient Armi/Armanum, but cf. Archi 2011, who prefers to seek this city further north (Samsat?).

8 Sanlaville 1985, 82. The material collected was MB, Roman, and Neolithic. A clear example of the MB material is fig. 14 (p. 151), 3.

9 Cf. photos of the site in Sanlaville 1985, 47 and fig. 7 (p. 89). A group of animal bones from the cut Neolithic layers is presented in the same volume,163-5. Sherds collected are said to be of Pottery Neolithic, EBA, Roman, and Islamic date. We have not observed any clear examples of the later material, but quite likely the lower part of the site had some post-Iron Age occupation.

10 Yet other types of "monument", intra-site, and from the Early MB period, have been exposed at Umm el-Marra and Ebla (Schwartz *et al.* 2012). These rather enigmatic structures seem related to ritual and cultic activities.

11 Given the very tentative nature of this idea it seems pointless to suggest a specific aggressor. For a summary of political and military dynamics in late 3rd millennium Upper Mesopotamia I refer to Sallaberger 2012.

12 The 2008 survey at Qala'at Halwanji is presently being prepared for publication and scheduled to appear in a future volume of PIHANS (Leiden).

Bibliography

Archi, A. (2011) In Search of Armi. *Journal of Cuneiform Studies* 63, 5–34.

Archi, A., Pecorella, P.E. and Salvini, M. (1971) *Gaziantep e la sue regione*. Rome, Edizioni dell'Ateneo.

Bagg, A.M. (2012) *Die Assyrer und das Westland*. Orientalia Lovaniensia Analecta 216.

Butterlin, P. (2007) Tell Medhouk et Mari. *Akh Purattim* 2, 213–214.

Bunnens, G. (2010) Tell Ahmar in the Middle and Late Bronze Age. In P. Matthiae, F. Pinnock, L. Nigro, and N. Marchetti (eds) *Proceedings of the 6th International Congress of the Archaeology of the Ancient Near East. Volume 2: Excavations, Surveys and Restorations: Reports on Recent Field Archaeology in the Near East*, 111–122. Wiesbaden, Harrassowitz.

Charpin, D. (1993) Données nouvelles sur la poliorcétique à l'époque paléo-babylonienne. *MARI* 7, 193–203.

Cooper, L. (2006) *Early Urbanism on the Syrian Euphrates*. Abingdon, Routledge.

Del Olmo Lete, G. and Montero Fenollós, J.-L. (eds) (1999) *Archaeology of the Upper Syrian Euphrates: The Tishrin Dam Area*. Barcelona, AUSA.

Durand, J.-M. (2005) *Le culte des pierres et les monuments commémoratifs en Syrie amorrite*. Paris, Mémoires de N.A.B.U. 9 (FM VIII).

Eidem, J. (2013) Qala'at Halwanji (North-Western Syria), 2008–2009. *Anatolica* 39, 1–24.

Eidem, J. and Pütt, K. (1999) Tell Jurn Kabir and Tell Qadahiye: Danish Excavations in the Tishrin Dam Area. In G. del Olmo Lete and J.-L. Montero Fenollós (eds) *Archaeology of the Upper Syrian Euphrates: The Tishrin Dam Area,* 193–204. Barcelona, AUSA.

Eidem, J. and Pütt, K. (2001) Iron Age Sites on the Upper Euphrates. *Annales Archéologique Arabes Syriennes* 44, 83–96.

Grayson, A. K. (1996) *Assyrian Rulers of the Early First Millennium BC II (858–745 BC).* Royal Inscriptions of Mesopotamia 3. Toronto, University of Toronto Press.

Hogarth, D. G. (1909) Carchemish and its Neighbourhood. *Annals of Archaeology and Anthropology* II, 165–184.

Ishaq, E. (2013) Figurines en terre cuite de Qala'at Halwanji. *Anatolica* 39, 25–31.

Jacobsen, D. (2011) *Tell Aushariye in the Middle Bronze Age.* Unpublished MA thesis, University of Copenhagen.

Kehlet, R. (2004) *The Upper Syrian Euphrates Area in the Early Iron Age. An Analysis of the Early Iron Age Pottery from Jurn Kabir and Environs.* Unpublished MA thesis, University of Copenhagen.

Kepinski, C. (2010) Tilbeshar, A Major City of the Early and Middle Bronze Ages, West to the Big Bend of the Euphrates (South-Eastern Turkie): Result from 2005 and 2006 Seasons. In P. Matthiae, F. Pinnock, L. Nigro, and N. Marchetti (eds) *Proceedings of the 6th International Congress of the Archaeology of the Ancient Near East. Volume 2: Excavations, Surveys and Restorations: Reports on Recent Field Archaeology in the Near East,* 303–315. Wiesbaden, Harrassowitz.

Lawrence, T. E. (1986) Crusader Castles. London, Haag.

Maqdissi, M. (2013) Notice sur la poterie de l'Age du bronze de Qala'at Halwanji (Fouilles Syro-danoises). *Anatolica* 39, 33–52.

McClellan, T. (1998) Tell Banat North: The White Monument. *Subartu* 4/1, 243–271.

Marti, L. (2005) Les monuments funéraires-*birûtu.* In J.-M. Durand, *Le culte des pierres et les monuments commémoratifs en Syrie amorrite,* 191–200. Paris, Mémoires de N.A.B.U. 9 (FM VIII).

Otto, A. (2006) Archaeological Perspectives on Naram-Sin's Armanum. *Journal of Cuneiform Studies* 58, 1–26.

Otto, A. (2009) Historische Geographie im Gebiet des Mittleren Euphrats zwischen Karkemish und Tuttul zur Mittleren und Späten Bronzezeit. In E. Cancik-Kirschbaum and N. Ziegler (eds) *Entre les Fleuves I. Untersuchungen zur historischen Geographie Obermesopotamiens im 2. Jahrtausend v. Chr,* 167–179. Berlin, PeWe-Verlag.

Peltenburg, E., Wilkinson, T. J. Ricci, A. Lawrence, D. McCarthy, A. Wilkinson, E. Newson, P. and Perini, S. (2012) The Land of Carchemish (Syria) Project: The Sajur Triangle. In R. Matthews and J. Curtis (eds) *Proceedings of the 7th International Congress on the Archaeology of the Ancient Near East, 12 April – 16 April 2010, the British Museum and UCL, London,* 191–203. Wiesbaden, Harrassowitz Verlag.

Postgate, N. (1985) Review of K. Nashef, Die Orts – und Gewässernamen der mittelbabylonischen und mittelassyrische Zeit. *Archiv für Orientforschung* 32, 95–101.

Sachau, E. (1883) *Reise in Syrien und Mesopotamien.* Leipzig, Brockhaus.

Sallaberger, W. (2012) History and philology. In M. Lebeau (ed.) *ARCANE* I: *Jezirah,* 327–342. Turnhout, Brepols.

Sanlaville, P. (ed.) (1985) *Holocene Settlement in north Syria: résultats de deux prospections archae archéologiques effectuées dans la région du nahr Sajour et sur le haut Euphrate syrien.* Oxford, BAR S238.

Sayce, A. H. (1911) Notes on an unexplored district of Northern Syria. *Proceedings of the Society for Biblical Archaeology* 33, 171–179.

Schwartz, G. (2007) Status, ideology and memory in third millennium Syria: 'Royal' tombs at Umm el-Marra. In N. Lanieri (ed.) *Performing Death: Social Analyses of Funerary Traditions in the Ancient Near East and the Mediterranean,* 39–68. Chicago, IL, Oriental Institute Seminars 3.

Schwartz, G., Curvers, H. Dunham, S. Weber, J. (2012) From urban origins to imperial integration in western Syria: Umm el-Marra 2006, 2008. *American Journal of Archaeology* 116, 157–193.

Sertok, K. and Kulakoğlu, F. (2002) Results of the 2000 Excavations at Saraga Höyük. In N. Tuna, J. Öztürk, and J. Velibeyoğlu (eds) *Salvage Project of the Archaeological Heritage of the Ilisu and Carchemish Dam Reservoirs, Activities in 2000,* 362–381. Ankara, METU, TAÇDAM.

Tenu, A. (2009) *L'expansion médio-assyrienne – approche archéologique.* Oxford, BAR S1906.

Weideman, S. (2011) *The 2008 Surface Survey at Qala'at Halwanji: The Ceramics.* Unpublished MA thesis, University of Copenhagen.

Ziegler, N. (2009) Die Westgrenze des Reichs Samsī-Addu's. In E. Cancik-Kirschbaum and N. Ziegler (eds) *Entre les Fleuves I. Untersuchungen zur historischen Geographie Obermesopotamiens im 2. Jahrtausend v. Chr.,* 181–209. Berlin, PeWe-Verlag.

Carchemish in the 3rd millennium: a view from neighbouring Jerablus Tahtani

Edgar Peltenburg

Our knowledge of the history of Carchemish is patchy at best. Most information, be it textual or archaeological, comes from relevant data of the 1st and 2nd millennia BC, but as demonstrated by schematic sections of the Acropolis mound, more than 10 m of occupational deposits had accumulated before the start of the 2nd millennium (Woolley and Barnett 1952, 209, fig. 84). Prior to that time, it fell temporarily under the control of Ebla (Archi 1990), but otherwise, reconstructions have had to be based on inferences from very deficient excavated material, and these have naturally led to differences of opinion. One of the most contentious is the timing of the growth of the site to its *c.* 44 ha size, and the relationship of probable urbanization to its emergence as a major political and economic centre (see below and this volume Chapters 4, 5 and 8). Current excavations will hopefully provide much needed stratified and well-dated evidence on these earlier periods of its history (Marchetti 2012, 2014), but meanwhile the neighbouring site of Jerablus Tahtani furnishes us with indirect clues to early developments. University of Edinburgh excavations at the site from 1992 to 2004 within the framework of the Tishrin Dam International Salvage Programme have yielded a detailed record for the Early Bronze Age, and so in this paper I will focus on some implications of discoveries there for our knowledge of 3rd millennium Carchemish.

Jerablus Tahtani was known to Woolley and others as Tell Alawiyeh. He viewed it as part of a defensive network of sites that protected Carchemish to the south:

> "Carchemish stood at the north end of the plain which stretches down the right bank of the river … it … commands the head of the rich hollow land … At the valley's farther end just where the Srisat hills close in to fall in high cliffs to the water, stands tell el Amarna, blocking the southern entrance; between it and Carchemish, the little Tell Alawiyeh forms a central link on the river front, and, where the chief of the tributary valleys give easy approach of the western upland, the tell of Tashartan protects the flank". (Woolley 1921, 36–38)

Lawrence also thought of it as an outpost (Lawrence 1955, 156). Apart from a predisposition to treat sites as geopolitical chess pieces typical of 19th century western politics, there is a strong presumption of an invariable degree of relative importance through time. While such retrospective projection is clearly an assumption to be proven rather than fact on which to build arguments, the relationship between the two sites must have been strong throughout history.

Carchemish and Jerablus Tahtani, both on the right bank of the Euphrates River, are intervisible across 5 km of the flat Jerablus Plain (Fig. 7.1). Woolley aptly described the plain: "Level with Jerablus the limestone hills fall back in a great arc, leaving between themselves and the Euphrates a plain some nine kilometres long by five wide" (Woolley 1921, 35). Both sites were founded on slight natural eminences, but there the physical similarities stop. Carchemish is situated in a fold of hills at the junction of a small stream (the Değirmen Su) and the Euphrates, so low that it cannot be seen from a kilometre inland. Cultivable land was circumscribed in this topographic niche. In contrast, Jerablus Tahtani, the only Early Bronze Age site on the Jerablus Plain, stands out as a 17 m high mound surrounded by flat fields given to agriculture (Figs 7.1 and 7.2). The plain, consisting of Pleistocene terraces, lies *c.* 10 m above the Euphrates River level (Wilkinson *et al.* 2012, 146, fig. 3). It was renowned amongst early travellers for its fertility. In the late 17th century, Henry Maundrell remarked on its exceptional character: "we came to a fine fruitful Plain covered with extraordinary Corn, lying between the Hills and the River *Euphrates*" (in Boese 2006, 53). For Irene Winter (1983,

Fig. 7.2 View from east to the fields of the Jerablus Plain with Jerablus Tahtani centre and the modern course of the Euphrates River in the foreground

Fig. 7.1 View from summit of Jerablus Tahtani (foreground) across the Jerablus Plain to Carchemish with the Inner Town rampart just visible below the Acropolis mound partly in shadow

177–179) it constituted the essential economic basis for the city of Carchemish. Their contrasting but complementary physical situations meant that the fortunes of the adjacent settlements were entangled, and that when the population of Carchemish grew significantly beyond the Acropolis mound, if not before, Jerablus Tahtani is likely to either have been annexed in order that the subsistence needs of Carchemish could be assured or to have prospered in a market setting for agricultural surpluses. Access to the adjacent Jerablus Plain was essential for the growth of an urban population at Carchemish. Lacking similar large tracts of cultivable land, most other sites in the Middle Euphrates Valley were denied the necessary sustaining conditions to underpin such growth.

Long-distance communication routes may also have structured the close association of the two sites. The railway bridge that strikes across the Euphrates River from the south-east corner of the Inner Town rampart gives a false impression that Carchemish was situated for easy river crossing. In fact, twentieth century engineering overcame what were otherwise undependable river conditions here. As Woolley noted, the 300 m wide Euphrates sweeps along the foot of the citadel mound, and channels on the other side fill up in spring when they submerge islands "in one turbid hurrying race" between cliffs and crumbling banks (Woolley 1921, 34). Because of the existence of the Water Gate, there is no doubt that river traffic existed to and from Carchemish, but this may have essentially been up and down the river, as attested in later Mari letters (Michel 1996). The location of its assumed quay, or trading entrepôt, derived from the name of Carchemish (*kar-kamiš*, quay of (the god) Kamiš) is unknown (Hawkins 1976–80, 426; Michel 1996, 417). In addition, it lacks a key feature of thriving cross-river links indicative of long-distance overland communication

systems, the twinned towns on opposite sides of the river (Wilkinson 2004, 182–186). Several EBA examples of twinned towns exist in the Carchemish sector of the Euphrates valley, but little is known of the occupational phases at a small site opposite Carchemish by the village of Zormaghara (Wilkinson *et al.* 2012; see Chapter 5 this volume). Woolley called attention to the existence of tombs similar to EBA types elsewhere at the same village (Woolley 1914, 92). The nearest securely identified EBA settlement site on an easterly route towards ʿAin al ʿArab is 15 km from the left bank of the Euphrates at Tell Auḥan (Einwag 1993, 30). Indeed, so constrained is the location that as soon as the railway line reaches the eastern bank of the river it has to swing sharply northwards in order to circumvent the hills.

What Carchemish lacked, Jerablus Tahtani had in the form of contemporary Shiukh Fawqani on the opposite side of the river, conveniently located below the southern end of the Beilun cliffs (Bachelot and Fales 2005). A ferry crossing existed between these paired sites, one now replaced by a new bridge (Sanlaville 1985, 70; destroyed 6 March 2015). It may have served as a communication hub on the outskirts of Carchemish as early as the 4th millennium. Leading from it towards the Gaziantep-Nizip plain and on toward Aleppo was a route of sites with diagnostic Uruk material not found in adjacent areas (Wilkinson *et al.* 2012, 161, fig. 16, 177; Lawrence and Ricci, Chapter 4 this volume). Ample traces of bitumen processing at the site, presumably for caulking riverine craft, suggest that it connected this east-west Uruk alignment with riverine traffic (Peltenburg *et al.* 1996, 3–5). Algaze (1999, 550–551) posits inter-regional contacts, especially trade, as a driver for nucleation and urbanization in the mid-3rd millennium. If so, Jerablus Tahtani would have been of added importance to Carchemish.

As we see, the strategic location of Jerablus Tahtani meant that it played a key role in the economy and perhaps the security of Carchemish. The premise of this paper, therefore, is that major developments at Jerablus Tahtani in the 3rd

Table 7.1 Chronological concordance chart of developments at Jerablus Tahtani and Carchemish in the 3rd and 4th millennium BC. Carchemish developments from Falsone and Sconzo (2007)

General Period	Jerablus Tahtani				Carchemish	
	Period	Area II	Area III	Main features	Citadel Mound	Inner Town
EME 5				Abandonment	?	Domestic architecture
EME 2-4	IIB	4	2-4	Latest occupation inside fort; Tomb 302 Phase 3		
		5		Intrusion into T 302		
		6		Tomb 302 Phase 1; inundations		
		7	5	South Terrace		
EME 1-2	IIA	8	5	Fort expansions, glacis addition	Cist graves, upper pot burials	Early levels, burials
		8/9	6	Construction of fort		
			7	Final pre-fort structures, burnt		
			8	Curvilinear pit phase		
			9			
LC 4/5 (Mid-Late Uruk)	IB	9	10	Rectilinear pits and structures	Buildings, lower pot burials, bevelled rim bowls	-
		unexcav	11			
			12	Building and secondary burial		
			13			
LC 3	IA		14	Post and other structures		
			natural			

millennium are likely to have impacted on Carchemish or were a result of policies directed from Carchemish. Four developments are evaluated here: the destruction of Jerablus Period IIA, followed by the construction of the IIB fort; intensification of production in late Period IIB; evidence for increasing major flood events; and abandonment of the site *c.* 2250 BC (Table 7.1).

Establishment of a fort

During the 4th millennium, Jerablus Tahtani comprised a core settlement area surrounded by satellite occupations or activity zones, ones that probably persisted into the 3rd millennium (Wilkinson *et al.* 2007, 227–229). No surrounding wall was found in the core area, but there were only limited exposures of this deeply buried component of the mound. A succession of open, pitted levels and buildings in Area III belong to the early 3rd millennium (Peltenburg 1999). Area III, Level 7 of that period was burnt and in subsequent Level 6 a massively built curvilinear wall on stone foundations was placed over the destruction deposits (Fig. 7.3). The same wall rested on burnt deposits in Area I on the other side of the mound (see Fig. 7.4 for location of Areas). It was also evident on the north side in Area IV. Destruction-construction events are radiocarbon-dated to 2825–2720 cal BC at 68% probability (Peltenburg 2015). A degree of site nucleation, therefore, took place at the end of the first quarter of the 3rd millennium when scattered

Fig. 7.3 Exterior of Period IIB fort wall (Area III Level 6) on the remains of the Period IIA buildings on a different orientation (Area III Level 7); 2 m ranging poles

activities on the surrounding plain were concentrated inside the 4–5 ha. mound (see Chapter 4 this volume). It was encircled by a disproportionately heavy wall that was quickly raised and enhanced by a *c.* 12 m wide glacis (Fig. 7.4). The wall was but one element in a comprehensively planned infrastructure from the outset since planners incorporated the drainage system for the internal buildings in its foundations.

Falsone and Sconzo (2007, 90) regard fortified Jerablus

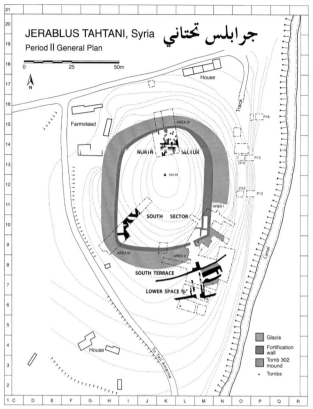

Fig. 7.4 General plan of the Period IIB fort with reconstructed wall and glacis between three exposures

as 'champagne' burials after the high stemmed bowls that proliferated together with metalwork inside the cists. Their character and location shed light on the nature of Carchemish about this time.

Cist graves in context

At least 15 EB I cist graves with uniform assemblages were found on different parts of the Acropolis mound at Carchemish (Woolley and Barnett 1952, 219–226; Falsone and Sconzo 2007). According to the published account, four were on the south-east mound (KCG 1–4), four on the north-east (KCG 6–9) and one on the north-west (KCG 11). In general, Woolley associated them "with the earliest fortification of the mound and the erection on it of official buildings" (Woolley and Barnett 1952, 223). In detail, he was of the opinion that they preceded, were contemporary with and later than the first recovered wall that surrounded the Acropolis. Thus, he states that most were found below the "heavy stratum of mud-brick debris which represents, more or less, the ground-level connected with the building of the first (mud-brick) fortification-wall round the Acropolis," (Woolley and Barnett 1952, 222; see also Woolley 1921, 40). But he also allows that "the lowest are either pre-fortification or contemporary" (Woolley and Barnett 1952, 223, n. 2). Others lie so high or in disturbance that their ground-levels are lost. An apparently late cist, KCG 3 was cut into the brickwork of the sally port, which in turn, was cut through three successive [defensive] walls the last of which precedes or is contemporary with the 'champagne' graves (Woolley and Barnett 1952, 225). Without meaningful sections or dates for the walls, it is not possible to securely relate the graves to the walls or to determine if the cists belonged to a settlement or a cemetery that straddled the Acropolis. Woolley associated them with buildings (Woolley and Barnett 1952, 214-5, 218), Laneri (1999, 232) places them within the walls of the town and Becker (2007, 226) leaves the question open. On the other hand Honça and Algaze (1998, 104) and Palumbi (2007/8, 156) assert the existence of a cemetery, although without stating reasons. Elsewhere, cist graves are characteristic of cemeteries (Cooper 2007).

Palumbi argues that the cist burial custom was derived from the expansion of the Kura-Araks culture where examples may be dated to the last quarter of the 4th millennium (Palumbi 2007/8, 141–149). Stone cists comprise orthostats, that is, slabs placed on edge in an upright position to line a pit or form a box (Fig. 7.5). Mud brick cists are more common in the Jezireh (Valentini 2011, 268). Neither have entrance shafts or portals, since access was usually required only once after which the top was sealed by capping stone(s). Those graves described as cists at Titriş, but with dromoi and entrances to facilitate multiple interments, are best treated as chamber graves, even if their sides are lined

Tahtani as one of a series of military outposts established by Carchemish at about the time of the Palace G archives of Ebla, but the walls of the Jerablus fort, as we have seen, antedate that period by several centuries. Porter (2012, 196), on the other hand, explains the appearance of massive enclosure walls around many small sites in the region as the result of territorial instability following the breakup of the Uruk system. This may have been an added incentive for the fortification of Jerablus Tahtani. Can we be more specific in this instance? The characteristics of the fort are quite out-of-keeping with the modest nature of differently oriented architecture of Area III, Level 7 and its precursors. Because of its size and sophistication, it may be argued that the wall is unlikely to have been created by the local inhabitants, nor is there reason to believe that the mobilisation of pastoralists, a strategy used to explain enormous undertakings at Titriş Höyük, would furnish the necessary planning ability for such an initiative (cf. Algaze *et al.* 2001). If it was not an autonomous development, then the most likely instigator was Carchemish whose assembly or rulers sought greater control of a strategic facility. But was Carchemish so large or powerful then that it could implement such a plan? The only secure, roughly contemporary evidence from the site are pot and cist graves, the latter sometimes referred to

Fig. 7.5 Unopened cist grave 1575 showing the unworked slabs used for the stone 'box'; 50 cm scale

Table 7.2 Contexts of cist burials at Jerablus Tahtani (C: Child)

Grave	Burial	Level	Context
795	C	Area IV unstratified	tell slope
871	C	Area IV unstratified	above Gr 956 of Level 3
1369	C	Area IV. 4?	below surface of tell
1383	C	Area I.3	extra-mural
1575	C	Area IV.5	insecure relationship with buildings
1709	C	Area IV. 4?	insecure relationship with buildings
2375	C	Area II.4	extra-mural
2523	C	Area IV.6	insecure relationship with buildings
2541	C	Area IV.6, below hearth	antedates structure

with uprights (Honça and Algaze 1998). Cists hosted single or, infrequently, multiple interments. Where the evidence is clear, they were used for burials in cemeteries, not within settlements.

An early remarkable example beyond the Kura-Araks core is the isolated "royal tomb" at Arslantepe, ascribed to level VIB2 at the start of the 3rd millennium. Frangipane (2007/8, 176) notes how burials at this time lay outside settlement areas, but the exact date of the "royal tomb" is debated. Porter (2012, 196) allows that it could belong to VIB1, contemporary with the wattle-and-daub structures of a seasonal encampment, Palumbi (2007/8, 150) to between VIB1 and VIB2 when there may have been no settlement at Arslantepe.

Further south in Turkey the cist burial rite first appears during the EB I period as well as later at Nevali Çori, Lidar, Hassek Höyük, Titriş Höyük, Hacınebi, Horum Höyük, Tilbes Höyük, Birecik, Gre Virike and Şeraga Höyük (Becker 2007, 216–224; Hauptmann 1993; Honça and Algaze 1998; Sertok and Ergeç 1999; Palumbi 2007/8, 156–159). The Lidar, Titriş Höyük, Şeraga Höyük, Gre Virike and Birecik cists occur in cemeteries or extra-mural situations. At Horum Höyük they were used for neonates under house floors, a widespread custom normally employing simple pits or pots (Marro et al. 2000, 265). The stratigraphic relationship of cists with habitation areas or ephemeral occupation at the other sites is unclear.

They also occur in diminishing numbers in the Middle Euphrates Valley south of Carchemish. There too, cists are mainly found in cemeteries or in extra-mural situations, as at Amarna, Hammam Kebir, Dja'de el Mughara, Shamseddin, Tell el 'Abd and Tawi (Woolley and Barnett 1952, 224; Cooper 2007, 65, table 4.1; Coqueugniot et al.1998). The context of a possible cist in the city at Tell Banat, Tomb 9, is unclear (McLellan and Porter 1999, 108, 114, fig. 3).

Exceptions include Qara Qûzâq, Tell Ahmar and Jerablus Tahtani. While a preliminary statement concerning Qara Qûzâq refers to early 3rd millennium child burials in small cists under floors (Valdés Pereiro 1999, 120), we have more information on the other two sites.

In the case of Tell Ahmar, some five cists were found in the vicinity of the hypogeum on the mound, some of them apparently cut into walls or in the corner made by walls. It is not possible now to state if they were contemporary with settlement, even if the grave goods are broadly similar in date to those in the hypogeum (Thureau-Dangin and Dunand 1936, 108–110). In more recent excavations, no cists were found amongst the four graves located in rooms adjacent to the hypogeum and most likely contemporary with activities in those rooms (Dugay 2005).

Of the nine cist graves recovered in excavations at Jerablus Tahtani, there were two that could be securely contextualised, and both were extra-mural (Table 7.2). All were reserved for children.

It is clear from these c. 20 sites that the overwhelming majority of cist graves belonged to extra-mural cemeteries and that where they have been recovered from a built environment, relationships have been difficult to establish with certainty. The latter may be graves that belong to a cemetery within a settlement but bearing no relationship to buildings, what Italians refer to as intra-moenia. The difficulty in establishing stratigraphic relationships may often be the result of the erosion of surfaces from which the graves were cut. Where there are potential intra-mural relationships, as at Horum Höyük and Jerablus Tahtani, interments are confined to children or neonates.

This brief survey of cist graves in Euphrates valley sites in Turkey and Syria indicates that cists normally belong to cemeteries. The exception is the use of cists for neonates or small children buried under house floors. Apart from two unusually small cists at Carchemish, KCG 1 and 2 (av. length 1.05 m), the others with published measurements have an average length of 1.88 m, more suitable for adults. Woolley reports the presence of adults and these are typical of cemeteries or, as at Arslantepe and perhaps Hassek Höyük (Behm-Blancke et al. 1981, 49–51), in more isolated positions. Where the burial rite has altered from a single-to a multiple-burial system for adults below house floors, the cists require entrance passages and doorways, and they are more usually referred to as chambers. There are no indications of entrance passages or portals in the published descriptions and illustrations of cist graves at Carchemish (Woolley and Barnett 1952, 218–222, fig. 85, pl. 56a), hence they were not designed to facilitate repeated entrance as befits mausolea in houses as at Titriş and later at sites like Ugarit (Honça and Algaze 1998; Salles 1995).

Annexation or independence?

If the Acropolis accommodated a cemetery and so was at least partly uninhabited at the time of the cist graves, we might infer that Carchemish was not a powerful centre then. Its post-Uruk development may mirror that of Arslantepe which went from an urban centre with Uruk connections to a burial place (Frangipane 2007/8). Settlement at Hacınebi also followed the same pattern in becoming a burial ground during EB I (see Chapter 4). Most cists at Carchemish are dated to EB I/EME (Early Middle Euphrates period) 1–2, that is, *c.* 3100–2750/2700, with a preference for *c.* 3000–2800 BC (Gerber 2000, 244; Becker 2007, 83, fig. 43; Falsone and Sconzo 2007, 78; Sertok 2007, 241–2).

As mentioned above, calibrated radiocarbon dates for the destruction of Jerablus Tahtani IIA and the building of the fort place the events *c.* 2825–2720 at 68% probability (Peltenburg *et al.* 2015). While the comparative chronology allows for both options considered here, namely, independent fortification or seizure by Carchemish, there is perhaps slightly more scope in the date ranges for the installation of a defensive wall soon after the cist grave horizon at Carchemish. A critical argument in favour of a Carchemish takeover hypothesis in the 28th century BC is the evidence for destruction together with continuity of material culture at Jerablus. The last settlement prior to the construction of the fort was destroyed and burnt, and there is no recognizable gap in ceramics, stratigraphy or radiocarbon dates between the settlement and earliest levels of the fort. That destruction tends to rule out an internal, peaceful transformation of the site and to favour hostile action. Also, the continuity of local ceramics between the settlement and fort implies local actors. One possible conclusion from this limited evidence is that an emergent centre of power at Carchemish forcibly incorporated its strategic neighbour and created a strong secondary centre to secure its immediate hinterland, the agriculturally rich Jerablus Plain, as well as an important river crossing.

Since its outpost was provided with enclosing walls and glacis, surely Carchemish itself must have been walled now, like such sites as Early Jezireh period (hereafter EJ) 0-1 Tell Chuēra (Meyer 2011, 129–130). Indeed, it could be argued that the expertise and labour for the unified fort

plan described above involved central administration from Carchemish. Presumably only the Acropolis mound was enclosed in the 28th century, not the Inner Town with its imposing ramparts, even if structural features are common to both sites. It has yet to be established if the development seen at Jerablus Tahtani, where an emerging centre such as Carchemish created a small strong outpost, was repeated elsewhere in the region, so perhaps accounting for references in the later Ebla texts to a proliferation of small forts in this borderland (Peltenburg 2013).

The Carchemish trajectory of centre-and-outpost bears similarities to developments in the Khabur, an area previously considered distinct from the Euphrates valley. Porter (2012, 178) has drawn attention to close correspondences amongst single room shrines, or "houses for the ancestors" in both regions, some located in specialized small sites along the mid-Khabur. These Ninevite 5 sites form a network that appeared about the same time as the introduction of the fort at Jerablus Tahtani (Akkermans and Schwartz 2003, 218–224). Some had enclosure walls with an additional glacis as at EJ 2 Rad Shaqrah, a site slightly larger than Jerablus Tahtani. At Tell Raqa'i Level 4, a Rounded Building was imposed on the site, and it seems to have been largely reserved for grain storage. So impressive are the fortified enclosure walls, glacis and platforms that, in the absence of a nearby major centre, Schwartz (1994, 30–31) believes outside architects and brick-layers from a distant complex polity were involved, in the manner suggested for Jerablus Tahtani above. Most other sites of the network were also devoted to grain storage, to such an extent that questions have been raised about the purpose of these sites in a marginal environment. Porter (2012, 226–227) believes that they were pilgrimage sites that wrought ties between mobile and sedentary components of society by collecting and redistributing grain. Hole suggests storage for pastoralists in the region, and Pfälzner contends that they were community storage facilities for local households (Pfälzner 2002). In support of his proposal that Raqa'i is an outpost, Schwartz points to the enclosure walls and the presence of administrative technology:

> "the specialized activities of the middle Khabur sites were conducted for the benefit of elites based at larger centres outside the middle Khabur, who collected agricultural surpluses to support their dependent personnel." (Schwartz 1994, 28; cf. Meyer 2011, 135)

The non-local and pastoralist are compatible perspectives, but for our purposes, the appearance of small, enclosed, specialised sites at some distance from larger centres and before fully fledged urbanization is significant. The phenomenon may be part of a broader pattern. Small, walled sites with features similar to those in the Middle Khabur also occur to the north-west of Hasseke, and Schwartz (1994, 29) notes other small specialized communities in the Hamrin, considered by some to be military outposts, but also for the storage of grain.

If the Middle Khabur and other small sites are regarded as outposts for the provision of distant emerging urban centres, then the Carchemish pairing of centre-and-outpost is far from unique. It is unlikely to have catered exclusively for pastoralists. The key evidential difference is the destruction that precedes the establishment of the fort at Jerablus Tahtani, since it would appear that no such destructive context is linked to the establishment of the small places in the Jezireh and Hamrin regions. What remains strikingly similar is that these small establishments appeared before urbanization and with only the slightest signs of complex societies with elites, attached specialists and central bureaucracies in northern Mesopotamia at that time.

During initial stages of urban formation in many parts of Mesopotamia, the populations of villages and hamlets in their immediate environs were absorbed into the growing centres and land was intensively farmed from the central settlement (e.g. Algaze 1999, 548; Ur *et al.* 2011, 8; Wilkinson 1994, 488). Commuting distances to fields are usually thought of as some 3-4 km unless "some very powerful constraining reason...prevents the establishment of farmsteads nearer the land" (Adams 1981, 87, quoting Chisholm). In our case, cultivable land around Carchemish was skewed to its south, to the Jerablus Plain, so necessitating a presence beyond the 3–4 km commute. Thus, there were compelling reasons to maintain a strong presence in such a strategic locale (above), especially if it is shown that the pervasive occurrence of fortified settlements in the Middle Euphrates Valley was due to endemic rivalry that necessitated the protection of vital resources (*cf.* Peltenburg 2013).

The proposal that a polity, in this case Carchemish, established overt control of its immediate hinterland is one that researchers often equate with integrative dynamics characteristic of emerging states and urbanization. Control might be exercised by tribute, alliance or force. There are several models of rural-centre interaction at the time of urban growth, ranging from centres maximizing outputs by "siphoning off as many assets as possible, while stopping short of undermining rural infrastructure" (Schwartz and Falconer 1994, 3), to urban or state elites taking over an independent community to administer it directly (Hayden 1994, 203). In our case, a complete transformation took place, one in which a corporately structured village was fortified, perhaps as an outpost of Carchemish.

In spite of these models, the implication that Carchemish was an emerging urban or state polity in the 28th century BC is unwarranted. Indeed, there are counter-arguments that urbanization did not take place in the Middle Euphrates Valley at any time in the 3rd millennium (*e.g.* Frangipane 2010, 82). We have few indications of socio-political structures of the earlier part of that millennium, but what exist are clearly out of keeping with the presence of urban elites and institutions of state. Although graves are rich in metal, the material is evenly spread (Squadrone 2007). An exception is grave L.12 at Qara Qûzâq, located near a temple (Valdés Pereiro 1999, 120–121). The association suggests that ritual authority was important at this time, a conclusion supported by the recurrence of shrines (Porter 2012, 178–185). Even if these very modest buildings are rather interpreted as village reception halls, they represent the most elaborate non-domestic buildings of the period (Morandi Bonacossi 2000, 1109). Mortuary and architectural evidence, therefore, point to the existence of limited complexity rather than stratified polities. It should be noted, however, that conquest and control of local labour existed in complex rank societies, even if the creation of a fort like Jerablus Tahtani might be regarded as an unusually elaborate example (*e.g.* Earle 1991, 6–8). Control of the countryside, therefore, may precede urbanization and state formation.

The alternative interpretation is that the fort was an autonomous development, with preceding destruction attributed to internal upheaval. Centralisation, architectural and planning sophistication and mobilisation of considerable labour are all innovatory characteristics unattested in earlier Period IIA levels of the site. But rather than see these as indicative of non-local transformations, it could be argued that to do so underestimates the capabilities of political figures in ranked societies to initiate large projects, attract labour from kin, some from archaeologically less visible pastoralist groups, and to pool skills in substantial co-operative works. The rapidity of the transformation may point to the charismatic authority of central persons, and the continued embellishment of the fort may herald the creation of an established elite. There are many instances of massive works undertaken by rank and other non-hierarchical societies (*e.g.* the megalithic monuments on North-west Europe), and more local examples exist of pre-urban large-scale building programmes. They include the 52.4 m^3 White Monument at Tell Banat and, more relevant, regional fortification systems that may have served as models to be emulated. Early 3rd millennium examples antedating Jerablus Tahtani include those at Tilbeshar (Kepinski 2007, 152–153), Habuba Kabira, Halawa B (Cooper 2006, 71) and Tell es-Sweyhat, now with radiocarbon dates (Danti and Zettler 2007, 177–179).

In support of her argument for a more heterarchical organization of Middle Euphrates Valley polities, Cooper (2006, 86–88) points to the segmented structure of the fortification walls, as if carried out by individual groups. It is a structural feature also noted at Jerablus Tahtani, and one that is consistent with the participatory communal labour inferred for the autonomous construction of the fort at Jerablus Tahtani. This alternative interpretation, therefore, is like Pfälzner's hypothesis for the independent capabilities of the inhabitants of the analogous Middle Khabur sites mentioned above (Pfälzner 2002).

Whichever hypothesis proves to be correct, annexation or independence, developments at Jerablus Tahtani demonstrate that the region of Carchemish underwent major social, economic and military transformations in the 28th century BC.

Intensification of production

The date of urbanization of Carchemish is vigorously debated. Pointing to its lowly status and infrequent mention in the Ebla texts, Bunnens (2007, 44–46) argues that it was still a minor centre of some 4 ha in the 24th century BC. Some time ago, Parr (1968) noted the similarity of its ramparts to MB II examples and dated the expansion of the site to 40 ha to that period. Following Parr's MB preference, Marchetti attributes the ramparts to shortly after or around 2000 BC (Marchetti 2012, 133, 141, fig. 19). The difficulty stems from early excavators' limited and very imprecise chronological data from the Inner Town and its massive ramparts. After reviewing this and other relevant evidence Algaze tentatively suggested that initial urbanization took place towards the end of the 3rd millennium (Algaze 1999, 552–553, 556, table 4). Subsequently, Falsone and Sconzo (2007) were able to demonstrate the existence of architecture of the second half of the 3rd millennium in the Inner Town. They concluded that the Inner Town existed by the time of the Ebla archives, a date supported by the inferred origin of EB pottery some 400–450 m from the Acropolis mound (Peltenburg 2010, 540; see Lawrence and Ricci, Chapter 4, this volume). There is circumstantial evidence, therefore, for occupation in the Inner Town during the later 3rd millennium BC (cf. Wilkinson *et al.* 2012, 144, table 2). If this extended to the ramparts, and the area so defined was inhabited at a nominal 100 persons per ha, then Jerablus Tahtani fell inside its catchment zone, as shown schematically by the larger "B" semicircle in Figure 7.6.

Models of large-scale population expansion, as we have seen, lead to the expectation of intensification of production and enhanced storage and processing equipment in the hinterlands of the central polity in order to meet the subsistence and other demands of the centre (*e.g.* Redman 1978, 216). In this case, a growing Carchemish would have been the driver for the changes at rural subsidiaries and above all at its adjunct, Jerablus Tahtani. While it was a supplier of impressive amounts of grain to Mari in Old Babylonian times (Durand 2011; Michel 1996, 393), it is doubtful that Carchemish had to provide grain as tribute earlier, when it was "in the hands" of Ebla. But it did send textiles, so there may have been pressure to produce additional barley for fodder for wool-bearing sheep (Lacambre and Tunca 1999, 591). The evidence from the Jerablus Tahtani Period IIB fort is consistent with such models, if not as full as is desirable. It includes frequency data from rubber and quern disposals,

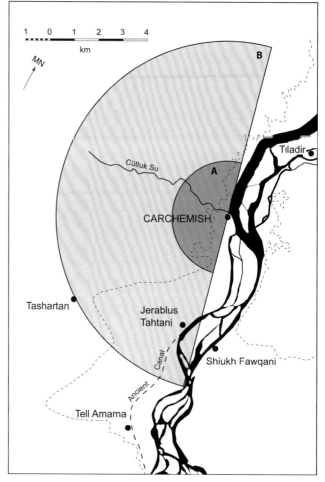

Fig. 7.6 Carchemish site catchment area on right bank of Euphrates River. A: area assumes occupation was confined to the Acropolis mound; B: area assumes occupation extended to the ramparts of the Inner Town. Note: this is a schematic rendering that does not take account of topographical restrictions on cultivable land in the north of the semicircle

special storage facilities, charred grain occurrences and increased numbers of administrative devices.

Area IV in the North Sector of the fort (Fig. 7.4) is a *c.* 150 m² cut through eight architectural levels. Levels 3–8 belong to the fort of Period IIB, c. 2825/2720–2250 BC. Rubbers and querns for grain processing occurred in each of these levels, starting with eight at the bottom. These are mostly spent rather than *in situ* tools, hence we are dealing with discard behaviour. Assuming that the behaviour did not change through those centuries, then the discard rate serves as a proxy for intensity of use of these vesicular basalt tools and by implication, potential changes in production rates. A total of 193 rubbers and querns were recovered from six levels. Discard was not at a steady pace. Figure 7.7 shows a gradual increase in Levels 8–5 followed by a steep rise in Level 4, much of it dated to the 24th century BC. Almost

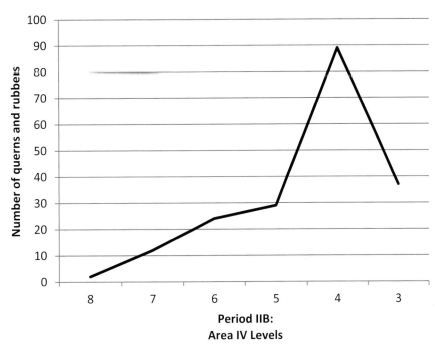

Fig. 7.7 Incidence of stone querns and rubbers in the fort levels of Area IV

half (46%) of the total were recovered from this level. Three contextual factors need to be borne in mind here. First, Level 4 was only preserved over half the area, the rest being denuded in tell slope erosion. Second, Level 3, which shows a marked depositional decline in Figure 7.7, only remained intact in a quarter of Area IV, hence the reduction may not have been as severe as shown. Lastly, for inter-level comparisons to be meaningful, each level should represent an equal block of time. The chronological controls are not refined enough to determine this, but Levels 3 and 4 contain only minor refurbishments to buildings, hence they do not represent a disproportionately lengthy period. The striking increase in Level 4 rubber and quern discards attests to the existence of a specialised crop processing area in the North Sector of the fort, one that could be interpreted in at least two ways. It may suggest that intensification of production was beyond the needs of local consumption, that it was organized for regional economies and that Carchemish probably played a determining role in its expansion. On the other hand, high discard/use rates may relate to local processing, and low rates to times when grain was transported to Carchemish for processing. The latter would have involved increased transport costs, but in either case the evidence points to intensified grain production and processing in the 24th century BC.

Grain storage facilities were incorporated within the limited confines of the small fort by using casemates within the fort wall (Fig. 7.8). Cells contained some charred grain and large amounts of straw-like silicates. In one

Fig. 7.8 Area I casemate room 1569 with two cell-like facilities below its floor; 50 cm scale.

case, the grain seems to have been introduced through an aperture that sloped into a room from inside the fort. Time prevented excavation of further stretches of wall here, but in comparable silo architecture in middle Khabur sites of the 3rd millennium, similar installations are repeated, so it is possible that more silos were embedded in the walls of the fort at Jerablus Tahtani (*cf.* Akkermans and Schwartz 2003, 218–221). As they formed part of the fabric of these walls, the cells were specialised, official facilities rather than domestic ones. They occur in an extension to the fort, hence they were not constructed in its earliest phases but were added when there was a need to expand facilities. The excavated sample is too small to allow estimates of the fort's storage capacity.

Preliminary analyses of archaeobotanical samples confirm the more specialised processing of barley in later levels of the fort (Murray 1996, 20–21). In pre-fort deposits, various cereals from processing wastes are typical, amongst them barley, emmer, einkorn, the free-threshing cereals, chaff, wild grasses and weeds. Inside the later fort, in Area IV Level 4 where there was such an abundance of rubbers and querns, samples were made up almost entirely of barley grains. Two samples are not the usual sieving wastes, but a cleaner product nearer the end of the crop-processing sequence. In this case, it is suggested that clean grain was brought here for final processing. Thus, intensification of specialised production occurred in later phases of the fort occupation, with different stages of barley production especially taking place in discrete localities.

Adams (1966, 46) argued that, in order to organise and account for various stages of production and exacted surpluses from villages, elites at urban centres needed institutional structures. If the fort was an appendage of Carchemish whose output was largely geared to the provisioning of that polity, then all the more reason to expect the presence of administrative devices. Seals, sealings and impressed jars are examples of appropriate mechanisms to control production, storage, transport and distribution (Fig. 7.9). Impressions occur on a variety of carriers, but the significant factors are that all but one come from Period IIB, the period of the fort, and that they occur with increased frequency during its later levels (McCarthy 2007).

Considered as a reflection of the expanding needs of nearby Carchemish, this combined evidence from the fort at Jerablus Tahtani points to the existence of a significant growth of population at Carchemish by the third quarter of the 3rd millennium BC. The abrupt increase of rubber and quern discards shown in Figure 7.7 is striking in this context. If caused by the pace and organisation of population growth at Carchemish, it suggests a sudden increase in demand in the 24th century, one consistent with a model of rapid population increments. Such rapidity is attested elsewhere. At Titriş, the process of urbanisation seems to have been a carefully planned operation by a central administration

0   2cm

Fig. 7.9 Cylinder seal impression on rim of storage jar, IT 3600, from Area II Level 5

whereby some streets, for example, were neatly laid out prior to the establishment of houses (Algaze 1999, 549–550). Its size increased through large scale redevelopment to some 43 ha. Elsewhere, in the Jezireh and Khabur regions, 3rd millennium urbanization is frequently seen as a rapid process, one that involved the mobilisation of considerable labour for the construction of massive city walls (*e.g.* Ur 2010, 404; but *cf.* Meyer 2011). Major sites such as Tell Leilan, Tell Mozan and Hamoukar grew from 15 ha to as much as 120 ha within a century (Ur 2010, 405). In other words, wherever the population was derived from, the initial emergence of urban centres in Upper Mesopotamia was often a deliberately planned transformation involving marked agglomeration of settlement. Evidence from grain production equipment and the palaeobotanical record of Jerablus Tahtani supports a similar reconstruction for Carchemish in the 24th century BC.

Major flood events during the 3rd millennium

Like Carchemish, 3rd millennium sites from the Enesh gorge south clustered along the Pleistocene terraces that flanked the Euphrates River. Overbank intrusions from the river have been found at several of these sites, from Ubaid times through the 3rd millennium. Those at Jerablus Tahtani have been considered elsewhere, so here we need only summarize the main aspects that may have had an impact on Carchemish (*cf.* Peltenburg 2007).

Outside the southern wall of the fort and a projecting built terrace, lay a high status above-ground tomb, T. 302. Its encasing mound was repeatedly gouged away by floods that left major channels filled with river gravels. Labourers constantly repaired the damage by laying more mound material over the channels. The wider significance of these events derives from the abnormally high levels of these flood waters. Earlier on, flood deposits occurred at much lower levels, so this represents more severe river instability. The highest preserved channel within the T. 302 mound reached a minimum of *c.* 3.20 m above the flat EB ground surface surrounding the tell, so that at times the site became an island. More investigations are needed to confirm this evidence, but taken at face value, flood waters must have covered significant parts of the flat Jerablus Plain. In all likelihood, this occurred during Euphrates spring high water as a result of upriver snow melt. We have seen that the dominant crop in the palaeobotanical record from the latest EB levels is barley. It ripens in May-June, and so was highly vulnerable when these floods took place. Since agricultural produce from the plain formed a mainstay of the subsistence needs of Carchemish, the population of that centre must have felt the impact of such misfortune.

The dating of these extraordinary flood events may be inferred from the history of the tomb. Two stratigraphically distinct use phases separated by a filling phase were detected in its main chamber. Phase 1 consisted of multiple interments followed by desecration in which the roof was dismantled. In Phase 3 people inserted commemorative deposits without burials high up in the main chamber. Any roofing then was probably ephemeral. Mound maintenance, as described above, preceded desecration. Once the roof was removed, the mound was allowed to erode into the main chamber together with domestic refuse during Phase 2. Radiocarbon dates indicate a range of 2400–2600 cal BC for Phase 1, so it is probable that major flooding of the Jerablus Plain took place during the mid-3rd millennium BC.

We may legitimately infer that unpredictable yields from its main catchment area affected the political economy of Carchemish at that time. No doubt coping measures were taken to mitigate the effects of these adverse conditions since, as far as we know, Carchemish continued to be occupied and over the long term to grow in importance. Communities under stress can react in a variety of ways. It may be that more flexible strategies were adopted such as recourse to safer, upland resources including hillside vinyards, ones that perhaps led to its valued wine production in the MBA (Michel 1996, 387–388). Alternatively, the impact may have hampered its growth and hence help to account for its relatively lowly status in the ensuing Ebla archive. Clearly, information on the nature of the impact on Carchemish requires investigation at the site itself or textual documentation.

Abandonment of Jerablus Tahtani

In an earlier consideration of the abandonment of Jerablus Tahtani in the last quarter of the 3rd millennium, I noted a rough correlation with flooding of the space outside its South Terrace and consequently the environs of the site (Peltenburg 2007, 254–258). While flooding may still have been a contributory factor, further analysis of the flood evidence in T. 302, the principal context for fluvial sediment deposition, has weakened the evidential connection (Peltenburg 2015). A shown above, it is now clear that flood repairs to the funerary mound took place only in Phase 1

and that the mound was allowed to erode into the tomb main chamber prior to Phase 3. Thus, direct evidence for the latest inundation ceases after Phase 1, well before the site was abandoned. Clearly, the community was sufficiently resilient for it to persist at the site after these flood events.

Bayesian modelling of Period IIB ^{14}C dates indicates that the site was abandoned *c.* 2270–2155 cal BC at 68% probability (Peltenburg 2015). Pottery from the latest Period IIB graves on the site has multiple correspondences with EME 4–5 pottery elsewhere, but the virtual absence of diagnostic EME 5 types like the collared-rim cup suggests that, stylistically at least, the fort did not extend far into EME 5 (*cf.* Sconzo 2015). It was probably abandoned earlier within the radiocarbon range, therefore, about the time of the destructions of Ebla and Mari or a little later according to Sallaberger's reduced Middle Chronology (Sallaberger 2011, 332–333). The final levels lack destruction evidence or artefacts in primary discard positions, suggesting that this was a planned abandonment.

Since Jerablus Tahtani was so closely related to Carchemish it is likely that its inhabitants went to that neighbour. The desertion is in contrast to occupational histories of sites beyond the 4–5 km radius of Carchemish (cf. Wilkinson *et al.* 2012, 164). Amarna, 10 km away at the south end of the Jerablus Plain, for example, continued to be occupied (Pons 2001). Secondary centres like 12 ha Tilader on the left bank of the Euphrates (Fig. 7.6) even seem to have grown at this time (Algaze *et al.* 1994, 15). This pattern is consistent with urbanization processes elsewhere. Adams (1981, 82–84) noted village implosion and centripetal forces in a radius of 5 km around emergent urban centres in South Mesopotamia. Similar changes are also recorded to the north, at Titriş and to the east at Tell el-Hawa where there was no settlement of any size within 4 km radius upon urbanization (Algaze 1999, 548; Wilkinson 1994, 488). Algaze's survey to the north of Carchemish indicates a short-lived major increase in sites and occupied area beyond the 5 km radius, a variation on the increases in site sizes throughout the more integrated systems at Leilan and Titriş at the time of urbanization (Algaze *et al.* 1994, 14–17; Algaze 1999, 548; Stein 1994, 14). It would seem likely, therefore, that the urbanization of Carchemish took place by the last quarter of the 3rd millennium BC, rather later than at most sites belonging to the so-called 'second urban revolution' in northern Mesopotamia (Akkermans and Schwartz 2003, 233–287).

The abandonment of Jerablus Tahtani may be part of a long-term development in the Middle Euphrates Valley. Presumably elites of Carchemish felt powerful enough in the final centuries of the 3rd millennium to control the immediate area to their south without the support of an outlier. This process of nucleation foreshadows developments in the MBA when more centralized political control at Carchemish entailed aggregation at the centre, a decline in settlement numbers regionally and use of outlying forts as a means of territorial control (Peltenburg 2010, 543–544).

Conclusions

It is argued that developments at Jerablus Tahtani and Carchemish in the 3rd millennium were closely intertwined because of the proximity of the two sites, with no intervening physical barriers, the relatively broad agricultural lands around Jerablus Tahtani in contrast to the circumscribed potentials in the immediate vicinity of Carchemish and the strategic location of Jerablus Tahtani for communications. Four key developments at Jerablus Tahtani were examined, all confirming the existence of a heterogeneous countryside rather than one populated by uniform villages, and that small sites were subject to radical transformations during the 3rd millennium BC.

Text-free archaeology is poorly equipped to identify the authors of specific actions such as the creation of a heavily walled fort at Jerablus Tahtani. Two possibilities are considered here. The first is that Carchemish was responsible, even if there is no compelling evidence that it comprised a state or urban entity at that time. In favour of this hypothesis are the burnt deposits intercalated between the last buildings of Period IIA and the foundations of the Period IIB fort, the lack of any discernible time gap between the two, so suggesting a causal link, the continuity of local ceramics, and the impressive construction. The second possibility is that it was an autonomous initiative. Reasons were given for not under-estimating the ability of small-scale society to undertake elaborate, labour intensive projects. This would imply that Carchemish remained a minor centre in the mid-3rd millennium and that the intensification of production and storage at Jerablus Tahtani was for surplus production for local exchange purposes. In this autonomous scenario, the subsequent abandonment of the site during the 23rd century BC might signal a time when Carchemish began to exercise unchallenged authority in its supporting area, leading to "urban implosion" (cf. Adams 1981, 82–84). There is no magic threshold at which point we can recognize urban status, but it may be no coincidence that the abandonment of Jerablus Tahtani occurred at about the same time as the destruction of Ebla. This must have led to greater instability in its sphere of influence, including the region around Carchemish, and such re-configuration of power may have freed the elites of Carchemish who had previously been in the hands of Ebla to implement independent expansionary policies. That did not necessarily translate into inter-regional political power, however, since it did not even figure as a second rank centre in Ur III texts pertaining to northern Mesopotamia (Sallaberger 2007, 434–441).

Obviously, inferences for the history of Carchemish from the four Jerablus Tahtani developments outlined here need to be tested against evidence from Carchemish itself or textual documentation, but hopefully they furnish researchers with tangible lines of enquiry worth pursuing.

Acknowledgements

Grateful acknowledgement is tendered to all those who generously supported the excavations at Jerablus Tahtani, especially the British Academy, the British Museum, the Council for British Research in the Levant and the Jennie S. Gordon Memorial Foundation. I am grateful to Tony Wilkinson for helpful comments on this paper. Photos: Edgar Peltenburg; Fig. 7.4: Lindy Crewe.

Bibliography

Adams, R. (1966) *The Evolution of Urban Society: Early Mesopotamia and Prehispanic Mexico*. Chicago IL, Aldine.

Adams, R. (1981) *Heartland of Cities:Surveys of Ancient Settlement and Land Use on the Central Floodplain of the Euphrates*. Chicago IL, University of Chicago Press.

Akkermans, P. and Schwartz, G. (2003) *The Archaeology of Syria: From Complex Hunter Gatherers to Early Urban Societies (ca. 16,000–300 BC)*. Cambridge, Cambridge University Press.

Algaze, G. (1999) Trends in the archaeological development of the Upper Euphrates Basin of South-eastern Anatolia during the Late Chalcolithic and Early Bronze Ages. In G. del Olmo Lete and J.-L. Montero Fenollós (eds) *Archaeology of the Upper Syrian Euphrates, the Tishrin Dam area: proceedings of the International Symposium held at Barcelona, January 28th–30th 1998*, 535–572. Aula Orientalis-Supplement 15. Barcelona, AUSA.

Algaze, G., Breuninger, R. and Knudstad, J. (1994) The Tigris-Euphrates Archaeological Reconnaissance Project, final report of the Birecik and Carchemish Dam survey areas. *Anatolica* 20, 1–96.

Algaze, G., Dinckan, G., Hartenberger, B., Matney, T., Pournelle, J., Rainville, L., Rosen, S., Rupley, E., Schlee, D. and Vallet, R. (2001) Research at Titris Höyük in Southeastern Turkey: the 1999 season. *Anatolica* 27, 23–106.

Archi, A. (1990) Imâr au IIIeme millénaire d'après les archives d'Ebla. *MARI* 6, 21–38.

Bachelot, L. and Fales, F. M. (eds) (2005) *Tell Shiukh Fawqani 1994–1998*. History of the Ancient Near East Monograph VI (1–2). Padova, S.A.R.G.O.N.

Becker, J.A. (2007) *Nevali Çori. Keramik und Kleinfunde der Halaf unf Frühbronzezeit.* Mainz am Rhein, Von Zabern.

Behm-Blancke, M., Becker, H. Boessneck, J., von den Driesch, A., Hoh, M.R. and Wiegand, G. (1981) Hassek Höyük, Vorläufiger Bericht über die Ausgrabungen den Jahren 1978–1980. *Istanbuler Mitteilungen* 31, 5–93.

Boese, J. (2006) Karkemisch A. D. 1699: Die älteste Stadtplan und ein "barocker" Löwe. *Mitteilungen der Deutschen Orient-Gesellshaft zu Berlin* 138, 43–55.

Bunnens, G. (2007) Site hierarchy in the Tishrin Dam area and third millennium geopolitics in Northern Syria. In E. Peltenburg (ed.)

Euphrates River Valley Settlement. The Carchemish Sector in the Third Millennium BC, 43–54, Levant Supplementary Series 5. Oxford, Oxbow Books.

Coqueugniot, E.A.J., Montero Fenollós, J.-L. and Anfruns, J. (1998) Une tombe du Bronze ancien à Dja'de el Mughara (Moyen Euphrate, Syrie). In J. Cauvin (ed.) *Cahiers de l'Euphrate* 8, 85–114. Paris, Éditions Recherche sur les Civilisations.

Cooper, L. (2006) *Early Urbanism on the Syrian Euphrates*. London, Routledge.

Cooper, L. (2007) Early Bronze Age burial types and social-cultural identity within the Northern Euphrates Valley. In E. Peltenburg (ed.) *Euphrates River Valley Settlement. The Carchemish Sector in the Third Millennium BC*, 55–70. Levant Supplementary Series 5. Oxford, Oxbow Books.

Danti, M. and Zettler, R. (2007) The Early Bronze Age in the Syrian north-west Jezireh: the Tell es-Sweyhat region. In E. Peltenburg (ed.) *Euphrates River Valley Settlement. The Carchemish Sector in the Third Millennium BC*, 164–183. Levant Supplementary Series 5. Oxford, Oxbow Books.

Dugay, L. (2005) Early Bronze Age Burials from Tell Ahmar. In P. Talon and V. Van der Stede (eds) *Si un homme ... textes offerts en hommage à André Finet*, 37–50. Subartu 16. Turnhout, Brepols.

Durand, J.-M. (2011) Le commerce entre Imâr et Mari sur l'Euphrate. Un nouvel exemple du début du règne de Zimrî-Lîm. *Revue d'assyriologie et d'archéologie orientale* 105, 181–192.

Earle, T. (1991) The evolution of chiefdoms. In T. Earle (ed.) *Chiefdoms: Power, Economy and Ideology*, 1–15. Cambridge, Cambridge University Press.

Einwag, B. (1993) Vorbericht über die archäologische Geländegehung in der Westgazira. *Damaszener Mitteilungen* 7, 23–42.

Falsone, G. and Sconzo, P. (2007) The 'champagne-cup' period at Carchemish. A review of the Early Bronze Age levels on the Acropolis Mound and the problem of the Inner Town. In E. Peltenburg (ed.) *Euphrates River Valley Settlement. The Carchemish Sector in the Third Millennium BC*, 73–93. Levant Supplementary Series 5. Oxford, Oxbow Books.

Frangipane, M. (2007/8) The Arslantepe "royal tomb": new funerary customs and political change in the Upper Euphrates Valley at the beginning of the third millennium BC. In G. Bartoloni and M.G. Benedettini (eds) *Sepolti tra i vivi. Evidenza ed interpretazione di contesti funerari in abitato. Atti del Convegno Internazionale (Università degli Studi di Roma "La Sapienza" 26–29 Aprile 2006)*, Scienze dell'Antichità 14 (1), 169–193.

Frangipane, M. (2010) Different models of power structuring at the rise of hierarchical societies in the Near East: primary economy versus luxury and defence management. In D. Bolger and L. Maguire (eds) *The Development of Pre-state Communities in the Ancient Near East. Studies in honour of Edgar Peltenburg*, 79–86. Oxford, Oxbow Books.

Gerber, J. (2000) *Hassek Höyük III. Die frühbronzezeitlichen Keramik*. Istanbuler Forschungen Band 47. Tübingen, Ernst Wasmuth.

Hauptmann, H. (1993) Vier Jahrtausende Siedlungsgeschichte am mittleren Euphrat. *Archäologie in Deutschland* 1, 10–15.

Hawkins, J. D. (1976–80) Karkamiš. *Reallexikon der Assyriologie und Vorderasiatische Archäologie* 5, 426–446.

Hayden, B. (1994) Village approaches to complex societies. In G. Schwartz and S. Falconer (eds) *Archaeological Views from the Countryside. Village Communities in Early Complex Societies*, 198–206. Washington DC, Smithsonian Institution Press.

Honça, M. and Algaze, G. (1998) Preliminary report on the human skeletal remains at Titris Höyük: 1991–1996 seasons. *Anatolica* 24, 101–139.

Kepinski, C. (2007) Dynamics, diagnostic criteria and settlement patterns in the Carchemish area during the Early Bronze period. In E. Peltenburg (ed.) *Euphrates River Valley Settlement. The Carchemish Sector in the Third Millennium BC*, 152–163. Levant Supplementary Series 5. Oxford, Oxbow Books.

Lacambre, D. and Tunca, Ö. (1999) Histoire de la vallée de l'Euphrate entre le barrage de Tišrīn et Karkemiš aux IIIe et IIe millénaires av. J.-C. In G. del Olmo Lete and J.-L. Montero Fenollós (eds) *Archaeology of the Upper Syrian Euphrates, the Tishrin Dam area: proceedings of the International Symposium held at Barcelona, January 28th–30th 1998*, 587–603. Aula Orientalis-Supplement 15. Barcelona AUSA.

Laneri, N. (1999) Intramural tombs. A funerary tradition of the Middle Euphrates valley during the 3rd millennium BC. *Anatolica* 25, 221–241.

Lawrence, M.R. (ed.) (1955) *The Home Letters of T. E. Lawrence and his Brothers*. Oxford, Blackwell.

Marchetti, N. (2012) Karkemish on the Euphrates. Excavating a city's history. *Near Eastern Archaeology* 75, 132–147.

Marchetti, N. (ed.) (2014) *Karkemish. An Ancient Capital of the Euphrates*. OrientLab 2. Bologna, Ante Quem.

Marro, C., Tibet, A. and Bulgan, F. (2000) Fouilles de sauvetage de Horum Höyük (province de Gaziantep): quatrième rapport préliminaire. *Anatolia Antiqua* 8, 257–278.

McCarthy, A. (2007) Is there a Carchemish regional glyptic style? Reflections on sealing practices in the northern Euphrates region. In E. Peltenburg (ed.) *Euphrates River Valley Settlement. The Carchemish Sector in the Third Millennium BC*, 214–221. Levant Supplementary Series 5. Oxford, Oxbow Books.

McClellan, T. and Porter, A. (1999) Survey of Excavations at Tell Banat: Funerary Practices. In G. del Olmo Lete and J.-L. Montero Fenollós (eds) *Archaeology of the Upper Syrian Euphrates, the Tishrin Dam area: proceedings of the International Symposium held at Barcelona, January 28th–30th 1998*, Aula Orientalis Supplement 15, 107–116. Barcelona, AUSA.

Meyer, J.-W. (2011) City planning. In M. Lebeau (ed.) *ARCANE I. Jezirah*, 129–136. Turnhout, Brepols.

Michel, C. (1996) Le commerce dans les textes de Mari. In J.-M. Durand (ed.) *Amurru I. Mari, Ebla et les Hourrites. Actes du colloque international (Paris, mai 1993)*, 385–426. Paris, Éditions Recherches sur les Civilisations.

Morandi Bonacossi, D. (2000) The beginning of the Early Bronze Age at Tell Shiukh Fawqani (Tishreen Dam Area) and in the Upper Syrian Euphrates Valley. In P. Matthiae, A. Enea, L. Peyronel and F. Pinnock (eds) *Proceedings of the First International Congress of the Archaeology of the Ancient Near East*, 1105–1123. Rome, Università degli Studi di Roma "La Sapienza".

Murray, M. (1996) Preliminary archaeobotanical report, 1995.

In E. Peltenburg, D. Bolger, S. Campbell, M. Murray and R. Tipping, Jerablus-Tahtani, Syria, 1995: preliminary report. *Levant* 28, 20–21.

Palumbi, G. (2007/8) From collective burials to symbols of power. The transition of role and meanings of the stone-lined cist burial tradition from Southern Caucasus to the Euphrates Valley. In G. Bartoloni and M.G. Benedettini (eds) *Sepolti tra i vivi. Evidenza ed interpretazione di contesti funerari in abitato. Atti del Convegno Internazionale (Università degli Studi di Roma "La Sapienza" 26–29 Aprile 2006)*, 141–167. Rome, Scienze dell'Antichità 14 (1).

Parr, P. (1968) The origin of the rampart fortifications in Middle Bronze Age Palestine and Syria. *Zeitschrift des Deutschen Palästina-Vereins* 84, 18–45.

Peltenburg, E. (1999) Jerablus-Tahtani 1992–1996: a summary. In G. del Olmo Lete and J.-L. Montero Fenollós (eds) *Archaeology of the Upper Syrian Euphrates, the Tishrin Dam area: proceedings of the International Symposium held at Barcelona, January 28th–30th 1998*, 97–105. Aula Orientalis Supplement 15. Barcelona, AUSA.

Peltenburg, E. (2007) Diverse settlement pattern changes in the Middle Euphrates valley in the later third millennium BC: The contribution of Jerablus Tahtani. In C. Kuzucuoğlu and C. Marro (eds) *Sociétés humaines et changement climatique à la fin du troisième millénaire : une crise a-t-elle eu lieu en Haute Mésopotamie ? Actes du Colloque de Lyon, 5–8 décembre 2005*, 247–266. Varia Anatolica 19. Istanbul, De Boccard.

Peltenburg, E. (2010) The emergence of Carchemish as a major polity: Land of Carchemish Survey (Syria) 2006. In P. Matthiae, F. Pinnock, L. Nigro and N. Marchetti (eds) *Proceedings of the 6th ICAANE Conference, May 5th–10th 2008, Rome*, 539–552. Wiesbaden, Harrassowitz.

Peltenburg, E. (2013) Conflict and exclusivity in Early Bronze Age societies of the Middle Euphrates Valley. *Journal of Near Eastern Studies* 72, 233–252.

Peltenburg, E. (2015) *Tell Jerablus Tahtani, Syria, I. Mortuary practices at an Early Bronze Age Fort on the Euphrates River.* Levant Supplementary Series 17. Oxford, Oxbow Books.

Peltenburg, E., Bolger, D., Campbell, S., Murray, M and Tipping, R. (1996) Jerablus-Tahtani, Syria, 1995: preliminary report. *Levant* 28, 1–25.

Pfälzner, P. (2002) Modes of storage and the development of economic systems in the Early Jezireh Period. In J. al-Ghailani Weir *et al.* (eds) *Of pots and plans. Papers on the archaeology and history of Mesopotamia and Syria presented to David Oates in honour of his 75th birthday*, 259–286. London, Nabu.

Pons, N. (2001) La poterie de Tell Amarna (Syrie) au BA IV et au BM I. Première approche et corrélations avec quelques sites clés. *Akkadica* 121, 23–75.

Porter, A. (2012) *Mobile Pastoralism and the Formation of Near Eastern Civilizations. Weaving Together Society.* Cambridge, Cambridge University Press.

Redman, C. (1978) *The Rise of Civilization: from Early Farmers to Urban Society in the Ancient Near East.* San Francisco CA, W. H. Freeman.

Sallaberger, W. (2007) From urban culture to nomadism: a history of Upper Mesopotamia in the late third millennium. In C. Kuzucuoğlu and C. Marro (eds) *Sociétés humaines et changement climatique à la fin du troisième millénaire: une*

crise a-t-elle eu lieu en Haute Mésopotamie? Actes du Colloque de Lyon, 5–8 décembre 2005, 417–456. Varia Anatolica 19. Istanbul, De Boccard.

Sallaberger, W. (2011) History and philology. In M. Lebeau (ed.) *ARCANE* I. *Jezirah.* 327–342. Turnhout, Brepols.

Salles, J.-F. (1995) Rituel Mortuaire et Rituel Social à Ras Shamra/Ougarit. In S. Campbell and A. Green (eds) *The Archaeology of Death in the Ancient Near East,* 171–184. Oxford, Oxbow Books.

Sanlaville, P. (ed.) (1985) *Holocene Settlement in North Syria: résultats de deux prospections archéologiques effectuées dans la région du nahr Sajour et sur le haut Euphrate syrien.* Oxford, BAR S238.

Sconzo, P. (2015) Ceramics. In U. Finkbeiner, M. Novák, F. Sakal and P. Sconzo (eds) *ARCANE* IV. *Middle Euphrates*, 85–202. Turnhout, Brepols.

Schwartz, G. (1994) Rural Economic Specialization and Early Urbanization in the Khabur Valley, Syria. In G. Schwartz and S. Falconer (eds) *Archaeological Views from the Countryside. Village Communities in Early Complex Societies,* 19–36. Washington DC, Smithsonian Institution Press.

Schwartz, G. and Falconer, S. (1994) Rural approaches to social complexity. In G. Schwartz and S. Falconer (eds) *Archaeological Views from the Countryside. Village Communities in Early Complex Societies,* 1–9. Washington DC, Smithsonian Institution Press.

Sertok, K. (2007) Fruit-stands and the definition of a cultural area around Carchemish. In E. Peltenburg (ed.) *Euphrates River Valley Settlement. The Carchemish Sector in the Third Millennium BC*, 238–249. Levant Supplementary Series 5. Oxford, Oxbow Books.

Sertok, K. and Ergeç, R. (1999) A new Early Bronze Age cemetery: excavations near the Birecik Dam, Southeastern Turkey. Preliminary report (1997–98). *Anatolica* 25, 87–107.

Squadrone, F. (2007) Regional culture and metal objects in the area of Carchemish during the Early Bronze Age. In E. Peltenburg (ed.) *Euphrates River Valley Settlement. The Carchemish Sector in the Third Millennium BC*, 198–213. Levant Supplementary Series 5. Oxford, Oxbow Books.

Stein, G. (1994) Segmentary states and organizational variation in early complex societies: a rural perspective. In G. Schwartz and S. Falconer (eds) *Archaeological Views from the Countryside. Village Communities in Early Complex Societies,* 10–18. Washington DC, Smithsonian Institution Press.

Thureau-Dangin, F. and Dunand, M. (1936) *Til Barsip.* Paris, P. Geuthner.

Ur, J. (2010) Cycles of civilization in Northern Mesopotamia, 4400–2000 BC. *Journal of Archaeological Research* 18, 387–431.

Ur, J., Karsgaard, P. and Oates, J. (2011) The spatial dimensions of early Mesopotamian urbanism: the Tell Brak suburban survey, 2003–2006. *Iraq* 73, 1–20.

Valdés Pereiro, C. (1999) Tell Qara Quzaq: a summary of the first results. In G. del Olmo Lete and J.-L. Montero Fenollós (eds) *Archaeology of the Upper Syrian Euphrates, the Tishrin Dam area: proceedings of the International Symposium held at Barcelona, January 28th–30th 1998*, 117–127. Aula Orientalis Supplement 15. Barcelona, AUSA.

Valentini, S. (2011) Burials and funerary practices. In M. Lebeau (ed.) *ARCANE* I. *Jezirah,* 167–286. Turnhout, Brepols.

Wilkinson, T. (1994) The structure and dynamics of dry-farming states in Upper Mesopotamia. *Current Anthropology* 35, 483–520.

Wilkinson, T. (2004) *On the Margin of the Euphrates. Settlement and Land Use at Tell es-Sweyhat and in the Upper Lake Assad area, Syria. Excavations at Tell es-Sweyhat, Syria* I. Chicago IL, Oriental Institute of the University of Chicago Publication 124.

Wilkinson, T.J., Peltenburg, E. McCarthy, A. Wilkinson, E. and Brown, M. (2007) Archaeology in the Land of Carchemish: landscape surveys in the area of Jerablus Tahtani, 2006. *Levant* 39, 213–247.

Wilkinson, T.J., Galiatsatos, N.. Lawrence, D., Ricci, A., Dunford, R. and Philip, G. (2012) Late Chalcolithic and Early Bronze Age landscapes of settlement and mobility in the Middle Euphrates: a re-assessment. *Levant* 44, 139–185.

Winter, I. (1983) Carchemish *ša kišad Puratti. Anatolian Studies* 33, 177–197.

Woolley, C.L. (1914) Hittite burial customs. *Liverpool Annals of Archaeology and Anthropology* 6, 87–98.

Woolley, C.L. (1921) *Carchemish Report on the Excavations at Jerablus on Behalf of the British Museum Part II: The Town Defences*. London, British Museum.

Woolley, L. and Barnett, R.D. (1952) *Carchemish Report on the Excavations at Jerablus on Behalf of the British Museum III: The Excavations in the Inner Town and the Hittite Inscriptions*. London, British Museum.

Investigations of Iron Age Carchemish:
the Outer Town survey of 2009 and 2010

Eleanor Barbanes Wilkinson and Andrea Ricci

Carchemish Outer Town Project: introduction

Archaeological history of the Outer Town

The site of Carchemish is by far the largest and best known site within the Land of Carchemish Project survey area. Being situated directly on the modern border between Turkey and Syria, Carchemish occupies a peculiar position geographically and politically. Systematic archaeological investigation of the site was prohibited in both countries from 1920 until the Land of Carchemish Project obtained permission to initiate a programme of archaeological survey on the Syrian side in 2009. On the Turkish side, the site has been the focus of renewed archaeological investigations since 2011. Under the direction of Nicolò Marchetti (Director, Bologna University) with Hasan Peker (Deputy Director, Istanbul University), many of the previously excavated areas are being re-examined and an extensive conservation and preservation plan is currently being implemented within the site in Turkey (Marchetti 2014). The geographical parameters of this discussion are limited exclusively to the area of the site in Syria which is referred to in the early 20th century field work reports as the Outer Town of Carchemish. Morphologically, the well-known plan published by Woolley in 1921 shows a site that is essentially tripartite; a 4 ha walled citadel crowns the northeast corner of a lower precinct of about 40 ha, referred to as the Inner Town. To the south and west of this, the Outer Town, encircled by a sizable rampart, extends the city by a further 55 ha. All together the site comprises about 100 ha. The site takes a shape that is roughly rectangular in the landscape, defined by a circuit wall of about 2400 m in length beginning at the north-west edge of the Inner Town earthen rampart, continuing around to join with a substantial stone wall that formed the eastern edge of the town. Woolley identified two

monumental gateways on the Outer Town ramparts; one on the west which was excavated, and one along the line of the Outer Town wall in the south-west quadrant which was identified only by surface remains. Hogarth, in a description of the site in 1912, recorded that the horseshoe-shaped embankment surrounding the Inner Town rose 30–50 ft (9.14–15.24 m) above the level outside (Woolley's Outer Town) and the citadel mound perched about 120 ft (36.58 m) above the Euphrates (Hogarth 1914, 1).

Carchemish has been bifurcated since 1922, when the Treaty of Lausanne was enacted, at which point the railway line running through the site just south of the Inner Town was designated the Turkish–Syrian frontier. Within Turkey are the citadel and Inner Town areas, where the excavated palaces and ceremonial spaces are located, as well as about 15 ha of the Outer Town. The greater proportion of the Outer Town, about 40% of the total site area, is situated within Syria. Currently, on the Syrian side the areas immediately adjacent to the border constitute a zone of prohibited access; a military base of the Turkish Armed Forces occupies the summit of the citadel in Turkey and watchtowers along the Turkish frontier directly overlook the Syrian side of the Outer Town. However, the greatest threat to the site in Syria today is the continued urban sprawl of the town of Jerablus, which long ago breached the ramparts of the ancient town. Today a sizable section of the southern part of site is subsumed by modern buildings and roads, and the intramural area up to the border is almost entirely given over to agricultural fields and orchards which have been heavily worked for centuries. In recent years the construction of number of private houses and other modern installations within the ancient site has increased at an alarming rate.

Carchemish was excavated by the British Museum during nine seasons between 1878 and 1920, and their work resulted in the publication of three major monographs (Hogarth 1914; Woolley 1921; Woolley and Barnett 1952).[1] From 1878 through 1881, P. Henderson, the British Consul in Aleppo conducted intermittent investigations on the south side of the citadel (or, acropolis) mound and in deep soundings on the north-west citadel slope. A programme of systematic excavations was initiated in March 1911 by D.G. Hogarth, assisted by R.C. Thompson and T.E. Lawrence. Further investigations continued for five more seasons from 1912 through to the spring of 1914, under the direction of C. L. Woolley, also assisted by T.E. Lawrence (Hogarth 1914, 8–12; Woolley 1921, preface; Hawkins 1980, 343–435). The outbreak of World War I caused the cessation of fieldwork, and the excavation materials stored in the expedition house, which included pottery and inscription catalogues along with excavated artefacts, were destroyed or otherwise lost. The site of Carchemish apparently suffered only minor looting during the war as it was protected by local guards associated with the expedition (Woolley 1921, preface). In 1920 investigations resumed, once again directed by Woolley, assisted by P.L.O. Guy. The town plan of Carchemish was produced during this last season and since then it has remained the only town plan by which the site has been known (Fig. 8.1).

In 1920, work at the site was once again interrupted, due to conflict between the Turkish National army and the occupying French forces. Many of the records and other material from this last season as well as previous ones were thrown away, destroyed or went missing when the expedition house was occupied by soldiers. (Woolley 1939, 11–12; Hogarth 1914, preface; Hawkins 1980, 434–435). Only the 1920 season was devoted to investigations in the Outer Town, but an enormous amount of work was completed by the team in a relatively short time. In addition to continued excavations elsewhere at the site, work in the Outer Town during 1920 included excavation of a gateway on the western ramparts (Woolley 1921, 73–81), some intramural burials (Woolley 1921, 133–134), and a number of structures that Woolley interpreted as eight domestic installations, designated Houses A-H (Woolley 1921, 118–132). One major component of this final season was the tracing of the Outer Town wall, an operation completed by Woolley with the assistance of P.L.O. Guy (Woolley 1921, 49–57, pl. 3). The artefacts retrieved from the British Expedition were distributed between the British Museum in London, the Anatolian Civilizations Museum Ankara, and the Archaeological Museums of Istanbul, with minor or single holdings also in the Museum of Gaziantep, the Ashmolean Museum in Oxford, the Louvre Museum in Paris, the Sadbırk Hanım Museum in Istanbul and the Vatican Museums in Rome (Marchetti 2014, 29–31).

While excavation had formed the basis for interpreting the nature of the citadel and Inner Town ramparts, the line of the Outer Town wall was reconstructed by Woolley mostly by means of surface survey, anchored by examination of a limited number of sondages along its length. Despite the detailed appearance of the town plan published by Woolley, he readily acknowledged that his rendering of the Outer Town wall was less a record of standing architecture than an extrapolation made "from the lie of the ground" (Woolley 1921, 51).

The Syro–Turkish border which cuts through the site had been systematically mined in 1956, but after Turkey signed the Ottawa Convention of 1996, the Turkish government began removing the mines from the area. The de-mining of Carchemish was completed in 2011. In the same year, the joint Turkish–Italian programme of excavation began within both the Inner and Outer Town areas and in an area of Neo-Assyrian cremation burials outside the city to the north-west. Investigations also included a section of the outer fortification wall on the north-west side of the site (Marchetti 2012, 2014). The areas of renewed excavation most relevant to this discussion of the Outer Town are their Area E (an excavation of roads and drains adjacent to the north-west Outer Town wall), and their re-examination of two previously excavated buildings; Woolley's House A, and the South Gate of the Inner Town, labelled Area D; in the latter, the new excavations produced a sequence dating from the 'Middle Ages' through Neo-Assyrian occupation levels (Marchetti 2012, 142). Excavated material from the 7th century BC testifies to the continued importance of the city as a centre for elites after the Assyrian conquest of 717 BC (Bonomo *et al.* 2012, 137; Bonomo and Zaina 2014). Based upon their published results, the excavators propose that the Outer Town expansion occurred during the 7th century BC (Marchetti 2012, 142), with the construction of the outer fortification wall dated at 700 BC (Marchetti 2012, 141, fig. 19). While archaeological work on the Syrian side of Carchemish has once again been interrupted, and the Land of Carchemish Project is postponed indefinitely, it is encouraging that operations on the Turkish side have been able to continue unabated.

The British Museum's excavations on the acropolis and Inner Town areas in Turkey, revealing occupation dating from the Chalcolithic through the Roman period, have been discussed at length elsewhere[2] and, as those two areas of the site were outside the remit of this project, those investigations are not included in this discussion. In the original British reports, the excavators subdivided the occupation levels from the later 3rd millennium BC through 600 BC into 'Early', 'Middle,' and 'Late Hittite' but subsequent analyses of the excavated material has resulted in a revised periodization for the site (see Table 8.1). Woolley considered the Outer Town a product of Neo-Hittite urban expansion and in the reports the outer ramparts and all excavated material from Outer Town was almost uniformly identified as 'Late Hittite;' as defined by Woolley this refers to the 600 years following the break-down of the Hittite Empire, or about 1200-600 BC (Woolley 1921, 49).

Table 8.1. Chronological chart of the occupation sequence at Carchemish (modified from Falsone and Sconzo 2007, 78, table 5.1)

	Revised periodization (Falsone & Sconzo)	Woolley's Periodization	Urban zone as defined by Woolley
A	Prehistoric Late Halaf/Ubaid	Neolithic	Acropolis
B	Late Chalcolithic (Middle/Late Uruk)	Chalcolithic	Acropolis
C	EBA I–II (champagne cup horizon)	Early Hittite (Early Bronze Age) 2200–1750 BC	Acropolis + wall
D	EB III–IV		
E	MBA I–II	Middle Hittite (Amarna horizon) 1750–1200 BC	Inner Town + wall
F	MBA II		
G	LBA		
H	IA	Late Hittite 1200–600 BC	Outer Town + wall

Project history and objectives

In May 2009, with the encouragement of the Directorate General of Antiquities and Museums in Syria (DGAM), the Land of Carchemish Project (LCP) initiated a programme of intensive on-site investigation within Carchemish. The primary objectives of the Carchemish Outer Town Project were essentially threefold: to reassess the published record of the Outer Town of Carchemish through the application of remote sensing and intensive survey; to delineate the visible limits of the ancient Outer Town while documenting any unpublished remains of ancient occupation and topographic features that might indicate earlier structures; and to identify the archaeological features at greatest risk from modern development. The immediate goal was to provide a detailed document that would assist the DGAM in the long-term conservation and management of the site and aid in addressing imminent threats from new building, utilities and industrial works, agriculture, and other potentially damaging development. At the same time, the loosening of security restrictions in this sensitive border zone, together with recent developments in remote sensing, presented an exciting opportunity for a new archaeological reckoning of this important site.

The main component of this new phase of investigations was the detailed archaeological assessment of the site. In May 2009, the first stage began with an intensive survey comprised of field walking, recording, and surface collection within the town walls of Carchemish and in the immediate site environs. These operations are summarized below, in the sections on Areas A, B and C, and they consisted primarily of the collection of a substantial amount of pottery, providing some indication of the occupation sequence in the Outer Town. In 2010, the programme was expanded to include: two

additional long surface collection transects traversing the intramural area from just outside the Outer Town ramparts up to the inaccessible zone close to the border; detailed recording of intra-site topography; recording of visible ancient remains; and recording of existing cut sections at key points along the western ramparts. A separate operation was devoted to stratigraphic analysis taking cores from sample areas within the Outer Town, and these results will be published once the samples are processed

Research questions

Since the completion of the British Museum's work in the Outer Town, a number of research questions have remained unanswered. Probably the most significant issue is that a full chronology for the Outer Town has not yet been produced, since the early Carchemish reports contain only very limited descriptions of any evidence potentially preceding or post-dating the Neo-Hittite period, the 'Late Hittite' era to which Woolley assigned the construction of the Outer Town. The Greco-Roman material which reportedly "littered" the site (Hogarth 1914, 1) received only scanty attention in excavations and consequently little is described in the reports. There has been a long debate as to whether the well-known Roman city of Europos was actually located at Carchemish (see Newson, Chapter 9 in this volume and Ricci 2014). In our investigations, therefore, any indications of occupation dating to the Roman period might be especially useful in determining the extent of the settlement at that time, and whether there is any archaeological support for the association of Carchemish with Europos. Moreover, although Woolley reported that some of the excavated buildings in the Outer Town contained features which clearly antedated the construction of the Outer Town ramparts, and therefore might be earlier than the Neo-Hittite period, the evidence presented for this was not very extensive, and it was not interpreted by Woolley as an indicator for occupation of the entire Outer Town in the periods preceding the Neo-Hittite city-states. The best examples of this potentially early architectural evidence, from excavations in buildings referred to as House C (Woolley 1921, 121) and House D (Woolley 1921, 125) will be discussed below. The artefact assemblages accompanying these intriguing bits of potentially early architecture were discussed in the reports as 'Late Hittite,' as were most of the artefacts from the intramural graves. Some pottery and other artefacts from the House sites, such as that from House D, are certainly post-Iron Age (Woolley 1921, 123, pl. 20, fig. d.8). Woolley did suggest the possibility of a squatter settlement within the Outer Town in the period immediately after the fall of the city to the Babylonians in 605 BC, a supposition largely based upon comparison with the burial style and contents of graves at Deve Höyük not associated with any architecture (Woolley 1921, 119, 1914a and b).

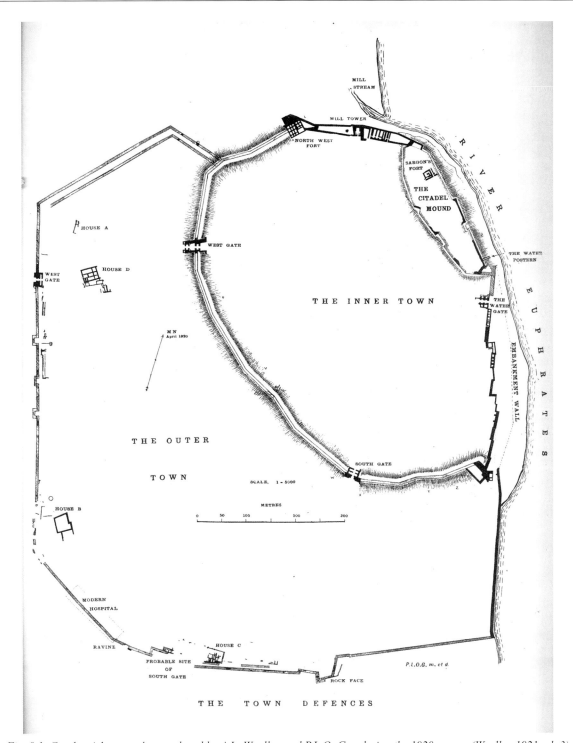

Fig. 8.1. Carchemish town plan produced by A.L. Woolley and P.L.O. Guy during the 1920 season (Woolley 1921, pl. 3).

Carchemish can be characterised as having experienced an atypically high degree of political and cultural continuity from the Late Bronze Age though the Iron Age (see discussions by Hawkins and Weeden, Chapter 2 and Brown and Smith, Chapter 3 in this volume), but given its history it would seem logical that some indication of three potentially transformative events might be found in the archaeological record of the site: the collapse of the Hittite Empire around 1200 BC, the takeover by Sargon II in 717 BC, and the capture of the city by Nebuchadnezzar in 605 BC. However, neither archaeological nor epigraphic evidence supports the destruction of the city of Carchemish in any of these episodes (see Hawkins 1980, 434, 446, and Chapter 2 in this volume). Nevertheless, the early British Museum excavators reported that signs of wholesale destruction dating to the fall of the Hittite empire were found "everywhere" they dug (Woolley 1921, 48), and in the Outer Town, evidence from House D in particular was interpreted as indicating destruction by a major fire and a "desperate struggle," which Woolley considered "definite proof" of the destruction of the city by the Babylonian army (Woolley 1921, 123–126). The British excavations also presented a case for the abandonment of Carchemish following the Babylonian takeover, a premise which has in the past gained acceptance.[3] The interpretation of this evidence remains debated. While it is probably impossible to identify destruction levels through surface survey alone, it is possible to identify chronological and spatial transitions from surface remains. A key goal of our project was to test the urban model for a Neo-Hittite urban expansion as presented by the earlier excavators, by attempting to determine the nature and extent of the city occupied during the Neo-Hittite period and the period following on from Assyrian takeover. While the early excavations in the Outer Town produced a substantial record of occupation during the late 8th–7th century BC, the period of Neo-Assyrian occupation on the citadel and Inner Town areas was relatively underrepresented in the published reports, though a small number of artefacts were identified as Assyrian by inscriptions on them or by stylistic features.[4] We were also interested in finding any evidence for the abandonment or contraction of the site after Nebuchadnezzar 's attacks in 605 and 596 BC (or in any case, the episodes of destruction referred to in the reports as being documented through excavated evidence by the early excavators[5]), and whether the Roman settlement also extended into the Outer Town. Finally, we hoped to obtain some insight into the urban evolution of the site: was the Outer Town defined by Woolley occupied at all times, or was it only partly occupied by dispersed habitations? Was it carefully planned as seems evident now in the Inner Town, and more generally, what variations in occupation existed in different historical periods?

Methodology

Because the ancient site is clearly threatened by modern development, the primary goal of the Outer Town project was to produce a thorough archaeological assessment of the site. From the onset, the project's premise was that in order to best protect the site, it was necessary to first gain an overview of the ancient remains relative to the impact of modern development. While excavation was a component of the project's future research design, it was considered that embarking on such a programme without a thorough assessment of the condition of the site would have been inadvisable. We chose instead to limit our operations to

non-invasive activities which would allow us to obtain the maximum amount of information with the least amount of impact to the site. This included surface survey and collection, topographic analysis, limited ground core sampling and, wherever possible, detailed examination of exposed ancient features. Remote sensing played a crucial part in the investigations. Our geographical data set included all relevant imagery, documenting the archaeological landscape as it has been recorded from the early 20th century through today, with the aim of obtaining the broadest possible view of the site transformation processes. In brief, the operations conducted by the Land of Carchemish Project in the Outer Town comprised the following research components:

- Recording of standing architecture and other ancient remains via photography, drawing, and location within a GIS framework, including the circuit of the ramparts and all ancient remains visible within the site and immediately outside the town walls
- Correlating the present site record with the earlier publications
- Recording topographic features that might indicate earlier structures or other occupation zones
- Collection of artefacts on the surface in sample areas to test for intra-site occupation variation and chronological sequence
- Topographic analysis through cross-site transects and core sampling
- Documentation of previously unrecorded details at several points along the Outer Town wall where modern agricultural activity had resulted in exposing the rampart's inner construction

While the LCP investigations corroborate Woolley's reports to a large extent, our results indicate a more complex rendering of the site's evolution than was originally proposed in the early 20th century. Moreover, our investigations have brought new data to bear upon certain long-held assumptions derived from the early excavation reports, allowing for a reassessment of the town plan and the phasing of its construction and occupation.

Geospatial resources

Recent developments in geospatial technologies presented the Project with the means for assessing a huge amount of information on Carchemish remotely. Concurrent to the fieldwork was a detailed study of the site relative to the development of the town of Jerablus using remote sensing techniques, in particular identifying the areas of archaeological significance that seemed to be obscured, damaged, or threatened by modern activity. To accomplish this we utilized a number of resources, from the earliest

Fig. 8.2 CORONA image 1038 (22 January 1967) showing the site of Carchemish transected by the railway line that forms the Syrian–Turkish border, with the modern town of Jerablus immediately adjacent to the Outer Town wall on the south. Note location of Outer Town wall and "Inner Anomaly"

published maps in the British Museum reports on Carchemish through the most recent satellite images and Geographical Information Systems. The recognition of key architectural elements of the Outer Town of Carchemish was aided by the use of recent high resolution satellite imagery such as Quickbird images from 2003 and 2008, and GeoEye imagery taken from 2009 to the present day. The oldest resource used was the set of topographic maps published in Hogarth's 1914 Carchemish report (Hogarth 1914, figs 4–6). Woolley's 1921 *Volume II, The Town Defenses,* was the main reference for the town plan and detailed architectural features recorded in the 1920 season. An additional historical perspective of the site was achieved by the use of CORONA satellite images taken in 1967–1969 (Fig. 8.2) as well as the latest high resolution images from ICONOS, Quickbird and GeoEye (Fig. 8.3).

2009 Investigations: surface collections, Areas A, B and C

Area A

The 1921 plan of Carchemish illustrates relatively little archaeological information in the south-east quadrant of the site. Woolley acknowledged that the visible remains of

the Outer Town wall and other features were so sparse that in this area the map was largely the result of topographic indicators and a certain amount of speculation (Woolley 1921, 56). In 2009 the LCP began investigations within three areas in the SE sector, between the walls of the Inner Town and the outer ramparts as defined on Woolley's town plan, designated LCP Areas A, B, and C (Fig. 8.4).

In this initial phase of investigation, the key criteria for the selection of these areas were the degree of accessibility on the ground and visibility on the available imagery. Each of the three areas were being worked by farmers but were only sparsely built upon, and they presented no particular security problem though some of the fields were contiguous with the Syrian–Turkish border. In order to obtain fixed points for use in the georectification of the imagery the team, composed of 3–5 people working for an average of 6 hours each day, took GPS readings using a hand-held device in a triangular area of cotton fields to the south of a modern road that cuts diagonally through the south-east sector of the Outer Town (Area A). The team also examined and recorded GPS points along the easternmost perimeter wall of Carchemish, referred to by Woolley as the "river wall" (Woolley 1921, 56–57 and pl. 5a), a section of worked stone wall which was well preserved for a length of about 100 m at the base of the embankment, which was designated Area C. Investigation in Area C illustrated that a considerable length

Fig. 8.3 1921 plan by Woolley/Guy (Woolley 1921, pl. 3) georectified with Panchromatic GeoEye image (10 November 2009) showing Carchemish and modern Jerablus on the south

Fig. 8.4 CORONA image of the site of Carchemish (22 January 1967). Circular points indicate the surface collection units and other field recording points made during 2009 in study areas A, B and C

of the river wall remained intact almost exactly as Woolley recorded it in 1920. No collection was undertaken in this area, but more will be said of this operation below. Of the three initial operations, Area B yielded the most significant new results and these will be discussed in detail.

Area A: Summary of collection assemblage

A limited surface collection was made in Area A, a triangular cotton field west of the river wall, just south of the modern road leading to a bridge across the Euphrates (shown on Fig. 8.4). The collection comprised just over 120 sherds and a few artefacts including a glass bracelet fragment. This ceramic corpus has not been illustrated, but it was analyzed in the field. The pottery generally consisted of very small abraded sherds, their poor condition most likely resulting from the continual agricultural activity in this sample area. Only about 20% of the collection was diagnostic. Chronologically, there appeared to be a mixture of common Iron Age wares and Greco-Roman wares. One of the most obvious and numerous indicators of Iron Age occupation here was a common jar form with a club-shaped rim, typically 10–20 cm in diameter, rendered in a light brown-buff fabric containing little chaff. Body sherds in this fabric dominated the collection. Other well-known Iron Age forms appearing in smaller numbers included bowls with everted rims, also in the light brown or reddish-brown buff fabric, and a few beakers in a very light grey fabric which might be Neo-Assyrian palace ware. However, among the diagnostics, post-Iron Age ceramics were dominant. These included at least two dozen clearly identifiable examples of fine ware, such as African Red Slip, Roman Phocaean, Sigillata, and a few Hellenistic and Eastern Mediterranean sherds, as well as a larger group of Roman Brittle Ware in the characteristic sandy orange-buff or reddish-brown buff fabric. Only a few showed signs of red-brown or black paint and a small number were gritty and corrugated. Despite the poor condition of the collection and the small proportion of diagnostics, it is still possible to conclude that this sample area was occupied sometime during the Iron Age from about 900–600 BC, though due to the long lifespan of the Iron Age forms present, a more specific chronological identification remains difficult. Moreover, although the collection may not indicate anything more than sparse settlement, it seems clear that some degree of occupation was present in this area within the mapped Outer Town walls well into the late Roman and perhaps Byzantine period. However, it is not possible to identify this area with certainty as 'intramural' settlement, since it is not certain whether the Outer Town ramparts were a functioning fortification system in these later periods. This point will be discussed in greater detail below.

Area B: Collection Transects 2, 4 & 6

Methodology

The CORONA satellite images from the 1960s proved to be a particularly useful resource for the Outer Town project, since they document the condition of the Carchemish before the extensive modern development obscuring the site today. In these images, variations of colour, density and texture in open areas could potentially signify subsurface evidence for human activity. This was especially the case in an area within the southern half of the Outer Town, immediately south of the railway line, a large open area in which no archaeological detail was recorded on Woolley's 1921 town plan. During our collections in 2009 and 2010 this area was given over to cultivation of pistachio trees. This area has been uniformly affected by the orchard planting, so any density variation is assumed to reflect underlying patterns. Investigation of the CORONA images showed a change in the soil colour across an area roughly 400 m by 100 m sq within the orchard. To determine the extent and nature of intra-site variation, this area was selected for intensive investigation and designated Area B. The area chosen for survey lay in flat ground immediately east of a slight rise that formed the edge of encroaching house gardens. Dressed blocks occurred on the surface along the rough perimeter of these properties, and were subsequently recorded in the 2010 mapping programme.

Survey in Area B consisted of the collection of diagnostic material in three major transects aligned on an east–west axis, each 420 m in length and spaced 10 m apart, plus three additional sample squares. Transects 2, 4 and 6 were the full 420 m in length, but to accommodate the spacing of the orchard trees, Transects 1, 3 and 5 consisted of only one sample square each. Each of the three main transects comprised 24 sample squares, each square 15 × 5 m in size. Archaeological material collected within each square was kept separate for analysis. GPS points were recorded at the south-east corner of each sample square. The 75 sample squares thus provided a total artifact sample retrieval from over 5400 m sq. between Woolley's House C and the Inner South Gate, yielding a total of 1044 sherds. Only the diagnostics (handles, rims, bases, decorated and unusual body sherds) were collected, and a representative sample has been drawn (see Figs 8.30–8.32). Chipped stone, fragments of grinding stones, tesserae, ceramic pipe fragments and ceramic figurine fragments were counted, and some of the figurine fragments were registered and drawn. Roof tiles, of a type typically associated with Greco-Roman architecture, were also found in some concentration.

Area B: Discussion of results, intra-site variation and urban organization

Artefact distribution rates varied considerably in Area B. A clear spike in sherd counts occurred about midway along all transects, but is most evident in transects 4 and 6, squares 9–13 (see Table 8.2). It is accompanied by moderate increases in roof tiles, ground stone and finds in transects 4 and 6. There were no masonry blocks that would support the

Table 8.2 Carchemish Outer Town, LCP Area B, Collection Transects 2–6: diagram showing number of sherds per sample square

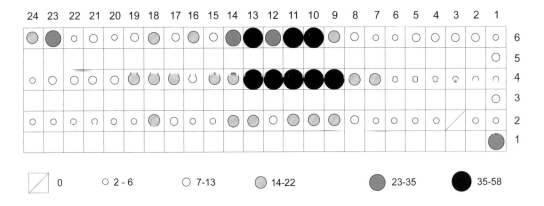

CARCHEMISH
AREA B
Collection Transects - Number of sherds per sample square

inference of a structure nearby, but the farmer has cleared heavier stonework from the orchard.

There is no obvious natural anomaly here to account for the discrete peak. However, some indication of relevant subsurface activity may be inferred from the CORONA satellite image from 1969, which illustrates that the area encompassed by the sample collection area is characterized by large patches of light-coloured soil (see Figs 8.2 and 8.4). These lighter patches may represent a diffuse matrix of occupational material, perhaps including decomposed construction debris, pottery and other aggregates resulting from modern activity, and perhaps overlying structural remains. The light patches are interspersed with darker stretches, which are perhaps indicative of moisture accumulation, which could signify open space beneath the overburden, perhaps streets or simply spaces between buildings. There is a pronounced linear stretch of dark material which takes the appearance of a road leading from the south gate of the Outer Town, in the south-east quadrant on Woolley's plan, up to through the south gate of the Inner Town, along the Processional Way of the Inner Town and on to the citadel. If the high concentration of artefacts present in the central transects does indicate subsurface construction, and the linear feature is indeed a road, then this area of survey may represent a neighbourhood built along the main route connecting the acropolis with the Outer Town and beyond. Other, less pronounced peaks in sherd densities are evident further to the west, particularly in the northernmost collection, in transect 6 (Table 8.2, squares 6/16, 18; 23–24), and there may be another concentration roughly midway along the western half of the transect line (Table 8.2, squares 6/18; 4/17–19, and 2/18).

These denser collections may indicate individual buildings. One further anomaly is a concentration of roof tiles in the extreme SE of the sample area (Table 8.2,

squares 2/1, 4/1, and 3) without commensurate increase in sherds. Within these three squares, a total of 32 roof tiles were recovered, while in the other sample squares typical totals ranged from zero to four tiles; perhaps there is a tile refuse area here or it is the edge of a structure with a tile roof. In any case, the results from this survey fill a gap in the earlier record of the site, by documenting an area which may have been occupied concurrently with settlement on the Inner Town and acropolis, if it can be concluded that the buildings and the road linking them with the upper areas are associated chronologically. The collection assemblage from this area contains artefacts from multiple periods, as will be discussed below.

Although some early 20th century accounts and the excavation reports contain many references to Roman architectural remains covering the Inner Town and citadel areas (Hogarth 1914; Woolley 1921; Bell 1924), the substantial overburden of later occupation found in these two areas of the site does not appear to have extended into the Outer Town. Woolley noted this contrast in 1920, remarking that the architecture in the Outer Town was largely in a poor state, while the "more grandiose" buildings in the Inner Town and citadel were executed in large dressed stone blocks (identified as Hittite) which appeared to have been obtained by the Roman builders from elsewhere in the site. This process of despoliation observed by Woolley was still continuing in the early 20th century, as soldiers occupying the site his day also utilized the stones from the Outer Town for their new barracks (Woolley 1921, 50).

Area B: Summary of collection assemblage
Analysis of the pottery collected in Field B of the Outer Town survey was only partially completed in the field seasons conducted thus far. Nevertheless, a fair amount of information can be gleaned from the representative sub-

set reviewed. The collection from Area B comprised 1044 diagnostic sherds and 683 of these, collected in 32 of the 75 sample squares, have been recorded in terms of formal attributes and probable date. This set, comprising over 65% of the total sherd count in Field B, provides the basis for the following discussion. It was possible to ascribe a date to almost 300 of the sherds. The analyzed pottery derives largely from the central area where the pottery was most dense, as mentioned above, although not each of these transect squares were among the highest yielding (Table 8.2). The intention of this recording strategy was to obtain

as broad a sample as possible of the pottery forms available on the surface, with the main objective of identifying the possible chronological range of the occupation in this area of the Outer Town, while testing for variations in spatial distribution. By comparing this assemblage with ceramic collections from relevant stratified excavations, some suggestions may be put forward concerning the possible chronological and perhaps functional parameters of this sample area of Carchemish. Bearing in mind the limited proportion of the collection sample that has been recorded so far, some obvious generalizations have emerged in the initial analysis.

The Area B collection appears to be a mixture of Iron Age and post-Iron Age material, the latter consisting of sherds dated to the periods from the Hellenistic though Islamic, with one or two possibly being Achaemenid (see Fig. 8.31, no. 25, and Table 8.3). The ceramic collection comprised predominantly small and somewhat weathered fragments, as is often the case with ceramics collected in surface survey. No complete vessels were found. In attempting to identify the pottery chronologically, we assigned a date only to sherds that were well-documented in published collections from stratified archaeological contexts. Over 50% of the collection was therefore deemed indeterminate in date. The largest proportion of dated pottery belongs to the Iron Age II/III, and a smaller amount of post-Iron Age ceramics is a clear indication of some degree of occupation in the Outer Town well into the later Roman/Byzantine period. A few sherds dated to the Islamic period, though extremely scarce, appeared as well (Table 8.4).

The number of plates or platters (Fig. 8.31, nos 15–20), as well as numerous cooking pots (Fig. 8.32, nos 30–34) might indicate a domestic function for Field B. Equally, the

Table 8.3 Carchemish Outer Town, LCP Area B: proportional breakdown of pottery reviewed (683 out of 1044 total count)

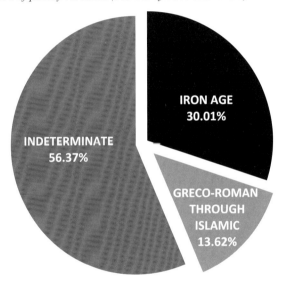

Table 8.4 Carchemish Outer Town, LCP Area B, Collection Transects 2–6: diagram showing relative proportion of dated sherds in each sample analyzed

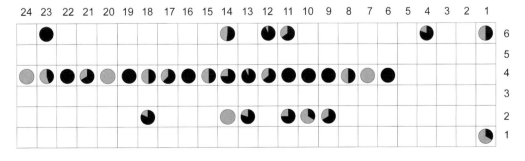

number of closed jars (Fig. 8.32, nos 45–53) does not seem to signify large amounts of transportable contents, but rather, jars tend toward the types most likely used for long-term storage, perhaps corroborating a domestic context, or at least a context in which the goods stored were being kept on a more permanent rather than in transit. It must be emphasized that these results derive from analysis of only the reviewed and datable portion of the Outer Town corpus. Moreover, several ceramic forms frequently appear in more than one level at comparative sites. It therefore seems prudent to ascribe the broadest dates of late 8th–7th centuries BC for the majority of the collection, with the acknowledgement of a small degree of Late Bronze and Early Iron Age settlement might be represented in a small number of sherds, indicating sparser occupation of the Outer Town in those periods. Equally indicating only sparse settlement or even scatter, are the less numerous indications for later and post-Iron Age settlement, possibly present as small numbers of pot forms which continue into the 6th and 5th centuries BC, and the 13% of the corpus dating within the Greco-Roman through Islamic periods. The periodization of the ceramics is discussed below.

Remarks on the Outer Town Ceramics: Iron Age

This discussion takes into account the most recent pottery report published by the Turkish–Italian team concerning their recent excavations of the Iron Age II–III levels in Carchemish and in the Yunus cemetery (Bonomo and Zaina 2014). Their preliminary report presents a combined Iron Age assemblage resulting from excavations completed in 2011 within many areas of the site, along with some comparative examples of Iron Age pottery published by the earlier British excavations (Woolley 1921; Woolley and Barnett 1952). The Turkish–Italian report illustrates pottery from a wide variety of contexts all together (domestic, religious, palatial, funerary and military) and categorizes all ceramics as Simple Ware, Kitchen Ware, or Preservation Ware. In our analysis the LCP does not adopt that interpretive scheme; instead we conform with the standard convention of identifying vessels according to vessel form; bowls, jars, cooking pots, etc. However, the numerous obvious comparisons between the two collections confirm that in terms of shape, fabric, and probable date, the Iron Age assemblage from the new investigations throughout the Turkish side of Carchemish is essentially the same material as that collected by the LCP survey in the Syrian side of the Outer Town. Apart from one or two exceptions, every vessel type illustrated from the new project in Turkey is replicated in the LCP Outer Town survey collection, including some which are not illustrated here, such as the newly-identified large pithos forms excavated mainly in the operations in the Lower Palace area and the Outer Town on the Turkish side (Bonomo and Zaina 2014, 143; fig. 6, nos 11–13).

The excavated ceramics from the British Expedition provide relevance for comparison for both the LCP and the Turkish-Italian excavations. In the early 20th century, Iron Age ceramics were found across both the Inner and Outer Town areas (Woolley 1921, 118–132) but the early British publications describe it only very superficially and with relatively few illustrations. From the Expedition field notes it is clear that a much more detailed programme of pottery recording was done than is reflected in the published record (Benati 2014). The reports tend to highlight the vessels of exceptional design or preservation, and today there is no trace of the large sherd collections which must have formed the basis for the ceramic typologies developed by Woolley, Lawrence, and rest of the British team (Marchetti 2014, 31). In those early days of excavation, much of the pottery was discarded, even whole undamaged vessels (Woolley 1921, 234–237, pl. 20). In terms of chronology, the Iron Age excavated ceramics were referred to by Woolley as 'Late Hittite' and the Iron Age ceramic sequence was far less developed than it is today, so it is understandable that the early British Museum reports contain scant ceramic evidence from the excavations that could be associated confidently with an Assyrian presence. The invisibility of key Assyrian type fossils is one of the most obvious features of the LCP Outer Town collection, a feature thus far shared by the excavated assemblage in Turkey. However, there are indications that the new excavations In Turkey are producing some direct parallels with excavated ceramics from Assyrian contexts further to the east, at sites such as Assur, and as more analysis is completed it can be assumed that more firm comparisons with known Assyrian wares will arise (Bonomo and Zaina 2014, 141; fig. 4 no. 8).

A brief review of the other Iron Age collections further west as far as Tell Afis and east as far as Nineveh suggests that the largest proportion of the survey collection from the Carchemish Outer Town survey can be dated within the Iron Age, and most of it appears to fall within the 7th century BC. Clear parallels for most of the sherds can be found in stratified Iron Age contexts published from other sites in the immediate region. The most useful excavated collection is to be found about 5 km downstream from Carchemish on the opposite bank of the Euphrates, at the site of Tell Shiukh Fawqani, under the direction of Luc Bachelot and Mario Fales (Bachelot and Fales 2005). This site, with stratified levels from all periods relevant to the Carchemish Outer Town and one of the closest in the region, provides the main comparison for this discussion. Firm comparisons with Shiukh Fawqani Areas E, F and G especially, seem to indicate that the majority of dated pottery from Field B in the Carchemish Outer Town survey can be placed within the Iron Age IIA, the 8th and 7th centuries BC. This is based in large part upon the many parallels with Shiukh Fawqani Area F, Levels IX and X and in Area G, Level IX, A and B (though there are fewer similarities with C, which is the earliest of the three occupation levels). The excavators propose that in Area F the settlement may date specifically from within the early 7th century BC through 600 BC, which might provide an appealingly more narrow range for the Carchemish Field B pottery if there were sufficient comparisons, but so far there are slightly more direct parallels with Shiukh Fawqani Area G rather than Area F. A lesser case can be made for comparisons found in other collections which point to a date later in the Iron III period, notably the pottery from Tell Jurn Kabir I, dated to the 7th century BC, Khirbet Khatuniyeh 3, and Khirbet Qasrij each of which include forms dated to the "post-Assyrian" period, *i.e.*, post-605 BC, the Babylonian takeover of the city.

This pottery report has also relied extensively on the published Iron Age collections from the sites of Tell Ahmar (Jamieson 2012) and Tell Jurn Kabir (Eidem and Ackermann 1999), both of which are nearby and have long Iron Age sequences. In terms of pottery associated with the Neo-Assyrian empire, in this analysis the most useful publications have been those of Nimrud (Lines 1954 and 1959), Nineveh (Lumsden 1995; Lumsden and Wilkinson forthcoming) and the sites in the Eski Mosul Survey area, namely Khirbet Khatuniyeh (Curtis and Green 1997), Qasrij Cliff and Khirbet Qasrij (Curtis 1989). In their (admittedly preliminary) report the new Turkish–Italian team similarly identify most of these sites as relevant in terms of comparative Iron Age assemblages, with the noteworthy exception of Shiukh Fawqani which provided the highest proportion of relevant IA II–III parallels for the LCP assemblage. One of the most significant features uniting the pottery collections from both the Turkish and Syrian sides of Carchemish is the close connection with excavated assemblages in the Middle and Upper Euphrates and sites further to the west. The links with these western sites, combined with the absence of certain wares, seem to provide strong evidence for a closer alignment with western ceramics than to those generally found at sites occupied by the Assyrians east of the Euphrates.

Of the Iron Age material, the major proportion of the sherd sample is characterized by grey–brown clay with medium to large sand temper. Mineral temper predominates; chaff temper is considerably rarer, though is still a measurable component of the sample. Many sherds have the appearance of a light cream slip on their exterior surfaces, an attribute common in 8th and 7th century BC Iron Age collections and most likely a result of the firing process rather than a decorative device (Oates 1959, 131). At Tell Ahmar, this affect is aptly referred to as self-slip, and this term is adopted here. Grey wares, of the type which are meant to imitate stone in terms of colour and texture, are absent from the sample. Certain classes of pottery, such as ring-burnished and Red Slip ware, are rare. While this is true of other Iron Age sites in the Euphrates as well including Tell Ahmar, Jurn Kabir, Tell Qadahiye and Tell Sheikh Hassan (Luciani

2005, 795), all of these sites have more of these types than were found in the Outer Town of Carchemish. There are, however, some examples of decorated wares, which include bands of incised lines and painting, which compare with other Iron Age collections, though the typically small size of sherds has meant that as yet no example is large enough to indicate more than a hint at the overall design pattern, so none have been illustrated here. The Turkish-Italian excavations identify more decorated pottery on the whole, particularly burnished and painted wares, though this may be the result of the qualitative differences between pottery from excavated contexts versus pottery that has been exposed on the ground surface for years before being collected in survey.

Certain bowl types which are often attested at sites with a known Assyrian presence are found at Carchemish. One particularly strong indicator of this class is the grooved rim bowl (Fig. 8.30, nos 1 and 2). In one example here, (Fig. 8.30, no. 1) the rim most closely duplicates examples of tripod bowls from at least two other sites in the Assyrian core (Nimrud: Oates 1954, pl. xxxviii, no. 1; and Khirbet Qasrij: Curtis 1989, fig. 30, no. 115) and though it is impossible to say whether the Carchemish example is a tripod, the grooved rim appears on standard bowls as well. In the Carchemish region, versions of this rim form appear commonly in bowls found at, for example, Tell Ahmar (Jamieson 2012: fig. 3.4/5) in Common Ware, though variations appears rendered in Fine Ware (Jamieson 2012:, fig. 3.26/1–2) and Grey Ware (Jamieson 2012, fig. 3.27/12), neither of which are present at Carchemish. Also at Jurn Kabir this type of grooved rim bowl ceramic occurs in the 7th century BC levels (Eidem and Ackermann 1999, fig. 8.10).

Another such bowl type well-represented at other sites with Late Assyrian occupation appears at Carchemish as well. This is a particular version of a bowl with inverted and thickened rim (Fig. 8.30, nos 5–11). Good parallels are also found at Tell Ahmar in the 7th century BC (Jamieson 2012, fig. 3.4). It does not appear to have been especially well-documented at Nimrud, and at Khirbet Qasrij this has been proposed as possibly post-Assyrian (Curtis 1989, 47, fig. 28). However, at Shiukh Fawqani they appear as early as the 8th century onwards (Makinson 2005, pl. 5) and it is fairly common in the early 7th century – 600 BC levels there as well. Although this form might be dated to seemingly quite late in the Iron Age, since it is clearly characteristic of the 8th–7th century BC, it is not necessarily a reliable indicator of post-Assyrian occupation. Other forms well-known throughout northern Mesopotamia and northern Syria from within Iron Age occupations include a type of Common Ware jar with handles flush with the rim (Fig. 8.32, nos 54 and 55; Bonomo and Zaina 2014, fig. 4, no. 2). Appearing in large numbers at Carchemish, this form occurs often at many sites in the area, and those closest to our examples can be found for example, at Shiukh Fawqani, where they are common in the 8th–7th century BC levels (Makinson

2005, pl. 23) and Tell Ahmar, where they are 7th century BC in date (Jamieson 2012, fig. 3. 2–5). As is the case with many Iron Age forms, this type of handle persists throughout many periods represented at Carchemish; a version is, for example, also considered a marker of Roman occupation and among the material for that period they were an important component. In our analysis only those examples which could be confidently distinguished by shape and fabric were assigned a probable date but despite the large numbers found, many of these handles were consigned to an indeterminate dating.

Certain ceramic forms present at Carchemish persist for long periods, presenting a challenge in distinguishing between sub-phases within the Iron Age, and this is not unique to Carchemish, but rather seems endemic to the region as well as to the period. At Tell Shiukh Fawqani, for instance, which shares the most similarities with the Carchemish assemblage, a similar problem has been noted; there, many types appear in the Iron Age I and II, and don't disappear in the 8th and 7th centuries BC (Makinson 2005, 432). A good example of one such type is the very shallow open bowl with simple rim, sometimes referred to either as large plates or platters. This type of vessel is quite numerous at Carchemish (see Fig. 8.31, nos 15–20 and see Bonomo and Zaina 2014, fig. 3, nos 1–4). Often present at sites with Neo-Assyrian occupation, at Shiukh Fawqani, they appear in levels from the Late Bronze (see Bachelot 2005, 335, pl. 2) well into the Iron Age (Luciani 2005, pl. 31; Makinson 2005, pl. 1). This is also the case further west, at Lidar Höyük, where they appear in levels dated to 1200–900 BC in fairly sizable numbers (Müller 1999, pls 2, 4, 7, 10) then less so in the levels dated to 850–725 BC (Müller 1999, pl. 15, 17). Closer to Carchemish, at Jurn Kabir, these are found quite early; they appear in Group A, Level III in that site, from the 11th-10th centuries BC (Eidem and Ackermann 1995, 314, fig. 4.9), though the excavators acknowledge in their publication that the dating of pottery from this level is provisional, as few published parallels exist. At Tille Höyük, it is represented in Early Iron Age levels (Blaylock 1999, 266, fig. 2). The LCP Carchemish examples show no indication of burnishing or decoration of any kind and can be described as coarse, gritty ware, typically of a light brown/buff fabric with the appearance of light yellow/cream slip, the closest parallel of which may be the Common Ware Bowl Type from Tell Ahmar, which is found in 7th century BC strata. (Jamieson 2012, 320, fig. 3.1). While we must consider the possibility that at least some of the examples collected represent occupation antedating the Assyrian takeover, we have quantified this type of vessel within the Iron Age material, as our examples are closer to most of the published later 8th–7th century BC examples in terms of fabric. Makinson has remarked that in the very persistence of these long-lived forms, especially the open forms such as these which are a continuation of the local IA II, the local

influence is most evident (Makinson 2005, 374), and this may be the case at Carchemish as well.

Fine wares, including Late Assyrian Palace Ware and most specialized common wares, do not appear as strong a component in the assemblage as might be expected, given the documentation confirming that Assyrian governors resided in the city following 717 BC (see Hawkins and Weeden, this volume Chapter 2; Hawkins 1980; Radner 2006–8, 58). Inscriptions also relate that the conquest of Carchemish was not accomplished solely by the imposition of administrators, but that Assyrian colonists were brought by Sargon to settle there (Hawkins 1980, 446). However, the possibility should be considered that the location where the Assyrians were settled was actually somewhere outside the walls of the city, a factor which might have contributed to the apparent scarcity of specifically Neo-Assyrian ceramic indicators in the Outer Town. The archaeological evidence for an Assyrian settlement to the north of Carchemish is discussed by Wilkinson in Chapter 5 of this volume. As mentioned above, noticeably absent from the Outer Town survey collection are most of the obvious type fossils commonly found in well-documented stratified contexts both within the Assyrian heartland and in the provinces (Hausleiter 2010). These include istikans, glazed wares, pipes, stands, cup-and-saucer lamps, tripod bowls. Bowls with internally and externally thickened rims, sometimes known as "hammerhead" types, appear, but only in very small numbers. At Khirbet Qasrij, the absence of some of these more representative forms contributed to the excavator's interpretation that the site was a post-Assyrian settlement, occupied after 600 BC but before the Achaemenid period (Curtis 1989, 51). However, at Carchemish the numerous parallels with other stratified Iron Age assemblages through the 7th century are considerable, so the obvious lack of these forms in the Carchemish Outer Town assemblage is not necessarily a strong indicator of post-Assyrian settlement. Imports, such as Cypro-Phoenician wares, are seemingly absent from the Outer Town survey, and the excavations on the Turkish side produced a similar absence of Cypriot Ware (Bonomo and Zaina 2104, 143). This is somewhat surprising, considering the many examples of imported wares illustrated by Woolley in the earlier reports (Bonomo and Zaina 2014, 141, fig. 5; Woolley 1939, pl. xiii, 5, 9), though it may be worth noting that many of the examples illustrated by Woolley seem to have been grave goods. This does not necessarily mean these imported wares are not present at Carchemish, but rather that they have not yet been recorded in any significant amount in the collection transects completed to date.

Due to the small size of the majority of sherds collected, the identification of specific vessel type was not always possible; when a vessel is represented only by a centimetre or two of rim or base fragment, distinguishing between bowls and jars is sometimes difficult. However, certain types of jars appeared with frequency in the Outer Town collection (Figs 8.32 and 8.33). As is the case with bowl types, the most relevant comparisons are again found at Tell Shiukh Fawqani in the 8th and 7th centuries BC and Tell Ahmar's 7th century BC levels, though only in the Common Wares; little evidence exists at Carchemish for specialized vessel types, and many forms appear with little variation over very long periods. The categorisation established for jar forms at Tell Ahmar provides an especially useful template for Jars at Carchemish. In this class, parallel forms include: jars with short or no neck and inverted rim (Jamieson 2012, 68, fig. 3.10/1–3); Jars with straight necks and ledge rims (Jamieson 2012, 69, fig. 3.11/1-2); Jars with restricted concave necks and externally thickened rims (Jamieson 2012, 65–66, figs. 3.7/7–9; 4.8/1–3; 4.9/1–7). While the most common jar forms found at Carchemish find their closest parallels at Tell Ahmar, especially those from Buildings C1A, C1B and C2, pointing to a 7th century date, since these forms are also appear earlier at other sites in the region, it would seem prudent to give them a more general date of 8th–7th century BC. The Turkish-Italian excavations report that jars, identified in their report as Simple Ware closed shapes, appear in a range of shapes and sizes similar to those from the LCP Outer Town illustrated here (compare Bonomo and Zaina 2014, fig. 4 with Fig. 8.32 this volume).

Remarks on the Outer Town collection: Greco-Roman through Islamic

The post-Iron Age material was dominated by Roman wares (see Newson, Chapter 9 in this volume). Examples of clearly defined Aramaean and Hellenistic forms were rare, and a small number of Early Islamic sherds appeared in the assemblage. Roman Brittle Ware was by far the most numerous, the sherds with characteristically red or orange–buff fabric and grey or black surface, always with a hard, gritty fabric. Many of these body sherds were corrugated. Although it sometimes appears that Greco-Roman pottery shares certain formal attributes with Iron Age ceramics, particularly certain bowl and jar rim shapes which look similar in shape, the later corpus differed from the Iron Age most obviously in its fabric; Roman material was frequently identifiable by a type of sandwich ware in orange/pale brown with white/yellow exterior slip or a red/brown or dark grey core with a brown/black surface, and typically rendered in a gritty hard fabric containing little or no chaff. Other well-known Roman wares included Roman Phocaean, with red sandy fabric and black surface, and Phocaean Red Slip, appearing in smaller numbers and including bowls with everted rims. The few Hellenistic and Eastern Mediterranean sherds represented a very small portion of the collection. Moreover, although the collection may not indicate anything more than sparse settlement, it seems clear that some degree of occupation was present in this area within the mapped

Outer Town walls well into the late Roman and perhaps Byzantine period. However, it is important to bear in mind that it is not possible to identify this area with certainty as 'intramural' settlement, since it is not certain whether the Outer Town ramparts were a functioning fortification system in these later periods.

The later corpus contained more examples of decorated sherds. Among the painted vessels, a few were distinguished by a bichrome design in yellow-white and black paint, and there is a particularly fine Eastern Mediterranean example of this style. The most common paint colours were red and black, though only a small number were sufficiently large to identify any patterning. There were a few examples of other decorative motives found mostly on body sherds, namely incised comb-pattern, fingernail type decoration, rope-impressed surfaces, the 'pie-crust' molded decoration present also in Iron Age wares, and one handle with a finger impression in a fabric which seemed to suggest a Roman or Islamic in date. Characteristic sherd forms included Roman strap handles, ring handles, amphora bases, and common bowl and jar forms. Along with 49 roof tile fragments, of recognized types characteristic of Roman and Byzantine periods (see Newson, Chapter 9 in this volume), one sample square produced a worked stone fragment with chisel scoring on its surface identifying it as a Greco-Roman artifact. Other diagnostic objects, which are possibly Iron Age in date, included a basalt curved platter and a molded rosette which could be either Roman or Islamic in date.

Mapping the Outer Town

The 'Inner Anomaly'

One of the most pressing issues of the 2010 season was the investigation of a major feature visible on the 1960s CORONA images but not mentioned in any of the early excavation reports. This feature does not appear on the town plan made in 1920, despite being identified as the outer town wall on one of the earliest maps of the site. On the CORONA (see Fig. 8.2), within the Outer Town, a light band is visible, running in parallel with the Outer Town rampart on the 1920 plan. As a built feature, it appears sufficiently sizable to be a town rampart. We termed this feature 'the inner anomaly,' since, although it had all the characteristics of a city wall (it is large, straight, and replicates the Outer Town wall in alignment), its functional identification was unknown.

It is likely that Woolley did encounter the inner anomaly in the course of excavations, as is clear from his description of the construction techniques used in House D, but he failed to realize that it was a distinct constructed component of the Outer Town, and that it had been already recognized as such by the British team who recorded the site in 1879 (see Fig. 8.5).

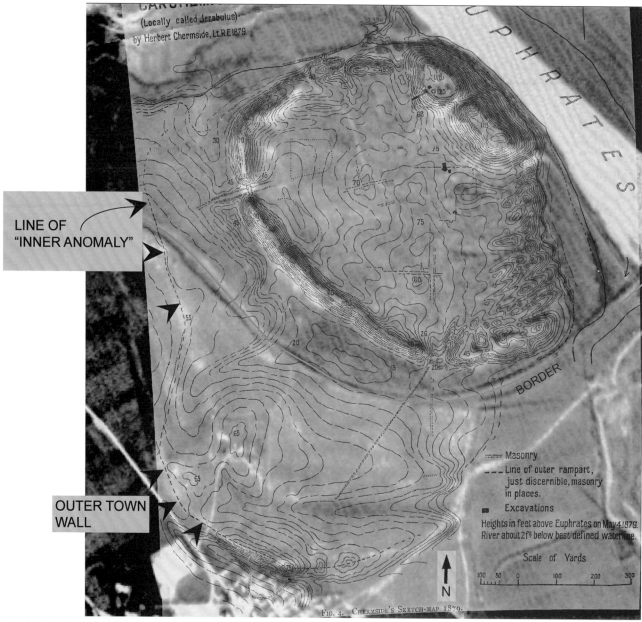

Fig. 8.5 Sketch map of the site of Carchemish produced by Herbert Chermside in 1879 (Hogarth 1914, fig. 4) georectified with CORONA image 1038 (22 January 1967)

The topographic sketch map produced by Herbert Chermside, dated 1879, which was published in *Carchemish I* (Hogarth 1914, fig. 4) records a feature then identified as the line of the outer rampart on the western side of the site, about 150 m west of the base of the Inner Town mound. Chermside describes this feature as: "Line of outer rampart, just discernible, masonry in places", but it does not correlate with the line of the outer wall which appears on the later town plan produced by Woolley and Guy in 1920. On the 1879 map this feature begins just south of the mill stream, and runs south-east for about 400 m before it turns

westward along a natural countour. It then runs south-west for another 250 m before changing direction again. It is only at this southwestern bend that the line of the rampart begins to correlate with the line of outer town wall documented by Woolley and Guy in 1920. The complete line of the outer rampart was in fact about 100 m further to the west, a fact which Woolley and Guy recognized and recorded. It is somewhat puzzling that Woolley did not record, or even make note of, the inner line of masonry recognized by Chermside, especially as it appeared on the earlier map, and particularly as this feature clearly runs directly beneath

Fig. 8.6 Carchemish Outer Town, 'Inner Anomaly' and Outer Town ramparts, looking west to east from atop the anomaly

Fig. 8.7 Carchemish Outer Town, 'Inner Anomaly' seen from the south, looking towards Jerablus football stadium

House D, excavated by Woolley's team in 1920 (see Fig. 8.1).

The only instance in Woolley's 1921 report which seems to refer to the inner anomaly appears in a discussion on construction techniques at Carchemish, although here Woolley seemed more concerned with the relatively unusual depth of the foundations found in the excavation of House D than the location on which it was situated:

> "Foundations vary greatly according to the nature of the soil on which the building stands: thus, sections of the outer West Wall, where the subsoil is of hard gravel, can show only a single course of cobble-stones and chippings below the brickwork, though this is a military work of defence over five metres thick; on the other hand the walls of House D, *built on a knoll of light soil,* have foundations nearly four metres deep ...". (Woolley 1921, 146)

It seems likely that the light soil knoll in which the foundations of House D were embedded is the linear feature now visible as the anomaly on the CORONA images. Woolley's inability to identify this feature on the ground, even when digging directly into it, is an indication of the subtlety of its topography and surface appearance within the agricultural fields in 1920. Although he recognized that the building sat on a knoll, without the benefit of remote sensing tools such as the CORONA images to provide a comprehensive overview of the entire site the feature was perceived as a localized natural phenomenon. Woolley's description confirms three important points about the inner anomaly: First, that the inner anomaly is in fact a three dimensional reality relative to the surrounding area, characterised by a distinctly light soil matrix as well as a change in topography; second, by being situated directly on top of the linear feature, House D is almost certainly related to it architecturally – if not in every building level then at least at some stage in its occupation; and third, with

foundations deeper, stronger, and perhaps older than any other building excavated in the Outer Town, House D may antedate the other buildings excavated in the Outer Town.

The true nature of this feature can probably only be determined by excavating a section through it. However, if one reconstructs the feature as a town wall, it delineates an area of roughly 40 ha, as compared with the 55 ha of the entire Outer Town mapped by Woolley. Including the Inner Town and acropolis, this would result in a site with a total area of 84 ha, as opposed to the 100 or so for Woolley's entire site. At 84 ha, Carchemish would still be considered large in comparison with other significant Iron Age centres, such as Til Barsip (47 ha) or Tell Halaf (51 ha). On the ground in 2010, the visibility of the inner anomaly varied widely within the site, although on the south it was much more obvious than even the Outer Town ramparts (see Fig. 8.6). In its most visible stretches, it is present in the form of a broad, diffuse change in soil colour and texture; as Woolley noted, it does appear lighter than the soil on either side of it. In some stretches it is defined by lines of stonework composed of both worked and natural stones of varying sizes; the largest of these found was 70 cm in length. For the most part, the stones are limestone, and the rare worked basalt stones were accorded individual GPS points. Other than appearing in a relatively straight line, the stones gave no indication of being bonded or fixed within a single construction; rather their appearance seemed more analogous to field clearing, except that they seemed to somewhat loosely form the edge of the anomaly, in that they sat at the highest position on the anomaly and there was generally lighter soil and more building debris on one side of the line rather than the other. Since the features of the anomaly are relatively subtle on the ground, it is easiest to see in relation to other structures. Its most obvious change in elevation can be seen in the SE quadrant of the Outer Town, east of the football stadium which partially sits on top of the highest point of the anomaly (see Fig. 8.7).

Fig. 8.8 CORONA image 1038 (22 January 1967) of Carchemish showing Topographic Transects A (= Collection Transect 7), B, C, D (= Collection Transect 8), and E

Transects: Topography (Transects A–E)

Five cross profiles, labelled Transects A–E, were made across the Outer Town to measure the degree of intra-site topographic variation and to estimate the height of occupational mounding (Fig. 8.8). The transects were laid out perpendicular to the inner anomaly and the Outer Town walls, extending from points outside the ramparts almost up to the border zone, as far as it was possible to walk within our survey area. In length they ranged from 148 m (Transect B in the north-west quadrant) to 247 m at the longest (Transect E, south-east quadrant). Figure 8.9 shows the degree of topographic variation illustrated in the surveyed transects. Plotted on a graph with condensed vertical exaggeration, the recorded points illustrate a pronounced rise within the Outer Town walls.

The rise is especially evident on the southern side of the Outer Town, as is illustrated in Transects D and E, while on the western side of the site, recorded in Transects A, B and C, the anomaly is much less distinct, although it is visible on the imagery. This fieldwork, in conjunction with evidence from the CORONA satellite images from the 1960s demonstrates

that the 'inner anomaly' is a major topographic feature with measurable three-dimensional characteristics. This topographic feature may have formed part of a previously unrecorded city wall or ramparts, perhaps now shrouded by occupational debris. Along Transects A (= Collection Transect 7) and D (= Collection Transect 8), a systematic collection of artefacts was undertaken, the results of which are discussed below.

Transects: Surface collection (Transects 7 and 8)

As well as defining the inner anomaly as a real topographic feature in the landscape, it was our objective to test the archaeological significance of the feature relative to the rest of the site by obtaining a sample collection of artefacts across the broadest possible area. Sample surface collections were therefore conducted along two of the Topographic Transects which had been laid out, one running east–west, and one north–south (Fig. 8.8). In the north-west area, Collection Transect 7 (= Topographic Transect A), 237 m long, consisted of nine sample squares, eight of which were

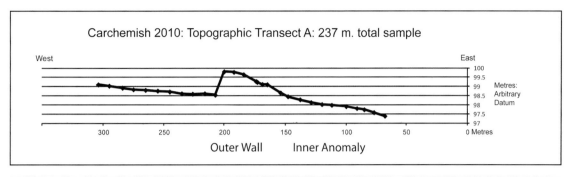

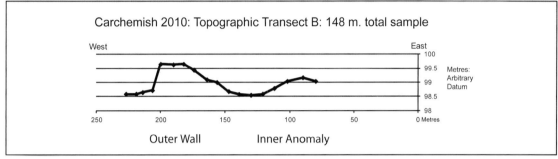

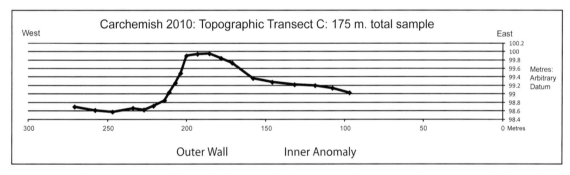

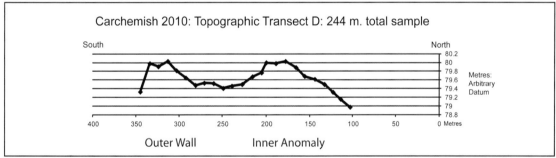

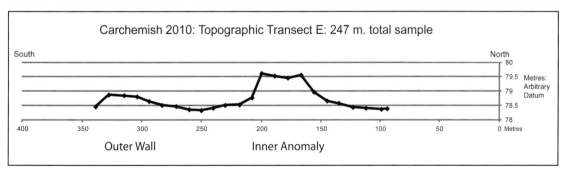

Fig. 8.9 Topographic survey points plotted on graphs with condensed vertical exaggeration to illustrate the degree of topographic variation of both Outer Town ramparts and 'Inner Anomaly'

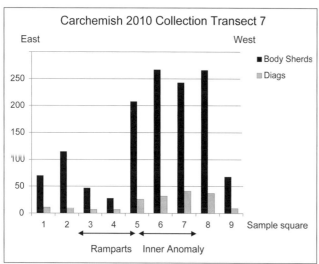

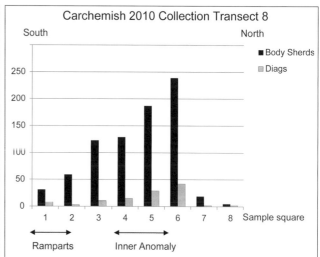

Fig. 8.10 *Sherd counts from sample squares along the N–W (Collection Transect 7) and E–W (Collection Transect 8) in Carchemish Outer Town*

Fig. 8.11 *LCP Cultural Inventory 2010: Original Woolley/Guy 1921 map georectified with 1967 CORONA image, with surveyed points recorded by the 2010 LCP cultural inventory indicated in red*

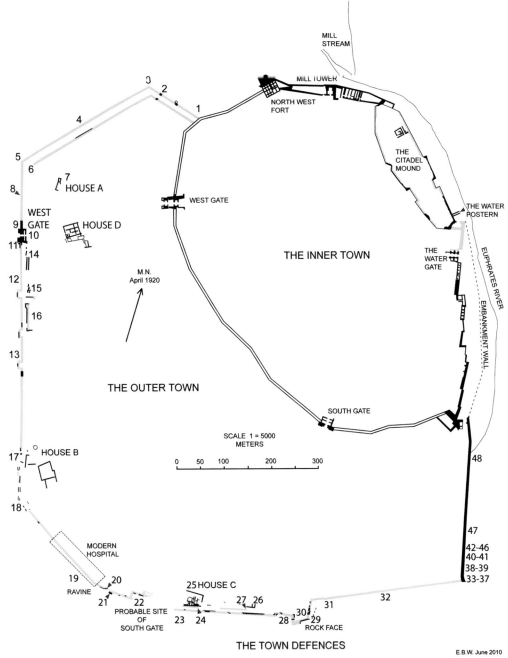

Fig. 8.12 Reassessing the original Woolley/Guy town plan: LCP town plan of Carchemish showing points recorded in 2010 located on the redrawn 1921 plan (after Woolley 1921, pl. 3). The walls rendered in blue represent conjectural reconstruction based on the original plan. Numbered points are described in Appendix 8.1 at the end of this chapter

10 × 10 m square, with one being 5 × 5 m square, laid at 40 m intervals. In addition to pottery, three small ceramic animal figurine fragments were found along this transect (LCP-10-33, 34, 35) and one stone tessera (LCP-10-36). The second Collection Transect, in the south-east quadrant, was designated Transect 8 (= Topographic Transect D) and along its 244 m length six sample squares of 10 × 10 m size and

two of 5 × 5 m were collected, also at 40 m intervals, the northernmost squares being close to the border zone. Two animal figurine fragments were included in this assemblage (LCP-10-31, 32). The surface collection was characterized in terms of artefact density as well as by period, and the visibility of artefacts relative to groundcover was recorded in case it was a factor in causing significant discrepancies in collection amounts. A GPS reading was taken at the north-east corner of each sample square. While ceramics were distributed across the entire Outer Town and into the area immediately outside its limits, the inner anomaly seems to function as the focus for the highest concentration of artefacts. The highest concentration of pottery was either on this feature or in its immediate vicinity, as illustrated in Figure 8.10.

Viewing the pottery in terms of its spatial distribution and chronological groupings, analysis thus far seems to indicate that within inner anomaly, Iron Age pottery is dominant. However, between inner anomaly and outer rampart, the collection consists of mixed Iron Age and later period wares. Outside the Outer Town wall, pottery was still collected but the lower number of sherds is more suggestive of field scatter than occupation. Equally, this small number of artefacts may be a result of the considerable amount of modern building works that have overtaken the southern half of the site. The dominance of Iron Age pottery within the inner anomaly may have implications in terms of the occupation sequence in the Outer Town; if a denser artefact concentration implies a longer period of occupation, then the area delineated by the inner anomaly might be older than the remainder of the Outer Town. Alternatively, the denser artefact distribution may be the result of density of settlement; in other words, more people lived within the inner anomaly than outside of it.

Thus far in our analysis, the Iron Age assemblage appears limited to the 8th–7th centuries BC and the sherds were chronologically consistent across the entire sample area, with no clear chronological concentrations identifiable in the three zones; inside the anomaly, just inside the Outer Town ramparts, or immediately outside of the city. Therefore, it is currently impossible to detect more refined settlement trends within the distribution pattern in the Outer Town. Some of the most representative Iron Age sherds from the Collection Transects are illustrated in Figure 8.33 (Transect 7, north-west quadrant) and Figure 8.34 (Transect 8, south-east quadrant). More intensive survey within all areas of the Outer Town would no doubt help clarify the potential chronological and spatial differences in occupation within the separate urban zones.

Reassessment of Woolley's town plan and cultural inventory

The LCP cultural inventory of the Carchemish Outer Town was completed in late July 2010 (Fig. 8.11). Our objective in this undertaking was twofold: First, to correlate the standing architecture and topography recorded in 1920 with the visible remains on site in 2010; second, to see whether new information could be gained by field walking to substantiate Woolley's reconstruction of the town plan. Our primary goal was to record all visible remains of archaeological

significance; in effect, creating a cultural inventory of the Outer Town. This work included field walking within the open areas of land within the town of Jerablus, and investigating the buildings, vacant lots, roads, and other installations which are in many instances now situated on top of the architecture illustrated on the 1921 plan. The locations visited by the LCP survey in 2010 are plotted on Figures 8.11 and 8.12, the latter of which illustrates the LCP's selection of points relative to the published town plan.

During this operation, many undocumented features were discovered within the modern fields, streets, yards and gardens that were accessible to the team. In some cases, the significance of the feature was less than clear, but we recorded it anyway. For instance, outside the Jerablus weather station we recorded walls of ancient, but unknown date jutting out from the fenced-in grounds of the station, and this appears in our inventory. We attempted to make note of any architectural features, however small or seemingly insignificant, including everything that appeared to antedate the 20th century, and even some features of a clearly more modern date but with potential historical significance. Many of these features were brought to our attention by local inhabitants. For example, in the unsheltered yard within the walls of one house compound near the stadium we were shown the well preserved remains of a polished concrete floor with an inscribed geometric pattern, which reportedly dated from the period of French occupation.

A major focus of the Outer Town project was a reassessment of the site plan published by Woolley in 1921. In terms of architecture, this included the Outer Town ramparts and the eight separate structures identified as houses A–H. In the 1921 report, the town plan (see Fig. 8.1) is accompanied by a narrative relating the survey process, with a succession of individual points along the town wall described in a fair amount of detail. A close reading of the report (Woolley 1921, 48–57) resulted in the identification of 48 key points along the ramparts and within the site which were deemed worthy of visiting, due to the strong likelihood for identification of those points on the ground based upon the specificity provided in the 1921 report. The original town plan was re-drawn, to clarify the difference between extant and conjectural features, and our 48 surveyed points were then situated on the new plan. (Fig. 8.12 and see Appendix 8.1).

The original town plan was re-drawn, to clarify the difference between extant and conjectural features, and our 48 points were then situated on the new town plan. The resulting map was then georectified and superimposed on a satellite image (Fig. 8.13). Using this new map and Woolley's narrative as a guide, the 48 points were visited on site. Woolley's descriptions were correlated with the points as they appear today, and the current state of preservation was recorded along with the geographical coordinates for each point, photos and in some cases, a sketch, particularly

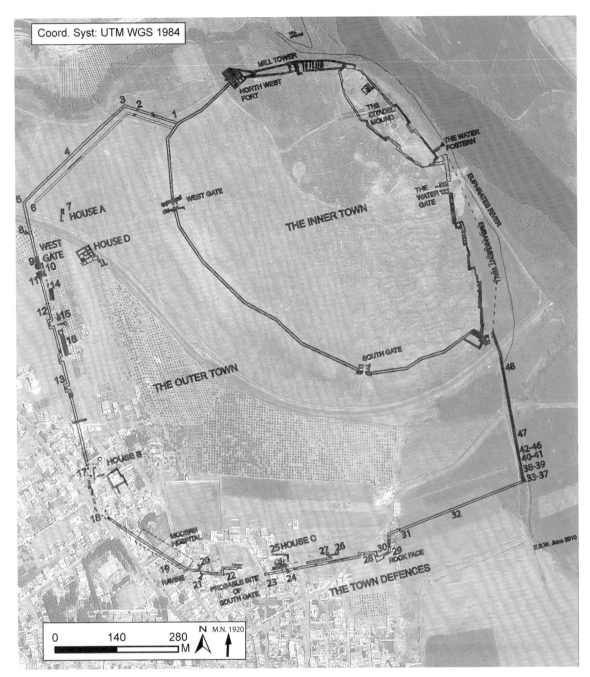

Fig. 8.13 Redrawn 1921 town plan of Carchemish (after Woolley 1921, pl. 3) georectified with GeoEye-1 image (2 March 2013) showing the site and modern Jerablus. Numbered points surveyed in 2010 are indicated

when topographic features seemed significant in the interpretation of the feature. In some instances Woolley's points were impossible to locate with any exactitude; in many cases the feature or location had been damaged, severely weathered, completely built over, or was inaccessible due to its proximity to the border. However, taken together, this recording represents a fairly detailed assessment of

the current state of visible remains in the major portion of the Outer Town, and many aspects of Woolley's urban reconstruction can now be better understood within the context of this new evidence.

Previously recorded key architectural features revisited as part of this inventory include:

  ○ House B: With the old excavation trenches now

obliterated by modern development, we were only able to identify its location within modern Jerablus.

○ House C, excavated by Woolley and Hogarth: vestiges of this feature still remain visible, but the excavation area is now partially covered by modern buildings to the south of the Jerablus football stadium

○ Houses D–H: the excavation trenches, with little visible architecture, were located in an open agricultural field. The unusual qualities of House D are worthy of reassessment in light of new evidence (see below).

○ The South Gate of the Outer Town: Currently invisible within the modern development of Jerablus, this architectural feature is also worthy of reassessment, due to the somewhat problematic nature of the original description in the report as well as new evidence from remote sensing, relating the fortification system to the ancient regional context of Carchemish (see the discussion by Wilkinson in this volume, Chapter 5).

○ The 'river wall' (our Area C). Forming the eastern perimeter of the Outer Town, this is the best preserved architectural feature in the survey; significant lengths of this prominent stone wall remain standing.

○ The Outer Town wall. Recording was completed of the entire circuit within Syria within the limits of the border zone. Assessments were made at key points along the visible stretches, as well as investigations along cuts made by agricultural activity on the western face. The investigation of the ramparts, being more detailed than the other previously documented features, is accorded a separate section, below.

○ The West Gate of the Outer Town, as excavated by Woolley. The location of the West Gate was found and recorded, although only a few of the dressed stone blocks now remain loose among the bulldozed soil. No new information was recovered from these trenches.

The 'House' sites

Many of the features recorded in 1920 were obscured or completely obliterated by modern construction or agricultural activities. The so-called House sites, in particular, have not fared well in the decades since their excavation. Within the Outer Town Woolley identified 8 separate structures interpreted as houses A–H. The excavation trench of House A (Woolley 1921, 188–119, fig. 36), just to the north of the railroad cutting and now in Turkey, was outside our survey area so is omitted from this discussion. It was re-excavated by the Turkish–Italian team beginning in 2011 (Marchetti

Fig. 8.14 An open lot in the town of Jerablus, showing an area between House B, excavated in 1920, and the Outer Town wall on the 1921 plan of Carchemish. In the foreground is a large worked limestone block, and the entire lot was littered with building debris, some of it certainly ancient

2012, 2014). House E was an annex of House D, and Houses F–H were represented by various architectural features either abutting or in the vicinity of House D, but all were interpreted originally as separate domestic structures. We were able to identify sizable trenches corresponding to the House D–H area in 2010 and while previously excavated mudbrick and stone rubble structures were visible on the surface, the remains were so deteriorated that distinguishing single structures was impossible at that time. The House D–H excavation area was situated very close to the border fence, which made it difficult to examine it in any detail, though we did manage to gain access to record the trench location with GPS points and photographs.

House B (Woolley 1921, 119–120, fig. 37)

House B was characterized by different walls assigned by the excavators to different levels, and there were additional walls and installations not connected to the house, including an unusual circular feature not identified (Woolley 1921, 120). Today the remains of House B are buried beneath a modern house and yard in Jerablus. In an adjacent open lot, a large dressed stone block (Fig. 8.14), clearly not in its original position, could be seen on the ground, and it may have originated in House B since similarly substantial stone architectural features were found in its vicinity during the original excavations. According to the excavation report, these included a column base, slabs of polished basalt, and dressed limestone doorjambs (Woolley 1921, 119–120).

House C (Woolley 1921, 121–123, fig. 38, fig. 54, pl. 18a, 18b)

In tracing the ancient remains throughout the village of Jerablus and within the fields, we discovered that some of

Fig. 8.15 Visible architecture in the 1920 excavation trenches of "House C", in the town of Jerablus, July 2010. The masonry and rubble wall in the foreground is probably the north wall of the structure, a detail of which was illustrated in the original report (see Woolley 1921, 146, fig. 55 and this volume, Fig. 8.16)

the features described by Woolley were extant almost exactly as they had been described in the earlier reports. This was the case in House C where, although situated in a densely built-up area of Jerablus, it was possible to match up a small section of the face of one wall in the standing architecture with the same section illustrated in the 1921 report, although the old excavation trenches were situated in an open lot in a densely occupied area of Jerablus (see Fig. 8.15).

The standing architecture here was recorded in plan and the site was recorded as a feature within the cultural inventory (see re-drawn plan, Fig. 8.16). House C is noteworthy because of the evidence presented in the original excavation report suggesting it may have antedated the Outer Town wall. The excavation of this structure is discussed in more detail below.

House D (Woolley 1921, 123–129, figs 39–49, pls. 19a, 19b)

Many of the characteristics of House D were remarkable in the context of the other so-called house sites excavated in 1920. None of the other house sites were comparable in terms of the quality of the construction and contents, and it was the sole context in the Outer Town in which Woolley found evidence of burning and destruction. Moreover, Woolley recorded only a single occupation level in this building, which he surmised was ultimately brought to an end with the Babylonian invasion of 605 BC. However, new information about the location of the building relative to the town's defences suggests that both its origin and its function may benefit from reanalysis. For these reasons, this building warrants more detailed discussion; see below (and see Fig. 8.17).

South Gate of the Outer Town

The assumption that there would need to be a monumental gate on the southern face of the Outer Town wall of Carchemish is logical, but in trying to locate reasonable evidence for such a building in 1920, Woolley was challenged by a similar situation as exists today, which is the encroachment of the town of Jerablus on the southern half of the site. The location of Woolley's South Gate in particular, could be construed as somewhat tenuous, considering the evidence provided in the report (Woolley 1921, 55). In an area in which his interpretation was confounded by the imposition of a modern hospital, house and road, Woolley extrapolated indications from the topography and fragments of architecture to construe the presence of a South Gate. The Gate does not appear on the 1920 plan as a discrete building, but rather as a collection of fragmentary architectural components which, combined with certain directional changes in the outer wall at that point, suggested to Woolley a monumental gateway. However, Woolley also commented in his report that the town wall foundations along this southern stretch of the ramparts on either side of the South Gate were on the whole "very shallow and feeble," in some places even sited on soft soil (Woolley 1921, 56. See below, Fig. 8.18)

The recorded architectural evidence for the South Gate seems to be comprised primarily of several individual elements which, to Woolley, suggested a situation similar to the "compartment-like wall which flanks the Water Gate of the Inner Town," and related components are described briefly as, "a small double re-entrant built of finely dressed basalt slabs either marked a recess in the wall line (as shown) or was part of the inside of a building whose outer (S.) face has fallen away: beyond this a solid buttress-salient occupied a slight projection of the rock bank" (Woolley 1921, 55). In 2010, we found the site of the South Gate area obliterated by a modern road and buildings, though within an open lot in the vicinity we recorded a number of large worked basalt and limestone blocks which could have been feasibly elements in the city wall, or a monumental gateway, but they were obviously not *in situ* (see location labeled "Probable site of South Gate" on Figures 8.13 and 8.18, LCP Points 20–22, and Appendix 8.1 for a description of those points). Moreover, the gateway at the point suggested by Woolley in the southern wall appears slightly off-set in relation to the major route way linking Carchemish with its region, a route discussed by Wilkinson in Chapter 5 of this volume. There is a street in the Inner Town leading though the area of unexcavated Roman remains up to the Processional Way on the citadel that is demarcated clearly on the GeoEye image by the remains of unexcavated Roman architecture (see Chapter 9, Fig. 9.2). As mentioned in Chapter 5, the major route running north–south to the south of Carchemish, which may be coincident with the Roman road, appears to meet the Outer Town ramparts where the modern road

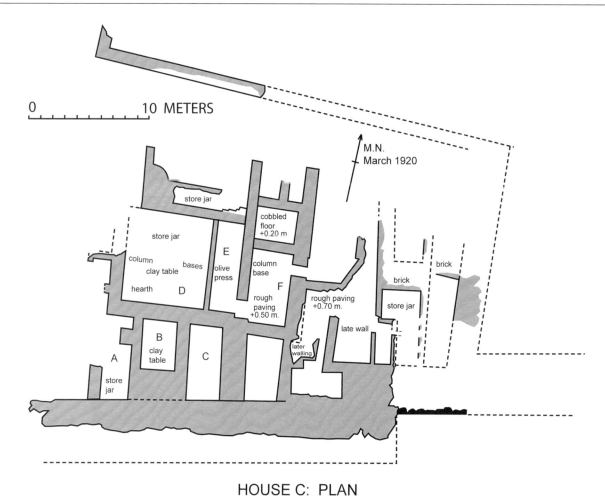

HOUSE C: PLAN

Fig. 8.16 Plan of "House C", Carchemish Outer Town (after Woolley 1921, pl. 18a). Walls rendered in lighter tone represent rubble masonry, while black indicates ashlar blocks

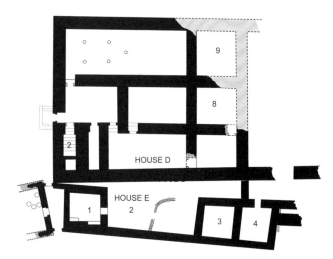

Fig. 8.17 Plan of "House D", Carchemish Outer Town (after Woolley 1921, pl. 19a). Lighter tone on this plan represents conjecture. The north and east external walls were brick resting on a single course of dressed stone block; all other walls were composed brick laid over stone rubble

intersects with a significant jog in the Outer Town wall. The area of this jog in the wall was described in the report of the survey of the Outer Town ramparts as a high, rocky outcrop of the Pleistocene terrace. Although Woolley found it worthy of note that this point along the outer wall offered a high, defensible position and was visibly aligned with the South Gate of the Inner Town, the architectural remains of the town wall here were too sparse to convince him that this was the site of a southern monumental gateway. Due to the degree of modern development in this southern sector, our investigations in 2010 could not confirm the presence of a southern gateway at this point along the ramparts, nor could we confirm a gateway at the location proposed on the Woolley/Guy town plan.

The river wall (LCP Area C)

Though referred to by Woolley as the 'river wall,'[6] the long straight stretch of stone masonry wall which forms the eastern perimeter of the Outer Town may have separated the

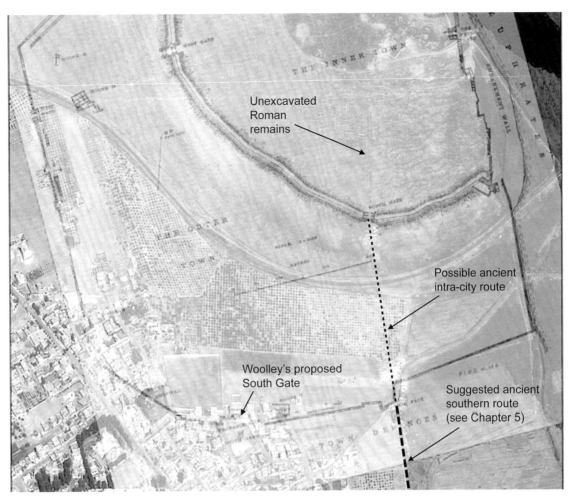

Fig. 8.18 LCP re-drawn plan of Carchemish georectified with GeoEye-1 image (2 March 2013) showing how an alternatively located southern gateway might have functioned in terms of linking the citadel mound and Inner Town with the greater N–S route system. Visible on the Geo-Eye image is the street or routeway within an area of unexcavated Roman architecture in the Inner Town, with linking the South Gate of the Inner Town with the acropolis. The suggested ancient route running N–S may have met the Outer Town ramparts as indicated

Fig. 8.19 The eastern face of the town wall of Carchemish, viewed from outside the site, at a point along the SE perimeter of the Outer Town (July 2010).

city not from the current of the Euphrates or a branch of it, but from a canal (Figs 8.18 and 8.19, and see Wilkinson, this volume, Chapter 5). On Woolley's town plan this wall joins with the southern perimeter wall, forming the south-east corner of the city. In 2009 the LCP assessed the state of the town wall on this eastern side and recorded GPS points along the visible north–south face and on the top ground surface bordering our collection Area A, where at least 13 large dressed stones were observed in a contiguous length lying three rows deep. In 2010 this feature was revisited, and more detailed recording was done along the accessible portions. A fair amount of the eastern stone circuit wall recorded in 1920 still stands today, and it is possible to correlate the extant remains with Woolley's description in the original report.

Constructed of well-dressed stone blocks with a rubble core, the north–south line of wall is the best preserved architectural feature in the Outer Town. Woolley noted that the carefully worked hammer dressed blocks in some parts of this wall, measuring up to 4.40 m long, were exceptional within the site (Woolley 1921, 146). Woolley reported that the extreme southern end of the river wall was "destroyed by the Germans during the war", and for the first 10 m the wall was only indicated by a few traces of filling (Woolley 1921, 56), which helps explain why no mention is made of any architectural evidence proving that this wall and the east–west perimeter wall intersected. A considerable amount of time was spent in 2010 searching for the south-east corner of the city, suggested by Woolley's plan, but its existence could not be verified.

The Outer Town ramparts: south sector

Considerable lengths of the Outer Town walls are now invisible in the landscape. In the southern quadrant, where modern Jerablus has encroached on the site, the town wall is either obscured by buildings and streets or appears as only a slight rise in the agricultural fields at the northernmost edge of the modern development (see Figs 8.6, 8.8, and 8.9, note appearance of Transects D and E). Limited lengths of it are indicated on the ground by copious amounts of scattered rubble, though this is often mixed with modern building material and differentiating between ancient and modern is often difficult, given the amount of construction that has impacted on the site's southern boundary. In the southern half of the site, topographic profiles recorded in July 2010 illustrate that the outer wall remains as a low topographic feature to the south-east of the Jerablus football stadium, extending east to a minor scarp revealed by a Pleistocene river terrace. Beyond the terrace to the east, through our Area A, Woolley's town plan projects a long, straight line of wall running east–west and forming a corner with the north–south line of the Outer Town rampart, the river wall. Woolley acknowledged that there was no particular evidence to support this line apart from some slight topographic indications and a few tumbled stone blocks, clearly not *in situ,* about half way along its length (Woolley 1921, 50, 56). No evidence of these blocks or this wall line was found in our survey, and the flat agricultural fields contained no topographic indicators of terracing or architecture. Therefore, the SE corner of the city as it is reconstructed remains essentially speculative.

The Outer Town Wall operations: north-west sector

On Woolley's plan, the Outer Town occupies a shape that is roughly rectangular in the landscape. Woolley reconstructed the entire Outer Town wall as one unified construction, and argued against multiple building phases, even though aspects

of it (specifically the double wall in the north-west quadrant) might suggest that it was built in successive stages (Woolley 1921, 52). While some of the defining characteristics of the wall are acknowledged as purely conjecture in the report, the Outer Town circuit wall is reconstructed as an ensemble despite the fact that, as recorded, the remains are not at all unified structurally. The ramparts are composed of a double wall system pierced by two monumental gateways, one on the west and one on the south. The 1920 plan shows projections along the outer face of the western wall, which Woolley interpreted as the foundations for 'salients,' or watchtowers, and in his narrative description (Woolley 1921, 55–56) he suggests that the entire perimeter wall was probably equipped with such salients at similar intervals, although other than the three on the western side, no others were actually located. One of the prime objectives of the LCP in 2010 was to investigate the visible evidence of the Outer Town wall, and in reassessing Woolley's descriptions relative to the extant evidence, we hoped to clarify some of the key characteristics only summarily described in the original report; specifically, features such as gates, towers, the double wall system, and details of construction. Our area of operation along the western Outer Town wall extended from the southern corner of the West Gate, close to the border zone, south to the junction of the modern road cutting east–west across the rampart that forms an approximate limit of the built-up area of Jerablus (see Fig. 8.20).

The 1921 report notes that a modern road ran along and over this stretch of wall, and that it was often difficult to distinguish between the ancient remains and the road metal (Woolley 1921, 55), a situation which still exists today. As opposed to the southern perimeter of the site, where the ramparts are not an obvious visible presence on the ground today, along the western perimeter the ramparts form a prominent topographic feature that defines the ancient site quite clearly. In the NW sector, our topographic profiles identified the remains of the Outer Town ramparts as an extensive feature now visible in a diffuse mound approximately 50 m wide and 1.5–2.0 m higher than the agricultural fields to the west, the width of the feature seemingly representing not just the architectural feature, but also the spread of its deteriorating debris and subsequent overburden. On this side of the city, the rampart mound is less visible on the interior, where the slope falls away gradually and is subsumed within the intramural agricultural fields (see Fig. 8.23 and Fig. 8.9, Transects A, B, and C).

Woolley's reconstruction of a double wall system at Carchemish was based largely upon the evidence he found only in this north-west sector. The architectural conditions recorded here were not replicated elsewhere along the wall circuit. Woolley reports tracing a patches of a double wall, composed of two parallel walls, each about 5 m in width, with about 9 m between them, resulting in a rampart originally 19 m in total width (Woolley 1921, 50–51). In

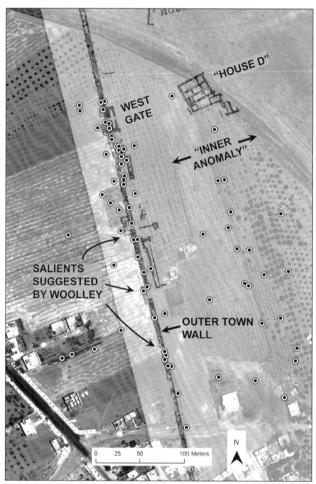

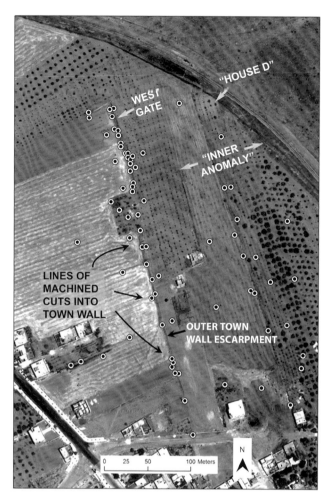

Fig. 8.20 Woolley/Guy 1921 town plan georectified with CORONA image 1038 (22 January 1967). The image shows the NW quadrant of the Carchemish Outer Town survey area including the Outer Town ramparts, West Gate, and House D, with LCP points surveyed in 2010 indicated as dots. Note location of the salients reconstructed by Woolley as projecting from the line of the wall on this side (scanty vestiges of the southernmost salient are not visible on reproduced plan)

Fig. 8.21 NW quadrant of Carchemish Outer Town survey area: CORONA image 1038 (22 January 1967), with LCP surveyed points indicated as dots. Straight lines visible in the field west of the site indicate ploughing or bulldozing which has cut into the Outer Town's western side, resulting in insets and projections in the western wall face. Compare with Fig. 8.20, showing Woolley's plan

the vicinity of the West Gate, especially, Woolley recovered sufficient evidence to suggest to him that the space between the two walls was given over to a series of inner chambers and corridors forming part of the fortification system (Woolley 1921, 54), and Woolley surmised that these were probably barracks or guard-houses which were sheltered by the height of the outer wall and towers (Woolley 1921, 50). The metalled road which runs along the top of the western scarp, and the houses built along it, have resulted in the disturbance of the ancient remains of the ramparts on this side, and our attempts in 2010 to locate any indication of these intramural chambers east of the outer wall face was thwarted. Several short stretches of wall lines composed of small cobbles were visible on the surface to the east of the rampart scarp, but as they were sometimes incorporated

within modern household installations, it was impossible to determine their age and their relationship to Woolley's plan.

Woolley acknowledged that the construction of the outer rampart seemed to vary depending on the nature of the topography; on high ground, over hard gravel, the foundations could be extremely shallow, but lower lying areas were filled in with deeper underlayment (Woolley 1921, 50). Here in the north-west sector, the ramparts were described in the report as a flimsy foundation of small stones and rubble. The passage in the report describing the wall length immediately north and south of the West Gate relates:

"… the foundations of the wall seem never to have been other than flimsy and shallow, a single course of small stones; the brick had entirely disappeared; the foundations survived only in patches; sometimes a face could be distinguished, but seldom with certainty". (Woolley 1921, 55)

Nevertheless, Woolley clearly considered the westernmost edge of the Outer Wall to be the actual wall face, reconstructing it as such in the town plan. He reconstructed the 300 m stretch of wall south of the West Gate as a straight run fortified with three projecting towers, each 20 m in width and spaced about 40 m apart. The interpretation of these three projections as towers caused Woolley to suggest that similar towers appeared probably along the entire circuit of the Outer Town wall (Woolley 1921, 54), though no others were found. Our investigation of this wall face suggests that these towers might not have been an architectural reality. Rather, by 1920, modern excavation may have created the impression of projections in the outer wall face. Much to the detriment of the archaeological integrity of the Carchemish, large-scale machined excavations have impacted severely on the western face of the town wall, in some areas cutting well into the wall structure and exposing the core of the ramparts. These cuts have been made for the extension of fields below the wall and for the extraction of gravel which, we discovered, is an abundant component of the rampart's construction.

The pattern of scarping is clearly visible on the most recent satellite imagery (compare Figs 8.20 and 8.21). On the CORONA image from 1967, one can see that the repetitive actions of the farmers' ploughs or bulldozers have cut into the hard matrix of the wall, leaving unploughed spaces in between where the machine turned, which appear to be projections from the wall face. When the 1920 town plan is georectified with the satellite image, the scalloped edge of the wall face closely aligns with Woolley's reconstruction of the stretch of wall containing the three tower projections. When measured on the ground, these 'projections' are almost exactly the same as Woolley's dimensions for the 'tower' width (about 20 m) and the intervals between them are roughly the same as Woolley's measurement (40 m).

Corroboration for the persistent pattern of agricultural scarping into the western ramparts may be indicated by two boundary stones which we discovered at points along the wall face (Fig. 8.22). We were informed by local inhabitants that these trapezoidal worked stones, measuring about 50 cm long and 20 cm wide and inscribed with a geometric pattern, are commonly recognized as markers of field ownership or usage, and are considered originally Ottoman in date. We found one such stone embedded into the top surface of the rampart escarpment, and one in the tumble below, further along the wall. In both cases, their location corresponded with existing boundaries indicated by a change in crops planted in the fields immediately adjacent to the wall.

It is possible that by the early 20th century, when Woolley's team recorded the rampart, this incremental cutting away of the western face of the perimeter wall

Fig. 8.22 Carchemish Outer Town, LCP 2010, NW quadrant, "Ottoman" boundary stone found directly below Outer Town wall, in the fields to the west of the rampart

Fig. 8.23 Carchemish Outer Town, LCP 2010, NW quadrant, view of the western (outer) face of the Outer Town wall, with Section 3 visible

by farmers had already been happening, perhaps even for centuries, but he failed to understand the dramatic impact it had made on the condition of the wall. One brief remark in the 1921 report may be an indication that Woolley saw, but did not recognize, that agricultural excavation was already reshaping the western wall face: Woolley states, "Along this west front it was noticeable that even when the rubble gave a more or less straight edge it seemed as if we were dealing less with an actual face than with the filling from behind such" (Woolley 1921, 53).

North-west sector: section recording along the Outer Town Wall

In addition to revealing factors affecting the preservation of the ramparts, the modern scarps allowed us to gain insight into the construction methods of the early builders. We examined four vertical section cuts already made along the outer face, conducting a concurrent surface survey to record any visible architectural characteristics and associated small finds (Fig. 8.23).

These sections demonstrate that the Outer Town wall in this north-west sector is not the flimsy, shallow, single-

course of stones that Woolley described on the western side (Woolley 1921, 50, 54), but is instead a sizable feature of dumped soil, Euphrates river gravels and broken limestone at least 2 m in height with a slope extending out at least 14–15 m from its top surface on the western side. Therefore, rather than being situated on top of a natural limestone bed, the fortification wall on this side of the city would have been resting on a substantial foundation, which could only have been produced with the investment of considerable labour and resources. There are also indications that the ramparts may have been erected in more than one episode: Just south of the West Gate, the successive agricultural scarps and gravel extraction pits have exposed within the wall core a length of mud brick wall approximately 14 m long which appears to be encased with the dumped matrix noted above. This feature is only visible in Section 3 (Figs 8.24 and 8.25). In Section 3, slightly further east than the other sections and therefore cut deeper into the rampart matrix, the exposed interior of the rampart revealed a distinctive construction feature. Here, delineated clearly in section was a length of mudbrick wall laid on top of another layer of medium-sized cobbles. It was unclear whether this wall was intended to serve as structural support for the loose gravel and loam layers on top of and around it, or whether it represented an earlier wall incorporated into the rampart. It did not seem completely continuous, and no other areas of mudbrick wall were found in the three other sections. Above the brick wall, an upper cobble stratum appears in this section, contained on one side by a stone revetment, indicating the intentional construction of the cobble layer. The LCP recorded masses

Fig. 8.24 Carchemish Outer Town, LCP 2010, NW quadrant, Section 3. Western (outer) face of Outer Town wall. Visible in the section is a 14 m. length of laid mudbrick, perhaps a previous wall or a mudbrick core

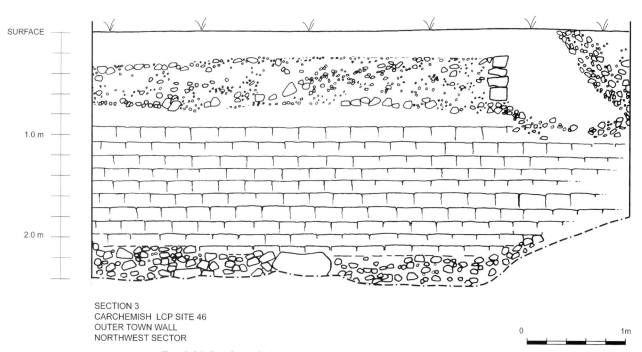

SECTION 3
CARCHEMISH LCP SITE 46
OUTER TOWN WALL
NORTHWEST SECTOR

Fig. 8.25 Carchemish Outer Town, LCP 2010, NW quadrant, Section 3

Fig. 8.26 Looking south from on top of the Outer Town wall in the NW quadrant of the site, showing the limestone cobbles described by Woolley in Carchemish II, which formed the uppermost layer of the massive defensive rampart and could have been the base for a stone or mudbrick superstructure

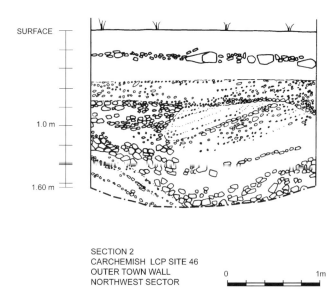

Fig. 8.27 Carchemish Outer Town, LCP 2010, NW quadrant, Section 2

of cobbles across a long stretch of the top of the rampart scarp (see Fig. 8.26), and it may have been this uppermost layer which gave Woolley the impression that in this stretch of the wall just south of the West Gate, "the foundations of the wall seem never to have been other than flimsy and shallow, a single course of small stones ..." (Woolley 1921, 55). While the cobbles are still a recognizable indication of the line of the rampart it appears that, in this part of the site at least, Woolley did not recognize the deep, multi-layered foundation levels lying beneath.

In terms of the processes of deposition, the primary construction feature is best visible in Sections 2 (Fig. 8.27) and 4 (Fig. 8.28). In both of these sections it is apparent that the rampart here is composed predominantly of successive layers of deposit on top of the natural consolidated gravel, or decomposed limestone.[7] On top of these gravel layers was the layer of cobbles described above, which Woolley took to be the foundation of a stone superstructure. The loose gravel and loam tip lines were visible in the sections, suggesting gangs of workers shovelling from different sides to create the supporting mound. The gravel is layered along with cobble layers, and in some cases larger stones. Examined in the field, these horizontal layers are clearly not the result of natural processes, and they are not sufficiently straight or consistent to be floor levels.

A small amount of pottery was retrieved from the section face in Section 1 (Fig. 8.29), and although it does not necessarily coalesce as an assemblage into one chronological period, we can at least suggest that Iron Age forms are possibly represented by a carinated bowl, a bowl with an externally thickened rim, and the ring bases, although the

few sherds recovered are not strong diagnostic indicators. If the deposition of the pottery can be associated with the construction of the wall, then it is possible that the pottery corroborates the extension of the Outer Town sometime during the Iron Age, though currently a more firm date for the origin of the ramparts is not possible from the evidence collected. At this point, within the mounding of the rampart no distinctly Hellenistic or Roman ceramics were identified and nothing obviously earlier than Iron Age. The absence of obvious post-Iron Age material in the Outer wall construction, together with the relatively low density of post-Iron Age sherds collected in all areas of the LCP Outer Town survey is noteworthy. Taken together, these factors seem to suggest that after the Iron Age, the main occupation of the city seems to have been relegated to the Inner Town and acropolis. As Newson discusses in Chapter 9 of this volume, Carchemish may have experienced resurgence in the Hellenistic period and enjoyed continued significance well into the Roman period, but the evidence does not correlate with urban expansion in these periods. On the contrary, pottery from the construction of the ramparts, surface survey, and remote sensing all indicate that in these later periods the Outer Town itself was probably given over to scattered low density suburban settlement. Although the ceramic evidence thus far suggests that the origin of the Outer Town wall could feasibly be ascribed to post-Assyrian occupation, until further investigations are completed it is impossible to assign an exact date to its construction, or to apply this evidence in determining a date for the extension of the Outer Town.

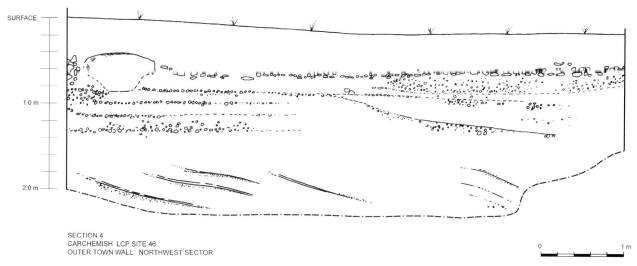

SECTION 4
CARCHEMISH LCP SITE 46
OUTER TOWN WALL NORTHWEST SECTOR

0   1 m

Fig. 8.28 Carchemish Outer Town, LCP 2010, NW quadrant, Section 4

General discussion of results

Urban development: reconsidering the Outer Town expansion based on the excavated evidence and the LCP results

As the 1921 Woolley/Guy town plan is the only architectural record of the site, this plan has long served as the basis for the accepted chronological model for the city's occupation sequence. This model is based upon Woolley's supposition that the Outer Town must have been built during a phase of expansion occurring sometime during the later Neo-Hittite period, when the political situation provided sufficient stability and resources, and the socioeconomic conditions necessitated an increase in urban space. The excavated buildings within the Outer Town provided Woolley with support for this hypothesis, but even though two excavated buildings, House C and House D, appear to have antedated the Outer Town wall, the original report does not accord this much significance. Instead, the evidence was interpreted as likely to be Neo-Hittite in date as well, only slightly earlier in the period. The Outer Town wall itself provided Woolley with little in the way of actual dating evidence. By the time Woolley recorded it, the brickwork had been almost thoroughly denuded, and most of the stone block work from the town wall was robbed out, apart from some sections of the river wall. So, Woolley's assertion that the wall was a Neo-Hittite construction was based on little direct evidence from the architectural characteristics of the wall itself, though a few artefacts found in its vicinity were reported, corroborating his hypothesis.[8] His interpretation of the Outer Town expansion as 'Late Hittite' (Neo-Hittite) in date seems to have depended on a chronological model in which the progressive extension of the city was coincident with specific sequential time periods; hence, the Outer Town

rampart was dated by him to the 'Late Hittite' period, the Inner Town ramparts were dated to the 'Middle Hittite' period (Woolley 1921, 41, 48), and the acropolis wall represented the 'Early Hittite' settlement (Woolley 1921, 40).

Outer Town Wall and the House sites: dating implications of the excavated evidence

Although Woolley uncovered evidence from buildings excavated in the Outer Town that clearly antedated the construction of the Outer Town ramparts, the evidence presented for this in the reports was not considerable, and it was not interpreted by Woolley as an indicator for extensive Outer Town occupation preceding the Outer Town wall. However, the few indications of multiple periods of occupation should, perhaps, be considered in detail in order to gain some insight as to the sequence of settlement within the Outer Town, in light of the new evidence obtained by the Land of Carchemish Project. The only examples reported of this potentially early evidence come from Houses C and House D.

In his report on the excavation of House C (see Fig. 8.16), Woolley stops just short of concluding that this house antedated the Outer Town ramparts. The evidence presented in favour of it preceding the rampart in origin seem fairly strong; the building's southern end had been obviously cut by the line of the outer rampart, and some of its rooms filled in solid after being reduced in size by the town wall's construction. Moreover, the walls and orientation of the building do not follow the orientation of the Outer Town wall, but are askew with it, and they abut the town wall jaggedly but do not bond with it, all indications that House C probably existed when the town wall was built. As Woolley suggests, if the town wall had been built first, its inner face would have been respected by the builder of House C, and in the immediate vicinity of the building, the inner face of the town wall consisted of excellent dressed stone blocks. The overall quality of the House C construction was poor. Multiple levels of foundations were composed typically of small, soft chunks of chalk mixed with larger blocks of limestone. One feature distinguishing this building from the others at Carchemish is a limestone olive press, found *in situ* in the middle of the house. Almost all distinct floor levels had been destroyed, and the pottery and artefact assemblage recovered was relatively small. Although the internal walls showed variation in depth and in details of construction, the contents were uniformly described by Woolley as 'Late Hittite' (Woolley 1921, pl. 20, c.6, d.7, d.8), the same period to which he attributed the Outer Town wall.

The report therefore implies that both House C and the Outer Town wall were roughly contemporaneous, both existing within the Neo-Hittite period. However, at least one recent analysis reports that the excavated pottery assemblage may in fact date to the 7th century BC.[9] If this is the case, then the contents of House C could post-date Woolley's date for the Outer Town wall by more than 100 years. This seeming contradiction between the date of the building and the date of its contents may be resolved by assuming that an older version of House C was in place at the time of the construction of the town wall, and it was partly destroyed at that time, but then subsequently re-occupied. However, the artifact assemblage was reportedly uniform in date, and there was no evidence to support an earlier origin for the structure. While Woolley presents substantial evidence indicating that House C pre-dates the town wall in origin, there is no discussion in the report of the possibility that the building and the town wall might belong to entirely different phases of expansion within the city's history, though that seems to be implied by the evidence and the discussion. If House C is dated by its contents uniformly to the 7th century BC, and it represents a single phase of occupation, then it may follow that the ramparts could have been constructed later, during the 7th century BC when the city was under Assyrian administration, or at any time thereafter. In sum, the spatial relationship between House C and the Outer Town wall seems to allow for the possibility that the Outer Town ramparts post-date House C, but without a more refined assessment of the contents of the building, which might point to occupation earlier than the 7th century BC that is hinted at by the variation in construction at different depths, it is difficult to determine whether House C represents evidence that the Outer Town was occupied well before the construction of the Outer Town wall.

As mentioned previously, many features of House D (see Fig. 8.17) distinguish it as unique within the excavated "house" sites in the Outer Town. In addition to being executed in "excellent hammer-dressed blocks of hard limestone"

(Woolley 1921, 123) and equipped with wooden columns and stone orthostats, the depth of its foundations, the quality of its construction and the fact that it may have been three stories high, are all qualities not found in any of the other buildings excavated by Woolley. Moreover, its occupation was limited to a single period, the later 7th century BC. Woolley presented the house and its contents as evidence for an occupation destroyed at the time of the Babylonian conquest, and this included indications of combat (numerous weapons) and burning (molten mudbrick, small piles of ash, and fused metal objects). Despite the substantial architecture and the rich and varied artefact assemblage found within and around the building comprising objects and features which could be interpreted as military in function and character (including a wide array of metal weaponry and the facilities to manufacture it), Woolley considered the building remarkable but nevertheless domestic in function. Among many features which lend House D a monumental quality, it is unusually large and well built, with an average wall thickness of 1.70 m and foundations of at least 3.75 m deep in places. Woolley identified similarities between the dressed stone blocks in this building and that of the South Gate of the Inner Town, part of the fortification system which he assigned to the "Middle Hittite" period (correlating to 1750–1200 BC). However, Hawkins and others have noted that the latest manifestation of the South Gate of the Inner town, to which Woolley was referring, probably dates to the Neo-Hittite period.[10] Nevertheless, in terms of size and layout, the comparison with the Neo-Hittite gate is striking, and perhaps more convincing than a comparison of this building with the other "House" sites. Woolley did acknowledge that the deepest levels in House D may have been built very early on in the Neo-Hittite period before the construction of the Outer Town wall, when it would have stood as an isolated extramural occupation outside the Inner Town. However, with foundations almost 4 m deep and characterized by stonework similar to a Neo-Hittite gateway, it is perhaps not implausible that the building's earliest occupation may extend back before the period of Neo-Assyrian occupation, and its origins may even belong in the Early Iron Age. Moreover, the position of House D directly on the line of the 'inner anomaly', as discussed above, also suggests a possible functional and temporal relationship between the original building and the fortification system that the 'inner anomaly' represents. Whether its association with the 'inner anomaly' would then support the function of House D as a gateway in the town's fortifications, and whether this fortification system represented a Neo-Hittite urban extension, will only be determined with further archaeological excavation.

LCP Outer Town results: the 'inner anomaly'

There is as yet no concordance on the dating of the Inner

Town ramparts. Whether the encircling rampart of the Inner Town can be attributed to a Hittite king has not yet been established with certainty. Sherds have been found within the earthen fill of the rampart dating as far back as EB III–IV (Falsone and Sconzo 2007), so the Inner Town wall might have preceded the Hittite occupation of Carchemish. The Hittite king Šuppiluliuma I conquered the city in about 1352 BC, and a Hittite text relates that when his army took the city, they plundered *the 'lower town'* and deported over 3000 of the inhabitants (Hawkins 1980, 429; Gütterbock 1956, 41 ff). The 'lower town' mentioned may refer to the Inner Town recorded on Woolley's town plan, even if the earthen rampart had not been erected at the time of the conquest. However, it is clear that the discovery of the 'inner anomaly', if it is a town wall, represents another phase in the sequence of urban expansion, and since it appears to have been superseded by the Outer Town wall, the possibility exists that it represents the limits of a Bronze Age city.

When Carchemish expanded beyond the acropolis to the limits of the Inner Town, urban space was increased by 40 ha. If the 'inner anomaly' is interpreted as a town wall, then it delineates a further expansion of about 40 ha, thereby representing almost a doubling of the previous urban size. If it is the case that Woolley's Outer Town was a phase of urban expansion subsequent to that delineated by the 'inner anomaly', then the Outer Town wall constitutes an increase of only about 15 ha of living space; hardly a substantial gain, in light of the considerable effort entailed in constructing such a feature. Functionally, fortifications are intended to provide a defensible barrier and secure the intramural area. However, when the gain in liveable space is only 15 ha, it seems necessary to consider the motives behind the erection of the Outer Town wall in the case of Carchemish. Lacking evidence obtained from excavation of the 'inner anomaly' itself, we can consider the evidence from the sample collections by the LCP by taken across the surface of the Outer Town.

Looking at the 'inner anomaly' relative to the collection sample from the LCP Outer Town survey reveals some interesting insights on the urban development of Carchemish. The fact that the anomaly is a relic of urban occupation is indicated by the higher concentrations of sherds found either on it or in its immediate vicinity. The majority of the collection sample has been dated to the 8th and 7th centuries BC, with a component of post-Iron Age material dominantly Roman in date which does not seem indicative of dense occupation (see Newson, Chapter 9). In terms of dating, the collection was the same both within the 'inner anomaly' and in the area extending closer toward the Outer Town Wall, where there was a noticeable reduction in sherd count. Inside the confines of the 'Inner Anomaly', in LCP collection Area B, there are areas of dense sherds of Iron Age and later date interspersed with open areas, plausible support for the identification of a neighbourhood

of buildings or perhaps refuse accumulation south of the South Gate of the Inner Town. As mentioned earlier, today the 'inner anomaly' is distinguished by broad spread of light soil containing copious amounts of building material, predominantly limestone gravel and hand-sized cobbles. The surface appearance seems to indicate a compositional matrix that recalls the construction framework recorded in sections along the western face of the Outer Town wall, characterized by a multi-layered amalgamation of small limestone block fragments and gravel. The subtlety of its topography, captured in the topographic transects completed in 2010, might be the result of continuous deterioration and weathering; there are no hard edges to define a wall, though it could plausibly represent a sizable foundation mound to support a monumental wall. Without further archaeological investigations in the site, it is impossible to conclude whether the 'inner anomaly' is the fortification wall which delineated the Bronze Age city (perhaps the "lower town" conquered by Šuppiluliuma), or whether it represents a phase of expansion that occurred during the Neo-Hittite period, only to be obliterated by subsequent occupation or intentional destruction.

Woolley seems to have discounted the possibility that the Outer Town extension might be associated with the period of Neo-Assyrian occupation of Carchemish, in large part because of the scanty evidence uncovered during excavations documenting the period on the acropolis and in the Inner Town, where he assumed official buildings of the imperial administration would have been located.[11] The early British excavations in these two areas revealed no complete buildings dated to the period of Neo-Assyrian occupation, apart from the building discussed above, initially mis-identified as a fort rebuilt by Sargon (as mentioned above) Woolley 1921, 40, pl. 3; Woolley and Barnett 1952, 211–213), and Woolley interpreted all of the buildings in the Outer Town as domestic. The excavators seem to have equated the absence of monumental architecture with an absence of Assyrian imperial investment in the city or, at the least, the absence of a vital Assyrian administration for which the expansion of the city might have been a requirement.

Woolley's overall interpretation of the chronological development of the urban fabric has remained essentially accepted since his 1921 publication. Convincing arguments have been made in support of a Neo-Hittite date for the Outer Town ramparts, and in recent decades, information gained though regional survey as well as additional textual studies has been employed effectively, to view the evolution of Carchemish within a wider historical context.[12] For example, Mazzoni has presented a convincing case arguing that the Iron Age expansion of Carchemish was part of a recognized trend in urbanization west of the Euphrates which had been in progress since 1000 BC, independent from the Assyrian push westward (Mazzoni 1995, 181–186). The evidence for a specifically western urbanization as presented by Mazzoni, combined with the relatively small number of inscriptions mentioning Carchemish after the Assyrian takeover (see Hawkins and Weeden, Chapter 2) may support the persistence of strong local cultural traditions in this region concurrent with Assyrian occupation. Moreover, both the pottery record from the Outer Town of Carchemish and the LCP regional survey results for Iron Age settlement appear to substantiate a high degree of local continuity in the material culture during the Iron Age, a point which will be discussed further in the next section of this chapter, and in Chapters 4 and 5.

LCP Outer Town results: topographic and collection transects

Mapping completed by the LCP has illustrated the 'Inner Anomaly' has significance as a topographic feature, and its importance as an urban feature is also evident in the record of artefact collection from the outer town sample areas. The absence of an entire class of vessels associated with an Assyrian imperial presence may be a critical point in the understanding of the role of Carchemish during the Iron Age, especially as it is so markedly different from the situation at Tell Ahmar, where they are much more apparent in the 7th century BC levels. This apparent invisibility of Late Assyrian ceramic type fossil could, for instance, be a manifestation of a difference in status between Carchemish and Tell Ahmar/Kar-Shalmaneser after 717 BC. The extensive Late Assyrian evidence from Tell Ahmar/Kar-Shalmaneser attests to that city's continued significance as a royal city and regional centre for the Neo-Assyrian kings well into the period after Sargon's conquest of Carchemish in ways that the ceramic record of Carchemish does not. As it appears to be more representative of a continuing local ceramic tradition rather than one introduced by the occupying power, the ceramic corpus from the Outer Town at Carchemish may reveal less of an Assyrian investment in the city relative to that found at Kar-Shalmaneser. This supposition accords with the results produced from the LCP regional survey, as discussed in this volume by Lawrence and Ricci, Chapter 4 and Wilkinson, Chapter 5. According to the survey data, the settlement pattern during the Iron Age indicates a persistence of the local occupations, especially on tells, even during the period when the Neo-Assyrian kings were actively transforming the socioeconomic structure of the Carchemish territory as areas were absorbed gradually into the imperial provincial system. In this process, it is possible that despite the considerable economic and geopolitical advantage which the conquest of Carchemish must have represented to the Assyrian kings, it was Kar-Shalmaneser, the royal city 20 km downstream at the well-documented crossing point on the Euphrates, which retained pre-eminence as the focus of Assyrian occupation; meanwhile, at Carchemish the local traditions of pottery manufacture and use persisted and were not really impacted

by the arrival of Sargon's colonists or the installation of an Assyrian governor on the acropolis.

It can be argued that within the context of the Assyrian consolidation of the western empire, Carchemish would have held immense strategic significance; as the ideological heir of the Hittite empire, as the regional centre of an extensive, lucrative trade network, and as an influential centre for cultural innovation (Winter 1983). In light of all of the evidence gleaned from investigations both within Carchemish and from survey in its hinterland, it seems important to consider the possibility that it was the Assyrians, and not the Neo-Hittites, who were responsible for expanding Carchemish to its maximum extent. At least two different scenarios could be considered as plausible, both based upon the supposition that the 'inner anomaly' represents the extent of the city encountered by the Assyrians at the time of the conquest by Sargon in 717 BC. The Assyrian king could have chosen to destroy the existing town wall (if the 'inner anomaly' is interpreted as such) as a symbolic gesture of conquest. From numerous instances documented in Neo-Assyrian texts and sculptural reliefs it is evident that the razing of city walls as a lasting gesture of triumph was enacted with some frequency by the Assyrian kings in their campaigns. The destruction of the city walls of Carchemish, if such an act was undertaken by Sargon in 717 BC, would have held tremendous symbolic resonance, especially given the enduring significance of Carchemish as a bastion of Hittite culture and power.

On the other hand, the removal of an earlier town wall could also have been simply a result of the need for more space. As mentioned previously, when Carchemish was finally annexed by the Empire, Assyrians were already settled there, so the need for more domestic space could have been a pressing factor in the expansion of the city and the erection of a new Outer Town wall. The relatively small area enclosed within the new ramparts might indicate a need for social separation in addition to the need for more space; a new fortified zone, even if only 15 ha in extent, could have provided the incoming denizens of the city with their own distinct quarter without displacing the existing inhabitants. The ceramic evidence certainly points toward extensive occupation in the Outer Town during the 8th and 7th centuries BC, both within and outside of the anomaly, with perhaps slightly denser occupation seen within the anomaly. The preliminary results from the renewed excavations on the Turkish side seem to corroborate the continuation of a local ceramic tradition with connections to sites both within the Middle and Upper Euphrates region west of the river, as well with the Assyrian core, but there is a marked lack of Assyrian type fossils in the Iron Age assemblage. There are no clear subdivisions within the Iron Age ceramics on either side of the border to allow for a more refined dating than Iron Age II–III. As yet, the ceramic evidence from within the Outer Town provides the capability for identifying neither sequential occupation within the Iron Age nor separate phases of social organization in the Outer Town in Syria. However, in terms of the sociocultural aspect of settlement within the Outer Town, while it is true that an architectural transformation was achieved with the construction of the Outer Town ramparts -- whenever they were built – the archaeological evidence from the Land of Carchemish Outer Town Project thus far seems to indicate that the local cultural traditions continued relatively unchanged by the impact of the Assyrian conquest.

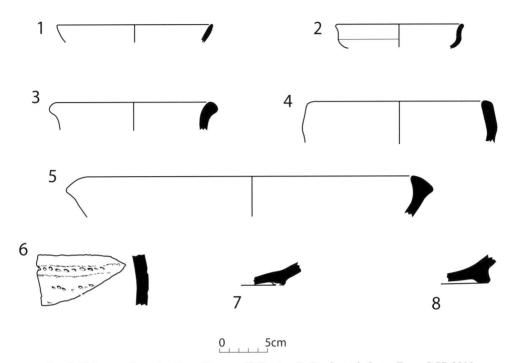

Fig. 8.29 Pottery from the Outer Town wall, Section 1, Carchemish Outer Town, LCP 2010

Table 8.5. Sherd descriptions for Fig. 8.29. Iron Age pottery from Carchemish Outer Town Survey, NW quadrant, Section 1

Fig.	Vessel	Fragment	Diam. (cm)	Color	Temper	Sherd Number	Remarks
1	Bowl/ Cup	Rim	16	Very light brown	Very fine sand	LCP10.46.Sec1.1	Palace Ware?
2	Bowl/ Cup	Rim	13	Very light reddish-brown	Fine sand	LCP10.46.Sec1.3	Exterior possibly burnished
3	Jar	Rim	16	Very light brown-buff	Abundant multi-colored medium grits	LCP10.46.Sec1.8	
4	Jar	Rim	?	Very light reddish-brown	Abundant fine-very large grits; Rare chaff	LCP10.46.Sec1.9	Self-slip exterior
5	Bowl	Rim	34	Medium orange-brown	Common medium grits	LCP10.46.Sec1.6	
6	?	Body	?	Very light reddish-brown	Fine sand	LCP10.46.Sec1.4	Exterior decoration: raised band with impressed finger nail marks
7	?	Ring Base	?	Light brown	Medium-large grits; rare chaff	LCP10.46.Sec1.2	
8	?	Ring Base	?	Medium reddish-brown	Common medium-large grits; abundant elongate voids	LCP10.46.Sec1.7	Sandwich temper (Post-Iron Age?)

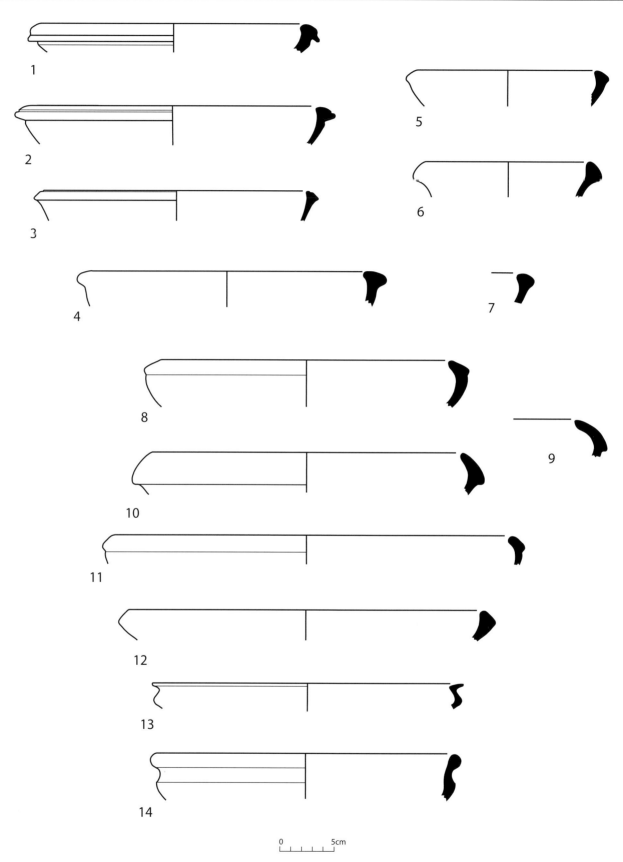

Fig. 8.30 Pottery from Area B, Transects 2-6, Carchemish Outer Town, LCP 2009

Table 8.6. Sherd descriptions for Fig. 8.30. Iron Age Pottery from Carchemish Outer Town Survey, Field B: Transects 2, 4 and 6

Fig.	Vessel	Fragment	Diam. (cm)	Color	Temper	Sherd Number	Remarks
1	Grooved rim bowl	Rim	24	Light reddish-brown	Common fine-medium sand	LCP09.46B.4.12.28	
2	Grooved rim bowl	Rim	26	Not described		LCP09.46B.2.12.10	
3	Grooved rim bowl	Rim	24	Very pale yellow-brown	Common fine-med sand; common chaff	LCP09.46B.4.11.18	Exterior slip or self-slip
4	Bowl	Rim	23	Very light brown buff	Common very fine sand	LCP09.46B.4.11.24	
5	Bowl	Rim	16	Very pale brown	Common fine sand	LCP09.46B.4.11.13	
6	Bowl	Rim	14	Very light brownish buff	Abundant fine-medium sand	LCP09.46B.4.12.15	
7	Bowl	Rim	?	Very light pink buff	Common fine sand	LCP09.46B.4.11.15	
8	Bowl	Rim	26	Very light reddish-brown	Rare medium grit; elongate voids	LCP09.46B.4.9.16	
9	Bowl	Rim	?	Very pale greenish brown	Very fine common sand	LCP09.46B.4.11.9	
10	Bowl	Rim	28	Very light brown	Common fine sand	LCP09.46B.4.11.5	
11	Bowl	Rim	36	Not described		LCP09.46B.2.12.4	
12	Bowl	Rim	34	Medium reddish-brown	Rare fine sand/grit	LCP09.46B.4.9.32	Glaze or paint on rim
13	Carinated bowl	Rim	28	Medium greyish brown	Circular voids, Common large grit	LCP09.46B.4.9.13	Burnished exterior; possibly post Iron Age
14	Carinated bowl	Rim	28	Pale brown	Abundant med-large sand & grit; occasional chaff	LCP09.46B.4.12.21	

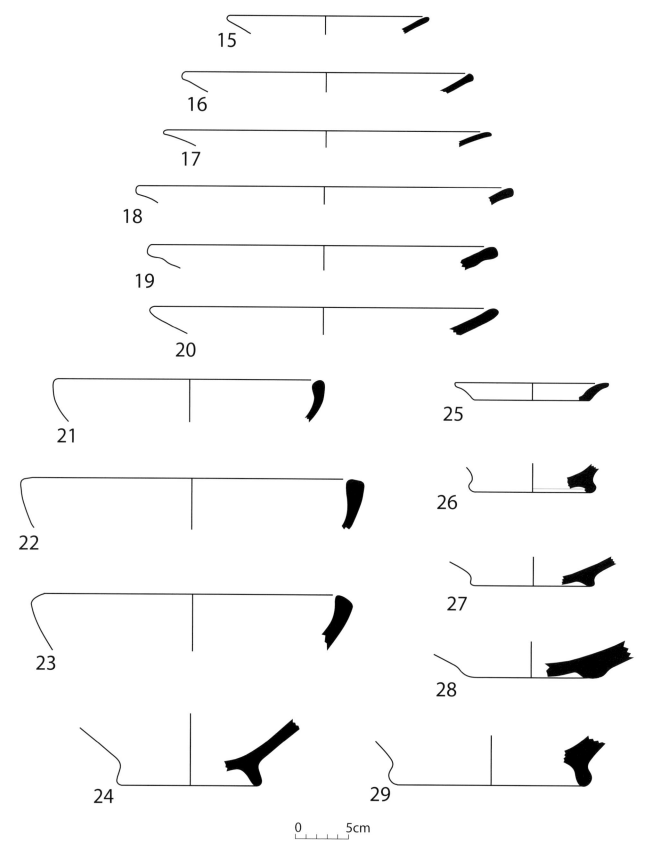

Fig. 8.31 Pottery from Area B, Transects 2-6, Carchemish Outer Town, LCP 2009

Table 8.7. Sherd descriptions for Fig. 8.31. Iron Age Pottery from Carchemish Outer Town Survey, Field B: Transects 2, 4 and 6

Fig.	Vessel	Fragment	Diam(cm)	Color	Temper	Sherd Number	Remarks
15	Open bowl/ platter	Rim	18	Not described		LCP.09.46B.2.12.2	
16	Open bowl/ platter	Rim	26	Light reddish-brown	Common fine-medium sand	LCP.09.46B.4.11.8	
17	Open bowl/ platter	Rim	30	light reddish-brown	Rare sand	LCP.09.46B.4.11.1	
18	Open bowl/ platter	Rim	34	Very light reddish brown buff	Abundant fine sand	LCP.09.46B.4.11.17	
19	Open bowl/ platter	Rim	30	Very light brown	Common white sand grits	LCP.09.46B.4.16.1	Self-slip exterior
20	Open bowl/ platter	Rim	32	Pale brown	Abundant fine-medium sand	LCP.09.46B.4.11.20	
21	Bowl	Rim	23	Very light brown buff	Very fine sand	LCP.09.46B.4.9.35	
22	Bowl	Rim	28	Very light orange-brown	Abundant fine sand	LCP.09.46B.4.12.13	
23	Bowl	Rim	26	Medium brown buff	Common fine sand	LCP.09.46B.4.12.17	
24	Bowl	Base	12	Not described		LCP.09.46B.2.12.9	
25	Shallow bowl	Complete profile	14	Medium greyish brown	Very fine sand; some voids	LCP.09.46B.4.12.53	Faint incised design on exterior; Possibly Achaemenid
26	Bowl	Base	10	Not described		LCP.09.46B.6.12.23	
27	Bowl	Base	10	Not described		LCP.09.46B.6.12.27	
28	Bowl	Base	?	Not described		LCP.09.46B.6.12.28	
29	Bowl	Base	16	Very pale brown	Common very fine sand	LCP.09.46B.4.12.52	

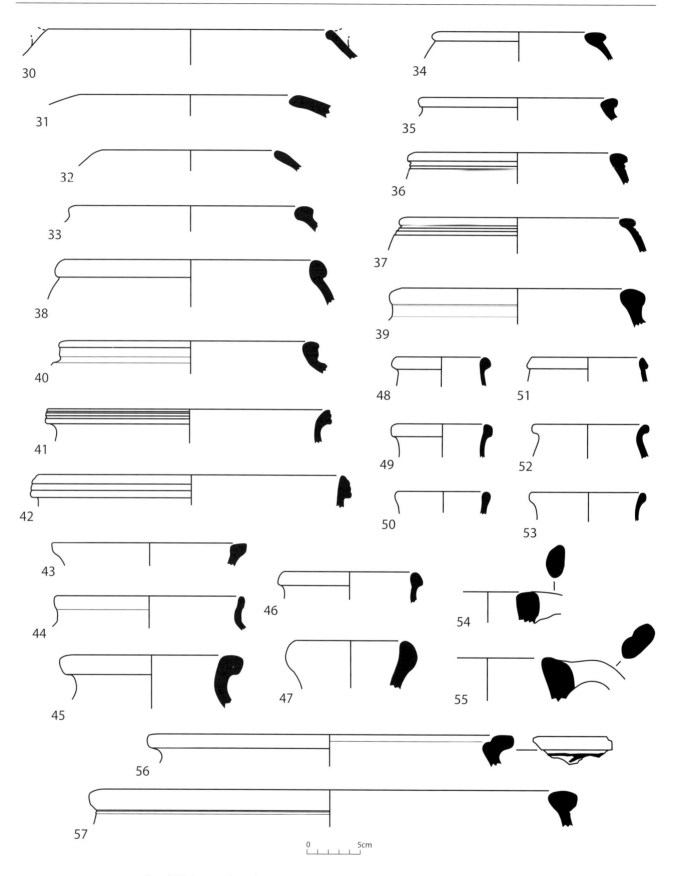

Fig. 8.32 Pottery from Area B, Transects 2-6, Carchemish Outer Town, LCP 2009

Table 8.8. Sherd descriptions for Fig. 8.32. Iron Age Pottery from Carchemish Outer Town Survey, Field B: Transects 2, 4 and 6

Fig.	Vessel	Fragment	Diam. (cm)	Color	Temper	Sherd Number	Remarks
30	Cooking pot	Rim	26	Dark greenish-brown	Medium-coarse sand; rare chaff	LCP09.46B.4.13.25	
31	Cooking pot	Rim	20	Not described		LCP09.46B.6.12.4	
32	Cooking pot	Rim	16	Not described		LCP09.46B.6.12.1	
33	Cooking pot	Rim	21	Not described		LCP09.46B.2.12.8	
34	Cooking pot	Rim	14	Very light brown-buff	Fine-medium common sand	LCP09.46B.4.11.3	
35	Cooking pot	Rim	17	Very light brown	Very fine common sand	LCP09.46B.4.11.7	
36	Jar	Rim	20	Pink	Sand; occasional fine voids; some mica	LCP09.46B.4.13.10	Grooved below rim
37	Jar	Rim	20	Very pale brown	Fine-medium common sand	LCP09.46B.4.13.2	groove below rim; slip or self-slip exterior
38	Jar	Rim	22	Light brown-buff	Very fine common sand	LCP09.46B.4.14.1	
39	Jar	Rim	20	Very light brown	Very fine occasional sand	LCP09.46B.4.15.4	
40	Jar	Rim	21	Light yellow-brown	Occasional fine-medium sand; occasional voids	LCP09.46B.4.14.3	
41	Jar	Rim	26	Not described		LCP09.46B.6.12.3	
42	Jar	Rim	28	Light reddish-brown	Common fine-medium sand & grit	LCP09.46B.4.11.23	Slip or self-slip exterior
43	Jar	Rim	18	Pale brown	Fine-medium sand	LCP09.46B.4.13.4	
44	Jar	Rim	17	Not described		LCP09.46B.2.12.1	
45	Jar	Rim	16	Very light reddish-brown	Abundant fine sand; rare voids	LCP09.46B.4.9.30	
46	Jar	Rim	12	Very light brown	Abundant fine-coarse sand & grit	LCP09.46B.4.11.22	
47	Jar	Rim	16	Pale brown	Abundant coarse sand; chaff	LCP09.46B.4.12.16	
48	Jar	Rim	8	Light brown	Abundant fine-coarse sand & grit	LCP09.46B.4.12.27	
49	Jar	Rim	8	Not described		LCP09.46B.6.12.5	
50	Jar	Rim	10	Not described		LCP09.46B.6.12.8	
51	Jar	Rim	10	Very pale reddish-brown	Common medium sand; occasional voids	LCP09.46B.4.13.17	
52	Jar	Rim	10	Very light brown-buff	Common fine-medium sand	LCP09.46B.4.12.29	Self-slip exterior
53	Jar	Rim	10	Not described		LCP09.46B.6.12.6	
54	Strap handled jar	Rim	?	Very light brown-buff	Very fine sand	LCP09.46B.4.23.7	
55	Strap handled jar	Rim	?	Very light greenish brown	Very fine common sand	LCP09.46B.4.12.34	
56	Jar	Rim	30	Very light brown-buff	Abundant fine-medium sand; small voids	LCP09.46B.4.12.30	Cream slip/paint on interior & cream slip/dark brown paint on exterior
57	Jar	Rim	42	Light brown	Abundant medium sand; chaff	LCP09.46B.4.12.7	

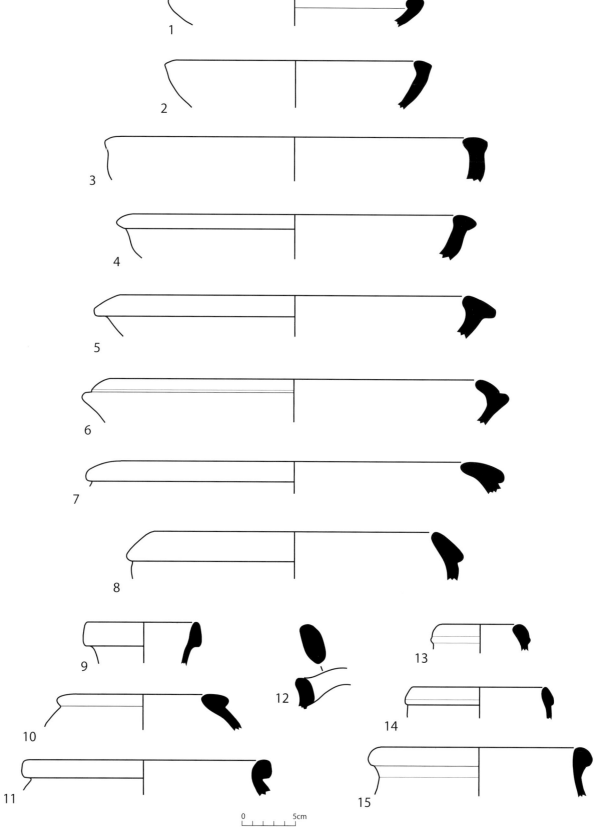

Fig. 8.33 Pottery from Collection Transect 7, Carchemish Outer Town, LCP 2010

Table 8.9. Sherd descriptions for Fig. 8.33. Iron Age Pottery from Carchemish Outer Town Survey, Transect 7

Fig.	Vessel	Fragment	Diam. (cm)	Color	Temper	Sherd Number	Remarks
1	Bowl	Rim	21	Light grey	Abundant medium sand	LCP10.46.7.8.8	
2	Bowl	Rim	22	Light yellow-brown	Fine-medium sand; some voids	LCP10.46.7.4.2	Heavily calcified exterior
3	Bowl	Rim	32	Dark greenish-brown	Fine sand	LCP10.46.7.5.3	Self-slip exterior
4	Bowl	Rim	30	Light reddish-brown	Very fine rare sand	LCP10.46.7.8.14	
5	Bowl	Rim	32	Light reddish-brown	Common very fine sand	LCP10.46.7.8.13	
6	Bowl	Rim	34	Medium brown	Medium common sand	LCP10.46.7.8.12	
7	Bowl	Rim	32	Very light brown	Very fine sand	LCP10.46.7.4.3	Self-slip exterior
8	Bowl	Rim	26	Light brown	Rare fine sand	LCP10.46.7.8.10	
9	Jar	Rim	10	Light reddish-brown	Abundant medium sand	LCP10.46.7.8.7	Heavily calcified exterior
10	Jar	Rim	12	Light reddish-brown	Rare fine sand	LCP10.46.7.8.9	
11	Jar	Rim	21	Very light greenish-buff	Common fine-medium sand & grits	LCP10.46.7.4.1	Heavily calcified exterior
12	Jar	Jar		Light Brown	Fine-medium sand	LCP10.46.7.5.4	
13	Jar	Rim	7	Very light brownish-buff	Common fine sand	LCP10.46.7.8.1	Subtle groove on rim
14	Jar	Rim	12	Very light brownish-buff	Common fine sand	LCP10.46.7.8.5	Subtle groove on rim
15	Jar	Rim	18	Very light brownish-buff	Common medium sand; chaff	LCP10.46.7.8.4	

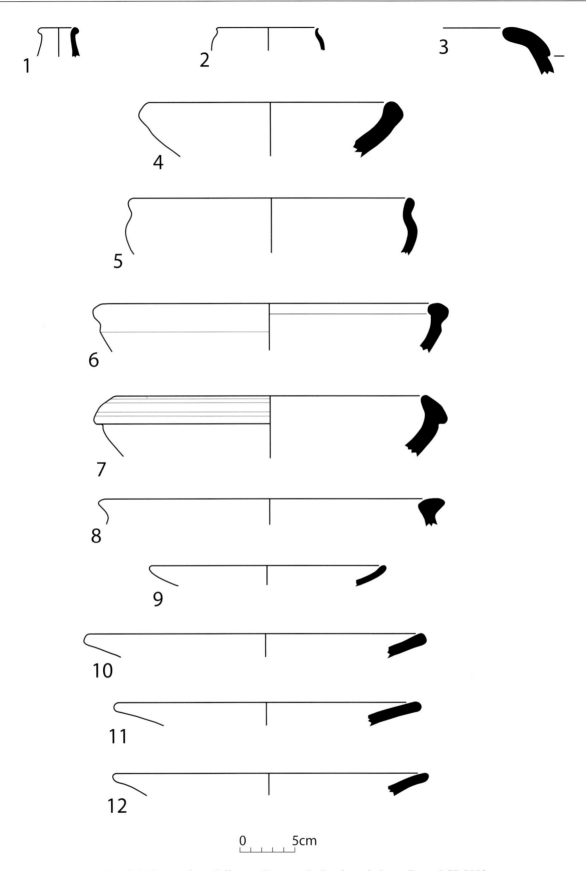

Fig. 8.34 Pottery from Collection Transect 8, Carchemish Outer Town, LCP 2010

Table 8.10. Sherd descriptions for Fig. 8.34. Iron Age Pottery from Carchemish Outer Town Survey, Transect

Fig.	Vessel	Fragment	Diam. (cm)	Color	Temper	Sherd Number	Remarks
1	Bottle/Cup	Rim	9	Color	Temper	Sherd Number	Remarks
2	Bowl	Rim	3	Very light grey-brown buff	Very fine sand	LCP10.46.8.6.1	Palace Ware?
3	Bowl	Rim	?	Medium reddish-brown	Abundant fine-medium sand	LCP10.46.8.6.2	
4	Bowl	Rim	22	Very light brown	Rare very large grits; elongate voids	LCP10.46.8.6.5	
5	Bowl	Rim	25	Very light brown-buff	Very fine sand	LCP10.46.8.6.8	
6	Bowl	Rim	30	Light reddish-brown	Abundant medium grits; chaff; elongate voids	LCP10.46.8.5.6	
7	Bowl	Rim	28	Very light reddish-brown buff	Abundant fine-medium sand	LCP10.46.8.6.3	
8	Bowl	Rim	30	Light reddish-brown	Abundant medium colored grits & sand	LCP10.46.8.5.7	Faint incised lines on rim
9	Open bowl/platter	Rim	21	Very light greyish-brown	Very fine common sand	LCP10.46.8.6.6	
10	Open bowl/platter	Rim	30	Very light brown	Common very fine sand; chaff	LCP10.46.8.5.1	
11	Open bowl/platter	Rim	27	Very light yellow-buff	Rare medium grits; sand; elongate voids	LCP10.46.8.5.4	
12	Open bowl/platter	Rim	28	Very light reddish-brown	Abundant very fine sand	LCP10.46.8.5.3	
				Very light reddish brown	Common fine-medium sand	LCP10.46.8.5.2	

Notes

1 For a more detailed summary of the early British excavations and methods see Benati 2014, 43–52.

2 Studies of the monuments of Carchemish are numerous, but the two most widely cited interpretative overviews remain Orthmann 1971, for the sculptural programme, and Hawkins 1980 (and 2000) for the inscriptions. Woolley published his views on the chronology of the monuments in *Carchemish III* (1952). See also Mazzoni 1995. A recent collection of papers concerning the development of the acropolis and the inner town from its beginnings through Late Bronze Age can be found in Peltenburg 2007.

3 Woolley states: "... the site yields ... evidence that ... from the day when Nebuchadnezzar destroyed the rebellious city, Carchemish was left virtually uninhabited until its resettlement in the Hellenistic age" (Woolley 1921, 95). In support of this statement, Woolley cites the absence of any pottery later than 604 BC, and the debris at Inner Town gate towers (1921, 79). For further discussion of the epigraphic and archaeological evidence post-717 BC, see in this volume, Hawkins and Weeden, Chapter 2, and Newson, Chapter 9.

4 Artifacts confidently dated to the period of Neo-Assyrian occupancy at Carchemish are discussed by Hawkins and Weeden in Chapter 2 of this volume, in the section dealing with the late 9th through 8th centuries BC.

5 For example, in the 1921 report the contents of House D, discussed below, were cited as evidence for the destruction of the city by the Babylonian army at the end of the 7th century BC. This evidence included indications of combat (numerous weapons) and burning (burned brick walls, burned contents within the molten mudbrick including fused metal objects, and small piles of ash interpreted as the burnt remains of wooden columns) (Woolley 1921, 123–129, pls 19a, 19b, figs 39–49). In addition to the evidence from House D, the excavators cited further evidence of destruction in the vicinity of the King's Gate, where the fragmentary appearance and disturbed context of some sculptural reliefs was attributed to an episode of deliberate destruction associated by the excavators to either Necho's Syrian conquests of 609 BC or those of Psamtik I ten years earlier (Woolley and Barnett 1952, 239–240).

6 The river wall is dealt with in two separate sections of Woolley's 1921 report; the part relating to the Inner Town is described in pp. 95–103, but the part forming the eastern perimeter of the Outer Town is described on pp. 56–57 of the report.

7 This is generally referred to in the original reports as "pudding stone."

8 In a sondage on the Outer Town's northern perimeter wall, Woolley recovered a jar and a bowl "against the wall," both identified as "typically Late Hittite" in the report. The jar with handle shown in the photo appears to be a type common to the Iron Age but also seen in later periods, with the handle flush with the rim (Woolley 1921, 53 and pl. 20.c.4), a form that recurred with regularity in the LCP Outer Town surface collections.

9 While Woolley identified all of the contents of the building as 'Late Hittite', Mazzoni has suggested the pottery from House C points to a late 7th century BC date (Mazzoni 1995, 186).

10 Hawkins and Peker (2014, 109) suggest that the latest sculpture from the South Gate fits stylistically within the late 8th century BC, and most likely should be credited to Pisiri, the last king of Carchemish, who was removed from the throne by Sargon II in 717 BC. See also Mazzoni 1997, 328–329.

11 In addition to the few artifacts discussed in this chapter (see above, this chapter, Research Questions), Chapter 2 in this volume presents the relevant epigraphic sources relating to the Neo-Assyrian period and the subsequent history of the site.

12 Collective opinion on the dating of the Outer Town extension has been thus far dominated by those favouring a Neo-Hittite date, but it must be emphasized that these interpretations arose in the years before the availability of remote sensing tools, and have preceded both the LCP work in the Outer Town in Syria and the recent joint Turkish-Italian excavations in Turkey. Previous discussion in favour of a Neo-Hittite date for the Outer Town walls can be found in Mazzoni (1995, 186, fn. 35), Hawkins (1980, 445–446) and Winter (1983, 194–195).

Bibliography

Bachelot, L. and Fales, F.M. (eds) (2005) *Tell Shiukh Fawqani 1994–1998*. History of the Ancient Near East Monographs VI/1–2. Padova, S.A.R.G.O.N.

Benati, G. (2014) The British Museum Excavations at Karkemish (1911–1914, 1920): A Summary of the Activities and of the Methods Employed. In N. Marchetti (ed.), *Karkemish. An Ancient Capital on the Euphrates*. Orient Lab 2, 52–65. Bologna, Ante Quem.

Bell, G. L. (1924) *Amurath to Amurath*. London, Macmillan and Co. Ltd.

Blaylock, S. R. (1999) Iron Age Pottery from Tille Höyük, South-Eastern Turkey. In A. Hausleiter and A. Reiche (eds) *Iron Age Pottery in Northern Mesopotamia, Northern Syria and South-Eastern Anatolia. Papers presented at the meeting of the international "table ronde" at Heidelberg (1995) and Nieborów (1997) and other contributions*. Altertumskunde des Vorderen Orients 10, 263–286. Münster, Ugarit-Verlag.

Bonomo, A. and Zaina, F. (2014) The Iron II–III Pottery Assemblage from Karkemish and Yunus. In N. Marchetti (ed.) *Karkemish. An Ancient Capital on the Euphrates*. Orient Lab 2, 137–144. Bologna, Ante Quem.

Bonomo, A., Guerri, L. and Zaina, F. (2012) Material Culture of the Urban Elites at Karkemish. In N. Marchetti, Karkemish on the Euphrates. Excavating a City's History. *Near Eastern Archaeology* 75/3, 137.

Curtis, J. E. (1989) *Excavations at Qasrij Cliff and Khirbet Qasrij*. London, British Museum.

Curtis, J. E. and Green, A. (1997) *Excavations at Khirbet Khatuniyeh*. London, British Museum.

Eidem, J. and Ackermann, R. (1999) The Iron Age Ceramics from Tell Jurn Kabir. In A. Hausleiter and A. Reiche (eds) *Iron Age Pottery in Northern Mesopotamia, Northern Syria and*

South-Eastern Anatolia. Papers presented at the meeting of the international "table ronde" at Heidelberg (1995) and Nieborów (1997) and other contributions. Altertumskunde des Vorderen Orients 10, 309–324. Münster, Ugarit-Verlag.

Fales, M.F. (1973) *Censimenti e catasti di epoca neo-assira.* Centre per le antichita e la storia dell'arte del Vicino Oriente: Studi economici e technologici 2. Rome, Centro per le antichita e la storia dell'arte del Vicino Oriente.

Falsone, G. and Sconzo, P. (2007) The 'champagne-cup' period at Carchemish. A review of the Early Bronze Age levels on the Acropolis Mound and the problem of the Inner Town. In E. Peltenburg (ed.) *Euphrates River Valley Settlement. The Carchemish Sector in the Third Millennium BC.* Levant Supplementary Series 5, 73–93. Oxford, Oxbow.

Gaborit, J. and Leriche, P. (1998) Géographie historique de la vallée du Moyen-Euphrate. In P. Arnaud and P. Counillon (eds), *Geographica Historica,* Seminaire Bordeaux 1994–1995, 167–200. Bordeaux-Nice, Ausonius.

Gütterbock, H.G. (1956) The Deeds of Suppliluluiuma, as told by his son Muršili II. *Journal of Cuneiform Studies* 10.

Hausleiter, A. (2010) *Neuassyrische Keramik im Kerngebiet Assyriens: Chronologie und Formen.* Wiesbaden, Harrassowitz Verlag.

Hausleiter, A. and Reiche, A. (eds) (1999) *Iron Age Pottery in Northern Mesopotamia, Northern Syria and South-Eastern Anatolia. Papers presented at the meeting of the international "table ronde" at Heidelberg (1995) and Nieborów (1997) and other contributions.* Archäologische Studien zur Kultur und Geschichte des Alten Orients 10. Münster, Ugarit-Verlag.

Hawkins, J.D. and Peker, H. (2014) Karkemish in the Iron Age. In N. Marchetti (ed.), *Karkemish. An Ancient Capital on the Euphrates.* Orient Lab 2, 107–110. Bologna, Ante Quem.

Hawkins, J.D. (2000) *Corpus of Hieroglyphic Luwian Inscriptions. Volume I: Inscriptions of the Iron Age.* Berlin, de Gruyter.

Hawkins, J.D. (1976–1980) Karkamiš. *Reallexikon der Assyriologie und Vorderasiatische Archäologie* 5, 426–446. Berlin, New York.

Hogarth, D.G. (1914) *Carchemish, Part I: Introductory.* London, Trustees of the British Museum.

Hogarth, D.G. (1911) Hittite Problems and the Excavation of Carchemish. *Proceedings of the British Academy* V, 1–15. London, Frowde-Oxford University Press.

Jamieson, A. (2012) *Tell Ahmar III: Neo-Assyrian Pottery from Area C.* Ancient Near Eastern Studies Supplement 35. Leuven, Peeters.

Lines, J. (1954) Late Assyrian Pottery from Nimrud. *Iraq* 16, 164–167.

Luciani, M. (2005) The Iron Age Productive Area (Period IX) and the Inhumation Cemetery (Period X). In L. Bachelot, and F. M. Fales (eds) *Tell Shiukh Fawqani 1994–1998.* History of the Ancient Near East Monographs VI/1–2, 719–993. Padova, S.A.R.G.O.N.

Makinson, M. (2005) La stratigraphie génénerale et l'occupation de l'Âge du Fer (architecture et matériel). In L. Bachelot, and F. M. Fales (eds) *Tell Shiukh Fawqani 1994–1998.* History of the Ancient Near East Monographs VI/1–2, 411–580. Padova, S.A.R.G.O.N.

Marchetti, N. (ed.) (2014) Karkemish. *An Ancient Capital on the Euphrates.* Orient Lab 2. Bologna, Ante Quem.

Marchetti, N. (2012) Karkemish on the Euphrates. Excavating a City's History. *Near Eastern Archaeology* 75/3, 132–147.

Mazzoni, S. (1995) Settlement Pattern and New Urbanization in Syria at the Time of the Assyrian Conquest. In M. Liverani (ed.) *Neo-Assyrian Geography.* Quaderni di geografia storica 5, 181–191. Rome, University of Roma.

Mazzoni, S. (1974) Sui rilievi di Karkemish dall'età di Sargon II al 605 av.Cr. *Rivista degli studi orientali* 47, 206–210.

Müller, U. (1999) Die eisenzeitliche Keramik des Lidar Höyük. In A. Hausleiter and A. Reiche (eds) *Iron Age Pottery in Northern Mesopotamia, Northern Syria and South-Eastern Anatolia. Papers presented at the meeting of the international "table ronde" at Heidelberg (1995) and Nieborów (1997) and other contributions.* Altertumskunde des Vorderen Orients 10, 403–434. Münster, Ugarit-Verlag.

Oates, J. (1959) Late Assyrian Pottery from Fort Shalmaneser. *Iraq* 21, 130–146.

Orthmann, W. (1971) *Untersuchungen Zur Späthetitischen Kunst.* Saarbrücker Beiträge zur Altertumskunde 8. Bonn, Rudolf Habelt Verlag.

Peltenburg, E. (2010) The Emergence of Carchemish as a Major Polity: Contributions from the Land of Carchemish Project (Syria), 2006. In P. Matthiae, F. Pinnock, and L. Nigro (eds) *Proceedings of the 6th International Congress on the Archaeology of the Ancient Near East, May, 5th–10th 2008, "Sapienza"- Università di Roma 2, Excavations, Surveys and Restorations Reports on Recent Field Archaeology in the Near East,* 539–552. Wiesbaden, Harrassowitz.

Peltenburg, E. (ed.) (2007) *Euphrates River Valley Settlement: The Carchemish Sector in the Third Millennium BC.* Levant Supplementary Series 5, Oxford, Oxbow.

Radner, K. (2006–8) Provinz C. Assyrien. In *Reallexikon der Assyriologie und der vorderasiatischen Archäologie* 11. *Prinzessin … Samug,* 43–68. Berlin, De Gruyter.

Ricci, A. (2014) Karkemish and its region in Late antique and Byzantine times. In N. Marchetti (ed.), Karkemish. *An Ancient Capital on the Euphrates.* Orient Lab 2, 119–124. Bologna, Ante Quem.

Ussishkin, D. (1967) Observations on Some Monuments from Carchemish. *Journal of Near Eastern Studies* 26/2, 87–92.

Winter, I. (1982) Art as Evidence of Interaction: Relations between the Assyrian Empire and North Syria. In H.J. Nissen and J. Renger (eds) *Mesopotamien und seine Nachbarn.* Berliner Beiträge zum Vorderen Orient 1, 355–382. Berlin, Reimer.

Winter, I. (1983) Carchemish ša kišad puratti. *Anatolian Studies* 33, 177–197.

Woolley, C.L. and Barnett, R.D. (1952) *Carchemish, Report on the excavations at Jerablus on behalf of the British Museum, Part III: The Excavations in the Inner Town and the Hittite Inscriptions.* London, Trustees of the British Museum.

Woolley, C.L. (1921) *Carchemish: Report on the Excavations at Jerablus on Behalf of the British Museum, Part II: The Town Defenses.* London, Trustees of the British Museum.

Woolley, C.L. (1939) The Iron Age Graves at Carchemish. *Annals of Archaeology and Anthropology* 26, 11–37.

Appendix 8.1: Land of Carchemish Project 2010 Cultural Inventory

(See Carchemish town plan (Woolley 1921, pl. 3) and Figs. 8.1 and 8.12 in this volume). Coordinates system: UTM WGS 1984 Zone 37N

LCP map ref point (Fig. 8.12)	Original description of point (Woolley 1921)	1921 Report pge pl./fig.	LCP July 2010 Remarks	Coordinates system: UTM WGS 1984 Zone 37N
1	The north part of the wall is practically non-existent: its course had to be guessed from the contours of the ground...supported by such scanty evidence as could be obtained...The point of junction of the built wall and the earth rampart of the Inner Town was fairly distinctly marked by an excrescence in the latter hardly to be explained in any other way.	53	In Turkey, not visited by LCP	
2	100 m from this (juncture of **Inner and Outer Town** walls) a modern irrigation trench had been dug and, just where the wall would be expected to run, had cut through a mass of fallen and decomposed brickwork...halfway visible above the surface a large and long limestone slab...may possibly mark the site of a north gate.	53	No mention is made of what appears to be standing architecture (shown on the 1921 plan in black) recorded between LCP Map Point 1 and the irrigation trench	
3	Beyond the irrigation trench the wall took a turn...	53	In Turkey, not visited by LCP	
4	...and here digging brought to light traces of the outer wall and a considerable stretch (40.00 m) of the inner line: the foundations only, of small stone were preserved. Against the wall were found a jug...(Pl. 20, fig. C.4) and a broken bowl, both typically Late Hittite.	53 pl. 20, fig. C.4	In Turkey, not visited by LCP	
5	The next angle had wholly disappeared.	53	In Turkey, not visited by LCP	
6	The railway cutting ran across the wall line, and on either side of it the ground surface which here sloped down to the head of a...tributary to the millstream...(was) so denuded by constant ploughing that nothing whatsoever could be found.	53	In Turkey, not visited by LCP	
7	The existence of House A showed that the town's limits must have been west of this line, but there was no more evidence than that.	53	In Turkey, not visited by LCP	
8	70.00 m from the supposed corner (*of the Outer Wall?*) a fragment of rubble foundation c. 2.00m long* lined up with the well-preserved section of walling which abuts on the west gate. Here there was no inner wall, but a few foundations remained of a building which may have replaced it.	53	No indication of this rubble wall fragment or the inner building foundations on Woolley's map.	
9	Near the West Gate the outer wall is of the normal thickness, 5.00 m wide, with very flimsy foundations of small rubble and pebbles one course deep...Along this west front it was noticeable that even when the rubble gave a more or less straight edge it seemed as if we were dealing less with an actual wall face than with the filling from behind such. In the north section, as to the south of the West Gate, no trace of brickwork survived.	53	Here the line of the wall runs over hard gravelly soil (Woolley: "decomposed pudding stone")	
10	The masonry of the gateway had been despoiled, in most places, down to almost foundation level...only the lowest course of rubble remained...	54	See detailed descriptions of buildings in this chapter	E: 411570 N: 4076304 (WP AR043)
11	...whereas on the north side the city wall was single, on the south side the two parallel walls of the double line abutted on the gate-tower, or, more exactly,...the outer wall abutted the tower, from the south-east corner of this a projection was run out to join up with the inner wall. This angle was so destroyed... that the actual junction had to be imagined. Between the two town-walls was a cobble-paved space...	54	In Turkey, not visited by LCP	

LCP map ref point (Fig. 8.12)	*Original description of point (Woolley 1921)*	*1921 Report pge pl./fig.*	*LCP July 2010 Remarks*	*Coordinates system: UTM WGS 1984 Zone 37N*
12	South of the (west) gate the wall ran in a virtually straight line for some 510.00 m....Here, as north of the gate, the foundations of the wall seem never to have been other than flimsy and shallow, a single course of small stones; the brick had entirely disappeared, and the foundations survived only in small patches; sometimes a face could be distinguished, but seldom with certainty. A modern road ran along and over the whole of this wall stretch...wall remains were often hard to distinguish from the road metal.	54,55	See text, section on LCP operations in the western quadrant	E: 411586 N: 4076186
13	In the north part of this stretch we could trace the remains of three salients, each having a frontage of roughly 20.00 m with a projection of 4.30 m along the whole circumference of the wall...	54,55	See text, section on LCP operations in the western quadrant	E: 411645 N: 4076021
14	The inner wall is more regular than the outer; its junction with the West Gate was broken away... a fragment of wall followed by a patch of...either paving or wall foundation(...out of line) led on to a comparatively well-preserved stretch of wall proper, 26.00 m long...not quite parallel to the other wall.	55	See text, section on LCP operations in the western quadrant	E: 411588 N: 4076249
15	(*south of previous point on inner wall*)...there was a gap, and when ruins of walling again occurred, behind the first salient of the outer wall, they were so confused as to assist but little the reconstruction...either a house on the wall line or else a salient of the inner wall...a long...thin wall running east-west had no connection with the other fragmentary remains.	55	See text, section on LCP operations in the western quadrant	E: 411604 N: 4076204
16	The inner wall was well preserved between this and the next salient on the outer wall, where it returned east and gave out: beyond this point all traces of it failed.	55	See text, section on LCP operations in the NW quadrant	Between: E:411607 N:4076153 And E: 4076153 N:4076186
17	Very scanty traces of wall followed along what the contours showed to be...the line of defenses...to opposite House B, where the remains were abundant...confused...of small value...in fact, little more than patches of cobbles...may or may not have been foundations. The only stretch of actual construction...belonged to a house built on the wall line.	55	Not located, below modern development. See text, section on LCP operations in NW quadrant and on House B	
18	A row of half a dozen fair-sized blocks gave the direction of the next stretch, which ran under the modern hospital....the line was fixed with certainty by the nature of the ground.	55	Not located, below modern development	
19	A narrow ravine with low but precipitous rock sides runs along beneath the south wall of the hospital and beyond it (making a slight turn) to where the pudding stone breaks down in a little cliff above the modern road to the village.	55	Not located, below modern development	
20	On the surface of the rock...traces of the wall were recovered; a small double re-entrant built of finely dressed basalt slabs either marked a recess in the wall line...or was part of the inside of a building whose outer (S.) face has fallen away.	55	Not located with certainty, see text section on LCP operations on the southern ramparts	
21	...beyond this (previous point) a solid buttress-salient occupied a slight projection of the rock bank. The ground from this point sloped rapidly downhill, there was but shallow soil above the rock, and remains were...scanty.	55	Not located with certainty, see text section on LCP operations on the southern ramparts	

LCP map ref point (Fig. 8.12)	Original description of point (Woolley 1921)	1921 Report pge pl./fig.	LCP July 2010 Remarks	Coordinates system: UTM WGS 1984 Zone 37N
22	42.00 m from the buttress the wall face seems to have been set back some 14.00 m; we found here parts of the face of a wall which at its east end developed into a compartment wall like that which flanks the Water-Gate of the Inner Town. Here the rock finally breaks down to the road, on the other side of which stands a modern house; here therefore excavations could not be carried out...here was the South Gate of the Outer Town	55	The 42.00 m seems measured from the southeast (outer) corner of the buttress. See section on Southern gateway. Not located with certainty.	
23	East of the modern building...a slight depression in the ground level, running in a straight line for about 180.00 m, represented the town ditch...along this ditch then ran the town wall. Its outer face had everywhere perished but considerable stretches of its inner face were preserved...foundations were...very shallow and feeble. No salients could be traced.	56	Note Woolley says considerable stretches of inner face preserved but also that inner wall evidence was less satisfactory. Not located with certainty.	
24	The evidence for the inner wall was less satisfactory......to the east of this (House C) were eight hammer-dressed blocks of hard limestone (giving a length of 5.90 m)...certainly part of the wall face, and two good blocks behind them which gave the thickness of the wall as 5.00 m. This seems to have been a recessed part lying 4.00 m behind the front wall of House C and some 8.00 m behind the next stretch for which evidence was forthcoming.	56	See detail plan of House C, Fig. 8.16 in this report. Rather than 'to the east' of House C, Woolley probably means 'in the east' of House C. See detailed plan of House C which makes this clearer. 'Behind' probably means 'west of'...	E:412101 N:412101
25	Just beyond the modern building were found the remains of House C, built upon the wall line itself and perhaps antedating the wall.	56	Below modern development? Not located with certainty.	
26	...where this next stretch came to an end, there were, behind its line, walls clearly belonging to another house and not to the town's defenses.	56	Below agricultural fields. Not located with certainty.	
27	East of this point the inner wall failed altogether and the outer wall became irregular...its remains were too scanty to afford...certain reconstruction.	56	Below agricultural fields. Not located with certainty.	
28	It (the Outer wall) seems to have been recessed for the length of 16.00 m and then to have been carried forward again...to enclose a small pudding-stone knoll on the line of the second scarp which drops to the lower river beach. The rock bank is here breached by the mouth of a wady, a continuation of that which skirts the hospital, and the edge of a miniature ravine has been cut artificially to an almost vertical face, above which rose the town wall.	56	The 16.00 m measurement seems to refer to the north-projection of the wall at this point rather than the east-west length described in the text. Rocky outcrop located but no ancient architecture visible.	E: 412316 N: 4075683
29	At the end of the ravine the wall seems to have returned north following the natural rock face and crossing a smaller and shallower wady - a mere dip in the rock's level,-the farther bank of which again was artificially scarped.	56	Rocky outcrop located but no ancient architecture visible.	E: 412352 N: 4075692
30	On the top of the rock foundations could be traced for about 3.00 m, but thereafter they failed: neither along the bank by the second wady nor on the flat ground immediately below could any signs of construction be discovered. It is possible that a wall did run along the rock edge to a point a little east of the South Gate of the Inner Town...but... there is little evidence...	56	Typographical error in the report? The north-south line which Woolley seems to be referring to here is more than 3.00 m long, closer to 30.00. Rocky outcrop located but no ancient architecture visible.	E: 412347 N: 4075716
31	The scarped edge of the second little wady gives a line which if produced hits the south end of the great embankment wall.	56	No mention is made of the evidence in the report for the location of this corner on the map, or of the little jog in the wall on this stretch after the corner.	

LCP map ref point (Fig. 8.12)	Original description of point (Woolley 1921)	1921 Report pge pl./fig.	LCP July 2010 Remarks	Coordinates system: UTM WGS 1984 Zone 37N
33	The extreme end of the river wall was destroyed by the Germans during the war, and for some 10.00 m there were only a few traces of filling...	56	Not located with certainty.	
34	Beyond this (first 10 m of filling) the first stretch runs on in a straight line for 14.00 m, having at the start three courses of stones which rose to six at the far end of the stretch; the courses are irregular, from 0.30 to 0.50 m high, and the stones are mostly rather small...from 0.40 to 1.20 m. The construction is of poorer quality than in the following stretch...presence of blocks taken from other buildings and worked into the wall anyhow, e.g. with the dressed face downwards, shows that it is of late date.	56, 57	Not located with certainty.	
35	The wall...makes a turn of 15 degrees and runs in a straight line for 253.00 m. It is more careful and more solid construction than before, the blocks are on average much larger...where the top course is preserved are well-dressed orthostats like those of the river wall of the Inner Town. The height of courses averages 0.70 to 0.95 m...blocks vary in length from 0.90 to 1.40 m.	57	Not located with certainty.	
36	There is a higher talus along the wall's base...of the four courses visible at the start the lowest corresponds to the fourth from the bottom in the previous stretch, i.e., seven courses would show if the wall face were cleared.	57	Not located with certainty.	
37	The top course is lost at 12.00 m, the second at 18.50 m, exposing a back (filling) course of similar big stones with a packing of small rubble and mud.	57	Not located with certainty.	
38	At 22.70 to 23.40 m...two blocks of the top course remain...then a wide gap up to 30.40 m lays bare a third row of big filling stones	57	Not located with certainty.	
39	Then the face reappears...four then five courses visible...the bottom course being the same as that in the first part of the reach; at 47.00 m three stones of a still higher course appear...the talus covers the course which had been the lowest part visible just before, so that only five courses show out of a probable nine (see Pl. 5)	57 pl. 5	Not located with certainty.	
40	At 48.50 m the wall breaks down to two (courses)...at 50.00 m to a single course...partly buried.	57	Not located with certainty.	
41	At 52.50 m it has two (courses) showing, is badly smashed up to 60.50 m, then becomes clear...	57	Not located with certainty.	
42	...and rises (at 67.00 m) to a total height of six courses, the sixth represented by one stone only.	57	Not located with certainty.	
43	At 74.50 m all the face is broken away or buried, and only the upper filling of the back part shows.	57	Not located with certainty.	
44	At 84.00 m it recovers with two, three, four...	57	Not located with certainty.	
45	At 92.50 m, five courses	57	Not located with certainty.	
46	At 96.50 m breaks down again to two courses and to one, retaining only the back filling. One to three courses remain as far as 106.50 m; filling here is of small unshaped stones so rough and roughly tumbled in that they can hardly be said to be in courses at all.	57	Not located with certainty.	
47	From 106.50 m onwards all facing stones have been removed by the Germans and only a little of the rubble is left; previous to this destruction the wall was stepped, each course being set back one stone's width from the front line of the course below, as in the embankment wall in front of the fort at the south-east corner of the Inner Town.	57	The description of the state of wall at this point, before its destruction by German soldiers, was in the 1921 report attributed to "the natives." Not located with certainty.	
48	At 253.00 m the wall disappears under the railway embankment, but its line is continued by the stepped embankment wall already mentioned.	57	Not located with certainty.	

The Carchemish region between
the Hellenistic and Early Islamic periods

Paul Newson

Introduction – the region from Hellenistic to early Islamic (Fig. 9.1)

Communications corridor

As with earlier periods, the development and settlement of the upper Middle Euphrates region was influenced hugely by the presence of the River Euphrates and its employment as a convenient and crucial conduit between the north and the south. Beyond the River Euphrates, the local environment provided sufficient levels of annual precipitation and reasonably fertile soils to support agriculture and a topography that was negotiable, all factors which encouraged settlement. Consequently, the upper Middle Euphrates region constituted part of the central section of the Fertile Crescent and formed a pivotal part of the overland communication link connecting the two horns of the Mediterranean littoral in the west and Mesopotamia in the east. Because of these factors the region was to be of vital importance throughout the centuries of what might be termed the Graeco-Roman period, a point emphasized in much of the literature (*e.g.* Clarke 1999b; Comfort and Ergeç 2001). At the same time as providing a useful north–south means of communication and trade, the physicality of the river, which is at many points at least 100 m wide and also was prone to intermittent flooding and shifting changes in course, presented a barrier to communications between either river bank; therefore cross-river communications were channelled to particular points which were fordable and where paired settlements developed (see Lawrence and Ricci, Chapter 4; Wilkinson, Chapter 5). In terms of the political geography, the period as a whole is characterized by heightened interactions between the east and the west beginning with the conquest of Alexander and the commencement of the Hellenistic period, and which then continued throughout the subsequent periods with the rivalry between Rome and a resurgent Persia of the Parthians and the Sassanians.

Settlement

The region of the upper Middle River Euphrates was relatively devoid of what might be characterized as urban settlements with large populations. Most of the bigger centres of population were to be found close to the river; the ancient site of Carchemish (LCP 46) itself was one such settlement, as were the twin towns of Zeugma and Apamea further to the north (Kennedy 1998). Probably the only substantial settlement inland during the Graeco-Roman period was the settlement of Hierapolis (the Holy City), modern day Membij. The larger settlements provided key services to the local region and usually also performed particular functions. In the case of Zeugma/Apamea, these twin towns acted as the bridgeheads for the most important crossing point of the Euphrates on the east to west road network, and so replaced Carchemish as a regional centre for the Euphrates during the late Hellenistic to Early Roman period (Waliszewski 2011, 220). Whilst it was no longer the main crossing point the archaeological evidence suggests the ancient site of Carchemish had something of a revival during the Graeco-Roman period, perhaps due to its continued strategic position beside the river at a point almost halfway between Zeugma and Hierapolis. As for Hierapolis, throughout the Graeco-Roman period, and almost certainly prior to this, as well as acting as a regional market town and travellers' rest, it also performed the function of a major regional religious centre with a sanctuary primarily dedicated to the goddess Atargatis. This sanctuary, which acted as a focus for festivals, processions and pilgrims was

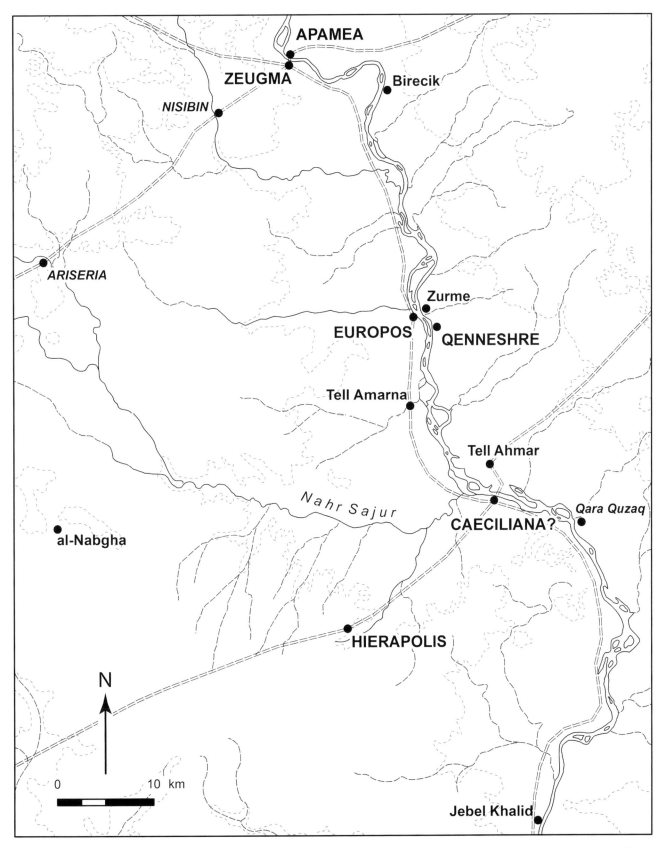

Fig. 9.1 The Middle Euphrates of the Hellenistic to early Islamic periods. Map shows the key settlements, communications routes and sites

celebrated for much of this period and these activities were elaborated at length by a local writer, Lucian of Samosata, in his surviving work on the goddess and her sanctuary, *De Dea Syria* (Lightfoot 2003).

The area of the Middle Euphrates to be considered is essentially framed by these three centres of population: Zeugma, Hierapolis and Carchemish. These three settlements were probably never huge in terms of population, being at their greatest extent in the Late Roman period, but they would have had a significant impact on the local region. The names of some other settlements within the region, smaller in size and importance, are known from ancient sources, usually as waypoints or stopping points in ancient geographies and itineraries such as that of Pliny or the Peutinger table (Talbert 2010). One notable settlement whose exact location is still disputed but which lay to the south of Carchemish is listed variously as Caecilia/ Caeciliana and served a subsidiary crossing point on the Euphrates (Clarke 1999b, 638; Comfort and Ergeç 2001; González Blanco 1999, 648; Waliszewski 2011, 217). Before tracing the development of the region as presented in the archaeological survey, it will be useful to reflect on what is known about the settlement of Carchemish, sketch its development and how it related, affected and interacted with its hinterland.

Carchemish

(see Wilkinson and Ricci, Chapter 8)

The site of Carchemish was undoubtedly a key urban centre for the Graeco-Roman period within the Upper Middle Euphrates region. Although it was always a relatively minor urban centre as far as it related to the rest of the Near East, during this period it served as the dominant urban site within the section of the Middle Euphrates designated as the Carchemish-Birecik enclave. Because it was a relatively minor urban centre, its position and history remain ambiguous and elusive to some extent. This situation has been amplified by many and varied additional factors, some of which relate to the settlement's position away from the main network of roads in antiquity and some to its recent past.

In terms of its recent history the archaeological investigation of the Graeco-Roman period at Carchemish has been given a low priority in view of the importance of its position as a bastion of the Neo-Hittite rulers. As has been mentioned in other places, the emphasis of the early excavators was to access these levels as quickly as possible so other periods of occupation were given scant regard (Clarke 1999b, 638). Furthermore, the actual circumstances of the first excavations, the great personalities of the archaeologists involved such as Hogarth and particularly the participation of Woolley and Lawrence, mixed with pre-war political intrigues and not

least the spectacular Neo-Hittite period finds, all conspired to push into the background the settlement of the Graeco-Roman and early Islamic period at Carchemish.

The location of Carchemish right on the border of the new countries of Turkey and Syria following the First World War placed the core of the site, that is the Citadel Mound and the Inner Town, beyond investigation for much of the twentieth century. This situation has recently been overturned with the opening up of the site to renewed investigation; however, these new investigations are again mainly concerned with the periods prior to the Hellenistic period (Marchetti 2012). In the course of the earlier excavations some indications of the material culture of the Graeco-Roman period were inevitably documented by Hogarth and Woolley; Hogarth notably recorded a number of inscriptions which shine some light on to the Graeco-Roman settlement, and Woolley published some indications of the Hellenistic period pottery (Bell 1911, 34, fig. 17; Clarke 1999b, 638).

Therefore until recently little material has been available with which to construct a detailed history of the settlement for the period from the Hellenistic to the early Islamic as a result of such factors as: the site's isolation in the liminal zone of the Turkish-Syrian border; the understandable emphasis of archaeological research on earlier periods at the site; along with few material indicators and brief mentions in the ancient sources. The resultant obscurity of the site has also insured its absence from many recent histories of the Roman Near East for example those of Millar and Sartre (Millar 1993; Sartre 2005). Modern satellite imagery and the latest archaeological survey of the outer town and renewed excavations in the inner town has allowed for some new analysis to be completed.

A second contention concerning Carchemish is its name during the Graeco-Roman period, which is a common problem for the settlements of the Euphrates region. So far no direct evidence from the site, such as an inscription, has allowed us to identify categorically the name for Carchemish during this period. Analyses of the ancient sources have indicated that its name was *Europos,* though some doubts continue to be raised as to this attribution (Gaborit and Leriche 1998, 195–196). However, as has been argued the name for the modern town Jerablus to the immediate south of the site would seem to be a possible distortion of Europos (Jones 1971, 243–244).

Carchemish context

For the Graeco-Roman period the town of Carchemish performed a number of functions which changed over time. From what is known of the history of Carchemish it appears the settlement regained some importance in the wake of the conquest of Achaemenid Persia by Alexander the Great. More particularly, following the death of Alexander with the establishment of the successor Macedonian controlled kingdom of the Seleukid Empire, of which this region formed a strategically important part.

The earliest record we have of the city of Europos is among a list of cities of the Euphrates region compiled by the naturalist-geographer Pliny the Elder at the time of Augustus (late 1st century BC) (Jones 1971, 262; Pliny *NH* V.87). Nevertheless several indications imply that the ancient settlement site of Carchemish received the name Europos during the Hellenistic period (Comfort *et al.* 2000, 119; Hogarth 1909, 167–169). The founder of the Seleukid kingdom Seleukos I Nikator realising the importance of the region, as the crucial bridge between the western half of the kingdom centred on the newly established capital of Antioch and the eastern half with its capital at Seleukia-on-the-Tigris in Babylonia, sought to secure this communication point by establishing colonies at key crossing points. In this regard Zeugma on the west bank and its twin settlement of Apamea on the east were established at a viable fording point of the Euphrates. At a point 30 km downstream a perhaps more ancient crossing at Carchemish was re-established as Europos with, according to Jones, a corresponding settlement called Amphipolis on the east bank (Comfort *et al.* 2000, 108; Jones 1971, 216).

The names of Europos and Amphipolis echo those of towns in Macedonia, which points strongly towards a foundation as colonies of Macedonians very early after the conquest of the region by Alexander. Shortly after this, these early colonies on the Euphrates were superseded in importance by the Seleukid-founded colonies of Seleukia-Zeugma and Apamea; settlements founded and favoured by Seleukos tended to be named after himself or members of his family (Grainger 1990, 50–52). It is known that Seleukos changed the name of Amphipolis to Nikatoris which according to Jones 'perhaps indicates a rise in status' (Jones 1971, 216). No evidence has been put forward to confirm the location of Amphipolis/Nikatoris although a source of the 6th century AD, Stephen of Byzantium, equated Amphipolis with a settlement called Turmeda which has been equated with the modern village on the east bank known as Zurme (Comfort *et al.* 2000, 119; Jones 1971, 442 n3). Recently, this identification has been challenged with the suggestion that Amphipolis should be equated with the next major Hellenistic period colony downstream from Carchemish at Jebel Khalid (Clarke 1999b, 639). As this Jebel Khalid settlement was only occupied during the Hellenistic period a sustained series of excavations has allowed us to envisage the nature and organisation of such colonies and to make inferences about the suspected colony at Carchemish (Clarke 1999a; Clarke *et al.* 2002; Connor and Clarke 1996–97).

Additionally, the Jebel Khalid excavations revealed features that were similar to another extensive Seleukid foundation even further downstream on the Euphrates and also named Europos – that of the settlement of Dura-Europos (Clarke 1999b, 639). Both these colonies possessed

an acropolis or fortified strongpoint, a long circuit of monumental city walls, a grid of streets with each block or *insula* filled with houses that occupied similar sized plots of land; all elements of Greek Macedonian military colonies. It follows Carchemish would have been no different in this respect with the ancient tell of Carchemish, the Citadel Mound, serving as the acropolis. As well as controlling the crossing point the colonies safeguarded both the major communication/trade route of the River Euphrates itself and the local region in which the colony was situated. The locations of the colonies were also carefully chosen to provide fertile farming land (Clarke 1999b, 638). In addition, Carchemish also may have served as a stopping off and trading point for waterborne travellers, for as with Jebel Khalid, it also possesses evidence for stone-built river walls which may have acted as wharves (Clarke 1999b, 639)

In the wake of the Roman takeover of what remained of the Seleukid Empire, Carchemish continued much as before as an urban market settlement serving the immediate region and as a trading waypoint on lines of inter-regional communication. Yet at this time only the west bank of the Euphrates was incorporated into the Roman province of Syria whereas the east bank became part of the Parthian empire. Thus, 'from the time of Pompey's establishment of the province of Syria in *c.* 65 BC, the Euphrates came to symbolize the boundary between Roman and Parthian interests in the Near East' (Edwell 2008, 7). In such circumstances the importance of Carchemish significantly increased not only strategically as a customs and communications control point but as an emblem of Roman culture and power. As a consequence of these factors, for the first two centuries of Roman rule the region acted as a springboard for aggressive actions by Rome against Parthia. In practical terms, it has been suggested this offensive policy meant there were no fortifications to monitor or mark out the border between the two empires along this stretch of the river (Dabrowa 1986, 96). Nonetheless, the crossing at Zeugma and its pre-eminence was emphasized by the permanent stationing of a legion at Zeugma from just after AD 18 to safeguard communications into Roman Syria and out to Mesopotamia (Dabrowa 1986, 96–97; Keppie 1986, 415).

From the Flavian period onwards, that is the AD 70s, this offensive policy changed with the steady transformation of the west bank into more of a fortified frontier. This entailed a change in the role of Carchemish to that of a defensive border post with a garrison of Roman soldiers. Evidence for this comes from a number of inscriptions from along the Euphrates. One of which, written in Latin for a Roman soldier, was found at the northern end of the Carchemish citadel during Woolley's excavations (Jalabert and Mouterde 1929, 84). While there is some doubt as to the exact meaning of the inscription, particular format and typographical indications point to a date in the 1st or early 2nd century AD. It could be that the soldier concerned was the *praefectus* (commander) of a regiment of auxiliary cavalry the *ala Commagenorum* (Jalabert and Mouterde 1929, 86–87, *IGLS* 137). Dabrowa (1986, 97) has suggested this process may have begun earlier with 'the presence of *ala I Bosphoranorum* near Europos on the Euphrates at the end of Claudius' reign' as indicated by an inscription from another funerary monument (Jalabert and Mouterde 1929, 88–89, *IGLS* 140). This monument was discovered *c*. 9.5 km to the south of Carchemish at Tell Amarna (listed as Tell el-Ganime by Jalabert and Tell el-Ghranim as described by Hogarth) (Hogarth 1909, 165; Jalabert 1929, 88–89). Significantly, as with Carchemish, Tell Amarna occupies a strategic and commanding position by the River Euphrates at the southern end of the Carchemish floodplain, controlling communications onto the plain and both along and across the Euphrates.

The discovery of an additional military tombstone 20 km to the south of Carchemish further hints at a regularised riverine presence. The stele commemorates, in Latin, a standard-bearer of an auxiliary cohort *cohors I Ascalonitanorum* (First Cohort of Ascalonites) a unit originally raised on the coast though the tombstone states the soldier was from Homs (Gatier 1994). The position of the find, just to the south of the confluence of the rivers Sajur and Euphrates and the suggested date of the tombstone, from the end of the 1st or the early 2nd century AD, helps to substantiate the notion of a greater military presence and a somewhat more defensive frontier in this section of the Middle Euphrates (Gatier 1994, 157). Further evidence for a frontier in the immediate vicinity has been weak as there is no firm evidence for forts or other military infrastructure such as towers. It is probably the case that the evidence is at present still to be found, as evidence for military structures including forts are certainly more visible along the Upper Euphrates, to the north and also further to the far south (*e.g.* Bridel and Stucky 1980; Waliszewski 2011, 221).

From all this circumstantial evidence it can be seen that as the first centuries of Roman rule in the region progressed there was an intensifying militarisation of the river zone, a consequence of the increasing recognition of the river as a realisable border between Rome and a resurgent Persia under the Parthians. The continued importance of Carchemish as a crossing point and its potential strategic importance are perhaps hinted at by it being the location of a major battle between the Romans and Parthian armies in the late 2nd century AD. The evidence for this comes from a reference by Lucian of Samosata, a contemporary writer of local origin, who claims that 70,000 Parthians were killed in the major battle at Europos at the time of war against the Parthians under Lucius Verus (Edwell 2008, 116; Lucian *Ver. Hist.* 20). Lucian wrote that the figure was exaggerated, but Edwell noted Lucian referred to the Europos battle on a number of occasions and complained that a contemporary source summarised the battle in only seven lines, all of which suggests the battle was a significant event (Edwell

2008, 112 n104, 116 n128). In later periods the continued strategic importance of Carchemish is underlined by the use of Europos as a military camp by the Byzantine general Belisarius in the war against the Persians in AD 542 (Procopius *Bell Pers.* II. xx. 24; Waliszewski 2011, 231).

Carchemish city plan

The archaeological evidence for the city of Carchemish for the Graeco-Roman period as a whole is fairly limited. It has long been known that there is evidence for a colonnaded street, at least within the 'Inner Town', and analysis of recent satellite imagery shows this very well. A number of building plans can be discerned from the imagery, of large houses and other public structures including a forum or agora to which the colonnaded street ran. Hogarth in his first report on the excavations mentions these structures as well as elaborately carved blocks of a major temple which he supposed dated to the 2nd or 3rd century AD at the south eastern end of the citadel mound (Hogarth 1914, 1–2).

One important problem has been the size of the Graeco-Roman settlement. Woolley mentioned the reuse of stone from the Hittite-built 'Outer Town' wall to construct 'Roman villas', which indicates some form of development in the vicinity of this wall and gives some impression of the extent of the city (Woolley 1921, 50). On this problem the Land of Carchemish Project (LCP) fieldwalking exercise in the southern sector of the 'Outer Town' has been able to provide substantial insights (see Wilkinson and Ricci, Chapter 8; E. Wilkinson *et al.* 2011). Of the large amounts of surface pottery collected from this exercise a significant quantity was of Roman date and included numbers of roof tiles. The distribution of these finds demonstrated signs of clustering, which would suggest low density 'suburban' development on the edges of the city core. On the whole the area of occupation for the Roman period can be seen to be confined to the area within the Inner Town walls giving a maximum size of *c*. 40 ha, plus suburbs. It is likely that the actual area occupied by buildings may well have been less than this. It is probably also the case that the size of the settlement oscillated, perhaps being at its greatest extent during the later Roman period.

The cumulative evidence gathered from the satellite imagery, the objects recorded and the surface survey of the 'Outer Town' thus provide good indicators of a smallish, but quite well-appointed and wealthy urban centre of the Roman period, with a population of some 4000–8000 based on estimates of 100–200 people per hectare. It is perhaps of some significance as an indicator of regional importance that at present there is no evidence to suggest that Roman period Europos ever produced coins. This is in contrast to the two other cities in the immediate vicinity, Hierapolis and Zeugma which struck their own coins from the early 2nd century AD (Jones 1971, 262).

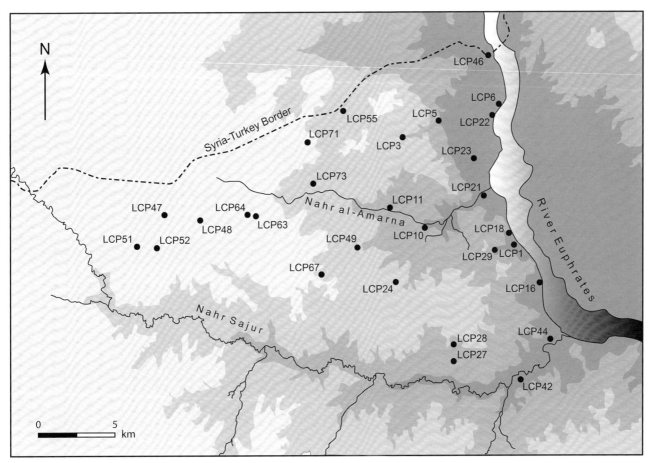

Fig. 9.2 Sites from LCP survey mentioned in the text

While there is clear visible and datable evidence for the monumental buildings of the Roman period, much less is known of the Byzantine and early Islamic settlement at Carchemish. Some of the many house structures may have been occupied during these periods, certainly the excavations of the north west part of the citadel would suggest domestic occupation from the Hellenistic to the early Islamic at least (Waliszewski 2011, 232; Woolley and Barnett 1952). In terms of monumental structures, Woolley's later excavation report does show a possible substantial Byzantine wall resting on a Roman foundation wall of the south west citadel temple (Woolley and Barnett 1952, 208, fig. 84). This Byzantine wall is important as a signifier for continued investment in the city and may date to a reinforcement of city defences in the region under the Byzantine Emperor Anastasius in AD 505 (Waliszewski 2011, 232).

The hinterland (Fig. 9.2)

In contextualising Carchemish within the region it is first important to consider the archaeological evidence of the Hellenistic to early Islamic period, evidence provided by survey work completed within the region between Carchemish and the Nahr Sajur prior to the LCP survey and summarised most recently in Waliszewski (2011). Major surveys include Sanlaville (1985) and the work of the University of Murcia (*e.g.* Egea Vivancos 2005; Matilla Séiquer and Gallardo Carrillo 1998). The Graeco-Roman period settlement distribution generated by this work has reinforced a particular characterization of the use and development of the region during the Graeco-Roman period as essentially confined to the areas adjacent to the River Euphrates. Away from the Euphrates the only other settlement, less dense in nature, has been seen to be concentrated wholly within tributary river valleys such as the Sajur. Such a settlement distribution, riverine in focus, has led to a foregrounding of the River Euphrates in its role as a major communication link, with any other functions being placed secondary to this.

A second issue to contend with is the dating of the evidence from surveys, which for the most part is based on surface pottery sherds. A particular concern regarding

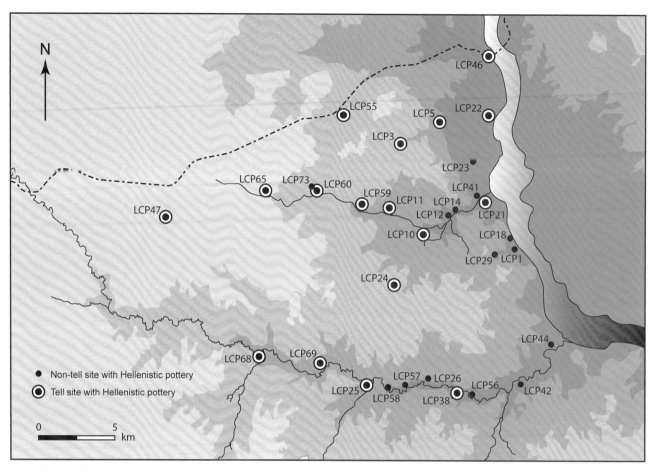

Fig. 9.3 The distribution of characteristic Hellenistic pottery sherds collected from tell and non-tell sites in the LCP survey

the pottery assemblages of the late 1st century BC is the difficulty in distinguishing the change from the rule of the Hellenistic Seleukids to that of Roman hegemony. The problem being that there is a continuation of much of the dateable pottery across this period of very different political rule. The same is true for the late Byzantine and early Islamic periods which share many pottery forms and fabrics, especially of the coarse wares (Newson 2014). In short, apart from a few high status fine wares and common, distinctive interregional wares, such as Brittle Ware, investigation of pottery of the Graeco-Roman period in the Near East is still at an early stage of development.

For this reason the survey data from the hinterland to the south and south west of Carchemish has been divided into three periods which are largely defined by fundamental changes in diagnostic pottery types. This simple system is also in line with other surveys in adjacent regions and categorizes the periods as: Hellenistic/Early Roman, Late Roman/Byzantine and early Islamic (Algaze *et al.* 1992; 1994; Wilkinson 1990). The three distributions generated using LCP data (Figs 9.4, 9.7 and 9.11) provide the foundation for making salient points of interest for individual

sites and underlying processes concerning the Hellenistic to early Islamic settlement. Besides providing insights into the settlement evolution of the Carchemish hinterland and its association to Carchemish itself, the distributions help to contextualise the region and its changing relationship to other regions of the Near East and beyond.

Hellenistic (Figs 9.3 and 9.4)

Recent understandings of the Middle Euphrates region of the Hellenistic period have implied the essential core of settlement development was that of the flood plain with little beyond this region apart from a few isolated and significant towns such as Hierapolis (Clarke 1999b, 638–639). In this way the Hellenistic period has been viewed through the prism of the colonies established by the Macedonian Greeks, with very little understanding beyond the role of these colonies. Some evidence from past excavations and surveys has hinted at Hellenistic occupation in other sites beyond the colonies. In this way it is known that a number of buildings were located on the summit of Tell Ahmar, a large tell situated on the east bank of the Euphrates some 20

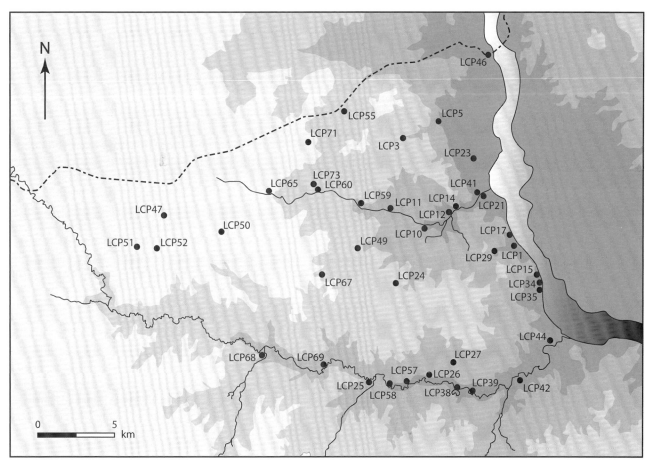

Fig. 9.4 Distribution map of sites from which surface sherds of the Hellenistic–Early Roman period were collected in the LCP survey

km south of Carchemish. Some of these structures have been investigated, including a small sanctuary, and are evidence of continued occupation of the tell site (Bunnens 1990, 3; Thureau-Dangin and Dunand 1936, 80–81). Again on the west bank of the Euphrates excavations by a Belgian team at Tell Amarna (LCP 21) have revealed Hellenistic period occupation, while to the north, Tell Jerablus Tahtani (LCP 22) also had evidence for buildings of the Hellenistic to the Roman period at several excavated locations across the tell (Peltenburg *et al.* 1995, 15–16; Tunca 1992, 24–29; Waliszewski 2011, 235).

In a casual analysis this evidence would suggest that Hellenistic period dwelling and activities outside the colonies were essentially limited, with settlement being restricted to tell sites situated along the edge of the Euphrates and principally in the zone of the Pleistocene Terraces Land Unit 2 (Wilkinson *et al.* 2012, 146–147). The pioneering surveys of Moore and Copeland in the late 1970s and early 1980s extended the region of settlement for the Hellenistic period with some indications of occupation at a number of tell sites along the valleys of the Sajur and Amarna rivers (Copeland and Moore 1985, fig. 10; Sanlaville 1985, 177).

One of the key results of the LCP survey work has been to extensively modify our knowledge of settlement during the Hellenistic period. As well as evidence for occupation of tells along the line of the Euphrates, the survey has shown there was substantial occupation of many of the tell sites closely linked to the subsidiary valleys, such as the Nahr Sajur and also shallow valleys which dissect the limestone of Land Unit 3, particularly that of the Nahr al-Amarna. Furthermore, the survey evidence has shown that a number of sites in the regions between such valleys were also occupied during the Hellenistic: characteristic Hellenistic period sherds were recorded at sites – LCP 3, 5, 24, 55 and 73. From an examination of the evidence presented by these sites it can be seen that Hellenistic occupation away from the valleys comes specifically from tell sites. Therefore, initial analysis suggests the settlement of the Hellenistic for the hinterland around Carchemish on the whole resembles past periods in being tell-focused (Chapters 4 and 5), with the densest region of settlement being located close to perennial supplies of water, though there is some limited occupation beyond these foci.

Late Hellenistic–Early Roman (Fig. 9.4)

As with other periods (particularly the Iron Age), the LCP survey has been able to show that beyond these tell sites new forms of site were being developed in the inter-tell spaces beginning in the Hellenistic period and increasing in number and location into the late Hellenistic and Early Roman periods. As mentioned Figure 9.3 compares the evidence for the occupation of tell sites against off-tell sites for the Hellenistic period, based on specifically diagnostic Hellenistic pottery wares and forms. Figure 9.4 shows the distribution of sites for the whole Hellenistic to Early Roman period. It can be seen that although the development of sites away from the tells themselves was not a new phenomenon, the scale of development in the Hellenistic period and the period after was much greater, than for example in the Iron Age (Wilkinson, Chapter 5). Some of the off-tell sites with evidence for Hellenistic occupation recorded by the LCP were on sites which had Iron Age and perhaps earlier occupational evidence (*e.g.* LCP 23). However, some of the Hellenistic period sites are undoubtedly new settlement sites and an example is the complex and widely dispersed site of LCP 18 (Fig. 9.5), the surviving remnant of which is positioned along the edge of the Land Unit 3 overlooking the River Euphrates floodplain (see Wilkinson, Chapter 5). These site vestiges are distinguished by walls and other structures within the floor of a shallow valley and by a number of elaborate rock-cut structures in the slopes above the site. Both the site and some of these rock-cut structures have pottery of the Late Hellenistic associated with them. These rock-cut structures, which are thought to be of Early Roman date, were probably originally constructed as tombs.

Fig. 9.5 View of site LCP 18 – the vestigial remains of which now lie immediately above the modern Lake Tishrin formed within the floodplain of the Euphrates valley. In the centre of the photograph can be seen the later abandoned cemetery of LCP 18C. The photograph was taken looking south from the entrance to the rock-cut monastery in Fig. 9.10

It would seem that one of these tombs was later re-cut and expanded for use as an early Christian monastery (Egea Vivancos 2005, 252–253).

The location of these off-tell sites would indicate that much of the expansion was restricted to the river valleys to begin with, revealing an intensification in development of these ancient areas with plentiful supplies of water and that were traditionally good for agriculture. They also reveal to some extent a reorganisation of this land from the traditional hierarchical tell-based society structure into a more complex diverse social organisation. In the later Hellenistic and particularly in the Early Roman period we begin to see an expansion of settlement onto the areas between the valleys. Figures 9.3 and 9.4 clearly show this general expansion along the shallow river valleys and later beyond.

The LCP survey of the Sajur valley has revealed a wide range of evidence for off-tell development of the Hellenistic period with a variety of smaller sites being recorded. Two example sites reflect this development. The first of these, LCP 42, yielded a number of high status pottery sherds of the later Hellenistic period including a Megarian moulded bowl (Newson 2014), while the Hellenistic–Early Roman pottery scatter of nearby LCP 44, closer to the confluence with the Euphrates, indicated an independent farmstead of some sort. This is a new development in the region: the appearance of small independent dwelling sites outside the nucleated settlement of the tells or even more recent off-tell sites of the Iron Age such as LCP 6. This combination of dwelling type and distinct material culture assemblage may reflect the entrance into the region of newcomers with different approaches and ways of living which could have affected local customs.

The material culture and buildings discovered in the excavations at Jebel Khalid suggested the people living here were just such outsiders from Macedonia and/or Greece and there were indications that intermarriage changed cultural practises in food preparation, changes which may have been apparent in other aspects of living (Jackson and Tidmarsh 2011, 518). Additionally, some settlements were established on virgin sites in new areas immediately adjoining the zone of occupation along the floodplain of the Euphrates river valley. Two such sites LCP 16 and 18 exemplify this new settlement variation positioned as they survive at the intersection of Land Unit 3 and Land Unit 2. These two sites have pottery dated to the Late Hellenistic and though some characteristic echinus bowls were also recovered in the surface collection these were produced at least into the Early Roman period (Jackson and Tidmarsh 2011, 14) (Fig. 9.6). The position of these sites at the juncture of the Euphrates floodplain with the abutting limestone terraces implies a strategy to maximise the acreage for profitable agriculture on the floodplain leaving the settlement to occupy the least profitable locations adjacent to this.

LCP08

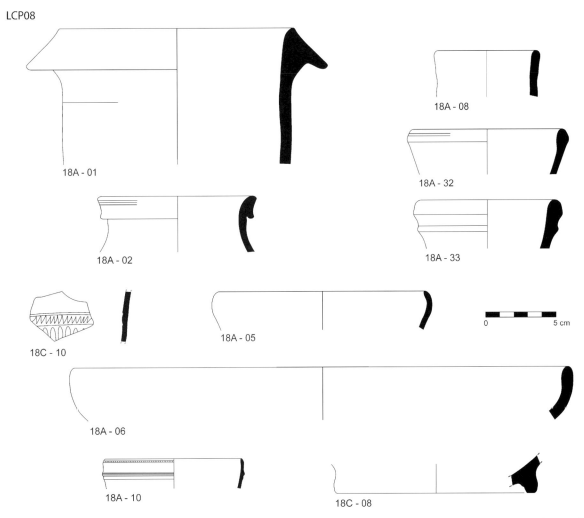

Fig. 9.6 Pottery from LCP 18. Profiles of Hellenistic to Early Roman pottery collected from south facing limestone slopes. The sherds represented include a semi-fine angled rim table amphora (LCP 18A-01); and a number of local Hellenistic fine ware bowls with incurved rims (LCP 18A-05, 06). Many of these fine ware sherds exhibited red and brown painted interiors. Late Hellenistic is the molded decoration fine ware sherd (LCP 18C-10). The Early Roman period is represented by a fine example of ESA in the shape of a hemispherical bowl Form 48 (LCP 18A-10) and by the base of a fine ware red-painted bowl (LCP 18C-08)

Roman–Byzantine (Fig. 9.7)

The processes of settlement change which begin with the Hellenistic (certainly the Late Hellenistic) accelerate, intensify and become more widespread during the Early Roman period and continue developing into the Byzantine. Firstly, the Hellenistic and Early Roman period is characterised by a significant shift in settlement form. The majority of tell summits which had been occupied were now being abandoned for the flat areas immediately below, adjacent to the tell foot. Some occupation of tells continues, but this appears to be less intense. This is a phenomenon observed at other sites in the vicinity in recent years at Tell Ahmar (Wightman 1990) and Tell Amarna (Tunca 1999). Further afield, surveys such as the Homs survey of central Syria (Philip *et al.* 2005, 31–34), and also excavations, as at the tell of Kamid el-Loz,

Biqa' Valley (Heinz *et al.* 2010), have shown substantial Hellenistic occupation on a tell summit was followed in the Early Roman period by a re-foundation of the core village settlement at the foot of the tell.

Secondly, there is a general and large-scale expansion of settlement into newer environmental zones most intensely in those regions which had not been previously populated so densely, if at all. The appearance of settlement is most visible in the Upper Plains of Land Unit 4 (see Wilkinson, Chapter 5). Here, large dense scatters of pottery sherds and roof tile can be discerned among the flat fields away from the previously dominant tell-linked settlement system. From the material evidence on the surface it emerges that much of this settlement dates from the Late Roman and into the Byzantine/early Islamic periods.

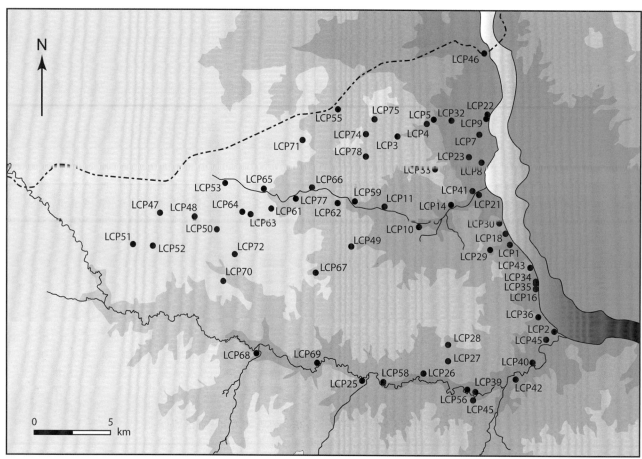

Fig. 9.7 Distribution map of sites from which surface sherds of the Late Roman and Byzantine period were collected in the LCP survey

Good examples of the move in the focus of settlement away from the tops of tells to the spacious flat areas at the foot of tells are provided at tell sites along the length of the Nahr al-Armarna. In collecting surface pottery from tell sites along the length of this shallow valley a particular collection strategy was tried which divided a tell into zones of collection: Zone A for the summit; Zone B for the sides; and Zone C + for the area(s) at the base of the tell. It was significant that the surface pottery in the three different zones of a tell generally belonged to different periods. For example, at tell sites LCP 10 and LCP 11 Zone A at each tell had predominantly Hellenistic period sherds with little from later periods while in Zone C there was a dense quantity of surface sherds of which a very high proportion were of the Late Roman and Byzantine periods and very few were of Hellenistic or earlier date (Wilkinson *et al.* 2007, 235). Table 9.1 reviews the surface distribution of pottery evidence for the Hellenistic to Medieval Islamic collected at other tells in the LCP survey area.

The extensive development of the upland plains is demonstrated by a series of sites located in the region between the al-Amarna and Sajur valleys of the LCP survey area. For example, by the size of the pottery and

tile scatters LCP 51 and 52 and LCP 63, 64 and 67 would represent flourishing villages of the Late Roman and early Islamic period (Fig. 9.8). Villages, whose populations may have furthered the deforestation of this previously sparsely populated upland region (Miller and Marston 2012, 98), and having recourse to wells and other water management systems, such as qanats, were now able to fully exploit the *terra rossa* soils. From the surface sherds collected, it is clear that this expansion had its beginnings in the Early Roman period as some sites had pottery of late Hellenistic forms (LCP 47, 48, 51 and 52) and ESA (Eastern Sigillata A) from one site (LCP 47). It also has to be remembered these recorded sites are just a sample of the settlements which exist on the high plains and it is likely that other sites of similar size and date exist. LCP 67 stands out amongst the upland sites for the very large numbers of roof tiles which characterized the surface material. The large-scale adoption of this non-indigenous architectural device into a rural context in this period is of interest in a region which even today tends to favour dwellings with flat roofs.

In addition to village sites of the Late Roman and Byzantine periods there is evidence for more isolated minor sites, perhaps small hamlets or farmsteads. A few examples

Table 9.1 The distribution of surface sherds at a range of tell sites in different demarcated areas of the tell in question. In each case Area A signifies the top of a tell, Area B signifies the slopes of a tell, Areas C, D, E etc are areas around the tell. However, for site LCP 50 the Areas B to F represent different sections of the tell slopes (see Appendix A for details). X represents clearly identified sherds of the period in question, while X? probable sherds of the period

LCP 47		A	B
	Class	X	X
	Hell		
	Hell-ER	X	X
	Rom		X
	Byz		
	LByz-EIsl		
	EIsl		
	Isl (Med)	X	X
	Other periods	X	X

LCP 50		A	B	C	D	E	F
	Class	X				X	
	Hell					X	
	Hell-ER					X	
	Rom						
	Byz						
	LByz-EIsl	X					
	EIsl						
	Isl (Med)		X				
	Other periods	X	X				

LCP 55		A	B	C	D
	Class	X	X		X
	Hell				
	Hell-ER	X	X		
	Rom		X?		X
	Byz				
	LByz-EIsl	X?			
	EIsl				
	Isl (Med)				
	Other periods	X	X	X	X

LCP 60		A	B	C	D	E	F
	Class	X	X	X			
	Hell	X	X	X			
	Hell-ER	X					
	Rom						
	Byz				X?	X?	X
	LByz-EIsl			X?	X?		
	EIsl						
	Isl (Med)	X	X	X			
	Other periods		X	X			

LCP 65		A	B
	Class	X	X
	Hell		
	Hell-ER	X	X
	Rom		
	Byz	X	
	LByz-EIsl	X?	
	EIsl		
	Isl (Med)		
	Other periods	X	

LCP 68		A	B	C	D
	Class	X		X	X
	Hell				
	Hell-ER	X		X	
	Rom				X
	Byz	X?	X?		
	LByz-EIsl			X	
	EIsl				
	Isl (Med)				
	Other periods	X	X	X	

of such sites were encountered and recorded during the fieldwork, specifically LCP 27, 28 and 49. Evidence for these appeared as concentrated pottery scatters over regions as small as 400 m² for LCP 49 or more dispersed over a larger area of 8800 m² in the case of LCP 28. As with the larger village settlements, there are undoubtedly many more such sites on the uplands and the sites recorded are just a small sample of the possible large numbers of smaller sites.

Helping to create a sense of the increasing impact on the landscape of people in the Late Roman and Byzantine periods an extensive number and range of rock-cut structures have been documented in recent years among the limestone terraces of Land Unit 3, especially within the region south of the Nahr al-Amarna (Egea Vivancos 2005; Matilla Séiquer and Gallardo Carrillo 1998). The majority of structures appear to be rock-cut tombs (*hypogea*) of various types and usually comprised a rectangular entrance chamber (*dromos*) around which were arranged (purportedly for single inhumation burials) three rock-cut niches (*arcosolia*) or several carved shelfs (*loculi*) or even a mixture of both. Though it is far from certain, such *hypogea* would seem to date from the 2nd century AD to the 6th or perhaps even the 7th century AD (Egea Vivancos 2005, 569; Sartre-Fauriat

2001, 91–94). The highest density of rock-cut tombs (*c.* 200 in number) has been documented among the steep terraces which surround the modern village of Kirk Mughara (LCP 16) (Egea Vivancos 2005, 123–208) (Fig. 9.9). Other locations have further clusters of such tombs, including Tell Amarna and in the environs of Khirbet Seraisat (especially the area delineated by LCP 1, 18 and 29) (Egea Vivancos 2005, 227–264; Matilla Séiquer and Gallardo Carrillo 1998, 285–288). Mixed in with the rock-cut *hypogea* at this location are other rock-cut structures which may be dwellings and/or stables for domestic animals.

Interestingly, on the edge of this complex of sites, in the vicinity of Khirbet Seraisat (LCP 1), is evidence for early monastic complexes focussed around rock-cut hermitages and possibly churches of two types either rock-cut or the more usual built basilica (Egea Vivancos 2005, 252–262, 637–638) (Fig 9.10). These monasteries are just a few examples of a large number in the region documented both archaeologically and referred to in the contemporary written sources that flourished from the 4th to the 7th centuries AD. The importance of Christianity to the population has been highlighted recently by the discovery of a late 4th–early 5th century basilica *c.* 700 m south of Tell Armarna

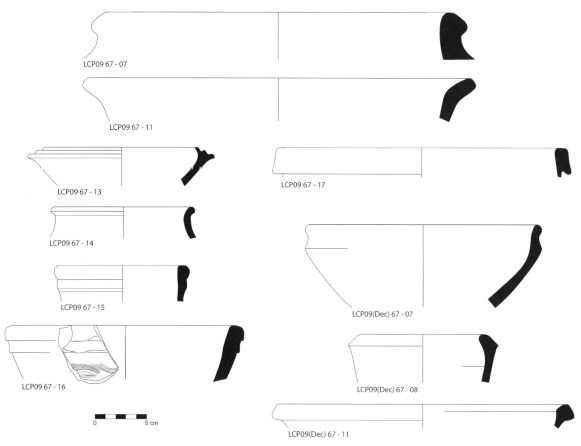

Fig. 9.8 Pottery from LCP67. Much of this pottery is characterised by coarse storage vessels including large jars (LCP09 67-09, 17), smaller jars (LCP09 67-14) and basins (LCP09 67-11, LCP09(Dec) 67-07, 11). LCP09 67-16 is a typical smaller basin of the Byzantine to early Islamic with combed decoration. LCP09-13 is a mortarium and LCP09 67-15 an amphora

Fig. 9.9 A typical rock-cut tomb (hypogeum) at the village of Kirk Mughara (LCP 16) featuring a rectangular entrance chamber (dromos), whose roof has collapsed, beyond which is the tomb chamber with three rock-cut burial niches (arcosolia)

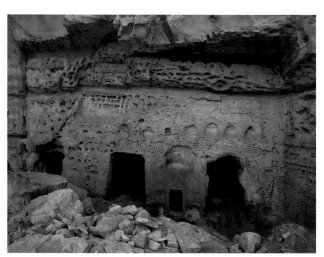

Fig. 9.10 The entrance to the so-called 'Staircase Monastery' which was situated in the cliff at the top of the slope to the immediate north of site LCP 18. This monastery was probably created by the adaption and extension of an earlier rock-cut tomb. It contains a number of linked chambers and niches and a rock-cut staircase leads from the monastery to the site of a basilica church on the plateau above the cliff

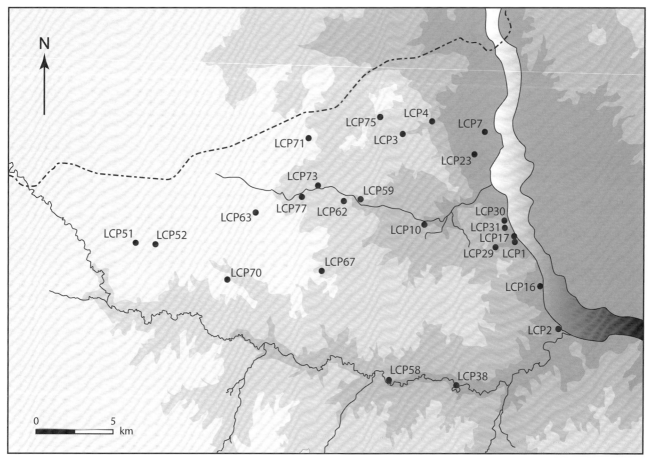

Fig. 9.11 Distribution map of sites from which surface sherds of the early Islamic period were collected in the LCP survey

(Waliszewski and Chmielewski 2000; Tunca *et al.* 2011) and by a church with the earliest Syriac Christian text in a mosaic dating to the early 5th century AD situated just to the west of the LCP survey area at the village of al-Nabgha (27 km WNW of Membij) (Chatonnet and Desreumaux 2011).

Associated with the increase in population and the development of settlement there is evidence for the increasing implementation of technologies to control water supplies. In regions associated with the higher land and the plateau this can be seen in the provision of elaborate qanat systems in the environs of Hierapolis. Along the length of the Sajur valley other evidence for water technologies was observed in the form of extensive networks of stone cut canals and channels which collected directed and distributed the surface and river flow to where it was needed along the valley (see Wilkinson, Chapter 5; Wilkinson and Rayne 2010, 128–129; Wilkinson *et al.* 2007, 235–239). Outside the Sajur valley additional intricate systems of water capture and distribution to centres of settlement have been documented, for example, the stone carved water channel management systems of Kirk Mughara village (LCP 16)(Egea Vivancos 2005, 209–210).

Early Islamic (Fig. 9.11)

The number of sites within the LCP survey recorded for the early Islamic period is much fewer than the previous Late Roman–Byzantine period. This is partly due to the under recognition of early Islamic pottery as some types continue in production and use across both periods; a key example being Brittle Ware which tends to be identified as purely Late Roman/Byzantine date, but was produced certainly into the Omayyad and in some forms up to the Abbasid (Vokaer 2007) (Fig. 9.12). Positively identified sites of this period are those which have clearly distinguishable early Islamic pottery, such as characteristic creamwares and green glazed forms found in other surveys and excavated contexts.

It was found that these identifiable early Islamic sites were sites which all had evidence for occupation in the Late Roman/Byzantine period. On the upland areas these included a number of the larger settlement sites that had appeared in the previous period on open ground away from traditional areas of settlement: LCP 67 and 71 are typical of such sites documented in the survey. It may be that some of the modern villages in this environment were also occupied

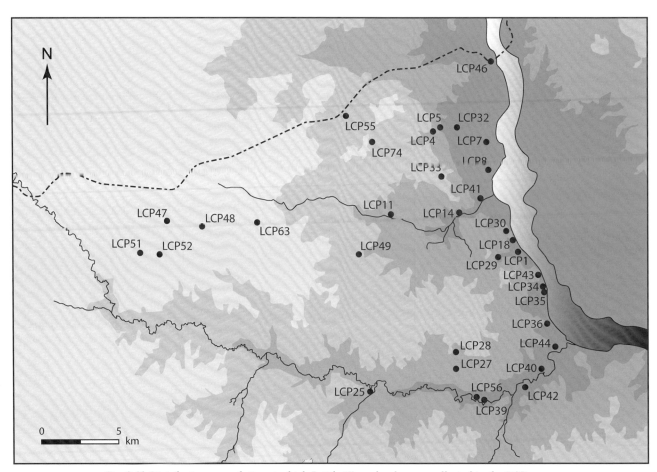

Fig. 9.12 Distribution map of sites at which Brittle Ware sherds were collected in the LCP survey

in this period, though this remains to be proven. That there was a continuity of population from the Byzantine into the early Islamic period is suggested by the important Syriac texts of the Qenneshre monastery whose half-buried but substantial remains are perhaps situated very near the east bank of the Euphrates just to the south of Carchemish/ Europos at a place called Naquta (LCP waypoint WP374: 414479; 4075332) (Egea Vivancos 2005, 645; Palmer 1990, 75) (Fig. 9.13). There is some evidence for the monastery continuing until at least AD 758 with the election of one of the Qenneshre monks as the Syriac Patriarch (Egea Vivancos 2005, 646; Palmer 1990, 174–175).

It has been argued that the non-monastic population was driven down over time, for it has been suggested that following the takeover of Edessa (modern Şanliurfa) and the region of Osrhoene on the east bank by Abu Ubaid in AD 637/638, the middle Euphrates region as a whole became a contested area between the Byzantines and Muslims, which may have had an adverse effect on the region's long-term prosperity (Algaze *et al.* 1991, 207–208; Waliszewski 2011, 226). Against this there are growing indications for the innovation of agricultural systems with botanical

Fig. 9.13 A view of exposed ashlar walls at Naquta on the east bank of the River Euphrates, the probable site of the important monastery of Qenneshre. Photo T.J. Wilkinson

remains from the upper Euphrates and Anatolia revealing the introduction of new crops such as cotton, rice and millet (Miller and Marston 2012, 102).

Graeco-Roman Carchemish in context

The Hellenistic period marks a turning point in the settlement history of the region with the arrival of Greek-speaking populations within Macedonian and Seleukid colonies established at Carchemish and elsewhere in the upper Middle Euphrates region. With the introduction of these new populations, profound changes were initiated, changes which would be amplified during the succeeding Roman period. Though the region had been part of the Persian Empire prior to its incorporation into the Hellenistic sphere there is little evidence for Persian influence, in part because of our lack of knowledge of the local pottery types of this time, as well as the continuity of Iron Age wares and forms. On the other hand the presence of Macedonian and other Greek colonists created new relationships and hierarchies within the region and new socio-economic links beyond, from the Mediterranean to Central Asia. The resultant modifications in culture and trade are manifested in the increasing diversity of settlement types and pottery assemblages. The Hellenistic also marks the beginning of the resurgence of Carchemish (*Europos*) as a regional centre.

In the Roman to Byzantine period, the broadening of settlement types, and also the distribution of new settlement in the previously little exploited high plain regions of Land Unit 4 reflects a continuance and growth of practices introduced in the Hellenistic along with a number of additional issues and processes. Many of the processes which operated within the landscape during the Late Roman/Byzantine period and subsequently can be seen as a direct consequence of the Roman takeover of the region and its *ad hoc* 'policy' towards first the Parthian and then later Sassanian empires. Fundamental to this incidental policy was the ever changing relationship with the people of the Osrhoene region on the east bank of the Euphrates (Sommer 2010).

Therefore, the major factor which most influenced developments in the region during the Roman period was the position of the frontier and all the features associated with it. For much of the first two centuries of Roman rule, the Euphrates formed the *de facto* frontier which increasingly became more formal as the 1st century AD progressed. This gradual structuring and institutionalising of the border affected the region of the upper Middle Euphrates in a number of ways. For example, the influx of soldiers stationed along the Euphrates would have necessitated their regular provisioning of basic foodstuffs grown locally and also the importation of substantial amounts of material equipment and foodstuffs not available locally.

In this way the local economy was stimulated to provide agricultural produce and other services for the army which then spent money in the region, some of which went into importing trade goods. As a consequence the local economy expanded, which stimulated the growth, over time, of both rural and urban populations. As with all frontier regions, it is possible that this growing population was augmented by retiring veteran soldiers who may have begun to establish isolated farmsteads at the edges of the settled areas. However, as yet, there are no indications for centuriation in the landscape around Carchemish, though there is evidence for the control of the River Euphrates through the use of canals which hints at the potential for large-scale modification schemes of the wider environment during the Graeco-Roman period (Wilkinson *et al.* 2007, 236). On the other hand the position of a population near a very porous and relatively open border ensured that settlement was focused on the top of tells and for the most part remained nucleated. The increasingly formalised border with garrisons and military infrastructure perhaps including some towers on strategic hilltops increased the sense of security during the 1st century AD.

The major change in the fortunes of the region came with the movement east of the frontier and the establishment of the Roman provinces of Osrhoene and Mesopotamia on the land to the east of the River Euphrates in the late 2nd and early 3rd centuries AD (Edwell 2008, 23–27). For the next few centuries the frontier was distant from the upper Middle Euphrates and so the army presence was significantly less. Subsequently there was a change in status and role for the region, from a border zone with emphasis on the military provision and as a communication route down the Euphrates to that of a regular provincial region with an increased sense of security and a stress on subsistence agriculture.

It is within this framework of the stable generic security of a non-border province that the population continued to increase and which led to a heightened exploitation of the higher plain areas in Land Unit 4. This phenomenon of extensive settlement development has been documented widely for the late Roman and Byzantine period in other rural contexts of the Near East (*e.g.* Foss 1997; Kennedy 2007; Philip and Newson 2014; Tate 1997). The idea that settlement expansion was all due to increased security is perhaps too simplistic a notion and it has to be the case that other factors and processes both political and economic were in operation as well. The evidence of the surface remains suggests the urban centre of Carchemish also prospered from the 2nd century AD, but it is unclear if the population of the city continued to expand into the Byzantine period as the LCP evidence suggests it did for the hinterland.

As with the Hellenistic, the influence of Rome and Byzantium within the hinterland of Carchemish can be seen in the adoption of new forms of material culture which were previously absent from this environment. The most obvious is the introduction of roof tiles which are commonly found on settlement sites particularly from the late Roman period onwards. While roof tiles are common there is an absence of stone or other building material at the sites. This suggests the walls of buildings continued to be constructed of traditional mudbrick, but that now it was common for houses to be roofed with ceramic tiles on pitched wooden-framed roofs. This represents one case of the many cultural changes that occurred during this period, though the use of roof tiles may, in part, reflect a more practical influence such as an increase in rainfall during the Late Roman/Byzantine periods (postulated in other regions: see *e.g.* Hirschfeld 2004; Kuzucuoğlu *et al.* 2011, 185–186; Neumann *et al.* 2007).

Recent synthetic work on the Late Roman sub-optimal regions of limestone to the west and long-term settlement modelling through time indicate future approaches that could be usefully developed (see Lawrence and Ricci, Chapter 4 and *e.g.* Decker 2009; Kennedy 2007; Wilkinson *et al.* 2012). In undertaking future work, a detailed comparative approach with the east bank area, which seems to have had a different settlement history in the Graeco-Roman period, would throw up some useful contrasts. For on the east bank of the upper Middle Euphrates there are indications of different tomb types, fewer larger settlements and no Greek inscriptions, only later Byzantine period Syriac inscriptions (Egea Vivancos 2005; Matilla Séiquer and Gallardo Carrillo 1998). For both areas, future work could be completed on the causes of the settlement expansion in the Late Roman/Byzantine periods, the diversity of forms in which this settlement was manifested, the relationship between the sedentary and pastoralist populations that may have existed and the extent to which these developments were a reflection of changing socio-political or environmental conditions (Miller and Marston 2012). The Land of Carchemish Project has provided new insights in settlement development through the amassing of detailed evidence with which to construct the settlement trajectories for the Graeco-Roman and early Islamic periods of the Carchemish hinterland. Furthermore, it can be seen that the project has also been able to successfully shine light on the regional importance and impact of the Graeco-Roman urban settlement of Carchemish (*Europos*) and its deep, interdependent relationship with its hinterland.

Ancient Sources

Lucian, *Verae Historiae (How to Write History)*. Translated by K. Kilburn. Volume VI. Loeb Classical Library. Cambridge, MA, Harvard University Press, 1968.
Pliny, *Naturalis Historia (Natural History)*. Translated by H. Rackham. Volume II. Loeb Classical Library. Cambridge, MA, Harvard University Press, 1969.
Procopius, *De Bello Persico* (*The Persian War: Book II*). Translated by H. B. Dewing. Volume I. Loeb Classical Library. Cambridge, MA, Harvard University Press, 1969.

Bibliography

Algaze, G., Breuninger, R., Lightfoot, C. and Rosenberg, M. (1991) Tigris-Euphrates Archaeological Reconnaissance Project: a preliminary report on the 1989–1990 seasons. *Anatolica* 17, 175–240.
Algaze, G., Mısır, A. and Wilkinson, T. (1992) Şanliurfa Museum/University of California excavations and surveys at Titriş Höyük, 1991: a preliminary report. *Anatolica* 18, 33–60.
Algaze, G., Breuninger, R. and Knudstad, J. (1994) The Tigris-Euphrates Archaeological Reconnaissance Project: Final report of the Birecik and Carchemish Dam survey areas. *Anatolica* 20, 1–96.
Bell, G.L. (1911) *Amurath to Amurath*. London, Heinemann.
Bridel, P. and Stucky, R.A. (1980) Tell el Hajj, Place Forte du Limes de l'Euphrate. In J.-Cl. Margueron (ed.) *Le Moyen euphrate. Zone des contactes et d'échange. Actes du Colloque de Strasbourg 10 à 12 mars 1977*, 349–54. Travaux du centre de recherche sur le Proche-orient et la Grece antiques 5. Leiden, Brill.
Bunnens, G. (1990) Tell Ahmar after fifty years. In G. Bunnens (ed.) *Tell Ahmar: 1988 Season*, 1–10. Abr-Nahrain Supplement series. Volume 2. Publications of the Melbourne University Expedition to Tell Ahmar. Volume 1. Leuven, Orientaliste.
Chatonnet, F.B. and Desreumaux, A. (2011) Oldest Syriac Christian inscription discovered in North-Syria. *Hugoye: Journal of Syriac Studies* 14 (1), 45–61.
Clarke, G.W. (1999a) Tell Jebel Khalid. In G. del Olmo Lete and J.-L. Montero Fenollós (eds) *Archaeology of the Upper Syrian Euphrates: The Tishrin Dam Area*, 227–236. Aula Orientalis Supplementa 17. Sabadel (Barcelona), Ausa.
Clarke, G.W. (1999b) The upper Euphrates Valley during the Hellenistic–Roman period. In G. del Olmo Lete and J.-L. Montero Fenollós (eds) *Archaeology of the Upper Syrian Euphrates: The Tishrin Dam Area*, 637–42. Aula Orientalis Supplementa 17. Sabadel (Barcelona), Ausa.
Clarke, G.W., Connor, P.J., Crewe, L., Frohlich, B., Jackson, H., Littleton, J., Nixon, C.E.V., O'Hea, M. and Steele, D. (2002) *Jebel Khalid on the Euphrates. Report on the Excavations 1986–1996. Volume One.* Mediterranean Archaeology Supplement 5. Sydney, Meditarch.
Comfort, A. and Ergeç, R. (2001) Following the Euphrates in antiquity: North–South routes around Zeugma. *Anatolian Studies* 51, 19–49.
Comfort, A., Abadie-Reynal, C. and Ergeç, R. (2000) Crossing the Euphrates in antiquity: Zeugma seen from space. *Anatolian Studies* 50, 99–126.
Connor, P.J. and Clarke, G.W. (1996–7) Jebel Khalid in North Syria: the first campaigns. *Mediterranean Archaeology* 9–10, 151–183.
Copeland, L. and Moore, A. M. T. (1985) Inventory and description of sites. In P. Sanlaville (ed.) *Holocene Settlement in North Syria: résultats de deux prospections archéologiques effectuées dans la région du nahr Sajour et sur le haut Euphrate syrien*, 41–98. Oxford, British Archaeological Report S238.
Dabrowa, E. (1986) The frontier in Syria in the first century AD. In P. Freeman and D. Kennedy (eds) *The Defence of the Roman and Byzantine East*, 93–108. Oxford, British Archaeological Report S297.

Decker, M. (2009) *Tilling the Hateful Earth: Agricultural Production and Trade in the Late Antique East.* Oxford, Oxford University Press.

Edwell, P.M. (2008) *Between Rome and Persia: the Middle Euphrates, Mesopotamia and Palmyra under Roman Control.* London and New York, Routledge.

Egea Vivancos, A. (2005) Eufratense et Osrhoene: Poblamiento romano en el Alto Éufrates Sirio. *Antigüedad y Cristianismo (Murcia)* 22, 23–784.

Foss, C. (1997) Syria in transition, A. D. 550–750: an archaeological approach. *Dumbarton Oaks Papers* 51, 189–269.

Gaborit, J. and Leriche, P. (1998) Géographie historique de la vallée du Moyen-Euphrate. In P. Arnaud and P. Counillon (eds) *Geographica Historica*, Seminaire Bordeaux 1994–1995, 167–200. Bordeaux-Nice, Ausonius.

Gatier, P.-L. (1994) Une inscription latine du moyen Euphrate. *Syria* 71 (1–2), 151–157.

González Blanco, A. (1999) Christianism on the eastern frontier. In G. del Olmo Lete and J.-L. Montero Fenollós (eds) *Archaeology of the Upper Syrian Euphrates: The Tishrin Dam Area*, 643–662. Aula Orientalis Supplementa 17. Sabadel (Barcelona), Ausa.

Grainger, J.D. (1990) *The Cities of Seleukid Syria.* Oxford, Clarendon Press.

Heinz, M., with Kulemann-Ossen, S., van Lengerich, L., Leschke, C., Nieling, J., von Rüden, C. and Wagner, E. (2010) *Kamid el-Loz. Intermediary between Cultures: More Than 10 Years of Archaeological Research in Kamid el-Loz (1997–2007).* DAAL Hors-Série VII. Beirut, Ministry of Culture and Directorate general of Antiquities of Lebanon.

Hirschfeld, Y. (2004) A climatic change in the early Byzantine period? *Palestine Exploration Quarterly* 136, 133–149.

Hogarth, D.G. (1909) Carchemish and its neighbourhood. *Annals of Archaeology and Anthropology, University of Liverpool* 2, 165–184.

Hogarth, D.G. (1914) *Carchemish. Report on the Excavations at Djerabis on Behalf of the British Museum. Part 1. Introductory.* London, British Museum.

Jackson, H. and Tidmarsh, J. (2011) *Jebel Khalid on the Euphrates. Volume 3: The Pottery.* Mediterranean Archaeology Supplement 7. Sydney, Meditarch.

Jalabert, L. and Mouterde, R. (1929) *Inscriptions grecques et latines de la Syrie. Tome premier: Commagène et Cyrrhestique.* Bibliothèque Archéologique et Historique T.12. Paris, Paul Geuthner. (*IGLS*).

Jones, A.H.M. (1971) *The Cities of the Eastern Roman Provinces* (2nd edn). Oxford, Clarendon Press.

Kennedy, D. (ed.) (1998) *The Twin Towns of Zeugma on the Euphrates: Rescue Work and Historical Studies.* Supplementary Series 27. Portsmouth RI., Journal of Roman Archaeology.

Kennedy, D. (2007) *Gerasa and the Decapolis: A 'Virtual Island' in Northwest Jordan.* Duckworth Debates in Archaeology. London, Duckworth.

Kenrick, P.M. (2013) Pottery other than transport amphorae. In W. Aylward (ed.) *Excavations at Zeugma Conducted by Oxford Archaeology. Volume II*, 1–81. Los Altos CA, Packard Humanities Institute. http://zeugma.packhum.org/toc (accessed January 12, 2014).

Keppie, L. J. F. (1986) Legions in the East from Augustus to Trajan. In P. Freeman and D. Kennedy (eds) *The Defence of the Roman and Byzantine East: Proceedings of a Colloquium Held at the University of Sheffield in April 1986*, 411–29. Oxford, British Archaeological Report S297.

Kuzucuoğlu, C., Dörfler, W., Kunesch, S. and Goupille, F. (2011) Mid- to late-Holocene climate change in central Turkey: The Tecer Lake record. *Holocene* 21 (1), 173–188.

Lightfoot, J.L. (2003) *Lucian on the Syrian Goddess.* Oxford, Oxford University Press.

Marchetti, N. (2012) Karkemish on the Euphrates. *Near Eastern Archaeology* 75 (3), 132–147.

Matilla Séiquer, G., and Gallardo Carrillo, J. (1998) Urbanismo: ciudades y necropolis. *Antigüedad y Cristianismo (Murcia)* 15, 247–298.

Millar, F. (1993) *The Roman Near East, 31 BC–AD 337.* Cambridge MA, Harvard University Press.

Miller, N.F. and Marston, J.M. (2012) Archaeological fuel remains as indicators of ancient west Asian agropastoral land-use systems. *Journal of Arid Environments* 86, 97–103.

Neumann, F.H., Kagan, E.J., Schwab, M.J. and Stein, M. (2007) Palynology, sedimentology and palaeocology of the late Holocene Dead Sea. *Quaternary Science Reviews* 26, 1476–1498.

Newson, P. (2014) Pottery of the '*Land of Carchemish*' project and the Northern Euphrates. In B. Fischer-Genz and H. Hamel (eds) *Roman Pottery in the Levant: Local Production and Regional Trade*, 3–19. Roman and Late Antique Mediterranean Pottery 3. Oxford, Archaeopress.

Palmer, A. (1990) *Monk and Mason on the Tigris Frontier.* Cambridge, Cambridge University Press.

Peltenburg, E., Campbell, S., Croft, P., Lunt, D., Murray, M.A. and Watt, M.E. (1995) Jerablus-Tahtani, Syria 1992–4: preliminary report. *Levant* 27, 1–28.

Philip, G. and Newson, P. (2014) Settlement in the Upper Orontes Valley. A preliminary statement. In K. Bartl and M. al-Maqdissi (eds) *New Prospecting in the Orontes Region. First Results of Archaeological Fieldwork*, 33–39. Orient-Archäologie Bd. 30. Rahden, DAI, Orient-Abteilung.

Philip, G., Abdulkarim, M., Newson, P., Beck, A., Bridgland, D., Bshesh, M., Shaw, A., Westaway, R. and Wilkinson, K. (2005) Settlement and landscape development in the Homs Region, Syria. Report on work undertaken during 2001–2003. *Levant* 37, 21–42.

Reynolds, P. (2013) Transport Amphorae of the First to Seventh Centuries: Early Roman to Byzantine Periods. In W. Aylward (ed.) *Excavations at Zeugma Conducted by Oxford Archaeology. Volume II*, 93–161. Los Altos, CA, The Packard Humanities Institute. http://zeugma.packhum.org/toc (accessed January 12, 2014).

Ricci, A. (2014) Karkemish and its region in Late Antique and Byzantine times. In N. Marchetti (ed.) *Karkemish: an Ancient Captial on the Euphrates*, 119–126. Orient Lab 2. Bologna, Ante Quem.

Sanlaville, P. (ed.) (1985) *Holocene Settlement in North Syria.* Oxford, British Archaeological Reports S238.

Sartre, M. (2005) *The Middle East Under Rome.* Cambridge MA, Belknap Press.

Sartre-Fauriat, A. (2001) *Des Tombeaux et des morts. Monuments funéraires, société et culture en Syrie du sud Ier S. av. J.-C. au VIIe S. apr. J.-C. Vol 2. Synthèse.* Bibliothèque Archéologique et Historique T. 185. Beirut, Institut français d'archéologie du Proche-Orient.

Sommer, M. (2010) Modelling Rome's Eastern frontier: the case of Osrhoene. In T. Kaizer and M. Facella (eds) *Kingdoms and Principalities in the Roman Near East,* 217–228. Stuttgart, Franz Steiner.

Talbert, R.J.A. (2010) *Rome's World: The Peutinger Map Reconsidered.* Cambridge, Cambridge University Press. http://www.cambridge.org/us/talbert/ (accessed August 1, 2013).

Tate, G. (1997) The Syrian countryside during the Roman Era. In S.E. Alcock (ed.) *The Early Roman Empire in the East,* 55–71. Oxford, Oxbow Books.

Thureau-Dangin, F. and Dunand, M. (1936) *Til-Barsib.* Paris, Paul Geuthner.

Tunca, Ö. (1992) Rapport préliminaire sur la 1ère campagne de fouille à Tell Amarna (Syrie). *Akkadica* 79–80, 14–34.

Tunca, Ö. (1999) *Tell Amarna. Présentation sommaire de sept campagnes de fouilles (1991–1997).* In G. del Olmo Lete and J.-L. Montero Fenollós (eds) *Archaeology of the Upper Syrian Euphrates: The Tishrin Dam Area,* 129–35. Aula Orientalis Supplementa 17. Sabadel (Barcelona), Ausa.

Tunca, Ö., Waliszewski, T. and Koniordos, V. (eds) (2011) *Tell Armarna (Syrie) V. La basilique byzantine et ses mosaïques.* Leuven, Paris and Walpole MA, Peeters.

Vokaer, A. (2007) *La Brittle Ware* byzantine and omeyyade en Syrie du Nord. In M. Bonifay and J.-Ch. Tréglia (eds) *Late Roman Coarse Wares 2: Cooking wares and Amphorae in the Mediterranean. Archaeology and Archaeometry. Volume II,* 701–13. Oxford, British Archaeological Report S1662.

Vokaer, A. (2011). *La Brittle Ware en Syrie. Production et diffusion d'une céramique culinaire de l'époque hellénistique à l'époque omeyyade.,* Collection des Mémoires de la Classe des Lettres in-4°, T.III (Fouilles d'Apamée de Syrie, 2). Brussels, Académie royale de Belgique.

Waliszewski, T. and Chmielewski, K. (2000) Tell Amarna: restoration and excavation, 2000. *Polish Archaeology in the Mediterranean* 12, 347–356.

Waliszewski, T. (2011) De Zeugma à Barbalissos. Archéologie de la région aux périodes romaine et proto-byzantine. In Ö. Tunca, T. Waliszewski, and V. Koniordos (eds) *Tell Amarna (Syrie) V: La basilique byzantine et ses mosaïques,* 215–57. Leuven, Paris and Walpole MA., Peeters.

Wightman, G. (1990) Area B – sounding in the Middle City. In G. Bunnens (ed.) *Tell Ahmar: 1988 Season,* 106–120. Leuven, Orientaliste.

Wilkinson, E.B., Wilkinson, T.J. and Peltenburg, E. (September 2011) *Revisiting Carchemish: the Land of Carchemish Project in Syria, 2009 & 2010.* http://www.antiquity.ac.uk/projgall/wilkinson329/ (accessed April 6, 2013).

Wilkinson, T.J. (1990) *Town and Country in Southeastern Anatolia, Vol. 1.* Chicago IL, University of Chicago, Oriental Institute.

Wilkinson, T.J. and Rayne, L. (2010) Hydraulic landscapes and imperial power in the Near East. *Water History* 2 (2), 115–144.

Wilkinson, T.J., Peltenburg, E., McCarthy, A., Wilkinson, E.B. and Brown, M. (2007) Archaeology in the Land of Carchemish: landscape surveys in the area of Jerablus Tahtani, 2006. *Levant,* 39, 213–247.

Wilkinson, T.J., Galiatsatos, N., Lawrence, D., Ricci, A., Dunford, R., and Philip, G. (2012) Late Chalcolithic and Early Bronze Age landscapes of settlement and mobility in the Middle Euphrates: a reassessment. *Levant* 44(2), 139–185.

Woolley, C.L. (1921) *Carchemish: Report on the Excavations at Jerablus on Behalf of the British Museum. Part II: The Town Defences.* London, British Museum.

Woolley, C.L. and Barnett, R.D. (1952) *Carchemish. Report on the Excavations at Jerablus on behalf of the British Museum, Part III. The Excavations in the Inner Town and the Hittite Inscriptions.* London, British Museum.

10

Sixty years of site damage in the Carchemish region

Emma Cunliffe

The Land of Carchemish Project, conducted south of the site of Carchemish, found a near-continuous spread of ancient settlement, which today is being damaged at an alarming rate. Whilst natural taphonomic changes have affected the condition of the sites, the area remained largely unchanged until the Tishrin Dam flooded large areas in the 1990s. No planned irrigation works were implemented but the new water level generated rapid expansions in agriculture, settlement, and the urban infrastructure required to support them, with a corresponding impact on the sites. Using Project data and comparative sequential satellite imagery from the 1960s to 2009, it is possible to study the changes on the sites. The results indicate that damage is not only still occurring, but is increasing in impact.

This chapter will begin by briefly describing the changes

to the region to contextualise the damage to the surveyed sites. A damage assessment will look at cause, extent, and location. Key trends are identified, and exploratory case studies are drawn from within the larger survey area to give specific local examples of damage patterns. The chapter concludes with final recommendations to address the problem.

The Carchemish region: context

The Project area is shown in Figure 10.1. There are four main land types (see Chapter 5). These are: 1) the river valleys of the Euphrates, the Sajur and the Amarna, and their flood plains (which are without archaeological sites); 2) the

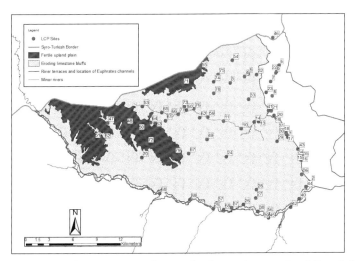

Fig. 10.1 Land of Carchemish survey area showing sites and major landscape features. Land Type 1 (the river valleys) which has no archaeological sites, is combined with land type 2, the terraces, for ease of scale

terraces of the Euphrates, Sajur and Amarna; 3) the eroded limestone terrain with thin soils which cover the majority of the area; and 4) the fertile upland plain to the west.

The early history of the region is well covered (Chapters 1–3, with the settlement and landscape surveys in 4 and 5, Carchemish Outer Town in Chapter 8 and the Roman-Byzantine Period in Chapter 9). Importantly, the earliest sites were small dispersed settlements along the rivers: these are now often eroded or buried. In the mid-3rd millennium BC, settlement expanded into new areas, followed by subsequent abandonment, re-growing in the Iron Age and again in the Hellenistic/Roman period, potentially damaging or erasing earlier features and sites. Certainly soil erosion from the latter period indicates increased farming (Chapter 5), which as will be shown can damage sites. The first evidence of settlement on the marginal soils of the limestone bluffs is also Hellenistic/Roman (although occupation during other periods cannot be ruled out) (Chapter 9). Later settlement remained small and dispersed, and Ottoman administration made little difference: the area remained sparsely populated. The Euphrates liwā (district) had only three settlements – a town and two villages: it was mainly populated by nomadic tribes (Göyünç and Hütteroth 1997). Even by the 20th century, settlement still consisted largely of small villages throughout the flood plain, most of which were flooded by the waters of Lake Assad and the Tishrin Dam, leaving the earlier relict landscapes unaffected by non-natural change.

The 1970s saw limited archaeological surveys, but after the Tishrin Dam plans were approved in the 1980s, rescue excavations ensued, concentrated on the soon-to-be-flooded valley floor (summarised in del Olmo Lete and Montero Fenollós 1999). From this sprang further survey work: the *Land of Carchemish Project* (LCP), part of the wider regional work of the Durham University Fragile Crescent Project (FCP). Four survey seasons (2006, 2008, 2009 and 2010) aimed to provide a more even and intensive coverage of settlement and landscape use and features south of Carchemish. Further fieldwork was unfortunately cancelled due to the political situation.

In addition to the LCP site visits, data for Tell Jerablus Tahtani (LCP 22) and Tell Amarna (LCP 21) was provided by excavation teams (Peltenburg 1999; Peltenburg *et al.* 1997; Tunca 1999; Tunca and Molist 2004, respectively; and Valdés Pereiro 2010). LCP 19 (Wadi Amarna) had also been excavated (Tunca and Molist 2004). Not all sites were surveyed as part of the LCP: the large citadel of Qala'at Halwanji was not visited and so was excluded here (but see Chapter 6). Excavations also restarted on the Turkish area of Carchemish (Marchetti 2012). However, these post-date the imagery available in this study, and were also excluded.

Sites can be split into three main types: hilltop settlements (varying from scatters to approximately a metre of cultural deposit); small, low sites of around 1 ha or less with less than 2 m of cultural accumulation; and large multi-period

tells. The region has never been intensely settled, and much of it is considered marginal land that was only occupied when population pressure demanded it. This implies that – with the exception of the river banks and terraces – sites will have been largely exempt from anthropogenic damage caused by later occupations (*e.g.* early farming). Most visible damage assessed in this study has therefore been from natural taphonomic causes or recent human impacts.

Studying damage: a methodology

Studies assessing site damage are becoming more common, and have informed the methodology used in this investigation (for example, Contreras 2010; Contreras and Brodie 2010; Darvill and Fulton 1998; Hritz 2008; Lasaponara *et al.* 2014; Parcak 2007; Stone 2008; van Ess *et al.* 2006). However, many require expensive high resolution multi-spectral satellite imagery or detailed field visits, which are not always possible, particularly when assessing large areas. Others gauged damage to site area, as if sites have no height, depth or volume. Carchemish citadel mound, for example, is 30 m high, and wells in the outer town revealed at least 2–3 m of sub-surface deposits (Wilkinson and Wilkinson 2010).

Defining sites

It is almost impossible to know the original (maximum) size of a site; however changes in extent can indicate damage. This can be complicated enough in the field, but it is particularly difficult on satellite imagery. It is usually assumed that the field definition of the site approximates the actual extent, but this is not always the case. Some sites appear larger on imagery than recorded during the survey, whilst others seem smaller. This was demonstrated in the Tell Beydar Survey area (TBS) of Syria. TBS 24 was described in the (unpublished)[1] field notes as a "rounded mound with steep north slope": recorded dimensions were 80 m north–south, 70 m east–west and a height of approximately 2 m. However, Corona imagery (which pre-dates major landscape changes) suggests that the true extent of the site is either much larger, or that it has experienced extensive attrition (or both). Later sets of imagery also imply that the site extends beyond the initial assessment (Fig. 10.2).

These discrepancies could be caused by multiple factors: erosion can reduce sites, or if site soil washes onto the surrounding earth, sites can appear larger; some soils or stone outcrops have similar reflectance signatures to sites; even new cultivation may degrade sites or bring them to the surface, altering their appearance. Imagery interpretation can also vary depending on image type and resolution, the enhancement method applied, and environmental factors.

If the extent is incorrectly estimated then subsequent analysis based on site area could be wrong. For example, a

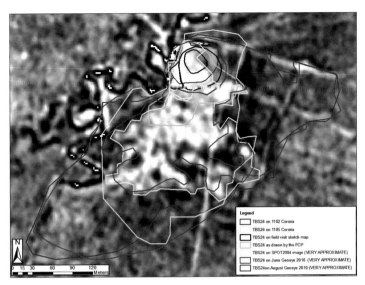

Fig. 10.2 Boundaries for TBS 24 according to different satellite images

road thought to pass by a site could actually pass through it, destroying archaeological material. However, as the transects undertaken during the LCP surveys testify, the field team were careful to look for possible site extensions (Wilkinson pers. comm. 2012), although this does not exclude the possibility of site removal via bulldozing, which cannot always be detected in the field. Given the complexities involved, for consistency the 78 sites studied here are defined as drawn in the field visit notes.

Defining and recording threats

Damage threats, and their effects on sites, were defined after the examination of satellite imagery and a comprehensive literature review (see Cunliffe 2013, chapter 3). Sixteen anthropogenic threats were identified (including erosion, as it can exacerbate and be exacerbated by cultural threats, and excavation, which is ultimately destructive). Not all threats are visible on imagery, but most can be assessed to some extent. Threats affect sites differently depending on their height and depth. Roads, for example, often cause minimal damage on large high sites, but can be extremely destructive to small flat sites. There was a concern that damage could be masked at sites which contained multiple site-types but which were recorded as one site, for example a tell and accompanying flat outer town (two parts). One part (for example, a flat outer town) might experience more damage than the other (for example, a high, densely compacted tell), and it was desirable to identify this. Six of the 78 sites were therefore separated out for analysis, giving 85 separate sub-sites: LCP1 (tell, outer town and industrial area: see case study), LCP5 (tell and outer town), LCP10 (tell and outer town), LCP 21 (tell and outer

Table 10.1. Sites covered on imagery in each area

	Upland plains	Dissected limestone terrain	River terraces	Total sites
Total sub-sites	21	48	16	85
Sub-sites covered by Corona	21	48	16	85
Sub-sites covered by Digital Globe	19	28	14	61
Sub-sites covered by Geoeye	21	39	15	75

town), LCP 46 (tell and outer town), and LCP65 (tell and surrounding area).

Sites were located in ArcGIS10 and Google Earth using GPS points collected during field visits. All sites had a central point, and many had points locating their outer boundaries and/or a sketch map. Sites were then examined on a series of sequential satellite images, supported by the field data. The earliest available imagery was FCP-supplied Corona imagery from the 1038 and 1102 missions (dated 22 January 1967 and 8 August 1968, respectively). This was compared to Digital Globe imagery (from 27 May and 2 September 2009), and Geoeye imagery (26 July, 22 September and 10 November 2009), available through Google Earth and the FCP[2]. Neither Geoeye nor DigitalGlobe covered the whole area (Table 10.1).

In order to deal with these complexities and the variable effects of threats on different site types, a series of relative ordinal categories were developed which would allow damage to be assessed, whilst avoiding inaccurate volumetric estimates. Damage was recorded as horizontal categories of extent across the site:

- None;
- Unknown;
- Intermittent/Fractional;
- Sectional/Partial;
- Majority/ Extensive;
- Total/Wholesale.

Damage to the height and depth of the site were recorded in vertical extent categories:

- None;
- Unknown;
- Site Buried;
- Pitted;
- Site Slightly Degraded;
- Upper Levels Damaged;
- Site Heavily Degraded;
- Site Destroyed To Ground Level;
- Site Destroyed.

(Categories are defined in Cunliffe 2013, chapter 4, and Cunliffe forthcoming b). These terms are formal terms and so are capitalised in the text to aid their identification. Where visible, damage on sites was then recorded in a database and analysed.

Site damage: results

Sites were not always visible on imagery, particularly when located in the dissected limestone terrain. About a quarter of sites became more visible on later higher resolution imagery, but a quarter become less visible, presumably because of the damage sustained. However, using the field notes and identified land covers, inferences about damage were still possible.

Site damage: land use

Sixteen different land uses/land covers which could potentially damage sites were counted around and on sites. Those included are not a comprehensive list of all types, but are tailored to reflect the goal of assessing damage. Land covers which do not damage sites are grouped into a single type (Bare/scrub). By counting land use types, it is possible to estimate how "busy" the land was in the 1960s, and how "busy" it became as time passed. Measurements of land use around and on sites, and the changing patterns can also act as an early warning of potential threats.

There was a clear increase in the number of threats through time: an average of 3.58 threats were identified around each site on Corona, 4.77 were visible on the DigitalGlobe sites covered, and 4.87 on covered Geoeye sites. This was not a result of increasing resolution: if the small features visible on the high resolution Geoeye were assumed to be present on Corona, then the average number

Table 10.2. Wilcoxon signed rank test results for change in land use on and around sites

Wilcoxon signed rank test	Analysis type	N	Z value	p value
Corona to DigitalGlobe 2003	Land use around sites	61	-4.753	<0.000
Corona to Geoeye 2009	Land use around sites	75	-5.606	<0.000
Corona to DigitalGlobe 2003	Land use on sites	61	-5.101	<0.000
Corona to Geoeye 2009	Land use on sites	75	-6.023	<0.000

of threats around sites on Corona was 3.75 (although this does not include sites that were not covered on Geoeye). An increase was visible even in the 6 years between the Digital Globe and the Geoeye acquisition. All increases are statistically significant (Table 10.2).

Increases in land uses on sites were even greater. 1.95 land uses were recorded per site on Corona, 3.02 land uses were recorded on DigitalGlobe, and 3.07 land uses per site were recorded on Geoeye. Again, all increases are statistically significant (Table 10.2). Sites with bare/scrub cover have decreased from 56 counts to 31 counts (66% of sites on Corona to 41% of sites on Geoeye). This demonstrates the increasing land uses of all types on and around sites: for example once agriculture and development abut a site, it is clear they will ultimately subsume it as the pressure for land increases.

Site damage: the main damage-causing threats

Damage to sites is increasing (Table 10.3). One hundred and forty-six damage threats were recorded on Corona and 224 on Geoeye, despite the fact that ten sites are not covered by Geoeye. (As described in the methodology, the formal terms for categories are capitalised in the following discussion).

Arable agriculture was recorded on three quarters of sites over the study period. It is the most common threat, and is a third again as prevalent as the next most common threat. By 2009 it accounted for a quarter of threats to sites. Even though many fields were converted to orchards, agriculture still increased between the 1960s and 2009, and crops were often farmed around the trees. Arable agriculture on Corona covered the Majority of the site in a third of cases, and in almost another third it Totally covered the site. In more than 85% of cases on Corona and Geoeye the affected vertical depth was in the Upper Levels. There was a large decrease in Peripheral agriculture over time as improved machinery has allowed the farming of sites. Double-cropping is now common, leading to additional disturbance from ploughing, and greater erosion. However, irrigation channels are rare and relatively small: water is machine pumped from rivers and wells.

Table 10.3. Counts of each damage cause on sites in all periods

Damage threat	No. sites	% of 85 identified Sub-sites (see Table 10.1)
Arable Agriculture	65	76.5
Bulldozing	12	14.1
Cuts	10	11.8
Development	26	30.6
Dumping Pits	3	3.5
Grave Pits	11	12.9
Irrigation Channels	5	5.9
Looting	15	17.6
Military Damage (*i.e.* Mines)	1	1.2
Mudbrick Pits	0	0.0
Natural Erosion	11	12.9
Orchards	30	35.3
Pits (Other)	7	8.2
Quarries	3	3.5
Railway	1	1.2
Roads/Tracks	47	55.3
Visitor Erosion/Vandalism	1	1.2
Water Erosion	10	11.8
Unknown	41	48.2

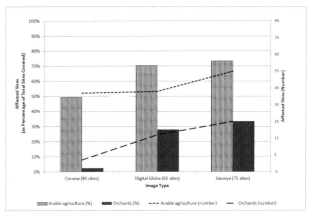

Fig. 10.3 Graph of increases in orchards and arable agriculture around Carchemish

Orchards are one of the fastest increasing threats to sites in this area (Fig. 10.3), and are predominantly located on flat sites. Only two were recorded on Corona, but 25 were recorded on Geoeye. Initially most were located on the upland plains, but the number on the limestone terrain more than doubled in 6 years. Most orchards covered only a Section across the site: two orchards covered sites entirely by 2009. Orchards were most likely to damage the Upper Levels of sites, but on particularly shallow sites (known from the field visits) the damage was far greater.

Increases in development mostly take the form of new isolated buildings rather than new settlements. Between 1967 and 2009, counts of development more than doubled. Almost half the sites on the plains and on the river terraces had buildings on them. The largest increase is on flat sites, where counts of development effectively tripled. Two-fifths of development affected Sections of sites in the 1960s: this number more than doubled by 2009. Development is almost always recorded as damaging the Upper Levels of sites as without excavation it is difficult to determine the depth of building foundations or how deep the site was.

Roads take three main forms: tractor tracks, gravel tracks, and tarmac roads. They were the second most common damage threat. 55% of sub-sites had a road or track through them, increasing from 29 on Corona to 42 on Geoeye. There are no correlations between roads and location or site type, nor were they placed to avoid sites: they were equally likely to affect the Periphery, a Fraction or a Section. Most roads on Corona were assumed to only Slightly Degrade the site (26 of 29 threats), as it was not always possible to tell if the road was covered by gravel, or by tarmac (the application of

which can cause significantly more damage). However, many were visibly improved over the study period. Whilst this rarely affected the horizontal extent, it increased the vertical depth of damage. By 2009, 13 roads were covered by tarmac, damaging the Upper Levels of sites; three Heavily Degraded sites, and two roads Destroyed sites to Ground Level.

Bulldozing is difficult to identify around Carchemish. Whilst it was usually determined from field notes, sometimes the ensuing cotton terraces were visible on imagery (Fig. 10.4). Bulldozing was recorded 12 times, all relatively recent: once on the upland plains, five times on the limestone hills, and five times on the river terraces (despite the fact that they cover a much smaller area). Bulldozing rarely destroys a site entirely: only one site was Totally bulldozed (LCP 45), and in most cases, only Sections were removed. Even though a large vertical extent is usually affected when sites are flattened, sub-surface remains are often preserved.

Looting was recorded on almost one in five sites, mostly on the limestone hills. It was never seen on Corona, perhaps due to the low resolution, but was recorded 12 times on Geoeye, and in three cases on field visits. Consecutive field visits and imagery both demonstrated increasing looting (Fig. 10.5). At most sites, only a fraction was affected, however large trenches were dug on some sites.

Cemeteries and graves were recorded on 11 sites, mostly on the limestone hills. One cemetery was visible on Corona, six on DigitalGlobe, and nine on Geoeye (with an additional cemetery known from field visits). There are almost no single graves: most cemeteries cover Sections of sites, and one covered a site entirely. In general, they protect the sites from further interference, but several are still in use, causing on-going damage and limiting field study.

Almost 30% of existing threats amplified between 1967 and 2009. Twenty-nine worsening threats were dated to between 1967 and 2003, and 40 worsened between 1967 and 2009. One in five threats grew worse between the 6

Fig. 10.4 Bulldozing at Tell Jerablus Tahtani: Top left: Three tiers of cotton terracing north-west of the tell. Image: July 2010 (author); Top right: Tell Jerablus Tahtani (LCP 22) on Geoeye November 2009 (FCP); Bottom left: Bulldozing to extend arable fields in the west of the tell. Image: July 2010 (author); Bottom right: Bulldozing to create cotton terraces to the SW of the tell. Image: July 2010 (author)

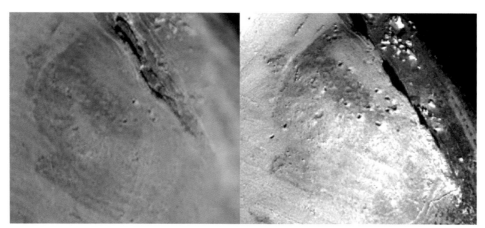

Fig. 10.5 Looting holes at Khirbet Seraisat on 2003 Digital Globe (Google Earth), and 2009 Geoeye (FCP)

year period 2003–2009. Only four damage threats decreased in the study period.

Case studies

Regional damage: limestone terrain

Land use is strongly associated with geographic region. Sites on the limestone hills and valleys were hardest to identify on satellite imagery, but the area was the least intensely occupied throughout history. There are fewer land

uses on and around sites there, however the rate of change is concerning: it may become more heavily utilized as time passes, increasing the risk to the sites. There is more evidence of bulldozing there compared to other areas: the hilly terrain and regular limestone outcroppings presumably interfere with land utilization. Looting is also far more common. Developments and roads have not increased more than elsewhere, so it is presumably not correlated with increasing access or population. Agriculture is the only other threat in this area to have increased so much (Fig. 10.6), suggesting a possible link.

In comparison, the river terraces have the most intensive

occupation history and saw the largest increase over time in numbers of threats. The greatest numbers of land uses were always on the sites in this region, which also witnessed the highest average number of threats per site. The upland plains had the largest number of threats around sites, and these have changed very little. This suggests that in intensively occupied areas, land pressure necessitated the incorporation of sites into land utilization strategies, whereas although the

fertile plains have a long history of farming, sites could be avoided, presumably as modern settlement density is lower.

The limestone terrain represents the increasing utilization of marginal land, which, in turn reflects intensifying occupation. Settlements continue to expand, but the rate of growth is not as great as in other areas. However, to focus on development as an indicator of human activity would be to miss the great changes occurring in the landscape.

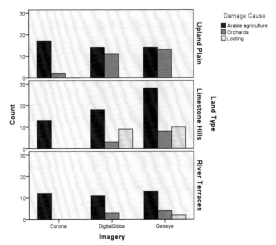

Fig. 10.6 Comparative graphs of increasing agriculture and looting by region

Case study: outer towns

Only five outer towns were recorded, therefore quantitative analysis was not possible. These were: Khirbet Seraisat (LCP 1), Tashatan (LCP 5), 'Ain al-Beida (LCP 10), Tell Amarna (LCP 21), and Carchemish (LCP 46). Tashatan's outer town was only observed from the tell, it was not visited by the field teams. The outer town of Carchemish, however, had an entire field season devoted to recording the archaeology as well as damage, which may further bias the results. A potential outer settlement was reported around Tell Jerablus Tahtani (Wilkinson *et al.* 2007): part of the Late Antique outer settlement lies within a modern cemetery, but parts of the Uruk period outer settlement were buried below sediment. As details regarding the size and condition of the settlement are limited, it was excluded. Three of the five outer towns were located on the limestone hills and two on the river terraces; none were identified around tells on the upland plains. All the outer towns were flat, and were compared to the other 33 flat sites recorded.

Outer towns experience significantly more threats than other flat sites (Table 10.4). By 2009, arable agriculture was the most common threat, affecting all five, compared to only 19 of the 33 flat sites. Three of the five also had orchards, compared to 12 of 33 flat sites, and most had roads over them too.

A Mann-Whitney-U test (Table 10.5) comparing damage

Table 10.4. Number of damage threats identified on outer towns

		Corona	Digital Globe 2003	Geoeye 2009
No. damage threats	Outer Towns	17	25	26
	Flat Sites	46	54	68
Average no. threats per site	Outer Towns	3.4	5.00	5.20
	Flat Sites	1.39	1.39	2.06

Table 10.5. Mann-Whitney-U test for differences in damage extents on outer towns and flat sites

Imagery	Count	U	p	Mean Rank: Outer Towns	Mean Rank: Flat Sites
Corona	Horizontal Damage	321.50	0.272	27.91	33.51
DigitalGlobe 2003	Horizontal Damage	581.00	0.295	36.24	41.74
Geoeye 2009	Horizontal Damage	687.50	0.080	39.94	50.39
Corona	Vertical Damage	382.50	0.889	32.50	31.82
DigitalGlobe 2003	Vertical Damage	606.00	0.398	42.76	38.72
Geoeye 2009	Vertical Damage	863.00	0.841	46.69	47.81

Table 10.6. Mann-Whitney-U Test for differences in damage extents over time

Location	Count	U	p	Mean Rank: Corona	Mean Rank: Geoeye 2009
Outer Town	Horizontal Damage	200.00	0.5.82	20.76	22.81
Outer Town	Vertical Damage	163.00	0.124	18.59	24.23
Flat Sites	Horizontal Damage	1516.00	0.775	56.46	58.21
Flat Sites	Vertical Damage	11200	0.005	47.86	64.02

extents on flat sites to outer towns suggests that there was no statistically significant difference. There was also no statistically significant difference in the amount of damage experienced over time on lower towns (Table 10.6), although damage depths increased in flat sites.

Although damage extents on outer towns are not increasing compared to similar sites, the high number of threats represents a substantial hazard. Traditionally, tells have been a major focus of excavation, but these figures illustrate the risk to understudied outer towns.

Case study: Khirbet Seraisat

Khirbet Seraisat (LCP 1) is a complex site on the limestone bluffs between the junctions of the Amarna, the Sajur and the Euphrates Rivers (Fig. 10.7). It consists of a tell (LCP 1.3 [C]), two flat areas beneath the cemetery to either side of the road (LCP 1.1 [A] and LCP 1.2 [B]), and the flat section between them and the tell (LCP 1.4 [D]). Ancient quarries and rock-cut tombs were recorded, and an industrial section along the wadi banks. That area was not numbered

during the survey, but is listed here as LCP 1.5. Sections 1, 2 and 4 (identified by a large pottery scatter) form one of the outer towns previously discussed (field notes 2006/8; Wilkinson *et al.* 2007).

Although the site is covered by all 4 sets of imagery, the tell is barely visible on Corona, and only the tell and some features (such as the quarries and the aqueduct) are visible on later imagery. Digital Globe coverage is partial (Fig. 10.8). Figure 10.7 shows the site as it appeared in 1967, superimposed over the 2003 Digital Globe imagery in order to demonstrate the site and surroundings, which are not clear on the Corona image. Figure 10.8 shows the site on Digital Globe: the boundaries are taken from the field visit descriptions and GPS way points taken in the field.

The initial field visit in spring 2006 recorded only one threat to the tell – looting holes at least 2 m deep. A cemetery, a road, and cereal cultivation were all noted on the outer town, and the wadi had caused "the obliteration of parts of

Fig. 10.9 Quarrying damage at Khirbet Seraisat in 2010 (author)

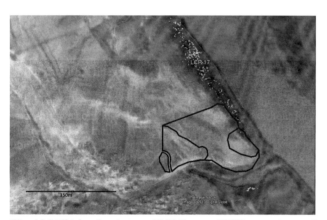

Fig. 10.7 Khirbet Seraisat on 1967 Corona (FCP), superimposed over 2003 Digital Globe image (Google Earth)

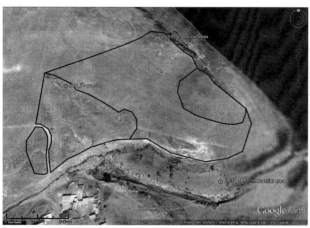

Fig. 10.8 Khirbet Seraisat on Digital Globe 2003 (Google Earth)

Fig. 10.10 Threats to Khirbet Seraisat on 2009 Geoeye image (FCP):1: Recent quarrying. 2: Upcast from road improvements. 3: New orchards. 4: Recent burials. 5: Increasing looting. 6: New orchard. 7: Arable agriculture. 8: New buildings

the industrial area" (Wilkinson *et al.* 2007), and buried other parts under 2–3 m of gravel. During a second visit in 2010, a recent quarry was noticed near the ancient quarry (Fig. 10.9).

A comparison of 2003 and 2009 imagery revealed the increase in these threats (Fig. 10.10), as well as other new or unrecorded threats. Looting holes at least doubled (Fig. 10.5); the number of graves increased; the road through the cemetery and outer town was widened and reinforced by tarmac – this was not present in 2003 or mentioned in the field visits. Another new orchard covers part of the tell. The village of Khirbet Seraisat has also expanded. Although the cemetery and orchard prevent it encroaching onto the tell from the east, the southern houses reached the wadi bridge by 2009. If the village continues to expand, the outer town and ultimately the tell could be threatened like other sites in this region.

This site is at great risk from multiple threats, although relatively speaking none of them have caused significant damage to the site. However, the more the site is incorporated into the intensifying land use strategies of the local community, the greater the risk to it. It is in a marginal area, but almost all parts of the land are utilised for agriculture, transport, burial, and artefact acquisition.

Case study: Carchemish

Khirbet Seraisat was a relatively unknown site in a marginal area. Carchemish, on the other hand, is a large, important site (LCP 46) on the intensely occupied river terrace. Although it consists of a large tell and an outer town, they are here considered together. Damage threats were identified on both 1102 Corona (22 January 1967, Fig. 10.11) and panchromatic Geoeye (November 2009, Fig. 10.12), and

ranked in terms of their severity to assess change over time (Tables 10.7 and 10.8).

After World War II, the tell and the Turkish part of the outer town were mined, although it was not possible to detect them using satellite imagery. In and of themselves, mines are small (3–15 cm), and are usually buried 0–30 cm deep, depending on the mine type and the soil type (Sai *et al.* 1998, 3). However, due to the risk (*i.e.* an explosion would cause serious damage), as they cover a large area, and because they deny access to large parts of the site, the mines are considered the main threat (Severity 1).[3]

The second most serious threat (Severity 2) – on both Corona and Geoeye – is the railway. It covers a smaller Section of the site than the mines, and is therefore ranked lower. Whilst it has a smaller horizontal extent and covers a smaller area than the arable agriculture marked as the next most serious threat on Corona (third), the vertical damage is much greater than that caused by agriculture (Site Destroyed to Ground Level). The ground was flattened and heavily disturbed, destroying any surface level remains, and some sub-surface remains. The depth of the disturbance is unknown, so the site was not recorded as Totally Destroyed (the next category).

On Corona, arable agriculture was the third ranked threat, covering almost the entire Syrian side of the outer town. The vertical damage extent was recorded as the Upper Levels, based on literature on plough types and methods. By the time the Geoeye image was taken, arable agriculture covered a much smaller section of the site, so this was considered only the sixth most serious threat visible in 2009. Most of the formerly-arable area was converted to orchards. These cover a large Section of the lower town and also damage

Table 10.7. Damage threats at Carchemish on Corona (identified on Fig.10.11)

Significance	Damage Cause	Horizontal Damage Effect	Vertical Damage Depth
1	Mines	Sectional/Partial	Upper levels damaged
2	Railway	Sectional/Partial	Site destroyed to ground level
3	Arable agriculture	Sectional/Partial	Upper levels damaged
4	Roads/Tracks	Intermittent/Fractional	Site slightly dispersed/degraded
5	Archaeological Excavation	Intermittent/Fractional	Upper levels damaged
6	Development	Peripheral	Site slightly dispersed/degraded
7	Water Erosion	Sectional/Partial	Site slightly dispersed/degraded

Table 10.8. Damage threats at Carchemish on Geoeye (identified on Fig. 10.12)

Significance	Damage Cause	Horizontal Damage Effect	Vertical Damage Depth
1	Mines	Sectional/Partial	Upper levels damaged
2	Railway	Sectional/Partial	Site heavily dispersed/degraded
3	Orchards	Sectional/Partial	Upper levels damaged
4	Development	Sectional/Partial	Site heavily dispersed/degraded
5	Bulldozing	Sectional/Partial	Site heavily dispersed/degraded
6	Arable agriculture	Sectional/Partial	Upper levels damaged
7	Roads/tracks	Sectional/Partial	Upper levels damaged
8	Irrigation	Intermittent/Fractional	Upper levels damaged
9	Pits (Other)	Intermittent/Fractional	Pitted
10	Archaeological Excavation	Intermittent/Fractional	Upper levels damaged

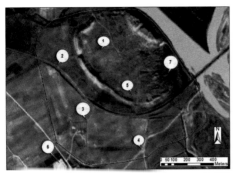

Fig. 10.11 Carchemish on Corona image (FCP)

Fig. 10.12 Carchemish on Geoeye image (FCP)

Fig. 10.13 Development of modern Jerablus over the outer town of Carchemish on Geoeye 2009 (Google Earth): the site of Carchemish (top) is outlined from Woolley's excavation map. The inner line of the town below indicates the extent of Jerablus in 1967, taken from 1038 Corona imagery. The outer line is the extent of Jerablus in 2009, from Geoeye imagery

the Upper Levels of the site. After the initial vertical hole has been dug (often at least 1 × 1 m), the growing roots cause further vertical and horizontal damage. Orchards also prevent archaeological excavation. This was therefore considered to be the third most significant threat recorded in 2009. However, the orchards protect the site from further expansion of the nearby town.

The fourth threat evident on Corona images was narrow roads: the recorded horizontal extent covers a Fraction of the site. The reflectance pattern suggests a gravel track, so the vertical extent is Site Slightly Degraded. By 2009, new, wider roads were built across the site, and the horizontal extent was accordingly increased to Sectional damage. Many (if not all) of the roads appear to be of tarmac, although they are not large enough to be major thoroughfares. The vertical extent was increased to reflect the fact that the road widening and application of tarmac will have damaged the Upper Levels of the site. However, other threats have also increased, so road building is only the seventh most severe threat in 2009.

The fifth threat on Corona was Hogarth and Woolley's archaeological excavations. These exposed some parts of the site, therefore the vertical extent is recorded as Upper Levels damaged. However, relative to the volume of the site, very little is affected so the horizontal extent is still only a Fraction. The excavated extents remain unchanged, but many other threats are now worse, so it is the tenth (i.e. the least serious) threat visible on Geoeye.

The sixth damage threat visible on Corona was from development, in the form of modern buildings and associated infrastructure, which abutted the outer town walls. The horizontal extent was therefore Peripheral: the vertical effect was Site Slightly Degraded. However, by 2009, development had increased markedly over parts of the outer town. The severity, horizontal and vertical extents were all increased accordingly. Development is the fourth most serious threat recorded on the site in 2009. It covers a large Section, and – as fieldwork has been completed to confirm this – it is known to Heavily Degrade the site (Wilkinson and Wilkinson 2010) (Fig. 10.13).

The last threat recorded on Corona was a rippled pattern consistent with water erosion damage on the south eastern side of the mound. This damage is old, but is recorded in the recent field notes (and on Chermside's 1879 map consulted during the LCP survey, see Fig. 8.5): it is therefore listed on the 1960s record, and as it is not on-going, it is not recorded on Geoeye.

Several new threats were recorded on the 2009 Geoeye. The fifth most serious was bulldozing. Fieldwork confirmed the affected horizontal extent was a Section along the outer town wall. Parts of the bulldozed section remained, albeit heavily damaged, so the vertical effect was Site Heavily Degraded. Two irrigation channels were visible in the arable fields to the south east of the site. These were small (a Fraction of the site extent, affecting the Upper Levels), and so were marked as the eighth threat to the site. Small gravel extraction pits were also recorded during survey (damage cause – Pits Other) (Wilkinson and Wilkinson 2010). These were too small to see or evaluate so they were accorded a low Severity (ninth) and minimal extents.

Whilst this study concluded in 2009, it should be stressed that site damage does not stop: it is an ongoing process. In the last three years, Carchemish, like many other areas of Syria, has been engulfed in the civil war. Of note, a new track has emerged across the lower town between Syria and Turkey, already deeply etched enough to be visible on Google Earth. In addition, the site has been affected by direct conflict.

> It: "became 'hell on earth' when fighters for the Islamic State of Iraq and Syria (ISIS) drove out secularist forces (in September 2013).
>
> 'Luckily, archeologists dig holes', Marchetti [excavating the Turkish side] told [journalist] Cerri. 'We dove in. We kept digging inside the deeper ones. The Turkish military kept telling us, stay down', though I rather doubt they needed reminding, as '[b]ullets were flying everywhere'. Eventually, the secularist fighters "surrendered" to the Turkish army and peace was restored; now, archaeologists and al-Qaeda fighters see each other across the border and 'do everything [they] can to ignore each other'." (in Hardy, 2013).

Evidence from elsewhere in Syria (Cunliffe forthcoming a) has shown that once conflict occurs on a site, its chances of experiencing significant damage increase rapidly as long as the fighting continues, suggesting the likelihood of further problems.

Recommendations and conclusions

The area south of Carchemish has undergone extensive change and modernization: the land is now utilized more intensively than ever before, resulting in damage to many of the sites. Sites are clearly being degraded: although no site has definitely been completely destroyed, some sites are almost gone. Only two sites appeared undamaged by cultural processes: the number of threats to sites has increased markedly. Most land is now cultivated, regardless of soil quality. Arable agriculture is the most common threat, affecting almost all sites: it is a slow, serious, on-going problem. Orchards have become common. Developments such as new buildings, have multiplied, and towns and villages have expanded, as have the road networks to accommodate them, and the associated infrastructure: new building methods require deeper foundations, pipes and electricity cables.

The arable expansion has led to a rise in related problems – looting, bulldozing, and roads and tractor tracks. The latter may not sound threatening, and in most cases it has only damaged the surface pottery, slightly disturbing the site, but in one case the bottom of a dried out wadi was bulldozed to create a tractor track. Many ancient water management features have been recorded along wadis in this area.

This is not the first time that the area has experienced intensive occupation and farming. These earlier instances, too, will have damaged the sites that went before them, just as they in their turn left the settlements that became the sites we study today. However, the destructive impact of modern urban and agricultural cultivation compared to that caused by the tools of earlier peoples cannot be understated. Damage in this region is occurring more quickly, and more destructively, than ever before, but it is clear that satellite imagery is of value in monitoring it.

It must be acknowledged that the types of damage discussed in this paper have now been over-taken by damage arising from the Syrian civil war, as seen at Carchemish and elsewhere. However, they will remain an increasingly serious problem for future generations. Responding to these longer-term issues facing the archaeological resource is the responsibility of both archaeologists and state agencies, and based on the identified risks, the following recommendations are made:

- Archaeologists need to design research questions considering attrition to the archaeological record, asking questions now that may not be answerable later.
- Further research is needed into the effects of different threats on site types, and the unique cultural and environmental context of each area.
- It is not possible to save every site, nor is it recommended. Modern people have just as much of a right to utilize the landscape as their ancestors did. However, a representative sample of sites of all sizes, periods and importance should be marked for protection to pass to our descendants.

Choices for protection must be based on an assessment of their condition, importance, uniqueness and representiveness on a local, regional and national scale. This requires a knowledge of the archaeological resource which is not currently available in Syria, or in many other countries.

- It is not possible to control every type of land use which may threaten sites. Recognition and encouragement should be given to those land uses which cause less damage to sites, or which act to protect them from greater damage.
- Future archaeological surveys should be combined with remote sensing to achieve more comprehensive investigations of the survey areas. We cannot save all the sites, but we can record them before they are destroyed. Copies of such records should be given to the governments of the respective countries.
- Surveys should also record the condition of the sites in more detail, and with greater accuracy and consistency. Site damage must move beyond the realms of the footnote.

Acknowledgements

Credit and thanks for this research must be given to Professor Wilkinson, who saw the site destruction occurring, and initiated and supported this study. Thanks are also due to Professor Philip for his support. This paper is based on AHRC-funded PhD research, and also could not have been completed without the generous financial support of the Global Heritage Fund Preservation Fellowship, Durham University's Department of Archaeology and Trevelyan College.

Notes

1   The sketch map boundary is taken from the unpublished field notes, kindly supplied by Professor Wilkinson.
2   The Corona imagery: Panchromatic, 2–3 m resolution, orthrectified and supplied by the Fragile Crescent Project. Digital Globe imagery: RGB composite, 05. × 0.6 m resolution, available on Google Earth. Google Earth do not specify whether they are hosting DigitalGlobe's WorldView imagery or their Quickbird Imagery. SPOT mosaic, RGB composite, 2.5 m resolution. Geoeye imagery: Pan-sharpened image, 0.5 m resolution, available on Google Earth. Additional copies of this imagery were supplied by the FCP: Panchromatic, 0.5 m resolution, orthorectified by the Dr Galiatsatos of the FCP.
3   De-mining was completed in February 2011, shortly after this analysis was conducted.

Bibliography

Contreras, D.A. (2010) Huaqueros and remote sensing imagery: assessing looting damage in the Virú Valley, Peru. *Antiquity* 84, 544–555.

Contreras, D.A. and Brodie, N. (2010) Quantifying destruction: an evaluation of the utility of publicly-available satellite imagery for investigating looting of archaeological sites in Jordan. *Journal of Field Archaeology* 35, 101–114.

Cunliffe, E. (2013) Satellites and Site Destruction: An Analysis of Modern Impacts on the Archaeological Resource of the Ancient near East. PhD Thesis, Durham University.

Cunliffe, E. (forthcoming a) Archaeological site damage in the cycle of war and peace: a Syrian case study. *Journal of Eastern Mediterranean Archaeology and Heritage Studies.*

Cunliffe, E. (forthcoming b) Remote assessments of site damage: a new ontology. *International Journal Heritage in the Digital Era* Special Issue on Metadata, Semantics and Ontologies for Cultural Heritage.

Darvill, T. and Fulton, A.K. (eds) (1998) *Mars: The Monuments at Risk Survey of England, 1995,* Bournemouth: School of Conservation Sciences, Bournemouth University/English Heritage.

del Olmo Lete, G. and Montero Fenollós, J.-L. (eds) (1999) *Archaeology of the Upper Syrian Euphrates: The Tishrin Dam Area.* Barcelona, Ausa

Göyünç, N. and Hütteroth, W.D. (1997) *Land an Der Grenze:*
Osmanische Verwaltung Im Heutigen Türkisch-Syrisch-Irakischen Grenzgebiet Im 16. Jahrhundert. Istanbul, Eren.

Hardy, S. (2013) *Turkey/Syria: Carchemish – Excavations on the Border of a Warzone.* In: *Conflict Antiquities Blog* [Online]. 18 November 2013 Available: http://conflictantiquities.wordpress.com/2013/11/18/turkey-italian-archaeologists-dig-under-the-eye-of-al-qaeda/ [Accessed 18 November 2013].

Hritz, C. (2008) Remote sensing of cultural heritage in Iraq: a case study of Isin. *Taarii Newsletter* 3 (1), 1–8.

Lasaponara, R., Leucci, G., Masini, N. and Persico, R. (2014) Investigating archaeological looting using satellite images and georadar: the experience in Lambayeque in North Peru. *Journal of Archaeological Science* 42, 216–230.

Marchetti, N. (2012) Karkemish on the Euphrates: excavating a city's history. *Near Eastern Archaeology* 75 (3), 132–147.

Parcak, S. (2007) Satellite remote sensing methods for monitoring archaeological tells in the Middle East. *Journal of Field Archaeology* 32 (1), 65–81.

Peltenburg, E. (1999) Tell Jerablus Tahtani 1992 – 1996: a summary. In G. Del Olmo Lete and J.-L. Montero Fenollós (eds) *Archaeology of the Upper Syrian Euphrates: The Tishrin Dam Area*, 97–105. Barcelona, Ausa.

Peltenburg, E.J., Campbell, S., Carter, S., Stephen, F.M.K. and Tipping, R. (1997) Jerablus-Tahtani, Syria, 1996: preliminary report. *Levant* 29, 1–18.

Sai, B., Morrow, P. and van Genderen, P. (1998) Limits of detection of buried landmines based on local echo contrasts. In *Workshop Proceedings of the 28th European Microwave Conference (EuMc) 9 October 1998: Workshop on High-Frequency Measurement Techniques for Interconnections and IC Packages used in Telecommunication and Computer Systems*, 121–125. Amsterdam, Miller Freeman.

Stone, E.C. (2008) Patterns of looting in Southern Iraq. *Antiquity* 82 (1), 125–138.

Tunca, Ö. (1999) Tell Amarna. Présentation Sommaire De Sept Campagnes De Fouilles (1991–7). In G. Del Olmo Lete and J.-L. Montero Fenollós (eds) *Archaeology of the Upper Syrian Euphrates: The Tishrin Dam Area,* 129–136. Barcelona, Ausa.

Tunca, Ö. and Molist, M. (eds) (2004) *Tell Amarna (Syrie) I: La Période De Halaf,* Louvain and Dudley MA, Peeters.

Valdés Pereiro, C. (2010) Tell Amarna on the Euphrates: new archaeological research. In P. Mattiae, F. Pinnock, L. Nigro, N. Marchetti and L. Romano (eds) *Proceedings of the 6th International Congress on the Archaeology of the Ancient Near East Vol I*, 743–754. Wiesbaden, Harrassowitz.

van Ess, M., Becker, H., Fassbinder, J., Kiefl, R., Lingenfelder, I., Schreier, G. and Zevenbergen, A. (2006) Detection of looting activities at archaeological sites in Iraq Using Ikonos Imagery. *Beiträge zum 18. AGIT-Symposium, Salzburg,* 2006, Heidelberg. Wiechmann-Verlag.

Wilkinson, T.J. and Wilkinson, E.B. (2010) Carchemish Outer Town Survey and Conservation Report: 2010. Report to the Global Heritage Fund. Unpublished, Durham University.

Wilkinson, T.J., Peltenburg, E.J., McCarthy, A., Wilkinson, E.B. and Brown, M. (2007) Archaeology in the Land of Carchemish: landscape surveys in the area of Jerablus Tahtani, 2006. *Levant* 39, 213–247.

11

Discussion

T.J. Wilkinson and Edgar Peltenburg

The particularistic nature of field monographs often results in them providing contributions to knowledge of a site or small area. However, because the Land of Carchemish Project was conceived to cover a relatively large area with a broad set of questions in mind, it might be expected to make wider contributions to knowledge.

A key research question raised in the original British Academy research design was: did the fact that archaeological research was constrained along the Euphrates distort our understanding of the nature of regional settlement (as noted in Chapter 1)? Certainly the results from the LCP clearly demonstrate that there was considerable settlement in the form of tells, low mounds and flat sites to the west away from the river, a situation which therefore limited the area of land that could have been used by nomadic pastoralists. However, this does not mean that such mobile communities did not operate in the region, but rather that their operating space was limited. Moreover, the extension of cultivation over virtually the entire landscape over the last 100 years, as discussed in Chapter 5, would have resulted in the destruction or dispersal of the ephemeral remains of mobile pastoral camps. Therefore, although we found no evidence of nomadic pastoralists, it does not mean that they were absent.

Within the triangle of terrain between the Sajur River and the Syrian–Turkish border, together with the lands north of that border within Turkey, the ceramic Neolithic provides the first evidence of individual sites, although there is no coherent pattern of settlement. It is therefore now apparent that "the Halaf period marks the beginning of recognizable settlement patterns across the area," (Chapter 4). That is not to deny the existence of such important PPNA and PPNB sites as Tell al-'Abr, Jerf el Ahmar and Halula in the region (Yartah 2004; Stordeur *et al.* 2000; Molist

1996), but arguably the Halaf must represent the founding period of tell formation and perhaps even the social and economic organizations that went with it. In other words, if the communities that occupied the tells also possessed and farmed the surrounding lands, the tell and its catchment could be regarded as a single unit (Wilkinson 2010). It can therefore be argued that this local corporate identity might extend back to the Halaf, and could have continued at least until the Iron Age or even the Hellenistic periods. Just how such a corporate identity may have manifested itself is less clear, but it probably included various aspects of communality (Roberts 1996, 35–37); since at least the 4th millennium BC, this meant the presence of fortification walls for defence (Peltenburg 2013) and the sharing of plough teams (Sherratt 1981; Van Driel 2001, 107; Widell *et al.* 2013). Unfortunately, it is difficult to simply project a local identity on a community without having sound evidence from the analysis of the material culture, burial practice and bio-archaeological data. However, not only was the duration of smaller tells often remarkable, in some cases extending over some 8000 years in what might be termed a landscape of rural resilience, it is now possible to recognize that the early development of tells has a deeper significance than them simply being long-lived formations.

The second half of the Early Bronze Age witnessed a substantial expansion of settlement in the region and the majority of these sites were tells (Chapter 4). Consequently, when tells are recognized beyond the limits of the survey area, but have not been dated by field survey, it follows, within a certain percentage probability, that they too were occupied in the EBA (Lawrence 2012). Few really large EBA sites were recognized in the survey area and until further excavations are conducted at Carchemish, the size of this site in the later third millennium BC (that is after the Ebla

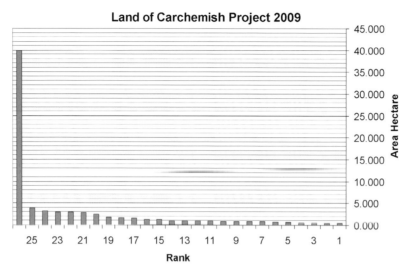

Fig. 11.1 Distribution of EBA sites according surface area. The estimate for Carchemish is approximate and based upon Falsone and Sconzo (2007), as well as earlier estimates by Algaze (1999) and McClellan (1999, 413)

royal archives) can only be estimated at *c.* 40 ha (Falsone and Sconzo 2007).

Overall, the results of the archaeological survey have underlined the significance of the excavations at Tell Jerablus Tahtani. This relatively modest site was not simply "One Bronze Age site among many" to paraphrase Dornemann (1988), but rather, being fairly typical, it can be taken as representative of the most common class of site in the whole region (Wilkinson *et al.* 2012).[1] The prevalence of small tells in the Middle Euphrates has already been recognized for the Kurban, Samsat, Titrish region in Turkey (Wilkinson *et al.* 2012, fig. 12) and a similar pattern is now evident in the LCP area (Fig. 11.1). Significantly, however, textual references to small fortified places, *bàd*[ki] - *bàd*[ki], and the increased prevalence of weapons at this time, suggests that many of these minor tells were probably accorded the status of small fortified strongholds (Peltenburg 2013; Wilkinson *et al.* 2014). These distinctive sites could therefore have been equivalent to the *dimtu* or *dunnu* settlements of the 2nd millennium BC, which are thought to have functioned as gathering places for the processing and storage of agricultural produce from the immediate area (Koliński 2001). Overall, the concentration of rescue excavations along the Euphrates has demonstrated the presence of fortifications at many small tells, and these numerous small fortified tells seem to imply the existence of a riverine culture of conflict (Peltenburg 2013, fig. 1). Furthermore, it can be suggested that similarly distinctive tells away from the river also acted as fortified strongholds.

The nature of the relationship between the small and seemingly stable tells and the EBA city of Carchemish remains difficult to determine, partly because of the uncertainties of the size of Carchemish itself. However, if the satellite tells were suppliers of surpluses and workers

to such expansive centres (Sollberger 1980, 134–135; Archi 1990, 18–19; Wattenmaker 2009, 119) it follows that because of their role as subordinate places (always giving, never receiving), the small tells would have been unable to grow beyond a certain size. Conversely, if Carchemish did attain some 40 ha in the Early Bronze Age, it would have been able to draw upon surpluses from more than 11 sites within 10 km radius (in all directions) or more than 28 sites within a 16 km radius.[2] Although it is not known how much surplus or labour would have been supplied from each satellite community, the growing site of Carchemish could have drawn upon substantial labour pools as well as considerable amounts of grain, animals and other supplies to provide a surplus as well as providing a buffer during times of shortfall (Chapter 7). Overall, when the size of Carchemish is considered in relation to the surrounding countryside: "It is interesting that the two phases of growth at Carchemish, namely the Middle EBA and Iron Age, were both characterized by a simultaneous rise in rural settlement" (Chapter 4). In other words, for the central city of Carchemish to be sustained it probably required a significant rural population to supply surplus foods. There is at least one major uncertainty, however, in the provisioning of Carchemish: given the role of the Euphrates as a boundary during several periods, the zones of supply may occasionally have been confined exclusively to the west side of the river (Chapter 7, Fig. 7.6).

During the survey, it was not always possible to demonstrate whether such walled sites continued after the EBA. However, there is a general and now familiar pattern of a tell-based landscape in the Chalcolithic and Bronze Age through until the Iron Age and even Hellenistic periods (Chapters 4, 5 and 10). Although sites like Tell Arab Hassan provide good evidence for fortification walls (Appendix,

LCP 68), their date of construction is difficult to estimate. Nevertheless, the excavation of the sites of Aushariye and Halwanji (Eidem, Chapter 6) as well as evidence from satellite images of the site of Khirbet al-Qana (Chapters 4 and 5) demonstrate the presence of walled strongholds of MBA, LBA and Iron Age date (although in these cases, not all are small, conical tells).

Because of their relatively small size, steep morphology and frequently vegetated surfaces, detailed patterns of occupation on the small tells have been difficult to recognize. On the other hand the *c.* 100 ha area of the main site of Carchemish was eminently sub-dividable into smaller units, although the dissection of the site by the Turkish Syrian border and the Berlin to Baghdad railway both have frustrated any overall sample scheme.

From the excavated record at Tell Jerablus Tahtani, it can be inferred that Carchemish expanded its territorial holdings around 2800 BC when a fort was constructed at the smaller site (Chapter 7). It can then be suggested that Carchemish received a population influx *c.* 2250 BC when Jerablus was abandoned. By the end of the EBA, forty sites within the aggregated survey areas had been abandoned (Chapter 4), and the total number of occupied sites halved, whilst the total settled area decreased by *c.* 25%. However, where these populations went is more difficult to say. Whether this late EBA decline was a result of adverse climate, political instability or a decline in inter-regional communications is unclear. Nevertheless, the abandonment of Tell Jerablus Tahtani around 2250 BC suggests that the crossing point with Tell Shiukh Fawqani was no longer of major significance.

From meagre textual evidence it is evident that Carchemish experienced a change of geopolitical status in the centuries following. At the start of this transition, in the 23rd century BC, it was barely acknowledged in the royal archives of Ebla, in spite of the fact that there are references to many important places much further afield than Carchemish. Its relatively lowly status may be explained by reference to it in the preamble to the treaty with Abarsal as "in the hand" of Ebla, a phrase denoting its subservience to that expansive state (Archi 1989). By the 18th century BC, however, the next time Carchemish appears in textual sources, it figures prominently as a major, independent polity in correspondence with Mari. It was renowned as a commercial centre with its *karum*, exporting wine, timber, grain, copper, bitumen and other products to that down-river metropolis (Michel 1996). To appreciate this fundamental transformation, it may be useful to consider it in the context of two significant changes that occurred during the interval between the Ebla and Mari references.

The first is that Ebla was destroyed *c.* 2300 B.C., and although it continued to be occupied, it seems to have had a reduced sphere of influence, one that may not have extended to this part of the Euphrates River valley (Archi

and Biga 2003). From its diminished role, we may infer that Carchemish gained a measure of independence at a time when profound re-arrangements of state interactions took place in Syria, ones that saw the eventual emergence of Amorite kingdoms. The second change more explicitly concerns inter-regional communications. Many sites in the Tabqa Dam area to the south of Carchemish grew to their largest size in the last quarter of the 3rd millennium, but then towards the end of that millennium several contracted and some were even abandoned (Chapter 4). The larger centres were heavily engaged in exchange networks, ones that seem to have led to a boom/bust trajectory amongst these so-called citadel cities (Wilkinson *et al.* 2012). Although the exact timing of the contraction of major Euphrates River valley sites and even of some outside the valley, like Umm el-Marra, is debated, it coincided with the interval in textual sources just mentioned (Kuzucuoğlu and Marro 2007). At the regional level, therefore, the de-urbanisation of trade competitors in the Banat-Tabqa region which lay between Carchemish and Mari may have furthered a concomitant political and economic expansion of Carchemish around the turn of the millennium. Its ability to do so may now be seen in the light of LCP and other survey evidence. Above and in Chapters 4 and 5 we have noted relative settlement stability north of the 300 mm isohyet approximately along the line of the Sajur, a continuity absent from the more marginal areas to the south around the Tabqa Dam. Our focus on survey evidence, therefore, provides another insight into possible reasons for the rise of Carchemish to prominence during this transitional period.

Taken together, the evidence points to conditions that may have precipitated the emergence of the city as a major centre in the Ancient Near East towards the end of the Early Bronze Age, as Algaze (1999, 552) argued for different reasons; a status it continued to hold in the 2nd and 1st millennium BC. Population nucleation at Carchemish may be one reason for the above-mentioned rural decline at the end of the third millennium BC (see above and Chapter 4), but a growing centre requires the regular intake of surpluses from its hinterland, a condition that would presumably demand continued occupation at many productive villages apart from those within walking distance from that centre. Historical contingency no doubt played a role in determining the decisions of various communities to move to Carchemish or to continue where they were. So, the multi-scalar changes that we see were not confined to demographics. They presumably involved greater centralisation of regional administrative mechanisms, the development of more effective communication systems and increased bulk storage facilities such as the special silos which appeared in abundance at Qara Qûzâq to the south of Carchemish at this time (Olávarri 1993, 4–5).

The 2nd millennium BC is difficult to interpret from the survey record, although as suggested in Chapter 4, there appears to have been a steady decline in the number of settled sites as well as aggregate settled area (here taken as a rough proxy for population). This shows a peak in the mid-late EBA, with a slight or significant decline in the MBA (see Chapter 4) to a minimum in the LBA, a trend which accords with the overall record of the Middle Euphrates in Syria where there was a general decrease in the number of settlements and in settlement size in the MBA (Cooper 2012, 83). The Sajur, which appears to have been rather sparsely populated during the EBA and the Late Chalcolithic, perhaps because it was a contested frontier zone, witnessed during the MBA a phase of strengthened settlement. This is manifest in the form of several major sites which were in use during the MBA, LBA or Iron Age, apparently to fortify the frontier (Chapter 6). Specifically, the excavated evidence from the remarkable hill-top fortification of Halwanji suggests that the MB II was a period of substantial military activity.

In his account of the excavations of the "acropolis mound" of Carchemish, Woolley reported that "the Roman leveling of the site swept away not only the Late Hittite but also all the Middle Hittite structures" (Woolley and Barnett 1952, 209). In the virtual absence of Late Bronze Age remains, it has even been suggested that the Hittite imperial seat was not situated at the site of the Iron Age city (Chapter 2). Nevertheless, in Chapter 2, Hawkins and Weeden also point out that the material evidence for a Late Bronze Age occupation is growing and the role of Carchemish may relate to its status as a rump state of the Hittite Empire in Northern Syria that survived the fall of the Empire. To complicate matters, political developments in the Amuq plain at Tayinat and Atchana as well as new readings of the dendrochronological data from Tille Höyük all suggest that the interpretations of the Late Bronze Age settlement record remain very much in flux.

Because of the rather undistinguished nature of LBA pottery in the Middle Euphrates Valley, the marked decline of settlement activity at this time should be viewed with caution (see Fig. 4.8). Although surveys in areas both north and south of the border clearly indicate a settlement decline at this time, this should not be taken as some sort of regional abandonment. This is because a significant number of large fortified centres were evident along the Middle Euphrates during the mid-late second millennium BC, both near Carchemish (Frangipane 2007, 137) and to the south (Einwag and Otto 1999, 180; Wilkinson *et al.* 2004, 188). On face value it therefore appears that the LBA was a period of significant reduction in the *rural* settlement, which perhaps built upon earlier decline in the MBA (McClellan 1992). In part, this was an outcome of the prevailing insecurity during this period of conflict between the Hittite, Mittanian, Assyrian (both Old and Middle) and Egyptian empires which resulted in rural areas becoming more insecure. Conversely, these circumstances also encouraged the concentration of population in fortified places such as Munbaqa and Bazi.

Therefore, although a period of ostensible settlement decline, the LBA was also a period when international exchange and interactions were also significant, and it was probably the larger fortified strongholds on the Euphrates that acted as the exchange hubs during such periods of political uncertainty.

The interpretation of political insecurity is inferred primarily from the historical record. However, in such a climatically marginal region the environmental record is also significant. Although there has been a tendency to focus on abrupt climatic change during the late third millennium BC, proxy records based upon oxygen and carbon isotopes demonstrate that, if anything, atmospheric drying intensified and continued throughout the 2nd millennium BC. This is evident at Lake Van which shows an oscillating decline from a peak moisture level in the 3rd quarter of the 3rd millennium BC through until the second millennium BC, which remained dry throughout (Lemcke and Sturm 1997). A similar long period of drier conditions during the 2nd millennium is recorded from Soreq Cave (Bar Matthews and Ayalon 2004) and Lake Kinneret (Rambeau and Black 2011, fig. 7.2). Unfortunately, these records are rather distant from northern Syria; however, recent analyses of Δ^{13} C in barley grains from sites in Syria and southern Turkey indicate a similar steady decline in atmospheric moisture through the MBA, reaching a minimum around the MB/LB boundary (Riehl and Deckers 2012, 18). Unfortunately, not all records from the Levant and Turkey are in accord, and the isotope record from barley grains shows considerable point-to-point variations (Riehl and Deckers 2012, 18).

The overall decline in settlement during the 2nd millennium BC accords quite well to the atmospheric drying during the same period. Although drier conditions lead to lower crop yields and potential shortfalls in food supply, it would be overly simplistic to equate such drying with diminished populations. This is because of the numerous coping mechanisms adopted by early populations as well as because trade, exchange and social interactions can address shortfalls (Wilkinson *et al.* 2014). In addition, the 2nd millennium BC is associated with the appearance of Amorite groups and mobile pastoralists in the Euphrates valley (Peltenburg 2007, 262; Cooper 2012, 87; Wossink 2009). Such populations, being frequently nomadic, would have left fewer material traces on the ground, especially in regions such as around Carchemish where extensive ploughing of the terrain in recent years will have removed much of the evidence of ephemeral occupations. A further debilitating factor was the increasing disengagement of people from exactions imposed by the palace economies of the 15th–13th centuries BC, leading to mass runaways and the growth of semi-nomadic groups reflected in the extradition clauses of LBA treaties (Liverani 1987).

Because the 2nd millennium BC was characterized by generally unstable conditions in the political economy

– due to of the presence of tribal groups as well as the environment, all of which tend to favour mobile groups – the prevailing sedentary settlement was sparse (see Fig. 4.14). As noted by Lewis (1987), however, during the Ottoman period settlement in climatically marginal regions increased during periods when the empire was strong, and diminished when it was weak. Consequently, the appearance of a strong central polity during the Iron Age, in the form of the Assyrian Empire, appears to have led to re-settlement. This was despite the rather arid conditions that prevailed in the early 1st millennium BC (Rambeau and Black 2011, fig. 7.2). In other words, settlement in the Middle Euphrates during the 1st millennium BC may have reflected both the strength of the local polities and the prevailing power of regional authorities such as the Assyrians, despite the fact that environmental conditions favoured either sedentary or mobile ways of life. Because there is no simple binary division between mobile and sedentary, mobile groups may settle and sedentary groups may become mobile depending upon circumstances. Under such conditions settlement would depend upon a tension between the power of competing polities, environmental conditions, and historical rights to the land as well as perceptions of various ethnic groups, especially the Amorites.

During much of the Holocene, most communities in the LCP area tended to live in settlements on tells, a pattern which continued well into the 1st millennium BC. If these long-lived communities did comprise the same communities through time, it can be inferred that local identities may also have continued. Although we don't currently have the data to demonstrate this, it suggests a tantalising possibility that such tell sites did belong to the same community which, if accepted, provides a powerful tool for interpreting the social geography of the region. Hence the observation that most Iron Age sites in the survey area were on tells provides a strong counterweight to the evidence from further east in the 'land of Assur' where Iron Age sites on low mounds formed part of a phase of deliberate colonization by deportees or sedentarizing mobile groups. Again, this underscores the importance of excavation of such small tells, because not only can excavation provide evidence on the function of such sites, it can also supply crucial data on changes in material culture and settlement sequences which, in turn, contributes to an understanding of local communities and their identities.

During the Iron Age, though the land of Carchemish was more densely settled than in the LBA, the region was still relatively sparsely occupied when compared with the Assyrian heartland in north-west Iraq and north-east Syria (Chapter 5). The data supplied in that chapter, together with the results of more recent investigations in Iraqi Kurdistan, suggests that the core regions of the Assyrian Empire were growing and becoming more densely populated at the expense of the peripheries.

To supplement the settlement evidence, the excavations at Aushariye on the Sajur provide vital information on the "Assyrianisation" of the region during the 1st millennium BC (Chapter 6). Not only did this valley form one of the preferred routes for the Assyrian army in its campaigns to the west, by circumventing the Land of Carchemish to the north, Shalmaneser III and other early 1st millennium BC kings could concentrate on pushing the imperial boundaries westward rather than getting ensnared with the Neo-Hittite kingdom of Carchemish.

Both the regional archaeological record and textual sources provide vital evidence about the geographical scale of the land of Carchemish in the Iron Age. As demonstrated in Chapter 3, the Land of Carchemish ranged in scale from a large state measuring 90 km north–south and 70 km east–west between 1200 and 1100 BC, down to a much diminished local polity of perhaps 50 km north–south × 30 km east–west at the time of its weakness in the 9th century BC (Fig. 11.2). Not only did the polity fluctuate in size around these figures, the discussion presented in Chapter 3 indicates that ancient polities could be remarkably dynamic, expanding and contracting depending upon the power of the king, the nature of threats from neighbouring states, and, in the case of Carchemish, the decisions of the central power of Assyria itself.

Whereas the small tells in the LCP varied little in size, remaining apparently stable over long periods, the main city of Carchemish exhibits numerous phases of growth (decline being difficult to demonstrate from the surface evidence). Although some phases might relate to the growth and decline of the territory of Carchemish, as demonstrated in Chapter 3, with currently available information such expansions of both city and territory cannot be synchronised.

Overall, the size of Carchemish through time appears to have been constrained or encouraged by various political, social and economic factors. For example, whereas the initial 4 ha tell represented by the citadel mound was fully self supporting within a short walking distance, the 40 ha ramparted Inner Town, although effectively self supporting within a 5 km radius, would have benefited significantly from the receipt of contributions or "taxation" from surrounding communities. Such communities would have supplied sufficient products (cereals *etc.*) to generate a surplus for the central city of the later EBA over and above the local production (Chapters 4 and 7). The subsequent expansion of the city in the Neo-Hittite period or the Iron Age to approximately 100 ha corresponded to the growth of the larger polity discussed in Chapter 3 (see also Fig. 11. 2). Moreover, the 100 ha Iron Age city was comparable in size to the maximum size of other Neo-Hittite cities such as Rifa'at (Casana 2013) as well as the 100–120 ha maximum of most EBA cities such as Mozan, Leilan, Hamoukar and Kasana Höyük. In other words the Neo-Hittite polities of the late 2nd and earlier 1st millennium BC may have been

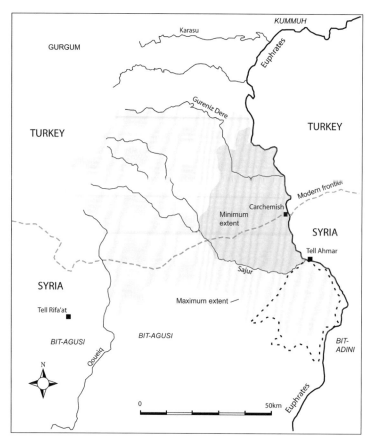

Fig. 11.2 The estimated maximum and minimum extents of the Land of Carchemish during the Neo-Hittite and Neo-Assyrian periods (based on discussion in Chapter 3, this volume. See Fig. 3.2)

constrained by similar factors of provisioning and political control as prevailed in the Early Bronze Age.

The surface investigations conducted in 2009 and 2010 supply confirmation on the Iron Age date of the Outer Town, and demonstrate that the outer ramparts were more substantial than suggested by the British Museum team (Chapter 8). Moreover, the recognition of what appears to be an alignment of inner ramparts (*i.e.* the 'inner anomaly', Chapter 8), together with a possible gateway (House D), suggests that there was an intermediate phase of ramparts between the Inner Town and the Outer Town Walls. How this can be fitted into the long history of the site remains difficult to say and:

> "without further archaeological investigations in the site, it is impossible to conclude whether the 'inner anomaly' is the fortification wall which delineated the Bronze Age city (perhaps the "lower town" conquered by Šuppiluliuma), or whether it represents a phase of expansion that occurred during the Neo-Hittite period, only to be obliterated by subsequent occupation or intentional destruction" (Chapter 8).

While it is tempting to see the Outer Town wall, as defined by Woolley, as resulting from an Assyrian expansion of the city beyond the limits defined by the inner anomaly, this is not clear from the field evidence. Although an expansion

of the Outer Town by such a small increment (*c.* 15 ha beyond the inner anomaly) may seem trivial, the addition of a similar narrow inter-rampart space at Ebla from EBA to MBA suggests that such additions did take place when circumstance demanded (Matthiae and Marchetti 2013, pl. 13, 2).

The LCP surface collection did not produce substantive distinctions between the dates or quantities of the Iron Age artefacts on either side of the "inner anomaly," so chronological and functional subdivisions within the Outer Town are not achievable with the current evidence (Chapter 8). In terms of the material culture of Iron Age Carchemish, the most noteworthy characteristic of the LCP sample is the obvious absence of most of the classic Assyrian type fossils found in seventh century BC contexts associated with the Assyrian heartland. This contrasts starkly with the east bank of the Euphrates, where the Assyrian stronghold of Tell Ahmar exhibits a solidly Assyrian assemblage. As with the settlement pattern, the west side of the river can be described therefore as decidedly provincial.

Although the settlement pattern of the LCP was relatively sparse during the earlier Iron Age, after 717 BC, when Carchemish was incorporated into the Assyrian empire, parts of the region became more densely settled and it is even possible to discern the hand of deliberate Assyrian re-settlement to the north of Carchemish (Chapter 5).

Long-term settlement trends, expressed as aggregate settlement area in 100 year increments (as discussed in Chapter 4), provide hints concerning the rise and fall of the component states as well as episodes of population growth. These trends show that, in addition to a general pattern of tell-based settlement in the Chalcolithic and Bronze Age and settlement diminution in the MBA and LBA, there was renewed growth in the Iron Age, although in the LCP this was relatively minor, except at Carchemish itself. This was then followed by a marked growth in settlement and/ or population accompanied by dispersal in the Classical and Roman periods. Whereas the minor EBA peak is barely visible in the LCP area, the more pronounced Classical Roman peak contains several components. Away from the Euphrates Valley, Hellenistic occupations were focused mainly on tell sites (Chapter 9), a situation which implies that local communities and identities may have persisted at least until the arrival of the Roman imperial administration. Although a minor movement away from tells was underway during the Roman period (*e.g.* at LCP 18), the process of dispersal was not really clearly evident until Late Roman and Byzantine times (Chapters 5 and 9). In other words: "The processes of settlement change which begin with the Hellenistic (certainly the Late Hellenistic) accelerate, intensify and become more widespread during the Early Roman period and continue developing into the Byzantine" (Chapter 9).

Because tell-based occupations continued during the Seleucid period, it is likely that traditional land use practices also continued. If so, it is possible that rain-fed cultivation around tells, with local vine and olive cultivation, may have predominated, and that some form of communal land distribution was also practiced. In other words there may have been:

> "a transition from a system where land was owned by a central authority figure and worked collectively, to a system more akin to what we consider private ownership today, [which] would have provided the incentive for people to stake their individual claims in the rural landscape (Casana 2007, 212–213)." Migliori 2013, 45

In addition, by the Classical-Roman period irrigation had become significant and the field evidence is eloquent in showing that every tributary wadi had its own water supply system. This not only enabled the land to be cultivated with increased intensity but also for a wider range of crops to be grown and greater taxation levied.

This phase of settlement expansion into the countryside appears to have contributed to more "flashy" flow regimes in the local wadis and an increase in valley floor colluviation and sedimentation. It is also likely (although unproven) that the constant abstraction of water resulted in the reduction of water in the tributary wadis. This, combined with the steady reduction of woodland in the area, suggests that human-induced degradation significantly increased over the past 2000–2500 years.

Unfortunately, hollow ways, which are so evident on satellite images in the Jazira to the east, are barely visible in the Carchemish area.[3] Nevertheless, possible crossing points of the Euphrates, as at Tell Shiukh Fawqani and Jerablus Tahtani, were probably linked to cross country routes. Therefore it is hardly surprising that the pairing of these two sites appears to have been connected to a remarkable alignment of Late Chalcolithic and Uruk sites across country to the west (Chapter 4). Although the long-held view that Carchemish lay on a major crossing point of the Euphrates is not entirely supported by field evidence, the alignment of significant landscape features (Chapter 5) does suggest that Carchemish was positioned on what must have been a long-distance route corridor running through Tell Rifa'at towards Alalakh and Tayinat to the south-west (Chapter 3). In other words, Carchemish was positioned in order to benefit from *a series* of crossing points, used successively through time, depending on prevailing socioeconomic, cultural and environmental factors. Overall therefore, landscape features, site alignments and paired sites at crossing points all contribute towards sketching the route pattern of the region, which appears to have fed to several crossing points, certifying the long-term significance of the city as a central point within an extensive transportation network.

Particularly vexing is our inability to bring together a meaningful link between aggregate data, as derived from the archaeological surveys, and historical evidence. Figure 11.3 shows how the specificity of historical information operates at an entirely different temporal resolution than the data derived from surface prospection. In other words, imprecision of the surface data, problems of dating pottery as well as surface recovery of artefacts, results in a somewhat fuzzy record of settlement change. Although valuable for suggesting long-term cycles, these data are less useful for illustrating short term changes, which results in a significant mismatch between the two types of information. Consequently the impact of, for example, Assyrian kings is effectively invisible, and Shalmaneser III would be disappointed to see how little affect he had on long-term archaeological trends or upon the landscape record. On the other hand, the spread of rural settlement that resulted from the incorporation of the region into the Seleucid, Roman and Byzantine empires is quite evident particularly from the significant peak of aggregate settlement area that is evident to both the north and south of the border.

In other words, at the scale of resolution of the surface data, structural transformations in settlement are more evident than the effects of human agency. Although hardly surprising, this mismatch needs to be understood and declared, otherwise our discussions that attempt to link

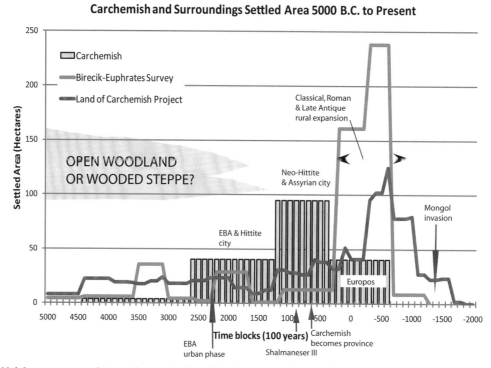

Fig. 11.3 Long-term trends in settlement for the LCP with selected historical trends arrowed. (Based on Fig. 4.14)

political cause and effect will be constantly frustrated. Therefore by laying out the information, as on Figure 11.3, we can start to suggest relationships that may be significant.

Overall, the presence of data sources of different temporal duration represents a classic Braudelian problem in which the long-wavelength features of several centuries or even millennia duration represent either *conjonctures* or *longue durée* events, whereas the historical records can be seen as equivalent to short-term *événements* (Braudel 1972; Bintliff 2004, 176). How the actual processes that operate at each time scale can be scaled up to the higher temporal scale remains difficult to demonstrate. However, an individual act of agency, such as the incorporation of Carchemish into the Assyrian empire in 717 BC by Sargon II, could have led to further developments, such as re-settlement programmes (either in the city or its countryside) which would then provide longer term consequents. In contrast, the numerous campaigns of kings such as Shalmaneser III, although enriching the coffers of the imperial centres, may have been less effective than hoped. This was particularly the case if subjected states to the west of the Euphrates "cast off the trappings of Assyrian sovereignty" and the frontier retreated back to the Euphrates leaving Til Barsip (Kar Shalmaneser) on the western boundary (Bryce 2012, 244). In other words the relentless campaigns of Shalmaneser may have amounted to little more than serious raids, so that they contributed little to long-term structural change that can be recognized in the regional archaeological record.

In contrast, specific types of landscape data more closely accord to historical evidence. For example, the desertion of Sazabe as a result of Shalmaneser's campaigns can be inferred from the archaeological record at the site, as can the rise and decline of Pitru (Chapters 5 and 6). Significantly, the suggested phase of Neo-Assyrian settlement north of the Turkish border (Chapter 5) fits approximately within the general framework of Assyrian policy, although it is not clear which king initiated such a programme. In 717 BC, when Carchemish was incorporated into the Assyrian empire, not only were the inhabitants of Carchemish deported to Assyria, populations from Assyria were also settled in Carchemish (or perhaps its region); but whether this was in the Outer Town of Carchemish or in the enclave of new settlement immediately to the north is not clear. Although Hawkins (1980, 445) states that re-settlement occurred "in the city" it is also possible to read "Carchemish" as the immediate territory of the city. On the one hand, the survey evidence suggests that there were no areas of significant re-settlement within the area of Carchemish within Syria. Even the significant phase of settlement north of the frontier is not immediately discernible on the aggregate settlement graphs (Fig. 11.3). On the other hand, the alignment of the field and historical records is more satisfactory in the realm of historical geography. Thus the details of Shalmaneser's campaigns through the Balikh and Til Barsip as well as at Burmarina (Tell Shiukh Fawqani), and up the Sajur valley can now be read with more local detail than before.

Moreover, by being able to recognize so many Assyrian and Aramaean place names, it is now possible to provide a much more richly contextualized archaeological and historical record and also to reconstruct the extent of the polity of Carchemish through time.

When interpreting the long-term historical trends it is evident that certain types of structural change are more visible in the archaeological record than others. In terms of the major cycle of Classical-Roman growth (see Fig. 4.14) the disparity between the records north and south of the border reflect two major events. First, the rise in Algaze's data around the 3rd century BC reflects a major turning point in the history of Syria when Seleucid and Greek colonists were settled in the region (Chapter 9). On the other hand, the second leap in aggregate settlement area, clearly visible in the LCP data around the 2nd century AD, relates to the first centuries of Roman control when the Euphrates became the frontier facing the Parthians to the east (Chapter 9; Migliori 2013, 43–44). However, the records to both the north and south of the border clearly show that even though the establishment of the frontier resulted in a burst of settlement, presumably as there was a need to provision the growing number of troops and other settlers (Chapter 9), the shift of the frontier further east after the 3rd century AD resulted in "the stable generic security of a non-border province" which resulted in the population continuing to increase as discussed in Chapter 9.

Although much more could be said about the combined analysis of long-term settlement trends with historical events, such analysis is not without its problems and contradictions. Nevertheless, the results from the Land of Carchemish surveys and the Carchemish Outer Town Project demonstrate that the results are to some degree coherent, and can be interpreted in terms of long-term historical processes. At the present state of resolution, however, rather than trying to force correspondences between such different data sets, it is better to "read" the results from each source on their own terms.

Unfortunately, because it proved impossible to continue fieldwork after the final field season in 2010, this investigation can hardly be regarded as complete. We had planned to undertake soundings in the Outer Town to establish the full stratigraphic sequence, to undertake topographic mapping of the some 40 ha remaining, as well as to perform more intensive surveys within the survey area. Although the Project had undertaken an overview of most of the triangular area identified by our permit, as indicated on Figures 4.1 and 4.2, the western apex was not surveyed at all, and survey intensity declined from east to west. However, thanks to the survey of Guillermo Algaze to the north of the border together with the surveys of Ozdoğan and Karul, as well as previous surveys by Copeland, Sanlaville, Moore, McClellan and Porter, much more is known, not just about the sites in the region (Appendix), but also about the layout of the polity of Carchemish, the social archaeology of the tell communities and new foundations, as well as how the city and its region fitted into the historical records. Nevertheless, much more needs to be done, because as demonstrated by Emma Cunliffe in her sobering contribution (Chapter 10), the archaeological record is being steadily destroyed during cycles of both peace and war.

Notes

1 Of course, not all tells may have served the same function.
2 These figures only include sites that have been surveyed in the field. If those sites that are only known from archival records or satellite images are included the number of satellite communities would probably be larger. Evidence of the close relationship between Jerablus Tahtani and estimates of the sustaining area are provided in Chapter 7 and Fig. 7.6.
3 Although faint examples are seen on CORONA images at Tell Ahmar, and in the western part of the LCP.

Bibliography

Algaze, G. (1999) Trends in the archaeological development of the Upper Euphrates Basin of South-Eastern Anatolia during the Late Chalcolithic and Bronze Ages. In G. del Olmo Lete and J.-L. Montero Fenollós (eds) *Archaeology of the Upper Syrian Euphrates: The Tishrin Dam Area*, 535–572. Barcelona, Ausa.

Archi, A. (1989) La ville d'Abarsal. In M. Lebeau and P. Talon (eds) *Reflets des deux fleuves: volume de mélanges offerts à André Finet*. Akkadica Supplementum 6, 15–19. Leuven, Peeters.

Archi, A. (1990) The city of Ebla and the organization of the rural territory. In E. Aerts and H. Klengel (eds) *The Town as Regional Economic Centre in the Ancient Near East*, 15–10. Leuven, Leuven University Press.

Archi, A. and Biga, M.G. (2003) A victory over Mari and the fall of Ebla. *Journal of Cuneiform Studies* 55, 1–44.

Bar-Matthews, M. and Ayalon, A. (2004) Speliothems as palaeoclimatic indicators: a case study from Soreq Cave located in the Eastern Mediterranean region, Israel. In R.W. Batterbee, F. Gasse and C.E. Strickley (eds) *Past Climate Variability in Europe and Africa*, 363–391. Dordrecht, Springer.

Bintliff, J. (2004) Time, structure, and agency: the Annales, emergent complexity, and archaeology. In J. Bintliff (ed.) *A Companion to Archaeology*, 174–194. Oxford, Blackwell.

Braudel, F. (1972) *The Mediterranean and the Mediterranean World in the Age of Philip II*. London, Fontana/Collins.

Bryce, T. (2012) *The World of the Neo-Hittite Kingdoms: A Political and Military History*. Oxford, Oxford University Press.

Casana, J. (2007) Structural transformations in settlement systems of the North Levant. *American Journal of Archaeology* 111 (2), 195–221.

Casana, J. (2013) Radial route systems and agro-pastoral strategies in the Fertile Crescent: New discoveries from western Syria and southwestern Iran. *Journal of Anthropological Archaeology* 32 (2), 257–273.

Cooper, L. (2012) Continuity and change in the Upper Euphrates region of Syria. In N. Laneri, P. Pfälzner and S. Valentini (eds) *Looking North: The Socioeconomic Dynamics of the Northern Mesopotamian and Anatolian Regions during the Late Third and Early Second Millennium BC*, 81–91. Wiesbaden, Harrassowitz.

Dornemann, R.H. (1988) Tell Hadidi: one Bronze Age site among many in the Tabqa Dam salvage area. *Bulletin of the American Schools of Oriental Research* 270, 13–42.

Einwag, B. and Otto, A. (1999) Tell Bazi, in G. del Olmo Lete and J.-L. Montero Fenollós (eds) *Archaeology of the Upper Syrian Euphrates: The Tishrin Dam Area*, 179–191. Barcelona, Ausa.

Falsone, G. and Sconzo, P. (2007) The 'champagne cup' period at Carchemish. In E. Peltenburg (ed.) *Euphrates River Valley Settlement. The Carchemish Sector in the Third Millennium BC*. Levant Supplementary Series 5, 73–93. Oxford, Oxbow Books.

Frangipane, M. (2007) Establishment of a Middle/Upper Euphrates Early Bronze I culture from the fragmentation of the Uruk world. New data from Zeytinli Bahçe Höyük (Urfa, Turkey). In E. Peltenburg (ed.) *Euphrates River Valley Settlement. The Carchemish Sector in the Third Millennium BC*. Levant Supplementary Series 5, 122–141. Oxford, Oxbow Books.

Hawkins, J.D. (1980) Kargamiš. In E. Ebeling and B. Meissner (eds) *Reallexikon der Assyriologie und Vorderasiatischen Archäologie*, 426–426. Berlin, Walter Gruyter.

Koliński, R. (2001) *Mesopotamian dimātu of the Second Millennium BC*. Oxford, British Archaeological Report S1004.

Kuzucuoğlu, C. and Marro, C. (eds) (2007) *Sociétés humaines et changement climatique à la fin du troisième millénaire: une crise a-t-elle eu lieu en Haute Mésopotamie? Actes du Colloque de Lyon, 5–8 décembre 2005*. Varia Anatolica 19. Istanbul, De Boccard.

Lawrence, D. (2012) Early Urbanism in the Northern Fertile Crescent: A Comparison of Regional Settlement Trajectories and Millennial Landscape Change. PhD Thesis. Durham, Durham University.

Lemcke, G. and Sturm, M. (1997) [18]O and trace element measurements as proxy for the reconstruction of climate changes at Lake Van (Turkey): Preliminary results. In H.N. Dalfes, G. Kukla and H. Weiss (eds) *Third Millennium BC Climate Change and Old World Collapse*, 653–678, NATO ASI Series: Global Environmental Change 49. Berlin, Springer.

Lewis, N. (1987) *Nomads and Settlers in Syria and Jordan 1800–1980*. Cambridge, Cambridge University Press.

Liverani, M. (1987) The collapse of the Near Eastern regional system at the end of the Bronze Age: the case of Syria. In M. Rowlands, M. Larsen and K. Kristiansen (eds) *Centre and Periphery in the Ancient World*, 66–73. Cambridge, Cambridge University Press.

Matthiae, P. and Marchetti, N. (eds) (2013) *Ebla and its Landscape: Early State Formation in the Ancient Near East*. Walnut Creek CA, Left Coast Press.

McClellan, T. (1992) The 12th Century B.C. in Syria: comments on Sader's paper. In W.A. Ward and M.S. Joukowsky (eds) *The Crisis Years: The 12th Century B.C. From Beyond the Danube to the Tigris*, 164–173. Dubuque, Kendall/Hunt.

Michel, C. (1996) Le commerce dans les textes de Mari. In J.-M. Durand (ed.) *Amurru I. Mari, Ebla et les Hourrites. Actes du colloque international (Paris, mai 1993)*, 385–426. Paris, Edition Recherches sur les Civilisations.

Migliori, J. (2013) Rural Settlement and the Euphrates Frontier in Roman Carchemish. MA thesis, Durham University, Department of Archaeology.

Molist, M. (1996) *Tell Halula (Siria). Un yacimiento neolítico del Valle Medio del Éufrates. Campanas 1991 y 1992*. Madrid, Ministerio de Educación y Cultura.

Olávarri, E. (1993) Tell Quzak, Informe Preliminar. Campaña IV (1992), *Orient Express* 1993 (1), 4–5.

Peltenburg, E. (2007) Diverse settlement pattern changes in the Middle Euphrates valley in the later third millennium BC: The contribution of Jerablus Tahtani. In C. Kuzucuoglu and C. Marro (eds) *Sociétés humaines et changement climatique à la fin du troisième millénaire: une crise a-t-elle eu lieu en Haute Mésopotamie? Actes du Colloque de Lyon, 5–8 décembre 2005*, Varia Anatolica 19, 247–266. Istanbul, De Boccard.

Peltenburg (2013) Conflict and exclusivity in Early Bronze Age societies of the Middle Euphrates Valley. *Journal of Near Eastern Studies*, 72(2), 233–252.

Rambeau, C. and Black, S. (2011) Palaeoenvironments of the Southern Levant 5000 BP to present: linking the geological and archaeological records. In S. Mithen and E. Black (eds) *Water, Life and Civilization: Climate, Environment and Society in the Jordan Valley*, 94–104. Cambridge, Cambridge University Press.

Riehl, S. and Deckers, K. (2012) Environmental and agricultural dynamics in Northern Mesopotamia during the Early and Middle Bronze Ages. In N. Laneri, P. Pfälzner and S. Valentini (eds) *Looking North: The Socioeconomic Dynamics of the Northern Mesopotamian and Anatolian Regions during the Late Third and Early Second Millennium BC*, 11–24. Wiesbaden, Harrassowitz.

Roberts, B.K. (1996) *Landscapes of Settlement: Prehistory to the Present*. London, Routledge.

Sherratt, A. (1981) Plough and pastoralism: aspects of the Secondary Products Revolution. In N. Hammond, I. Hodder and G. Isaac (eds) *Patterns of the Past: Studies in Honour of David Clarke*, 261–305. Cambridge, Cambridge University Press.

Sollberger, E. (1980) The so-called treaty between Ebla and "Assur". *Studia Eblaiti* 3, 133–134.

Stordeur, D., Brenet, M., Der Aprahamian, G. and Roux, J.-C. (2000) Les bâtiments communautaires de Jerf al Ahmar et Mureybit horizon PPNA (Syrie). *Paléorient* 26, 29–44.

Van Driel, G. (2001) On villages. In W.H. von Soldt (ed.) *Veenhof Anniversary Volume: Studies Presented to Klaas R. Veenhof on the Occasion of his Sixty-Fifth Birthday*, 103–118. Leiden, Nederlands Instituut voor het Nabije Oosten.

Wattenmaker, P. (2009) States, Landscapes, and the urban process in Upper Mesopotamia: Inter-polity alliances, competition and ritualized exchange. In S.E. Falconer and C.L. Redman (eds) *Polities and Power: Archaeological Perspectives on the Landscapes of Early States*, 106–124. Tucson, University of Arizona Press.

Widell, M., Gibson, M., Wilkinson, T.J., Studevent-Hickman, B. and Tenney, J. (2013) Household and Village in Early Mesopotamia. In T.J. Wilkinson, M. Gibson and M. Widell. (eds) *Models of Mesopotamian Landscapes: How small-scale processes contributed to the growth of early civilizations,* 112–129. Oxford, British Archaeological Report S2552.

Wilkinson, T.J. (2010) The Tell: social archaeology and territorial space. In D. Bolger and L. Maguire (eds) *The Development of Pre-state Communities in the Ancient Near East: Studies in Honour of Edgar Peltenburg,* 55–62. Oxford, Oxbow Books.

Wilkinson, T.J., Miller, N., Reichel, C. and Whitcomb, D. (2004) *On the Margin of the Euphrates: Settlement and land use at Tell es-Sweyhat and in the Upper Lake Tabqa Area, Syria.* Chicago IL, Oriental Institute Publications 124.

Wilkinson, T.J., Galiatsatos, N., Lawrence, D., Ricci, A., Dunford, R. and Philip, G. (2012) Late Chalcolithic and Early Bronze Age Landscapes of Settlement and Mobility in the Middle Euphrates: a re-assessment. *Levant* 44 (2), 139–185.

Wilkinson, T.J. Philip, G. Bradbury, J. Dunford, R. Donoghue, D. Galiatsatos, N. Lawrence, D. Ricci, A. and Smith, S. (2014) Contextualizing Early Urbanization: Settlement Cores, Early States and Agro-Pastoral Strategies in the Fertile Crescent during the Fourth and Third millennia BC. *Journal of World Prehistory* 27 (1), 43–109.

Woolley, C.L. and Barnett, R. (1952) *Carchemish Report on the excavations at Jerablus on behalf of the British Museum III: The Excavations in the Inner Town and the Hittite Inscriptions.* London, British Museum.

Wossink, A. (2009). *Challenging Climate Change: Competition and Cooperation among Pastoralists and Agriculturalists in Northern Mesopotamia (ca. 3000–1600 BC).* Leiden, Sidestone Press.

Yartah, T. (2004) Tell 'Abr 3, un village du néolithique précéramique (PPNA) sur le Moyen Euphrate. Premiere approche. *Paléorient* 30/2, 141–158.

APPENDIX A

Land of Carchemish Project, Syria, 2006–2010
Site Gazetteer

T.J. Wilkinson, D. Lawrence and A. Ricci

The following site catalogue was compiled from the site record sheets which included the field and lab assessments of the pottery types. These were then cross-checked against the Fragile Crescent Project data base. In each case, the site location is represented by a GPS Waypoint (WP), usually taken at the site centre (see Table A.1). Additional WPs defining site perimeters and other parts of the site are contained in the site archive. Cross references for site names and numbers according to the earlier surveys in Sanlaville et al. (1985) are provided in Table A.1.

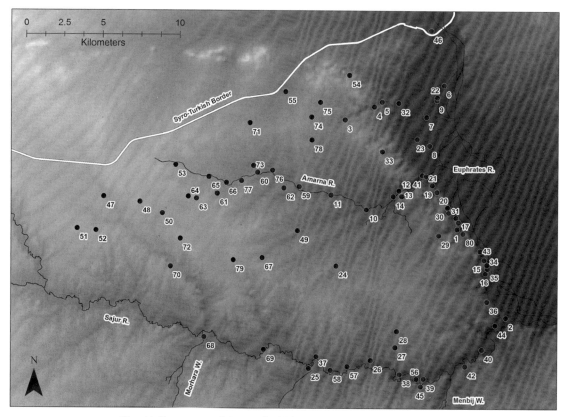

Fig. A1 Sites surveyed during the 2006, 2008 and 2009 field seasons

Table A.1: GPS coordinates of sites in the Land of Carchemish Survey

Site no.	Name	GPS: UTM 37R:	Comment	Reference, other surveys
1	Khirbet Seraisat	0414105 4063842		
2	Duluk (Aushariye)	0417052 405 8280	Area C	M. 19 (Moore, 52)
3	Tell Sha'ir (north)	0406699 4070624	Top	
4	Ain al-Abid	0408585 4071448		
5	Tashatan	0409023 4071708	Top	RCP 109 (Copeland, 70)
6	Jerablus Tahtani village	0413103 4072907	Well	
7	Khirbet Wadi Mansur	0412009 4070766		
8	Al-Jermideh	0412176 4069005		
9	Tell Jerablus Tahtani S	0412633 4071860		
10	Tell 'Ain al-Beida	0408101 4064980		RCP 40 (Copeland, 77)
11	Tell Ma 'zala	0405804 4065924		RCP 41(Copeland, 77)
12	Wadi al-Nagout	0410212 4066180		
13	Jebel al-Mitraz	0410384 4065837		
14	Nahr al-Amarna site	0409830 4065797		
15	Meshirfe	0415658 4061940		
16	Kirk Mughara	0415880 4060941		M.20 (Moore, 52)
17	No name	0414053 4064214		
18	Serai	0413898 4064521		
19	Wadi Amarna	0412404 4066582		
20	Mughar Seraisat	0412674 4066088		
21	Tell Amarna	0411916 4067119	North summit	M.21; RCP 103; (Moore, 52; Copeland, 71)
22	Tell Jerablus Tahtani	0412663 4072049		M. 22; RCP 96; (Moore, 53; Copeland, 70)
23	Jamel.	0411392 4069457		RCP 97 (Copeland, 71)
24	Tell Dabas	0406207 406 1449		
25	Tell Dadate	0404451 4055018		RCP 76 (Copeland, 74)
26	Tukhar Kabir	0408406 4055522		
27	al-Qarra	0410020 4056330		
28	Umm Dash	0410110 4057400	N end of site	
29	Rejem	0412854 4063428	E end	
30	Near Mughar Seraisat	0413365 4065126		
31	NW of LCP 18	0413426 4064802		
32	Near Tashatan	0410161 4071671		
33	Bayrzakli	0409122 4068620		
34	Near LCP 15	0415935 4061537		
35	Near LCP 15	0415975 4061366		
36	Near Kirk Mughara	0415947 4059199		
37	Dadate North	0404961 4055772	Main pottery area	
38	Tell Sha'ir (Sajur)	0410301 4054651		M.13 (Moore, 50)
39	Tukhur Saghir	0411869 4054342		M.14 Moore, 51)
40	Qirata	0415624 4056197		M. 18 (Moore, 52); Tell er-Resm
41	Tell Amarna cemetery	0411741 4067222		
42	No name	0414523 4055164		
43	Mishrife-2	0415480 4062406		
44	Aushariye west.	0416470 4057754	Summit	
45	Tukhar Saghir al-Janubi	0411707 4053879		
46	Carchemish SE	0411543 4076294	N end transect E	
47	Boz Höyük	0390992 4065767	Summit North	RCP 39 (Copeland, 78)
48	Kuelliye West	0393326 4065464		
49	NE of Bouldouq	0403699 4063647		
50	Koulliye	0394790 4064728	Tell Summit	RCP 45 (Copeland, 78)
51	No name	0389257 4063730	Near Ra´rsid Jows	
52	No name	0390572 4063733	Near Ra´rsid Jows NE corner	
53	No name	0395479 4067839	Bel Virane/ Zahiriyah, top of mound	
54	Hajaliyyeh / Kaklije	0406990 4073431	Top of mound	
55	Douknouk	0402842 4072363	Summit	
56	Tukhar Saghir W	0411385 4054370		
57	No Name	0406938 4055129	Near Tukhar Saghir W	
58	No Name	0405867 4054879	Near Tukhar Saghir W	
59	Yousuf Bek	0403795 4066427	Summit	RCP 42 (Copeland, 77)

Site no.	Name	GPS: UTM 37R:	Comment	Reference, other surveys
60	Koundouriye	0401068 4067307	Summit	RCP 43 (Copeland, 78)
61	Ghasaniyah	0398397 4065999		
62	No Name	0402581 4066294	SW of site	
63	Bel Virane	0397046 4065678		
64	No Name	0396523 4065765	SE depression	
65	No Name	0397926 4066897	Pistachio orchard	
66	Nahr Bash	0398994 4066662		
67	Al-Hadira	0401713 4062089	1 of 9 WPs	
68	Arab Hassan	0397579 4057065	Summit	RCP 32 (Copeland, 74)
69	Halwanji W	0401511 4056180	Summit	RCP 33 (Copeland 74)
70	No Name	0395162 4061448	N edge of site	
71	Jube al-Aswad	0400395 4070458	Top of mound	
72	No Name	0395999 4063127		
73	Koundouriye N	0400760 4067711	WP1194, SW	
74	No Name	0404564 4070786	Haimer N	
75	No Name	0405026 4071720	WP1205, SW	
76	No Name	0402061 4067433	WP 1214 centre	
77	No Name	0399998 4066726	WP1223 centre	
78	Haimer	0404582 4069371		
79	Hadhirah	0399435 4061828	Depression to N	
80	Khirbet Seraisat S	0414431 4063117	WP 876	
–	al-Qana	0385883 4060044	Tell to NE	RCP 79 (Copeland, 82)

References according to other surveys:
M: survey by A.M.T Moore (in Sanlaville 1985) with page number; RCP: survey by Sanlaville *et al.*; site catalogue by Copeland (in Sanlaville 1985), with page number; Note: only those sites which are distinct equivalents are stated here; less certain equivalents are omitted.

2006 Season

LCP-1 Khirbet Seraisat

Located immediately outside village of same name and between village and the Euphrates; extends mainly to E of tarmac road; to W of road site adjacent to small cemetery. Dimensions of main site: 150 × 150 m. Main artefact scatter extends over a little over 1 ha, but to E a series of quarries are evident, delimited by perimeter rock-cut channel either employed to channel excess run-off from quarries or to define next stage of ashlar cutting (D). Beyond, *i.e.* E of quarries, further sherd scatter recorded with graves on slopes beyond. Note that settlement continues on hill to SE which has excellent oversight over the site, the lower wadi and the Euphrates. Possibly a citadel area. The main part of site consists of moderate sherd scatter, occasional ashlar blocks and a small area of kiln waste in a recently excavated pit. Site subdivisions: A, cemetery W of road; B, E of tarmac road; C Tell, D, area between B and D above quarries. The tell (C) is *c.* 100 m diameter and *c.* 4 m high. Pottery is common over entire site area, and there are occasional weathered stones as well as one or two wall traces. Plunder pits by local people reveal up to 2 m of cultural deposits. Basalt querns occur frequently over surface. The sedimentary sequence in the "industrial area" along the wadi to the south is described in Chapter 5.
Pottery: Mid-EBA, Late EBA, MBA, LBA, Iron Age?, Late Roman, Byzantine and Early Islamic.

LCP-2 Duluk (Aushariye)

Immediately N of junction of Sajur with Euphrates, and immediately NE of village of Umm Rosa (Aushariye). Length (N–S) *c.* 240 m. Extensive site consisting of three areas: A, to SE, ploughed, and only a few metres above lake; B, upslope and to N of A; also ploughed. C, to W and upslope of road on low hill, extensive area ploughed and strewn with rubble and common sherds. Modern house on hilltop. An additional outlier of the site occurs to the west within the village where a scatter of Late Roman/ Byzantine tiles occur along road within village of Aushariye. Nearby a small group of shaft tombs pointed out by locals. WP 1033 taken in the area of these tombs. EBA sherds found in the spoil of the looting that has plundered some of these tombs.
Pottery: A, Late Roman, Byzantine; B, BRBs and Uruk; C, to NW, significant EBA including mid EBA. D, cut to NE within area B includes Uruk, LC 1–3 wares and 1 Ubaid painted ware.

LCP-3 Tell Sha'ir (North)

Small but prominent tell in valley to E of Jerablus, just outside and E of village of same name. Length, 90 m E–W, 60 m N–S, 10 m high. Includes cemetery on W slopes, but open and relatively un-vegetated on remaining slopes. Pottery fairly common on all slopes, especially south facing slopes. Base of mound cut by a series of pits (D). A, summit; B, S slopes of tell; C, N slopes; D, pits at base with BRBs.
Pottery: Ubaid, LC 1–2, Uruk, Early EBA, Mid/Late EBA, Hellenistic, Roman.

LCP-4 'Ain al-Abid

Small flat site located in Wadi Tell Sha'ir upstream of LCP 5, and NW of village of Tashatan, at the head of the ancient water channel. 100 m E–W, 75 m N–S. Also extends to E of small tributary wadi. N side of site bounded by a small quarry for ashlar stones; S side bounded by low cliff which overlooks the ancient rock cut water channel; this probably accounts for the name of the site downstream (LCP 5) namely Qanat (Copeland and Moore 1985). E end of site strewn with numerous Late Roman/Byz roof tiles. The association between the site and the quarries behind and also the rock-cut channel suggests that the quarries, site and channel head may all be of the same date.

Pottery: Late Roman-Byzantine, occasional to common; Early Islamic?

LCP-5 Tashatan (Marm al-Hajar)

The site of Qanat (according to Copeland and Moore 1985). On N side of Wadi 'Ain al-Nemla (or Sha 'ir) to NW of village of Tashatan. 140 m N–S, *c.* 80 m E–W; height 11.5 m (max). The tell is perched on a limestone hill to N of and overlooking wadi. The depth or height of the tell is difficult to estimate because the cultural deposits appear to be draped over the rock. A large limestone quarry threatens the site from the N. Pottery is abundant over all slopes of the site down to the base of the hill on the western side. There are several robber holes on the lower southern slopes. Part of Jerablus town is visible, but Carchemish is not; excellent views down the Euphrates valley, however. Outcrop of buildings noted towards base of slope to S. A lower site (B) is located to the E. on low hill on the left bank of the Wadi. EBA graves, recently plundered on S side of wadi opposite site (spoil includes curious hand-axe type flint implements). Areas (2008; in 2006 finds amalgamated): A: main mound; B lower site area to E.

Pottery: Halaf (1), Uruk, early EBA, Mid/Late EBA, MBA, Iron Age, Hellenistic, Roman.

LCP-6 Jerablus Tahtani Village

On low terrace (flood plain terrace) of Euphrates at S end of village, between the village and the new Euphrates bridge. 250 m N–S, 90 m E–W, 0.75 m high. Low, elongate site which appears virtually flat. Iron Age pottery common throughout; occasional large stones and querns (basalt); 1 fragment of vitrified clay from kiln within area B. Roughly 1/3 of site was exposed for collection as slightly weathered ploughed surfaces with moderate visibility. Remainder of site was obscured below young cereals. Although pottery was relatively common, these appear to be mainly body sherds; rims being fairly rare (perhaps because there was a predominance of storage jars. A: S end of site; B and C: field to N of A and N of E–W irrigation bund; D: Field at N end of site. Lion head (back cover).

Pottery: Iron Age, including LIA.

LCP-7 Khirbet Wadi Mansur

Small flat site of indeterminate size located on flood plain terrace overlooking slightly lower terrace of flood plain in the area of Hawi, SW of Tell Jerablus Tahtani. Immediately W of course of ancient canal. Late Antique and Early Islamic pottery was evident in cut along the NW side of the Wadi Mansur (*i.e.* canal), and from pottery scatters along field boundaries and local tracks. However the section was sufficiently deep (1.5 m) to show that the site has some depth, and surface pottery, with several tiles were quite common.

Pottery: Byzantine? Early Islamic.

LCP-8 Al-Jermideh

Located *c.* 1 km SE of village of Jemal. 130 m N–S, 80 m E–W, *c.* 1.00 m high. Low mound, crossed by dirt track and partly cut

by a 1.5 m high section running parallel to and below the track. GPS near centre of site where well penetrates through the northern part of the occupation. The section exposed a possible kiln with fragments of vitrified kiln waste (perhaps from firing of tiles), and several limestone wall foundations, one of which was associated with a limestone floor. One tile waster suggests that the site also functioned as a tile manufacturing area which is supported by the abundant pottery and tile on the surface.

Pottery: Abundant Late Roman/Byzantine pottery and tile (hence name Kermit/Jermideh).

LCP-9 Tell Jerablus Tahtani (S site)

Located on edge of floodplain terrace *c.* 200 m S of Tell Jerablus Tahtani. 60 m N–S, *c.* 70 cm deep in section. Small Late Antique site only evident in the cut running S from Tell Jerablus Tahtani. Footings of stone walls are evident at several places along a 60 m length of the section, and occasional clusters of roof tiles are evident in the upper section. There is one large ash-filled pit towards the S end of the site. What appears to be a high temperature kiln (with vitrified kiln waste) was evident in the section at WP 266, but whether it belongs to LCP 9 or to Tell Jerablus Tahtani is not clear.

Pottery: Byzantine.

LCP-10 'Ain al-Beida

Small, prominent tell *c.* 0.5 km W of village of 'Ain al-Beida. 100 m diameter, 18 m high. Lower town, probably mainly Late Roman-Byzantine, extends to the S and SE. Prominent steep-sided LC & MBA mound with Late Antique lower site. Pottery more evident on S-facing slopes; N-facing slopes covered in light grass. Cuts on SE side of base collected separately. To S and SE a scatter of pottery extending along field boundaries suggests the presence of a lower settlement. Additional tile and brittle ware is evident in the cut near WP 277. Seleucid/Hellenistic occupation was thick and abundant on the S-facing slopes of the tell, and this occupation probably obscured any underlying MBA occupation. Site revisited in May 2009 when a small pit was observed on the NW base of the mound (area D). At least 4 walls (2 of mud brick, 2 of stones) are visible on the S and E sections of the pit and deeper than the surrounding field.

A, main tell above level of cuts; B, cuts at the base of the lower slopes to SE. C, ?? D, pit, base of the mound. to NW.

Pottery: LC, early and mid EBA, MBA, ?LBA, Iron Age, Hellenistic, Roman, Byzantine.

LCP-11 Tell Ma'zala

Small, conical tell just NE of village of Ma'zala, and between the road and the Nahr Amarne. 80 m diam., 12 m high. Cemetery covers much of the S slope of the mound. There are no cuts on the mound, and pottery, especially large sherds, is very scarce over the entire mound.

Pottery: Mid-EBA, MBA channel base; Hellenistic sherds. Copeland and Moore suggest MBA for the site.

LCP-12 Wadi al-Nagout

Small prominent mound, part natural, to N of Membij–Jerablus road, just N of confluence of Nahr al-Amarna and Wadi al-Nagout. 24 × 20 m, height *c.* 30–40 cm in E facing section. Top layer of

natural low mound evident in E facing section, with surfaces of hardcore packed floors and flagstones, and possibly stone foundation walls. Pottery and a basalt quern fragment also seen in section, but cultural material occurs only above the underlying reddish calcium carbonate soil, in upper 30 cm of the mound.
Pottery: Hellenistic/Roman.

LCP-13 Jebel al-Mitraz

Scatter of chipped stone on summit of large natural steep-sided hill overlooking Nahr al-Amarna above and S of the confluence of the Nahr and Wadi al-Nagout, Diameter of scatter *c.* 80 m. No discernible structures or occupational materials evident. No burnt stones, but occasional sherds of late date (post-Hellenistic, one brittle ware). Two small chunks of vesicular basalt may be related to the sherd scatter rather than the lithics.
Chipped stone: includes pale brown, reddish, and dark blue-grey flint and although some (pale brown) may be from local source, the wide range of material suggests that some was imported. Small amounts of chipped stone also on N-facing slope of hillside. (Late Pleistocene/early Holocene?).

LCP-14 No name

Two small low sites to E and W of a small wadi which joins the Nahr Amarna from the N; *c.* 2 km E of 'Ain al-Beida. E area *c.* 70 × 35 m, 0.5 m high; W area *c.* 40 m diameter, 1 m high.
Area A: at confluence, on terrace above the wadi cut is a scatter of roof tiles and some pottery and at NE-most extent of site dislodged from the wadi section is a large ashlar block with both short, V-shaped chisel marks, and flatter chisel marks made with a chisel with parallel teeth. More roof tiles and pottery occur near side wadi and two rock-cut, partially capped canal channels are visible on either section of side wadi. E channel (65 cm wide) shows cut in surface of bedrock across wadi channel, joining continuation of capped channel on the N-facing section. W channel (75 cm wide, plaster-lined) which is higher and larger, is evident in both sections. Both channels cut into solid limestone on N side of wadi and appear to be built stone structures on the S side of wadi. Site 14A appears to be constructed over the underground channel. B: low mound with abundant limestone fragments on surface upstream of the two conduits in side wadi. Site under cereal, but common Late Antique pottery on surface. C, (July 2010) *c.* 1 ha of low mounding to N of road and merging down into area A. Abundant tile.
Pottery: A, mainly tiles, possible water pipe fragments; Byzantine; B, Hellenistic and early Roman; C, Byzantine.

LCP-15 Meshirfe

Small site with very low mounding *c.* 3 km N of village of Kirk Mughara. Located on limestone hill immediately adjacent to Euphrates River overlooking Lake Tishreen, and framed by shallow wadi to N and a more deeply incised wadi to S. About 100 m diameter. Shallow cultural deposits cover bedrock evident in section in the many *c.* 1 m diameter looter's cuts. In some looter's cuts possible stone wall foundations and pottery evident, indicating shallow stratigraphy (*c.* 30 cm). Extent of site *c.* 1 ha, determined by surface pottery scatter and cultural material in long pipe trenches cut into and down the hillside.
Pottery: Late Iron Age / early Hellenistic.

LCP-16 Kirk Mughara

Moderately large site just N of village of Kirk Mughara. Site covers *c.* 2 ha, divided into a lower component A, close to Lake Tishrin, and a high component on the hill to the west. 110 m N–S, 150 m E–W, height of mounding *c.* 1 m. Lower site is on a ploughed field of limestone-derived soil. The site is under immature trees and pottery is common to abundant and at least 1 quern was noted. On Area B on low hill to the W, blocks of rough limestone form low building mounds overlooking the remainder of the site. These may be of buildings of the same date as the remainder of the site; quarries common along the bluffs to N, also *c.* 200 m to the W in rocky side wadi near the track to Meshirfe.
Pottery: A: main area of lower site: Hellenistic jar rims; Hellenistic–Roman fishplates; also Roman, Late Roman through Early Islamic brittle wares (including Early Islamic lugged brittleware handle). B: upper site on hill to W, pottery scatter sparse and mainly Late Roman brittle wares; 1 Roman fine ware).

LCP-17 No name

On top of bluffs overlooking Euphrates/Lake Tishreen to the E. Extensive site *c.* 2 km NE of village of Khirbet Seraisat and extending over *c.* 100 × 30 m. At the N extent of the site, before the slope descends to the wadi below, a 25 × 25 m square building can be seen through the grass cover by the line of the wall tumble *c.* 2–3 m wide. Each of the 4 corners, (one dug through by a looter's cut) appears to comprise a tower of rubble and rough limestone blocks to a minimum of 7 courses deep. The building is of apparently similar date to the pottery scatter. In between these hilltop features (in total spanning *c.* 100 m N–S) and within the building were found pottery and tile scatters on the surface.
Pottery: Early Islamic.

LCP-18 Serai

About 1.5 km NE of village of Khirbet Seraisat and extending over >1 ha. Located on S facing limestone slopes overlooking a wadi with limited valley floor and mainly bare limestone outcrops on slope. Site includes an impressive complex of rock-cut tombs including a spectacular tomb with multiple burial chambers, a rock-cut stair-case and short length of rock-cut road. Pottery common on slopes. Revisited in March 2008 and sub-divided into 3 collection areas. Of these C is within an abandoned cemetery located at the junction of the wadi with the Euphrates. The section along the Euphrates revealed 2–3 m of cultural deposits of Hellenistic-Roman date with two ashlar walls. These indicate that a lower site at roughly flood plain level was the main area of occupation and the area on the S facing slopes represented the "back" of the site. Water supply appears to have derived from two sources: first, at least one (perhaps 2) underground channels with rectangular access shafts. The main alignment formed an arc-shaped configuration on the N side of the valley, and two additional shafts were evident on the S side. Second, two large bee-hive rock-cut cisterns within a flat area of limestone. These appear to have been fed by runoff from the limestone and adjacent slopes. An additional outlier of settlement occurred at the W end of the site (WP 799). The wadi intersected with several quarry-like features. The site was evidently much larger than was initially thought to be the case, and it appears to have extended at least on the upper part of the flood plain. Areas: A, S facing limestone slopes of the valley. B, small collection of sherds from a robbed-out tomb near the summit of the ridge above the site. C, lower settlement near the junction of the wadi and the Euphrates, beneath the cemetery.

Pottery: Hellenistic and earlier Roman: incurved rim bowls, fold-over rim jars; red-gloss wares.

LCP 19 Wadi Amarna

Located *c.* 1.5 km S of Tell Amarna, a short distance from the edge of the Euphrates flood plain. A small Halaf site located within an orchard and cut by a small wadi, previously investigated by a Belgian team. Wadi is dissected to *c.* 1.5 m depth, but with minimal channel deposits. Pottery (common) is eroding out of the top 70 cm of loam; wadi gravels contain occasional limestone pebbles. Site is poorly defined but may have extended over *c.* 1 ha. The site appears partly incorporated into the developing alluvial fan sediments and there were occasional sherds in soils exposed along the wadi.

Pottery: Halaf.

LCP-20 Mughar Seraisat

Neolithic site located on high limestone hill *c.* 2 km S of Tell Amarna. 60 m E–W, 30 m N–S. The small area of remaining midden gives an estimated depth of 0.5 m. Some plunder holes on summit. Located on high limestone hill *c.* 2 km S of Tell Amarna overlooking deep valley to S, LCP 19 to the N, and the Euphrates floodplain to E. Slight mounding of midden material on the summit of the hill, and around the outside limestone outcrops on most sides. The site appears small, but the slopes to the NE may either be wash and midden material from the site, but equally may represent the extension of the site on the slopes. Lithics are abundant, especially on the hill summit, and pottery is locally common. The stone footings of one wall are visible on the NW side of the site, and an alignment of rough limestone blocks around the E edge of the summit may represent another wall. Although no querns were observed on the main summit site, several were glimpsed on the NE-facing slope. One or two plunder holes are visible on the N side, and one shows cultural material penetrating to *c.* 80–100 cm. Below the hill summit and to the W extends a limestone spur upon which recorded a sparse lithic scatter (WP 369: 0412525 4066013). Re-visit in March 2008 defined the area on the slopes as extending *c.* 150 × 120 m. Lithics and some pottery continue down to base of slope to the level of Pleistocene terrace. Plunder holes *c.* 20 m from top of site reveal what appear to be limestone ashlars from tombs.

Pottery and Lithics: Late PPNB including Amuq-type points and Early ceramic Neolithic simple rims and bases (Wilkinson *et al.* 2007). Single painted Halaf/Ubaid sherd.

LCP-21 Tell Amarna

Large prominent tell at junction of Nahr al-Amarna and the Euphrates, excavated by Belgian team directed by Ö Tunca from 1991-1997 (Tunca 1999). Tell *c.* 200 × 130 m, 23 m high; Late Roman-Byzantine lower town to E and SE and building of similar date on hill to SE. Not collected by LCP team. LCP 41, within cemetery to NW may be small lower settlement.

Pottery: Halaf, Ubaid and LC, Uruk, Early EBA, Middle EBA. (not excavated), EB IV and MB I and II were excavated. Also Iron Age, Hellenistic, Roman and Byzantine (not excavated).

LCP-22 Tell Jerablus Tahtani

Small tell on W bank of Euphrates, *c.* 150 × 80 m, extended to *c.* 220 x 180 m by lower mounding to S, W and N; *c.* 16 m high. Lower activity area to W extends over *c.* 12 ha, but is sealed beneath alluvial silts. Excavated by the University of Edinburgh (Chapter 7).

Pottery: Halaf; LC 3; LC 4–5 (BRBs) and early EBA. Second lower settlement to SW within the cemetery is a Late Roman–Byzantine lower town. Overall occupations: Halaf, LC, EBA (excavated), Iron Age, Roman and Byzantine.

2008 Season

LCP-23 Jamel

On main terrace of Euphrates, W of the Jamel canal and the modern tarmac road. Low rounded mound *c.* 150 × 110 m, 2.5 m high, about half of which is under houses of outlier of Jamel village. Abundant pottery and limestone fragments on surface. A local man observed that a hole dug within the site had reached pottery down to a depth of *c.* 3 m.

Pottery: ?MBA; ?Iron Age; Hellenistic; Early Islamic and perhaps Byzantine.

LCP-24 Tell Dabis

On rolling limestone hills S of Jerablus-Menbij road. Ploughed and under thin cereal crop. Common limestone fragments on surface; thin soils. Low mound, *c.* 70 × 70 m, 1–2 m high;
visible from main road, with trig point on summit. Evident as a low terrace surrounding the mound on all sides which appears roughly square. Occasional – common pottery, and many querns noted. Tentatively interpreted as a Iron Age (and Hellenistic?) fort, now heavily ploughed away.

Pottery: 1 bowl (MBA/LBA or Iron Age), Iron Age bowl; some Hellenistic.

LCP-25 Tell Dadate

Steep sided, conical tell, *c.* 120 m diameter, 9 m high, outside and NW of village of Dadate. On low terrace on S side of Nahr Sajur where a tributary (Wadi Sa'in) enters. Approximately 2 m above level of flood plain. Tell has steep N-facing slope and gentler S facing slope. Pottery quite common on surface, which is under cereals. No clear lower town, but sparse scatter of Roman/L Antique material extends to W between tracks. A masonry structure by the adjacent wadi was described by local man as a device for getting water underneath the wadi (inverted siphon?).

Pottery: A (summit): LC; MBA/LBA; Hellenistic & Roman bowls. B, (N slopes): mid-/late EBA diagnostics including tri-lug and Hama goblet. Also possible Neolithic and LC. C, (S slopes): MBA jars; L Antique roof tile.

LCP-26 Tukhar Kabir

On river terrace on N bank of Nahr Sajur where wadi enters the valley just W of the site. Low mound *c.* 60 m diameter, 1–2 m high, almost entirely covered by cemetery. The site is bordered by tarmac roads to S and E, and village of Tukhar Kabir to W and N. The wadi E of the site has cut the E extension of the site exposing a section *c.* 2 m high, where stone walls, floors and a possible pit are visible.

Pottery: sparse, but careful collection revealed occasional small Hellenistic–Roman sherds.

LCP-27 al-Qarra

Located on rolling limestone hills with shallow soils, currently being converted to olive groves. Extensive views over rolling limestone hills. Small site, 70 × 50 m; A local farmer reported pottery fragments cast up in pits dug for the planting of olives; he also noted that stones from a wall foundation were also present. The name of the site appears to relate to a half-way point between two villages.

Pottery: sparse Hellenistic or Roman coarse-wares.

LCP-28 Umm Dash

On rolling limestone uplands and south of a wadi which until 8–9 years previously flowed with water from the spring of 'Ain Umm Dash to the N. Extensive site, *c.* 110 × 80 m, within fields of wheat or barley. Low relief morphology (c. 1 m) indicates the remains of individual low building mounds. Site continues on top of neighbouring hill.

Pottery: Late Roman/Byzantine pottery moderately common across the site.

LCP-29 Rejem

On S facing slopes of limestone hills to N of Wadi Seraisat (W of village of Khirbet Seraisat). Wadi is currently dry, but there is a possible rectangular water hole in wadi opposite the site. This was fed by a small seepage or spring above and connected to the depression by two small rock-cut channels. Extensive, flat site, 160 × 80 m, on gentle S facing slopes. Common pottery. Site partly ploughed and under fallow with some fields under cereals. A rock-cut tomb, 4 m wide, 2 m high, is cut in the escarpment that defines the back of the site (N). On crest of hill above a series of disturbed possible cairns appear to be some burial mounds (WP 773–774). One or two plunder holes in site suggest a depth of occupation of at least 1 m.

Pottery: Late Roman–Byzantine; 1 Late Roman C keel-rim bowl, 1 Islamic glazed ware; occasional brittle wares.

LCP-30 Mughar Seraisat-2

Near Mughar Seraisat, flat site, *c.* 50 m N–S × 30 m E–W. On S facing slopes in small Euphrates tributary. Within limestone hills to SSW of Mughar Seraisat village. Small site; occasional large stones on slope appear to be from eroded walls. Site defined by occasional sherds of brittle ware.

Pottery: 1 glazed sherd, 1 handle; brittle ware. Early Islamic or Byzantine.

LCP-31 Mughar Seraisat-3

On limestone plateau W of limestone bluffs, near Mughur Seraisat and NW of LCP 18. 130 m long, 80 m wide. W part of site overlooks upper tributaries of Wadi Serai which lead down to LCP 18. Includes large, square structure 42 E–W × 32 m N–S with a moderate scatter of pottery continuing to E. Building defined by a rock-cut face to W, and traces of walls to N and E, which form

a roughly rectangular space. Sparse scatter of pottery on W facing slopes to the W.

Pottery and Lithics: includes brittle ware. Occasional struck flints on slope, but no concentrations. Byzantine or Early Islamic.

LCP-32 Tashatan-2

Small, flat site, 15 × 15 m, on summit of hill immediately NE of village of Tashatan, within area of olive trees. Gently sloping hill N of Wadi Tashatan overlooking Euphrates floodplain, with a prominent limestone outcrop at the summit; soil thin and rocky. Site consists of a sparse to medium density sherd scatter, 1 tile fragment. Possibly a single building or farmstead.

Pottery: Late Roman/Byzantine brittle ware; occasional roof tiles in adjacent field below site.

LCP-33 Bayrzakli

Trace site, 30 × 25 m, on one of the highest peaks of the bluffs W of the Euphrates and W of village of Jamel. Cultivated soil under wheat; broken limestone and a few cairns (clearance?) present, especially under the triangulation point on summit. Consists of a low-density sherd scatter and a few chipped stones. No visible structures, although a few very small fragments of basalt groundstone. It is possible that this is a very low mound rather than a flat site, but cultivation has obscured this, and clearance cairns mask a good part of the site. Perhaps a small building or a threshing floor.

Pottery: Late Roman?

LCP 34

Trace site, 70 m (N–S) × 30 m (E–W), between Mishrife (LCP 15) and Kirk Mughara (LCP 16), N of LCP 35. On plateau on the N side of the wadi separating LCP 34 and 35; set back from cliffs overlooking Lake Tishreen. Heavily tilled field with mature olive orchard. Soil contains many broken up limestone chunks. Flat site identified by moderate to low-density sherd scatter.

Pottery: Late-Roman-Early Islamic brittle ware.

LCP-35

Between Mishrife (LCP 15) and Kirk Mughara (LCP 16), S of LCP 34. On plateau above cliffs overlooking Lake Tishreen. Flat site, 150 × 150 m, with moderate density sherd scatter. Located on the S side of the wadi separating LCP 34 and 35. No apparent mounding, visible features or other cultural material besides pottery. Effectively an extension of LCP 16.

Pottery: Late-Roman–early Islamic brittle ware.

LCP-36

Trace site between Kirk Mughara (LCP 16) and Duluk (LCP 2). Flat site 50 m (N–S), 30 m (E–W); on plateau above cliffs overlooking Lake Tishreen and 30 m E of the paved road between the villages of Kirk Mughara to the N and Aushariye (Duluk) to the S. The hilltop is framed on both N and S by deeply-incised wadis. Low density scatter of pottery.

Pottery: Late-Roman-Early Islamic brittle ware.

LCP-37 Dadate-North

On limestone bluffs overlooking Sajur flood plain, on N side of valley *c.* 1 km E of Membij–Jerablus road; the road to Tukhar winds

around the site on its N side. A wadi enters the Sajur valley and defines the site to the east. 140 m E–W × 120 m N–S. An extensive, apparently flat Iron Age site, with common pottery and occasional querns. Although the morphology of the site on CORONA images suggests the possibility of an outer wall, there was no evidence in the field. An estimated *c.* 1 m + depth of occupation deposits remains in place. Today the site lies entirely to S of the tarmac road to Tukhar, which appears to define it on its N site. To the SW of site the limestone bluffs have been cut into by a large quarry, which, in its upper part has carved parallel lines of small chambers, *c.* 30 cm high by 25 cm wide which may be pigeon lofts (*columbaria*) cut into earlier (Classical–Early Islamic) quarries.
Pottery: Iron Age, including large pithos rims.

LCP-38 Tell Sha'ir (Sajur)

E of village of Tukhar Kabir and immediately E of the hamlet of Tell Sha'ir on N bank of Sajur valley. 90 m diameter, *c.* 5 m high. The tell is situated on a low hill overlooking the Sajur valley and on N bank and immediately E of a N bank tributary wadi. Below, to S, is a *c.* 3 m diameter well and a single rock-cut wine press. Site ploughed and under barley. A deep plunder hole on the summit demonstrates the presence of at least 3 m of occupation with evidence of stone walls and carved stone blocks. Also evident are two limestone blocks which appear to be large door sockets. Pottery is common on surface; occasional querns. On the SW slope, near the well, are 1–2 rock-cut tombs. A revisit, in June 2009, revealed components of two complex water management systems. One, possibly more recent, is the earthen channel that runs from WP 1089 to LCP 56, paralleling the N margins of the Sajur alluvial plain. A second semi-subterranean system consists of qanat shafts and elongated rock-cut channels following the contours of the hill upon which LCP 38 is located. A tomb (WP 1070), to the E of LCP 38, is cut into the rock.
Pottery: LC, Mid-/late EBA, Iron Age, Hellenistic and Roman, Early and Middle Islamic.

LCP-39 Tukhur Saghir

Within SW part of Tukhur Saghir village on low N bank terrace of Sajur, which is some 4 m above the level of the Sajur flood plain. Low, rubble-covered mound, 90 m diameter, 1–2 m high, partly under modern cemetery. Pottery is sparse and mainly small, but larger fragments are evident in new exposures at E end of site. A large oil crushing basin of limestone, *c.* 1.5 m diameter, is evident at E end of site, and at least two graves have column drums as markers. In addition, two capitals and a single basalt rotary mill fragment were noted.
Pottery: Small collection of Late Roman-Byzantine pottery.

LCP-40 Qirata

Qirata (not Tell er-Resem, as stated in Copeland and Moore 1985) on N side of Sajur valley. A small N bank Sajur tributary wadi defines the site on the E side. Evident as very low mound, *c.* 50 m diameter; 1–2 m high site on low terrace on N side of Sajur. Partly obscured by old graves on eastern slopes. Pottery sparse; 1–2 ashlar blocks evident on W part of site. Currently has village to W; shops and village on E bank of tributary wadi; tarmac road on N side.
Pottery: Late Roman–Byzantine.

LCP-41 Tell Amarna Cemetery Site

On low terrace to NW of Tell Amarna. Located immediately W of Tell Amarna to the N of the Jerablus road and the Nahr al-Amarna within the modern cemetery. The Nahr al-Amarna flows to the S and E of the site. Within old cemetery a little below and E of the modern cemetery and extending over 130 m E–W × 75 m N–S; height *c.* 1 m. The surface scatter of stones, and graves includes various architectural elements as grave markers; these include 4 column drums, as well as several basalt querns and roof tiles (including concentration to S near the road). WP 911 is on the NE edge of a complex of Late Antique tombs on the N bank of the Nahr al-Amarna, N of the Jerablus-Dadate road; only the 3 eastern-most tombs were observed, but no sherds were found in their vicinity. The tombs might relate to both LCP 21 (Tell Amarna) and LCP 41. Pottery is moderately common on LCP 41 and their were occasional good quality lithics.
Pottery and Lithics: Lithics (Neolithic?), some chaff-tempered LC wares; sparse EBA and Iron Age; Hellenistic and Roman.

LCP 42 No name

Located 2 km E of the junction of the Wadi Membij and the Sajur, immediately W of a wadi joining the Sajur valley from S. Section in wadi to the north shows 1–2 m of coarse limestone gravel overlying reddish yellow silt-clay of relict flood plain perched several metres above the Sajur flood plain. The site, 80 m N–S × 50 m E–W, height *c.* 1 m, appears partially bull-dozed and deeply ploughed. Traces of building debris and associated cultural deposits are still evident on the ground surface and it appears that at least 2–3 buildings have been flattened.
Pottery: Occasional to common Hellenistic pottery includes 4–5 incurved rim bowls; flanged bowls; slipped/gloss wares; 2 amphorae bases.

LCP-43 Mishrife-2

Below Mishrife village on a promontory of limestone between 2 wadis, near where they meet Lake Tishreen. Small site, 50 m diameter, height 75 cm, which consisted of at least 1 building of rough-cut limestone blocks. 5–10 Late Antique roof tiles. Partly plundered with looting holes.
Pottery and Lithics: 1 micro-blade; occasional pottery, including 3–4 brittle wares. Late Roman–Byzantine.

LCP-44 Aushariye West

1 km W of Aushariye village on limestone hill and S facing slopes on N side of Sajur valley. A narrow, deep wadi is to the W. Consists of area A) upper area on summit of limestone hill within new orchard. B) on the lower limestone slopes immediately above the road, measures 60 m E–W × 50 m N–S. There is no obvious mounding, but there are one or two tiles on B.
Pottery: A, has occasional sherds, mostly coarse wares of storage jars; B, Hellenistic pottery more common with more fine wares including a Hellenistic incurved rim bowl.

LCP-45 Tukhar Saghir al-Janubi

On S side of Sajur valley, 1 km W of Tukhar Saghir al-Janubi. 60 m E–W, 50 m N–S; depth of deposit *c.* 1.3 m. On bench in limestone hill and on the N facing slopes of the Sajur valley, overlooking the village and site of Tukhar Saghir al-Shamali. Deep wadi to

the E. In 2008, this small Late Roman–Byzantine site consisted of a totally bulldozed platform of rubble with abundant masonry in debris. The common roof tiles and fine red bricks or tiles, had probably been used for intermediate tile courses. Although the site appears to have been bulldozed away, a hole along the southern edge of site indicated *c.* 1.3 m of occupation deposit.
Pottery: The sparse pottery included occasional brittle ware.

2009 Season

LCP-46 Carchemish

The main site in the area, consisting of a *c.* 4 ha citadel mound, a 40 ha Inner Town and a 55 ha Outer Town making up a total area of *c.* 100 ha. Cut by the Syrian–Turkish border leaving some 40% of the site (*i.e.* much of the Outer Town) within Syria. Surface collection of pottery was conducted in 2009 and 2010 within a limited area away from the border as per the request from the DGAM, Damascus.
Pottery: Halaf, Ubaid, LC, Uruk (LC 4–5), early EBA, middle EBA, late EBA, MBA, LBA, Early Iron Age, Later Iron Age, Hellenistic, Roman, Byzantine, Early Islamic. See Chapter 8.

LCP-47 Tell al-Akhbar (official Syrian name) Boz Höyük (Turkish)

A prominent tell, elongated on the N–S axis, situated at the SE fringes of the Gaziantep/Nizip plain (the upland plain), some 2 km S of the Syrian–Turkish border. To the E a fairly large wadi runs NW SE forming 1 of the 2 upstream tributaries of the Wadi Zourba which joins the Sajur at Arab Hassan (LCP 68). E of the village of Boz Höyük a bulldozed quarry along the course of the wadi reveals *c.* 3 m of gravel similar to that described in the Wadi Zourba sequence (Chapter 5), overlain by reddish yellow silty clay loam. The soil of the surrounding fields is reddish brown, fertile terra rossa. The paved road on the E and NE edges of the tell might have partly cut the slope on those sides. A prominent tell, 140 m N–S, 100 m E–W, 15.5 m high. The paved road on the E and NE edges of the tell might have partly cut the slope on those sides. Area A, the summit, *c.* 30 × 20 m, features a tripod triangulation station and a single modern tomb. The slopes of the tell (B) were steep on all 4 sides. The modern village of Boz Höyük/El Akhbar extends over the S, SW and W slopes, and is terraced for 2 houses. Clear views over the plain, including to Deve Höyük (in Turkey). Numerous chipped stones.
Pottery: Pottery Neolithic? LC 2–3; early and Mid-/Late EBA; MBA, LBA, Iron Age, Early Islamic.

LCP-48 Koulliye West

Located N of the Koulliye to al-Akhbar road on a low ridge. Forms a very low mound, *c.* 40 m diameter and 50 cm high. A carved stone, possibly a stone basin, remains in the middle of the low ridge. In addition to Late Antique pottery, several tiles and chunks of building material were evident. Possibly a small Late Antique farmstead.
Pottery: Late Roman, Byzantine.

LCP-49 No Name.

Small flat site located NE of the village of Bulduq on a hilltop between the Wadi Babinsi and a small tributary wadi. Forms a concentration of pottery on top of a ridge overlooking two wadis. On undulating limestone terrain with thin soil. The site is on a cropped field with olive/pistachio orchards to E. The site appears to be a small Roman or Late Antique farmstead.
Pottery: ?Late Roman–Byzantine?

LCP-50 Koulliye

A prominent tell, 130 m E–W, 85 m N–S, 8 m high, located at the NW edge of the modern village of Koulliye, at the SE margin of the upland plain. The extent is difficult to determine because of a large pit to the NE, a road to the NW and W which might have removed the slopes of the tell, and the modern village of Koulliye on the S and SE slope of the tell. Possible stone walls, of unknown age, are visible on the E, SE and S slopes; Ubaid and Halaf sherds have been collected from this section (area F). Large quantities of chipped stone were evident on the site and surrounding fields. Grindstone fragments were also present.
Areas: A, top of the tell; B, W slope; C, N slope; D, NE slope; E, SE slope; F, S slope.
Pottery: Halaf, Ubaid, LC 1–2, 3?Uruk early, middle and late EBA; Late Roman/Byzantine.

LCP-51 No Name

Some 700–800 m W of modern village of Rasid al-Jous, at the SE margins of the reddish brown soils of the Gaziantep/Nizip plain. The site has a clear 360° view of the surrounding plain and the Sajur Valley to the S. The site, 185 m N–S, 80 m E–W, height 3 m, forms a low tell with the E slope being the steepest; electricity pylon in middle of site. The road partly cuts the S edges of the site, which extends some 40 m S of the road. A few tiles and several basalt grindstones
Pottery and Lithics: Frequent chipped stone; Byzantine, Early and Middle Islamic pottery.

LCP-52 No Name

E of modern village of Rasid al-Jous and E of the paved road which runs through the village. Situated at the SE edges of the reddish hued Gaziantep/Nizip plain within a large pistachio orchard. A large flat settlement, 185 m NW–SE, 270 m NE–SW. The extent of the site was inferred from the pale soil, numerous white limestone fragments and the sherd scatter. Outside the site, where pottery was minimal, the soil was a typical "terra rossa". Numerous stone fragments and tiles suggest the presence of buildings. Also several fragments of basalt grindstones and carved basalt blocks.
Pottery and Lithics: Numerous chipped stones; pottery Byzantine (including 6th century AD) and Early Islamic.

LCP-53 No name

Some 2 km NW of the modern village of al-Zahiriya (Bir Wirane) at the headwaters of the Nahr al-Amarna, and on its right (S) bank. On gentle valley side slopes overlooking the Nahr al-Amarna Valley. Reddish brown topsoil cover. A very large settlement, with a core area of 120 m E–W and 105 m N–S; max. height, *c.* 5 m (A). The settlement is composed of several low mounds which created the impression of undulating terrain. Area A (WP 1030),

5 m high mound towards E end of site with moderately steep slopes to E and N, and a low, rounded profile. Animal burrows on E slope provided window into earlier (LC/EBA) deposits. Site mainly under harvested cereals providing moderate visibility. Common basalt, mainly vesicular, over A. Occasional Late Roman Byzantine pottery on summit. B, elongate mound to W of A, *c.* 3–4 m high. Field boundaries have numerous large limestone and basalt stones at intervals along them; these appear to have been dug out of the site. In general there are numerous fragments of basalt (grindstones, rubbers, pestles, carved blocks etc) as well as numerous fragments of roof tiles and other building materials. Overall, the site appears to be an extensive Late-Roman/Byzantine site with an earlier mound at A.
Pottery: A: LC, Uruk, EBA; B: Late Roman, Byzantine and remainder of site.

LCP-54 al-Hajalliya

Strategically located on top of a conical limestone hill, immediately SE/S of the modern village of Hajalliya. Small hilltop mound, 90 m N–S, 50 m E–W, 8.5 m high (but not all cultural deposit). Consists of a distinctive summit mound (A) of archaeological debris with traces of stone wall foundations on the top and a lower bench (B), which, although possibly archaeological, more likely is a dipping limestone bed. A cave cut into a coarse limestone breccia halfway up the N side is partly cemented with travertine / flowstone. The limestone bench (B) has a moderate sherd scatter and occasional large stones presumably derived from buildings. On the SE slope (WP 1053), emerging wall foundations may belong to a single building. The site summit has views in all directions especially towards the Euphrates Valley, but Carchemish and Jerablus are not visible. Possibly a small fortress or citadel. A qanat in the wadi below (WP 1034 through WP 1043; except WP 1041) is parallel with both the wadi and the road below. One limestone cut shaft retains its original form but the others are concreted over.
Pottery: Mid-/Late EBA; Iron Age.

LCP-55 al-Hilwaniya (Duknuk)

About 200 m NW of the modern village of al-Hilwaniya (Duknuk), 300 m SE of the Turkish border. The site is situated at SW edge of a fertile plain, with reddish brown soil, that stretches to N and NE. A prominent tell, 250 m N–S, 130 m E–W, 21 m high. The tell stands in isolation in this small plain and is clearly visible from a distance. It is located by a wadi which flows along the W side of the site and then along the Syro–Turkish border until entering the Milli Dere, before the Turkish village of Karchemish. The tell is conical with a flat top (A) and steep slopes (B).
Along the N edges of the tell summit are stone wall foundations *c.* 3 m long, oriented NE-SW. At the bottom of the tell, along the NW side, were pits in-filled with soil-wash (C: WP 1057). Area D is the field N of the tell.
Pottery: Halaf, Ubaid, LC, LC 5 (Uruk), with band-rimmed bowls, Mid-/Late EBA, MBA, Iron Age, Hellenistic, Roman, Late Roman, Byzantine.

LCP-56 Majra Saghir W (al-Tukhar)

Located W of the modern village of Majra Saghir, on the N side of the Sajur River, on the 1st terrace above the alluvial plain. Today this 75 m diameter site is flat, but farmers (Dec. 2009) say that this was originally a tell, bulldozed some 15 years previously. It is possible that the site extended to the S, but it has been cut by bulldozing to create a terrace for agriculture. A few meters NE of the bridge an exposed section revealed a stone wall of no obvious orientation, made of roughly-dressed stone blocks (WP 1060). This possibly belonged to a water management system, and today an earthen channel runs W–E, parallel to Sajur River along the N margin of the Sajur alluvial plain. This earthen channel runs from WP 1089 (NE of LCP 38) to LCP 56 which is cut by this hydraulic feature along its W, SW and S edge. This channel was first recognized as a rock-cut feature (WPs 822 and 823) and from the CORONAs it appears that the earthen channel made a sharp curve in this area.
Pottery: 1 late EBA bowl rim, MBA, LBA, Iron Age, Hellenistic, Roman/ Byzantine.

LCP-57 Majra Kebir W (al-Tukhar)

Located *c.* 200 m S of the road between Majra Kabir and Dadate, N of the Sajur River and W of the modern village of Majra Kabir/ Tukhar Kabir. The site, roughly 50 m N–S × 40 m E–W, is flat and is on slightly sloping terrain towards the Sajur. Only a few diagnostic sherds and several fragments of basalt grind stones and rubbers. Small Hellenistic farmstead?
Pottery: Hellenistic handle and jar rims.

LCP-58 Majra Saghir W (al-Tukhar)

About 700 m S of the road between Tukhar Kebir and Dadate; N of the Sajur, and W of the modern village of Tukhar Kabir. The site is 40 m diameter and flat, and is on terrain that slopes slightly towards the Sajur. Immediately W of the site the ground has been bulldozed to a depth of some 30–40 cm, which might have removed the W part of the site. Possibly a small farmstead.
Pottery: Hellenistic, Roman/Late Roman, Early Islamic.

LCP-59 Yousuf Bek

Tell, 110 m diameter and 14 m high, located within the village of Yousuf Bek and NW of the paved road to Tell Sha'ir. On gentle slopes immediately N of the Nahr al-Amarna. The site is conical with fairly steep slopes, less steep to E. The houses of the village extend on all four slopes of the mound, except for a small portion on the SW slope. The flat summit of the tell is only *c.* 12 × 8 m therefore there were no collection subdivisions. A few tiles and basalt fragments (not collected).
Pottery: LC, early and mid-EBA, LBA, Iron Age, Hellenistic, Roman, Late Roman, Early and Middle Islamic.

LCP-60 Koundouriye (al-Ghoundariya)

Located in the valley of the Nahr al-Amarna River immediately N of the river and adjacent to the modern village of al-Ghoundariya. A prominent tell, conical in form, standing in isolation with no modern construction on it. A major site, 230 m NW–SE, 140 m NE–SW, 26 m high, situated beside the Amarna River and with a long sequence of occupation. The tell has a flat summit with very steep slopes. Gullies and sparse vegetation result in very good visibility on all 4 slopes. Possible stone wall foundations are visible on the surface at the top and along the slopes. Area A: mound summit; Area B: slopes; Area C: base of tell with pits/cuts; Area D: fields W of tell; Area E: fields N of tell; Area F: fields

E of tell. Although the pottery scatter in areas D–F is relatively sparse and decreases away from the tell, field assessments suggest that occupation had occurred in part of the surroundings. Finds include 1 pithos, possibly *in situ* (Area A); 3 figurine fragments; a Canaanean blade; a few tiles, basalt fragment (of which one pestle), abundant chipped stones.
Pottery: Halaf, Ubaid, LC, Uruk, Mid-/Late EBA, MBA, Iron Age, Hellenistic, Roman, Late Roman, Byzantine, Early and Middle Islamic.

LCP 61 Ghasaniya

The site, which originally might have been a tell, is located in the middle of the village of Ghasaniya, at its highest point and surrounded by houses. The village lies on a low limestone rise above the surrounding plain. Sherds were found in a field and in the alleyways that lead up to the highest point of the village, where a residual of soil *c.* 5 × 3 m and 1 m high containing mud-bricks and stone block fragments was noted. This could be either the remains of a tell or the result of bulldozing that piled up the soil. It is impossible to determine the extent of the site.
Pottery: 2 Mid-/Late EBA (tri-lug and ring base) and Late Roman–Byzantine.

LCP-62 Yousuf Bek SW

Immediately N of the 'Ain al Beida–Koundariye paved road, within a hamlet, SW of the modern village of Yousuf Bek. Immediately S and SW of a tributary wadi of the Nahr al-Amarna River and SW the Nahr, on gently undulating hill slopes towards the river valley. An extensive site, 360 m NW–SE × 330 m NE–SW, flat. Located on flat limestone terrain with thin brownish topsoil; no apparent mounding. The 4 WPs indicate the extent of the site at its edges. The slightly hummocky nature of the site might indicate the presence of cultural deposits; but no section exposed. Despite low visibility, pottery and roof tiles are abundant as well as several basalt stone fragments. Also 1 basalt column noted within the hamlet. The farmer pointed out 1 basalt column, ovoid in section, brought from the fields into the hamlet. The farmers say that tombs and old wells were found while the hamlet was built.
Pottery: 1 Iron Age? storage jar; mainly Late Roman, Byzantine.

LCP-63 al-Zahiriya (Bir Wirane)

Located in the village of al-Zahiriya (Bir Wirane) within its SW extension. Pottery mainly in village cemetery which measured some 100 × 80 m. However, the extent of the site could not be determined. The cemetery lies on a low ridge, rising *c.* 1 m above the surrounding ground. Numerous carved basalt and limestone fragments found on the cemetery and in the village. Pottery was collected in the alleyways and, more abundantly, from the village cemetery. A house stands on the highest point of the cemetery, but it remains unclear if the cemetery stands on a low tell because no sections are exposed and modern constructions have deeply altered the original context. Numerous carved basalt and limestone fragments, found on the cemetery and in the village, include: 2 fragments of basalt column shafts; 1 basalt capital with shaft; 3 basalt basins; 2 basalt olive presses; 1 limestone olive press.
Pottery: Byzantine, Early and Middle Islamic; Ottoman?

LCP-64 No name (W of al-Zahiriya)

Located W of the village of Zahiriya, S of the paved road that leads to Zorhar. This flat site, 100 m NW–SE, 50 m SW–NE, lies at the SE margins of the Nizip–Gazientep upland plain with its reddish soil. The site consists of 2 depressions, 40 m in diameter, and the surrounding areas. The 2 depressions are irregularly rounded in form with slopes of moderate gradient, and the SW side is slightly straighter than the other sides. In the SE depression cemented conglomerates outcrop, whereas limestone occurs in the NW depression at its N edge. The function of the depressions is unclear and there is no evidence of a quarry. Although the depressions appear on CORONA images (Jan 1967), they could be the result of an earlier bulldozing phase which removed the site. There is no evidence of up-cast soil around the depressions. There are a few roof tile fragments.
Pottery: Late Roman–Byzantine buff handles and bowl of similar date.

LCP-65 Nahr Bash West

Tell, 160 m NW–SE, 125 m NE–SW, 7 m high, situated immediately S of the Nahr al-Amarna on terrain that slopes gently towards the river valley; *c.* 1 km NNE of the village of Ghasaniya. A minor tributary of the Nahr al-Amarna runs to the S of the site. Tell has a rounded profile, and gentle slopes that rise some 7 m above the surroundings; a house occupies the summit. The N part has been recently planted with fruit trees. A few basalt fragments were noted immediately S of the Nahr al-Amarna. When soil had been removed from holes for tree planting, pottery was particularly abundant. The tell (area A) yielded the majority of pottery; in particular an Uruk sherd and numerous chaffy sherds. Area B consists of the fields extending S, SE and E of the tell where a few sherds of pottery were collected and kept separated. However, it is possible that these sherds had moved down from the tell and dispersed into the nearby field by modern ploughing. No pottery was found in the surrounding fields to W, N and NE.
Pottery: LC, Uruk, Early EBA; Iron Age, Hellenistic, Roman, Late Roman, Byzantine.

LCP-66 Nahr Bash

The site, 75 m E–W, 55 m N–S, is located on a low natural ridge at the small hamlet of Nahr Bash, W of Koundoriye. It is immediately N of the Nahr al-Amarna and is situated on terrain that slopes towards that river; it is essentially flat. In the backyard of a house an entire column base of limestone was noted; although possibly Hellenistic/Roman in date, there was no Hellenistic/Roman pottery. Therefore the base may have been moved from its original context. *Pottery:* mainly chaff-tempered sherds of the LBA, with squared rims, platters and pithoi, plus possible Iron Age and MBA types.

LCP-67 Al-Hadhira

Situated in a small valley immediately S of the modern village of al-Hadhira. A paved road, that connects al-Hadhira to Umm Sousse, runs along the E edge of the site and divides it into 2 parts. The site extends across an extensive area of land between two wadis and is intensively planted with adult pistachio trees. The limits of the site, *c.* 630 m NE–SW, 320 m NW–SE (flat), were inferred by the dispersion of roof tiles (literally thousands!). At least 2 types

of tile were noted: 1) with lower, narrower ridges along the sides, 2) with thicker, shallower ridges; some exhibited 3 digit wavy imprints along the diagonal. Sherds were much less common.
Pottery: Late Roman/Byzantine; Early Islamic types include flanged bowls; Late Antique handles, Late Roman C, Early Islamic comb-incised wares.

LCP-68 Arab Hassan

A prominent tell immediately E of the junction between the Sajur River and its S bank tributary, Wadi Morhara. Situated NW of the modern village of Arab Hassan Kabir and E of a dirt track that connects Arab Hassan Kabir with Arab Hassan Saghir. The site measures 290 m NW–SE, 210 m SW–NE, 38 m high (27 m lower tell; 11 m upper tell). Between the inner high mound and the outer wall are gentle slopes of archaeological debris. There appears to be little direct evidence of outer walls or ramparts, but the large stones of limestone and basalt to the N might indicate the remains of a N gate (note that the RCP survey of Copeland and colleagues report: "Cyclopean masonry consisting of huge basalt blocks at base of west side", (Copeland 1985, 74). A number of large masonry blocks outcrop on the summit mound (A), and these appear to be part of a small citadel structure. The site can be conceived of as 2 superimposed tells: 1st, a larger mound (B) elongated NW–SE, rising *c.* 27 m above the surrounding fields. The lower part of this mound has been cut by the field terraces along the W edges of the site and this lower area was designated as Area C. Between WP 1126 and WP 1127, several carved limestone blocks were visible and belong to an architectural feature that runs NE–SW, perhaps being the ruins of a retaining/enclosure wall at the N margins of the tell. A 2nd, smaller tell, rising *c.* 11 m above the lower main mound, was collected as Area A. This upper tell, elongated with NW–SE axis, has steep slopes to the N and E. On both satellite images and the ground, the site appears to consist of an oval outer wall or rampart with the inner high tell (A) concentric within it. Occasional large stones outcrop along the E edge of the lower mound (B), but these are not sufficient to demonstrate the existence of a wall. The shape and position of the upper tell (A) has the form of a citadel built on a bulky lower settlement (B). At the NW of the apex of area A, five carved limestone blocks (the biggest *c.* 80 × 60 × 30 cm) are visible on the surface and may belong to a wall foundation forming the remains of a fortress. At the S edge of the upper tell a dressed and carved basalt block with a rectangular depression (15 cm in depth) was noted. The low natural vegetation offered good visibility, and the impression was gained that the MBA or later layers might have blanketed the more ancient/prehistoric part of the tell. A few roof tiles and basalt fragments were observed. Area D, located NE of the tell in fields on the alluvial plain, yielded occasional sherds.
Pottery: Mid-/Late EBA, MBA, LBA, Iron Age, Hellenistic, Roman, Byzantine (see Table 5.5 for full sequence).

LCP-69 Hilwanji Tahtani

Located on the first alluvial terrace of the Nahr Sajur River and on the N side of the river on terrain that slopes gently towards the river. Between the modern villages of Hilwanji, to the E, and Mahnsanli, to the W. It is NW of Qala'at Hilwanji, on the opposite side of the Sajur River (not surveyed; see Chapter 6). A tell, 110 m NE–SW, 100 m NW–SE, rising some 10 m above the surrounding

fields and with rounded profile. The slopes are gentle on all sides and the W part of the tell has been bulldozed to a depth of *c.* 3 m to expose an irregular N–S section; however, no archaeological features were evident. Visibility on the entire tell was fairly good.
Pottery: Late EBA, MBA, Iron Age, Hellenistic, Roman, Byzantine.

LCP-70 No name (Wadi Zourba)

Situated on a hill-top overlooking the Wadi Zourba to the E; S of Saboundji. A flat site, partly on *terra rossa* soils. The site extends along the hill-top from NW to SE over some 60 × 30 m. The site overlooks the wadi valley whereas to the W extend rolling hills dissected by wadis. Two small basalt stones of indeterminate shape and a few roof tiles, were noted, particularly on the N side. Under cereals, and although stony, the visibility was excellent; some robber trenches. Two chamber tombs at the S end have been extensively dug by grave robbers.
Pottery: Late Roman, Byzantine, Early Islamic.

LCP-71 Jub al-Aswad

Between the villages of Bir Fawqani and Bir Tahtani. Situated on a fertile plain, with dark reddish brown topsoil. A wadi runs from W to E in the central part of the site. A large and complex site, 600 m N–S, 500 m E–W, with a 120 m diam., 5 m high mound. The extent of the site was difficult to determined due to poor visibility. The tell is located in the N part of the site. Numerous roof tiles and basalt fragments noted. Two transects, N–S and E–W, were collected to determine the edge of the site. The site exhibits undulating or hummocky morphology probably created by sub-surface architectural/archaeological features. The following features were noticed: A tell (WP 1171) is located in the N part of the site on slopes that dip towards a wadi. The tell is rounded in shape with gentle slopes. WP 1172 identifies a rounded depression to the SW, some 60 m in diameter and 2 m deep. WPs 1169, 1170, 1173 and 1174 identify an area where the soil changes in colour. In addition, WP 1173 appears to stand on ground some 50/80 cm above the surroundings. Common basalt stones evident on the surface along the wadi, may have given rise to the name "Jube al Aswad", but whether this indicates the presence of an artificial channel is unclear. Very large collection and all collected sherds were labelled as LCP 71.
Pottery: Early EBA (1 reserved slip); EBA III (foot base sherd); Roman, Late Roman, Early and Middle Islamic.

LCP-72 Shoukhra

Located W of the village of Shoukhra, SE of Koulliye, at the margin of the upland (Nizip) plain with its reddish brown soils. E of the Wadi Zourba, the site and its immediate vicinity are cultivated with crops and olive/almonds/pistachio trees. The site is on grey soil which forms a slight rise above the surrounding fields near a low limestone outcrop. The site scatter includes pottery, a few roof tiles and basalt grindstone fragments. Visibility poor due to straw cover. Collection interrupted, but site area estimated as 2 ha.
Pottery: Byzantine (brittle wares and buffware handles).

LCP-73 Koundouriye North (al-Ghoundariya)

Located NW of LCP 60 (Tell Koundouriye), W of a paved road. The site, 100 m E–W, 70 m N–S, is within a pistachio orchard and the visibility was good. Situated on a gentle slope that overlooks

the Nahr al-Amarna valley from the N, with a tributary wadi of the Amarna immediately W, SW and S of the site. The site is on a low ridge that rises some 2 m above the surrounding fields. Pottery was more abundant on the S and SE sides of the low mound where the slopes are steeper. Some basalt stone fragments, but no roof tiles.
Pottery: Hellenistic red and grey wash wares; incurved-rim bowls and jars.

LCP-74 al-Haimar North

The site, estimated at 80 m E–W × 60 N–S, and flat, is *c.* 1.5 km N of the village of al-Haimar. A paved road is passes W of the site. No anthropic deposit was noted and there was no change in soil colour. Sparse sherds were also observed in the fields surrounding the site. When pottery was checked they were seen to be uniformly stained brown, unlike the pottery from other sites. This suggests the sherds had resided in the natural mineral soil and had been coated or infused with clay minerals. They may therefore represent field scatters which were ploughed to the surface.
Pottery: Late Roman–Byzantine.

LCP-75 Tell Sha'ir NW

Located *c.* 1.7 km NW of the village of Tell Sha'ir (LCP 3). The site is within a fertile plain, with reddish brown soils, which contrast with the greyish brown on-site soil. Forms a low tell (1.5 m high), 205 m, E–W × 150 m N–W, on undulating terrain rising *c.* 1.5 m above the surrounding fields. Numerous roof tiles and basalt fragments; 2 cream chert mosaic tesserae.
Pottery: Byzantine and Early Islamic, with buff-ware handles and many brittle wares.

LCP-76 Koundouriye NE (al-Ghoundariya NE)

Immediately N of the Amarna River, on the left bank, within the broad alluvial plain. The site is *c.* 1 km NNE of LCP 60 (Tell Koundouriye). Consists of a 90 m NW-SE x 65 m, NE-SW area of scattered potsherds on a rise 0.50 m above the surrounding fields; soil colour used to define site in field. In addition to a few roof tiles, basalt stone fragments were noted, but not collected. Possibly a rural farmstead.
Pottery: Middle Islamic coarse cooking pots (sub-brittleware) and handles, but lacking true brittle wares or glazed wares.

LCP-77 Koundouriye E (al-Ghoundariya)

Between the al-Ghoundariya-Koulliye road and the Nahr al-Amarna; *c.* 700 m ESE of the village of al-Ghoundariya. On the ENE side of a limestone ridge, the site consists of a thin anthropic deposit rising to 1 m above the surrounding fields. Forms a shallow mound extending over 290 m N–S × 270 m E–W. The highest point of the mound corresponds to WP 1223. Along the NE and NW of the site, bulldozing exposed 2, 2 m sections. Common roof tile fragments.
Pottery: Byzantine and Early Islamic brittle wares including handles (some with crescent lugs); also L Roman C and buff-ware handles.

LCP-78 al-Haimar

Small, low mound, 80 m N–S, 65 m E–W, 3.5 m high, within village of al-Haimar. The village is located on a limestone upland with very limited water resources and low agricultural potential.

Area A is within a walled compound created after a conflict in the village resulted in the departure of some of population. B is the area around the compound within village to N. The site was used for a cereal crop at the time of collection (2009); moderate visibility. Common pottery, with frequent stones and some modern rubbish. Occasional basalt querns and Late Antique tiles.
Pottery: LC3 Uruk (including BRBs), Early and Late EBA, Iron Age, Byzantine.

LCP-79 Hadhira South

Near the village of Hadhira, on a slightly undulating high upland plain. The site (visited 26 Dec. 2009) appears to extend over *c.* 4 ha, or less, but the main cultural deposit extends over *c.* 100 × 100 m. Site consists of two depressions 1–2 m deep (WP 1321 & 1322) with a surrounding area of moderately dense pottery scatter, becoming denser in the W of the site where a very low mound and artefact scatter appears to represent the remains of a single building. The surrounding fields show a field scatter of moderate density. Occasional tile and basalt fragments; 1 dressed limestone block.
Pottery: Late Roman to Early Islamic; includes Late Roman C, 2 glazed wares, brittle wares and buffware handles.

LCP-80 Seraisat South

Very small site located to S of the Wadi Seraisat on a limestone ridge above bluffs overlooking the Euphrates. Noted in 2008 as sparse scatter of Late Antique pottery and tile with sparse lithic scatter to S, but not allocated a site number. Subsequently recognized on CORONA imagery as a site from its distinctive morphology. Area estimated from imagery: 0.79 ha. WP 876 (2008).
Pottery: Byzantine.

References

Copeland, L. (1985) The survey of RCP 438 in 1979. In P. Sanlaville (ed.) *Holocene settlement in north Syria: résultats de deux prospections archéologiques effectuées dans la région du nahr Sajour et sur le haut Euphrate syrien*, 67–98. Oxford, BAR S238.

Copeland, L. and Moore, A.M.T. (1985) Inventory and description of sites. In P. Sanlaville, P. (ed.) *Holocene settlement in north Syria: résultats de deux prospections archéologiques effectuées dans la région du nahr Sajour et sur le haut Euphrate syrien*, 41–98. Oxford, BAR S238.

Sanlaville (ed.) (1985) *Holocene Settlement in North Syria: résultats de deux prospections archae archéologiques effectuées dans la région du nahr Sajour et sur le haut Euphrate syrien.* Oxford, BAR S238.

Tunca, Ö. (1999) Tell 'Amarna. Présentation sommaire de sept campagnes de fouilles (1991–1997). In G. del Olmo Lete and J.-L. Montero Fenollós (eds) *Archaeology of the Upper Syrian Euphrates, The Tishrin Dam Area*, 129–36. *Aula Orientalis Supplementa* 15. Barcelona, Editorial Ausa.

Wilkinson, T.J., Peltenburg, E.J., McCarthy, A., Wilkinson, E.B. and Brown, M. (2007) Archaeology in the Land of Carchemish: landscape surveys in the area of Jerablus Tahtani, 2006. *Levant* 39, 213–247.